# Contents

# Discover the
# Florida Gulf Coast

Stretching more than 700 miles from Pensacola to Everglades National Park, the Florida Gulf Coast is one of the most beautiful and captivating places on earth. Along most of the coastline you will find sugar-white sands and warm emerald waters – these beaches bring millions of travelers each year to the Sunshine State's western shore and hundreds of islands.

The Gulf Coast is comprised of diverse landscapes and cultures and an extremely wide variety of destinations suitable for any traveler's taste and budget. In Naples and Sarasota you can spend the morning shopping at upscale boutiques before driving 45 minutes to the Everglades for a kayak excursion through winding mangroves. There are flawlessly manicured, world-class golf courses in abundance on the Paradise Coast and a sprawling wilderness of forests, rivers, and freshwater springs along the Nature Coast. In Apalachicola you can enjoy a quiet morning of fishing with only a few other locals casting in the bay, while right down U.S. 98, the vacation towns of Destin, Pensacola, and Panama City are packed with sunbathers.

You can start the day touring Tallahassee, charmed by the Southern architecture and accents, and in four hours find yourself in Tampa's

historic Cuban district, Ybor City, munching on a Cubano sandwich before enjoying a night of flamenco dancing. The culture of the Gulf Coast's people and cities is a fusion of the Southerners, Northerners, and Spanish, Cuban, Native American, and Cajun people that have settled in the area.

For travelers interested in history, there are Native American sites all along the coast, as well as military forts, sunken Spanish ships, Civil War sites, plantations, and colonial-era destinations. For outdoor adventures, the Gulf Coast boasts thousands of miles of coastline, rivers, and pristine springs to paddle, swim, and dive. There are countless coastal and forested sites for camping, hiking, and exploring – not to mention some of the best offshore and inshore fishing in the world.

The Gulf Coast of Florida evokes a sense of wonder and curiosity and a desire to explore the beaches, the islands, and the waterways. Along the way, you might just discover your own idea of paradise.

# Planning Your Trip

## ▶ WHERE TO GO

### The Paradise Coast

Located at the southwestern tip of Florida's Gulf Coast, Naples swarms with upscale resorts, high-end restaurants, cultural amenities, and more golf courses per capita than anywhere else on the Gulf Coast. Marco Island, just south, the northernmost island in the string of what is called the Ten Thousand Islands, is in a similar vein, with tall resort hotels and condos rising up on a long crescent of white-sand beach. Everglades City provides a paddler's and outdoorsman's paradise at one end of the Everglades backcountry, the famous Wilderness Waterway route linking Everglades City to Flamingo.

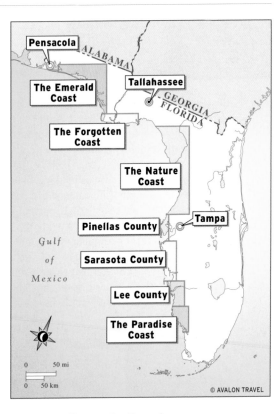

### Lee County

Lee County comprises Fort Myers, Sanibel Island, and Captiva Island. Fort Myers is the largest and oldest city in southwest Florida, set on the banks of the Caloosahatchee River. Sanibel is a casual, low-rise beach town with just enough to do (visit the J. N. "Ding" Darling National Wildlife Refuge and the Bailey-Matthews Shell Museum) to keep the whole family entertained. There's less to do on neighboring Captiva Island, and that's just the way residents and visitors like it. The superlatives heaped upon it include "exclusive," "romantic," and "tranquil"—all accurate.

### Sarasota County

Sarasota has been recognized as Florida's cultural capital, home to a professional symphony, ballet, and opera. There are theaters, art galleries, the John and Mable Ringling Museum of Art, and the Van Wezel Performing Arts Hall. A chain of narrow barrier islands sits offshore to the west. Lido and St. Armands Keys are fairly urban extensions of downtown Sarasota, connected by a causeway. Longboat Key to

## IF YOU HAVE . . .

- **A WEEKEND:** Visit Tampa and Pinellas County.

- **FOUR DAYS:** Add Sarasota and Fort Myers, including the barrier islands of Sanibel, Captiva, and Siesta Key.

- **A WEEK:** Add Naples, with a kayak tour of the Everglades.

- **TWO WEEKS:** Tour the entire length of the Gulf Coast by car.

the north and Siesta Key to the south are destinations in their own right, the former lined with upscale resort hotels and condominiums, the latter a more casual and fun, low-rise beach getaway.

## Tampa

Busch Gardens, Ybor City, the Florida Aquarium, Tampa Bay Buccaneers, Tampa Bay Devil Rays, and Tampa Bay Lightning. But notice I didn't mention the beach. Tampa fronts Tampa Bay, not the Gulf of Mexico. A huge port city—the largest pleasure and industrial port in the southeast—it

doesn't have any beaches to speak of. Before you fret, though, it's an excellent family vacation destination. There's a perfect convergence of warm weather, affordable accommodations, professional sports, kids' attractions, and upscale shopping that seems to suit every taste.

## Pinellas County

Easygoing and relaxed, the city of St. Petersburg exerts its pull with a vibrant downtown of pastel art deco buildings and cultural attractions like the Salvador Dalí Museum, Florida International Museum, the symphony at Ruth Eckerd Hall, or theater at American Stage. But on the Gulf side of the peninsula, Clearwater Beach and St. Pete Beach are welcoming shores of Gulf water lapping at white sand, backed by restaurants, souvenir shops, and boogie-board-and-bikini stores. Caladesi Island, Honeymoon Island, and Fort De Soto Park are all favored Pinellas beaches.

## The Nature Coast

The Nature Coast includes Homosassa and Crystal River in the south, both famous for their tarpon fishing and manatee habitat. South of that, and worth a day's excursion,

kayaking a calm Gulf of Mexico along the Paradise Coast

is Weeki Wachee Springs with its historic mermaid show and incredible high-magnitude spring. To the north, the small fishing communities of Cedar Key and Steinhatchee require a little extra effort to get to, but the payoff is big. Each is like a look back into Florida's past, populated by anglers, some great bars, relaxed motels, and plenty of guides eager to take you out into the beauty of the Nature Coast.

## Tallahassee

Its inclusion in this book may seem quirky, as Tallahassee doesn't really lie on the Gulf Coast but sits inland a bit. Still, the city of Tallahassee is the gateway to the Panhandle and the seat

fishing from a canoe in Tallahassee

of state government, and as such, it stays in the picture. It's strongly Southern, more so than most cities on the Gulf Coast, with the country's largest concentration of original plantations (300,000 acres, 71 plantations) between here and Thomasville, Georgia, 28 miles away. Refined and rooted in history, the top attractions are the two capitol buildings, new and old.

## The Forgotten Coast

With 200 historic homes and buildings on the National Register, and a downtown of repurposed 1850s brick cotton warehouses, Apalachicola has antebellum charm to burn. The Apalachicola National Estuarine Research Reserve, historic Grady Market, and the sweet John Gorrie State Museum, which celebrates the inventor of modern refrigeration—there's enough here to occupy visitors for at least a couple of days, but then top it off with incredible nearby beaches on St. George Island, and St. Joseph Peninsula, or a view into Franklin County's oystering business in Eastpoint.

## The Emerald Coast

The Emerald Coast—Fort Walton Beach and Destin, Beaches of South Walton, Panama

City Beach—got its name from the deep green color of its water that laps against its glinting white-sand beaches. But this is nearly all that the communities along this stretch of coast share. Its easternmost section, Panama City Beach, is a densely populated beachside playground, especially favored by college kids on spring break. Farther west, the Beaches of South Walton feature quieter, more luxurious beachside enjoyments. And still farther west, fishing is what put Destin on the map, and that continues today with anglers arriving from all over the planet to get a crack at the local marlins, sailfish, and spearfish.

## Pensacola

If you're looking for a very relaxed, fun, and casual place to explore beautiful beaches where you will be welcomed with warm Southern hospitality, then Pensacola is the place to go. A city of 412,000, Pensacola has finally recovered from the devastating hurricane season of 2004 and looks better than ever. Its long stretches of white beaches are a popular summer destination for Floridians and tourists across the nation as the temperature tends to stay a bit cooler in this northwestern Panhandle destination. It is known

Pensacola is home to the Blue Angels.

as the City of Five Flags, as it has been occupied at different times by Spain, France, England, the Confederacy, and America, and as the "Cradle of Naval Aviation," being home to the Naval Air Station Pensacola and the Blue Angels, or even "America's first European settlement" (the Spanish tried to colonize Pensacola in 1559).

## ▶ WHEN TO GO

Florida is a year-round destination, but each broad geographical area along the Gulf Coast has its own peak season, off-season, and in-the-know in-between times.

Southwest Florida sees a huge influx of "snowbirds" in the winter months. These northerners come after Thanksgiving and stay just through Easter, generally speaking, bumping up the populations in Naples and Fort Myers up through Sarasota and Bradenton. The timing isn't arbitrary—March and April along much of the Gulf Coast are magical: temperatures in the high 70s, a little breeze, low humidity, little rain, and Gulf water just warm enough for swimming. That said, if you visit before the snowbirds arrive in the spring or after they depart in the fall, you'll find plenty of accommodations, unoccupied tables in restaurants, and room to roam the beaches.

The Central West region encompasses the southern portion of Florida's Nature Coast, as well as the popular vacation destinations of Tampa, St. Petersburg, and Clearwater. Again, Thanksgiving to Easter is the peak visitor time, but it's less clear-cut here. A huge family draw, partly because of its proximity to Orlando and Walt Disney World, the area is at its busiest during school vacations, including the hot, steamy summer one.

On the Panhandle, which has colder winters and more moderate summers than elsewhere on the Gulf Coast, it's busiest during the summer. Many of the summer-season tourists here are Florida residents from elsewhere hoping to improve upon the high temperatures and humidity of their hometowns.

For college kids, the time to visit the Gulf Coast, and specifically Panama City Beach, is spring break, which falls during the months of March and April.

# ► BEFORE YOU GO

## What to Take

Florida is casual and what to pack is mostly about being comfortable.

If you're spending time in Naples, Sarasota, or Tampa's Hyde Park, bring something a little more formal, preferably in a tropical style, to wear in the evening. Elsewhere, the name of the game year-round is layering. For women, a twin set and slacks is a good dressy outfit, for men a polo shirt and khakis. You will need several pairs of shoes: something for dinner, sneakers for hiking (ones that can get wet and possibly muddy, repeatedly), and swim shoes or sandals.

Even if you're visiting the Gulf Coast in the summer, bring a sweater. Most places keep the air conditioner going strong. You'll appreciate this when you first step inside from the relentless heat, but if you plan to spend any length of time indoors you'll end up getting cold, especially when the cold air-conditioning is coupled with sweat on the skin. In the winter, a long-sleeved pullover with light slacks is usually fine unless you're up north on the Panhandle and in the Tallahassee area, where the temperatures can drop near and very occasionally below freezing during the winter months of January and February. During these times you will want to layer your tops, maybe bring a fleece or other good jacket and a pair of warm pants or jeans.

Bring sunscreen, binoculars, polarized sunglasses (for seeing depth when you fish and to better spot dolphins), a bird book, snorkel, swim flippers, a good novel, more bathing suits than you think you can use, bug spray, flip-flops or sandals, a digital camera, maybe a disposable waterproof camera, and your cell phone (it will work in almost every part of Florida these days, except a very few rural parts of the Nature Coast, especially with Verizon service).

A car is an essential tool in most of the area, but visitors can also rent bikes, scooters, skates, strollers, beach chairs, boogie boards, surfboards, skimboards, fishing equipment, motorboats, personal watercraft, kayaks, canoes, sailboards, and sailboats.

## What It Will Cost

This information is hard to nail down: What it costs depends upon what you're willing to spend. If I averaged the prices at all the restaurants of

sugar-white sands and emerald-green waters along the Emerald Coast

kayaking through Everglades wetlands

the Gulf Coast, I'd say a restaurant dinner for one person costs $20. If I were to do the same thing for accommodations, I might find an average hotel room costs $100. But are those numbers really helpful? It's a range, with significant variation, on both counts.

Travel costs are at their most expensive during peak season, which for the Florida peninsula is December–April; for the Panhandle it's June–August. What's helpful to know is the Gulf Coast is less expensive the farther north and west you go, and also in Tampa. Top-dollar honors go to Naples, where an average dinner for one is about $30 and an average room is about $125 per night mid-season. Then it gets cheaper and cheaper as you drive up I-75 and west along U.S. 98. Cheapest place on the Gulf Coast? Panama City Beach, where lots of bargain hotel rooms on the beach bottom out at $30. Pensacola is a very affordable town; Sarasota, not so affordable.

Beaches on the Gulf Coast are free, maybe a few dollars for parking and sunblock. What you do at them may cost more—a half-day offshore fishing trip will run at least $250, an ecotour kayak trip $50, a brief Wave Runner rental $40. Of the attractions, everything pales financially by comparison to a day at Walt Disney World. Still, Busch Gardens in Tampa, Asolo Theater tickets in Sarasota, and snorkel-with-the-manatees charters in Homosassa are all pretty expensive.

If you can stay for a week, which I recommend, you can cut costs: A totally luxurious multibedroom beach house rental on St. George Island or even North Captiva Island will cost you less per night than a swanky single room in Naples. In a rental house, you can be even more fiscally prudent by preparing your own breakfasts and picnic lunches. Splurge on dinners.

With attractions, check their websites for free or reduced-rate days or nights. Museums tend to admit people free on Thursday nights or Sunday mornings, primarily to lure locals, but you can benefit. It's worth it to visit the local chambers of commerce or convention and visitors bureaus, not only for the information, but also for the coupons.

# Explore the Florida Gulf Coast

Pure, white, crystal quartz beaches that fade into the warm emerald waters of the Gulf of Mexico lure millions of tourists each year to Florida's Gulf Coast, a sunshine state where sandals, shorts, and sunglasses are the local attire. But Florida's Gulf Coast is much more than sandy beaches and small tropical bungalows. The larger cities on the Gulf Coast like Tampa, Pensacola, Sarasota, Naples, and Tallahassee offer all the excitement and amenities you could ask for and are about as similar as the Westminster dog show and a rodeo. In Tampa you find a bustling city with a modern skyline of glass skyscrapers gleaming in the Florida sun, and in Pensacola you find a relaxed and casual historic city that captures the spirit of old-Florida charm and Southern hospitality.

When you look at it all, though, I have to say the best place to go on the Gulf Coast is out on the water. On the water is where life is happening on the Gulf Coast. Whether you are sunbathing on Pensacola Beach with a piña colada in your hand, swinging the club on a beautiful waterfront golf course in Naples, body surfing alongside a giant winged manta ray, shopping at upscale oceanfront boutiques in St. Petersburg, collecting fresh scallops in the spring-fed waters of Apalachicola Bay, exploring the winding maze of mangrove islands in Everglades National Park, sailing a yacht through the canals of Tampa, or sitting down to a dinner of fresh crab cakes, raw oysters, and a bowl of seafood gumbo, you are experiencing the Florida life that so many have come to love, enjoy, and return to year after year. This is the life on Florida's Gulf Coast: a life with sand between your toes, sunshine, and adventure, in a state whose true borders extend far beyond land and reach deep into the dark blue waters of the Gulf of Mexico.

Pensacola Beach's pristine white sands are perfect for a lazy day by the water.

# ▶ THE BEST OF THE FLORIDA GULF COAST

In the late 1800s Harriet Beecher Stowe described her home state of Florida as "a tumble-down, wild, panicky kind of life—this general happy-go-luckiness which [is] Florida." I don't know about the panicky, but the rest of it nails why so many Americans have made regular pilgrimages to the Sunshine State since before Stowe was born—Florida represents freedom and possibility, the final American frontier. But even along the Gulf Coast, much of that frontier has been prettified, codified, condo-fied. Where's Stowe's Florida?

You can still find it traveling from the Nature Coast to up around the Big Bend all the way to Apalachicola. Nature seems more natural, historic sites less mediated and sanitized for tourists. These "Real Florida" allures are really the best and most distinctive the area has to offer.

## Day 1

Start your tour in the capital city of Tallahassee, spending a day at the Old and New Capitols, driving the city's fabled canopied roads, maybe eating a little barbecue or fried fish and sweet iced tea. After you're satisfied and full, drive due south of the city for 15 miles on Highway 363 to Wakulla Springs State Park. Nestled amongst a pristine forest lush with tropical plants and animals you'll find an amazing blue-water spring feeding clear, clean water into the Wakulla River. Take the glass-bottomed boat tour of what is said to be the world's largest and deepest freshwater springs. Then settle in for the night at the historic Wakulla Lodge. The springs were also the location for shooting *Creature from the Black Lagoon* and a couple of Tarzan movies. So just for fun, find a vine and swing on it while beating your chest and yelling as loud as you can.

## Day 2

Continue south on Highway 363 a few miles and take a right onto U.S. 98, heading west for 60 miles. You'll drive through the fishing town of Carrabelle and the oystering town of Eastpoint. Continue west to Apalachicola and try a dozen oysters on the half shell with a squirt of fresh lemon juice, cocktail sauce, and a heap of horseradish. Then take the historic home walk around downtown Apalachicola for a tour of antebellum, Greek Revival, and Victorian homes on wide, tree-lined streets. You could stay at one of Apalach's historic inns, but better to get back in the car and head over the new St. George Bridge to St. George Island. Word of its first-class fishing and fabulous beaches has not been disseminated widely, which means much of the year you'll be

pitcher plants in Apalachicola

sunset over the water and an old fishing house in Cedar Key

walking alone in the 1,900-acre beachfront St. George Island State Park. The island has hundreds of beach house rentals, many of the homes large enough for family reunions or large group gatherings and also an incredible campground, if this is more your style.

## Day 3

Feeling rested and mellow, cross back over onto the mainland and head back east the way you came on U.S. 98, maybe taking a quick jog out of your way to see the sweet towns of Sopchoppy and Panacea. You'll drive about 95 miles along U.S. 98 as it skirts the Big Bend and joins with U.S. 19 at the town of Perry. Now head south along the Florida peninsula for 28 miles and drive eight miles west to the coast along Highway 51. The town of Steinhatchee has long been renowned in fishing circles for its trout and redfish. Splurge a little and stay at the nicest place in town, the Steinhatchee Landing Resort, then figure out if you're going to go fishing offshore for black grouper or amberjack or stay closer in for redfish in the grass flats. If you visit between

July 1 and September 10 you can try your hand at scalloping. It's also nice to just drift in a canoe along the Steinhatchee River.

## Day 4

Next stop is Cedar Key. It's not far as the crow flies, but you have to head back inland on Highway 51 for eight miles, go south on U.S. 19 for 45 miles, then cut back out west to the coast on Highway 24 for 21 miles. The town is actually a constellation of tiny islands that juts three miles out into the Gulf of Mexico, its downtown a collection of weathered wooden buildings up on stilts. What to do: fish, kayak, hike, sit. Cedar Key's lack of fancy attractions is part of its attraction.

Finish up your trip by swimming or snorkeling with the West Indian manatees in Homosassa or Crystal River, both towns about 40 miles south along U.S. 19. Snorkel or just splash around in the warm waters of Kings Bay in Crystal River or the Blue Waters area of the Homosassa River, observing these endangered marine mammals that also seem inexorably drawn to "Real Florida."

## SOAK IT ALL UP

Sponge diving had been a family business in Greece at the end of the 19th century, with naturally adept swimmers assisted by rubber suits and heavy copper helmets to which air was pumped via hose. John Corcoris brought the apparatus to **Tarpon Springs** around 1900 and persuaded friends and family, sponge divers all, to relocate from Greece to this little Florida backwater. Tarpon Springs was the largest U.S. sponge-diving port in the 1930s, but a sponge blight and new synthetic sponge technology caused business to dry up. The town is still more than a third Greek, and sponges are everywhere. It's well worth an afternoon of your time.

### SPONGEORAMA
A little down at the heels, the shop/attraction has mannequins dressed as sponge divers and shows an old crackly movie called *Men and the Sea*, which you view before wandering around the little sponge museum with dioramas of sponge-diving history (one gory diorama depicts a diver dying of the bends — kids hang out for a long time in front of this one). Spongeorama is located at 510 Dodecanese Blvd., 727/943-2164, and is open 10:30 A.M.-6 P.M. Monday-Saturday and 11:30 A.M.-6 P.M. Sunday. Admission is free.

natural sponges in Tarpon Springs

### ST. NICHOLAS BOAT LINE
If you're still angling for more sponge action, this boat line offers a fun 30-minute narrated boat cruise through the sponge docks, with its own sponge-diving demonstration. St. Nicholas is located at 693 Dodecanese Blvd., 727/942-6425. Cruises are $6 for adults, $2 for children 6-12, and free for kids under 6.

## ▶ BEST BEACHES

Some people say "You see one beach, you've seen 'em all." Well, not on the Gulf Coast of Florida. Most Gulf Coast beaches are entirely unique. There is a diverse amount of sand types, sealife, and natural settings and an equally wide range of waterside activity. In Florida you'll also find an extremely large number of barrier islands off the coast of the mainland. Many times these barrier islands are very thin and in a few minutes time you can walk from the beaches of the Gulf Coast to the beaches on the bayside, two very different and equally interesting and beautiful environments.

### Day 1
Start in Naples at Naples Municipal Beach & Fishing Pier, an urban downtown beach that fronts Naples's famous Millionaires' Row. At the center of the gorgeous strand a 1,000-foot structure juts into the Gulf, a pier that has been knocked down and built again,

in 1910, 1926, and 1960. It's really the heart of downtown Naples, a short walk from restaurants, shopping, and entertainment.

## Day 2

The next day, head north on U.S. 41 (the Tamiami Trail) for 10 miles, then take County Road 865 northwest for 14 miles into Lee County and try two of the best beaches on the same day. At Lovers Key State Park in Fort Myers Beach on Estero Island, walk or take a tram through a bird-filled forest of mangroves to a gorgeous, unspoiled beach occupying four little barrier islands. The park offers 90-minute sunset ecotours most days, on which you'll see roseate spoonbills and snowy egrets. Lover's Key is a serious shelling beach for those in the know.

The same can be said of Cayo Costa State Park, known for its lack of people and abundance of starfish, conchs, and sand dollars. Accessible only by passenger ferry or private boat, Cayo Costa in Lee County is the least-visited state park in Florida. It may be you all by yourself on this 2,132-acre barrier strip of sand, pine forest, oak hammock, mangrove swamp, and grasslands.

Beachcombing on Cayo Costa yields serious shell treasures.

## Day 3

Get up early the next day and do it all over again, only this time farther north in the St. Petersburg/Clearwater area. You'll drive 100 miles north on fast and easy—but scenery-free—I-75, then cut over to I-275 in Tampa and head north to reach Pinellas County. Caladesi Island State Park in

The beaches at Fort De Soto Park are a favorite among campers and day-trippers alike.

# GONE FISHIN'

From sea bass to billfish, stone crabs to blue crabs, and redfish to red snapper, there are many popular species of fish to hook in the Gulf and surrounding waters. You can fish for some species year-round in Florida, but most fish generally run during specific months and the peak fishing season shifts out of the summer months and into the spring, fall, and winter the farther south you go. In north Florida from Pensacola to Cedar Key, the best season for fishing runs April to October. Once you reach the Everglades, the peak season runs from October to March.

The Gulf Coast offers some of the best fishing in the entire state with the cities of Pensacola, Destin, Apalachicola, Cedar Key, Sarasota, and Everglades City drawing fishing enthusiasts from all over the world. So grab your polarized sunglasses and a camouflage visor (just to fit in better with the locals) and reel in the fun on Florida's Gulf Coast.

## PENSACOLA

Fish offshore for snapper, grouper, triggerfish, and amberjack or head into deeper waters in search of blue marlin, white marlin, tuna, wahoo, and mahi. For exceptional **pier fishing**, try your luck at the **Bob Sikes Fishing Bridge** that used to connect Pensacola with Gulf Breeze and the **Pensacola Beach Fishing Pier.**

## DESTIN

Offshore **deep sea fishing** dominates the Destin area. Known as the **"World's Luckiest Fishing Village,"** Destin is lucky indeed – its position on the Gulf Coast places it closest to the **100-Fathom Curve,** where the sea shelf abruptly drops and provides habitat for deep sea fish species. Red snapper, grouper, amberjack, king mackerel, sailfish, and blue marlin are the favorite target species from Destin.

## APALACHICOLA

The **oyster** is king in the Apalachicola area. A combination of nutrient-rich and spring-fed waters has made Apalachicola Florida's capital for harvesting oysters. Charter services, primarily embarking from downtown Apalachicola, offer oyster harvesting trips as well as exceptional **flats fishing** in Apalachicola Bay and **offshore fishing** in the Gulf of Mexico. Speckled trout, flounder, tarpon, and redfish are popular catches in the flats and bays. Cobia, mahi, and snapper are easy to hook in the Gulf of Mexico and **scallops** are harvested around Apalachicola from July to September.

## CEDAR KEY

**Redfish** and **speckled trout** are abundant in the shallow waters surrounding **Cedar Key.** The island-dotted bay is not very well marked and can be hard to navigate without a guide, but the fishing in this area is legendary. **Cobia, mackerel, grouper,** and **snapper** are the usual suspects when fishing offshore in the Gulf.

## SARASOTA

There's not much need to go offshore when the inshore fishing for **snook,** redfish, trout, pompano, and bluefish around **Siesta Key, Longboat Key,** and **Sarasota** is so good. The narrow and winding mangrove channels in this area give inshore **fly fishing** and light tackle trips a wilderness backcountry feel. Offshore trips mostly target grouper, amberjack, and snapper.

## THE EVERGLADES

Fishing the sheltered waters and mangrove islands throughout **Everglades National Park** and surrounding **Everglades City** is one of the most rewarding and unique fishing experiences to be had in the entire state of Florida. Snook, redfish, trout, and tarpon are popular targets in the Everglades, and Everglades City is regarded as the capital for harvesting **stone crabs.** The season for collecting the juicy clawed crabs runs from October to May.

Clearwater Beach and Fort De Soto Park in St. Petersburg often make people's lists of top beaches in the world.

## Day 4

Today it's another road trip to the north, this one nearly five hours as you traverse the Nature Coast and around Florida's Big Bend to the Panhandle, which itself is essentially a long, uninterrupted stretch of perfect beach. With Apalachicola as your home base, you can visit St. Joseph Peninsula State Park and St. George Island State Park on the same day, the former a trip over a causeway west off Highway 30 in Port St. Joe, the latter over a bridge in Eastpoint on U.S. 98 onto St. George Island.

## Day 5

Drive another three hours west on U.S. 98 and finish your tour of Gulf Coast beaches on Pensacola Beach, at the pristine beaches of the National Seashore with nearly seven miles of preserved beach and wilderness between Pensacola and Navarre. The National Seashore's allure includes great fishing in the Gulf and Pensacola Bay, a hiking trail through beautiful dunes, and a fantastic paved bike and running trail along the Gulf front road for the length of the park.

# ▶ TOP TENT AND RV CAMPGROUNDS

Florida has some of the best campgrounds in the country and a few of them are right on the Gulf. So whether you're a tent-staking, fire-making, s'mores-eating, backcountry-camping purist or a modern-day road warrior coasting the coast in a 40-foot RV with a hot tub and gourmet kitchen, these campgrounds will accommodate and appease you with their range of amenities, natural beauty, and proximity to some of the best beaches on the Gulf Coast.

Siesta Key, home to Turtle Beach Campground

# FOR THE BIRDS

It's an exciting time for birders in Florida. The **Great Florida Birding Trail** (GFBT) is a 2,000-mile trail through the state, its numerous sites selected for their excellent bird-watching or bird-education opportunities. The trail is split into four sections – the east, the west, the Panhandle, and South Florida – and trail maps can be downloaded from the GFBT website (www.floridabirdingtrail.com). Even if you focus your energies on the western or the Panhandle sections of the trail, there's too much area to cover in a single trip. Pick a smaller section of either one, or play it fast and loose and hit a few spots in each, like these.

## LOWER SUWANNEE NATIONAL WILDLIFE REFUGE

The Lower Suwannee National Wildlife Refuge extends north and south along the Gulf Coast from the Nature Coast town of Suwannee and is one of the largest undeveloped river delta-estuarine systems in the United States. The refuge headquarters is on Highway 347, 16 miles west of U.S. 19, with a nearby river trail and boardwalk from which to see migratory songbirds. Citrus County is home to 250 bird species, with red-cockaded woodpeckers, Bachman's sparrows, American white pelicans, and Florida scrub jays among the more rare. The county has its own birding website at www.citrusbirdingtrail.com.

## CEDAR KEY SCRUB STATE RESERVE

You can see a more dense concentration of Florida scrub jays at Cedar Key Scrub State Reserve, one of the fastest-disappearing habitats in Florida. The park has 12 miles of marked walking trails. Also in Cedar Key, the **No. 4 Bridge and Fishing Pier** affords great views of the tidal flats in the channels between the islands, flats in which you're likely to see snowy egrets, great blue herons, white ibis, terns, gulls, shorebirds, black skimmers, and brown and white pelicans.

## SANIBEL ISLAND

Once on this island in Lee County, you can do a little birding warm-up, looking for some of the many resident bird species. You'll find rare

The Gulf Coast is a bird lover's paradise, with 500 bird species, including a number of species of egrets.

white pelicans hanging out in Pine Island Sound and ospreys and eagles nesting on telephone poles above the bike paths and along Sanibel-Captiva Road. The lighthouse area of Sanibel is a good place to see birds, as are the mangrove islands off Pine Island Sound, as is Tarpon Bay on Sanibel.

You're going to hit pay dirt at **J. N. "Ding" Darling National Wildlife Refuge,** which takes up half of Sanibel Island. It's serious birder territory; everyone is equipped with high-powered binoculars and huge camera lenses. There's a naturalist-led tram ride on which you're bound to see rare species, colorful species, important life-list species. There are more than 238 species in the refuge, among them tricolored and little blue herons, black-crowned night herons, ibis, wood storks, peregrine falcons, roseate spoonbills, and anhingas. The best time to go is early morning, about an hour before or after low tide.

## Grayton Beach State Park

This beautiful campground puts you right in the heart of the incredible beaches of Walton County. You won't have to rough it out here, though, because the idyllic New Urbanist villages of Seaside and Watercolor are right down the road. After spending the day sunbathing and relaxing on the perfect, bright white beaches of the state park, you can meander over to Seaside for an escape to a casual pedestrian wonderland of upscale seafood restaurants, high-fashion shopping, and a little bit of coastal nightlife fun. If you're not into including all that comfort and city life in your camping trip, the park has miles of hiking trails and beaches to explore. The campground has 34 sites that can accommodate tents or RVs.

## St. Joseph Peninsula State Park

This is one of my favorite parks in the state. The two campgrounds at the park are located right on the Gulf. The extensive boardwalk that connects the two campgrounds gives you an opportunity to explore all of the ecosystems represented in the park and the miles of beach that stretch to the tip of the peninsula can keep you intrigued for days. The park has some of the largest sand dunes anywhere on the Gulf Coast and the fishing, crabbing, and scalloping in Apalachicola Bay is out of this world. The park has backcountry camping throughout the peninsula and 119 campsites. I recommend camping in the Shady Pines campground, which offers private campsites surrounded by stands of pine trees and separated by strips of thick shrubs and palmetto ferns.

## Turtle Beach Campground

The golden rule of real estate is location, location, location, and the same should be said for campgrounds on the Gulf Coast. And for location, Turtle Beach Campground

camping under the stars in the Everglades

has all the competition beat. It is right on the Gulf in incredibly beautiful Siesta Key. What more could you ask for? The campground may be small, but the 40 campsites are well designed with fences providing a bit of privacy and noise reduction between the sites. About a block away is the public beach access point, and the campground is a short drive to the city center, with plenty of fun restaurants, bars, and shops to keep you entertained. The park even has Wi-Fi for all of the sites, so this isn't roughing it by any means.

## Fort De Soto Park

As you get past Tampa, finding a decent place to camp becomes increasingly difficult. There are quite a few places you can get to by ferry or boat, but this isn't going to help RV campers very much. One exceptional anomaly is Fort De Soto Park, run by Pinellas County. Fort De Soto Park has a whopping 236 campsites, with

86 reserved for tent, van, or pop-up campers only. The park is over 1,136 acres and is made up of five interconnected islands. It has miles of beautiful white sand beaches and hiking trails, a sprawling fort area to explore, 13 artificial reefs to dive and snorkel, and a large network of paddling trails. The park is just off the coast of St. Petersburg, if you find yourself in need of an escape to the city, and just south of all the urban beach excitement of St. Pete Beach.

## Everglades National Park

The Everglades is the granddaddy of camping on the Gulf Coast. The Flamingo campground is a little isolated from anything else on the coast, being 38 miles from the entrance to the park in Everglades City, but it is the best choice for RV and tent camping in the area. It gives you access to the surrounding national park from its 234 drive-in sites and 64 walk-in sites. The campground is open all year, but I recommend visiting between October and March. The other parts of the year are too hot and buggy. Park ranger–guided canoe and kayak tours launch from the campground, which is equipped with showers and restrooms, a marina store and gas station, bike rentals, and a visitor center with a museum.

# ▶ KIDS' STUFF

A family vacation on the Gulf Coast should start in Tampa—first, because it boasts a big, easy airport with lots of flights; second, because it's only an hour away from Walt Disney World and all the other excitement in Orlando; and third, it's where Busch Gardens is!

## Day 1

Tampa really has family fun dialed. First stop, as I said, must be a day at Busch Gardens for a ride on the Montu, the SheiKra, the Kumba, the Python, and the tooth-rattling Gwazi, in descending order of priority. It's a park for all ages, with a mix of big, scary coasters and cool animal attractions.

## Day 2

Right across the street from Busch Gardens is Tampa's Museum of Science and Industry (MOSI), probably the best science museum on the Gulf Coast. It's nearly impossible to see this the same day as Busch Gardens, so visit MOSI on your second day, and spend the other half of the day wandering at either the Florida Aquarium (with a stop-off for lunch across

A family favorite along the Gulf Coast is a day at Busch Gardens in Tampa.

the street at the portside dining/entertainment complex of Channelside Bay Plaza) or the Lowry Park Zoo. Both of these attractions are midsize, thus very walkable and requiring less

Kids will find plenty of water activities along the Gulf Coast.

than four hours to fully explore. Before you get out of Tampa, take one of the aquarium's Wild Dolphin Ecotours out into the bay to eagle-eye dolphins, manatees, and migratory birds.

## Day 3

Start heading north along the coast on U.S. 19. Get excited about seeing the manatees (submerged mammalian cows with flippers), but before that, stop off and visit the mermaids (about an hour north of Tampa on U.S. 19). Some people insist that Weeki Wachee Springs is pure camp and nostalgia, but I think those mermaids put on a good show. The show is brief, and afterward the family can cool off at the attached Buccaneer Bay water park, fed by a natural spring. This is a warm-up for the manatees, about another 30 miles north on U.S. 19.

## Day 4

You may need to stay overnight in Homosassa or Crystal River to get a jump on the day. You're going to hang out with the West Indian manatee, still listed as an endangered species. From October 15 to March 31 you'll find hundreds of these gentle giants swimming in the warm waters of Kings Bay

in Crystal River and the Blue Waters area of the Homosassa River. They are herbivores, huge and playful. Manatee Tour & Dive or Bird's Underwater will take whole families out for snorkel trips with the manatees. If you find yourself and your family along the Nature Coast when manatees aren't in season, there are still good reasons to get wet. From July 1 to September 10, scalloping in Steinhatchee is lots of fun.

## Day 5 and Beyond

So far this family vacation has been action-packed. You'll need a couple of extra days to cool down—keep driving north up and around the Big Bend for 300 miles on U.S. 19/98. Apalachicola is a historic town filled with more adult attractions (antebellum homes, fine dining), so head instead over the St. George Island Bridge for a few days of fishing, beachcombing, and relaxing on St. George Island. It's very family-focused, with comfortable beach houses (many with bunk-bed rooms and private pools), biking paths the length of the island, and a tremendous 1,900-acre state park that encompasses the whole eastern end of the island.

# THE PARADISE COAST

Many people describe this part of Florida as the Paradise Coast. This is not terribly descriptive, it seems to me, as one person's paradise is another's episode of *Survivor*. And, really, the three cities that make up the paradise in question couldn't be more different. Naples satisfies more worldly tastes with upscale shopping, fine dining on Fifth Avenue, and more first-rate golf courses than you can swing a club at. A little farther south you find Marco Island, a relaxed and sunny barrier island that has become a beach vacation destination for families and other travelers who would like to be away from the bustling and expensive world of Naples. And if outdoor adventure is what you seek, head out to Everglades City and the surrounding wilderness areas. Strap some kayaks and fishing rods

to your roof and drive all the way south to Everglades National Park.

Take a luxury boat tour through the canals that make up the backyards of the multimillion-dollar homes of Naples's Port Royal, then pilot your own canoe quietly through the mangrove jungle of Big Cypress Preserve and you'll see: Paradise is in the eye of the beholder.

The Calusa people were the first to recognize paradise, settling in southwest Florida centuries before Spanish explorers found their way here. But even after the Spanish had evicted and killed off these first residents, the land lay virtually empty until the late 1800s. Survey teams brought back news of the beauty of the wilds of southwest Florida, sparking the imagination of General John S. Williams, a senator from Louisville, and Walter N. Haldeman,

COURTESY OF NAPLES, MARCO ISLAND, EVERGLADES CVB

# HIGHLIGHTS

**◖ Naples Municipal Beach and Fishing Pier:** Some of the area's top beaches here are a little more urban than in other parts of the Gulf Coast. Naples Municipal Beach features a 1,000-foot fishing pier considered the heart of the city, flanked on either side by a wide swath of beach and the length of upscale houses known as "Millionaires' Row" (page 31).

**◖ Corkscrew Swamp Sanctuary:** Head north out of Naples to this wildlife sanctuary. You'll see wood storks with faces only a mother could love and a strange plant called a Resurrection Fern that comes back from the botanically deceased (page 33).

**◖ Naples Museum of Art:** A recent addition to the Philharmonic Center for the Arts complex, the museum packs quite a bit in its three-story, 30,000-square-foot building. It features 15 galleries and spectacular chandeliers by acclaimed glass artist Dale Chihuly (page 38).

**◖ Naples Zoo:** Families visiting Naples usually find their way here, with good reason. Little ones enjoy the gator-feeding show, the Panther Glade, the big cats show, and the boat ride out to see the antic monkeys on their little islands. Parents, on the other hand, will appreciate the park's incredible native and exotic plants, as well as the adult humor of the animal handlers (page 39).

**◖ Third Street South:** Some of Florida's most upscale boutiques, antiques shops, and galleries line both sides of Naples's main drag. There's even a street concierge to help get you oriented (page 40).

**◖ Tigertail Beach:** Against the backdrop of Marco Island's tall skyline of resort hotels, Tigertail Beach draws a fun-seeking crowd. For some, fun is Jet Ski rentals and water sports, others seek a cutthroat game of beach volleyball, and still others linger equipped only with a pail and shovel (page 48).

**◖ Boat Tour to Calusa Shell Mounds:** Take a boat tour through the deep backwater with Florida Saltwater Adventures. You'll motor out through the tiny mangrove islands near Marco Island, stopping to walk around, peering to find remnants of this Native American culture (page 49).

**◖ Everglades Eco Adventures:** Paddle through the Ten Thousand Islands and part of Everglades National Park with the Everglades Rentals and Eco Adventures Company. A guide glides with you through mangrove tunnels, drifting by wading birds, rare orchids, and gators of all sizes (page 58).

**◖ Totch's Island Tours:** There are other ways to get out and explore the area's exotic "walking trees." Don a pair of protective headphones and hop aboard a backcountry or open-water airboat tour of mangrove islands with Totch's Island Tours (page 58).

Corkscrew Swamp Sanctuary ◖
Bonita Springs
Naples Municipal Beach and Fishing Pier
Naples Museum of Art
◖ Naples Zoo
Naples Third Street South
Marco Island
◖ Tigertail Beach
Boat Tour to Calusa Shell Mounds
Everglades Eco Adventures
Everglades City
Gulf of Mexico
Totch's Island Tours
0    5 mi
0    5 km
© AVALON TRAVEL

LOOK FOR ◖ TO FIND RECOMMENDED SIGHTS, ACTIVITIES, DINING, AND LODGING.

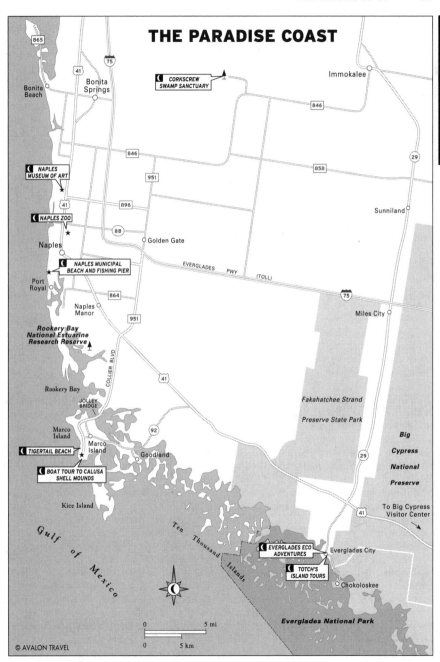

# THE PARADISE COAST

865

75

41 Bonita
Springs

Bonita
Beach

Immokalee

846

( CORKSCREW
SWAMP SANCTUARY

846

858

( NAPLES
MUSEUM OF ART

951

29

896

41

( NAPLES ZOO

Sunniland

88

Naples

Golden Gate

EVERGLADES    PWY    (TOLL)

( NAPLES MUNICIPAL
BEACH AND FISHING PIER

75

Port
Royal

864

Naples
Manor

Miles City

951

*Rookery Bay
National Estuarine
Research Reserve*

Rookery Bay

41

*Fakahatchee Strand*

*Preserve State Park*

JOLLEY
BRIDGE

*Big*

Marco
Island

92

*Cypress*

( TIGERTAIL BEACH

Marco
Island

Goodland

29

*National*

( BOAT TOUR TO CALUSA
SHELL MOUNDS

*Preserve*

Kice Island

To Big Cypress
Visitor Center

41

*Ten    Thousand*

*Gulf*

*of*

( EVERGLADES ECO
ADVENTURES

Everglades City

*Mexico*

*Islands*

( TOTCH'S
ISLAND TOURS

Chokoloskee

*Everglades National Park*

0          5 mi

0          5 km

© AVALON TRAVEL

owner of the *Louisville Courier-Journal.* The men chartered a boat and came to look, mesmerized by the miles of white-sand beaches. Not long after, in 1886, the Naples Town Improvement Company was formed, purchasing 3,712 acres between the Gulf of Mexico and what is now known as Naples Bay.

The group had big plans. The name alone says quite a bit: These founders were modeling the new Naples on the cultured and thriving Italian seaport city (heck, if you squint, the Florida peninsula even looks a little like the Italian peninsula, right?). They built a pier, blocked out plans for a city, built their own homes on the beach—and then the Naples Town Improvement Company ran out of money. It was sold at a public auction in 1890 to the only bidder, Walter Haldeman, who now owned 8,600 acres of land, the swanky Naples Hotel, the pier, and a steamship that brought guests to and from Naples. Instead of making him rich beyond his wildest dreams, Naples was more of an avocational interest, a financially draining hobby for Haldeman. In fact, in the early 1900s, the area that is now Collier County was mostly populated by feisty herds of scrub cattle that grazed the open prairies.

The city chugged on with minimal growth until rail service came to Naples in 1927 and Memphis-born millionaire Barron Collier's Tamiami Trail was completed the next year. Poised at the verge of vigorous expansion, the city's growth was quashed by the Great Depression, followed swiftly by World War II. A direct hit by Hurricane Donna in 1960 devastated Everglades City but bolstered growth in Naples—not long after the storm, the county seat was transferred from Everglades City to East Naples.

Since then, Naples has experienced an enormous population boom, mostly amongst Midwestern and northern retirees (it's funny, but every other person you meet here used to live in Chicago, Milwaukee, New York, and so forth), such that it was deemed the fastest-growing community in the country in the 1980s. It's got the look of many monied, sunny American cities (Santa Barbara, Palm Springs): lawns that seem maintained round the clock with tweezers and nail scissors, and fancy new Mercedes everywhere, their gleaming bumpers sporting "I'd rather be golfing" stickers.

As for Marco Island and Everglades City, differences go deeper. Much of Marco Island has modest, ranch-style homes built a couple of decades ago, before the Deltona Corporation began building and the island heated up as a vacation destination. The heat is focused on the beach, where tall resort hotels and condos stretch for two miles along the strand on Collier Boulevard. Vacationers (often families) may never see much of the island, their eyes focused continuously on the gorgeous warm water of the Gulf, the maze of mangrove islands just to the south, and whether their tans are even.

Everglades City and the little town to the south called Chokoloskee (chuck-uh-LUSK-ee, not chock-oh-losk-ee) are the end of civilization before you run into Everglades National Park. Some of the mystery and wildness of that park has rubbed off on these little towns, or maybe it's just that the residents are a free-spirited bunch. Hang out at the Rod and Gun Club, or paddle a kayak through the quiet tunnels of mangroves, and you'll feel like you've entered the Wild West—only with gators.

## PLANNING YOUR TIME

If you threw open the suitcase of someone about to travel the entire length of the Paradise coast, you would know it right away from the sheer variety of clothes. There would be smart slacks, polo shirts, and dress shoes or little black dresses and heels for Naples; swimming trunks or bikinis, sandals, and sunscreen for Marco Island; and an old pair of sneakers, durable zip-off outdoors pants, vented long-sleeve shirts, and an enormous can of bug spray for Everglades City and the surrounding wilderness. To travel down the Paradise Coast and comfortably enjoy all it has to offer, without sticking out like a sore thumb, you'll need exceptionally diverse attire.

Where you should stay depends on what

you're looking to do while visiting the area. Most of Naples's accommodations are considered upscale and expensive, and the ones that are not are generally overpriced for what you get compared to the surrounding areas, as are those on Marco Island. Everglades City attracts more outdoorsmen and -women and therefore most of the accommodations are simple, down-to-earth, relaxed places that are much less expensive. A couple of suggestions for romantic travelers would be dinner at a nice restaurant and a walk on the beach in Naples or a paddle trip on a kayak for two on the bayside of Marco Island, depending on your idea of romance.

Family travelers are welcomed most on Marco Island, with many of the large hotels offering programs for kids.

Peak season in and around Naples is roughly December 23–April 16. Rates for hotels reflect this, and you may save a bundle visiting instead in the late spring or early fall (when the weather in Naples and on Marco Island is really nice). Everglades City, on the other hand, is best to visit November–February. The thick heat, the wet blanket of humidity, and dense fog of mosquitoes and other insects act as a real enthusiasm damper during the hotter months in the Everglades.

# Naples

Naples has been dubbed "the Palm Beach" of Florida's Gulf Coast. With nearly 90 golf courses, Naples has one of the highest ratios of greens to golfers in the United States. Beyond the links, Naples is known for world-class shopping, dining, and a preponderance of beautiful people. Although a stroll of trendy Fifth Avenue is certainly reminiscent of the posh Atlantic Coast resort, the analogy breaks down as soon as one sees Naples's tranquil beauty, which begins just five miles out of town: the Rookery Bay National Estuarine Research Reserve (with sprawling mangroves and a high diversity of rare birds), Big Cypress National Preserve to the east, and the untamed mystery of Everglades National Park.

And then there are the nine miles of sun-soaked, white-sand beaches. A locus of sun-worshipping these days, the Naples shorefront was once populated by the Calusa people. In the late 1860s, Roger Gordon and Joe Wiggins were the area's first white settlers, drawn to the abundant fish and mild climate—a climate that was often compared to the bay in Naples, Italy (thus the name). In 1887, a group of wealthy Kentuckians, led by Walter N. Haldeman, owner of the *Louisville Courier-Journal,* purchased enormous parcels of land in the town of Naples. Quickly gaining a reputation as

a winter resort, Naples boasted a glamorous social life that revolved around the exclusive Naples Hotel, a magnet for celebrities at the turn of the 20th century.

As their first civic act, Haldeman and the Naples Town Improvement Company set to work building a 600-foot-long wooden pier in a T shape to allow large ships to dock easily. First completed in 1888, the pier was destroyed and rebuilt three times (most recently demolished by Hurricane Donna in 1960) and remains the center of the town's fishing activity.

At the western end of 12th Avenue South, locals and visitors alike congregate at the pier, but the city has a number of other draws broadly distributed around town. The shopping district on the nearby Gordon River is called Old Marine Market Place or Tin City. For more upscale commerce, walk along Fifth Avenue, between Third and Ninth Streets South, full of stylish shops, restaurants, and cafés. Not far from there, in the center of town, the 13 acres of the **Conservancy of Southwest Florida** (9 A.M.–4:30 P.M. Mon.–Sat., noon–4 P.M. Sun., $9 adults, $4 kids 3–12) provide opportunities for canoe tours and nature hikes, as well as aviaries and a serpentarium (that's a snake house). Its Discovery Center has just undergone extensive renovations, replacing the

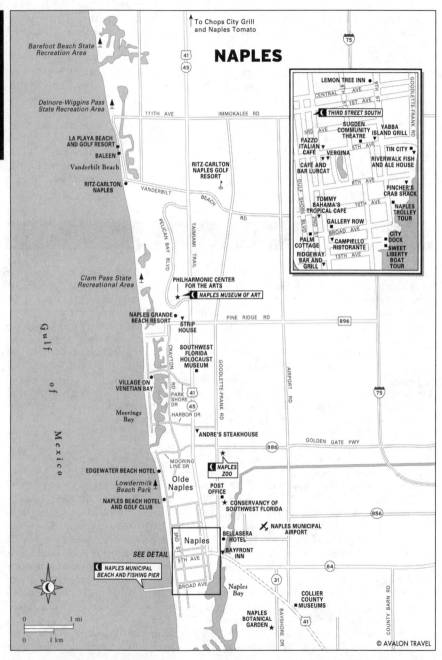

**NAPLES**

To Chops City Grill
and Naples Tomato

Barefoot Beach State
Recreation Area

Delnore-Wiggins Pass
State Recreation Area

LA PLAYA BEACH
AND GOLF RESORT
BALEEN
Vanderbilt Beach
RITZ-CARLTON,
NAPLES

RITZ-CARLTON
NAPLES GOLF
RESORT

Clam Pass State
Recreational Area

PHILHARMONIC CENTER
FOR THE ARTS
NAPLES MUSEUM OF ART

NAPLES GRANDE
BEACH RESORT
STRIP
HOUSE

SOUTHWEST
FLORIDA
HOLOCAUST
MUSEUM

VILLAGE ON
VENETIAN BAY

Moorings
Bay

ANDRE'S STEAKHOUSE

GOLDEN GATE PWY

NAPLES
ZOO

POST
OFFICE

CONSERVANCY OF
SOUTHWEST FLORIDA

EDGEWATER BEACH HOTEL
Lowdermilk
Beach Park
NAPLES BEACH HOTEL
AND GOLF CLUB

Olde
Naples

MOORING
LINE DR

BELLASERA
HOTEL
BAYFRONT
INN

NAPLES MUNICIPAL
AIRPORT

Naples

SEE DETAIL

NAPLES MUNICIPAL
BEACH AND FISHING PIER

BROAD AVE

Naples
Bay

COLLIER
COUNTY
MUSEUMS

NAPLES
BOTANICAL
GARDEN

0      1 mi
0      1 km

*Gulf*

*of*

*Mexico*

111TH AVE
IMMOKALEE RD

VANDERBILT

PELICAN BAY BLVD

TAMIAMI TRAIL

BEACH

RD

PINE RIDGE RD

CRAYTON

RD

PARK SHORE DR

HARBOR DR

3RD ST

5TH AVE

GOODLETTE-FRANK RD

AIRPORT RD

BAYSHORE DR

COUNTY BARN RD

**Inset detail map:**

LEMON TREE INN
CENTRAL   AVE
THIRD STREET SOUTH
SUGDEN
COMMUNITY
THEATRE   YABBA
ISLAND GRILL
PAZZO
ITALIAN
CAFÉ   VERGINA
TIN CITY
CAFÉ AND
BAR LURCAT   RIVERWALK FISH
AND ALE HOUSE
PINCHER'S
CRAB SHACK
TOMMY
BAHAMA'S
TROPICAL CAFÉ   NAPLES
TROLLEY
TOUR
GALLERY ROW   CITY
DOCK
BROAD AVE
PALM
COTTAGE   CAMPIELLO
RISTORANTE   SWEET
LIBERTY
BOAT
TOUR
RIDGEWAY
BAR AND
GRILL   13TH AVE

GOODLETTE-FRANK RD

GULF SHORE BLVD

1ST AVE ST
3RD ST
5TH AVE
6TH AVE
10TH AVE

© AVALON TRAVEL

aquatic touch tank and constructing a brand new Florida panther exhibit, which shows the endangered Florida panther in its natural environment.

Boosters often describe Naples as the crown jewel of southwest Florida. The jewel that sparkles brightest may just be the downtown beach, arguably the finest city beach in Florida. Accessed at the Gulf end of each avenue—the downtown is a grid, with streets running north and south, avenues east and west—the beach has ample metered parking. (The parking meters on the roads near the beach are $3 per hour and take quarters only; if you don't mind walking five blocks or more, you can park downtown for free and walk to one of the beach access points.) There you may find a loggerhead sea turtle nest, a swirl of prehistoric-looking pelicans, or any of the other lures that have made Naples a top vacation spot for the past 150 years.

## SPORTS AND RECREATION
### ❿ Naples Municipal Beach and Fishing Pier

For an urban beach experience, stroll along Naples Municipal Beach and Fishing Pier (access the pier at 12th St. and Gulf Shore Blvd., just south of downtown, 239/213-3062, open 24 hours, no fee, metered parking

© KALENKOV/123RF.COM

**Naples Municipal Beach and Fishing Pier**

near entrance). Known locally as The Pier, the 1,000-foot structure that juts into the Gulf attracts anglers, new and old (best fishing months: May–July and Sept.–Oct.). There's a bait house, fish-cleaning tables, chickee shelter, restrooms, and concessions on the pier, which was originally built in 1888 as a freight and passenger dock. The pier is a symbol of the locals' tenacity and civic pride, having been damaged repeatedly by fire and hurricanes and rebuilt in 1910, 1926, and 1960. It's perhaps the most photographed spot in Naples, the emerald green Gulf water and wide swath of beach flanking it on either side. The beach's proximity to downtown (and the stretch of fancy houses known as Millionaires' Row) makes it ideal for a moonlit stroll after dinner or even a sandy escape after an afternoon in the city.

### Clam Pass Beach Park

At the south end of Naples, you'll find Clam Pass Beach Park (at the end of Seagate Dr., 239/254-4000, 8 A.M.–sunset daily, $6 parking). Clam Pass consists of 35 acres of mangrove forest, rolling dunes, and 3,200 feet of white-sand beach. There's a three-quarter-mile boardwalk from a high-rise development through the mangroves and out to the beach. It's easily walkable (and you're likely to see eagles, ospreys, and waddling, pillbug-like armadillos along the way), but you can also take a fun, free tram that runs continuously throughout the day. Once at the beach, there are kayak, canoe, sailboard, and catamaran rentals. The water is shallow and the surf mild, a perfect combination for a family day at the beach. Clam Pass also contains a concession area and picnic pavilions.

### Delnor-Wiggins Pass State Park

To the north end of the city, Delnor-Wiggins Pass State Park (11135 Gulfshore Dr., five miles west of I-75, Exit 17, 239/597-6196, 8 A.M.–sunset daily, $6 parking, five parking areas) regularly makes Dr. Beach's (a.k.a. Dr. Stephen Leatherman of the University of Maryland) top 20 list of America's best beaches. On Delnor-Wiggins you'll find the white-sand swath

# TEE TIME

Naples isn't called the golf capital of the world for nothing. Here are the courses available to visitors, plus the driving ranges and pro shops. All of the greens fees quoted fluctuate seasonally and according to the time of day. Call ahead.

## THE COURSES

### Arrowhead Golf Course
2205 Heritage Greens Dr., 239/596-1000
Semiprivate, 18 holes, 6,832 yards, par 72, course rating 73.1, slope 130
Greens fees: $37 7-11 A.M., $28 11 A.M.-3 P.M., $22 after 3 P.M.

### Cypress Woods Golf and Country Club
3525 Northbrook Dr., 239/593-3392
Semiprivate, 18 holes, 6,330 yards, par 72, course rating 71.7, slope 136
Greens fees: $35 7-10 A.M., $28 after 10 A.M., cart included

### Eagle Lakes Golf Club
18100 Royal Tree Pkwy., 239/732-0034
Public, 18 holes, 7,150 yards, par 71, course rating 71.1, slope 122
Greens fees: $39 for 18 holes

### Hibiscus Golf Club
5375 Hibiscus Dr., 239/774-0088
Public Course, 18 holes, 6,476 yards, par 72, course rating 71.7, slope 128
Greens fees: $30 summer, $80 winter

### Lely Flamingo Island Club
8004 Lely Resort Blvd., 239/793-2223
Classics Course: private, 18 holes, 6,805 yards, par 72, course rating 72.4, slope 128
Flamingo Course: resort, 18 holes, 7,171 yards, par 72, course rating 73.9, slope 135
Mustang Course: resort, 18 holes, 7,217 yards, par 72, course rating 75.3, slope 141
Greens fees: $49-162 depending on the month for both Flamingo and Mustang courses, cart included

### Marco Island Marriott Beach Resort, Golf Club & Spa
400 Collier Blvd. S., Marco Island, 239/389-6600

Resort, 18 holes, 7,152 yards, par 72, course rating 75.2, slope 145
Greens fees: $89 7:30 A.M.-11:59 A.M., $69 noon-2:59 P.M., $39 after 3 P.M.

### Naples Beach Hotel and Golf Club
851 Gulf Shore Blvd. N., 239/261-2222
Resort, 18 holes, 6,488 yards, par 72, course rating 71.2, slope 129
Greens fees: $65 before noon, $45 after 1 P.M., $35 after 3 P.M.

### Naples Grande Golf Club
7760 Golden Gate Pkwy., 239/659-3700
Resort, 18 holes, 7,102 yards, par 72, course rating 75.1, slope 143
Greens fees: $59 before noon, $39 after noon

### Quality Inn and Suites Golf Resort
4100 Golden Gate Pkwy., 239/455-9498
Resort, 18 holes, 6,564 yards, par 72, course rating 70.8, slope 125
Greens fees: $55 before 2 P.M., $40 after 2 P.M., $30 after 3:30 P.M., cart included

### Riviera Golf Club of Naples
48 Marseille Dr., 239/774-1081
Public, 18 holes, 4,090 yards, par 62, course rating 60.4, slope 95
Greens fees: $50, $38 after 2 P.M., cart included

### Tiburon Golf Club
2620 Tiburon Dr., 239/594-2040
North Course: resort, 9 holes, 3,693 yards, par 36, course rating N/A, slope N/A
South Course: resort, 9 holes, 3,477 yards, par 36, course rating N/A, slope N/A
West Course: resort, 9 holes, 3,500 yards, par 36, course rating N/A, slope N/A
Greens fees: $280 before noon, $235 after noon, $170 after 3 P.M.

### Valencia Golf Course
1725 Double Eagle Trail, 239/352-0777
Public, 18 holes, 7,145 yards, par 72, course rating 74.3, slope 130
Greens fees: $85 before noon, $65 after noon, cart included

**DRIVING RANGES**
**Coral Isle Golf Center**
4748 Championship Dr., 239/732-6900

**Ferguson Golf Center**
9100 Immokalee Rd., 239/352-4996

**PRO SHOPS**
**Edwin Watts Golf**
3980 Tamiami Trail N., 239/403-0615

**Fix Up Stix**
1101 Sun Century Rd., 239/591-3743

**For the Love of Golf**
9765 Tamiami Trail N., 239/566-3395

**Golf Balls Galore & More**
2181 J&C Blvd., 239/597-6528

COURTESY OF NAPLES, MARCO ISLAND, EVERGLADES CVB

Greater Naples is a world-renowned golf destination.

**Naples Golf Co.**
5091 Tamiami Trail E., 239/643-5577

**Pro-Am Discount Golf & Tennis**
13000 Tamiami Trail N., 239/597-1222

framed by picturesque sea oats, sea grapes, and cabbage palms. Delnor-Wiggins is on a narrow barrier island separated by a maze of mangrove swamp and tidal creek, and it boasts a nature trail and observation tower from which to spy on the abundant wildlife. It's a superior shelling beach, and Wiggins Pass generates much enthusiasm amongst anglers. Again, the water is shallow, with a gentle slope and calm surf suitable for swimming. There are picnic facilities, a lifeguard on duty, and a boat ramp. (Caution: Stay out of the dunes and don't pick the sea grass, which is protected due to its important role as a sand stabilizer.)

## Other Beaches

Other beaches in the area would be star attractions anywhere but here, but the wealth of possibilities make **Lowdermilk Beach Park** (Gulf Shore Blvd. S., 239/213-3029), **Vanderbilt Beach** (near the Ritz-Carlton at the end of Vanderbilt Dr., 239/254-4000), and **Barefoot Beach Preserve,** also known as **Lely Barefoot Beach** (take U.S. 41 to Bonita Beach Road and head west, 239/591-8596) less popular here in Naples. All of them have restrooms

and picnic facilities, are open sunrise–sunset daily, and charge $6 for parking. In addition, Lowdermilk has lively sand volleyball courts, and Vanderbilt offers exceptional bird-watching. Barefoot boasts a learning center with exhibits on sea turtles and shorebirds, as well as a nature trail; it was ranked No. 10 among American beaches by Dr. Beach in 2006.

## ◖ Corkscrew Swamp Sanctuary

The greater Naples area offers several outstanding opportunities to explore the exotic and wild natural world of the area—easily accessible to those with disabilities, seniors, or the stroller-bound.

In Collier County, huge swaths of bald cypress forest stood until right around World War II. Logging quickly decimated most of it, with just one virgin stand of cypress left in southwest Florida—the Corkscrew Swamp near Immokalee, now Corkscrew Swamp Sanctuary (375 Sanctuary Rd. W., Naples, 239/348-9151, open 7 A.M.–7:30 P.M. daily April 11–Sept. 30, 7 A.M.–5:30 P.M. daily Oct. 1–April 10; entrance fee $10 adults, $6 college students, $5 Audubon Society members,

COURTESY OF NAPLES, MARCO ISLAND, EVERGLADES CVB

There are many secluded and private beaches tucked away along the waterways of the Paradise Coast.

$4 children 6–18, children under 6 free). It offers visitors a 2.25-mile raised boardwalk—there's also a one-mile trail if the longer one sounds daunting, and benches and rain shelters along the way—through four distinct local environments: a pine upland, a wet prairie, a cypress forest, and a marsh. Interpretive signs along the boardwalk give you the basics, but the guide-led tours are tremendous, and there's a field guide and a kids' activity book that you can pick up at the admissions desk. There's a birders' checklist and a white board for birders to jot down what they've seen for the benefit of those who've just arrived. It's also a great place to see gators and rare orchids. To get there, take I-75 to Exit 111, go approximately 15 miles, and turn left on Sanctuary Road.

## Rookery Bay National Estuarine Research Reserve

Another worthwhile day trip is to be had about 13 miles south of Naples at Rookery Bay National Estuarine Research Reserve (300 Tower Rd., 239/417-6310, 9 A.M.–4 P.M. daily,

$5 adults, $3 children 6–12, children under 6 free). Rookery Bay and Ten Thousand Islands estuarine ecosystem is one of the few pristine mangrove estuaries in North America, with 110,000 acres of forest, islands, bays, interconnected tidal embayments, lagoons, and tidal streams that are home to bald eagles, pink roseate spoonbills, and lots of other birdlife. You can explore the estuary on your own by kayak or with a guided kayak excursion through Rookery Bay's mangrove estuary (offered twice per month). There are also frequent naturalist-led one-hour historical walks (hourly at 10 A.M., 11 A.M., noon, 1 P.M., and 2 P.M. Tues.–Sat.), on which visitors learn about the mighty Calusas and the pioneering families of the Little Marco Settlement. A 16,500-square-foot Environmental Learning Center opened in 2004, with 5,000 square feet of interactive exhibits and a visitors center, four marine research laboratories, a coastal training center, and five aquaria; an authentic Seminole chickee was added in 2007. (The big fish at the entrance, by the way, is a polka-dot batfish.) The

# WALKING TREES

This area owes much of its landmass to the mangrove tree. They are often called walking trees because they hover above the water, their arching prop roots resembling so many spindly legs. The mangrove is one of only a handful of tree species on planet Earth that can withstand having its roots sitting in ocean water, immersed daily by rising tides, and that thrives in little soil and high levels of sulfides. The mangrove's hardiness is just one among its many idiosyncrasies, however.

Mangroves are natural land builders. Seed tubules about the heft and length of an excellent Cuban cigar sprout on the parent tree, drop off, and bob in the brackish water until they lodge on an oyster bar or a snag in the shallows. There, the seed begins to grow into a tree, its leaves dropping and getting trapped along with seaweed and other plant debris. This organic slurry is the bottom of the food chain, supplying food, breeding area, and sanctuary to countless tiny marine creatures. In addition, it is the foundation upon which a little island or "key" begins to take shape, this buildup of sediment and debris creating a thick

layer of organic peat upon which other plant species begin to grow. This first tree drops more seed tubules, which get stuck in the soft mud around the base of the parent tree and begin to grow. Soon, it's an impenetrable tangle of trees and roots extravagant enough to support birdlife and other animals.

Three types predominate in the Everglades and Ten Thousand Islands: The red mangrove forms a wide band of trees on the outermost part of each island, facing the open sea. The red mangrove encircles the black mangrove, which in turn encircles the white mangrove at the highest, driest part of each mangrove island (they are the least tolerant of having their roots sitting in saltwater). The mangroves' leathery evergreen leaves fall and stain the water a tobacco-colored tannic brown, but in fact the mangroves and all of the species dependent upon them do much to keep the waters clean and pure.

For all these reasons, mangrove trees are protected by federal, state, and local laws. Do not injure, spindle, mutilate, or even taunt a mangrove or face steep penalties.

coolest part of the center is the climb-in "bubble" that allows visitors to observe the many creatures that live among the roots of a 14-foot mangrove in the center aquarium.

## Big Cypress National Preserve

This part of Florida also boasts the first national preserve in the national park system, the Big Cypress National Preserve (Oasis Visitors Center, midway between Naples and Miami on U.S. 41, 239/695-1201, www.nps.gov/bicy, 9 a.m.–4:30 p.m. daily, free admission), contiguous with Everglades National Park and just about as big. The preserve encompasses 720,000 acres of the Big Cypress Swamp of southwest Florida—terrain is varied, with swamp, freshwater marshes, forests of slash pine and palmetto, and wet prairies containing abundant wildlife. But how best to investigate this vast area? There are two terrific choices.

**Hike it.** There's a public boardwalk located at the **Kirby Storter roadside pull-off** that allows you to walk into a cypress dome without getting your feet wet. If this sounds too training-wheels, the **Florida Trail** stretches across the state from Gulf Islands National Seashore through the Big Cypress National Preserve. It's wonderful hiking, which the park rangers divide into three logical sections. Part 1, **Loop Road to U.S. 41** (7.8 miles one-way) begins at Loop Road about 13 miles from its east end on U.S. 41. The other end is across from the **Big Cypress Visitors Center** (53 miles east of Naples on U.S. 41). The easy path meanders through dwarf cypress and prairies and crosses through Robert's Lake Strand (can be very wet during rainy months). Part 2, more for the seasoned backpacker, **U.S. 41 to I-75** (30 miles one-way) has trailheads on U.S. 41 near Big Cypress Visitors Center and on I-75 at the rest area at mile marker 63. A harder hike (for which you'll need to pack in all your own water), it takes you through hardwood hammocks, pinelands, prairies, and cypress. There is high-ground camping at the 13-mile mark. Part 3, **I-75 to Preserve North Boundary** (7.6 miles one-way) follows an old oil road through hardwood, prairie, and pine forest.

**Canoe it.** The park's main canoe trail begins at U.S. 41 and follows the **Turner River** until it ends in Chokoloskee Bay (about a five-hour paddle). You can also put in at the Everglades National Park Gulf Coast Visitors Center. There's another trail called the **Halfway Creek Canoe Trail,** for which you can put in at Seagrape Drive and paddle south past Plantation Island.

Big Cypress also accommodates camping, hunting, biking, and sightseeing by car. You'll need to go to the visitors center (or visit the National Park Service website at www.nps.gov/bicy) to see an informative 15-minute movie about the preserve, view a small wildlife exhibit, and pick up literature and books about the preserve.

## Naples Botanical Garden

If you would like to experience all of the incredible plant life that the Big Cyprus Preserve has to offer in a less wild and more cultivated setting, the Naples Botanical Garden (4820 Bayshore Dr., Naples, 239/643-7275, 9 A.M.–5 P.M. daily, $7 adults, $4 children 6–12) won't disappoint. It's a living botanical museum within minutes of downtown. The garden has recently expanded dramatically growing from a meager 1.5-acres to a 170 acre tropical garden. And in the fall of 2010 the garden added another 50-acres of cultivated garden and 90 acres of native preserve where you'll spot gopher tortoises and bald eagles. Also don't miss the butterfly house, history exhibitions, the great lecture series and nice garden store.

## Boat Tours

There are many ways to get out on the Gulf and Naples Bay, to wind through the Ten Thousand Islands, and to idle along the one of

the area's many rivers. Here's just a sampling of the tours to be had. The **Sweet Liberty** (Naples City Dock, 880 12th Ave. S., 239/793-3525) is a 53-foot sailing catamaran available for public tours and private charters. Departing from Boat Haven, the boat offers three tours (each $29.50 adults, $15 children): shelling tours (9:30 A.M.–12:30 P.M.), sightseeing tours (1:30–3:30 P.M.), and two-hour sunset tours. On all of the cruises, the boat is usually trailed by a playful pod of dolphins, and you'll have an opportunity to see the large homes of Port Royal.

The **Lady Brett** (departing from Tin City, 1146 Sixth Ave S., 239/263-4949, 10 A.M., noon, 2 P.M., 4 P.M., and one hour before sunset, daily, $30 adults, $15 children under 12) offers five one-hour narrated cruises daily out on the usually calm and beautiful waters of Naples Bay, and the double-decker **Double Sunshine** (departing from Tin City, 1200 Fifth Ave. S., 239/263-4949, 7:45 A.M. and 1 P.M., $70 adults, $55 children under 12) takes folks out on half-day deep-sea fishing trips (for grouper, snapper, kingfish, mackerel, and cobia) aboard a 45-foot vessel equipped with bathrooms. Rod, reel, bait, and fishing license are included, but bring your own drinks and lunch. If you want to wet a line in the Ten Thousand Islands (think snook, sheephead, redfish, snapper, and trout), **Captain Paul** (departing from Tin City, 1200 Fifth Ave. S., 239/263-4949, $70 adults, $35 children under 12) takes people on half-day bay fishing trips on a comfortable pontoon boat.

A fancier experience, the **Naples Princess** (departing from Port-O-Call Marina, 550 Port-O-Call Way, 239/649-2275, $30–60) has narrated lunch cruises and sunset buffet dinner cruises on a 93-foot, air-conditioned luxury yacht that can accommodate 149 passengers.

Or make yourself useful: The **Dolphin Explorer** (Marco River Marina, 951 Bald Eagle Dr., Marco Island, 239/642-6899, www.dolphin-explorer.com, $54) is a 30-foot catamaran that takes up to 28 passengers out for a laidback dolphin-watch cruise that is actually part of the Ten Thousand Islands Dolphin

Project, an ongoing scientific dolphin research study, the only one in the country that involves the public on a daily basis. Passengers work with a naturalist on board to identify the resident dolphin population and to catalog their activities. Dolphins are identified by their dorsal fins, as unique as human fingerprints, and if a passenger spots a dolphin not already catalogued in the study, he or she gets to name it. Cruises depart at 9 A.M. and 1 P.M. and include a stop at a barrier island for shelling and beach walking.

## SIGHTS
### Trolley Tours

A good place to start and orient yourself in Naples is with a long ride aboard a **Naples Trolley Tour** (1000 10th Avenue S., 239/262-1914, hourly 8:30 A.M.–5 P.M., $25 adults, $12.50 children). The open-air trolley has a narrated tour of more than 100 local places of note, including historic Naples Pier and Tin City. The tour itself lasts about two hours, but you can embark and disembark to explore, catching the next trolley when it suits you. Tickets are available at all boarding stops, but to get oriented you might want to begin at the Experience Naples depot, the welcome center

for the Naples Trolley, Segway and Everglades van tours offered by Naples Transportation, Tours, and Event Planning.

There are two guided Segway tours available in downtown Naples. One departs from the Charter Club Resort on Naples Bay and the other from the Experience Naples store, which is also the Naples Trolley depot. Both offer insight into the history of downtown Naples and are a fun way to get oriented to the area.

### Galleries

Collier County had 134 commercial art galleries at last count, wedged in among the shops of downtown, largely congregated along the length of **Third Street South,** on what is called "Gallery Row" on Broad Avenue off Third Street South, and along **Fifth Avenue** (many between the 600 and 800 blocks).

Naples was selected as the No. 1 small art town in America by author Robert Villani in his fourth edition of *The 100 Best Art Towns in America.* He cited the area's "amazing range of natural splendor," along with its "sophistication and serious art galleries," art fairs, community arts centers and theaters, and the Philharmonic Center complex. *American Style Magazine* also named Naples in the top 25 arts

A real draw for Naples is its art.

destinations in the United States, with good reason. Most of the galleries are found downtown, and to see the work of many local artists, stop in at the **von Liebig Art Center** (585 Park St., next to Cambier Park, 239/262-6517, 10 A.M.–4 P.M. Mon.–Sat., free admission). It houses the Naples Art Association and features changing exhibitions in five galleries.

## Naples Museum of Art

The Naples Museum of Art is the crown jewel of Naples's cultural attractions, located at the incredible $19.5 million Philharmonic Center for the Arts (5833 Pelican Bay Blvd., Naples, 239/597-1900, www.thephil.org). Museum hours are 10 A.M.–4 P.M. Tuesday–Saturday, noon–4 P.M. Sunday June–October; it's closed July–September, and open until 5 P.M. November 2–May 1. General admission is $8 adults, $4 students, but higher admission may be charged for special exhibitions. The visual arts center, opened in 2000, is a three-story, 30,000-square-foot museum with 15 galleries. Exhibits are varied and expertly curated, from a small antique walking stick show to the underwater-phantasmagorical blown glasswork of Dale Chihuly, from an Andy Warhol print show to one of the largest collections of Mexican art in the Southeast. Beyond the permanent collection and visiting shows, the space itself is a work of art with a huge glass-domed conservatory, interesting entrance gates by metal artist Albert Paley, and an impressively cool Chihuly chandelier. There are also educational programs and art lectures held at the museum—many of them sell out, so buy tickets early on the museum's website.

## Collier County Museums

Five minutes east of downtown Naples, history enthusiasts flock to the Naples site of the Collier County Museums (3301 Tamiami Trail E., 239/252-8476, 9 A.M.–5 P.M. Mon.–Fri., until 4 P.M. Sat., free admission). There are three other locations of the museum— the Museum of the Everglades in Everglades City, the Immokalee Pioneer Museum at the home of the Robert Roberts family, and the

newly renovated Naples Depot historic train station on Fifth Avenue South—but it's the Naples main museum that's worth the most time. Established in 1978, the museum offers interpretive exhibits that illuminate the history, archaeology, and development of this part of Florida, as well as a five-acre botanical park with a native plant garden, orchid house, two early Naples cottages, a logging locomotive, swamp buggies, and, somewhat strangely, a World War II Sherman tank. The museum holds the **Old Florida Festival** every year on the first weekend in March—a good time for people who like historical reenactments.

## Palm Cottage

Another walk through Naples history can be had at Palm Cottage (137 12th Ave. S., 239/261-8164, $8 donation suggested). On the National Register of Historic Places, it's the second-oldest house in Collier County, built by Henry Watterson, the editor of the *Louisville Courier-Journal*. It reopened recently after a significant facelift that includes new woodwork, a new roof, and improved landscaping. The house is one of the few remaining "tabbie mortar" structures in the area—a mortar goo made from burned seashells mixed with lime and seawater. The Palm Cottage is now home to the Naples Historical Society. Tours of the house are offered 1–3:30 P.M. Monday–Friday. (You may get a broader historical picture by picking up a copy of the pictorial history titled *Naples,* published in early 2005 and compiled by the former Naples Historical Society executive director, Lynne Howard Frazer. It contains fascinating pictures and oral histories and is available at most local bookstores.)

## Holocaust Museum of Southwest Florida

Growing out of an exhibit created by Golden Gate Middle School students in Naples, the Holocaust Museum of Southwest Florida (4760 Tamiami Trail N., 239/263-9200, www.hmswfl.org, 1–4 P.M. Tues.–Sun., $8) is another small history museum. The students collected more than 300 death camp and Holocaust artifacts, which constitute the bulk of the exhibit. Docents lead tours for individuals as well as local school groups. The museum has also embarked on an oral history project with local survivors, liberators, and others, and it installs traveling Holocaust exhibits in local schools as well.

## C Naples Zoo

Adults will be able to while away days in Naples with the sophisticated pleasures of dining, shopping, the arts, and so forth. But as every parent knows, the kids must be entertained with regularity, or mutiny is assured. The single most mutually agreeable family attraction in Naples is Naples Zoo at Caribbean Gardens (1590 Goodlette-Frank Rd., 239/262-5409, www.napleszoo.com, 9:30 A.M.–5:30 P.M. daily, $18.75 adults, $10.50 children 4–15, children 3 and under free).

It began as a botanical garden, founded by botanist Henry Nehrling in 1919. The original garden was expanded in the 1950s by Julius Fleischmann, and the Tetzlaff family introduced the rare animals in 1969. In 2004 the zoo acquired nonprofit status after local taxpayers opted to tax themselves to save the zoo land from being sold to a developer. Since then this quickly expanding zoo has been able to add a new exhibit every year.

The zoo has recently greatly increased the number of species in the presentations and has included raptors and dozens of native and exotic venomous reptiles, from diamondback rattlesnakes and Gila monsters to an African puff adder and Komodo dragon, as well as South American poison dart frogs and bushmaster snakes. Other notable exhibits are The Panther Glade and Leopard Rock, which separate you from the big cats by a thrillingly thin sheet of glass, and the three rare and beautiful Malayan tigers, the only such cats in Florida (the Naples Zoo is attempting to bring in more Malayan tigers soon).

Kids will prefer the baby alligator–feeding shows and the fossa exhibit (which the kids will instantly recognize from the movie *Madagascar*). The zoo recently shifted the alligator-feeding area from an elevated deck to a beach area, where zookeepers hand-feed the alligators, which has added more excitement and up-close action to the feedings. Be sure to catch the Planet Predator and Meet the Keeper live animal shows. Seeing these animals up close inspires a certain amount of awe, and the keepers' banter keeps the shows very entertaining. There's also a wonderful short boat ride; a fourth boat was recently added to help reduce wait times. The ride takes you past a bunch of tiny islands, from which you can view various species of primates. Recently, the zoo welcomed five young giraffes; their new exhibit is expected to open in 2012.

## Family-Friendly Attractions

If the weather is nice during your visit, which it doubtless will be, kids enjoy a round of mini golf at **Coral Cay Adventure Golf** (2205 Tamiami Trail E., one mile east of Tin City, 239/793-4999, 10 A.M.–11 P.M. daily, $9.50 adults, $8.50 children 5–11, $3.50 children 4 and under), with its exotic tropical setting featuring caves, reefs, and a waterfall. There's a snack bar, slushies, and ice cream, and a game room as well.

**North Collier Regional Park** (15000 Livingston Rd., 239/252-4000, 6 A.M.–10 P.M. daily, free admission) is a great destination for families, with eight tournament soccer fields, five tournament softball fields, an interactive playground and Calusa fossil dig play area for children, an exhibit hall with ranger-led tours, and a recreation center. For visitors, the more salient part is the **Sun-N-Fun Lagoon Water Park** (239/252-4021, 10 A.M.–7 P.M. daily during the summer, weekends only during the spring and fall, $12 for those taller than 48 inches, $5.50 for children less than 48 inches tall, free children 3 and under), with one million gallons of good times for children and their handlers. Opened in 2006, the center features water-dumping buckets, water pistols, four pools (a family pool, a "tadpole" pool for kids six and under, Turtle Cove for kids seven and up, and a lap/diving pool), and Sunny's River, a lazy river attraction with three waterslides.

Also worth a couple of hours of investigation is the Conservancy of Southwest Florida's **Naples Nature Center** (1450 Merrihue Dr., 239/262-0304, 10:30 A.M.–4:30 P.M. Mon.–Sat., noon–4 P.M. Sun., $9 adults, $4 kids 3–12), just a few blocks from the Naples Zoo. The center is currently undergoing an impressive expansion, and the new center is expected to open in early 2012. Until then there are education programs and lectures on the common areas deck (11 A.M.–3 P.M.), talks about the aquatic life found in the areas bays and gulf at the touch tank (every half hour 10:30 A.M.–3:30 P.M.), and electric boat cruises through the mangrove habitat on the Gordon River (hourly noon–3 P.M. Mon.–Fri., 11 A.M.–3 P.M. Sat.). The renovation will add two new buildings, the Sugden Gomez Environmental Planning Center and the von Arx Wildlife Clinic, to the 21-acre center. Three previously existing buildings, the Dalton Discovery Center, Eaton Conservation Hall, and the Ferguson Interactive Learning Lab, are undergoing extensive renovations. The center is also completing environmental restoration work on several filter marshes on the property that will enhance Gordon River and the Naples Bay water quality. Kudos to the Naples Nature Center.

## ENTERTAINMENT AND EVENTS

The **Philharmonic Center for the Arts** (5833 Pelican Bay Blvd., 239/597-1900, www.thephil.org, box office hours 10 A.M.–4 P.M. Mon.–Fri., ticket prices and show times vary) is an outstanding venue hosting more than 400 events a year, including world-class dance, opera, classical, and popular music, and traveling Broadway musicals. The center contains a 1,425-seat main hall and a 283-seat black box theater. The **Naples Philharmonic Orchestra** (239/597-1111) performs here with more than 120 concerts per year including classics, pops, chamber orchestras, and numerous educational performances. As of 2010 the **Sarasota Opera** is in residence performing four programs with the Naples Philharmonic during the season.

There isn't any professional theater company in Naples, although the **Sugden Community Theatre** (701 Fifth Ave. S., 239/263-7990) is home to the 40-year-old **Naples Players,** a fairly amateurish community theater troupe that stages around 14 musicals, comedies, dramas, and children's productions annually (it also hosts a program called KidzAct with musical theater workshops for kids). The Sugden also screens a "Films on Fifth" series, mostly independent and art house films.

And for mainstream movies, head to the 20-plex **Regal Hollywood 20** (6006 Hollywood Dr., 239/597-9494), the **Towne Centre 6 Theater** (3855 Tamiami Trail E., 239/774-4800), **Pavilion Cinemas** (833 Vanderbilt Beach Rd., 239/596-0008), or **Marco Movies** (599 Collier Blvd., Marco Island, 239/642-1111), where you can dine on Greek salad, beer, or wine with your movie popcorn.

## SHOPPING

Of anyplace along the Gulf Coast of Florida, Naples really stands out as a top-notch shopping destination. Comparisons are often made to Rodeo Drive and some of the United States' other prime shopping spots, but Naples may win for sheer diversity.

### ◖ Third Street South

Third Street South is where to start, with exquisite clothing and giftware shops, chic restaurants, and dozens of galleries. Just a couple of blocks from the beach and Naples Pier, the street was Naples's real core at the turn of the last century. Don't know where to begin? Consult the **street concierge** (1203 Third St. S., 239/434-6533, 10 A.M.–6 P.M. Mon.–Sat., noon–5 P.M. Sun.) located just opposite the Fleischmann Fountain for help navigating the area's shops and restaurants.

### Fifth Avenue South

Not far from there, Fifth Avenue South (239/435-3742) is another huge draw. Seminoles once sold their crafts from a stand on Fifth, and before that Calusas used this area as a canal connecting Naples Bay with the Gulf. The Ed

**Fifth Avenue South is an upscale shopping and dining destination in Naples.**

Frank Garage was the first commercial building—erected in 1923—and growth puttered along organically for decades (maybe a hardware store, then a gas station). Then, as in so many cities around the country, the birth of the mall heralded the death of downtown.

In 1996, savvy civic planners had Fifth Avenue South join the Florida Main Street Program, and a master plan was created with the help of Miami urban planner Andres Duany. The upshot was that dilapidated one-story storefronts were razed and replaced with sleek Mediterranean two- and three-story buildings (with room for people to live above). Today, Fifth Avenue encompasses 12 blocks and 50 buildings (including the Bayfront and Tin City shopping and dining complexes), with such a crafty mix of shops, dining, and nightlife possibilities (as well as a strange preponderance of brokerages and realties) that the length of it is busy at most hours. There is free street entertainment the second Thursday of the month during Evenings on Fifth, tucked at intervals along the banyan- and flowering poinciana–bedecked avenue.

### Village on Venetian Bay

Equally fancy-pants is the Village on Venetian Bay (4200 Gulf Shore Blvd., 239/261-6100), with a kind of Venetian canal-side vibe. You'll find lots of independent clothing boutiques (plus familiar faces like Sunglass Hut, White

House/Black Market, and Chico's), a couple of high-end shoe stores, a handful of restaurants (plus Ben & Jerry's), and some home interior shops.

### Tin City

More overtly touristy, but really fun, Tin City (U.S. 41 E at Goodlette Rd., 239/262-4200, www.tin-city.com), at the eastern end of downtown, was built in 1976 on the site of a 1920s clam- and oyster-processing plant. It incorporated the crusty waterfront buildings, with oodles of rustic maritime charm, into a shopping emporium (surf shop, bikini shop, and plenty of Jimmy Buffet–themed items) with a few restaurants (Riverwalk Fish & Ale House, Pincher's) worthy of your money. The Naples Trolley drops you right here, and it's an easy walk from Fifth Avenue South.

### Waterside Shops

The Waterside Shops (5415 Tamiami Trail N., in Pelican Bay, 239/598-1605, www.watersideshops.com) are anchored by huge draws such as Saks Fifth Avenue, Nordstrom, Tiffany & Co., Gucci, Coach, Hermès, Polo Ralph Lauren, MaxMara, Pottery Barn, Banana Republic, and the like. It's a classic, high-end mall with covered walkways and restaurants like California Pizza Kitchen.

### Other Shopping Areas

Before you start getting fatigued by all this shopping, let me put in a word for the boutiques along the **Dockside Boardwalk** (corner of 11th St. and Sixth Ave. S) and **Crayton Cove** (at the historic City Dock, off 10th St.). If you need a good old-fashioned JCPenney or Sears to offset all the glitz, there's the **Coastland Center Mall** (1900 Tamiami Trail N., 239/262-2323), with Macy's, Dillard's, and new restaurants including Kona Grill, Ruth's Chris, and the Cheesecake Factory.

## ACCOMMODATIONS
### Under $150

My favorite midpriced hotel in Naples is the ◖ **Lemon Tree Inn** (250 Ninth St. S.,

239/262-1414, www.lemontreeinn.com, $89–199). The owner recently remodeled the 35 rooms, adding new carpeting, linens, and bedroom furniture. Some rooms have mahogany four-poster beds. There's a sweet little gazebo and swimming pool surrounded by lush tropical landscaping, where breakfast is served each morning. But the real draw is the people—the owner is incredibly warm, as are all the people he employs. It has an Old Florida charm married with a sophisticated Naples aesthetic and an ideal location in the heart of downtown Naples. Just around the corner is the upscale dining and shopping district of Fifth Avenue. A short walk past the galleries, boutiques, and beautiful homes will take you to the happening beach hangout surrounding the Naples Municipal Pier. There's even free lemonade in the office, very thirst-quenching after a long day of beach-bumming.

In terms of other decent midpriced options, **The Holiday Inn Naples** (3837 Toll Gate Blvd., 239/348-1700, $85–145) is in a good location with pleasant rooms, a nice pool, and easy access to the beach and shopping; **Bayfront Inn on Fifth** (1221 Fifth Ave. S., 239/649-5800, $95–325) has spacious rooms, tropical decor, a very central location, and a full-service marina; and **Hampton Inn** (2630 Northbrooke Plaza Dr., 239/596-1299, $125–175) is off Exit 111, closer to I-75 and Corkscrew Sanctuary Swamp.

## Over $150

Where to even begin? Naples is lousy with luxury hotels—so much so, in fact, that the Ritz-Carlton boasts not one property, but two in town. Once you enter the luxury accommodation price point, where to stay depends largely on your priorities. If you want an urban experience, so you can roll out of bed and be wandering the downtown shops within minutes, consider ▌ **The Inn on Fifth** (699 Fifth Ave. S., 239/403-8777, www.naplesinn.com, $150–200), a boutique hotel filled with Mediterranean charm. The 87 rooms are beautiful, with sliding French doors to a balcony or terrace. The common space features splashing fountains, courtyards, and nice gardens—all at the center of downtown. The inn features the Asian-influenced **Spa on Fifth.**

On a slightly more residential street downtown, the **Trianon Old Naples** (955 Seventh Ave. S., 239/435-9600, www.trianon.com, $220–500) is another small luxury hotel with a pool, a lounge, off-street parking, and complimentary continental breakfast served in the lobby (although there's no on-site restaurant, thus no room service). The 55 roomy guest rooms and three large one-bedroom suites have all the usual fine amenities with balconies, multiline phones, computer data ports, and easy access to Tin City and Fifth Avenue South.

The **Bellasera Hotel** (221 Ninth St. S., 239/649-7333, $240–475) was named one of the "top 10 hidden gems in the U.S." in the Travelers' Choice awards on TripAdvisor. It features 100 luxurious studios, one-, two-, and three-bedroom suites with kitchens and spacious living and dining areas, all with bold Tuscan-style architecture and decor. It's a AAA Four Diamond award-winner just far enough removed from the bustle of Fifth Avenue to seem restful. A heated outdoor pool, fitness center, Zizi Restaurant & Lounge, meeting space, and business center round out the amenities.

If your favorite time is tee time, there are several golfy wonderlands. The **Naples Beach Hotel & Golf Club** (851 Gulf Shore Blvd. N., 239/261-2222, www.naplesbeachhotel.com, $439–600) is a 125-acre beachfront resort with 318 guest rooms and suites, on-site championship golf, an award-winning tennis center, large beachside swimming pool, fitness center and spa, complimentary kids' program, four restaurants, an open-air beach bar, and a handful of lovely boutiques. The hotel recently completed its $5 million beachfront pool complex, which includes a free-form pool, as well as a secluded oval-shaped pool for adults. This all-new pool complex follows the completion of the 319-room resort's multimillion-dollar renovation and remodeling of its guest rooms and suites in January 2010.

**LaPlaya Beach & Golf Resort** (9891 Gulf Shore Blvd. N., 239/597-3123, $225–1,000) had a multimillion-dollar makeover in 2002 that turned an already incredible property into one of the best in the area. The 189 spacious guest rooms and suites are well decorated, with goose-down pillows and Frette linens. There are extremely comfortable waffle-weave bathrobes, marble bathrooms with jetted tubs, a tremendous spa, twice-daily maid service—and there's golf. You have to drive a little over three miles from the hotel, but enthusiasts say the Bob Cupp–designed course is worth it. It's an 18-hole, par 72, 6,907-yard championship layout with a driving range, practice area, and 12,000-square-foot clubhouse.

Not to be outdone, the **Ritz-Carlton Naples Golf Resort** (2600 Tiburon Dr., 239/593-2000, $250–1,000) has received kudos from *Golf Digest* as one of the best golf resorts in North America. And in fact all of the 295 guest rooms manage to look out on the sweeping vistas of the Greg Norman–designed Tiburon Golf Club. Guests can also enjoy the amenities at the sister Ritz-Carlton in town.

And if your aim is to have sand in your bed, or at least the beach within walking distance, there are several wonderful luxury hotels that fit the bill. The **Edgewater Beach Hotel** (1901 Gulf Shore Blvd. N., 239/564-1508, $200–900) is an intimate, 126-suite boutique hotel right on the beach. All suites, the lobby, and pool deck area had a hip redecoration in 2006. It's another AAA Four Diamond property, with a deliciously edgy lobby restaurant called Coast. Guests also have dining and recreational privileges at the Naples Grande Beach Resort, its sister property.

Speaking of the **Naples Grande Beach Resort** (475 Seagate Dr., 888/722-1267, www.naplesgranderesort.com, $164–869), it was one of the area's most beloved landmarks when it was known as the Registry. This property has undergone a complete transformation in the past few years. A sweeping granite lobby leads to the new Aura restaurant and bar, complete with a South Beach–style, draped Chill Out Lounge. Naples Grande is surrounded by 200 acres of tropical mangrove preserve, with beach access and three swimming pools. The newest additions are the Golden Door Spa, the first Golden Door to open in the eastern United States, and a Strip House steakhouse restaurant.

The other **Ritz-Carlton, Naples** (280 Vanderbilt Beach Rd., 239/598-3300, $300–799) is a Mobil Five-Star, AAA Five Diamond resort, all 463 rooms with stunning views of the Gulf of Mexico. There are seven on-site restaurants, tennis courts, a 33-treatment-room spa with fitness center, two pools, championship golf nearby at Tiburon, and white sand as far as the eye can see.

If you want to totally and completely get away from it all, there's **Key Island Estate** (847/526-0154, www.keyislandestates.com, $2,000/day for up to 14 people). You get your own private island. Located on the eight-mile-long barrier Keewaydin Island between Naples and Marco Island, it's accessible only by boat and overlooks the Rookery Bay Reserve on one side and the Gulf of Mexico on the other. There's a master suite and two separate wings for additional guests, wraparound porches, huge open kitchen, and great detailing throughout. It's something to think about for weddings, corporate retreats, or big family getaways.

## FOOD

Naples has an extremely active restaurant scene that is continually evolving. It is one of those few cities that takes dining extremely seriously. It's a place where top chefs open up another branch of their namesake kitchen and green chefs fresh out of culinary college come to cut their teeth. There are lots of restaurants competing for the diner's dollar, and when there is competition as stiff as you find in Naples it means only great restaurants can stay open. Despite the abundance of great choices, in high season, you will need to make a reservation at most of the spots that have become hip for the moment.

At the beginning of May, make sure not to miss the annual **Taste of Collier** in Naples.

Here you can sample all of the top restaurants in the area as they showcase their best flavors in a one-day, family-friendly festival.

## Fifth Avenue South

There are a few exceptionally dense concentrations of wonderful restaurants in downtown Naples; Fifth Avenue has the greatest embarrassment of riches, assembled between Ninth Street and Third Street. The gamut is impressive, from trendy to fancy continental, covering a range of prices and ethnicities. The best ones are listed here from east at Ninth (the beginning of downtown) to the west as it reaches the Gulf.

**St. George & The Dragon** (936 Fifth Ave. S., 239/262-6546, 11 A.M.–10 P.M. Tues.–Sat., $14–50) isn't trying to keep up with any of the trendy places nearby. It does what it's been doing best for more than 30 years, with moody lighting, a reason to get dressed up, and nostalgic continental fare like fat escargots redolent of garlic and dripping butter, or creamy Delmonico potatoes. Nearby **Pazzo Cucina Italiana** (853 Fifth Ave. S., 239/434-8494, 5–10 P.M. weekdays, until 11 P.M. weekends, $15–28) presents diners with an instant conundrum—sit in the lovely modern dining room with its open bar and kitchen, or settle into one of the sidewalk tables through open French doors and watch the world stroll by? Pazzo makes a mean Bellini, champagne and peach nectar cocktails that are the height of festivity, and lots of elegant spins on familiar Italian dishes. Worth trying are the grouper saltimbocca and the Vincenzo, a molten chocolate cake oozing its way into soft vanilla ice cream and raspberry coulis. Practically next door is one of downtown's most happening places, **Chops City Grill** (837 Fifth Ave. S., 239/262-4677, 5–10 P.M. weekdays, until 11 P.M. weekends, $15–34). The menu possibilities might sound a bit schizophrenic, but it all works. Try the tuna three ways (citrus seared tuna tataki, shrimp and tuna sushi roll, and tuna summer roll), or an order of Mongolian beef satay with an addictive peanut sauce and five-spice apple slices, and a stacked tomato-Napoleon salad

with a precarious avalanche of Roquefort crumbles. Singles: Dine at the long food bar and you won't be alone long. Everyone's friendly, and the look of the place is hip.

A block down you'll find the other hippest, waitlist-for-miles place, **Yabba Island Grill** (711 Fifth Ave. S., 239/262-5787, 5–10 P.M. weekdays, until 11 P.M. weekends, $15–30). It's no coincidence, really, as Pazzo, Chops, and Yabba are all owned and operated by the same folks. It's an island-themed menu with items like sugarcane-skewered grilled chicken with sweet and spicy barbecue sauce, and sautéed plantain and macadamia-encrusted black grouper with rum butter sauce. Just plain good and inventive tropical fusion in an upbeat and island-inspired atmosphere.

From here, take your appetite to the more upscale **Vergina** (700 Fifth Ave. S., 239/659-7008, 11:30 A.M.–11 P.M. Tues.–Sat., $15–25). Again, there's wonderful outdoor seating in a sheltered plaza and a soaring indoor space with a long, inviting bar. The food is all familiar Italian, with a bold Caesar salad and hearty seafood pastas.

A fun and rollicking Irish hangout lies just across the street. **McCabe's Irish Pub & Grill** (699 Fifth Ave. S., 239/403-7170, $10–25) is in the lobby of the Inn on Fifth, and while the atmosphere is all jovial Irish pub (live, brogue-dripping singers, heavy on the Guinness), the food is fairly sophisticated, from a grilled swordfish with a capery lime beurre blanc to an apple-cranberry cobbler with slowly melting vanilla bean ice cream.

A recent addition to the strip, **⬛ Café and Bar Lurcat** (494 Fifth Ave. S., 239/213-3357, 5–9:30 P.M. Sun.–Thurs., until 10 P.M. Fri. and Sat., $11–32) has been knocking people's socks off with its New American cuisine and über-stylish atmosphere. It's owned and managed by D'Amico & Partners, which also owns Campiello, on Third Street. The first floor is the bar, with live music and a small plate approach, and the upstairs is the more formal dining room. The wine program is quirky and thoughtful, with good suggestions on food and wine pairings. And what food it is: pot roast braised in cabernet sauvignon with roasted veggies; foie gras with roasted pears; buckwheat crepes with smoked Kentucky ham and figs.

There are plenty of other fine choices along Fifth—walk and peer in, reading menus as you go. For a casual sandwich, coffee, or ice cream, try **Cheeburger Cheeburger** (505 Fifth Ave. S., 239/435-9796), **PJ's Coffee & Tea** (599 Fifth Ave. S., 239/261-5757), and **Regina's Ice Cream Pavilion** (824 Fifth Ave. S., 239/434-8181).

## Third Street South

Third Street South was once the central business district of Old Naples, and these days it's fairly overrun with galleries, high-end boutiques, and antiques shops. There aren't as many restaurant choices as on Fifth, but a few of Naples's absolute best restaurants line up along Third.

**◖ Campiello Ristorante** (1177 Third St. S., 239/435-1166, 11 A.M.–3 P.M. daily, 5–10 P.M. Sun.–Thurs., until 10:30 P.M. Fri. and Sat., $17–38) is a favorite around town. It's got a healthy and fresh Cal-Ital bistro approach to the menu, but the atmosphere reminds you of power-lunch restaurants of the 1980s. Bite into a spit-roasted pork sandwich with red onion and smoked mozzarella, or sample the housemade chicken sausage and gorgonzola pizza slices. The food is good and presentations are simple. The produce is very fresh and well selected and the slow-roasted meats steal the show.

A totally different vibe, but equally popular, is **Tommy Bahama's Tropical Café** (1220 Third St. S., 239/643-6889, 11 A.M.–2:30 P.M. Mon.–Sat. and 5–10 P.M. daily, $12–35). It's the same company as the clothing line, the "purveyor of island lifestyles" (who *is* this Tommy Bahama anyway?), and as one might expect this means an upscale island cuisine— great jerk chicken, tropical fruit cocktails— served under slowly rotating bamboo-blade fans and a palm frond thatched-roof. Tommy Bahama's also has live music most nights, so it's a good place to stop in for a drink (I recommend Tommy's Bungalow Brew) and lively conversation.

A longtime Naples institution, **Ridgway Bar & Grill** (1300 Third St. S., 239/262-5500, 8 A.M.–10:30 P.M. Mon.–Sat., 11:30 A.M.–10:30 P.M. Sun., $16–30) actually closed up a while back and then was reborn. Owner Tony Ridgway is something of a legend in Naples, having brought one of the first restaurants using a traditional gourmet approach to Naples 30 years ago. He owns a small cooking school as well as **Tony's Off Third** (1300 Third St. S., 239/262-7999) gourmet deli and wine shop next door; the restaurant's wine offerings reflect this close proximity, with more than 600 bottles on the far-reaching list. The food is mostly American, with a bit of French flavor here and there.

## Tin City

Tin City Waterfront Marketplace is a waterside indoor shopping center with about 40 mostly nautical-theme upscale shops and several good restaurants. The complex is on U.S. 41 at Goodlette Road. The most casual of the restaurants is **Cafe Europa** (1200 Fifth Ave S. #19, 239/262-5911, 10 A.M.–9 P.M. daily, $5–12), where you'll find good sandwiches, hamburgers, and subs at fair prices. A little more upscale is the lively **Riverwalk Restaurant at Tin City** (1200 Fifth Ave S., 239/263-2734, 11 A.M.–10 P.M. daily, $14–28), serving local seafood and classic American grill selections. And then there's the brand new **Pincher's Crab Shack** (1200 Fifth Ave S. #8, 239/434-6616, 11 A.M.–10 P.M. weekdays, until 11 P.M. weekends, $10–90), the newest location in the southwest Florida family of restaurants as famous for their fresh-caught Gulf grouper and snapper as for their cheesy crab dip. Right across from Tin City is a casual joint called **Kelly's** (1302 Fifth Ave. S., 239/774-0494, 4:30–10 P.M. Mon.–Sat., $15–25). It's one of the oldest restaurants around here, and where you'll find the city's best stone crabs.

## Downtown and Vicinity

The rest of the area's top restaurants are fairly spread out, although there's a dense concentration of fine eats north of downtown on the Tamiami Trail (U.S. 41) between about Golden Gate Parkway and Pine Ridge Road. **Andre's Steakhouse** (2800 Tamiami Trail N., 239/263-5851, 5–10 P.M. daily, $24–35) falls squarely in the luxury American steakhouse idiom. Try the porterhouse for four people, like something from the *Flintstones,* with a bottle from the wine list that contains 4,000 bottlings.

If you love French food, the French way of life, or menus that you can't understand, visit Chef Claudio Scaduto's **Cote D'Azur** (11224 Tamiami Trail N., 239/597-8867, 5–10 P.M. Tues.–Sun., $18–36). At this intimate restaurant, you'll find what you're looking for with dishes like *loup de mer Antibois* (Mediterranean sea bass) and *noisettes d'agneau peillois* (roasted spring lamb loins).

Back downtown, next to Sugden Theater, **Trulucks** (698 Fourth Ave. S., 239/530-3131, 4–10 P.M. daily, $15–34) is a newer addition to the dining scene, part of a small chain out of Texas, but the seafood is pretty darned good. Especially the crab, and there's lots of it: Northwest Dungeness crab, Florida stone crab, Alaskan Norton Sound Bairdi crab, and red king crab.

North of town almost to Bonita Springs is **Naples Tomato** (14700 Tamiami Trail N., 239/598-9800, 11:30 A.M.–11 P.M. daily, $10–30). This is the first Florida restaurant to install the self-serve, ATM-style Enomatic wine system. Just buy your wine "debit" card and sample either a 2-, 4-, or 6-ounce pour of any number of boutique wines. Opt for the classic lasagna, several signature seafood dishes,

grilled fish, or selections from the antipasti bar. The restaurant has expanded in recent years to provide more dining area and has a full liquor license as well.

## Hotel Restaurants

These are all upscale and expensive restaurants, suggesting reservations and dress attire. Starting at the top, **The Grill** (The Ritz-Carlton, 280 Vanderbilt Beach Rd., 239/598-3300, 6–10 P.M. daily, $30–55), formerly Artisans in the Dining Room, features "aged prime meats and fresh seafood paired with rare vintages." Nightly entertainment and a very cozy fireplace are attractions.

Naples Grande Beach Resort now features the **Strip House** (475 Seagate Dr., 239/598-9600, www.striphouse.com, 5–11 P.M. Mon.–Thurs., until midnight Fri. and Sat., 5–10 P.M. Sun., $35–52), created by the Glazier Group of Monkey Bar and Twenty-Four Fifth fame. The well-marbled steaks are paired with decadent sides like potatoes fried with foie gras and black truffle–laced creamed spinach.

**Baleen** at LaPlaya Beach & Golf Resort (9891 Gulf Shore Dr., 239/598-5707, 7 A.M.–11 P.M. daily, $25–40) is also a favorite among visitors and locals livin' large. The dining room has wonderful indoor-outdoor seating that overlooks a perfect swath of beach and Gulf of Mexico. The menu contains some Asian-inspired fare as well as more continental dishes: seared sea scallops with a lo mein noodle cake and charred scallion-miso butter, alongside a roquefort-crusted filet mignon with potato puree and red wine sauce.

# Marco Island

Marco Island is a beach vacation spot that especially caters to families. It is the largest and northernmost of the Ten Thousand Islands, with an average annual high temperature of 85 degrees and an average low of 65, so most of the year it's very enjoyable to be outside. Unfortunately, it doesn't have the best civic planning and development in the area; in some areas on the island the high-rise hotels block all view of the ocean for very long stretches of the coast, and there is a lack of public beach access and parking. But, Marco Island has lots going for it—gorgeous sunsets, gentle Gulf breezes, a subtropical lushness, not to mention easy access to Naples just to the north and the western gateway to the mysterious Everglades National Park just to the south. Beyond the beaches, there are several fine private and semi-private golf courses; lots of good snook, redfish, and pompano fishing; and access to more tiny, wonderful islands than you can count. Most of the residents who live on Marco reside in the low-rise, ranch-style homes on the bridge end of the island. The rest of the island is given over to a luxury-resort paradigm.

Marco Island is a family-oriented beach vacation destination.

© JOSHUA LAWRENCE KINSER

The island used to be two separate landmasses—one part of it a shell mound raised by generations of shellfish-eating Calusas. Their detritus, along with some more recent swamp dredging, yielded the current-day 6,800-acre island with its rolling sand hills, beaches, and slash pine forests. It's accessed easily from Exit 101 off of I-75, heading south on Collier Boulevard for 20 miles until you cross Jolley Bridge.

The island was named La Isla de San Marco, the Island of St. Mark, by the Spaniards shortly after they landed on these shores in 1513 (around the time the Calusa disappeared). The island's history dates back much further, though—archaeology enthusiasts and history buffs flock to the island's historic markers and wealth of artifacts. A dozen markers around town chart Marco Island history, including one of the most significant excavations in North America—the priceless Key Marco Cat, the first known North American example of a half man-half animal figurine. The cat itself is now at the Smithsonian, but the small sculpture was unearthed here in 1896 and is thought to be more than 3,000 years old (there's a replica in the historical society museum).

Despite all that ancient history, W. T. Collier is credited with founding Marco Island in 1870—the northern end was called Key Marco, the southern end Caxambas. Not too long after that it was incorporated as Collier City. But it wasn't until the 1960s, when the Deltona Corporation got big ideas about the island's potential as a resort and leisure destination, that Marco became recognizable as the place it is today. A mad scramble of residential and commercial building turned the sleepy town of a few thousand into a beachy retreat for more than 14,000 people in high season.

# SPORTS AND RECREATION
## ◖ Tigertail Beach

Marco Island boasts a four-mile crescent of white sandy beach. Not too far from the long stand of tall condominiums and resort hotels, Tigertail Beach (entrance at Spinnaker Dr. and Hernando Dr., 8 A.M.–sunset daily, parking $8) is pretty much all things to all people. There's a rental stand for water sports and toys, umbrellas, and chairs; volleyball nets that see heavy action; a concession stand, showers, and restrooms; and children's play area. You'll see little Sand Dollar Island out across the lagoon, which was Tigertail's sandbar only 10 years ago, a perfect place for shelling and sand castle–building at low tide. The 32-acre beach park is also a birder's favorite for watching shorebirds (but the bird sanctuary nearby is off-limits to visitors).

## Marco South Beach

Marco South Beach (walkway access from Collier Blvd. north of Cape Marco, sunrise–sunset daily, parking $4) is a residents' beach, which has public parking and access. This beach has no facilities but is a good place to beachcomb for Florida sand dollars, whelks, fighting conchs, lion's paws, calico scallops, and others of the more than 400 types of seashells found on the island. Be sure to leave all live shells on the beach. Pets are prohibited on Marco Island beaches.

## Fishing

Island visitors and locals surf cast for black drum and sheepshead; they take boats out in the backcountry mangrove flats to fish for tarpon, snook, and redfish; or they head into deeper water offshore for grouper, amberjack, snapper, and kingfish. A number of species in the area have gamefish status, and are thus more exotic and often the most sought after. This means redfish, snook, tarpon, bonefish, and sailfish are illegal to buy or sell (that's why you don't ever see them on restaurant menus), and many of them have very low catch limits and specific seasons. For instance, in the Gulf of Mexico and the Everglades, open season for snook (the

# THE STINGRAY SHUFFLE

It's not a dance, exactly.

It's strictly anecdotal, but Marco Island seems to have more than its share of flat, seafloor-living stingrays. Visitors occasionally step on these creatures, their winglike fins hidden in the sandy shallows. When trod upon, a stingray flips up its tail in self-defense and delivers a nasty stinging puncture with its barb. To avoid this, drag your feet along the sandy bottom (as opposed to stepping up and down). The "shuffle" may not look too swift, but it alerts stingrays to your approach. They are just hanging around the shallows to catch shellfish and crustaceans, and they'd rather not waste their time on stinging you.

If you are unlucky enough to be stung, it's important that you clean the wound with freshwater immediately (other bacteria in seawater can infect the area). As soon as you can, soak the wound in the hottest water you can stand for up to 90 minutes to neutralize the venom. The pain can be severe, often accompanied by weakness, vomiting, headache, fainting, shortness of breath, paralysis, and collapse in people who are allergic to the venom. You may want to see a doctor, who might add insult to injury with a tetanus shot.

Always report stingray injuries to the lifeguard on duty.

period of time you are allowed to harvest a fish) is now limited to the months of March, April, September, October, and November. Fish must be between 28 and 33 inches to keep, with one snook allowed per person. If you catch a snook during December–February or May–August the fish must be released alive. Don't wet a line until you've studied up on what you can catch, how many, and when.

If you want to head out fishing with an expert, Marco Island, as with much of the Gulf

Coast, has many specialists willing to show you the way. Specializing in light tackle and fly-fishing, **Captain Gary Eichler** (239/642-9779, www.marcoislandcharters.com, $395–800, depending on the boat and location) has a number of boats from which to choose, lots of experience in the area, and a fun website on which you and your trophy catch can be immortalized. He does individual private charters (no split charters) with six passengers at the most.

Captain Bill Walsh takes visitors out with his company **Dawn Patrol** (Marco River Marina, 951 Bald Eagle Dr., 239/394-0608, www.dawnpatrolcharters.com, $300 for four people for a half day), known for fishing the nearshore artificial reefs and ledges. Dawn Patrol specializes in family trips and will tailor a fishing trip to include a mix of shelling, fishing, and sightseeing so even non-anglers in your group are entertained.

Specializing in fly-fishing and light tackle angling is **Everglades Angler** (810 12th Ave. S., 239/262-8228 or 800/57-FISHY, www.evergladesangler.com, $375–950 depending on the length and type of trip), which has a number of boats and captains from which to choose, lots of experience in the area, and is ORVIS endorsed.

If you want to go it alone, **Marco River Marina** (951 Bald Eagle Dr., 239/394-2502) rents out the largest array of boats on the island including center consoles, deck boats, and pontoons. Boats at **Cedar Bay Yacht Club** (705 E. Elkcam Cir., 239/642-6717, www.cedarbayyachtclub.com) all come equipped with a bimini (sun top), plastic cooler stocked with ice and drinks, VHF radio, USCG equipment, and an easy-to-navigate color chart of the local waters. They're endlessly patient with beginners, too. Deck boats are $285 for full day, $210 for half; pontoon boats $260 for full day, $195 for half; center consoles $260 for full, $195 for half. The Marco River Marina is also the debarkation point for **Sea Key West Express** (239/394-9700, roundtrip is $119 for adults, $75 children under 12, $109 for seniors 62 and over, departs 8:30 A.M. and

5 P.M.), a three-hour cruise to Key West; this is a very affordable way to explore Key West without having to fly.

## Golf

Guidebooks all bandy about the statistic that Naples has more golf courses per capita than anywhere else. Many of these are in East Naples, and many are private. On Marco Island there are several notable private courses—**Hideaway Beach Club** (250 Beach Dr. S., 239/642-6300), **Island Country Club** (500 Nassau Rd., 239/394-6661), and others—but only a couple of public possibilities. The Marco Island Marriott's **Rookery Golf Club** (3433 Club Center Blvd., 239/793-6060), designed by Joe Lee, is an 18-hole, par-72, Scottish links–style course built on 240 acres of rolling terrain and featuring several mounds coming into play around the greens. The signature hole is No. 16, a 165-yard par 3, requiring a tee shot over water to a peninsula green. Swing tune-ups for experienced players as well as beginners' lessons are available at the Marriott's Faldo Institute located at The Rookery at Marco.

Despite its name, the **Marco Shores Country Club** (1450 Mainsail Dr., Naples, 239/394-2581) is in Naples, but very close by. The course has long, wide fairways and well-maintained greens blended seamlessly into the native mangroves and waterways of the Ten Thousand Islands. With four separate tees, Marco Shores accommodates all skill levels.

## ◖ Boat Tour to Calusa Shell Mounds

The Calusa (kah-LOOS-ah) tribe lived on the coast and along the inner waterways in this area. They were tall and fierce and regularly battled with neighboring tribes. They did not farm, but rather fished and hunted for their sustenance from the bountiful bays, rivers, and Gulf (these were so bountiful, in fact, that as many as 50,000 Calusas may have been living here at a time). They controlled much of the southwest coast of Florida, and many other tribes justifiably feared their aggression. This is all ancient history, though, as the Spanish settlers ran them off or killed them off, either actively or passively with the introduction of smallpox and other diseases, starting soon after the Spanish arrived in the 1500s. By the 1700s the tribe was wiped out, the remaining handful of Calusas purportedly lighting out for Cuba when the Spanish turned Florida over to the British in 1763.

The impact of the Calusas on the area and their unique way of life are still apparent today, however. They built homes on stilts with palmetto leaf roofs and no walls and fashioned nets from palm tree fiber to catch mullet, catfish, and pinfish. But their most ingenious work was with shells. Shellfish was a staple in the Calusa diet—then once the succulent meat was removed, the shells were used to make jewelry, utensils, spearheads, other tools, and vast heaps upon which other things could be built. Little mangrove keys, uninhabitable on their own, became homes or sacred places with the addition of a few thousand carefully piled shells.

These shell mounds are literally the building blocks for Marco Island and many of the Ten Thousand Islands. If you want to spend a day exploring the remnants of Calusa mounds, **Florida Saltwater Adventures** (239/595-7495, $270 for a three-hour trip for up to six people, $350 for four hours, $425 for five, reservations necessary) offers wonderful ecotours. Captain Alex Saputo takes small groups out on his 24-foot boat, weaving in and out of the Ten Thousand Islands while pointing out wildlife and explaining in detail the horticultural and local history. He's extremely knowledgeable about the Calusa and Seminole peoples and history, and his enthusiasm is infectious as you tramp around a shell mound, crouching to see a fat whelk shell once used as a hammerhead or other tool. And on the way back, watch for dolphins that leap in the wake of the boat—they're either playing or "drafting" off the boat's speed (even dolphin experts disagree about why they do it)—but it's about as close as you'll ever get to dolphins outside of Sea World.

## SIGHTS

History enthusiasts have a couple of tiny yet illuminating museums on-island. Marco Island Historical Society operates the **Museum at Olde Marco** (168 Royal Palm Dr., 239/389-6447, www.themihs.org, 11 A.M.–3 P.M. Thurs.–Sat., free admission) next to the oldest building on the island, the Olde Marco Island Inn. The focus is on archaeological finds of the area with an emphasis on Calusa culture. There's even a sweet life-sized diorama of a Calusa household.

The second museum, the **Key Marco Museum** (in the lobby of the Board of Realtors office, Waterway Ct., 9 A.M.–4 P.M. Mon.–Fri., free admission) covers some of the same ground, with Calusa treasures displayed prominently. But it moves forward in time to capture moments of pioneer history and early island industries, up into the 20th century. Both museums are unstaffed, but a guided tour can be arranged by calling ahead. There are also maps at the museums for a self-guided tour of Marco Island's 13 historical markers, including that of the Cushing Archaeological Site from 1895, said to be one of the most historically significant excavations in North America (it unearthed a renowned statue known as the Key Marco Cat). It doesn't take long to zip through the tour, either by car or bike, and it's a good orientation to the island.

## SHOPPING

Marco doesn't have as many upscale shops as Naples to the north, but it certainly has more shopping than you'll find in Everglades City to the south. There are a few concentrated areas: The **Esplanade** (740–760 Collier Blvd. N., 239/394-7772) is a newer development with clothing and home decor stores, a few restaurants, and a nice day spa. It's also the only place on the island with a Starbucks (and a Cold Stone Creamery). Beyond that, there's a collection of shops at the **Marco Town Center Mall** (on Collier Blvd. N at Bald Eagle Dr.) and a number in **Mission Plaza** (on Collier Blvd. across from the Hilton). Adjacent to the Olde Marco Island Inn at the northern tip of the

## CHICKEES

What is a chickee, you ask? You'll see the term a lot around here. It's a Seminole word for an open, handmade structure made up of cypress poles and a roof of palm fronds. Historically, there was an art to erecting chickees, the cypress stripped in a process called "draw knife" and the fronds nailed in a particular pattern to keep out the area's heavy rains. A chickee is now more broadly defined as any open-air structure, but usually ones in which boozing and general merriment occur.

island, the **Shops at Olde Marco** (100 Palm St., 239/475-3466) complex has a couple of boutiques, gourmet food shops, and the inn's spa and fitness center.

But for the big kahuna of shopping you have to drive just north off the island. The **Prime Outlets** (7222 Isle of Capri Rd., 239/775-8083, 10 A.M.–8 P.M. Mon.–Sat., 11 A.M.–6 P.M. Sun.) has more than 40 stores, most of them big names, with designer clothes and shoes, books, and housewares at up to 70 percent off retail prices.

## ACCOMMODATIONS
### Under $100

There's not much on Marco Island for the budget traveler. However, satisfaction is just a couple of minutes away. Goodland is a little town adjacent to Marco Island that's about a mile square and boasts a few hundred residents, mostly fisherfolk, and a bunch of down-home bars. There has been a shift toward more up-scale development in the recent years, but you can still find casual and reasonably priced accommodations at the **Pink House Motel** (310 Pear Tree Ave., Goodland, 239/394-1313, $59), a historic family-owned waterfront motel with boat docking, efficiency kitchens, laundry facilities, and the Marker 7 Marina and Tackle Shop. In a similar vein on Marco Island, but a little pricier, the **Boat House Motel** (1180 Edington Pl., 239/642-2400, www.

theboathousemotel.com, $78–290) is a little more glamorous—two stories with a gazebo and boat docks—but still really a straightforward low-rise motel.

### $100-150

**Marco Island Lakeside Inn** (155 First Ave., 239/394-1161, $95–315) has 10 one-bedroom, 2 two-bedroom units and 7 studio efficiencies located on Marco lake one mile from the beach. There is a pool area with a thatched-roof gazebo and gas grill overlooking the lake, an Italian steakhouse, and full bar on-site.

There are also hundreds of vacation rental homes and condominiums on Marco Island. Many of these rent only by the week, especially in high season, and most work out to less than $150 per night. Several rental companies have nice websites from which you can peruse properties: **Coldwell Banker** (800/733-8121, www.marcoislandvacations.net) seems to rent largely in high-rise condos, **Holiday Homes of Marco Island** (239/389-9940, www.marco-island.com) represents a number of single-family homes, and **Prudential Florida Realty** (239/642-5400, marcobeach-rentals.net) offers a wide range, from fancy high-rise condos to individual homes right on a golf course.

### Over $150

Maybe it's an "if you can't beat 'em, join 'em" mentality, but if you're going to stay on Marco Island you might as well pony up the dough and stay at one of the "Big Three." Three beachfront resorts dominate the most coveted piece of shoreline. Each has lots of amenities, good restaurants on-site, and a broad price range to accommodate different budgets.

Having experienced a $187 million renovation in recent years, the **Marco Island Marriott Beach Resort, Golf Club, and Spa** (400 Collier Blvd. S., 239/394-2511, www.marcoislandmarriott.com, $135–850) may be best suited to a romantic golf-and-pampering getaway, with more than 700 rooms and lavish resort activities and facilities, the 24,000-square-foot Balinese-themed spa, a new tiki pool, and the Rookery at Marco—the resort's newly upgraded golf course.

The **Marco Beach Ocean Resort** (480 Collier Blvd. S., 239/393-1400, www.marcoresort.com, $279–1,000) opened in 2001 with 98 one- and two-bedroom suites, a spa, upscale Italian restaurants (Sale e Pepe's chef is so exacting that he imports flour for pasta from his hometown in Italy), and a stunning rooftop swimming pool with a panoramic view of the Gulf.

And the 25-year-old **Hilton Marco Island Beach Resort** (560 Collier Blvd. S., 239/394-5000, www.marcoisland.hilton.com, $99–379) is a luxury resort that consistently wins four-diamond status and so forth for its large guest rooms with Gulf-view private balconies, lighted Har-Tru tennis courts, vast amoeba-shaped pool, and other amenities. An incredible new luxury spa opened in 2008 with spacious massage and relaxation rooms all designed in a stylish and bold Greco-Roman theme.

Right out the back door of all three hotels you can rent aqua trikes and personal watercraft with **Marco Island Ski & Watersports** (239/642-2359) which also offers parasailing, banana rides, and dolphin-watching tours on the Gulf.

For a more historic, small inn experience, try **Olde Marco Island Inn & Suites** (100 Palm St., 239/394-3131, www.oldemarcoinn.com, $90–600), a 116-year-old Victorian in the historic district. It features one- and two-bedroom suites with roomy screened lanais. There are six luxurious penthouses and a much-lauded restaurant. It's a convenient location, near beaches, shopping, and golf, and guests enjoy complimentary use of the inn's 38-foot catamaran.

## FOOD

All the times listed below reflect peak season hours. If you're dining here during the off-season, it's best to call for hours of operation.

### Casual

Originally called the Snook Hole for the wealth of snook you could catch right off the dock,

the **Snook Inn** (1215 Bald Eagle Dr., 239/394-3313, 11 A.M.–10 P.M. daily, $13–20) was first a sprawling, casual restaurant that catered to the Deltona Corporation's construction workers who built up Marco Island in the 1960s. Right on the Marco River, the Snook Inn is a fun indoor-outdoor joint with live music and long lines. Locals and visitors seem to come for the grouper and the vast salad bar with a really neat old-fashioned pickle barrel. The garden courtyard is a great locale to get creamy seafood chowder or tackle a pile of peel-and-eat shrimp (if you aren't wild about seafood, the jerk chicken quesadilla is quite good). There's docking available for more than 20 boats near the chickee.

Most of the island's other restaurants are lined up along Collier Boulevard. You'll see a lot of locals at **Bimini's** (657 Collier Blvd. S., 239/394-7111, 11:30 A.M.–10:30 P.M. daily, $10–20), who swear by the eatery's housemade bread and the Capt. Bimini's platter of broiled grouper, shrimp, and sea scallops. You can also hang with the locals while tucking into a thick-crust pizza at **Joey's Pizzeria** (257 Collier Blvd. N., 239/389-2433, $10–15).

Or browse the range of possibilities at the Marco Town Center Mall: **Crazy Flamingo** (1035 Collier Blvd. N., 239/642-9600, 11 A.M.–2 P.M. daily, $10–20) is a lively raw bar with good fish entrées, and **Susie's Diner** (1013 N. Collier Blvd., 239/642-6633, 7 A.M.–2 P.M. Mon.–Sat., 7 A.M.–1 P.M. Sun., $5–15) is the locals' favorite for breakfast and lunch. Go early for fresh housemade biscuits, waffles, pancakes, and omelettes in the morning. Lunches are a good deal as the price includes beverage and dessert.

### Upscale

**Marek's Collier House** (1121 Bald Eagle Dr., 239/642-9948, 5:30–10 P.M. daily, $25–35) gets the nod from local publications nearly every year for upscale and romantic continental dining. It's partly due to the setting—the restaurant is nestled in Captain Bill Collier's beautiful historic home—and partly because of chef/owner Peter Marek's tasteful take on rich seafood dishes. This guy is a triple gold medalist at the World Culinary Olympics—yes, there is such a thing—and his lamb chops, swordfish in green peppercorn sauce, and veal scaloppini with blue crabmeat all score a solid 9.8.

The restaurant at the **Olde Marco Island Inn** (100 Palm St., 239/394-3131, 4–10 P.M. daily, $25–35) is another expensive favorite in the area for those looking for a nice bottle of wine and a perfectly prepared steak. There are five individual dining rooms, each with a slightly different feel, so try to wander through each before settling on a table (there's also an upper dining deck that looks out over the inn's gardens).

**Arturo's Italian Restaurant** (844 Bald Eagle Dr., 239/642-0550, 5–10 P.M. daily, $15–25) opened in 1994 and serves a justifiably famous stuffed pork chop, a range of hearty pastas, and an extensive wine list.

### Dining with a Twist

Dine one of several ways aboard the 74-foot **Marco Island Princess** (departs from the marina, 951 Bald Eagle Dr., 239/642-5415, www. marcoislandprincess.com, $35–60), sister ship to the *Naples Princess*. There's the Sea Breeze lunch buffet cruise, a sunset hors d'oeuvres cruise, or a sunset dinner cruise. Head out on the luxury yacht as it glides along scenic Marco River into the Gulf of Mexico with leaping dolphins in hot pursuit. The ship itself is beautiful, as is the scenery, either by day or with a sunset casting its warm glow. The food is pretty good, but the cash bar is expensive. The ship gets busy for holidays (Valentine's Day, Mother's Day, New Year's Eve) and is often rented out for private parties, so reserve early if you can.

Marco boasts another unusual dining experience. An evening at **Marco Movies** (599 Collier Blvd. S., Ste. 103, 239/642-1111, $8–14) is the oldest date-night one-two punch in the books: dinner and a movie, but both at the same time. A small, family-owned four-screen theater, it shows first-run movies (there's always at least one family-appropriate pick) and serves food and alcoholic beverages. A sampling of the menu includes Greek salad, good sweet-potato fries, several tortilla-wrapped sandwiches, beer, wine, cocktails, and of course popcorn.

# Everglades City

In the late 1970s, there were maybe 550 residents in the little town of Everglades City—tough, independent-minded folks who mostly made their living off the Gulf waters, shrimping and fishing. In those days you were likely to see a small shack with a Maserati out front and a shiny Cessna 206 parked out on the back 40. Seeing something like that in a small sleepy town like Everglades City would send up a red flag for almost anyone, and it certainly didn't get past the United States Drug Enforcement Agency.

After law enforcement agents launched Operation Everglades in 1981, one of the biggest stings the state had ever seen, more than 125 residents were carted away in yellow school buses. The police had been watching the residents of Everglades City smuggle large amounts of marijuana up from Colombia and elsewhere through the maze of mangrove islands. And when the dust had settled, kids at the high school, carpool moms, busboys—most people in Everglades City at the time seemed to somehow be involved in the trafficking.

In fact, Everglades City seems to have a knack for attracting illegal and sordid activities. The first white settlers arrived just before the Civil War, many of them evading conscription or the law. Many of them squatted, not comfortably given the heat, humidity, mosquitoes, and awkward nature of mangrove islands (no dirt, lots of knotty roots dipping down into murky, tannin-tinged water). Farming was hard-won (tomatoes, cucumbers, peppers, Florida avocados, pineapple, and sugarcane grew adequately thanks to hard labor), but the

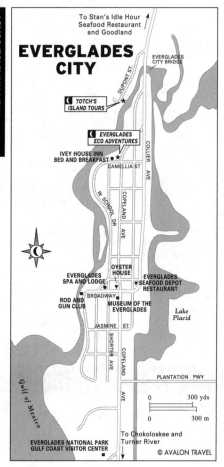

# EVERGLADES CITY

To Stan's Idle Hour
Seafood Restaurant
and Goodland

EVERGLADES
CITY BRIDGE

TOTCH'S
ISLAND TOURS

EVERGLADES
ECO ADVENTURES

IVEY HOUSE INN
BED AND BREAKFAST

CAMELLIA ST

COLLIER AVE

COPELAND AVE

W. SCHOOL DR

DUPONT ST

OYSTER
HOUSE

EVERGLADES
SPA AND LODGE

EVERGLADES
SEAFOOD DEPOT
RESTAURANT

ROD AND
GUN CLUB

BROADWAY

MUSEUM OF THE
EVERGLADES

JASMINE ST

SHORTER AVE

COPELAND AVE

Lake
Placid

PLANTATION PWY

Gulf of Mexico

0        300 yds

0        300 m

EVERGLADES NATIONAL PARK
GULF COAST VISITOR CENTER

To Chokoloskee and
Turner River

© AVALON TRAVEL

fishing was good. Mullet, a significant export at the time, was caught by net, salted down, and barreled for sale in Key West.

Seminoles and the new white settlers mostly kept to themselves, as did the descendants of the fabled Calusa in these parts. John Weeks and William Smith Allen are said to be the area's first permanent residents, settling sometime around 1870 along the Allen River (now the Barron River), the latter building himself a home on the site of the present-day Rod and Gun Club. George W. Storter, Jr. opened the

first general store and trading post in 1892, in which the locals traded alligator hides, furs, and plumes for ammo and such.

The area's biggest growth spurt came when wealthy businessman Barron G. Collier made it the headquarters for his Tamiami Trail road-building company in 1923. He purchased more than a million acres in southwestern Florida, promising the Florida legislature he'd complete the half-finished Tamiami Trail (linking Tampa with Miami through the swamp) in return for the creation of Collier County. Collier got to work dredging to make land and then paving over it to make the first real roads in the area, but his efforts eventually petered out and the state stepped in to finish the job.

The trail was finished in 1928, and improved access made the area's cattle ranching, commercial fishing, and produce farming more viable. For a while it was the county seat, but storms, along with Collier's decision to move his headquarters up to Naples, sealed Everglades City's fate as the sleepy mile-long mangrove island at the highway's dead end. In the 1940s many locals made their living sponge diving; after that came shrimping, stone crabbing, gator skinning, and sportfishing when wealthy outdoorspeople came to the "wilderness" for a little R&R.

Today, Everglades City's year-round population is as teeny as it ever was, its residents as self-reliant and wary of authority. It's a locus of ecotourism, with canoe tours, airboat rides, fishing guides, and other nature-based businesses capitalizing on the mystery and majesty of the million acres of mangrove jungle just to the south. It's significantly more rustic than swanky Naples to the north—there are no Ritz-Carltons, tux-clad waiters, or turndown service with mints on the pillow anywhere near, but Everglades City is a must for adventure seekers. A couple of days of paddling Everglades National Park will have you gliding past 12-foot gators, beautiful orchids and epiphytes (air plants) dotting the swamp with color, and birds engaged in a strenuous call-and-response—it's an exceptionally wild and beautiful park, best

COURTESY OF NAPLES, MARCO ISLAND, EVERGLADES CVB

Everglades City is an anglers' paradise.

explored by kayak or canoe, that is well worth extensive exploration.

## EVERGLADES NATIONAL PARK

Everglades National Park (mailing address: 40001 Hwy. 9336, Homestead, FL 33034-6733, 305/242-7700; in Everglades City: Gulf Coast Visitor Center, 815 S. Copeland Dr., 239/695-3311, 8 A.M.–4:30 P.M. daily mid-Nov.–mid-April, 9 A.M.–4:30 P.M. mid-April–mid-Nov., no entrance fee on this side of the park) is the third-largest park in the continental United States and has been designated a World Heritage Site, an International Biosphere Reserve, and a Wetland of International Importance. It's the only subtropical preserve in North America, containing both temperate and tropical plant communities. Really, it's the only everglade in the world.

Still, I don't think any of this conveys exactly what's so cool. The Seminoles called the park "grassy water," because it is essentially a wide, shallow river with no current, no falls or rapids, that flows very slowly southward along the subtle slope of the land, eventually meeting open water

in Florida Bay 100 miles away. This river flows along sawgrass prairies, mangrove and cypress swamps, pinelands, and hardwood hammocks. Everywhere there are wading birds, alligators, dense and exotic tropical plantlife. But the U.S. government looked on all this as a dud, a big goose egg. In 1850, the federal government passed the Swamp and Overflowed Lands Act, which essentially gave people the latitude to manhandle this delicate ecosystem in any way they saw fit in an effort to make the land "useful." By the 1880s developers started digging drainage canals that eventually caused major silting problems. And in the early 1900s the first of several South Florida land booms saw the transforming of huge swaths of wetland to agricultural land crisscrossed by canals and new roads. Unsightly mangroves (essential for the maintenance of shorelines in these areas) were removed in favor of more picturesque palms.

Everglades boosters Ernest F. Coe and Marjory Stoneman Douglas (author of *The Everglades: River of Grass*) eventually brought their case for conserving the area to President Harry S. Truman and convinced him to

# THE EVERGLADES

*The Everglades proper is the mainland, about 4,000 square miles of flat prairie grass that slopes southward at one-fifth of a foot per mile. The rainfall averages fifty-five inches, June through October. In rainy season, the most southwest part near the mangroves gets anywhere from a few inches up to two or three feet under water.... The strip of mangrove mainland has many little rivers not much wider in the narrows than a rowboat, running all the way to the grasslands of the Glades. In rainy season these rivers slowly drain the rainwater off the Glades into the Islands. As the rainwater from the Glades mixes with the saltwater coming in from the Gulf, it becomes brackish. Most all the fish and a big portion of the wildlife, especially the saltwater birds, do most of their breeding and feeding in the brackish water here.*

*The fish and the wildlife all follow the brackish water line. In the driest of the season, April and May, the brackish line is at the very head of the rivers near the Glades, and so are the fish and game. As the rains come on, the brackish line slowly drifts down the rivers into the Islands and eventually to the coast.*

*– Loren G. "Totch" Brown, from Totch, A Life in the Everglades*

He would know. He spent most of his life finding ways to eke out a life in this lush, junglelike wilderness at the bottom of the state of Florida.

## THINGS THAT CAN KILL YOU IN THE EVERGLADES

Eastern diamondback rattlesnake, dusky pigmy rattlesnake, cottonmouth, and coral snake all fall under this category. Alligators very, very seldom attack adults, even if you're thrashing about in the water. Dogs and small children are less safe from them. Keep both away from water's edge unattended. Do not, under any circumstances, feed the alligators, even if it's entertaining. It teaches them bad habits. You don't want to see a gator sit up and beg. Crocodiles, on the other hand (there are fewer of these in the Everglades), are larger and more ferocious.

## THINGS THAT CAN REALLY BOTHER YOU IN THE EVERGLADES

Mosquitoes are pretty fierce in the summer (always bring bug spray and long sleeves to thwart them as best you can). Information on mosquito levels during the summer is available at 305/242-7700. Also, there are a few poisonous plants: poison ivy, poisonwood, and manchineel tree. You might want to research these plants' leaf shape so you can avoid brushing up against them.

## WHERE TO SEE GOOD STUFF

The Anhinga Trail (at Royal Palm) and Eco Pond (a mile past the Flamingo Visitor Cen-

dedicate the vast swath as Everglades National Park in 1947. The park is still being rerouted, uprooted, and damaged in a variety of ways, but the wilderness is being increasingly protected and restored and is very much worth visiting.

The Everglades region is mild and pleasant December–April, rarely reaching freezing temperatures, and mostly without a drop of rain. Summers are hot and humid, with temperatures hovering around 90°F and humidity at a fairly consistent, steamy 90 percent. And, as with most places along the Gulf Coast, there are tremendous afternoon thunderstorms in the summer.

## SPORTS AND RECREATION
### Canoeing and Kayaking

Everglades National Park is America's only subtropical wilderness, a third of it given over to marine areas and shallow estuaries easily

COURTESY OF NAPLES, MARCO ISLAND, EVERGLADES CVB

**Clusters of red mangrove form the Ten Thousand Islands of Everglades National Park.**

ter) are good for birding. There's also a train tour at Shark Valley that birders enjoy. Canoeists like paddling into Chokoloskee Bay (Gulf Coast) and Snake Bight (near Flamingo) to see the waterbirds feeding on mudflats.

For freshwater canoeing, try Nine Mile Pond. Serious canoeists tackle the Wilderness Waterway, the backcountry route linking Everglades City to Flamingo. Check at the Gulf Coast Visitor Center for canoeing maps, directions, and rentals (there's no launch fee at the Gulf Coast Visitor Center). A quick and easy way to get a sense of the immensity and majesty of the Everglades is to take one of the 90-minute boat tours (from the Gulf Coast Visitor Center, 239/695-2591, on the half hour 9 A.M.–4:30 P.M., no reservations necessary).

### CAMPING

Even if you're planning on doing primitive camping, backcountry permits are required (they're free; they just help keep track of visitors). There's established beach camping in the Everglades, chickee (little cabin structures) camping along the rivers and bays, New Turkey Key camping, Plate Creek camping, and camping at South Lostmans. Go to the visitors center to get a map and detailed description of all of the established campsites and more primitive options. Camping at park campgrounds is $16 per night, and a backcountry camping permit costs $10 per night (plus $2 per person per night, maximum 14 days).

### OTHER ACCOMMODATIONS

Lodging is available in communities that border the park, including Homestead, Florida City, Miami, Everglades City, and Chokoloskee.

paddled by rookie or seasoned kayakers or canoers (in my experience, a kayak seems easier to navigate through these sometimes-tight quarters). The mangroves form canopied tunnels through the swamp, through which you pick in a peculiar way: Often the flat of your paddle is used to gently push off from the tangle of mangrove roots when it's too tight to actually dip into the water. In this way you pole through the tight spots, the nose of your craft

sometimes hitching up in the roots, necessitating backward paddling to disengage.

Mosquitoes are surprisingly not a real problem until the summer, when you absolutely don't want to be paddling through the steamy swamp anyway due to the heat and humidity. Still, you'll need bug spray, water, sunglasses, a flotation device (required by law), shoes you don't mind getting wet or muddy, comfortable clothes, a hat—and a plan.

Check at the **Gulf Coast Visitor Center** (815 S. Copeland Dr., 239/695-3311, 8 A.M.–4:30 P.M. daily mid-Nov.–mid-April, 9 A.M.–4:30 P.M. mid-April–mid-Nov.) for maps and directions, and you can rent canoes downstairs from the visitors center at **Everglades National Park Boat Tours** (239/695-2591, $35/day). It's fairly daunting to head off by yourself the first day, so the visitors center and Everglades National Park Boat Tours both offer guided tours on a first-come, first-served basis. For more advanced paddlers, there's a trip that departs at 9:30 A.M. Saturdays that lasts seven hours; a Sunday morning trip more for beginners is only four hours.

After that, if you want to push off on your own, put in at the canoe ramp next to the visitors center or the ramp next to Outdoor Resorts on Chokoloskee Island. As everyone will tell you: Don't overestimate your abilities, and time your trip with the tides (a falling tide flows toward the Gulf of Mexico; a rising tide flows toward the visitors center). If you want to pick up a nautical chart, No. 11430 covers the Chokoloskee Bay area. There are also detailed descriptions to be had at the visitors center and other local shops of how to traverse the **Wilderness Waterway,** a 99-mile canoe trail that winds from Everglades City over to the Flamingo Visitor Center at the southeast entrance to the national park. It's about an eight-day excursion, to be undertaken only after lots of diligent preparation.

Collier County has completed Phase I of the Paradise Coast Blueway, a system of GPS-marked paddling trails in the Ten Thousand Islands region, which will eventually extend north to Bonita Springs. There is a main trail route from Everglades City to Goodland, as well as six day-trip routes ranging 2–10 hours of paddling time. If you only have time to do one section of the trail I would highly recommend reserving a campsite at Rabbit Key through the Everglades National Park Visitor Center and camping out on the sandy, palm-lined, private beach for the night. The paddling trip embarks from the Outdoor Resorts center on Chokoloskee Island and is about five miles

to Rabbit Key. It can easily take an entire day depending on your skill level, strength, and the speed and weight of your kayak or canoe. It is especially important to check the tides when paddling in the Ten Thousand Islands region of the Everglades as they are dramatic and can leave you stranded in water too shallow to paddle in, with nowhere to camp. You should also bring a GPS and use the GPS waypoints posted on the Paradise Coast Blueway website for ease of navigation, as it is very easy to get lost amongst the literally thousands of mangrove islands that look extremely similar. Visit www.paradisecoast-blueway.com for more information and detailed downloadable route maps.

## ◖ Everglades Eco Adventures

**Everglades Rentals & Eco Adventures** (Ivey House Bed and Breakfast, 107 Camellia St., 239/695-3299, $95–750) offers spectacular half-day, full-day, and overnight guided canoe, kayak, and boating adventures led by naturalist guides who have a clear passion for the abundant natural beauty of the area. You will stop occasionally to view unusual orchids, alligators sunning, and eagles overhead. Paradise, really, with the dense lushness and lack of human marks that make one feel as if you've fallen somehow into a prehistoric jungle. Substitute pterodactyl babies for the osprey fledglings you see peering from that huge nest above, and the illusion's complete.

One of the trips it offers launches into the water off U.S. 41 at the old Turner River, quickly passing into narrow mangrove tunnels, then out into lagoons and past sawgrass prairies and into Turner Lake. The company runs its tours November 1–April 30 and offers a range of specialty tours for small groups, from photography workshops to night paddles. It also rents equipment you can take out on your own.

## ◖ Totch's Island Tours

Lots of airboat companies offer competent tours with nature-focused narration, but the most historically significant is Totch's Island Tours (929 Dupont St., just before the Everglades

City Bridge, 239/695-2333, 30-minute, 1-hour, and 1.5-hour tours, $20–40). Loren "Totch" Brown, author of *Totch: A Life in the Everglades* (a must-read if you are interested in the crusty, taciturn folks who've eked a living out of the Everglades over the past 100 years), grew up on an island near Chokoloskee during the Depression.

As a young man he fought in World War II before going home to work variously as a pompano fisherman and stone crabber (legally) and an alligator poacher and marijuana smuggler (illegally). You can see a picture of the local legend in Smallwood's Store, a tiny museum on Chokoloskee Island (150 acres made entirely of shells by the Seminoles), or catch a glimpse of him in the 1955 film *Wind Across the Everglades* with Christopher Plummer.

Totch died in 1996, but his tour company consists of his family members and a number of fourth- and fifth-generation Everglades residents. They'll take you out either in backcountry or open water to Totch's Island to see his rustic family cottage on a tiny mangrove island. Along the way, you'll be trailed by pelicans, catch glimpses of manatees lumbering along the brackish shallows beneath you, and see alligators (big ones), wild pigs, ospreys, and incredible plantlife.

## Other Boat Tours

You've seen them. They're the embodiment of Newton's Third Law: Those tall boats propelled by air whooshing through their giant fans—with no outboard motor and rudder for propulsion and control, these boats can scoot through extreme shallows on their flat bottoms, perfect for swamp exploration. It's an Everglades cliché, and a loud one, but fun (although they're not allowed in Everglades National Park proper, they scoot around the edges in the Ten Thousand Islands).

One successful airboat company is **Captain Doug's Florida Boat Tours** (102 Broadway, at the Captain's Table Resort, 800/282-9194, www.captaindougs.com, $37.75 adults, $22.95 children, children 3 and under free). The airboat tour groups are small and the tour is one hour of meandering through the mangrove forest backcountry and a sawgrass wetland. Back at the headquarters, visitors are treated to a free alligator show and are welcome to walk around a replica of a Native American village.

**Wooten's Airboat Tours, Swamp Buggy Rides and Animal Sanctuary** (32330 Tamiami Trail E., Ochopee, five miles south of Everglades City, 239/695-2781, www.wootensairboats.com, 9 A.M.–4:15 P.M. daily, $25.44 adults for either tour, $21.20 for kids, $8 for the farm) is a little farther afield. It's fairly famous in these parts, but to my mind the 30-minute airboat ride through the mangroves and marshlands is very similar to that of the others (and it's a less intimate group, taking up to 18 people at a time). Much neater are the 30-minute swamp tours on the swamp buggy. You'll travel through spooky cypress swamp and spot alligators (as well as North American crocodiles—the Everglades being the only area you'll find these guys in the United States), deer, snakes, and tons of birds. Wooten's also has a little "farm" with native Florida creatures brought in expressly for your excitement (Florida panthers, bobcats).

A quieter ride, with a more overtly ecotourism piety, the **Everglades National Park Boat Tour** (at the ranger station on the causeway between Everglades City and Chokoloskee Island, 239/695-2591, every 30 minutes 9:30 A.M.–4:30 P.M., $16 adults, $8 children) is a wonderful two-hour motorboat tour departing from the Gulf Coast Visitor Center. The cruise is slower, following a loop through a dizzying number of the Ten Thousand Islands. Along the way tour-goers are likely to see manatees, frisky bottle-nosed dolphins, bald eagles, and loads of smirking alligators.

**Everglades Area Tours** (238 Mamie St., Chokoloskee Island, 239/695-3633, www.evergladesareatours.com, $95 and up) provides year-round, half-day, guided kayak ecotours assisted by a motorboat shuttle that carries kayaks and up to six passengers. Aptly named the Yak Attack, the tour strategy allows you to quickly get to the most remote and beautiful paddling areas. All tours are guided by experienced naturalists. Motorboat ecotours, sea kayaking and camping trips, backcountry charter boat and kayak fishing trips, bicycle tours, and aerial tours in the winter season are all on offer.

## SIGHTS
### Big Cypress Gallery
East of Everglades City, famous black-and-white landscape photographer Clyde Butcher has a photo gallery worth the drive. **Clyde Butcher's Big Cypress Gallery** (52338 Tamiami Trail, Ochopee, 239/695-2428, 10 A.M.–5 P.M. daily) features Butcher's own work on local themes—he is to Big Cypress and the Everglades what Ansel Adams was to Yosemite—as well as the work of other nature-inspired photographers. If you happen to be in the area around Labor Day, the gallery sponsors a huge party with a naturalist-led swamp walk, music, and more.

### Museums
The dire economic climate of Reconstruction after the Civil War prompted some robust families to move to the southwest Florida frontier, a "grass is always greener" hopefulness that didn't necessarily pan out as planned. They came, cleared the land on little islands (many of them now named after the original family inhabiting them), built rough-hewn cabins of pine and cypress, and hunted, fished, and farmed. Stoically, they made do in the wilderness, many of them visiting their neighbors by boat only infrequently. Then Ted Smallwood opened Chokoloskee Island's first general store in 1906. There, white settlers and the remaining Seminoles would bring in their hides, furs, and produce in exchange for sugar, coffee, ammunition, and other of life's essentials.

Today, **Smallwood Store** (three miles south of Everglades City, 360 Mamie St., Chokoloskee, 239/695-2989, 10 A.M.–5 P.M. daily, $2.50) is preserved as a 1920s-era general store with its original structure and its last stock of merchandise. The small museum provides stirring insight into the hard lives of the pioneers who settled at the edge of this vast

Glide over the swamps searching for gators on an airboat ride.

wilderness, and the isolation borne of living on tiny, remote mangrove islands. The store was placed on the National Register of Historic Places in 1974 and reopened as a museum by Ted Smallwood's granddaughter in 1989.

Just off the circle in the center of Everglades City, the little **Museum of the Everglades** (105 W. Broadway, 239/695-0008, 9 A.M.–4 P.M. Tues.–Sat., $2 suggested donation) is in the town's Old Laundry, a building that dates to the 1920s, when Everglades City was Barron Collier's "company town," during the construction of the Tamiami Trail. The focus is more on the area's Seminoles and other tribes who inhabited the area before white settlers arrived. The building is of note for the history buff—listed on the National Register of Historic Places, it's the only unaltered original building in town. Don't just visit the museum, though, make sure to get a sense of the area's unique history by chatting with the locals or gliding through the mangroves in a canoe. And if it's a rainy day, put aside an hour or two for the museum.

## EVENTS
### Everglades Seafood Festival
The annual Everglades Seafood Festival in Everglades City draws thousands the first weekend in February with the promise of stone crabs (they say Everglades City is the world's capital, with more than 400,000 pounds of crab claws harvested Oct. 15–May 15), fish chowder, gator nuggets, fresh Gulf shrimp, grouper, and fish of all local vintage,

along with live country music, rides, and arts and crafts.

## SHOPPING

There's a squat nondescript building in the middle of nothing near where the road ends in the Everglades. You can buy ice, bait, gas, and a small assortment of groceries here. It's called the Chokoloskee Mall. I'm sure it's a joke the locals play on tourists, but that about sums up the shopping options in this edge-of-the-wilderness area. Head back up into Naples if the retail bug bites.

## ACCOMMODATIONS
### Under $50

Camping opportunities are abundant around here but not recommended in the hot, wet season. According to the National Park Service, the rainy season runs June–October. The hot season is definitely a bit longer, with the temperature averaging 87 degrees in May. Temperatures can easily climb to above 90 degrees in April and May. For a sure bet to beat the heat and the bugs, I feel the best time to visit the Everglades is November–February. The park and surrounding areas get pretty busy during the week between Christmas and the New Year. The slowest season to visit, when there is still cool weather and few bugs, is the last week in October or the first week in November and the last week in January before all the outdoorsy spring breakers come out for paddling trips.

If you do want to camp in Everglades National Park, stop off at the Gulf Coast Visitor Center for an overnight pass. There are two campgrounds accessible from the Homestead entrance of the park. The Long Pine Key campground is located six miles from the Ernest Coe Visitor Center in Everglades City and the Flamingo campground is located near the Flamingo Visitor Center near the shores of Flamingo Bay. Both accommodate RV and tent campers and offer a limited number of group sites. They both cost $16 a site per night, free during the rainy season. For reservations call 877/444-6777 or make them online at www.recreation.gov.

The nearby Big Cypress Preserve also offers many campgrounds that are generally closed during the wet season June–October. More information on these sites and a listing of open campgrounds can be found though the Oasis Visitor Center (239/695-1201).

RV campers have an appealing option at **Outdoor Resorts of America** (at the entrance to Chokoloskee Island, 239/695-2881, $49–69). Tent and van camping are prohibited, but the RV campsites are nice. The campground offers cabin rentals ($70–90) along with kayak rentals (at the dock), 16-foot skiff rentals for $150 a day, showers, laundry, and a small convenience store. It may be the quickest route from under the covers to steering through the magical Ten Thousand Islands. Pets are welcome.

### $50-150

There are three wonderful places to stay in Everglades City, and all are significant pieces of local history and legend. The white clapboard **Rod and Gun Club** (200 Broadway, 239/695-2101, www.evergladesrodandgun.com, $85–125, no credit cards) was built in 1850 on the site of the first homestead in Everglades City. It has hosted movie stars, U.S. presidents, and lots of other celebs needing to get away from it all. The Rod and Gun Club was, for years, where local and visiting sportspeople gathered to tell big fish stories or share hunting information. A long, low lodge, it contains 17 comfortable rooms, a waterfront restaurant, and dock space.

The **◖ Ivey House Inn Bed and Breakfast** (107 Camellia St., 239/695-3299, $70–155) is my absolute favorite. The property consists of three accommodation options. There is the historic Ivey House, which was first built as a recreation hall for workers on the Tamiami Trail and then converted to a boarding house. Today it is a lodge with seven rooms and a great choice for anglers or large family and group gatherings. It has a very welcoming and comfortable gathering room with a casual old-Florida style. Next door you'll find the Ivey House cottage. This is definitely the best deal

The Ivey House Inn Bed and Breakfast offers a relaxing refuge.

two-story property offers 32 one-bedroom and studio suites. Some are fully equipped with kitchens, and all include televisions, refrigerators, microwaves, a private balcony or patio, and high-speed Internet available in the lobby area. The pool area is well landscaped with local tropical plants, and the adjacent marina is convenient for boaters who would like to sail up to their accommodations for the evening. The on-site restaurant and bar are very casual and comfortable, with a friendly staff and a great breakfast buffet with omelette chef.

in town. You can rent this two-bedroom, fully equipped cottage and have access to all of the Inn amenities and breakfast for only $116 April 19–December 16; the rest of the year it is only $174. The Inn part of the property was built in 2001 and added 17 spacious rooms all centered on a beautifully landscaped screened pool and waterfall area. A delicious breakfast accommodating to all tastes is served in the morning, and complimentary coffee is available throughout the day. The inn is committed to sustainable environmental practices that earned them Florida Green Lodge certification.

The inn's staff is a wealth of information on the area, there's an Everglades library on-site, and the complimentary bikes make familiarizing yourself with the area a snap (take a bike and ride all the way to Chokoloskee Island for a coffee at Big House). The Ivey House is also the headquarters for Everglades Rentals & Eco Adventures, with exemplary naturalist-led charter trips and canoe and kayak rentals. Staying at the Ivey house gets you 20 percent off kayak rentals and guided eco-adventures. You can paddle through the mangrove tunnels of the Big Cypress Preserve during the day or take a sunset tour and paddle through the Everglades at night if you're feeling exceptionally bold and adventurous.

Just outside of Everglades City and closer to the expansive Fakahatchee Strand Preserve and Big Cypress Preserve you'll find the classic old-Florida **Port of the Islands Resort and Marina** (2500 Tamiami Trail East, 239/394-3101, $79–99). This affordable and beautiful

## FOOD

Dining in Everglades City is unilaterally casual, but with no fast food and very few ethnic restaurants. All the times listed below reflect peak season hours. If you're dining here during the off-season, it's best to call for hours of operation. Several spots are outstanding, both for the food and the convivial ambience. **◖ Big House Coffee and Gumbo Limbo Gallery** (238 Mamie St., Chokoloskee, 239/695-3633, 10 A.M.–4 P.M. daily, Thurs. until 10 P.M., call for summer hours, $10–15) has a bohemian vibe—not exactly hippie, but a free-spirited something like that. The cute little coffeehouse and shop (great array of books on the Everglades and lovely local handicrafts) was established circa 1890 as C. G. McKinney Store and looks today like a sprawling, comfortable house with extra tables set up in the side yard under a papaya tree. This is the place to go in the Everglades for Internet access and a peek at newspapers and periodicals. Enjoy homemade key lime pie, brownies, and coconut cream pie with a cup of organic coffee or a glass of fresh limeade.

The **Oyster House** (901 S. Copeland Ave., 239/695-2073, 11 A.M.–9 P.M. daily, Fri. and Sat. until 10 P.M., $10–19) is a fun and sprawling place with model boats, murals, and mounted largemouth bass and the like. They have fresh fried fish platters, and stone crabs are a house specialty—eat them like the locals, chilled with mustard sauce—as is fried gator tail. And here's a must after lunch or dinner: take the walk up to the top of the Ernest

Hamilton Observation tower right behind the restaurant. This is a 75-foot-tall structure built in 1985, with a panoramic view of Chokoloskee and the Ten Thousand Islands.

At the **Everglades Seafood Depot Restaurant** in the old train depot opened in 1928 (102 Collier Ave., 239/695-0075, 10:30 A.M.–9 P.M. daily), try the deep-water lobster or stone crabs (their season is Oct. 15–May 15), and at the **Rod and Gun Club** restaurant (200 Broadway, 239/695-2101, 11 A.M.–2:30 P.M. and 5–9:30 P.M. Mon.–Sat., $12–25, no credit cards) set your sights on the conch fritters, gator nuggets, hushpuppies, or blue crab claws. At **Triad's Seafood Market and Cafe** (401 School Dr., 239/695-2662, 10:30 A.M.–9 P.M. daily, $7–15) try the crab cakes, grouper sandwiches, fried shrimp platters, and homemade peanut butter pie. If you've really worked up an appetite after a day of Everglades adventure, order up the all-you-can-eat Stone Crab.

Anyplace that's known for a dance called the Buzzard Lope and that throws the biggest annual party around in honor of mullet is worth some investigation. **( Stan's Idle Hour Seafood Restaurant** (221 Goodland Dr. W., Goodland, 239/394-3041, 11 A.M.–6 P.M. Tues.–Sun., $14–25) is on the tiny island of Goodland, in between Marco Island and Everglades City, connected by causeways. Sunday afternoons are the time to go to Stan's—heck, anytime's a good time to go to Stan's—when a fair percentage of the island's 200 or so residents show up for some live music, pitchers of beer, peel-and-eat shrimp, and fried oysters. (For fisherfolk, Stan's also has a "you caught 'em, we cook 'em" policy.) The weekend after the Super Bowl every January brings the Mullet Festival to Stan's, with lots of rowdy fun and festivities to enjoy.

# Information and Services

Naples and environs are located within the **Eastern time zone.** The telephone area code is **239,** but it used to be 941 (unfortunately, some guides and brochures still list the old area code, and the automatic call-forwarding expired in 2003).

## TOURIST INFORMATION

The **Naples Daily News** (239/262-3161, www.naplesnews.com) may be the best way to find out about local events and entertainment (it also produces the *Bonita Daily News,* the *Marco Island Eagle,* and the *Bonita Banner*). Kiosks are pretty much everywhere, and it will run you $0.53. For visitor information, stop in at the **Chamber of Commerce Visitors & Information Center** (2390 Tamiami Trail N., Naples, 239/262-6141) to pick up brochures, maps (there's a good city one that's worth the couple of bucks it costs), and lots of coupons. The **Convention and Visitor Bureau** (800/688-3600) maintains a tremendous visitor information website at www.paradisecoast.com.

Golfers have lots of local publications at their fingertips, such as the freebie *Golf Naples Times* (www.golfnaplestimes.com).

Marco Island events and information can be found easily in a copy of *Marco Island Sun Times* (239/394-4050), the widely distributed free community paper. For Everglades City information, call the **Everglades Area Chamber of Commerce** (239/695-3941, www.florida-everglades.com), or visit it at the junction of U.S. 41 and County Road 29, where there's a nice little gift shop and lots of good books on the area.

## POLICE AND EMERGENCIES

As always, if you find yourself in a real emergency, pick up a phone and dial 911. For a nonemergency police need, call or visit the **Naples Police Department** (355 Riverside Circle, 239/213-4844, www.naplespolice.com). The **Marco Island Police Department** can be reached at 239/389-5050, and the sheriff in **Everglades**

City can be reached at 239/695-3341. In the event of a medical emergency, stop into the **Naples Community Hospital** (350 Seventh St. N., 239/436-5000) or **Marco Healthcare Center** (40 S. Heathwood Dr., Marco Island, 239/394-8234). To fill a prescription there are nine CVS pharmacies in the Naples area, the most central to downtown being at 294 Ninth St. S., 239/261-8610. The **Island Drug** (1089 Collier Blvd. N., #409, Marco Island, 239/394-3111) has met Marco Island's pharmaceutical needs for 30 years.

### RADIO AND TELEVISION

For when you feel like cranking a little music around here, turn to **100.1 FM** for smooth jazz, **96.1 FM** for classic rock, **99.3 FM** for new music, **102.9 FM** for an eclectic "we play anything" format. Turn to **770 AM** for sports talk, and either **1240 AM** or **1270 AM** for news talk.

And on the television, **WBBH Channel 2** out of Fort Myers is the NBC affiliate, **WEVU Channel 8** out of Naples is the UPN affiliate, **WINK Channel 11** out of Fort Myers is the CBS affiliate, **WZVN Channel 7** out of Fort Myers is the ABC affiliate, and **WGCU Channel 30** out of Fort Myers is the PBS affiliate.

### LAUNDRY SERVICES

If you're staying at one of the upscale hotels, condos, or inns on Marco Island or in Naples, most offer their own laundry services to guests. There's also a cool **24 Hour Laundromat** (4045 Golden Gate Pkwy., Naples, 239/590-4800) that doesn't use coins. You stick in bills and it issues you a card, which you then stick in the washer or dryer. In Everglades City it's a little trickier—the Ivey House and a few other accommodations have laundry services for their guests.

# Getting There and Around

### BY CAR

Main driving access to the area is via I-75, either from the north or straight west across the bottom of the state (this section of I-75 is known as Alligator Alley, with ample cause). From I-75, you may take Exit 101 to Highway 84, which leads to downtown Naples (best if your aim is to do a little shopping or dining along Fifth Avenue South or Third Street South, or if you want to amble along the Naples Pier). The new Exit 105 is best to reach Naples Zoo and Naples Municipal Airport. Exit 107 (Pine Ridge Rd.) takes you directly to U.S. 41, otherwise known as the Tamiami Trail, the best exit for reaching Clam Pass and Vanderbilt Beach parks and beaches. National Audubon Society's Corkscrew Swamp Sanctuary is easiest accessed by Exit 111 (Immokalee Rd.), which also takes you to North Naples.

To get to Marco Island, take Exit 101, then follow Collier Boulevard (Hwy. 951) west to the island. And to reach Everglades City, continue south from Naples on U.S. 41.

If you're coming from Miami, take U.S. 41 the whole way. The Tamiami Trail is a little slower than I-75, but it offers more sightseeing possibilities, as it has been designated a National Scenic Byway and Florida Scenic Highway. The route celebrated its 75th anniversary in 2003 and takes you right through the Everglades and Big Cypress National Preserve.

### BY AIR

By air, the closest large airport is **Southwest Florida International Airport** (239/768-1000, www.flylcpa.com), 40 minutes to the north in Fort Myers. Most major domestic airlines serve the airport, and there are international flights from Germany and Canada. The airport has enjoyed enormous growth recently, finishing an expanded terminal and new runway opening in 2005. There is a little commuter airport in Naples, the **Naples Municipal Airport** (239/643-0733, www.flynaples.com), which offers nonstop jet service from Atlantic Southeast Airlines as well as regular flights to Key West on Yellow Air Taxi.

Private jets constitute much of this airport's daily traffic. Private planes can also fly into Marco Executive Airport, Immokalee Regional Airport, and Everglades Airpark in Everglades City.

**Alamo** (800/327-9633), **Avis** (800/831-2847), **Budget** (800/527-0700), **Dollar** (800/800-4000 domestic, 800/800-6000 international), and **National** (800/227-7368) provide rental cars from Southwest Florida International Airport. From the Naples Municipal Airport, there is a convenient **Naples Airport Shuttle** (888/569-2227).

## BY TRAIN AND BUS

**Amtrak** (800/USA-RAIL) offers train service as far south as the Fort Myers station, located 40 miles or so north of Naples, but you'll have to drive from there. Also, **Greyhound Bus Line** (239/774-5660) provides regular service into Naples, and Collier Area Transit operates a reliable network of city buses ($3 for a daylong pass).

One of the most pleasant sightseeing opportunities in Naples is the **Naples Trolley** (1010 6th Ave. S., 800/592-0848, day passes $25 for adults, $12.50 for children 4–12, free for children under 4). The narrated tour covers over 100 local points of interest and offers a nice historical overview of the area. You can disembark whenever something captures your interest and then hop the next trolley that comes shuffling by.

# LEE COUNTY

The area between Sarasota and Naples was inhabited for 2,000 years by the fierce, tall Calusas. They were not agriculturalists, but hunters and gatherers who primarily relied on the good fishing and the even better shell-fishing in the area. For a while Lee County had a slick ad campaign that read: "Ancient cultures once used shells as currency. Guess this place must have been Fort Knox." It seems to have retired the campaign, but the fact remains: The long stretches of beach in this area are spectacular for their sand, their birds, their sunsets, and, most strikingly, for their shells. Lightning whelks are abundant in the area (an anomaly in the mollusk world, opening to the left and not the right), and shell hunters are commonly seen searching for perfect Florida fighting conchs along the water's edge.

Gold-seeking Spanish conquistadores all but wiped out the Calusa and then never really settled here with any impressive numbers. The nearly unpopulated barrier islands became a hideout for pirates, most famously José Gaspar, the "last of the buccaneers." Whether fictional or not, in 1783 Gasparilla, as he called himself, commandeered a Spanish ship, the *Floridablanca,* and roamed the Gulf Coast waters plundering treasure and capturing beautiful women (his "captives," it is said, were held captive on Captiva Island).

The area, called the Beaches of Fort Myers and Sanibel (its county, Lee County, was named after Confederate general Robert E. Lee), was the site of one of the southernmost land battles of the American Civil War. It was fought in Fort Myers on February 20, 1865,

COURTESY OF LEE COUNTY CVB

# HIGHLIGHTS

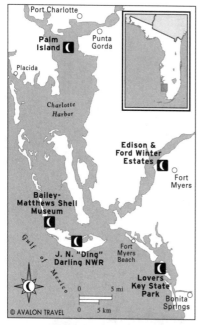

◖ **Lovers Key State Park:** Lee County beaches are ranked some of the best in the nation for shelling, with more varieties found Lovers Key State Park gives you the widest range of recreation options, including shelling the 2.5-mile stretch of beach and five miles of bike trails (page 70).

◖ **Edison & Ford Winter Estates:** Thomas Edison, who spent 46 winters in Fort Myers, is considered the most inventive man who ever lived, holding 1,097 patents for everything from light bulbs, cement, and phonographs to the natural rubber he made from goldenrod. His estate and that of his buddy Henry Ford are fascinating (page 74).

◖ **J. N. "Ding" Darling National Wildlife Refuge:** Occupying more than half of Sanibel Island, this refuge is home to a tremendous array of birdlife (page 85).

◖ **Bailey-Matthews Shell Museum:** It's a crash course in Neptune's treasures, a must if you want to know which species you're painstakingly unearthing along the shoreline (page 89).

◖ **Palm Island:** If you have the resources of time and money, a day or two on Palm Island is good for the soul, and most of your other parts, too. It's an unbridged barrier island paradise (page 98).

LOOK FOR ◖ TO FIND RECOMMENDED SIGHTS, ACTIVITIES, DINING, AND LODGING.

with both sides claiming victory (the confusing event is celebrated annually in North Fort Myers with a battle reenactment during its Cracker Festival). The county was named following the war, when it separated from nearby Monroe County in 1887.

Lee County's draw for the visitor is sheer variety. The city of **Fort Myers,** in large measure due to its most famous residents, Thomas Edison and Henry Ford, is culturally rich, with attractions spread along the banks of the Caloosahatchee River. It is the oldest and largest city in southwest Florida and, as such, dense

with history. Nearby, the barrier islands offer tropical island getaways.

The most well known of this group of islands are **Sanibel** and **Captiva.** Once connected to each other at what is now Blind Pass, the siblings bear a family resemblance but have vastly different personalities. Both cater to mostly wealthy winter visitors, but Sanibel is more accessible (financially and physically), with miles of bike paths and low-rise, independently owned inns and smaller hotels. Living here is casual; a tremendous wildlife refuge takes up nearly half of the island, with

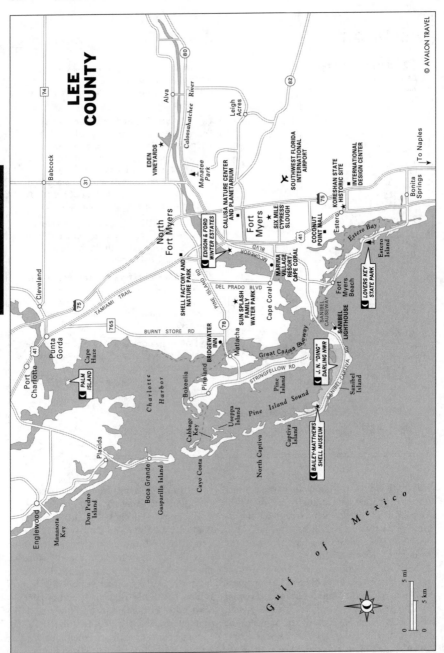

white-sand beaches on the Gulf side and picturesque mangrove forests on the eastern side. Captiva, to the north and connected by a causeway, is the playground of the even more affluent. Many people own homes on Captiva (you won't see it, but artist Robert Rauschenberg had an unassuming white, beachfront mansion and studio on the island), most tucked down driveways shielded from prying eyes by lush foliage. There's less to do on Captiva; there are fewer places to stay, fewer tourist amenities. But that's how people on Captiva like it.

Then there are the other barrier islands, each with its own character. Fort Myers Beach is on the long strip of coast-hugging land known as Estero Island. It's the closest thing this area has to a spring break–type beach, with affordable motels and crowded, family-friendly beaches. Gasparilla Island has made a name for itself as the tarpon capital and host to American presidents and a wide array of fish-seeking celebrities. Its town of Boca Grande is worth the quick boat ride or slightly longer car ride (you've got to go north and then out a causeway) to see. Cabbage Key, North Captiva, and Useppa are accessible only by boat but make a beautiful day trip. And Pine Island is the largest of the barrier islands in this area, mostly residential, with the charming maritime towns of Matlacha, Bokeelia, Pineland, and St. James City. Anglers know it for its "Fishingest Bridge in the United States."

## PLANNING YOUR TIME

The area could entertain the troops for a week or more. The budget traveler will make his or her home base in Fort Myers or Fort Myers Beach, slinking over the very expensive causeway ($6) to Sanibel and Captiva for a day of rejuvenating beach therapy. The Edison & Ford estates in Fort Myers will occupy much of a day, as will the J. N. "Ding" Darling National Wildlife Refuge on Sanibel. The rest of the area's attractions are more fleetingly entertaining (although the beach never gets old). Families will spend a fair amount of time at the kids' water park and attractions to the north in Cape Coral; history buffs will likely occupy themselves at one of several Calusa museums; the outdoors enthusiast will choose fishing, canoeing, sailing, or all of the above. The Great Calusa Blueway Paddling Trail is a truly remarkable, newly charted route for beginning or advanced paddlers—well worth a half day's exploration for even the most timid boater.

The end of each October and beginning of November, the **Calusa Blueway Paddling Festival** (www.calusabluewaypaddlingfestival. com) is another event around which to plan an outdoors-oriented trip. Lee County has been recognized as one of the best U.S. kayaking destinations by both *Paddler* and *Canoe & Kayak* magazines. Paddlers, competitors, families, and outdoors enthusiasts enjoy nine days of festivities including competitive canoe/kayak races, a pro-am kayak fishing tournament, paddling clinics and demonstrations, seminars, family activities, archaeological and environmental events, guided tours, a speakers' series, and more celebrations along the Great Calusa Blueway.

Fall is beautiful here, while summers are extremely hot and humid. If your aim is winter, it's cheaper to visit in the first two weeks of December. Rates generally increase for high season during the third week of December, and the large crowds arrive in February and March. In early December, you'll find lots of accommodations and nominal traffic (which can be frustrating on Sanibel and Captiva in March).

# Fort Myers

A hurricane in the 1840s drove the soldiers out of Seminole War Fort Dulaney at the mouth of the Caloosahatchee. The evacuation had an upside. First Lt. John Harvie found a safer, more sheltered place for a fort, which he named Fort Myers in honor of that war's Col. Abraham C. Myers. Retired soldiers came back to the area after the war, making use of the picturesque Caloosahatchee to ship cattle to Cuba. Fort Myers was a sleepy cowpoke town, not even on the beach, when Thomas Alva Edison visited and fell in love with it in 1885.

Fort Myers was incorporated that same year, and the banks of the Caloosahatchee Intercoastal Waterway started to be settled by intrepid northerners. Edison talked his buddy Henry Ford into exploring the area, and Ford promptly bought the house next door on McGregor Boulevard. Because of Edison's gift to the city of hundreds of royal palms, its nickname is "City of Palms."

These days, Fort Myers is Lee County's working center, the biggest urban center in southwest Florida (well, nearby Cape Coral has greater landmass). There are attractions, restaurants, and hotels centered on the bustling downtown historic district and along the riverfront, and a recent downtown city renovation designed by famous New Urbanist architect Andrés Duany is under way, promising a major renaissance in the near future.

Its easy access to nearby barrier islands (Sanibel, Captiva, Pine Island, and Gasparilla), combined with its wealth of family-friendly attractions, makes it an obvious home base for the dynamic traveler. There are full-service marinas connected to several of the hotels along the river, so boaters can pull right up.

The city of Fort Myers is beachless, but you can head down to Fort Myers Beach on Estero Island for fun in the sun and sand—its gentle slope and lack of steep drop-offs make it a safe beach for young swimmers or waders. At the north end of the island a casual beach village offers a cluster of restaurants and shops, and at Estero's southern end Lovers Key State Park is a huge draw, with a number of nearby resort hotels.

## SPORTS AND RECREATION
### Beaches

**Fort Myers Beach** is actually on the island of Estero, connected to Fort Myers by a causeway. There are several worthwhile beaches here. **Bowditch Point Regional Park** (50 Estero Blvd., 239/765-6794) is a 17-acre park that fronts both the Gulf and the bay at the northern tip of Estero Island, with a boardwalk over to a beach with beautiful views of nearby barrier islands. It recently added 10 boat slips for day use that can accommodate boats up to 28 feet in length and a paddle craft launch providing access to the Calusa Blueway Paddling Trail. Parking is available behind the bathhouse (nice showers and changing rooms), and there's a $0.25 trolley from the Main Street parking lot. Just a bit to the south and on the Gulf side, **Lynn Hall Memorial Park** (950 Estero Blvd., 239/765-6794, parking $2/hour) is a great family beach and a teen hangout. There's also a fishing pier here, heavily frequented by opportunistic pelicans. (If you happen to hook a pelican or other bird while fishing, reel the bird in slowly, cover its head with a towel to calm it, cut the line close to the hook and remove all monofilament from wings and body, then call **Clinic for the Rehabilitation of Wildlife,** C.R.O.W., 239/472-3644, a local nonprofit bird rescue organization.)

### ◖ Lovers Key State Park

Lovers Key State Park (8700 Estero Blvd., Fort Myers Beach, 239/463-4588, 8 A.M.–sundown, $5/car up to eight people, single occupancy car $3, pedestrians and bicyclists $1) is one of the newest of Florida's state parks and actually occupies four small barrier islands (Black Island, Long Key, Inner Key, and Lovers Key) between Fort Myers Beach and Bonita Beach to the south. The park contains a 2.5-mile stretch

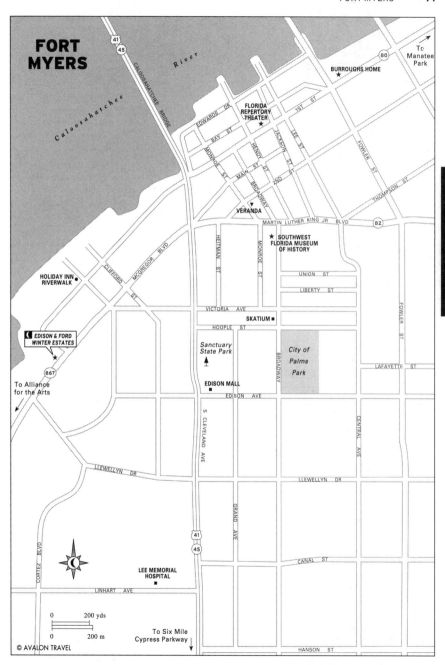

© AVALON TRAVEL

COURTESY OF LEE COUNTY CVB

The beaches of Lovers Key State Park are secluded and surrounded by preserved forest.

of beautiful beach and five miles of bike trails (bike, canoe, and kayak rentals available on-site), including the Black Island Trail through a maritime hammock. There are brand-new picnic facilities at the New Lovers Key Bayside area on Estero Boulevard. There's free tram service to the beach (9 A.M.–5 P.M. daily).

In addition to roseate spoonbills, snowy egrets, and American kestrels, birders will see active osprey nests and a couple of bald eagle nests. The park offers one-hour sunset ecotours (239/594-0213, $25 adults, $15 children ages 3–12) Tuesday, Thursday, and Saturday at 5 P.M., and there is a dolphin cruise every Thursday and Saturday, 8:15–9:15 A.M.

### Six Mile Cypress Slough
Six Mile Cypress Slough (7751 Penzance Crossing, Fort Myers, 239/533-7550, www. leeparks.org, 8 A.M.–sunset daily, parking $1/ hour) is a fabulous wild spot in south Fort Myers, easily accessible to those on the way to or from the airport. You'd never know you were in a county of a half million people. There are

ongoing free guided nature walks (twice daily during high season at 9:30 A.M. and 1:30 P.M.) along a 1.5-mile fully accessible boardwalk trail through a wooded wetland, as well as monthly nature programs in which children and adults learn to identify animal tracks, evening moonwalks, summer camps for kids, and wilderness exploration camps for teens. In 2010, the Six Mile Cypress Interpretive Center, Lee County's first LEED-certified green building, opened on-site.

### Manatee-Watching
Spend a little time on the Orange and Caloosahatchee rivers, and chances are you'll see a West Indian manatee. Take a two-hour boat tour with **Manatee World** (16991 State Road 31, Fort Myers, 239/693-1434, www. manateeworld.com, 11 A.M. daily, $20 adults, $10 children 12 and under) and the odds get even better that you'll see a few of these mammals, related biologically to the elephant and, unlikely though it may seem, the aardvark. The narrated ecotour provides insight into the

life of the area's most famous species, as well as information about how they are threatened by outboard motors and habitat destruction. Manatees seem to congregate in the Orange River in the winter, basking in the waters warmed by the outflow of the nearby power plant. This is a good family adventure, and if you are extremely interested by these gentle sea cows, you can head on over to **Manatee Park** (10901 Hwy. 80, 1.5 miles east of I-75, North Fort Myers, 239/481-4600, 9 A.M.–4 P.M. daily, parking $1/hour, kayak rentals $15/hour). There are three observation decks for viewing and hydrophones so you can listen in (I don't speak manatee, but even scientists are unsure how they make these chirps, whistles, and squeaks). A cow and her calf are especially talkative, vocalizing back and forth. The park rents kayaks in winter and on summer weekends, with kayak clinics the second Saturday of the month and free guided walks through the native plant habitats at 9 A.M. every Saturday.

Discovery Day at Manatee Park is always the last Saturday in January, drawing 3,000 people to ecotourism activities, butterfly gardening, manatee-viewing, and kayaking on the Orange River.

## Golf

The greater Fort Myers area has around 100 public and semiprivate golf courses, the egalitarian nature of which makes the city duly proud. The city of Fort Myers itself maintains two professionally designed golf courses. **Fort Myers Country Club** (3591 McGregor Blvd., 239/321-7488, public, 18 holes, 6,414 yards, course rating 70.5, slope 118, par 71, greens fee $25–55, depending on season and time of day) was designed by the great Donald Ross in 1916 and opened in 1917—one of the oldest courses on the Gulf Coast. It hosts the pro-am Coors Open tournament every year in January and is only a mile from downtown. **Eastwood Golf Course** (4600 Bruce Herd Lane, 239/321-7487, public, 18 holes, 6,772 yards, par 72, course rating 73.3, slope 130, greens fee $20–40) reopened in December 2007 after a $1.5 million renovation that included 84 new bunkers,

54 new tee grounds, new irrigation, resurfaced cart paths, and a new driving range. Golfers will also enjoy the recently added $2 million clubhouse.

## Tracking School

North and east of Fort Myers is a little town called Alva. Not much to do there amongst the dense Florida live oak, slash pine, and palmetto, unless you want to learn to be a tracker. New Jersey–based **Tom Brown, Jr.'s Tracker School** (Caloosahatchee Regional Park, 18500 North River Road, Fort Myers, www.tracker-school.com, 908/619-3809, about $950 for one week) relocates part of the year to this lush stretch of Florida wilderness. Students spend a week learning how to observe nature, track animals, and survive in the wilderness. Brown started his tracking school in 1978, on the heels of a number of successful books including *The Tracker, Tom Brown's Field Guide to Wilderness Survival,* and *Grandfather.* The Florida school site has swimming holes, trails, and camping areas, all dense with local plants and animals. If you need a hair dryer and a dry pair of socks, this may not be for you.

## Spring Training

The Boston Red Sox have certainly made New England swell with pride in recent years. If you're a fan and you want to do some extra gloating, take in a **Boston Red Sox Spring Training** (City of Palms Park, 2201 Edison Ave., Fort Myers, 877/REDSOX9, www.redsox.com, $10–46) game. It's a great little ballpark into which Lee County has poured tons of money—a good place to see a Grapefruit League home season game, and to get a preview of what the Sox are capable of this season. Spring training games are the whole month of March at 1:05 P.M.

**Minnesota Twins Spring Training** (Hammond Stadium, 14400 Six Mile Cypress Pkwy., Fort Myers, 239/768-4210, www.miraclebaseball.com, $16–18) also takes place locally at the Lee County Sports Complex, recognized widely as one of baseball's top five spring training facilities. Games

Hammond Stadium plays host to the Minnesota Twins for spring training.

are at 1:05 P.M. all of the month of March, and after that, in April, fans can watch the Miracle League, a minor-league affiliate of the Minnesota Twins and member of the Florida State League.

## SIGHTS
### ◖ Edison & Ford Winter Estates
Thomas Edison arrived in Fort Myers on March 20, 1885. Not one to be indecisive, evidently, he purchased 13-plus acres along the Caloosahatchee River within 24 hours, with the aim of building his winter home.

Seminole Lodge was duly built in pieces in Maine from his designs and then sailed to Florida and assembled. The home served as the winter retreat and workplace for the prolific inventor until his death in 1931. It's encircled with large overhanging porches; grand French doors encourage a cross breeze. There are electric chandeliers—"electroliers"—designed by Edison. It's a fascinating house, deeded to the city for $1 by Edison's widow, Mina.

Edison's close buddy Henry Ford must also

have fallen in love when he visited Fort Myers in 1915. He bought the house next door. Called The Mangoes, it became another top destination for the country's elite—Harvey Firestone, naturalist John Burroughs, Nobel Laureate Alexis Carrel, and Charles Lindbergh all made their way to this Florida paradise. For quite a while it was essentially Fort Myers's biggest tourist destination.

Edison & Ford Winter Estates (2350 McGregor Blvd., Fort Myers, 239/334-7419, www.efwefla.org, 9 A.M.–5:30 P.M. daily) raised $10 million in the past few years through a laudable public-private partnership, restoring the houses and grounds and repositioning the attraction as a community and cultural center.

The two estates encompass 14 acres of botanical landscaping, the two titans' historic homes and guest cottages, Edison's laboratory, a museum containing his famous inventions and exhibits, a museum store, a garden shop, and an outdoor café. It's worth at least a couple of hours of wandering through the gorgeous

COURTESY OF LEE COUNTY CVB

Tour Thomas Edison's laboratory and winter home in Fort Myers.

environs, but the real draw is peeking into the lives of these fascinating men.

Poke your head into the laboratory and the museum of Edison's inventions and artifacts, spend a little time in Ford's garage, then walk through the tropical botanical garden. Edison planted it as an experimental garden with more than 1,000 species, focusing on the byproducts of plants (rubber for his buddy Firestone's tires, for instance). Later, Mina Edison prettied it up by adding roses, orchids, and bromeliads.

In the painstakingly restored houses, the year 1929 was chosen as the "period of interpretation," the interiors accurately reflecting the decor and accoutrements of that time. (Edison's lab is undergoing renovation in 2011; call ahead to ensure the lab will be open when you would like to visit the Edison estate.) It's fun to mosey on your own with the electronic audio tour, but the staff-led tours are a must, giving the place context and depth.

You can dispel Edison myths (alas, the light bulbs burning in the estate are not Edison's originals), hear funny stories (Henry Ford stuffed the seats of his first Model T imprudently with local Spanish moss, which prompted the first automotive recall when little chiggers started crawling out and biting drivers on the butts), or just learn a little about the quirks of these American legends (Edison hated paparazzi, so he disembarked from the train before the station and walked the rest of the way).

The very young may be underwhelmed by all the Edison-Ford-obilia, but everybody feels a sense of awe when navigating the huge banyan tree out front. Its circumference spans more than 400 feet, making it one of the largest in the country, a gift to Thomas Edison from Firestone.

A combined tour of the estates is available 9 A.M.–5:30 P.M. daily, with the last tour leaving promptly at 4 P.M.; cost is $20 adults, $11 children 6–12, free for children 5 and younger. Botanical tours are offered at 9 A.M. Thursday and Saturday; you'll pay $24 adults, $10 children 6–12.

## McGregor Boulevard

Fort Myers is sometimes called the City of Palms. Why? Edison and Ford's estates are poised just at the edge of McGregor Boulevard, which is lined on both sides by 60-foot-tall royal palms. The original 200 or so, from Cuba, were gifts from Thomas Edison to the city. The idea caught on, and now more than 2,000 palms flank the roadside of stately McGregor Boulevard. Drive the length of the 15-mile boulevard and the city's nickname seems fairly apt.

## Museums

### Southwest Florida Museum of History

(2300 Peck St., 239/321-7430, www.cityft-myers.com, 10 A.M.–5 P.M. Tues.–Sat., $9.50 adults, $5.50 with student ID, $8.50 seniors and children 12 and under) is a quirky mix of stuff, but its wide net gathers a broad catch. The history of the Calusa and Seminole people, as well as that of this area's Spanish explorers, is a major focus of the museum, and more broadly the history of Fort Myers. Set in a restored Atlantic Coastline railroad depot built in 1924, the museum houses photographs and memorabilia; there's an 84-foot-long Pullman rail car built in 1929 and a replica of a late 1800s Cracker house.

A changing exhibit lends a different flavor to the museum every few months. The museum also runs 90-minute architectural and historic downtown walking tours in Fort Myers on Wednesdays and Saturdays at 10 A.M. ($5 adults, $3 children, reservation required).

## Koreshan State Historical Site

Hands-down winner of Weirdest Attraction in the Area prize is the Koreshan State Historical Site (U.S. 41 at Corkscrew Rd., Estero, 239/992-0311, 8 A.M.–sundown, $5/car, $2 for walkers or bicyclists, $26 camping, $5/hour canoe rentals). It commemorates an eccentric religious sect begun by Dr. Cyrus Teed in 1894 after he had a spiritual "great illumination." It seems he and his followers believed the world is a hollow globe, with mankind residing on the inner surface, gazing into the universe below.

The Koreshan followers (at its peak there were 250) gave their commune to the state if it would be maintained as a historic site in perpetuity. Now the site is a compound of buildings and a theater, but visitors also avail themselves of the park's fishing, camping, nature study, and picnicking. There's a boat ramp and canoes for rent, and guided walks and campfire programs are offered seasonally.

## Family-Friendly Attractions

Cape Coral, north of Fort Myers, isn't among the area's biggest draws for adults. As soon as children get a say, however, you may find yourself driving north with regularity. On a hot day, the kids will help navigate you to **Sun Splash Family Waterpark** (400 Santa Barbara Blvd., 239/574-0558, www.sunsplashwater-park.com, open March 12–Sept. 25, mostly 10 A.M.–6 P.M., Thurs. and Sat. until 9 P.M. in the summer, $16.95 adults, $14.95 children under 48 inches tall, $8.95 seniors, $4.95 age two and under), on the shore of Lake Kennedy. It's not huge, but there are two new tall water flume rides, a big family pool, a tot playground, a "river" tube ride, a café, and a superfast ride called the Electric Slide, which is an enclosed tube in which you twist and turn at high speed. Not far away is **Mike Greenwell's Family Fun Park** (35 Pine Island Rd., Cape Coral, 239/574-4386, 10 A.M.–10 P.M. Sun.–Thurs., Fri. and Sat. until 11 P.M., $3–6.50 for miniature golf, $6 for 24 pitches in batting cages, plus $1 equipment rental, $3–6.50 for go-carts, $15 for paintball). It fills in the gaps, with miniature golf, batting cages, four go-cart tracks, a maze, an arcade, a sweet fish-feeding dock, and paintball.

Located in downtown Fort Myers, another bad-weather delight for little kids comes at the **Imaginarium Hands-On Museum** (2000 Cranford Ave., 239/321-7420, www.imaginar-iumfortmyers.com, 10 A.M.–5 P.M. Mon.–Sat., noon–5 P.M. Sun., $12 adults, $10 seniors, $8 children 3–12, under 3 free). It's a calm hands-on museum in which kids can fly and be free. A hurricane simulator, fossil dig, miniature TV weather studio—it's hard not to get

# GET OUT OF TOWN

Something to think about: If you have an extra day and nothing on the docket, why not pop off to Key West? Explore the country's southernmost city just for the day. There are high-speed shuttles from Fort Myers, a welcome alternative to driving (about seven hours) or flying (usually several hundred clams).

**Key West Express** (239/394-9700, $128 adults, $118 seniors, $68 children 6-12, $3 children 5 and under, but prices fluctuate by season and there are sometimes coupons in local papers) has a couple of boats that head out of Fort Myers.

The company currently operates four vessels, the 130-foot *Whale Watcher*, the 140-foot *Atlanticat* catamaran, the 155-foot *Big Cat* catamaran, and the brand new 170-foot *Key West Express* catamaran. The catamaran ferry zips over to Key West in 3.5 hours.

Most seating on the boat is contoured, airplane-like chairs, but there are also plush couches with tables. Although the floor-to-ceiling windows provide plenty of entertainment (and there's a full outdoor deck upstairs), there are six plasma-screen TVs showing movies, sports, and more. The *Key West Express* catamaran from Salty Sam's Marina (2500 Main St., Fort Myers) features two enclosed cabins, a sun deck, satellite TV, slot machines, and full galley and bar. The ships depart Fort Myers Beach 9 A.M., arrive Key West 12:30 P.M.; depart Key West 6 P.M., arrive Fort Myers Beach 9:30 P.M. That gives you five hours or so to noodle around town. Alternatively, you can find a hotel or inn, stay overnight, and come back on the next day's ferry for no additional ferry fee. This tiny three- by five-mile island, 100 miles from the coast, has the only living coral reef in the United States, not to mention great restaurants and nightlife. And for 10 days in October, Fantasy Fest makes Key West the biggest party around.

---

engrossed. There's also a fairly nice aquarium here, with cool moray eels and a lively coral reef tank.

Bigger kids have a couple of similar options in Fort Myers, with science and nature centers more suited to school-age kids and adults. The **Calusa Nature Center & Planetarium** (3450 Ortiz Ave., Fort Myers, 239/275-3435, www.calusanature.com, museum and trail 9 A.M.–5 P.M. Mon.–Sat., 11 A.M.–5 P.M. Sun., $9 adults, $6 children 3–12) enables people to learn about southwest Florida's natural history in a number of ways. There are nature trails on boardwalks through pine flatwoods and cypress wetlands, on which you'll pass a Seminole village replica, a live bobcat, and a native birds-of-prey aviary for permanently injured birds. Dogs are welcome on the trails the first Sunday of the month. Inside the nature center, there are live animals and exhibits about their habitats. The best parts of the center are the regularly scheduled guided walks and animal lectures (cool stuff about snakes,

gators, and Florida's endangered species). The center also has a planetarium, in which you can learn about the Hubble telescope and the night sky or just chill out while watching a laser light show.

The kind of Old Florida tourist draw people get nostalgic for, the **Shell Factory & Nature Park** (2787 Tamiami Trail N., North Fort Myers, 239/995-2141, www.shellfactory. com, free admission, miniature golf and boat rides $5) adopts a something-for-everyone approach (and has been doing so since the 1950s). There's a lot of kitschy shell-themed merchandise to check out while kids get into the miniature golf, bumper boats, batting cages, and a video arcade. Supposedly it has the world's largest collection of rare shells and coral, but the glass-blowing artisans are more entertaining to watch (there's also a funny little History of Glass Museum on-site). Outdoors you'll have to visit the nature park with a petting zoo (camels, llamas, donkeys, potbellied pigs, goats), trails, and a botanical garden. Sounds like a lot under one roof, huh? This is the kind of place where you simply have to give in and consume a batter-dipped hot dog followed by a pound of fudge.

After the fudge, you may need to get the blood flowing at Fort Myers's **Skatium** (2250 Broadway, Fort Myers, 239/321-7510, www. fmskatium.com, public skating 1–3 P.M. and 7:30–9:30 P.M. Sat. and Sun., $7 adults, $6 children 12 and under, $3 for skate rentals), a 72,000-square-foot facility with an ice-skating rink, an inline rink, laser tag arena, and video arcade. Most of the time, the rink is given over to local youth hockey and figure skating. If your kids are more into outdoor inline skating or skateboarding, the **Fort Myers Skate Park** (13499 S. Cleveland Ave., downtown Fort Myers, 239/461-4445, 3–9 P.M. weekdays, 11 A.M.–9 P.M. weekends, $3/day, helmets mandatory) is right next door, the area's premier street-style course with wood and galvanized steel ramps surfaced with Skatelite Pro sitting on a 15,000-square-foot base.

## ENTERTAINMENT AND EVENTS
### Wine-Tasting
About 10 miles east of Fort Myers you'll run across the southernmost bonded winery in the continental United States. **Eden Vineyards** (19709 Little Ln., at Exit 141 off I-75, Alva, 239/728-9463, www.edenwinery. com, 11:30 A.M.–3:30 P.M. daily, free) makes six wines (all around $12), none of them identified by varietal. They're made of hybrid grapes that have proven themselves capable of withstanding the Florida sun and heat. It's fun to do a little tasting in an area not known for its wine—and these fruity, low-alcohol wines suit the climate.

### Music and Theater
The **Barbara B. Mann Performing Arts Hall** (on the campus of Edison College, 8099 College Pkwy., 239/481-4849, www.bbmannpah.com) is the center of arts activity for Fort Myers. The full-sized and fully equipped stage hosts traveling Broadway musicals,

popular music, and **Southwest Florida Symphony** (4560 Via Royale, 239/418-1500, www.swflso.org) concerts. The professional symphony orchestra offers classical and pops series annually (its chamber orchestra series takes place in Schein Hall at BIG Arts on Sanibel Island).

The **Florida Repertory Theatre** (Arcade Theater, 2268 Bay St., 239/332-4488, www. floridarep.org) is a 10-year-old ensemble-based company with a year-round season. Split between musicals, comedies, and serious dramas, the professional repertory's season features nine productions, staged in a great restored 1908 Victorian movie house.

Broadway musicals and family-friendly comedies are the mainstay at **Broadway Palm Dinner Theatre** (1380 Colonial Blvd., 239/278-4422, www.broadwaypalm.com), which has a main stage as well as a more intimate black-box theater (in which Off Broadway Palm stages smaller-scale comedies and musical revues, as well as children's theater). Some of the performers are local, and they occasionally bring in talent from farther afield. Performances are accompanied by cocktails, salad bar, and a buffet.

### Visual Arts
Lee County isn't the visual arts smorgasbord of Naples to the south. Still, there are several nice galleries and the local arts center. The Lee County **Alliance for the Arts** (10091 McGregor Blvd., 239/939-2787, www.artinlee.org, 9 A.M.–5 P.M. Mon.–Fri., 9 A.M.–noon Sat., free admission) is a multipronged arts organization founded in 1975. On a 10-acre campus, the organization contains the Frizzell Cultural Center of galleries, classrooms, a 175-seat indoor theater, and an outdoor amphitheater. The adjacent Charles Edwards Building houses local artists and arts groups. Local, regional, and national art and crafts are displayed in the public galleries, and the theaters host live theatrical performances and festivals throughout the year. Locals use the facility for adult and youth art classes of all kinds, from glass fusing to acrylics.

The densest concentration of crafts and fine arts in the area is to be found on the main drag of Matlacha on Pine Island. Many of the galleries are in little houses painted in a variety of sunset colors. Leoma Lovegrove's work is on display at **Matlacha Art Gallery** (4637 Pine Island Rd., 239/283-6453), and you'll find the metal sculptures of Peggy McTeague next door at **Wild Child Art Gallery** (4625 Pine Island Rd., 239/283-6006, 10 A.M.–5 P.M. Tues.–Sat., noon–4 P.M. Sun.), with a dozen or so other whimsical galleries within walking distance of the Matlacha drawbridge. So visitors can tour a number of these small galleries, Art Nights are held the second Friday of each month November–April, with the artists on hand to discuss their work.

## SHOPPING

Downtown Fort Myers is the city's entertainment district, but east of **Centennial Park** there is a strip of nice shops, galleries, and cafés perfect for exploring on a walk. Strictly a driving route, the **Tamiami Trail,** or U.S. 41, is lined with the basic businesses that cater to locals. You'll also find chain restaurants of all stripes along the busy road.

Serious shoppers will head to **Tanger Outlets** (20350 Summerlin Rd., 239/454-1974), which has more than 60 shops stocking deeply discounted clothing, housewares, and gifts. It's nothing you haven't seen before, including Polo Ralph Lauren, Liz Claiborne, Mikasa, Jones New York, Gap, Dana Buchman, Ellen Tracy, Nine West, Easy Spirit, Greg Norman, Bass, Coach, Van Heusen, Izod, Koret, Swim Mart, and Zales.

A more pleasant shopping experience, capitalizing on the area's glorious weather, is the **Bell Tower Shops** (13499 U.S. 41 SE, 239/489-1221). It's an outdoor mall anchored by Saks Fifth Avenue with the usual upscale chains (Banana Republic, Ann Taylor, Williams-Sonoma) and a 20-screen movie theater.

**Edison Mall** (4125 Cleveland Ave., 239/939-5464) is more of a workhorse mall serving the local community, with Macy's, Dillard's,

JCPenney, Sears, and lots of little mall stores. It's the biggest mall in southwest Florida.

**Fleamaster's** (4135 Dr. Martin Luther King Blvd., 239/334-7001, www.fleamall.com, 8 A.M.–4 P.M. Fri.–Sun.) is a serious hoot. It's a vast, 400,000-square-foot indoor flea market with something like 900 vendors—perfect for a rainy day exploration. From hardware to bath soap, this place sells some of everything.

The **Moromar Design Center** (10800 Corkscrew Road, Estero, 239/390-5111, www.idcfl.com) opened in 2007 as an interior design resource for fine furniture, accessories, fabrics, wall coverings, lighting, kitchen and bath products, flooring, and antiques. More than 80 internationally known showrooms (Agostino's, Ann Sacks Tile & Stone, Clive Christian, Gallery on Fifth, Paris Ceramics, and Stickley, for example) anchor the three-story center.

Another newcomer in Estero, **Coconut Point** (23106 Fashion Dr., Intersection of U.S. 41 and Coconut Rd., 239/992-9966, www.simon.com) is an open, Main Street–style shopping destination with Mediterranean architecture. The property includes 90,000 square feet of office space, residential units, and 1.2 million square feet of retail space. There you'll find Dillard's, West Coast Surf Shop, Coldwater Creek, Z Gallerie, Old Navy, Muvico Theatres, and restaurants like Bice Grand Café, Ruth's Chris Steakhouse, California Pizza Kitchen, and Blue Water Bistro.

And the **Gulf Coast Town Center** (9903 Gulf Coast Main Center Dr., Fort Myers, 239/267-0783, www.gulfcoasttowncenter.com) is another new shopping center with some of the usual suspects, but its real calling card is the hugely buff **Bass Pro Shops Outdoor World** (www.basspro.com), a 75,000-square-foot retail center that includes Islamorada Fish Company Restaurant and a boat showroom along with outdoor gear, clothing, and accessories for hiking, backpacking, wildlife-viewing, camping, outdoor cooking, and hooking those bass. Kids will be entertained by the indoor aquariums and water features stocked with native fish species.

## ACCOMMODATIONS
### Under $100

For not a lot of money, you can get just about everything at **Rock Lake Resort** (2937 Palm Beach Blvd., 239/332-4080, www.bestlodgingswflorida.com, $63–105). The nine little cottages (18 units) encircling a small lake were built in 1946. Canoeing, lighted tennis courts, a nature trail, barbecue facilities, and comfortable porches overlooking the water—it all sits on Billy Creek, which allows direct access for small boats to the Caloosahatchee River. Rock Lake isn't fancy, but it's just a short drive to the beach and half a mile from downtown. Rooms are wheelchair accessible, and there are also rooms for the hearing-impaired. Pets are welcome.

### $100-150

At Matlacha Pass right near the drawbridge on Pine Island, we bedded down one night at the funky **Bridge Water Inn** (4331 Pine Island Rd., Matlacha, 800/378-7666, $109–175). Some multitasking enthusiasts have been known to throw a line right out their motel window into the water off the west deck below—fishing and catching the football game simultaneously. You can watch the late-night snook anglers battling catfish for their bait right out the window.

On Fort Myers Beach, a natural family destination, there are lots of midpriced hotels and motels that fit the bill. **Sandpiper Gulf Resort** (5550 Estero Blvd., 239/463-5721, www.sandpipergulfresort.com, $90–245) is a fairly big, fairly low-rise hotel set in a few buildings. Opened in 1969, the resort has 63 large guest suites, some of them recently remodeled. There's a big pool surrounded by tropical gardens and the beach just beyond.

### Over $150

Not far away from the Sandpiper, the **Outrigger Beach Resort** (6200 Estero Blvd., Fort Myers Beach, 239/463-3131, www.outriggerfmb.com, $160–330) is a fun, tropical-themed, casual, high-rise hotel. It is a great choice for families and couples, located on a very wide stretch of beach where there will be plenty of room to stretch out during the busy summer months. All of the rooms are efficiencies with a king or two double beds, an additional sleeper sofa, and a full kitchen with stove, oven, and microwave. A comfortable living room adjoins to a dining room with a private balcony. The pool area is surrounded by thatched-roof cabanas and a lively tiki bar.

Significantly costlier but still a good deal, **Gull Wing Beach Resort** (6620 Estero Blvd., 239/765-4300, www.gullwingfl.com, $165–649) is another high-rise hotel on the quiet south end of Estero Island. There are 66 comfortable and spacious one-, two-, and three-bedroom family suites, with a lovely Gulf-side swimming pool, tennis courts, outdoor spa, barbecues, and gazebo area. Its parent company, SunStream Hotels & Resorts (800/625-4111, www.sunstream.com), is headquartered in Fort Myers Beach and has a number of other luxury properties locally.

The **DiamondHead Beach Resort** (2000 Estero Blvd., Fort Myers Beach, $200–420) offers one-bedroom, one-bath suites with Gulf, island, or pool views. All suites are 700 square feet, and some have been recently upgraded with granite countertops, flat screen TVs, new furnishings, flat kitchen cooktops, and an interactive computer in each room that allows communication to the front desk, room service, and multimedia concierge services. The resort has free wireless Internet, private balconies, refrigerator, and microwave and an additional queen-size sofa sleeper. There is a large heated pool, two hot tubs, and a fitness facility on-site.

The **Pointe Estero Beach Resort** (6640 Estero Blvd., Fort Myers Beach, $151–529) is the best pick for families and groups. All of the two-bedroom suites offer wraparound balconies where each room has a nice view of the Gulf. One-bedroom units are available upon request only. The resort features spacious kitchens, dining room seating for six people, two full baths with a marble jetted tub in every master bathroom, and a spacious living room with an extremely large wraparound couch and

180-degree views of the Gulf of Mexico from the floor-to-ceiling windows that surround the room. The property also has tennis courts, a heated pool, a trolley service around town, and water-sports activities on the beach. This property is also more family-oriented, with a kids' program and playroom.

One of the most stylish and well-appointed resorts in the area is the new **Resort at Marina Village** (5951 Silver King Blvd., Cape Coral, 259/541-5000, $129–349). The resort offers studio, one-bedroom, two-bedroom, and three-bedroom suites that range up to 2,225 square feet with views of the surrounding Caloosahatchee River, San Carlos Bay, and Gulf of Mexico. The on-site Tarpon Point Marina has a depth of 8–12 feet that can accommodate cruising boats of almost any size. The on-site restaurants and bars include lunch and dinner at the fun, outdoor tiki bar called the Nauti Mermaid with exceptional happy hour menu and drink specials; fine dining at Marker 92, specializing in seafood; and delicious brick oven–fired pizza. The pool area, with surrounding fountains and hot tub, is not to be missed, nor is the exceptional spa and fitness center.

**Sanibel Harbour Resort & Spa** (17260 Harbour Pointe Dr., Fort Myers, 239/466-4000, www.sanibel-resort.com, $150–600) had a huge renovation and reopened in 2005 with updated guest rooms, lobby, meeting space, and restaurants (including a good Chicago-style steakhouse). This is a big place, with 240 hotel rooms, 107 more elite and very private accommodations complete with concierge services at Grande Bay, and waterfront condominiums as well. It's just about the most luxurious resort-style spot in Fort Myers, with two gorgeous pools, restaurants and lounges to suit all needs, and a spa.

Bonita Springs is a nice residential area of Florida's Gulf Coast, and one of the draws for the visitor is ◖ **Hyatt Regency Coconut Point Resort & Spa** (5001 Coconut Rd., Bonita Springs, 239/444-1234, $255–600), halfway between Fort Myers and Naples in Bonita Springs. It's a deluxe, destination-

Boaters can sail right up to the Resort at Marina Village.

style hotel with 454 elegantly appointed guest rooms and lots of amenities on-site, including a Raymond Floyd–designed championship golf course, a day spa, and views of beautiful Estero Bay (beach not far away). Golf packages ($225–425 for a standard room) include accommodations, one round of golf at 18-hole Raptor Bay per night stay, a golf cart, unlimited range balls, a yardage book, and a golf club bag tag.

## FOOD

Fort Myers is awash in chains, from Carrabba's to Olive Garden to T.G.I. Friday's. You have to look a little to find the unique, independent gems.

### Breakfast

For traditional American breakfast, **Mel's Diner** (4820 S. Cleveland Ave., 239/275-7850, 6:30 A.M.–10 P.M. Sun.–Thurs., until 10:30 P.M. Fri. and Sat., $4–8) gives you all the diner staples. Mel's biscuits and sausage gravy will give you the get-up-and-go for a day at the beach, and kids love it here. It's a regional chain.

A delicious short stack of banana nut pancakes can be had for a very affordable price at **The Island's Pancake House** (2801 Estero Blvd., Seagrapes Plaza off Estero Blvd., Fort Myers Beach, 239/463-0033, $1.50–7.50), along with a wide variety of essential pre-kayaking breakfast foods.

Fort Myers residents swear by the hangover special at **Oasis Restaurant** (2260 Martin Luther King Jr. Blvd., 239/334-1566, 7 A.M.–3 P.M. Mon.–Fri., 8 A.M.–2 P.M. Sat. and Sun., $5–9), of three fluffy eggs enfolding cheese, sausage, and sautéed veggies, instrumental in the post-booze, saturated-fat-induced flushing, topped off by 26 ounces of Gatorade in the car on the way back to the hotel to take a nap. It serves breakfast all day—very casual—near the Edison & Ford estates.

## Casual

With live piano and jazz singers nightly, **Biddle's Restaurant & Piano Bar** (Sanibel Beach Plaza, 12984 S. Cleveland Ave., 239/433-4449, 11 A.M.–2 A.M. daily, $19–36) is a fairly chic hangout: faux-painted walls, richly upholstered booths, and a Pacific Rim fusion menu at dinner (macadamia-crusted grouper). The weekend brunch is great and à la carte, with excellent shrimp and grits and nice outdoor seating.

If you find yourself at the Bell Tower shopping center, you can't go wrong with a stop at **Blue Pointe Oyster Bar & Seafood Grill** (13499 S. Cleveland Ave., 239/433-0924, www.bluepointerestaurant.com, 11:30 A.M.–10 P.M. Mon.–Thurs., until 11 P.M. Fri. and Sat., noon–9 P.M. Sun., $17–33). It's a New England–style fish restaurant with excellent broiled swordfish and Florida black grouper, a nice crab cake, and good but slightly pricey oysters on the half shell.

Also at the Bell Tower, **Bistro 41** (13499 S. Cleveland Ave., 239/466-4141, 11:30 A.M.–10 P.M. Mon.–Fri., until 10:30 P.M. Sat., noon–8 P.M. Sun., $15–35) seems to be a local business favorite, upscale with an American seafood-and-steaks menu. Beware the daily specials' prices, which can run close to $40. Otherwise, it's a pleasant, something-for-everyone kind of place with a nice outdoor patio.

On Fort Myers Beach on Estero Island, lots of casual beachfront restaurants make great use of the location and purvey mostly seafood-centric cuisine. **Matanzas Inn Restaurant** (416 Crescent St., 239/463-3838, 11 A.M.–10 P.M. daily, $15–23) has a great deck and a nice fried grouper plate. **Chloe's on the Beach** (2000 Estero Blvd., 239/765-0595, 7:30–11 A.M. and 5–9 P.M. Mon.–Sat., 7:30 A.M.–1 P.M. Sun., $16–32) is in the DiamondHead Beach Resort, with more upscale continental cuisine and gorgeous water views. Make sure to check out the daily frozen drink special. And **Beach Pierside Grill** (1000 Estero Blvd., next to the pier, 239/765-7800, 11 A.M.–11 P.M. daily, $12–20) is more family friendly, featuring ribs, fried seafood platters, and the fat beach burger.

## Fine Dining

A favorite fancy restaurant in Fort Myers is **Veranda** (2122 2nd St., 239/332-2065, 11 A.M.–4 P.M. Mon.–Fri., 5:30–10 P.M. Mon.–Sat., $25–37), partly because it's set in two stately 100-year-old homes joined by publishing heir Peter Pulitzer in the 1970s for his buddy Fingers O'Bannon, who ran the restaurant then. So, it's the history, but the Veranda also seems like a happening place. The menu at Veranda is traditional but with contemporary touches, meaning pan-seared local grouper with wilted spinach, New York steak covered in gorgonzola, and artichoke fritters stuffed with blue crab.

The new Coconut Point Mall in Estero has introduced a number of upscale eateries to the local restaurant scene, the best of which are probably the hip **Blue Water Bistro** (23151 Village Shops Way, 239/949-2583, www.blue-waterbistro.net, 5:30–9:30 P.M. Mon.–Thurs., 5:30–10 P.M. Fri. and Sat., 4:30–8:30 P.M. Sun., $11–30) and the ubiquitous **Ruth's Chris Steakhouse** (239/948-8888, 4:30–10 P.M.

Mon.–Sat., until 9 P.M. Sun., $15–30)—worth a visit, especially if you're planning on being at the mall anyway. Otherwise, check out the recently opened **H2 Tapas and Wine Bar** (2214 Bay St., Fort Myers, 239/226-1687,

4–11 P.M. Mon.–Sat., $15–25), or a selection from the huge salad bar and then the slow-roasted prime rib at **Charley's Boat House Grill** (6241 Estero Blvd., Fort Myers Beach, 239/765-4700, 5–9:30 P.M. daily, $17–30).

# Sanibel Island

LEE COUNTY

There are more than 100 small barrier islands that flank the coastline of the greater Fort Myers area. Of these, Sanibel stands out—literally, because it bucks the system and lies east–west in a gentle, shrimp-shaped curve, and figuratively, because it is so well known and widely trafficked. The single biggest draw is nothing the chamber of commerce had any control over. The island's orientation, coupled with the fact that there are no offshore reefs, means that Sanibel is the recipient of the Gulf of Mexico's beneficence: more than 400 varieties of shells have been found along the 16 miles of white-sand beaches. The gently sloping sea floor, the patterns of tides and water circulation—it means that crown conch, lion's paw, angel wings, alphabet cones, and sand dollars wash up whole at your feet.

Birders would take issue with the shellers, though, on top draw. The birding on Sanibel is impressive for breadth as well as sheer numbers. More than half the island is encompassed by the J. N. "Ding" Darling National Wildlife Refuge, 6,354 acres of preserved subtropical barrier island habitat for Florida's native wetland, part of the largest undeveloped mangrove ecosystem in the country. Either on foot, biking, canoeing, or with a narrated tram ride, naturalists and sightseers observe wading birds, wetland birds, and the array of other Sanibel wildlife.

Connected to the mainland by a three-mile-long scenic drive across a causeway, Sanibel is a comfortable island. It welcomes families and traveling couples with a friendly, easy charm and fairly reasonable prices. It isn't the kind of island on which you'll find gigantic resort hotels. Most accommodations are low-rise; in

fact, buildings on the island can be only as tall as the tallest palm. There are no traffic lights, no street lamps, and no motorized water sports (such as Jet Skis or Ski-Doos).

Sanibel's main street is Periwinkle Way, a picturesque thoroughfare that, pre–Hurricane Charley, was canopied by a tall stand of Australian pines (not native) and palms. A massive replanting effort in recent years has made it fully leafed once again (but no pines). Shops, small inns, and casual restaurants punctuate the road from the Sanibel Lighthouse to Tarpon Bay Road. Fort Myers is where to have your home base if you want museums, spectator sports, and attractions; Captiva is where to go for a slow pace and lots of quiet relaxation. Sanibel is like the middle child who likes to mix it up a little—there are things to do beyond beach walking, with friendly restaurants and a great shell museum.

## SPORTS AND RECREATION
### Beaches

Sanibel is unusual among barrier islands due to its east–west orientation. Because of this, the surf is gentle and the shells arrive whole and pristine. The beaches along East, Middle, and West Gulf Drive slope gradually, making the shallows vast and safe for young waders and beachcombers. There are some beach rules to follow: Pets must be on leashes and cleaned up after (no pets at all on Captiva beaches); no alcoholic beverages on the beaches November–May; no open fires; and no collecting live shells. All public beach access areas on the island have restrooms, some with concessions and picnic tables. Beach parking is $2 per hour.

# SEA TURTLES

From the beginning of May to the end of October, the beaches of Sanibel play host to a different kind of visitor. Loggerheads, the most common sea turtles in Florida, make their way out of the Gulf and up the beaches to lay their eggs. An estimated 14,000 females nest in the southeastern United States each year, many of them from the northern tip of Fort Myers Beach to the Lee-Collier border of Bonita Beach. Called loggerheads because of their big heads, they can reach 200-350 pounds and measure about three feet long.

**More than 90 percent of the loggerheads that nest in the United States nest on Florida beaches.**

Female loggerheads return to the beaches on which they were born to lay their own eggs. They painstakingly dig nest cavities with their rear flippers, deposit about 100 golf ball-sized eggs, cover them up, and head back out to sea. And two months later the two-inch hatchlings break out and flap their way toward the moonlit sea. Sanibel has a lights-out policy on beaches so the little turtles aren't confused in their mission, stumbling toward a brightly lit condo instead.

According to the Florida Fish and Wildlife Research Institute, the number of known nesting loggerheads between the years 1998 and 2010 declined by 25 percent. Currently the impacts of the BP oil spill on loggerheads and other sea turtle populations in the Gulf are being studied. The oil spill, collision with boats, habitat destruction, drought, hurricanes – all of these contribute to the dismal numbers. While loggerheads are currently listed as threatened, petitions have been drawn up to suggest their status should be changed to the more dire endangered.

What you can do to help:

• Pack up your beach trash, monofilament fishing line, and especially plastic bags and plastic six-pack holders. Turtles mistake this stuff for tasty sea creatures undulating in the water, and they often get snarled in fishing line.

• Observe nesting turtles only from a distance. That goes for your curious pets, too. Dogs must be leashed on Sanibel, and do so even at night when no one's around to enforce the regulation. Last year a dog on one of the local beaches wiped out 67 hatchlings with one exuberant gambol.

• Stack up beach chairs or other items that might impede the baby loggerheads' progress toward the water.

• If you're staying in a beach house, close your drapes or blinds after dark. If you use exterior lights, make sure they are 25-watt yellow bug lights. Don't use flashlights, fishing lanterns, or flash photography on the beach.

• Leave nest identification markers in place. To report a wandering hatchling or a dead or injured turtle, call the **Florida Fish & Wildlife Conservation Commission** (800/ DIAL-FMP) or the volunteer organization **Turtle Time** (239/481-5566).

If you have to pick two beaches to visit from among the 14 miles of sand, start with **Lighthouse Beach & Fishing Pier** (turn left on Periwinkle Way, the first stop sign as you enter the island, and follow Periwinkle Way, which terminates at the parking lot for the boardwalk) and **Bowman's Beach** (off Sanibel-Captiva Rd.; turn left on Bowman's Beach Rd.). The heart of the former is the **Sanibel Lighthouse Boardwalk** (1 Periwinkle Way, Sanibel, 239/472-6397), the most frequently photographed landmark on the island. It's been here since 1884 on the eastern tip of the island, near the bay side. The beach has a lovely T-dock fishing pier and a boardwalk nature trail through native wetlands. Bowman's Beach is more remote and quiet. Park in the lot and walk over a bridge to secluded white beach. It offers showers and barbecue grills.

Beyond these, **Gulfside City Park** (mid-island on Algiers Ln. off Casa Ybel Rd.), **Tarpon Bay Beach** (also mid-island at the south end of Tarpon Bay Rd. at W. Gulf Dr.) and the **Causeway Beaches** (adjacent to the causeway on both sides) are inviting.

## ◖ J. N. "Ding" Darling National Wildlife Refuge

J. N. "Ding" Darling National Wildlife Refuge (1 Wildlife Dr., Sanibel, 239/472-1100, www.fws.gov/dingdarling, 7:30 A.M.–sunset, closed Fridays, $5/vehicle, $1 walkers or bicyclists, $10 tram ride) takes up more than half of Sanibel Island. The refuge was named for Pulitzer Prize–winning cartoonist Jay Norwood Darling, the first environmentalist to hold a presidential cabinet post (during FDR's administration), and it is an absolute marvel. It contains a visitors center, a five-mile driving tour route, hiking trails, tram service, canoe and kayak rentals, and guided interpretive programs.

The 6,354-acre refuge is made up of a variety of estuarine and freshwater habitats. You'll see mudflats and mangrove islands, wide swaths of seagrass and open water, West Indian hardwood hammocks and ridges, and places poetically described as spartina swales. But the real draw is birds.

Ordinarily I'd advise walking or biking through a refuge like this, 2,825 acres of it designated as wilderness area—you know, go at your own pace, get a close-up look at things. But then you'd miss out on the naturalist-narrated tram ride full of competitive birders.

An up-close look at birders is half the fun of a day at "Ding" Darling. On the tram ride, listening to these birders, you can learn to recognize black-crowned night herons and immature ibis and see wood storks, peregrine falcons, and a wealth of the 238 bird species that hang out in the refuge. The best birding time is early morning, about an hour before or after low tide, when you'll see birders equipped with cameras set up on tripods. Watch what they're watching, and ask questions. You'll see things rare and magnificent. The wildlife observation tower is a superb place to hang out any time of the day, and the education center (open 9 A.M.–5 P.M. daily Nov.–Apr., until 4 P.M. the rest of the year) provides a little guidance to the rookie.

**Tarpon Bay Explorers** (900 Tarpon Bay Rd., Sanibel, 239/472-8900), which runs the tram tour, also offers a 90-minute kayak trail tour ($30 adults, $20 children) along the Commodore Creek water trail and a sunset paddle ($40 adults, $25 children) out to the rookery islands in the refuge. You'll see hundreds upon hundreds of egrets, herons, anhingas, and ibis, all bedded down in the treetops for the night.

## Shelling

Beaches are the most magnetic draw on Sanibel, with wide lengths of white-sand beaches and some of the best shelling in the world. Some say 400 species of seashells dot the beaches here, from polka-dotted junonia to lacy apple murex and fat lightning whelks.

The most fruitful time to shell is early morning, at low tide, and after a storm, especially after the big-wave coastal storms in January and February. Other experts say the peak season for shelling is May–September. Walk slowly and look for seashells hidden just beneath the surface of the sand where the surf breaks, about where the water comes up to your knee. Wear polarized sunglasses so you can see into the water, bring a bag or fanny pack for your treasure, and don't take any shell that's inhabited.

The south side of Sanibel has a wide shallow beach that seems to attract shells without battering them—they stay whole and perfect. You're more likely to find good ones where the competition isn't too fierce—the less populated the stretch of beach, the better. (The beaches of North Captiva and Cayo Costa islands are known, among aficionados, for their lack of people and wealth of starfish, conchs, and sand dollars.) Generally, smaller shells are found closer to the Lighthouse Beach end, with larger shells the closer you get to Captiva. Common shells include lightning whelk, cockle, scallop, murex, tulip, olive, little coquina, and conch. If you find a junonia, hang on to it for the bragging rights.

If you're coming up empty-handed, turn it over to the professionals, with one of the local shelling charters. **Duke Shells** ('Tween Waters Marina, Captiva, 239/472-5462) customizes three- and four-hour trips to include nature tours and shelling. **Captain Mike Fuery's Shelling Charters** ('Tween Waters Marina, 239/466-3649, www.mikefuerystours.com, private charter for up to four passengers is $250 for a two-hour trip) is another famous shelling outfit, its tours featured in *National Geographic, Southern Living, Martha Stewart,* and other magazines. Shelling trips for romantic couples seem to be a specialty.

## Kayaking

The **Great Calusa Blueway Paddling Trail** is a 100-mile mapped-and-markered route for paddlers of all skill levels to explore. Following the trail of the area's early fishermen, the Calusa people, it runs along Lee County's coastal waters from Cayo Costa and Charlotte Harbor south through Pine Island Sound and Matlacha Pass to Estero Bay and the Imperial River in Bonita Springs.

If you're not an outdoorsy type whose idea of fun is an Eskimo roll in fierce white water, you can enjoy a couple of days of nice, easy kayaking, with stops for lunch and bird-watching, and a comfy bed at the end of each day.

The website (www.greatcalusablueway.com) gives details on the routes, what you'll see along the way, where to launch or stop, maps, GPS coordinates, and more, but you will still need to pick up a kayak or canoe. Outfitters offer guided trips (even some moonlight excursions), and there are numerous rentals and launch areas if you want to head out on your own.

You start the first day on the Pine Island Sound–Matlacha Pass section of the paddling trail. Crunching over the gravel at the Fish House Marina, you find your way to **Gulf Coast Kayak** (4530 Pine Island Rd., Matlacha, 239/283-1125, single kayak $30 half day, $40 full day). You get paddles, life jackets, trail maps, and kayaks and put in just at the drawbridge at Matlacha Pass.

The second segment to be mapped, the Pine Island Sound trail is gentle and sheltered. You can see small black crabs scoot along red mangrove trunks, and great blue herons wade in their shade as you meander through backwaters and mangrove tunnels from marker 84 to marker 89. A few hours later you realize paddling makes you hungry.

From here you head back down through Buzzard Bay until you reemerge at the Old Fish House. Lunch here is local shrimp quesadillas, local smoked mullet, and a novelty food: fried mullet gizzard (it seems that the mullet, mostly vegetarian, is like a chicken in that it has no stomach but a crop and a gizzard). Order at the counter, eat at picnic tables, and watch the snook and needlenose gar churn the water down below.

On day two you put in at Fort Myers Beach, which is actually on the island of Estero, connected to Fort Myers by a causeway. There are several worthwhile beaches here (Bowditch Point Regional Park, Lynn Hall Memorial Park), but we set our sights on **Lovers Key State Park** (8700 Estero Blvd., Fort Myers Beach, 239/463-4588, 8 A.M.–sundown, $8/ car up to eight people, $4 single occupancy car, $2 pedestrians and bicyclists), another

COURTESY OF LEE COUNTY CVB

Kayaking the 100-mile Great Calusa Blueway Paddling Trail is a great way to become familiar with the beaches and islands of the area.

key embarkation point on the Great Calusa Blueway.

From here you head to the **Nature Recreation Management** concessionaire (239/765-7788, www.naturerecreationmanagement.com, single kayak $20 for half day), pick up paddles and gear, then headed to the launch spot to put in your kayaks. Using a Blueway map, you can make your way from marker 8 to markers 13 and 22. In parts the water is shallow, maybe a foot deep, and you quietly make your way out to congregations of ibis, egrets, and herons. If you keep paddling you can make it to **Mound Key** (Estero Bay, 239/992-0311, daylight hours, free), a complex of Calusa mounds made of shells, fish bones, and pottery. Thought to be a sacred ceremonial center for the native people, in 1566 it was settled by the Spanish and became the site of the first Jesuit mission in the Spanish New World. That didn't last long, as the Calusa weren't thrilled with the settlers.

The shell construction contains mounded platforms, ceremonial mounds, ridges, substantial carved-out canals, and open water courts—evidence of a fairly elaborate community some 2,000 years ago. There are not a lot of interpretive markers or signs here, but it's a nice place for a picnic.

**Adventure Sea Kayak** ('Tween Waters Inn Marina, 14000 Captiva Dr., Captiva, 239/822-3337, www.kayak-captiva.com, $40/person) conducts kayak tours, its specialty being interactive trips that focus on the wildlife, ecology, and history of the barrier islands. Also based in Captiva, **Captiva Kayak Company & Wildside Adventures** (11401 Andy Rosse Ln. at bayside McCarthy's Marina, Captiva, 239/395-2925, www.captivakayaks.com) offers rentals, instruction, and sunrise, sunset, and starlight tours. On Sanibel, **Tarpon Bay Explorers** (900 Tarpon Bay Rd., Sanibel, 239/472-8900, www.tarponbayexplorers.com, $15–180) has a range of services, from canoe, kayak, and bike rentals to guided tours. And if you just want to rent a kayak or canoe, try **Gulf Coast Kayak** (4530 Pine Island Rd., Matlacha, 239/283-1125, www.gulfcoastkayak.com, single kayak or canoe $30 half day, $40 full day) or farther south with **Estero River Canoe & Tackle Outfitters** (20991 S. Tamiami Trail, Estero, 239/992-4050, www.all-florida.com/swestero.htm), which offers 300 canoes and kayaks, all different kinds.

## Sea School

The newly opened **Sanibel Sea School** (414 Lagoon Dr., 239/472-8585, www.sanibelseaschool.org) is dedicated to teaching children and adults about marine ecosystems. It uses the setting of the barrier island habitats of Sanibel and Captiva as an opportunity to touch, feel, and understand. Adult classes might focus on bivalves, gastropods, local history, and natural history, with field trips to study mollusk distribution, fish seining, investigating the mangroves at Blind Pass, and exploring the island on Indigo Trail and the Bailey Tract hikes. Call for a schedule of classes and drop-in events.

## Biking

It's an island pastime partly because it's relatively safe (there are 25 miles of wide, paved biking path) and partly because you can cover serious ground on these pancake-flat islands. You can take an extremely enjoyable bike ride from the eastern tip of Sanibel to the northern tip of Captiva, stopping occasionally to take a swim in the Gulf. You can also bike on the main drags, Sanibel-Captiva Road and Periwinkle Way, or swing through a stretch of the J. N. "Ding" Darling Wildlife Refuge, or skirt the water's edge along Gulf Drive. The **Sanibel-Captiva Islands Chamber of Commerce** (1159 Causeway Rd., Sanibel, 239/472-1080) has a free bike path map.

Many inns on Sanibel and Captiva offer complimentary bikes to their guests—ask before you set up a rental elsewhere. The oldest bike shop on Sanibel is **Billy's Rentals** (1470 Periwinkle Way, 239/472-5248, www.billysrentals.com, 8:30 A.M.–5 P.M. daily, two-hour bike rentals range $5–10, also daily and weekly rentals).

Billy's offers regular hybrids, but a range of unique stuff as well, from adult trikes to recumbent bikes, Segways, and these cool multiperson surreys. You can also rent jog strollers and motor scooters at Billy's. **Finnimores Bikes & Skates** (2353 Periwinkle Way, 239/472-5577, www.finnimores.com, 9 A.M.–4 P.M. daily, four-hour rentals $9–14) is another wonderful shop, with no charge for delivery and pickup for a multiday rental. It also has inline skates (they come with free helmet and pad rentals), umbrellas, fishing equipment, boogie boards, and most other essential fun-in-the-sun beach gear.

## Birding

Birds just like it here. Some live here year-round, other migrating species choose this island as a stopover or a convenient flyway terminus. J. N. "Ding" Darling National Wildlife Refuge is a wealth of avian splendor, but the rest of the island is a birder's paradise, too. Sanibel boasts so many habitats—freshwater wetlands, brackish mangrove estuaries, beaches, woodland—that 240 different species feel at home here.

The ornithologically inclined have websites and chat groups devoted entirely to bird trails and spots on Sanibel. One of the local papers even has a regular bird column, and traffic stops fairly regularly for the recalcitrant crossing heron or egret.

Part of the thrill is the chase, tramping around with your binoculars trained on the treetops or water's edge at low tide. Here's where to look: rare white pelicans hang out in Pine Island Sound; ospreys and eagles nest on telephone poles above the bike paths and along Sanibel-Captiva Road; wood storks troll for snacks in roadside ditches in the winter; burrowing owls dig tunnels in shopping center parking lots; sandhill cranes walk gracefully across expanses of lawn in groups of three. The lighthouse area of Sanibel is a good place to see birds, as are the mangrove islands off Pine Island Sound and Tarpon Bay on Sanibel. The little clumps of island off the causeway area attract lots of species as well. For an absolute sure thing, you'll hit pay dirt in Periwinkle Park, which has an aviary for lovebirds, toucans, flamingos, and talking birds.

## SIGHTS
### ◖ Bailey-Matthews Shell Museum

Slippersnail. White baby ear. Ponderous ark. All of these are the beautiful names of shells. The Bailey–Matthews Shell Museum (3075 Sanibel-Captiva Rd., Sanibel, 239/395-2233, www.shellmuseum.org, 10 A.M.–5 P.M. daily, $7 adults, $4 children 5–16, children 4 and under free) will make a shell collector out of most people. It's not a vast museum—it will occupy a pleasant 90 minutes or so—but it equips you to go out there and get yourself some of Neptune's treasures. Shells are arranged in thematic groupings from around the world, with an emphasis on the local offerings, and there are anthropological exhibits on humanity's relationship to shells (did you know that Native Americans' use of conch shells as weapons was the origin of the expression "conk on the head"?). There's also a video called *Mollusks in Action* shown five times each day.

### Sanibel Historical Village and Museum

Sanibel Historical Village and Museum (950 Dunlop Rd., Sanibel, 239/472-4648, 10 A.M.–4 P.M. Wed.–Sat., $5 adults, children 17 and under free) is a celebration of the local history of the island. This little cluster of historic buildings dragged from all over the island includes pioneer Clarence Rutland's original island home from the early 1900s, the Burnap Cottage built in 1898, Miss Charlotta's Tea Room restored to its 1930s look, Bailey's General Store, the original Sanibel post office, an old schoolhouse, an antique Model T, a Sanibel Lighthouse display, archived newspaper articles, and photos. The on-site town historian is a wealth of information and a wonderful storyteller.

### Old Town

For more historical sightseeing, the East End village of Old Town was originally a fish camp

built by Cuban fishermen in the 1860s, prior to construction of the lighthouse in 1884. The Sanibel Historical Society has a walking and biking tour map of 19 historic sites along a stretch of about 2.5 miles. You can pick up a copy of the map at the chamber of commerce (1159 Causeway Rd.) or at the Sanibel Historical Village and Museum.

## ENTERTAINMENT AND EVENTS
### Theater and Cinema

The **Schoolhouse Theater** (2200 Periwinkle Way, Sanibel, 239/472-6862, www.theschoolhousetheater.com, 8 P.M. Mon.–Sat., $30 adults, $25 children 16 and under), an institution in town, moved in 2004 to a larger, 160-seat theater. The little community group puts on crowd-pleasing musical revues. With a grand piano on stage, the theater does all-music performances. The restored 1896 one-room schoolhouse that used to house the theater has been hauled over to the Sanibel Historical Village and Museum to add another element to the little cluster of historic sites.

If you're just itching to be entertained, catch a flick at the **Island Cinema** (535 Tarpon Bay Rd., in Bailey's shopping center, 239/472-1701). It shows first-run mainstream films.

### Festivals

The biggest festival in the area takes place peak season, in March, but it's still worth considering. Sanibel hosts an annual **Shell Fair** (www.sanibelcaptivashellclub.com), usually held at the Sanibel Community House (2173 Periwinkle Way). The largest and longest-running shell festival in the country, it draws serious shell collectors from around the world. For more information, contact Anne Joffe at 239/472-3151.

## SHOPPING

Sanibel's shopping is as low-key as the island itself. **Periwinkle Place** (2075 Periwinkle Way, www.periwinkleplace.com) boasts 28 attractive shops, a tropical bistro called Gully's, and the enjoyable Sanibel Day Spa, all connected by covered walkways and shaded by banyan trees. Its clothing shops are mostly geared to beach- and sportswear; there are nice toy and swimsuit shops. **Olde Sanibel Shoppes** (630 Tarpon Bay Rd., 239/472-2783) is another cluster of gift shops, clothing, and jewelry, with a couple of casual restaurants thrown into the mix. The **Village Shops** (2340 Periwinkle Way) has roughly a similar lineup, and the 15 shops arrayed in the low pink buildings of **Tahitian Gardens** (1975–2019 Periwinkle Way) sell artisan candles, bright cotton clothing, jewelry, bathing suits, T-shirts, and giftware. This center also contains one of the island's best breakfast spots, the Sanibel Café.

None of this will rock your world—for a real one-of-a-kind island shopping experience, browse a while in **She Sells Sea Shells** (2422 Periwinkle Way, 239/472-8080). The funky shop contains shells from all over the place, but many are the same species you'll see stooped enthusiasts mining for (some even have lighted miner's hats in the early mornings) along Sanibel beaches.

And if you need a regular old grocery store, **Bailey's** (2477 Periwinkle Way, 239/472-1516, 7 A.M.–9 P.M. daily) is the biggest local market.

### Galleries

Now, Sanibel has got some galleries worth investigating. It seems to attract residents of artistic temperament, many of them opening shops that feature their work. **Tower Gallery** (751 Tarpon Bay Rd., 239/472-4557, www.towergallery-sanibel.com) is a good place to start, and it's hard to miss in an electric blue and green building. It's a cooperative of 23 local artists. Representing all media and a real mix of styles, the work in the gallery is all juried. Right nearby you'll find another small cooperative called the **Hirdie Girdie Gallery** (2490 Library Way, 239/395-0027, www.hirdiegirdie.com, 10 A.M.–4 P.M. Wed.–Sat.), and next door to it the **Tin Can Art Gallery** (2480 Library Way, 239/472-9002), with the eccentric work of artist Bryce McNamara.

Sanibel's **BIG Arts** (Barrier Island Group for the Arts, 900 Dunlop Rd., 239/395-0900) is a community cultural arts organization that has a center for island arts. It has two galleries open to the public (1–4 P.M. Mon.–Fri.), a sculpture garden, and performance space. Exhibits change monthly, and there are frequent workshops, lectures, films, and concerts.

## ACCOMMODATIONS

There's very little on Sanibel Island that's dirt cheap. On the other hand, nothing is extremely upscale. It's the kind of place where you get a sweet apartment, hotel, or motel rental a few steps from the beach, and you don't worry about whether there are luxurious amenities because you have the Gulf of Mexico at your doorstep.

If you're thinking about staying for a whole week it makes sense to rent a condo or cottage. **Cottages to Castles of Sanibel & Captiva** (2427 Periwinkle Way, 800/472-5385, www.cottages-to-castles.com) has a number of intimate and affordable one-week rentals; it also offers the enormous seven-bedroom pink house called Sandhurst that was featured as the 2004 MTV Summer Beach House. The rates on the condos are very reasonable offseason ($600–1,750 weekly).

My two favorites on the island have a subtle Old Florida nostalgia to them. Both have nice interiors and modern amenities like Wi-Fi, but they have a historic feel, the kinds of places you could imagine visiting for decades. The 【 **Island Inn on Sanibel Island** (3111 W. Gulf Dr., 800/851-5088, www.islandinnsanibel.com, $140–660) in fact opened in 1895. Look at the scrapbook of clippings to get a sense of who has roamed this compound of lovely little cottages and larger lodges on 10 acres, with 550 feet of unobstructed beachfront. Draws include shuffleboard, table tennis, and bike rentals, but it's the warmth of the staff and other guests that seems anachronistic. The same can be said of 【 **West Wind Inn** (3345 W. Gulf Dr., 239/472-1541, www.westwind-inn.com, $190–375), a beachfront place in the quiet part of the island. Rooms have kitchenettes, but don't skip breakfast at its Normandie Seaside Restaurant, which seems to be a locals' morning hangout. West Wind's 500-foot stretch of beach is a marvel for stargazing. The lush landscaping surrounding the large heated pool captures the essence of this tropical destination. The inn is casual and comfortable, with a touch of old Florida styling in the rooms and a focus on traditional elegance in the dining room. The staff goes out of their way to ensure superb customer service and provide a unique level of attention to their guests' needs.

**Shalimar Resort** (2823 W. Gulf Dr., 239/472-1353, www.shalimar.com, $165–385 per night, $2,095–2,625 per week) is another favorite getaway, with 33 one- and two-bedroom cottages, apartments, and motel efficiencies spread around a huge property right on the Gulf. All units have full kitchens, and the pool is beautiful.

**Sundial Beach Resort** (1451 Middle Gulf Dr., Sanibel, 239/472-4151, www.sundialresort.com, $179–749) has 270 one- and two-bedroom suites that all have a condo vibe, complete with full kitchens. It sits in 33 acres of tropical landscape right along the beach and has a tremendous weekday camp for children 4–11. **Sanibel Inn** (937 E. Gulf Dr., Sanibel, 239/472-3181, www.sanibelinn.com, $189–589) is smaller, with 94 hotel rooms and one-bedroom suites. Outside, the inn sits in the shade of more than 600 palms, with butterfly gardens all around and complimentary use of the inn's bikes. Inside, bamboo flooring and shades of green, blue, and light brown give the rooms a relaxed style. The Sanibel Inn also offers a wonderful children's educational/entertainment program. For adults, the Dunes Golf & Tennis Club is nearby.

## FOOD

The restaurants of Sanibel are mostly fun, casual locations that serve lots of delicious seafood. Expect menu prices on Sanibel to be slightly higher than most other areas along the Gulf Coast. You're mostly paying for the view and expensive location, but you can cut the cost by doing the early-bird special before 6 P.M. offered at many restaurants and happy hour at the bars. Plus, there are a few really good deals on the island.

### Breakfast

**Lighthouse Cafe** (362 Periwinkle Way, 239/472-0303, breakfast served 7 A.M.–3 P.M. daily, open 5–9 P.M. in the winter months, $5–9 for breakfast) usually beats the early-morning competition, hands down, whether you're a fan of the seafood Benedict or the blueberry whole-wheat hotcakes.

### Lunch

Novelist Randy Wayne White is about the biggest booster this area has. Although I know when he was young he was a light tackle fishing guide right in this neighborhood, I'm not quite sure how often he's in residence at the restaurant named for the main character of many of his books set in these parts. Wayne White is actually purported to be a good cook, with a seafood cookbook to his name. Regardless of who's cooking, **Doc Ford's Sanibel Rum Bar & Grille** (975 Rabbit Rd., 239/472-8311, 11 A.M.–10 P.M. daily, $11–30) is a blast, with lots of TVs blaring the game, good sandwiches, and great drinks. The food—panko-breaded fried shrimp, Cuban sandwiches, pulled pork—is better than you might expect for such a laid-back setting.

**Sanibel Café** (2007 Periwinkle Way, 239/472-5323, 7 A.M.–3 P.M. daily, $8–17) seems like a locals' hangout, unpretentious and friendly. Go for the fat blue-cheese hamburgers.

### Dinner

The menus at the following three places seem cut from the same mold. At **McT's Shrimp House & Tavern** (1523 Periwinkle Way, 239/472-3161, 4–10 P.M. daily, $12–22) the draw is the Sanibel Steamer, a huge tray of steamed seafood, or the all-you-can-eat shrimp and crab platters. It's lively and casual. The same can be said of **Island Cow** (2163

Periwinkle Way, 239/472-0606, 7 A.M.–9 P.M. daily, $8–16), which occasionally has a mooing contest among the guests, the winner of which gets a T-shirt in addition to deep and abiding respect. There's also live music, a wonderful outdoor patio, generous seafood baskets with fries—and they serve a great breakfast, too. It's a wonderfully fun restaurant, with excellent food, where you can save a lot of "moooo-lah." And **Jacaranda** (1223 Periwinkle Way, 239/472-1771, 5–10 P.M. daily, $16–32) has a funky bar and a screened patio (good for when the bugs are biting). The Jac has music nightly (reggae on the weekends), sweet oysters from the patio raw bar, and a fairly extensive late-night menu.

**Matzaluna** (1200 Periwinkle Way, 239/472-1998, 4:30–9:30 P.M. daily, $11–17) is more traditional. The wood-fired pizzas get top honors, with hearty baked pasta dishes (lasagna, stuffed shells) placing a close second. Like many island spots, it offers drink specials during happy hour and really good $0.99 pizza slices at the bar.

# Captiva Island

Sanibel's northern neighbor, Captiva Island, is smaller, only about a half-mile wide and five miles long. It is at once more laid-back and more exclusive, perfect for a solitary getaway or romantic escape. Captiva has less commerce, fewer hotels and inns, fewer people in general. A fair percentage of the island's houses, all recessed behind dense pines and thick foliage, are the beach retreats of wealthy and often absentee owners, contributing to the island being quieter than Sanibel.

Captiva, with Captiva Drive running its length, has a relaxed downtown area of beach bars, restaurants, and gift shops that draw their inspiration from the beaches of Key West and the lyrics of Jimmy Buffet tunes. Captiva Village uses colorful and upbeat pastels, and some of the restaurants (such as the Bubble Room (such as the Bubble Room) adopt a fun and eccentric approach to decorating. Things are casual without being run-down—which lets much more upscale accommodations seem proper on Captiva. South Seas Island Resort dominates a whole section at the northern tip of Captiva, where it breaks before the island of North Captiva (once attached). Its sprawling charm and incredible beach set a tone for the island.

There are few attractions on the island, although much to do. Walk, run, fish, canoe, sit and read, or just sit. Anne Morrow Lindbergh was so inspired by Captiva's tranquility that it's where she wrote her best-selling book, *A Gift from the Sea*.

## SPORTS AND RECREATION
### Beaches
Captiva's beaches are less populated than those on Sanibel, for a couple of reasons. First, there are more private homes on Captiva, visited sporadically by their affluent owners. Thus, there are just fewer feet to churn the sand and rustle the packs of waterbirds. Second, the shelling is better on Sanibel. But Captiva's waters are clearer and the swimming slightly better. **Captiva Beach** (at the end of Captiva Dr., free but limited parking) is a case in point—beautiful sand, lovely clear water, and only a few people in sight. It's a great place from which to watch the sunset. Because of fairly swift currents, don't count on swimming at **Turner Beach** (Sanibel-Captiva Rd. at Blind Pass Bridge), but it's still a favorite among fisherfolk and shellers.

Gulf-side beach erosion has been a problem in recent years, exacerbated by recent storms. Private and public funds have been raised to restore beaches by pumping in sand from offshore.

### Fishing
The South Seas Island Resort hosts the annual **Caloosa Catch & Release Tournament**

on Captiva each June. This one is known as the largest single-site public flats tournament in Florida, with more than $120,000 in cash and prizes in 2010. People here are serious about fishing, and not just about the seasonal giant tarpon.

What are you likely to catch? Redfish is a pretty steady catch in these parts, some over 10 pounds. The species has rebounded since the New Orleans blackening craze made them a hot commodity. They can be fished on the flats. Snook is best in the springtime, and the season is closed December 15–January 31 and June–August. You'll catch lots of speckled trout in the winter when they're especially large; they tend to hang out in three to five feet of water near the edges of the grass flats and sand holes. Tarpon are the area's biggest draw, huge fish that range 100–150 pounds with lots of fight in them. (Some say the very first tarpon ever taken on rod and reel was in southwest Florida, near Punta Rassa across San Carlos Bay from Sanibel in 1885.) Tarpon season runs from the latter part of April through August. Then there are cobia (here Feb.–July, but best in April and May), tripletail, and jacks for much of the year on the flats, and black grouper far out in the Gulf. Commercial catches of grouper have been limited recently, so sportfishers might benefit from increased numbers.

Fishing charters start at around $200 for a half-day trip, and the charter captain provides the boat, fishing license, fishing gear, equipment, and bait. Sometimes the client pays an additional fee for gas—ask about this. As a matter of etiquette, a tip of $20–50 is customary, as is buying your captain and crew a meal or drinks at the end of your fishing trip. Many guides will clean and fillet your edible catch—if you don't want all the fish, give it to whomever seems interested dockside. As for mounting and taxidermy: Big fish are largely catch and release, so have a picture taken of yourself with your catch before you release it. Then, one of the new breed of high-tech taxidermists will create a lifelike plastic model of your prize.

Figure out whether you want to do deepwater fishing, cast in the flats, or maybe take a fly-fishing lesson, then visit the marinas to ask around about charter captains, prices, what people are catching, and where. **Capt. Jim's Charters** ('Tween Waters Marina, 15951 Captiva Dr., 239/472-1779, $225–350) does back-bay fishing; **Capt. Joe's Charters** (Castaways Marina, Sanibel-Captiva Rd., Sanibel, 239/472-8658, www.captjoescharters.com, $250–400) does back-bay and fly-fishing; **Captain Van Hubbard/Let's Go Fishin'** (239/697-6944, www.captvan.com, $400–600) does sight casting for giant tarpon and snook seasonally; **Soulmate Charters** (17544 Lebanon Rd., Fort Myers, 239/851-1242, www.soulmatecharters.com, $350–550) offers backcountry fishing with light spin tackle and fly-fishing. The list goes on, with more than 50 charter captains willing to help you wet a line.

## Sailing

Take the three-day certification program with **Offshore Sailing School** (16731 McGregor Blvd., Fort Myers, 888/454-7015, www.offshore-sailing.com, courses for beginners, racers, and cruisers, basic keelboating class tuition $895). It's a tremendous amount of fun, three days on the water with an instructor and three other students, plus hours of classroom time learning all the sailing jargon, parts of the boat, points of sail, etc. At the end of the class you take a fairly difficult 80-question test, and you get out and show your sailing chops to your teacher, complete with man-overboard demonstrations and doing a quick stop by "shooting" into the wind.

If you're a goal-oriented person, it's a great activity to build a vacation around. You learn on a midsize daysailer, a Colgate 26, designed specifically for training and chosen by the U.S. Naval Academy to replace their training fleet. From here, you can take any number of other courses designed for more advanced sailors—performance sailing, live-aboard cruising, or a camp for racing sailors. At the very least you'll be able to tie nautical knots as a party trick.

Classes are held at the Pink Shell Beach

Resort & Spa in Fort Myers Beach and the South Seas Island Resort on Captiva. Call for information.

## SHOPPING

Hand-painted souvenirs and shell trinkets can be found along Sanibel-Captiva Road and in the Captiva Village area along Andy Rosse Lane, at the only four-way stop on Captiva. A popular shop here is **Jungle Drums** (11532 Andy Rosse Ln., 239/395-2266), a collection of wildlife, island, and environmental art in a variety of media.

## ACCOMMODATIONS
### Under $150

If you want to be where the action is, **C Captiva Island Inn** (11508 Andy Rosse Ln., 239/395-0882, www.captivaislandinn.com, $99–300) is a wonderful bed-and-breakfast right in the middle of teeny Captiva Village. There are traditional B&B rooms, one- and two-bedroom cottages, a loft, and a suite. The owners also have a four-bedroom house with 4.5 baths for big gatherings.

Jensen's has two options—one more fishing-focused, the other beachier. **Jensen's on the Gulf** (15300 Captiva Dr., 239/472-4684, www.gocaptiva.com, motel suites $150–300, apartments $175–400, houses $300–600) has nine units directly on the Gulf. **Jensen's Twin Palm Cottages** (15107 Captiva Dr., 239/472-5800, one-bedroom $110–180, two-bedroom $125–190), on the other hand, are spread out along the bayside marina and fishing action. You can rent a boat right here, grab some bait, and be out on the water before your pajamas have had time to miss you. The 14 cheerful tin-roofed cottages have kitchens and screened porches.

### Over $150

The biggest game in town in recent years has been **C South Seas Resort** (5400 Plantation Rd., Captiva, 239/472-5111, www.southseas.com, $229–1,259) at the northern tip of the island, which closed after Hurricane Charley in 2004 for a massive $140 million renovation. Set in 330 acres of mangroves, the resort, which has an ownership time-share complex too, is casual but spectacular, with beautiful rooms and added draws such as a popular children's program, world-renowned sailing, pools, kayaking, a fishing pier, 2,100 feet of dockage for boats up to 130 feet long, and Gulf-edge golf.

The main pool area at the resort offers sleek cabanas for rent with a private attendant and spa services. The Point restaurant overlooking the pool offers casual Caribbean fare, and an upscale bar upstairs provides grand views of Pine Island Sound. The renovation includes 24,000 square feet of meeting space complete with high-speed Internet access, video and data projectors, and new sound and lighting systems. Captiva Golf Club was redesigned by Chip Powell as one of the Top Five Short Courses in the world.

**'Tween Waters Inn Beach Resort** (15951 Captiva Dr., Captiva, 800/210-5594, www.tween-waters.com, $155–650) is another heavy-hitter on the island, with a huge resort complex that stretches from the bay side to the Gulf side. The inn dates back to 1926, when the collection of cottages hosted Teddy Roosevelt, Charles and Anne Lindbergh, Roger Tory Peterson, and J. N. "Ding" Darling. There are 137 water-view rooms, suites, and cottages; Olympic-sized and children's pools; tennis courts (free to guests); a day spa; four restaurants; and a full-service marina. The rooms are very attractive, and there's a nice complimentary breakfast for guests, but it's all the cool amenities that make this a great experience. Rent a canoe or kayak and head out for the day.

## FOOD

Most of the restaurants here are casual and reasonably priced, set in pastel-colored cottages with outdoor seating. There's a nice, fun beachy style and a funky charm.

The **C Bubble Room** (15001 Captiva Dr., 239/472-5558, 11:30 A.M.–2:30 P.M. and 5–10 P.M. daily, $15–28) is definitely fun and entirely eccentric. The waiters and bartenders are in scouting uniforms, with patches of their own devising meticulously sewn on. They wear neckerchiefs and mischievous grins. The

# TROPICAL FRUIT

Jackfruit, carambola, mamey sapote, sapodilla, lychee, longans, pineapple, and papaya are the kinds of fruits you imagine eating on a far-flung tropical island. Fling a little closer, and you've got Pine Island. Just west of Cape Coral, it is the largest island along the southwest coast of Florida and the producer of some of the state's most exotic fruits. Not the usual Florida orange, Pine Island's king of fruits is the mango. Its reign is so celebrated that there is an annual two-day festival, the **Pine Island MangoMania Tropical Fruit Fair** (239/283-0888) in July with mango-inspired foods, entertainment, and lots of fragrant fruits and plants for sale.

From late May to about Labor Day, enthusiasts can also stop into the tent-covered **Pine Island Tropical Fruit Market** in Bokeelia (10 A.M.–4 P.M. Fri.-Sun.) for a wide array of tropical fruits. The **Fort Myers Downtown Farmers' Market** in Centennial Park offers a fair sampling of the local exotic fruits (7 A.M.–2 P.M. Thurs.). Even the local **Eden Vineyards** applauds the local fruits with one of its wines, made from carambola.

But what is a carambola, exactly?

**Carambola** is another word for starfruit, that light yellow, ribbed, ovoid fruit that, when sliced, has star-shaped cross-sections. The flesh is yellow, crisp, juicy, and not fibrous, ranging from very sour to mildly sweet.

**Mamey sapote** is a large, football-shaped fruit that grows on an ornamental evergreen. The brown skin has a rough texture – rougher than a kiwi. The flesh is either creamy pink or salmon color, and it has a big avocado-like pit. The flavor is described as a combination of honey, avocado, and sweet potato. Closely related, the **sapodilla** has soft brown flesh that tastes a little like very sweet root beer. The sapodilla tree is also the source of chicle, a chewing gum component.

**Lychee** are nubby red fruits with pearly white flesh and the texture of a grape. The flesh is sweet but tart, and with a very strong scent. Experienced lychee eaters bite lightly through the skin of the top and then squeeze the fruit out. The **longan** is known as the little brother of the lychee. They look alike, only the longan is smaller. The flesh is whitish and translucent like the lychee, but less strong smelling and a little muskier.

**Jackfruit** is the fruit for the intrepid. It is the largest tree-borne fruit in the world, up to 80 pounds, and the unopened fruit has a strong, disagreeable smell. The exterior is spiky and green, and the inside has large edible bulbs that taste like a cross between banana and papaya. You may not want to bother with jackfruit, but check out the rest of Lee County's tropical bounty.

interior is like something out of Santa's workshop, with toy trains and elves and hobbyhorses, but then add in 2,000 movie stills and glossies, lots of Betty Boop memorabilia, and a long list of other stuff. The food is definitely good, from fried shrimp to grilled fish cooked with a pineapple/ginger marinade.

Andy Rosse Lane, the area often called Captiva Village, has a cluster of fun places. The **Keylime Bistro** (in the Captiva Island Inn, 11509 Andy Rosse Ln., 239/395-4000, 8 A.M.–10 P.M. daily, lounge until 1 A.M., live entertainment daily) is a great place to hear musicians performing great island music like Jimmy Buffet covers. The kitchen serves an excellent grouper sandwich, as well as a delicious sausage sandwich with onions and peppers; at dinner, choose shrimp scampi or grouper piccata. Good margaritas, and there's a Bloody Mary bar for Sunday brunch.

**RC Otter's Island Eats** (11506 Andy Rosse Ln., 239/395-1142, 8 A.M.–10 P.M. daily, $8–20) is right across the street, with a vast menu of accessible American staples, with care put into vegetarian options. It serves wine as well as a housemade beer. Depending on the weather, you can sit indoors, on the covered veranda, or out on the patio, where there's usually live island music. **Mucky Duck** (11546 Andy Rosse Ln., 239/472-2388, 11:30 A.M.–3 P.M.

and 5–9:30 P.M. daily, $18–28) is more of an English pub vibe, only set right on the beach. The only thing on the menu that might be construed as English is fish and chips, but no matter when the seafood platter is so good. Every night at sunset, revelers convene on the beachside patio to watch the colorful show.

The **'Tween Waters Inn** (15951 Captiva Rd., 239/472-5161) is something of an institution around here, going from the bay side to the Gulf side across the island, and with a couple of restaurants on-site. For my money, I'd skip the fine-dining **Old Captiva House** (7:30–11 A.M. and 5:30–10 P.M. daily, $18–34) and head for the ℂ **Crow's Nest Island Pub** (5:30–10 P.M. daily, cocktails until late, $8–15). Not that the former isn't good—it often wins Florida's Golden Spoon Award, with swordfish saltimbocca, jerk grouper, seafood jambalaya, and key lime pie served in an intimate, special-occasion kind of space (sit in the Sunset Room). It's more that the latter is so much fun, with good drink specials, fine bar staples, and a band Tuesday–Sunday. But you cannot miss the NASCrab races, 6 P.M. for families, 9 P.M. for adults. Pick your hermit crab, the one who looks most like Dale Earnhardt Jr. or Jeff Gordon, and line him up. The competition is ESPN-worthy drama. For lunch at 'Tween Waters, opt for the **Canoe and Kayak Waterfront Restaurant** (11 A.M.–6 P.M. daily, $7–10) on-site, where you can eat a fat deli sandwich while watching the marina's commotion.

When you're looking for a cocktail and a place to watch the sun go down, the **Green Flash Bayside Bar & Grill** (15183 Captiva Dr., 239/472-3337, 11:30 A.M.–3:30 P.M. and 5:30–9:30 P.M. daily, $13–20) is the place. At the site of the longtime island favorite called The Nook, the two-story restaurant is situated on Roosevelt Channel and overlooks Buck Key and Pine Island. What you need to know about the menu is what is written at the top:

*A green flash occurs because sunlight spreads out in air of increasing density, just like water vapor creates a rainbow. The atmosphere refracts the light into a spectrum with the longest (red-orange) wavelengths at one end and the shortest (violet-blue-green) at the other. The dispersion is greatest at sunset and sunrise because that's when sunlight takes a long, low path through the atmosphere. The blue-green light is bent toward the top of the sun, but usually it is scattered by air molecules. But sometimes only the blue is scattered, leaving the root of the bent light – the green part – visible once the sun sets. The chances of seeing the green flash are better in tropical or desert areas since an observer has more opportunities to view a horizon free from clouds and haze. Experts recommend watching a sunset from the beach on a calm day with a horizon free of clouds. A yellow sun, rather than a red one, will have the best potential for a green flash.*

# Charlotte Harbor and the Barrier Islands

From Charlotte Harbor south past Fort Myers, there is an incredible number of great little islands in the waters of Lee County and Charlotte County. A long line of curves and dots on the map between the Gulf waters and the Intracoastal Waterway, some of these islands are accessible by causeway, others just by boat. What unifies them is unbelievable natural beauty and romanticized, often pirate-related histories. Sailboating outfits, fishing charters, regularly scheduled ferries, and water taxis head out to these barrier islands. One of the area's first tourists was Spanish explorer Ponce de León, who ended up taking a Calusa arrow and dying in these waters. The natives are friendlier now.

## CHARLOTTE HARBOR
Most people hadn't heard of Florida's Charlotte Harbor and Punta Gorda until Hurricane

Charley blew through and over them on August 13, 2004. Punta Gorda took one of the category IV storm's worst beatings, with loads of people months later still trying to decide whether to renovate or rebuild.

The area not only rebounded, but went further and added an estimated 500 new hotel rooms, a $5.5 million new Bailey Airport Terminal at Charlotte County Airport, and the $46 million rebuilt and expanded sports arena that now hosts the Tampa Bay Rays for spring training. The whole area is worth exploring, especially for the ecotraveler. Charlotte Harbor is the second-largest estuary in the state, encompassing 270 square miles. It has 365 miles of canals: 190 miles of them saltwater, 175 miles of freshwater. Most of the area bordering the harbor is preserved land, with parks, 53 blueway trails, and the largest undisturbed pine flatwoods in southwest Florida.

The area has been featured on *Sail* magazine's list of the "10 Greatest Places to Sail in the United States" and was ranked by *Golf Digest* as the "Third Best Place to Live and Play Golf in America." Charlotte Harbor annually hosts the Oh Boy! Oberto Redfish Cup, broadcast by ESPN, the nation's premier saltwater fishing championship; the field of anglers is limited to 40 professional two-man teams, representing the very best.

If you're visiting Lee County, don't skip **Punta Gorda.** It's worth the drive north from Fort Myers to visit **Babcock Wilderness Adventure** (8000 Hwy. 31, Punta Gorda, 800/500-5583, tours by reservation 9 A.M.–3 P.M., $19.95 adults, $12.95 children 3–12, also special group and seasonal prices) for a swamp buggy ride in which you are bumped and jostled in an open vehicle through an exhilarating 90-minute tour through the Babcock Ranch, Telegraph Cypress Swamp, and the 90,000-acre Crescent B Ranch. Guides offer narration on birds, animals, plants, and the cattle and horses raised on the ranch. You'll see Florida panthers (okay, not wild, exactly), big gators, white-tailed deer, wild turkeys, and ornery-looking Florida Cracker cattle that are raised on the ranch. It's thrilling, especially for kids.

Out of Fisherman's Village in Punta Gorda, **King Fisher Fleet** (1200 W. Retta Esplanade, 941/639-0969, cruises range $12–23 adults, half price for kids 3–11, free under 3, back-bay fishing $450/day, deepwater $650/day) pays equal attention to sightseers and anglers. It offers sightseeing cruises to the out islands, ecotours, full- and half-day cruises, sunset cruises, and harbor tours. Or you might want to take a kayak trip with **Grande Tours** (12575 Placida Rd., Placida, 941/697-8825, www.grandetours.com). After a workout on the kayaks, you can visit one of Punta Gorda's two excellent day spas, **Spago Day Spa** (115 Taylor St., 941/205-3030) and **Bisous at the Spa** (321 Taylor St., 941/575-6363).

At Christmastime, all of the houses and boats along the canals in Punta Gorda are decorated lavishly for the holidays. King Fisher offers a charming evening cruise along the canals to check out the lights and holiday festivities.

If you want to learn to sail or cruise in the sheltered waters of Charlotte Harbor, **Florida Sailing & Cruising School** (Burnt Store Marina on Charlotte Harbor, 800/262-7939, www.flsailandcruiseschool.com) offers live-aboard sailing beginning at $595 for a two-day basics class.

And the little town of Englewood, west of Charlotte Harbor and north of Cape Haze, is definitely worth the drive. A great place for an evening barbecue is the covered pavilion on the downtown beachfront at **Chadwick Park.**

There's also the 135-acre **Oyster Creek Regional Park** in Englewood, located on the greenway waterway corridor known as the Oyster Creek–Lemon Bay Aquatic Preserve–Ainger Creek waterway.

Lemon Bay is at the north end of Cape Haze peninsula, where evidence suggests early Floridians lived well from about 1000 B.C. to A.D. 1350. You can see their faint evidence at **Paulson's Point** (Orange St., 941/474-3065, dawn–dusk daily, free), also known as the Sarasota County mound. The tall shell-mound park features helpful interpretive markers and

**LEE COUNTY**

a beautiful, easy walkway around and through the Native American mound.

## Food

The area has a number of worthwhile restaurants. There's **Amimoto Japanese Restaurant** (2705 Tamiami Trail, Punta Gorda, 941/505-1515, 11:30 A.M.–2:30 P.M. and 5:30–9:30 P.M. Mon.–Sat., $15–22), serving sushi presented very artistically. It is a great lunch spot. Also popular in Punta Gorda are the restaurants of **Fisherman's Village** (1200 W. Retta Esplanade, www.fishville.com), including **Village Oyster Bar** (941/637-1212, 11:30 A.M.–8 P.M. Sun.–Thurs., until 9 P.M. Fri. and Sat., $16–25) and **Bella Luna** (941/637-1212, 11:30 A.M.–8 P.M. Sun.–Thurs., until 9 P.M. Fri. and Sat., $16–30).

Then in the town of Englewood, classy water-view dining can be had at **Gulfview Grill** (2095 N. Beach Rd., 941/475-3500, 3–9 P.M. Sun.–Thurs., until 10 P.M. Fri. and Sat., Sun. brunch 10 A.M.–2 P.M., $12–32). Get the stone crab claws if they're in season.

Undoubtedly the best restaurant in the area is **The Perfect Caper** (121 East Marion Ave., Punta Gorda, 941/505-9009, 11:30 A.M.–9 P.M. Tues.–Thurs., until 10 P.M. Fri. and Sat., $20–40), where James and Jeanie Roland take a fresh approach to California-Asian fusion. Jeanie, a CIA grad, is very strict about the ingredients. Her passion for the season's best can be seen in starters like fried jumbo prawns wrapped in phyllo and served with avocado relish and blood orange vinaigrette, and entrées of grilled venison tenderloin with roasted purple potatoes.

The nearby **Swiss Chocolate** (403 Sullivan St., 941/639-9484, 10 A.M.–5 P.M. Mon.–Sat., $3–15) is a stunning shop filled with utterly tempting chocolates and European pastries. Also nearby, hearty breakfasts are to be had at **Pies & Plates** (2310 Tamiami Trail, Suite 3117, 941/505-7437, 9 A.M.–5 P.M. Mon.–Sat., $3–9). The little café also does cooking classes—a perfect getaway endeavor.

## ◖ PALM ISLAND

Almost everything on Palm Island revolves around **Palm Island Resort** (7092 Placida Rd., Cape Haze, 941/697-4800, www.palm-island.com, $300–1,200), one of the best places to stay on the entire Gulf Coast. Start by driving to Cape Haze, for which the directions are a little tricky: Take I-75 29 miles north from Sanibel. Take the County Road 768 W exit (Exit 161) toward Punta Gorda. Almost immediately, turn right onto Taylor Road (County Road 765A), which then runs into the Tamiami Trial (U.S. 41 N). Follow this nine miles, then turn left onto El Jobean Road (Hwy. 776 W). Follow this eight miles, turn left onto Gasparilla Road (County Road 771), and drive another eight miles. Turn right onto Placida Road (County Road 775), go two miles, and you're there. Then you wait in line in your car for the car ferry. It comes, you drive on, and about 60 seconds later the ferry lands on Palm Island. Then you're in paradise. Nice young men in shorts greet you, take all your stuff, and tell you where to ditch your car; you get your own golf cart, and you motor over to your unit along gravel roads.

The island is really due north of Boca Grande, with about 200 private homes, plus 15 more private homes within the resort. Resort guests stay in 154 one-, two- or three-bedroom villas right on the Gulf. In clusters of low-rise buildings, spacious units reflect a real range of tastes, from beachy casual to swanky contemporary—be specific about your tastes and needs when you call. There are several pools, tennis courts, a comfy restaurant called the Rum Bay, children's programs, and kayak rentals. Make sure to bring your own groceries from the mainland, as the prices at the little on-island market are exorbitant.

Beautiful beaches, clear green-blue waters, amazing sunsets, an abundance of sea oats—it's all worth the price of admission, making Palm Island a perfect getaway that everyone will appreciate.

## GASPARILLA ISLAND

Named for the infamous pirate José Gaspar, who may have hidden out (and buried his treasure, never to be found) on this island in the 1700s with his band of adventurous men,

The Boca Grande Lighthouse is now a state park and museum.

Gasparilla Island has had a much more posh and refined recent history. Connected to the mainland by a short causeway near Punta Gorda, the island was founded as a vacation retreat and fishing spot by the DuPont family in the late 1800s. Its town of **Boca Grande,** at the mouth of Charlotte Harbor, is filled May through mid-July with tarpon fishers; the opening between Cayo Costa and Gasparilla Island has been called the "Tarpon Fishing Capital of the World." Tarpon are sparser in the pass and the estuarine waters of Pine Island Sound these days, but during peak season the dense cluster of fishing boats still pull into port to try their luck. There is driving access to the island via the Boca Grande Causeway, the causeway at County Road 775, and at Placida.

Boca Grande is on the southern tip of Gasparilla Island and has a quaint fishing village feel that really appeals to anglers and is complemented by a number of upscale shops and restaurants (George W. Bush has been a regular guest). While there, walk around **Boca Grande Lighthouse Park** (Gasparilla Island State Park, 880 Belcher Rd., Boca Grande, 941/964-0375, 8 A.M.–sunset, $3/car). The wooden Boca Grande Lighthouse was built in 1890 and is a maritime landmark. The lighthouse is open to the public 10 A.M.–4 P.M. the last Saturday of the month, and there's a little lighthouse museum ($2), gift shop, and the Armory Chapel. The waters in these parts have strong currents—not great for swimming, but you'll see people sailboarding.

The **Gasparilla Inn and Club, Boca Grande** (500 Palm Ave., 941/964-4500, www.gasparillainn.com, $173–748) completed renovations in 2007 and received designation as a Historic Hotel of America. Built in 1912 and opening to guests in 1913, the historic pale-yellow wooden frame, white-pillar entrance, and Victorian-style gable roofs define this grand resort, its main hotel surrounded by cute cottages. With a major Old Florida feel, it sits on 156 acres of well-manicured grounds with great views of the Gulf of Mexico and Charlotte Harbor. A Pete Dye–designed golf course, croquet lawn, two pools, fishing, spa, and 200-slip marina are some of the reasons it's been a Bush family favorite over the years. It's also pet-friendly.

## USEPPA ISLAND

Across from Cabbage Key is Useppa Island, which pirate José Gaspar supposedly named for one of his more favored captives, a Mexican princess named Joseffa. Calusas may have lived here as far back as 5000 B.C., discarding their oyster and clam shells to create a greater amount of dry land. Barron Collier, for whom Collier County is named, bought the 100-acre island in 1912 and built a resort there in his own name that lured fishing enthusiasts from all over. The island is really a private residential club called the Useppa Island Club, with a couple of places on-island for visitors to stay. The **Collier Inn** (239/283-1061) offers seven stylishly decorated suites, and there are also a number of cottages for rent. The **Useppa Marina** accommodates visitors' boats and the **Tarpon Restaurant** is basically the only place to eat. The Useppa Island Historical Society's little **Useppa Museum** (239/283-9600, noon–2 P.M. Tues.–Fri., 1–2 P.M. weekends, $5 suggested donation) is a very worthwhile museum, full of an odd assortment of things. There are uniforms here from Cuban leaders who participated in the doomed Bay of Pigs invasion of the Bay of Pigs. These leaders were chosen in secrecy on Useppa by the CIA. And there's a forensic restoration of the "Useppa Man," taken from a skeleton unearthed during an archaeological dig in 1989. Other finds reflect the Paleo nomadic hunter-gatherer people who must have hung out here 10,000 years ago when the island was part of the mainland.

If you'd like to visit the island, **Captiva Cruises** (239/472-5300, 10 A.M.–3:30 P.M. Tues.–Sun., $30 adults, $15 children) has a luncheon cruise to Useppa that includes a visit to the museum.

## CABBAGE KEY

The **Cabbage Key Inn** (Intracoastal Waterway, marker 60, Pineland, 239/283-2278, www.cabbagekey.com, $119 rooms, transient dockage available), built by writer Mary Roberts Rinehart and her son in 1938, has two very tempting draws for the visitor. Apparently it was here that Jimmy Buffet drew his inspiration for "Cheeseburger in Paradise." And indeed, the inn serves a great burger. The second reason is the **Dollar Bill Bar,** located in the inn, which rides atop a 38-foot Calusa shell mound. The pub is lined with dollar bills, a custom that began in 1941 when a fisherman autographed and taped his last dollar to the wall for safekeeping (assuring a beer on his return). Since then, people sign and date a buck, and tack them up—more than 30,000 $1 bills are taped to the walls, ceilings, and woodwork, providing a historical collage. (It's illegal to deface currency, but no one in this live-and-let-live bar will tell on you.)

Cabbage Key is accessible only by boat, helicopter, or seaplane, located directly across from mile marker 60 on the Intracoastal Waterway. It doesn't really have sandy beaches or many amenities, but it's a great day or overnight trip. **Captiva Cruises** (239/472-5300, 10 A.M.–3:30 P.M. Tues.–Sun., $30 adults, $15 children) also offers a narrated cruise to Cabbage Key, and there are regularly scheduled water taxis every day from Pine Island, Captiva Island, and Punta Gorda.

## CAYO COSTA

It's one of the quietest, unbridged barrier islands in the chain, but one of the largest. Immediately to the west of Cabbage Key, stretching from Boca Grande Pass to Captiva Pass, it offers eight miles of pristine beach and unspoiled beauty. **Cayo Costa State Park** (P.O. Box 1150, Boca Grande, 941/964-0375, 8 A.M.–sunset, $1 honor system) is the least-visited state park in Florida, but it's because there are no cars, no electricity, and no hot water, not because it's not worthy. It is where Hurricane Charley made landfall in October 2004, but the landscape has bounced back entirely.

Calusas occupied the island for hundreds of years, then in the early 1800s Cuban fishermen landed here, and in 1848 the U.S. government started managing the land. There are 20 private homes on the island, only a couple of them lived in year-round. Really, it's a place to tent camp ($18/night) or overnight in one of 12 rustic cabins ($30), all on the northern end of the island. There are a small pioneer cemetery and a fair number of wild pigs—other than that it's sea creatures, birds, and swaths of sun-warmed sand.

Cayo Costa is accessible only by passenger ferry or private boat. Call **Tropic Star of Pine Island** (239/283-0015, $150 for up to six passengers) to make reservations.

## NORTH CAPTIVA ISLAND

Once a part of Captiva Island, this island was severed during the hurricane of 1926. And then the right eyewall of Hurricane Charley in October 2004 passed over North Captiva Island and severed it into two parts (not surprisingly, folks call it Charley Pass). But all has been set right in the past six years—lost rooftops, demolished docks, and uprooted trees are merely a memory.

The island has maintained a reputation as a remote retreat for the super wealthy. There are four miles of state-owned beaches—the state bought 350 acres, almost half of the island, in 1975. At the turn of the 20th century the island contained a vast tomato plantation; after that it was the processing plant for the Punta Gorda Fish Company. In recent years there have been about 50 year-round residents on the island, most of them on the northern part in an enclave known as the Island Club, with the rest of the island given over to affluent vacationers driving golf carts and strolling the sparsely populated beaches.

## PINE ISLAND

Pine Island is one of the largest islands off the Gulf Coast of Florida and consists of Matlacha (mat-la-SHAY), Pine Island Center, Bokeelia (bo-KEEL-ya), Pineland, and St. James City. It's a great fishing retreat (the tarpon fishing craze started here in the 1880s) and a lovely place from which to observe wildlife, such as the bald eagle nesting sites.

**Matlacha** is a funky fishing village, with a drawbridge over Matlacha Pass that has seen a

COURTESY OF VISIT FLORIDA

LEE COUNTY

The barrier island beaches are lush tropical settings shaded by palm trees and carpeted with beautiful shells.

lot of fishing action in its day. If you want to wet a line, there are plenty of bait and tackle shops and boat rentals at the **Olde Fish House Marina** and **Viking Marina. Pine Island Center** is the island's commercial district, where shopping, the school, fire station, ball fields, and community pool are located.

**Bokeelia** is the home port for many of the island's commercial fishing boats and the agricultural part of the island (you'll see mangoes and a whole bunch of only vaguely familiar-looking tropical fruits: carambola, longan, loquat). This part of the island contains a few historic buildings, including the **Museum of the Islands** (5728 Sesame Dr., Bokeelia, 239/283-1525, www.museumoftheislands.com, 11 A.M.–3 P.M. Tues.–Sat., 1–4 P.M. Sun., in the winter only Tues.–Thurs., $2 adults, $1 children 12 and under), with exhibitions on Pine Island pioneers.

**Pineland** is home to the **Randell Research Center** (13810 Waterfront Dr., Pineland, 239/283-2062, www.flmnh.ufl.edu/RRC,

$7 adults, $4 children), one of the main historical sites of Calusa mounds. You can spend a day paddling the Calusa route and explore the Calusa Heritage Trail, a series of artistic signs interpreting the Calusa way of life and religious beliefs.

There are also guided tours out of Pineland Marina (13921 Waterfront Dr., Bokeelia, 239/283-3593) on Wednesday at 10 A.M. Also in Pineland you'll find one of the country's smallest post offices and boat rentals and fishing charters out of Pineland Marina.

The Randell Research Center is within a stone's throw of celebrated Florida author Randy Wayne White's house; it also happens to be just across the street from the **Tarpon Lodge** (13771 Waterfront Dr., Pineland, 239/283-3999, $140–170), where we stopped for dinner. Blue crab and roasted corn chowder, followed by fat Gulf shrimp scampi over linguini, were all served graciously in a historic house (which for a bit was an alcohol rehab center).

**St. James City** is Pine Island's residential community, with about two-thirds of the island's population living here. Most homes are located on canals with easy access to Pine Island Sound, San Carlos Bay, and the Gulf of Mexico.

# Information and Services

Lee County is located within the **Eastern time zone.** The area code is **239,** but it used to be 941, an area code now used farther north.

## TOURIST INFORMATION

For visitor information, the **Lee County Visitor & Convention Bureau** (12800 University Dr., Ste. 550, Fort Myers, 239/338-3500 or 800/237-6444, www.FortMyersSanibel. com) has an absolutely tremendous website, with well-written text and good graphics—an easy resource for planning a trip. Its office is less convenient for walk-ins. The **Sanibel & Captiva Islands Chamber of Commerce** (1159 Causeway Rd., Sanibel, 239/472-1080, www.sanibel-captiva.org) maintains a visitors center on Causeway Road as you drive onto Sanibel from Fort Myers. The chamber gives away an island guide and sells a detailed street map for $3.

This area has a fair number of small newspapers that serve Lee County, but no big metro paper. The **Fort Myers News-Press** (239/335-0233) is the daily in these parts. In Fort Myers Beach, look for the **Fort Myers Beach Observer** (239/765-0400), a weekly newspaper distributed every Wednesday. The **Island Reporter** (239/472-5185) is the newspaper of record for Sanibel and Captiva

Islands, and there's also a magazine covering Sanibel called **Times of the Islands Magazine.** On Boca Grande, look for the weekly **Boca Beacon.**

## POLICE AND EMERGENCIES

As always, if you find yourself in a real emergency, pick up a phone and dial 911 or the local **Emergency Management Office** (239/533-3622). For a nonemergency police need, call the **Sheriff's Office** (239/477-1000), **Florida Highway Patrol** (239/278-7100), **U.S. Coast Guard** (239/463-5754), or **Florida Poison Information Center** (800/222-1222).

Sanibel and Captiva medical facilities serve the local community during business hours. For emergency medical needs, **HealthPark Medical Center** (16131 Roserush Ct., Fort Myers, 239/433-7799) and **Lee Memorial Hospital** (2776 Cleveland Ave., Fort Myers, 239/343-2000) are full-service hospitals on the mainland with 24-hour emergency service. For your pharmacy needs on the islands, **CVS** (2331 Palm Ridge Rd., Sanibel, 239/472-0085) is convenient. If your pet has a medical problem, there's **Coral Veterinary Clinic** (1530 Periwinkle Way, Sanibel, 239/481-4746).

## RADIO AND TELEVISION

If you're looking for NPR radio, turn to **WGCU 90.1 FM**. For local music programming, **WARO 94.5 FM** is classic rock; **WCKT 107.1 FM** is country music; **WDRR 98.5 FM** has smooth jazz; **WINK 96.9 FM** offers adult contemporary programming; **WJBX 99.3 FM** is alternative rock; **WOLZ 95.3 FM** is, of course, oldies; **WRXK 96.1 FM** gives you classic rock; and **WXKB 103.9 FM** is Top 40 radio.

And on the television, **WBBH Channel 2** is the NBC affiliate, **WINK Channel 11** is the CBS affiliate, **WZVN Channel 7** is the ABC affiliate, **WGCU Channel 30** is the PBS affiliate, and **WFTX Channel 4** is the FOX affiliate out of Cape Coral.

## LAUNDRY SERVICES

Large hotels and beach rentals often have laundry services of one sort or another. If you need to throw in a load of wash, launderettes are limited on the islands. Try an RV park along the route. In Fort Myers the laundry options are much broader. There are three **60 Minute Cleaners** locations (12842 S. Cleveland Ave., 239/936-3616; Cypress Trace Shopping Center, 239/481-1900; and 16970 San Carlos Blvd., 239/466-5115). In Fort Myers Beach, there's **Beach & Bubbles Coin Laundry & Dry Cleaners** (7205 Estero Blvd., 239/765-1771), a garden-variety coin-op laundry.

## FISHING LICENSES

Fishing licenses are sold at all county tax collectors' offices and at many bait-and-tackle shops, or by phone (888/347-4356). On Sanibel, you can buy a license at the **Bait Box** (1041 Periwinkle Way, Sanibel, 239/472-1618); at **Bailey's** (239/472-1516), at the corner of Tarpon Bay Road and Periwinkle Way; at **Tarpon Bay Explorers** (900 Tarpon Bay Rd., Sanibel, 239/472-8900); and at all the marinas. Also pick up the Florida Marine Fisheries Commission's publication about size and bag limits. You do not need a license if you are fishing from a boat that has a valid recreational vessel saltwater fishing license, if you are under 16, or if you are a Florida resident fishing from a pier, a bridge, or on shore.

LEE COUNTY

# Getting There and Around

## BY CAR

Lee County is along southwest Florida's Gulf Coast between Naples and Sarasota. The biggest north–south driving routes are I-75 and U.S. 41. East–west major arteries include Alligator Alley (I-75) and U.S. 41 (where it jogs east at around Naples).

To get to Fort Myers, you can take either I-75 or U.S. 41. In town, McGregor Boulevard runs alongside the Caloosahatchee River and is also called Highway 867. Highway 865 (also known as Hickory Boulevard, Estero Boulevard, and San Carlos Boulevard, depending on where you are) is the route south to Fort Myers Beach on Estero Island.

To get to Sanibel from I-75, take New Exit 131 or Old Exit 21 (Daniels Parkway) west to Summerlin Road, approximately seven miles.

Turn left on Summerlin Road and drive approximately 15 miles to the Sanibel Causeway (a $6 toll). Drive across and onto Sanibel Island. At the four-way stop at Periwinkle Way, either a right or a left turn will lead you to beaches, shops, and accommodations. Sanibel Island has a couple of main roads that parallel each other: Periwinkle Way, the main business route, and Gulf Drive, segmented into East, Middle, and West Gulf Drive. Tarpon Bay Road connects Sanibel-Captiva Road with Periwinkle Way at its west end. And Sanibel-Captiva Road—most folks call it San-Cap—goes by most of Sanibel's attractions before crossing over a short bridge at Blind Pass, where it becomes Captiva Drive on Captiva Island.

So, to reach Captiva, turn right on Periwinkle Way, drive two miles, turn right onto Tarpon Bay Road, and at the next left turn onto Sanibel-Captiva Road. Drive for approximately eight miles, cross Blind Pass Bridge, and you're there.

Driving into Florida from the north via Jacksonville, take I-95 south to I-4 to I-75, and then follow the directions above.

## BY AIR

By air, the area is served by **Southwest Florida International Airport** (16000 Chamberlin Parkway, Fort Myers, 239/768-1000, www.flylcpa.com). The airport's Midfield Terminal Complex opened in 2005, with three concourses and 28 gates. The terminal is one of the first in the United States to be built with new security equipment and procedures incorporated into the design. The $438 million project focused on passenger convenience with a lovely subtropical look and permanent photography collection of the work of Florida photographer Alan Maltz.

Most major domestic airlines serve the airport, and there are international flights from Germany and Canada. The airport, opened in 1983, currently serves: Air Canada, AirTran, American, Continental, Delta, Jet Blue, Northwest, Southwest, United, US Airways, and many smaller carriers, as well as German airlines Condor and LTU International.

**Alamo** (800/327-9633), **Avis** (800/230-4898), **Budget** (800/227-5945), **Dollar** (800/800-3665), **Enterprise** (800/736-8222), **Hertz** (800/654-3131), **National** (800/227-7368), and **Thrifty** (800/847-4389) provide rental cars from Southwest Florida International Airport. Enterprise and Thrifty offices are directly across the street from baggage claim.

## BY BUS AND TRAIN

**LeeTran** (239/275-8726, www.rideleetran.com) has hourly service 6 A.M.–10 P.M. to a transfer point at Daniels Parkway and U.S. 41, with connections to other routes.

**Greyhound Bus Line** (239/774-5660) offers bus service to the Fort Myers station, but from here you really need to rent a car. Public transportation to and between the islands is limited to taxis and limousines.

# SARASOTA COUNTY

Sarasota took its time becoming the culturally rich city it is today. Centuries after Ponce de León, Panfilo de Narvaez, and Hernando de Soto came through this part of the Gulf Coast, the area went unnoticed by white settlers. Even after the United States acquired Florida in 1821, the only white men to linger here were a handful of entrepreneurial fishermen who supplied salted fish and live turtles from the area for export to Cuba. In 1842, William Whittaker homesteaded in the area, planting some orange trees. Not many followed suit, perhaps because the local Seminoles' reputation for fierceness was widely acknowledged.

In fact, it was the brutal seven-year Seminole War that brought Whittaker and a stalwart few to town as part of the Armed Occupation Act, which deeded 160 Florida acres and six months'

provisions to any person who agreed to carry arms and protect the land for five years.

Forty years later, as a means for drumming up some new residents, the Florida Mortgage and Investment Company started talking up Sarasota, with a few serious exaggerations, in Scotland. Sixty Scottish families arrived in 1885 to find a waterlogged Main Street and a decided lack of amenities. Being Scottish, they promptly built a golf course (possibly America's first) and then got to work making it a real town. Because there was no overland transportation, sailing ships and steamboats were the only connection to the outside world. In 1902 came the railroad, which connected Sarasota to Tampa; electricity and paved roads followed not too long after.

An influx of wealthy socialites settled

# HIGHLIGHTS

**☾ Spring Training at Ed Smith Stadium:** Take me out to the ballpark. Ed Smith Stadium is the spring-training home of the Baltimore Orioles, with all the Grapefruit League teams cycling through in preparation for the summer season. It's thrilling to see big-league teams in such a small-town setting. Tickets are cheap and the hot dogs are good (page 109).

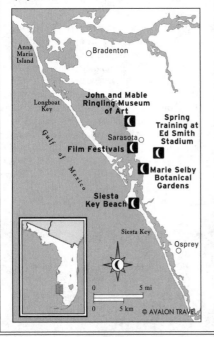

**☾ Marie Selby Botanical Gardens:** You don't have to be a master gardener or skilled horticulturalist to enjoy a day here. In 11 bayfront acres, the open-air and under-glass museum has more than 6,000 orchids and more than 20,000 other plants, many of which have been collected in the wild by the gardens' research staff. Most impressive is the vast array of otherworldly epiphytes, or air plants (page 113).

**☾ John and Mable Ringling Museum of Art:** This museum is a must-see for fans of Flemish and Italian baroque art, with room after room of canvases, the most impressive of which is a series by Peter Paul Rubens known collectively as *The Triumph of the Eucharist* (page 114).

**☾ Film Festivals:** Time a trip to Sarasota to catch one of the city's two film festivals, the Sarasota Film Festival and the Cine-World Film Festival. The former is in April, the latter in November – both are a citywide excuse for a party, in between two-hour popcorn-eating stints at the city's many movie theaters (page 121).

**☾ Siesta Key Beach:** Beaches are a central draw of this area, with a couple of world-class contenders. Siesta Key Beach, with its pure-quartz white sand (it's more like powdered sugar than granulated sugar), usually gets top honors (page 130).

LOOK FOR ☾ TO FIND RECOMMENDED SIGHTS, ACTIVITIES, DINING, AND LODGING.

the area starting around 1910, establishing Sarasota as a winter resort for affluent northerners. It was during this time that Sarasota's performing and visual arts institutions were established, to entertain those first hoity-toity tourists. Among the early tourists to be smitten by the town was circus magnate John Ringling. He scooped up property all around Sarasota, moving the circus's winter home here, building himself a winter residence, art museum, circus museum, and college.

The population doubled in the Florida land boom of 1924–1927—it was Roaring Twenties indeed for Sarasota, with tourist hotels, tourist attractions, and a causeway over the bay sprouting up to accommodate the surge in interest.

Growth in neighboring towns (Bradenton, Venice, North Port), as well as along the chain of narrow barrier islands (from north to south: Anna Maria Island, Longboat Key, St. Armands Key, Lido Key, Siesta Key, and Casey Key) was slower, largely due to limited access.

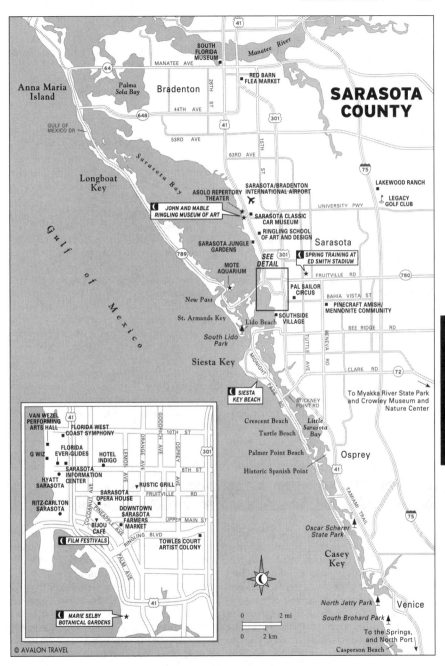

SARASOTA
COUNTY

Anna Maria
Island

Longboat
Key

Gulf

of

Mexico

Palma
Sola Bay

Bradenton

Sarasota Bay

SOUTH
FLORIDA
MUSEUM

MANATEE AVE

RED BARN
FLEA MARKET

44TH AVE

53RD AVE

63RD AVE

SARASOTA/BRADENTON
INTERNATIONAL AIRPORT

ASOLO REPERTORY
THEATER

JOHN AND MABLE
RINGLING MUSEUM OF ART

SARASOTA JUNGLE
GARDENS

MOTE
AQUARIUM

New Pass

St. Armands Key

South Lido
Park

Lido Beach

Siesta Key

SARASOTA CLASSIC
CAR MUSEUM

RINGLING SCHOOL
OF ART AND DESIGN

UNIVERSITY PWY

LAKEWOOD RANCH

LEGACY
GOLF CLUB

Sarasota

SEE
DETAIL

SPRING TRAINING AT
ED SMITH STADIUM

FRUITVILLE RD

PAL SAILOR
CIRCUS

BAHIA VISTA ST

PINECRAFT AMISH/
MENNONITE COMMUNITY

SOUTHSIDE
VILLAGE

BEE RIDGE RD

CLARK RD

To Myakka River State Park
and Crowley Museum and
Nature Center

SIESTA
KEY BEACH

Crescent Beach

Turtle Beach

Palmer Point Beach

Historic Spanish Point

Little
Sarasota
Bay

Osprey

Oscar Scherer
State Park

Casey
Key

North Jetty Park

South Brohard Park

To the Springs,
and North Port

Casperson Beach

Venice

GULF OF
MEXICO DR

GULF OF MEXICO DR

Midnight Pass Rd

Stickney
Point Rd

Tamiami Trail

Tuttle Ave

Beneva Rd

26TH ST

15TH ST

VAN WEZEL
PERFORMING
ARTS HALL

FLORIDA WEST
COAST SYMPHONY

G WIZ

FLORIDA
EVER-GLIDES

HOTEL
INDIGO

HYATT
SARASOTA

SARASOTA
INFORMATION
CENTER

RUSTIC GRILL

RITZ-CARLTON
SARASOTA

SARASOTA
OPERA HOUSE

DOWNTOWN
SARASOTA
FARMERS
MARKET

BIJOU
CAFE

FILM FESTIVALS

TOWLES COURT
ARTIST COLONY

MARIE SELBY
BOTANICAL GARDENS

10TH ST

GOODRICH AVE

ORANGE AVE

OSPREY AVE

LEMON AVE

6TH ST

FRUITVILLE RD

COCOANUT AVE

PINEAPPLE AVE

UPPER MAIN ST

RINGLING BLVD

PALM AVE

0   2 mi

0   2 km

© AVALON TRAVEL

SARASOTA COUNTY

Tourists gradually settled their sights on the keys, noticing the 35 miles of glistening white-sand beaches that fringe their Gulf side.

Because of this head start, the city of Sarasota is the undisputed cultural center of the area, with theater, opera, symphony, ballet, art museums, and restaurants to rival those in much bigger cities. Each of the keys maintains its own identity, with glorious beach access being the central unifying theme. Lido and St. Armands are really just extensions of down-town Sarasota, connected by a causeway and fairly urban. Started as a quiet fishing village, Longboat Key is now extremely upscale, with tall resort hotels and condominiums and an abundance of golf courses. Siesta Key is much more low-rise, with a personality to match. It's relaxed, laid-back, with a fun and colorful is-land atmosphere. It's the most youthful spot on this part of the Gulf Coast. Casey Key is less of a tourist draw, dotted with single-family homes.

## PLANNING YOUR TIME

A typical vacation in this area is about a week. This is partly because there's a week's worth of things to do, and partly because many of the beach houses and condos rent only by the week, especially in high season. Staying down-town in Sarasota is a little cheaper than stay-ing beachside. Downtown streets and roads run east–west; avenues and boulevards run north–south.

From downtown, go east across the John Ringling Causeway to access St. Armands Circle and Lido Key (St. Armands is a shopping and restaurant destination of note). Continue north to Longboat Key, where there's not a lot of draw beyond swanky hotels, golf courses, a few restaurants, and slightly inconvenient beach access and parking. To reach Siesta Key, head south on U.S. 41 (also called the Tamiami Trail), then take a right onto either Siesta Drive or Stickney Point Road—the former takes you to the northern, residential section of the key; Stickney takes you closer to the funky Siesta Village. The public beaches on Siesta Key are among the finest in the state.

The area's peak season begins in February and continues until Easter (average tempera-tures around 75°F). During that time, prices are hiked and reservations are necessary for ac-commodations. What travel agents call "the value season" is pretty much all summer in Sarasota, June–September. The Gulf waters are bathwater temperature during much of the summer—and as gentle and safe to swim in as your bathtub, too. On a hot day (in the summer, this means about 90°F with a lot of humidity), the water temperatures aren't ex-actly refreshing, but that's the price to pay for a peaceful, sparsely populated day at the beach. Many of Sarasota's cultural institutions (sym-phony, ballet, opera, theaters) take a hiatus during the summer months, another drawback to visiting then.

# Sarasota

The circus built Sarasota. Sure, the 361 days of sun each year and the exotic subtropical plants and animals brought people to the area. But it was when circus impresario John Ringling snapped up real estate that others started giv-ing this rural orange grove and celery farm another look. And in the 1920s, as Ringling began amassing huge numbers of baroque paintings in his new mansion, Cà d'Zan, so too did Ringling's cohorts begin assembling

collections of their own for a little winter rest and relaxation. Soon the opera, theater, and symphony orchestras took root.

Beyond Ringling's generous gift of his house and museums to the city, the Circus King gave Sarasota a tradition of arts patronage. Sarasota's population of 54,000, with a little help from twice that number of winter visitors, supports a vast number of arts events along with an equally strong restaurant and shopping scene.

The striking thing is that it's all set in an incredible natural environment. It is home to world-class beaches and all the fun beach activities, with easy access to outstanding state parks and outdoor fun.

## SPORTS AND RECREATION
### Beaches

**North Lido Beach** is just northwest of St. Armands Circle, off of John Ringling Boulevard on Lido Key (which itself is just a 2.5-mile spit of beach from Big Sarasota Pass to New Pass). It's a short walk from shops or restaurants, and fairly secluded. There are no lifeguards, swift currents, nor real amenities. In the other direction from St. Armands Circle, southwest, you'll run into **Lido Beach,** which has parking for 400 cars, cabana beach rentals at the snack bar, playground equipment, and bathrooms. It's a good hang-out-all-afternoon family beach. It's more crowded than North Lido. The third beach on Lido Key is called **South Lido Park,** on Ben Franklin Drive at the southern tip of Lido Key. The park is bordered by four bodies of water: the Gulf, Big Pass, Sarasota Bay, and Brushy Bayou. It has a nature trail, and the beach offers a great view of the downtown Sarasota skyline. There's a nice picnic area with grills, as well as volleyball courts. Kayakers use this area to traverse the different waterways.

### Golf

Sarasota is Florida's self-described "Cradle of Golf," having been home to the state's first course, built in 1905 by Scottish colonist Sir John Hamilton Gillespie. The nine-hole course was located right at the center of what is now Sarasota's downtown. That first course is long gone, but there are more than 1,000 holes to play at public, semiprivate, and private courses in Sarasota, at all levels of play and most budgets. Of the top southwest regional courses as voted by the readers of *Florida Golf News* (a nice resource, www.floridagolfmagazine.com), many are in the Sarasota area.

## ◀ Spring Training at Ed Smith Stadium

Sarasota's Ed Smith Stadium has been an exciting part of the Grapefruit League's spring training program for years. The New York Giants arrived back in 1924, followed by the Red Sox and then the White Sox. These days, Sarasota's Ed Smith Stadium (2700 12th St., at the corner of Tuttle Ave., 941/954-4101, box seats $14–16, reserved $12–14, general admission $9) is the spring training home of the Baltimore Orioles (the Boston Red Sox now train a bit to the south in Fort Myers, and the Pittsburgh Pirates play in nearby Bradenton). To reach the stadium from I-75, take Exit 210, Fruitville Road.

The little 7,500-seat stadium provides intimate access to big-league play in a small-time venue. Cheap tickets and up-close seats make for a perfect outing on a warm Sarasota spring evening, even if baseball's not your sport. Day games start at 1:05 P.M. and night games at 7:05 P.M.; practices begin at 9 A.M. Many spring-training games sell out, so you might want to buy tickets in advance. For more information, visit http://baltimore.orioles.mlb.com.

### Polo

There are scads of spectator sporting opportunities in Sarasota, but polo trumps a fair number of them. Games are enormous fun, the horses racing around tearing up the lush sod of the polo grounds while their riders focus fiercely on that pesky little ball. Polo is amazingly physical and exciting to watch, whether you're in your fancy polo hats or your weekend jeans. **Sarasota Polo Club** (Lakewood Ranch, 8201 Polo Club Ln., 941/907-0000, 1 P.M. Sun. mid-December–early April, $10, children 12 and under free) is in its 17th year, with professional-level players coming from around the world to play on the nine pristine fields. Bring a picnic or buy sandwiches and drinks once you there. Gates open at 11:30 A.M., and dogs on leashes are welcome. You can also take polo lessons at Lakewood Ranch.

# SARASOTA'S GOLF COURSES

Call for tee times and greens fees, as they vary wildly by time of day and time of year.

**Bobby Jones Golf Complex**
1000 Circus Blvd., Sarasota, 941/365-4653
6,039 yards, par 71, course rating 68.4, slope 117

**Heather Hills Golf Course**
101 Cortez Rd. W., Bradenton, 941/755-8888
3,521 yards, par 61, course rating 58.6, slope 96

**Imperial Lakes Golf Course**
6807 Buffalo Rd., Palmetto, 941/747-GOLF
7,019 yards, par 72, course rating 73.9, slope 136

**Legacy Golf Club at Lakewood Ranch**
8255 Legacy Blvd., Bradenton, 941/907-7067
Semiprivate, 7,069 yards, par 72, course rating 73.8, slope 130

**The Links at Green Field Plantation**
10325 Greenfield Plantation Blvd., Bradenton, 941/747-9432
6,719 yards, par 72, course rating 72, slope 130

**Manatee County Golf Course**
6415 53rd Ave. W., Bradenton, 941/792-6773
6,747 yards, par 72, course rating 71.6, slope 122

**Palma Sola Golf Club**
3807 75th St. W., Bradenton, 941/792-7476
Semiprivate, 6,264 yards, par 72, course rating 68.4, slope 115

**Palmetto Pines Golf Course**
14355 Golf Course Dr., Parrish, 941/776-1375
5,358 yards, par 72, course rating 68.4, slope 92

**Peridia Golf & Country Club**
4950 Peridia Blvd., Bradenton, 941/753-9097, www.peridiagcc.net
3,344 yards, par 60, course rating 55.0, slope 76

**Pinebrook/Ironwood Golf Club**
4260 Ironwood Circle, Bradenton, 941/792-3288
3,706 yards, par 61, course rating 59.9, slope 101

**River Club**
6600 River Club Blvd., Bradenton, 941/751-4211
7,026 yards, par 72, course rating 74.5, slope 135

**River Run Golf Links**
1801 27th St. E., Bradenton, 941/747-6331
5,825 yards, par 70, course rating 67.9, slope 115

**Rosedale Golf and Country Club**
5100 87th St. E., Bradenton, 941/756-0004
6,779 yards, par 72, course rating 72.9, slope 134

**Sarasota Golf Club**
7280 N. Lee Wynn Dr., Sarasota, 941/371-2431
6,585 yards, par 72, course rating 72.9, slope 122

**Terra Ceia**
2802 Terra Ceia Bay Blvd., Palmetto, 941/729-7663
4,001 yards, par 62, course rating 67.9, slope 99

**Timber Creek Golf Course**
4550 Timber Lane, Bradenton, 941/794-8381
2,086 yards, par 27 (9 holes), course rating 35.1, slope 117

**University Park Country Club**
7671 Park Blvd., University Park, 941/359-9999
4,914-7,247 yards, par 72, course rating 67.8-74.4, slope 113-138

**Village Green Golf Course**
1401 Village Green Pkwy., Bradenton, 941/792-7171
2,735 yards, par 58, course rating N/A, slope N/A

**Waterlefe Golf & River Club**
1022 Fish Hook Cove, Bradenton, 941/744-9771
6,908 yards, par 72, course rating 73.8, slope 145

## Cricket

Polo's not the only game in town…cricket, anyone? The **Sarasota International Cricket Club** (Lakewood Ranch, 7401 University Pkwy., just east of Lorraine Rd., 941/232-9956) was founded in 1983 and has 42 playing members who play about 35 matches a year with clubs from around the Southeast. The season runs weekends from late September through the end of May, and watching is free. Call for a game schedule.

## Lawn Bowling

Are you starting to see a theme? Vast expanses of perfect grass, a ridiculous number of beautiful sunny days—people in Sarasota clearly love to spend their days outside. The **Sarasota Lawn Bowling Club** (809 N. Tamiami Trail at 10th St., 941/316-1123, beginning at 9 A.M. weekdays May–Nov., beginning at 12:50 P.M. Nov.–Apr., $7/day to play) is the oldest sporting club in Sarasota, with three greens, $1 *boule* (ball) rentals, and free lessons. Wear flat shoes if you want to play.

## Pétanque

Similar to lawn bowling but a little more obscure, pétanque is played at **Lakeview Park** (7150 Lago St., 941/861-9830, 9 A.M. Sun., free to watch). Players toss and roll a number of steel balls as close as possible to a small wooden ball called the *cochonet* (the piglet). Pronounced PAY-tonk, it's another great spectator sport, especially when accompanied by a wide blanket, a nice bottle of wine, and a tasty picnic. The Sarasota Club de Pétanque has 30 members of all skill levels, from beginners up to the national singles champion, and they bring extra *boules* and are happy to give instructions. Lakeview Park, which is adjacent to Lake Sarasota, also contains an enclosed dog park—even if Rover stayed at home, visitors find it fun to just watch all that canine enthusiasm. It's open daily 6 A.M. until dark.

## State Parks and Nature Preserves

If you want to spend a day outdoors, the **Myakka River State Park** (nine miles east

Myakka River State Park is one of Florida's oldest, largest, and most diverse state parks.

of Sarasota, 13208 Hwy. 72, 941/361-6511, 8 A.M.–sunset daily, $6 per vehicle up to eight people) has a lot of activities to offer. The 28,875-acre park offers hiking, off-road biking, horseback riding, fishing, boating, canoeing, camping, and airboating. Both part of Florida Division of Forestry's Trailwalker Program, the North Loop (5.4 miles) and South Loop (7.4 miles) are fairly easy but scenic marked trails. Beyond these, there are 35 miles of unmarked trails open to hikers, mountain bikers (rentals $15 for two hours, or rent cool four-person quads for $35 for one hour, great for a family), and equestrians (BYOH—that's bring your own horse). If you just want to breeze in for a few hours, a ride on the Myakka Wildlife Tours Tram Safari (10151 Sommers Road, Sarasota, 941/377-5797, runs Dec.–May only, $10 adults, $5 children 6–12, children 5 and under free if held in lap) takes visitors on a whirlwind tour of the park's backcountry, through shady hammocks, pine flatwoods, and lush marshes.

The 14-mile stretch of the scenic Myakka River has fairly easy-to-follow canoe trails (bring your own or rent at the Myakka Outpost; rentals $20 for first hour, $5 each additional hour). Canoes and kayaks can be launched at the bridges, fishing area, other picnic areas, or at the boat ramp. During periods of low water (winter and spring), you'll have to portage around the weir at the south end of the Upper Lake. If you don't want to travel under your own paddle power, the park has a boat

**SARASOTA COUNTY**

# HOPE SPRINGS ETERNAL

Nine million gallons of warm mineral water flow daily at the **Warm Mineral Springs** (12200 San Servando Ave., North Port, 941/426-1692, 9 A.M.–5 P.M. daily, weather permitting, $20 adults, $14 seniors, $9 students, $8 children 12 and under, $18 AAA members), with a higher mineral content than any other spring in the United States. Eighty-seven degrees year-round, it's thought to be Ponce de León's fabled Fountain of Youth.

North Port isn't exactly a tourist destination. It's a fairly rural, unsexy town that looks like it needs a cash transfusion if the patient is to be saved. The big draw is this natural wonder, an hourglass-shaped sinkhole, 1.4 acres around and 230 feet deep, filled with heavily mineralized water, believed by some to have healing powers.

You'll learn quickly upon exiting your car that heavily mineralized water stinks. The sulfurous stink of a really rotten egg. Also, the water's mineral content makes it slimy and viscous-feeling. Also, it's not that warm.

But here's the thing: Russians and other international visitors come from across planet Earth to splash around in this particular sinkhole. The snack bar is the proof: It's an all-Russian menu – goulash, something called Russian ravioli, pictured with descriptions beneath, written *in Russian*.

Because the spring contains no dissolved oxygen, organic matter that gets into the springs stays more or less intact. In 1973, a scientist named Wilburn A. Cockrell brought up a nearly complete skeleton of an adult Paleo-Indian male that was dated at 11,000 years old. Dated to nearly the same time period, part of a saber-toothed cat was also found. In a few thousand years, divers may pull up an order of Russian ravioli and just scratch their heads and wonder what it was doing here in a rural Florida backwater.

tour that runs every 1.5 hours ($12 adults, $6 children, 941/365-0100), and a couple of the world's largest airboats, the *Gator Gal* and the *Myakka Maiden,* are available for guided one-hour tours on the mile-wide and 2.5-mile-long Upper Myakka Lake (serious gator territory).

One unique park feature opened in 2004 in conjunction with Marie Selby Botanical Gardens; the Canopy Walkway, the first of its kind in North America, is an 85-foot-long observation deck suspension bridge that hangs 25 feet in the air in the midst of a subtropical forest canopy. Perched in the tops of live oaks, laurel oaks, and cabbage palms, your perspective on birdlife and animal life is unparalleled.

The park offers primitive camping ($5) and more equipped campsites ($26 per night including water and electric), but the neatest option might be one of the five palm log cabins built in the 1930s. They're pretty comfortable, with two double beds, linens, blankets, and kitchen facilities. The fee is $70 per night for up to four people (call 800/326-3521 to reserve far in advance).

Adjacent to the state park you'll find the **Crowley Museum and Nature Center** (16405 Myakka Rd., 941/322-1000, 10 A.M.–4 P.M. Thurs.–Sun. May–Dec., Tues.–Sun. Jan.–Apr., $8 adults, $3 children 5–12, children under 5 free), a 190-acre wildlife sanctuary and education center. A couple of hours here dovetails nicely with time spent hiking or paddling in Myakka River State Park—there's a short nature trail, a boardwalk across Maple Branch Swamp, and an observation tower overlooking the Myakka River. To give more of a historical context to the area, the Crowley's real core is a pioneer museum tricked out with a rustic one-room cabin, a restored 1892 Cracker house, a working blacksmith shop, and a little sugarcane mill. The museum sponsors Pioneer Days every December, an annual antiques fair, a folk music festival in October, and a yearly stargazing night with high-powered telescopes.

It won't knock your socks off with stunning

topography or habitats, but **Oscar Scherer State Park** (1843 S. Tamiami Trail, Osprey, 941/483-5956, 8 A.M.–sundown daily, entrance fee $5 per vehicle) is a local hangout for birders and families who want to spend an afternoon in nature without a lot of hassle. Much of it is a classic Florida flatwoods (scrub pine and sawtooth palmetto populated with animals like scrub jays, gopher tortoises, and indigo snakes). The park has several marked trails open to hikers and bikers (it's sandy terrain, most suitable for mountain bikes), and kayakers paddle around South Creek (bring your own canoe or kayak or rent canoes from the ranger station for $5/hour, $25/day), launched from the South Creek Picnic Area. Birders may want to join the informal Thursday morning bird walks at 8 A.M., the Friday morning ranger-led walks at 8:30 A.M., or canoe tours on Wednesdays at 9 A.M. Check in at the park's nature center.

## SIGHTS
### ◖ Marie Selby Botanical Gardens
Much has been written in recent years about the mystery of orchids, bromeliads, and other epiphytes: *The Orchid Thief, Orchid Fever,* and the more historical *The Orchid in Lore and Legend.*

The word epiphyte comes from the Greek roots "epi," meaning "upon," and "phyton," meaning "plant." Beginning their life in the canopy of trees, their seeds carried by birds or wind, epiphytes are air plants, growing stubbornly without the benefit of soil on the branches or trunks of trees. Orchids, cacti, bromeliads, aroids, lichens, mosses, and ferns can even grow on the same tree, a big interspecies jamboree.

And if you want to see some beautiful and alien epiphytes, spend a long afternoon at Marie Selby Botanical Gardens (811 S. Palm Ave., 941/366-5731, www.selby.org, 10 A.M.–5 P.M. daily, $17 adults, $6 children 6–11, children under 6 free). The nine-acre gardens on the shores of Sarasota Bay are one of Sarasota's absolute jewels. Marie Selby donated her home and grounds "to provide enjoyment for all who visit the gardens." There's a lot of enjoyment to be had meandering along the walking paths through the hibiscus garden, cycad garden, a banyan grove, a tropical fruit garden, and thousands of orchids. The botanical gardens also host lectures and gardening classes and

© JOSHUA LAWRENCE KINSER

Explore the exotic and lush orchid exhibits at Marie Selby Botanical Gardens.

have a charming shop (beginners should opt for a training-wheels phalaenopsis—very hard to kill—or an easy-care bromeliad) with an exhaustive collection of gardening books (80 on orchids alone). Spend an hour gazing at epiphytes in the tropical greenhouse and you'll become a fan, I promise. Kids get fairly bored here, with a brief flurry of interest around the koi pond and butterfly garden. I would tend not to bring them unless they're really into plants or stroller-bound.

## ◖ John and Mable Ringling Museum of Art

John Ringling's lasting influence on Sarasota is remarkable, but the John and Mable Ringling Museum of Art makes it simply undeniable (5401 Bay Shore Rd., 941/359-5700, www.ringling.org, 10 A.M.–5 P.M. daily, $25 adults, $20 seniors, $10 children 6–17 and Florida teachers and students with ID).

In 2007, the museum's six-year, $140 million master plan came to fruition, marking the completion of a most extraordinary transformation. It's now one of the 20 largest art museums in North America. Since 2006, the Ringling Museum has opened four new buildings: the Tibbals Learning Center, the John M. McKay Visitors Pavilion, The Ulla R. and Arthur F. Searing Wing, and the Education/Conservation Building, as well as the restored Historic Asolo Theater.

The whole museum complex is spectacular, but the art museum is definitely worth its fairly hefty admission price. It was built in 1927 to house Ringling's nearly pathological accretion of 600 paintings, sculptures, and decorative arts including more than 25 tapestries. The Mediterranean-style palazzo contains a collection that includes a set of five extremely large paintings by Peter Paul Rubens, many other Spanish works of art, and the music room and dining room of Mrs. William B. Astor (Ringling bought all this in 1926 when the Astor mansion in New York was scheduled to be demolished). The permanent collection is spectacular, with Van Dycks, Poussins, and lots of other baroque masters, but there are

shows such as a recent one on surrealism and another on the photos of Ansel Adams and Clyde Butcher that enter into at least the 20th century.

The complex also houses the **Museum of the Circus,** a peek into circus history. It achieves a certain level of overstatement in the interpretive signs when it parallels the ascendance of the circus with the growth of the country. Still, the museum's newspaper clippings, circus equipment, parade wagons, and colossal bail rings make one nostalgic for a time and place one probably never knew.

The single most impressive thing about the museum, the thing that caused rampant loitering and inspired commentary like, "Whoa, cooool," is the Howard Bros. Circus model. It takes up vast space—the world's largest miniature circus, after all—and is a three-quarter-inch-to-the-foot scale replica of Ringling Bros. and Barnum & Bailey Circus at its largest. The model itself takes up 3,800 square feet, with eight main tents, 152 wagons, 1,300 circus performers and workers, more than 800 animals, a 57-car train, and a zillion wonderful details.

Fully restored and reopened in 2002, John Ringling's home on the bay, **Cà d'Zan** (House of John), is also open to the public, an ornate structure evocative of Ringling's two favorite Venetian hotels, the Danieli and the Bauer Grunwald. Completed in 1926, the house is 200 feet long with 32 rooms and 15 baths. It is truly a magnificent mansion.

## Sarasota Classic Car Museum

What's your dream car? DeLorean? Ferrari? Mini Cooper? The Sarasota Classic Car Museum (5500 N. Tamiami Trail, 941/355-6228, www.sarasotacarmuseum.com, 9 A.M.–6 P.M. daily, $8.50 adults, $7.50 seniors, $6.50 children 13–17, $4 children 6–12, children under 6 free) has examples of everyone's favorite wheels. A recent renovation has greatly improved the collection of more than 100 vehicles, from muscle to vintage to exotic cars. You'll see a rare Cadillac station wagon, one of only five ever made, and the gift shop has collectibles for most automotive preoccupations.

The Ringling estate contains many buildings including the Cà d'Zan, the Museum of the Circus, and the original art museum building.

The museum rents out some of its cars if you want to make a grand entrance somewhere, and the cars are also available for photo ops.

## Historic Spanish Point

History buffs may want to visit Historic Spanish Point (337 N. Tamiami Trail, Osprey, 941/966-5214, www.historicspanishpoint.org, 9 A.M.–5 P.M. Mon.–Sat., noon–5 P.M. Sun., $10 adults, $8 Florida residents, $9 seniors, $5 children 5–12), operated by Gulf Coast Heritage Association. Bordered on its western edge by Little Sarasota Bay and by pine flatlands to the east, the 30-acre site tells the story of life in the greater Sarasota area going back many generations. Interpretive markers and an "Indian village" show how early Floridian natives fished and hunted here, building middens, or shell mounds, and a burial mound (an archaeology exhibit in the main hall gives you the background on this). Then there's a restored pioneer home and chapel, revealing the story of the early white settlers here, the Webb family. After that, you'll stroll the gardens of heiress Bertha Matilde Honore Palmer's winter estate on Osprey Point. The site has a butterfly garden to add to the mix, showing the larval and nectar plants for monarch, zebra longwing, swallowtail, and other butterflies native to the area.

## South Florida Museum

The South Florida Museum (201 10th St. W., Bradenton, 941/746-4131, 10 A.M.–5 P.M. Mon.–Sat., noon–5 P.M. Sun., $15.95 adults, $13.95 seniors, $11.95 children 4–12) is worth a short drive north to Bradenton for the history buff. There are Ice Age dioramas with animals and natural history exhibits that trace the state's ancient history. The Spanish explorers are covered with nice detail, and the museum houses the Tallant Collection of artifacts, an assemblage of loot from Floridian archeological sites.

## Farmers Market

Despite the fact that Florida is a huge agricultural state (citrus, sugarcane, tomatoes, strawberries), much of the Gulf Coast doesn't have serious farmers markets. Sarasota is an exception. Every Saturday morning year-round you'll find all the sights and smells unique to the local Florida farmers market: stacked produce; the cookie lady; a band of musicians passing the hat; babies in strollers, smiling a mouthful of gummed peach; wind chimes and handicrafts; and bromeliads, orchids, and cut flowers filling the bulging bags of nearly every shopper. The **Downtown Farmers Market** has been going on for 30 years, the tents and tables of 50 or so vendors erected Saturday mornings by 7 A.M. and broken down around noon. It used to be located on South Pineapple Avenue, but now it sets up each week on Lemon Avenue at the intersection of Main Street.

## Tours

One of the more popular tours in the area, is a 2.5-hour guided tour of downtown Sarasota on a Segway Human Transporter in Sarasota with **Florida Ever-Glides** (1370 Blvd. of the Arts, Ste. C, 941/363-9556, www.floridaever-glides. com, tours 8–11 A.M. and 5:30–8:30 P.M., $88, no kids under 15), zipping along the bayfront and arts community. The two side-by-side wheels (as opposed to a bike or motorcycle, in which the two wheels are in a line) are self-balancing, and you stand above the wheels on a little platform and steer the electric-powered vehicle with the handlebars. With speeds of up to 12 mph, they can be used in pedestrian areas and are a perfect way to cover serious ground at a pace slow enough to really appreciate things. Tours are limited to 12 people, and there are weight limitations.

If your passion is architecture, you won't need to be told that Sarasota is the birthplace of a certain strain of American modernism. (If this is news to you, pick up a copy of the excellent *The Sarasota School of Architecture, 1941–1966,* by John Howey.) The **Sarasota Architectural Foundation** (P.O. Box 3678, Sarasota, FL 34230-3678, 941/365-4723, www.saf-online.org) hosts architectural tours, educational events, film screenings, exhibits, and parties for architecture lovers who travel to Sarasota to see its architecture up close and personal. A list of tours is posted on the website.

After indulging in several of Sarasota's cultural attractions, you need to clear your head and take a **Walk on the Wild Side** (3434 N. Tamiami Trail, Ste. 817, 941/351-6500, www.walkwild.com, $30–65). The very friendly tour providers tailor trips, taking small groups kayaking, canoeing, day hiking, backpacking, camping, auto touring, bird-watching, or wildlife-viewing, according to people's interests and mobility. You don't need prior canoeing or kayaking experience (guides instruct you, but you still have to be fairly fit to work that paddle) to go out on the area's bays, estuaries, and rivers, pointing out birds, dolphins, gators, and manatees along the way. You can choose where you go and for how long (half day, full day, or overnight), but the most romantic is the sunset canoe outing with wine and cheese.

Several companies offer boat tours on Sarasota Bay and into the Gulf of Mexico. **Enterprise Sailing Charters** (2 Marina Plaza, 941/951-1833, www.sarasotasailing.com, 8 A.M.–8 P.M. daily, $40 for two hours, $55 for three hours, $70 for four hours, group and child discounts) takes people out on a tall-masted three-sail ketch. **Key Sailing** (2 Marina Jack, Bayfront Plaza, 941/346-7245, www.siestakeysailing.com, two-, three-, and four-hour sails daily, $48–80) offers charters and sailing

instruction aboard a sleek 41-foot Morgan Classic II. **LeBarge Tropical Cruises** (U.S. 41 at Marina Jack, 941/366-6116, 9 A.M.–6 P.M. daily, $20 adults, $15 for children 4–12) offers two-hour cruises of Sarasota Bay, either a dolphin watch narrated by a marine biologist, a narrated sightseeing cruise, or a tropical sunset cruise with live entertainment.

## Family-Friendly Attractions

My favorite family attraction in Sarasota is **Sarasota Jungle Gardens** (3701 Bay Shore Rd., 941/388-4441, 10 A.M.–5 P.M. daily, $15 adults, $14 seniors, $10 children 3–12, children under 3 free), but then I'm a sucker for quirky Old Florida attractions. Once part boggy banana grove, part universally agreed-upon "impenetrable swamp," the subtropical jungle was purchased in the 1930s by newspaperman David Lindsay. He brought in tropical plants, trees, and bird species. It opened in 1940 as a tourist attraction, and it puttered along through a couple of ownership changes until it ended up in the hands of the Allyn family. Every elementary student within 100 miles has made the trek by school bus to sit and watch the short birds of prey show (there's also a show that features animals linked only, I think, by their universal repugnance to human beings—things like giant Madagascar hissing cockroaches, I kid you not), and then wander along the paths through the lush formal gardens, the farmyard exhibit, the tiki gardens, and the flamingo area. The zoological gardens are home to about 100 animals, many of them abandoned pets, so it's an odd assortment. Another section of the park, however, has nothing to do with plants or animals—in one back corner you'll find the Gardens of Christ. It's a series of eight two-dimensional dioramas by Italian-born sculptor Vincent Maldarelli depicting important events in the life of Jesus Christ.

The **Mote Marine Laboratory and Aquarium** (1600 Ken Thompson Pkwy., City Island, 941/388-2451, 10 A.M.–5 P.M. daily, $17 adults, $16 seniors, $12 children 4–12, children under 4 free) is an enjoyable small aquarium that also serves as a working marine laboratory. For kids, the coolest parts are the 135,000-gallon shark tank and the "immersion cinema" state-of-the-art theater with a 40-foot wide, high-definition screen with Dolby Surround sound. Visitors get their own interactive consoles that change the outcome of the game or movie on the screen. Children will also like the underwater microphone in the Marine Mammal Center, which allows visitors to hear the resident manatees chirping at each other and methodically munching the heads of romaine lettuce that bob at the top of their tank. There's a touch tank, where you'll see parents cajoling their small ones to feel up a sea urchin, starfish, horseshoe crab, or stingless stingray, as well as nicely interpreted exhibits of eels, puffer fish, sea horses, and extraterrestrial-looking jellies.

The more impressive part of the Mote is not really open to the public—the Mote Marine Laboratory is known internationally for its shark research and more locally for its research on red tides or algal blooms, which occasionally adversely affect Sarasota's summer beach season with fish kills.

**Sarasota Bay Explorers** (941/388-4200) works in conjunction with Mote Marine Laboratory and runs their science boat trips out of the facility. They offer several wonderful styles of ecotours, all perfect for a fun yet educational family outing. There are narrated **Sea Life Encounter Cruises** ($35 including aquarium admission, $28 children), backwater **guided kayak tours** ($50 adults, $40 children), and private charters aboard the 24-foot Sea Ray Sundeck *Miss Explorer* ($295 for a three-hour trip, $445 for a five-hour trip).

If fate hands you a foul-weather day during your visit, a lovely family afternoon can be had at **G. WIZ** (1001 Boulevard of the Arts, 941/309-4949, 10 A.M.–5 P.M. Tues.–Sat., noon–5 P.M. Sun., $10 adults, $9 seniors, $7 children 3–18). It stands for the Gulf Coast Wonder & Imagination Zone, but it could best be described as a 33,000-square-foot facility of interactive science-focused exhibits. There are traveling shows, and the permanent exhibits are compelling. Kids can fly and be free as they zoom through the EcoZone (snakes, box turtles, and other native Florida creatures), the EnergyZone (with exhibits on electricity, sound, light, and neat building materials made out of magnets), the TechZone (where you can design a robot or create an animated video), and the BodyZone (exhibits on human anatomy, strength, endurance, and flexibility). Which is handy, as parents will need some strength and endurance of their own to keep up with their scampering progeny. The G. WIZ also offers programs for school groups and summer day camps.

Sarasota has a nice paint-your-own-pottery center, **S'Platters Pottery Painting Place** (2110 Gulf Gate Dr., 941/926-3070, 11 A.M.–6 P.M. Tues., Wed., and Sat., 11 A.M.–9 P.M. Thurs. and Fri., noon–5 P.M. Sun., prices start at $7, most pieces $12–25, which also includes paint, studio time, and firing), which makes another satisfying bad-weather family activity. S'Platters has jumped on a couple of current trends in kids' entertainment, offering a build-your-own-teddy-bear option, a bead-painting option so you can make your own beaded jewelry, and some neat mosaic-making kits. You can also take your favorite photo from your family vacation and have it fired onto a ceramic piece as a keepsake of your trip.

# ENTERTAINMENT AND EVENTS

Sarasota describes itself as the "cultural coast" of Florida. It starts getting monotonous when you enumerate all the professional arts options in Sarasota, but I suppose that's what I'm getting paid to do.

## Theater

Celebrating over 50 years of professional theater in Sarasota, the **Asolo Repertory Theatre,** until 2006 called the Asolo Theatre Company (5555 N. Tamiami Trail, 941/351-8000, www.asolo.org, curtain times generally 2 P.M. and 8 P.M. Nov.–June, prices vary), is a professional company that performs primarily in the

The Asolo's resident company performs in rotating repertory on the historic mainstage at the Mertz Theatre.

500-seat Harold E. and Esther M. Mertz Theatre at the Florida State University Center for the Performing Arts, a theater originally built as an opera house in 1903 in Dunfermline, Scotland. There's a second, smaller 161-seat black-box Jane B. Cook Theatre on-site for performances of the conservatory season and smaller productions of the Asolo. Students also present a series of original works known as the LateNite series, and the FSU School of Theatre presents a variety of other special events and performances. Recently, the Asolo Rep and the Conservatory perform one show each in the Historic Asolo Theater, located in the Ringling Museum's Visitors Pavilion. All of this means more shows and more variety for Sarasota's theatergoers.

Because the Florida State University Conservatory for Actor Training's graduate-level program yields so many newly minted thespians in Sarasota, the whole theatrical playing field has been elevated. Worthwhile community and professional theater troupe efforts include the contemporary dramas and comedies at **Florida Studio Theatre** (1241 N. Palm Ave., 941/366-9000). They perform mostly Broadway musicals at **Golden**

**Apple Dinner Theatre** (25 N. Pineapple Ave., 941/366-5454, www.thegoldenapple. com). Enjoy six annual musical productions with **The Players of Sarasota** (838 N. Tamiami Trail, 941/365-2494, www. theplayers.org), dramas in the summer with **Banyan Theater Company** (at the Asolo's Jane B. Cook Theatre, 941/358-5330), the more avant-garde readings of **Infinite Space** (different locations, 941/330-8250, www.in-finite-space.org), and even the small community productions on two stages of the **Venice Little Theatre** (140 W. Tampa Ave., Venice, 941/488-1115).

## Music and Dance
The oldest continuously running orchestra in the state of Florida, **Florida West Coast Symphony** (Beatrice Friedman Symphony Center, 709 N. Tamiami Trail, box office 941/953-3434, www.fwcs.org, prices and times vary) offers a wide array of more than 75 symphonic and chamber music concerts in a 37-week annual season. It also hosts the internationally recognized Sarasota Music Festival each June, an intense three-week event of chamber music, master classes, and concerts, with the coaching and performance of chamber music as its primary priority. Seven Masterworks programs are presented by the symphony throughout the season, as well as a four-concert Composer's Series and a set of six Great Escapes programs of light classics and pops on Thursday, Friday, and Saturday evenings and Friday mornings. The symphony also occasionally presents Symphonic Pops concerts with special guests.

But even if you're not a huge symphonic music fan, it's a good excuse to check out Sarasota's most distinctive landmark, the **Van Wezel Performing Arts Hall** (777 N. Tamiami Trail, 941/953-3368, www.vanwe-zel.org, times and prices vary). Designed by William Wesley Peters of the Frank Lloyd Wright Foundation, the building riffs on a seashell found by Frank Lloyd Wright's widow, Olgivanna, near the Sea of Japan.

It has an eye-popping lavender/purple color scheme, and it looks accordion-folded, like a scallop shell (supposedly to maximize the space's acoustical possibilities). Love it or hate it, the Van Wezel presents a wonderful range of Broadway productions, world-class dance, music, comedy, and popular acts, as well as being the home base for many of the local arts organizations.

For instance, the **Sarasota Ballet of Florida** (5555 N. Tamiami Trail, 941/359-0099, www.sarasotaballet.org, times and prices vary) splits its performances between the Van Wezel and the Asolo, offering a combination of treasured classical works and contemporary and modern dance. The ballet was founded as a presenting organization in 1987 by Jean Allenby-Weidner, former prima ballerina with the Stuttgart Ballet. Through community support, it became a resident company in 1990. The ballet often works collaboratively with other local arts organizations on productions—in 2005 it staged a ballet with Circus Sarasota that tells the story of John Ringling's life, complete with aerialists, clowns, and such. (The Sarasota Ballet also runs the Sarasota Ballet Academy; The Next Generation, an award-winning scholarship program for youth at risk; and an international summer school.)

The **Sarasota Opera** (61 N. Pineapple Ave., 941/366-8450, ext. 1, www.sarasotaopera.org) presents concerts year-round, but its much-anticipated (often sold out) repertory season is every February and March, housed in the beautifully restored 1926 Mediterranean Revival–style Edwards Theatre. The opera house underwent an extensive renovation in 2007. It also offers youth outreach, and Sarasota Youth Opera receives all kinds of recognition for its productions.

It's an endurance event, one that takes grit and a good pair of opera glasses: The Sarasota Opera's **Winter Opera Festival** draws opera buffs from all over the country for a compact season of four productions, which can be enjoyed nearly at one sitting for the especially enthusiastic. The festival provides a good program of obscure operas as well as the big

crowd-pleasers. While you're hanging around in the striking art deco lobby during intermission, look up: The chandelier is from the movie *Gone with the Wind.*

Sarasota also has an annual chamber music festival each April, **La Musica International Chamber Music Festival** (rehearsals in Mildred Sainer Pavilion of New College of Florida, performances in the Edwards Theatre, 61 N. Pineapple Ave., 941/366-8450, ext. 3, www.lamusicafestival.org, 8 P.M., $35 single tickets, $50 pass to all the rehearsals). The public is welcome to watch rehearsals for $10 each, to see the musicians work their way through complicated pieces by Tchaikovsky, Schubert, Mendelssohn, Prokofiev, Brahms, Mozart, and others. Before the actual evening performances there are short lectures about the pieces.

## Circuses

Five of the seven sons of August and Marie Salomé Ringling of Baraboo, Wisconsin, ran away and joined the circus. Or, rather, they invented their own. In 1870, they premiered their show and charged a penny admission, building it year by year from a modest wagon show (its first "ring" a strip of cloth staked out to form a circle) to a major national show that traveled via rail from town to town. Meanwhile, circus titans P. T. Barnum and James A. Bailey teamed up in 1888 to create "The Greatest Show on Earth," blowing away all the competition with their glitz, animals, and death-defying acts. It was Bailey's untimely death in 1906 that led the "Greatest Show" to be bought out by the Ringling brothers. The two circuses ran separately until 1919, when they were joined to form the mega-huge **Ringling Bros. and Barnum & Bailey Circus,** and the rest is history.

In the 1920s, John Ringling and his wife Mable built a spectacular Venetian-style estate on Sarasota Bay, called Cà d'Zan (House of John in Venetian dialect). They built an art museum to house their bursting-at-the-seams collection of 17th-century Italian paintings, Flemish art, and works by Peter Paul Rubens. But it was in 1927 when Sarasota became an

## CLOWNING AROUND

Ringling Bros. and Barnum & Bailey Circus, the oldest — in addition to being the greatest — show on earth, reinvents itself every two years, with two totally different traveling units. The Red Unit and the Blue Unit each tour North America 11 months out of the year for two years before going back to winter quarters (now in Tampa, but historically here in Sarasota) and preparing a new edition. The Red Unit presents the odd-numbered editions, the Blue Unit presents the even-numbered editions (so, for instance, if you see the 140th edition Blue Unit this year, you'll see the 141st edition Red Unit next year).

So one year the show's centerpiece might be the Living Carousel, an assemblage of 105 people, 27 animals, and more gold lamé than a Liberace concert, with something like two million rhinestones and elephant blankets inset with 81,000 mirrors turning the whole arena into a disco-ball fantasy.

Or it's the Globe of Steel, a 16-foot steel globe, into which ride eight members of the Torres Family, riding a complicated routine of loops around the interior, reaching speeds of 65 mph, and then someone gets in and stands there, daring one of them to flub up. Talk about extreme sports.

Or maybe sixth-generation circus performer Taba (no last names please), the "tiger whisperer," who quietly persuades four different types of Bengal tigers to romp around the center ring. Then there are always the high-wire acts, the classic Clown Alley, and an incredible live band performing the zany circus music.

But the circus has its work cut out for it. It may be the greatest show on earth, but these days it's definitely not the only show in town. Ringling Bros. and Barnum & Bailey Circus comes to town in this new millennium with its usual pageantry and death-defying acts, and it has to lure audiences from other popular traveling shows like Cirque du Soleil and persuade them to choose the big top over the big screen — not an easy task.

To get a sense of how much the magic of the circus means today and meant in the past, you only need to visit the **Museum of the Circus** (5401 Bay Shore Rd., 941/351-1660, 10 A.M.-5:30 P.M. daily, $19 adults, $16 seniors, $6 students and children 6-17, $6 Florida teachers and students with ID). It was John Ringling who brought the circus to Sarasota, moving the winter quarters of the Ringling Bros. and Barnum & Bailey Circus from Bridgeport, Connecticut, to Sarasota in 1927 — thus changing this part of Florida forever. The museum documents, preserves, and exhibits the history of the circus with props, rare handbills, parade wagons, tent poles, and memorabilia.

official circus town—the Ringling Bros. and Barnum & Bailey Circus's winter quarters were moved here, giving the sedate Florida town a firsthand look at the oddity, eccentricity, and glamour that is the circus.

Many of the circus performers who acted in the *Wizard of Oz* and that ultimate non-PC film *Terror of Tiny Town* (a musical western starring all little people) called Sarasota home, with specially built homes in a section of town called, unsurprisingly, **Tiny Town** (you can visit this area on Ever-Glide guided tours).

Today visitors get a sense of Sarasota's circus history at the **Museum of the Circus** on the Ringling grounds, but during February and March the circus comes alive with **Circus Sarasota** (8251 15th St. E., 941/355-9335, ringside $40, section C $20). Founded in 1997 by Ringling Bros. alums Pedro Reis and aerialist Dolly Jacobs (she's a second-generation circus performer—her father was the famous clown Lou Jacobs), it's a single-ring, European-style circus that changes every year. Reis and Jacobs often perform an aerial pas de deux, and there are tightrope acts, trained horses, aerial acrobats from China, clowns, tumbling, contortionists, and so forth, all performed in an intimate setting.

Despite the fact that Ringling Bros. circus now makes its winter home to the north in Tampa, Sarasota is still training the next generation of circus performers. **PAL Sailor Circus** (2075 Bahia Vista St., 941/361-6350, 11:45 A.M. and 7 P.M., $16 adults, $12 children) has been thrilling audiences for more than 50 years, educating kids 8–18 in the circus arts and then letting them put on a show. In 2004, the program was on the verge of closing. With the assistance of Sheriff William F. Balkwill, the Police Athletic League took over the Sailor Circus as one of its after-school programs. About 90 students participate in the twice-annual training sessions, where they learn circus skills like clowning, tumbling, high-wire, flying trapeze, unicycling, juggling, rigging, and costuming. Then, in March and the end of December, the students perform for the public in an exciting four-ring circus.

### ◖ Film Festivals

Sarasota supports not one, but two film festivals. By far the more famous of the two is the **Sarasota Film Festival** (multiple venues, box office is located in the Main Plaza at 1991 Main Street, Suite 108A, adjacent to the Regal Hollywood 20 Theatre, 941/364-9514, www.sarasotafilmfestival.com), which happens every April. The fastest-growing film festival in the country, it showcases 200 independent feature, documentary, narrative, and short films. The event usually includes a Shorts Fest, a couple of family-oriented events, and lots of panel discussions with industry leaders and symposiums with guest stars. And every November there's the Sarasota Film Society's 10-day **Cine-World Film Festival** (Burns Court Cinemas, 506 Burns Ln., 941/955-3456), which showcases Florida film artists in addition to presenting the best of the preceding Toronto, Cannes, New York, and Telluride film festivals.

### Festivals

February's not a bad month to visit, because you can catch the monthlong annual run of the European-style **Circus Sarasota.** Sarasota is the self-described "circus capital of the world," after all. Music lovers may want to come in February or March for the repertory season

of the **Sarasota Opera,** although in April there's **La Musica International Chamber Music Festival.** April also brings the weeklong **Florida Wine Fest & Auction.**

If you're visiting the area strictly for the white, powdery sand, you might think of coming in May for the pro-am **Sand Sculpting Contest** on Siesta Key Beach. **Fourth of July** fireworks over the Gulf are wonderful from the vantage spot of Siesta Key Beach.

## NIGHTLIFE
### Bars

Downtown has a few nightspots that really stand out. **Zoria** (1991 Main St., 941/955-4457, 11 A.M.–2 P.M. Mon.–Fri. and 5–10:30 P.M. Mon.–Sat., bar menu 10:30 P.M.–midnight, 5–9 P.M. Sun., $19–31) has a vital bar scene with a remarkable by-the-glass wine list.

For a more rarefied experience, head to the **Cà d'Zan Lounge** at the Ritz-Carlton (1111 Ritz-Carlton Dr., 941/309-2000, 5 P.M.–midnight Mon.–Thurs., until 2 A.M. Fri. and Sat., 1 P.M.–midnight Sun. $10–25). Overstuffed couches, clubby leather chairs, hickory wood walls, and an outstanding specialty drink menu.

Beyond these, there are refreshing drinks and good times to be had many places here, including the **Beach Club** (5151 Ocean Blvd., Siesta Key, 941/349-6311, www.beachclubsiestakey.com, noon–12:30 A.M. daily) in Siesta Key Village and **Sharky's** (1600 Harbor Dr S., Venice, 941/488-1456, www.sharkysonthepier.com, 11:30 A.M.–10 P.M. Sun.–Thurs., until midnight Fri. and Sat.), beachfront on the Pier in Venice. Local sports bars include the **Sports Page** (1319 Main St. Sarasota, 941/365-0469, 11 A.M.–2:30 A.M. daily), **Findaddy's** (935 N. Beneva Rd., Suite 601, Sarasota Commons Shopping Center, 941/953-6356, 11 A.M.–midnight daily), in Sarasota for watching the big game, and **8 Ball Lounge** (3527 Webber St., Sarasota, 941/922-8314, noon–2 A.M. daily), for when you feel like working on your own game.

### Dance and Music Clubs

For when you're ready to get on the dance floor, the **Five O'Clock Club** (1930 Hillview St.,

941/366-5555, www.5oclockclub.net for concert schedule, happy hour noon–8 P.M. daily, small cover charges change nightly depending on band) in Southside Village has what the mechanic ordered. There's live music seven nights a week, with national and local rock/blues/pop bands taking the stage at 10 P.M. The 5-O draws a 30s and 40s crowd, and just a smattering of college kids. The **Gator Club** (1490 Main St., 941/366-5969) is another longtime nightlife haunt. There's live music every night, often of the Jimmy Buffet–cover variety, plus pool tables upstairs and an impressive single-malt selection.

For something totally different and un-booze-centric, track down the **Siesta Key Drum Circle** on Sunday evenings, a drop-in party in which everyone adds their own beat. It all gets under way about one hour before sunset, just south of the main pavilion between lifeguard stands 3 and 4.

## SHOPPING

The shops of **St. Armands Circle** on Lido Key have been a primary retail draw in Sarasota for a long time, historically known for high-end boutiques. These days the shops cover familiar ground—chains like **Chico's** (443 St. Armands Circle, 941/388-2926), **Tommy Bahama** (300 John Ringling Blvd., 941/388-2446), **Fresh Produce** (1 N. Boulevard of the Presidents, 941/388-1883), and **White House/Black Market** (317 St. Armands Circle, 941/388-5033)—and a handful of up-scale, independently owned boutiques. You can also explore the circle's novelty and giftware shops: **Fantasea Seashells** (345 St. Armands Circle, 941/388-3031), **Wet Noses** (472 John Ringling Boulevard, 941/388-3647) for pet stuff, or **Kilwin's** (312 John Ringling Blvd., 941/388-3200), offering ice cream and fudge.

**Towles Court Artist Colony** (Adams Ln. or Morrill St., downtown Sarasota) is a collection of 16 quirky pastel-colored bungalows and cottages that contain artists working furiously and the art they've been working furiously on. You can buy their work and watch them in action 11 A.M.–4 P.M. most Tuesdays through Saturdays, or visit Towles Court on the third Friday evening of each month for Art by the Light of the Moon.

**Palm Avenue** and **Main Street** downtown are lined with galleries, restaurants, and cute shops, and historic **Herald Square** in the SoMa (south of Main Street) part of downtown on Pineapple Avenue has a fairly dense concentration of antiques shops and upscale housewares stores. Also on Pineapple you'll find the **Artisan's World Marketplace** (128 S. Pineapple Ave., 941/365-5994), which promotes self-employment for low-income artisans in developing countries worldwide by selling their baskets, clothing, and handicrafts.

**Westfield Shoppingtown Southgate** (3501 S. Tamiami Trail, 941/955-0900) is a pretty standard mall, with several anchor stores (Saks Fifth Avenue, Dillard's, Macy's) and many of the usual suspects (Ann Taylor, Talbots, Pottery Barn, Banana Republic, Gap, Gymboree, and The Disney Store). For when you need to make those credit cards sizzle, you have to head north on I-75 to the **Prime Outlets** in Ellenton (5461 Factory Shops Blvd., Ellenton, 941/723-1150). There are more than 130 stores (Ralph Lauren, Gap, Geoffrey Beane, Tommy Hilfiger, Nike, Off Fifth) with deep, deep discounts.

And if your mantra is "reduce, reuse, and recycle," you'll find all kinds of used goods at the more than 400 covered booths of the **Red Barn Flea Market** (1707 1st St. E., Bradenton, 941/747-3794), in Manatee County to the north. Go on the weekend for the greatest number of vendors and the widest variety of things, from collectibles and antiques to out-and-out junk.

## ACCOMMODATIONS

There are scads of condos and beachfront rentals in the greater Sarasota area, but most of these rent only by the week. If that's your time frame, the weeklong rentals often are a more financially prudent choice. Try giving **Argus Property Management** (941/927-6464) a call, or visit **Vacation Rentals by Owner** (www.vrbo.com). There are also golf resort condo communities such as **Heritage**

**Oaks Golf and Country Club** (4800 Chase Oaks Dr., 941/926-7602) and **Timberwoods Vacation Villas & Resort** (7964 Timberwood Cir., 941/312-5934) that rent by the week. If you're only in for a few days, hotels and motels run the gamut from moderately priced and no-frills to truly luxurious. Generally speaking, beachside places are pricier than mainland or downtown accommodations, and winter rates are highest, dropping down usually by a third in summer. Listed here are Sarasota and Lido Key accommodations—Longboat Key, Siesta Key, and Venice are covered in *The Keys* section of this chapter.

## Under $100

The **Cadillac Motel** (4021 N. Tamiami Trail, 941/355-7108, $42–58) is a no-frills, clean, single-story motel. It's a bit away from all the action of downtown (about a mile), but there's a sweet little pool and shuffleboard to entertain you. For a simple room, efficiency, or apartment, rented by the day or by the week, try **Southland Inn** (2229 N. Tamiami Trail, 941/954-5775, www.southlandinn.com, rooms starting at $50). Rooms have been recently remodeled, most with kitchens, and there's a large heated pool. It is near the Ringling School of Art and Design.

## $100-150

The three-story **La Quinta Inn & Suites Sarasota** (1803 Tamiami Trail N., 941/366-5128, $129–299) is not far from Ringling School of Art and Design, a few minutes' drive from downtown. Rooms are midsize, some with sofa beds, and those on interior hallways have desks. There's an outdoor pool, a pleasant complimentary breakfast, free parking, and pets under 30 pounds are accepted.

Business travelers enjoy **Springhill Suites by Marriott** (1020 University Pkwy., 941/358-3385, $149–189), a moderately priced, all-suites hotel fairly close to the airport. All rooms have a king or two double beds with separate sleeping, eating, and working areas. There's also a pullout sofa bed, a pantry area with mini refrigerator, sink, and microwave, and a big desk with fancy chair and two-line telephones with data port. The free continental breakfast isn't an afterthought, offering items like sausage, eggs, oatmeal, and make-your-own waffles.

**Courtyard by Marriott** (850 University Pkwy., 941/355-3337, $149–199) is a mostly business, recently renovated three-story hotel directly across from the airport. It's convenient to both Bradenton and Sarasota. This is a great hotel for business trips or family vacations. There's wireless high-speed Internet throughout the hotel, and a hot breakfast buffet.

## Over $150

It was controversial when it opened, but the **Ritz-Carlton Sarasota** (1111 Ritz-Carlton Dr., 941/309-2000, reservations 800/241-3333, www.ritzcarlton.com, $410–719), a 266-room, 18-story luxury hotel right downtown, has managed to blend in beautifully, as if it has always been here. Ritz-Carlton's signature warm and efficient service, spacious rooms with balconies and marble baths, and great amenities make it the top choice among business and other travelers looking for upscale amenities. The downtown location is convenient to restaurants (although there are two laudable ones on-site) and attractions; there's a lovely pool, and the wood-paneled Cà d'Zan Bar & Cigar Lounge is always hopping.

The Ritz has a spa open to guests and members only, and the Members Golf Club located 13 miles from the hotel offers a Tom Fazio–designed 18-hole championship course. It is a par 72, located on 315 acres of tropical landscape with no real estate development.

**Lido Beach Resort** (700 Benjamin Franklin Dr., 941/388-2161, www.lidobeachresort.com, $209–449), formerly a Radisson, is a favorite among families vacationing in the area. The 12-story south tower is newer than the north and comprises one- and two-bedroom suites with kitchens. The hotel has two beautiful free-form pools and three hot tubs all right on the beach, and one of Sarasota's few beachside tiki bars. It's a brief walk out the door to Lido Beach and St. Armands Circle shopping/dining area, 10 minutes to downtown, and 15–20 minutes to the airport. The hotel offers beach volleyball, a free shuttle to St. Armands, dry cleaning, laundry, business services, and meeting rooms.

At the end of April 2008, the 12-story **Hyatt Sarasota** (1000 Boulevard of the Arts, 941/953-1234, $229–439) completed a $22 million transformation, with a full makeover of guest rooms, lobbies, corridors, meeting space, fitness center, business center, restaurants, and bars. It's a big convention hotel right downtown with easy access to Van Wezel Performing Arts Hall, the Municipal Auditorium, and other attractions. It's right in the downtown business district, but waterside, with its own private marina, a floating dock, and a beautiful lagoon-style pool. The 294 guest rooms all have a view of the bay or marina, most with little balconies.

One of the trendiest and hippest hotels to open in recent years is the **Hotel Indigo** (1223 Boulevard of the Arts, 941/487-3800, www.hotelindigo.com, $199–233). Guest rooms have wall-size murals and fabrics in bold blues and greens—altogether it's a fun, contemporary alternative, right in the thick of things. The onsite café is called the Golden Bean, there's a little wine bar called Phi, and a fitness studio called, well, Phitness Studio.

If you think small is beautiful, you may want to take a gander at **The Cypress, a Bed & Breakfast Inn** (621 S. Gulfstream Ave., 941/955-4683, www.cypresbb.com, $180–279), with only four distinctly decorated rooms. Set in a 1940s tin-roofed cypress home, the four suites are kitted out with American and European antiques, paintings, and artifacts, and the house's common space is charming. Room rates include an extravagant breakfast and an afternoon social hour with hors d'oeuvres and refreshments. The inn is across the street from Bayfront Park and down the block from Marie Selby Botanical Gardens. No children or pets are allowed.

## FOOD

Strips of chain restaurants pop up on the Gulf Coast of Florida like mushrooms after the wet season. In fact, many chains, such as Outback Steakhouse and Hooters, call the Gulf Coast home, and new chains are often market-tested first in the urban areas along this part of Florida. Why, I ask myself? It's demographics. In an area that still has a fairly dense concentration of retirees, the newest growth segment is young families. And what do the elderly and young families have in common? They like to eat out, but they want things to be familiar. They want to go to Chili's and eat the same thing they ate last time.

Well, Sarasota restaurants are fighting the creeping encroachment of chains. Twenty-eight independent restaurants in town joined together not long ago to build public awareness of the importance of the community's unique cuisine. They formed the Sarasota Originals, the first Florida Chapter of the Council of Independent Restaurants of America (CIRA). For the visitor, this is good news. The city has a superabundance of unique restaurants and the diners who love them.

### Downtown

I'll start with the heavy hitters. A recent addition to the Sarasota culinary landscape, **Derek's Culinary Casual** (514 Central Ave., 941/366-6565, 11:30 A.M.–2:30 P.M. Tues.–Fri., 5–10 P.M. Tues.–Sat., $19–29) is the brainchild of chef/owner Derek Barnes, former chef at 5-One-6 Burns. In a much larger, high-ceilinged space, he has brought exciting, contemporary American cuisine to Sarasota's Rosemary District. Treats like tuna gnocchi, and duck two ways (a seared breast paired with pecan-crusted leg confit, German spaetzle, and bitter greens) aim to bring a new twist to classic French/Italian/Californian dishes. The wine list is similarly ambitious and fairly priced, but small.

Located in the historic Florida Citrus Exchange, **Rustic Grill** (400 N. Lemon Ave., 941/906-1111, 5–10 P.M. Sun.–Thurs., until 11 P.M. Fri. and Sat., $24–34) has a spectacular Tuscan villa interior and nice selection of art and antiques. Chef Clinton Combs' open kitchen and wood-burning grill add a nice touch to an inventive array of small plates and large plates. The waiters need

## TABLE HOPPING

In the off-season, Sarasota's many culinary pearls are yours for the plucking – and during June that plucking gets all the more delicious with a 10-day **Savor Sarasota restaurant week.** In a city with one of the highest concentrations of *Zagat*-rated restaurants in Florida, dozens of restaurants have banded together to offer the public value-priced, three-course, prix fixe menus.

"We're offering our prix fixe lunch for $15, $25 for dinner," says Jeremy Saccardi, chef de cuisine at the Ritz-Carlton Sarasota. That's right, I said the Ritz-Carlton. "For us in particular it's a chance to see some people who wouldn't normally come into the restaurant, who would consider us out of their budget. We were so busy during the restaurant week last year that we had to extend it another week."

Alright, it's a bargain, but what's in it for the restaurants? According to Michael Klauber, proprietor of Michaels on East and one of the instigators of the restaurant week, "The original idea came from the local convention and visitor's bureau. They got a few of us restaurateurs together to talk about it. We thought this would be a great way to showcase the restaurants, and it gives the restaurants an opportunity to explore something different with a special menu. I hope it can become a destination event, and that hotels and resorts will see an influx of people."

Some restaurants include interactive cooking demonstrations; others feature live music. Many of the restaurants offer several choices for appetizer, entrée, and dessert, some with suggested wine pairing flights. At core, though, it's not complicated: Pick a participating restaurant, make a reservation, dine, pay ($15 for lunch, $25 for dinner). Repeat. For more information about participating restaurants, events, and pricing, visit www.savorsarasota.com.

stamina to explain each dish: Grilled local grouper comes with baby fennel confit, haricots verts, kalamata tapenade, roasted tomatoes, English pea emulsion, and a blistered red pepper coulis. Whew. Grilled meats are the star of the show, from the bone-in strip loin to a smoky pork tenderloin.

Sarasota's 🄲 **Bijou Cafe** (1287 1st St., 941/366-8111, 11:30 A.M.–2 P.M. Mon.–Fri., 5–9:30 P.M. Mon.–Thurs., until 10:30 P.M. Fri. and Sat., until 10 P.M. Sun., $19–36) has been a local gem since 1986, making everyone's top 10 list and bringing praise from *Zagat, Bon Appetit* and *Gourmet.* It's what you'd call Continental-American fare, presided over by chef Jean-Pierre Knaggs and his wife, Shay. Located a couple of blocks from Ritz-Carlton Sarasota in a 1920s gas station turned restaurant, the vibe is special-occasion or big-time-business dining. A 2004 renovation (after a fire) brought a bar, lounge, private room, and outdoor dining courtyards. The wine list features a number of South African wines (Knaggs is South African),

and the menu contains dishes like shrimp and crab bisque, roast duck with orange-cognac sauce, and crab cakes with Louisiana rémoulade. And don't miss the crème brûlée.

Opened in 2003, **Mattison's City Grill** (1 N. Lemon Ave., 941/330-0440, 11 A.M.–11 P.M. Mon.–Thurs., until midnight Fri. and Sat., until 10 P.M. Sun., $17–25) is casual, hopping, with Italian-ish small plates and pizzas. It feels more urban than many of the other downtown restaurants, with great outdoor seating, cool wine events and cigar dinners, and live jazz nightly. It's been so successful that owner Paul Mattison has a virtual empire in the area now: Mattison's Riverside, Mattison's Steakhouse at the Plaza, Mattison's Forty One, and a catering business—all fun, all fresh dining experiences.

Another longtime downtown favorite has nightly live music but a totally different feel. **Marina Jack's** (2 Marina Plaza, 941/365-4232, 11:30 A.M.–1 A.M. daily, main dining room closed 2–5 P.M., $8–36 depending on which dining room you choose) is all about casual waterside dining, with a few different ways to eat with the water in view. Choose from the second-level Bayside Dining Room, the Portside Patio, or a cocktail at the Deep Six Lounge and Piano Bar. If you still don't feel aquatic enough, there's the *Marina Jack II* yacht, which wines you and dines you in the bay. Back on land, the menu leans to crowd-pleasers like crab-stuffed mushrooms, conch fritters, steaks, and grilled grouper.

In a similar style (fun, casual, seafood joint), but with no water views, **Barnacle Bill's** renovated in 2005 in its downtown location (1526 Main St., 941/365-6800, 11:30 A.M.–9 P.M. daily, with a small-plate menu only 4–5:30 P.M., $12–24). The Main Street location is the chain's white-tablecloth establishment with choices like crab cakes, fried popcorn shrimp, or stuffed flounder. Other locations: 3634 Webber St., 941/923-5800 (this one was just renamed Chef D's Italian Fisherman); 5050 N. Tamiami Trail, 941/355-7700; and 8383 S. Tamiami Trail, 941/927-8884.

It's not exactly downtown, but just slightly south. Still, any list of important downtown restaurants has to include ◖ **Michaels On East** (1212 East Ave. S., 941/366-0007, 11:30 A.M.–2 P.M. Mon.–Fri. and 5:30–10 P.M. daily, $18–31). It's won best-of-Florida accolades from nearly everyone since its opening at the beginning of the 1990s—and it's kept up with all the newcomers, consistently pushing the envelope and wowing diners with its "New American" take and lavish interior. During the day it's a power-lunching crowd enjoying Wendy's warm chicken salad with dried cranberries, goat cheese, and candied pecans in honey-lemon-basil vinaigrette; at night, romantic dinners include a grilled duck breast paired with Bermuda onion and shiitake fondue, and fig and pecan risotto, all flavors showcased with a nice selection of wine.

For when you're tired of fish, ◖ **Patrick's** (1400 Main St., 941/952-1170, 11 A.M.–midnight daily, $9–18) gets top honors for Sarasota's best burger. It's a casual spot, with no reservations accepted, and the bar scene is fun. Patrick's has an extensive lunch and dinner menu with an exceptional variety of burgers, steaks, seafood, salads, and traditional bar fare favorites like chicken wings and jalapeño poppers. The burger selection is creative and original—try the Bronx burger with grilled onions, Swiss cheese, and barbecue sauce or the Cajun burger with jalapeños, Cajun spices, and Monterey jack cheese. The wine list contains around 20 well-selected wines and the beer selection focuses on stout ales and Irish varieties.

Located just a few steps from the Burns Court Cinema, with a monumental banyan tree marking the sweet little Old Florida cottage, **5-One-6 Burns** (516 Burns Court, 941/906-1884, 11:30 A.M.–2 P.M. Mon.–Fri. and 5:30–10 P.M. daily, $12–28) is a locals' favorite. The location is great, but this solid restaurant is prized primarily for its inventive American bistro fare. The menu explores the food of many countries; choices include sweet-and-sour shrimp broth with shrimp, shiitake mushrooms, and scallions and grilled Alaskan halibut with grilled peach and lemon-and-mint salsa. The wine list is ambitious, focusing on lesser-known producers and boutique wineries.

Just want a quick, inexpensive bite? Head to downtown's **Cafe Epicure** (1298 N. Palm Ave., 941/366-5648, 11 A.M.–10:30 P.M. daily, $5–25). It's a cool bistro/deli/market, an easy place to hang out on the patio and write postcards while having a drink and enjoying a great sandwich or salad. If you're feeling bold, try the surprisingly good octopus salad with potatoes and string beans.

Best breakfast? It's a chain, but this location is without a doubt the best of the breed. **First Watch Restaurant** (1395 Main St., 941/954-1395, 7:30 A.M.–2:30 P.M. daily, $5–12) serves Sarasota's finest quick, no-fuss, inexpensive breakfasts with bottomless coffee and cheery service. Investigate the Greek Fetish omelette (roasted red peppers, feta cheese, and spinach, topped with black olives and red onions) or the cranberry nut pancakes. Lines can be long, but they move quickly. If you just can't wait, walk south along Central Avenue and stop into one of the sidewalk coffeehouses.

## St. Armands Circle and Lido Key

In 1893, a Frenchman named Charles St. Amand bought a little mangrove island off Sarasota, homesteading in the usual way with fishing, hunting, and growing a little produce. In the land deeds his name was misspelled, so it stuck when circus magnate John Ringling bought the property in 1917 (well, it's rumored he won it in a poker game). He planned for St. Armands Key to be a residential and shopping development laid out in a circle, bringing people over first by steamer and then via the John Ringling Causeway completed in 1926 (the major lifting done by circus elephants). The area has had a fairly consistent commitment to becoming as upscale as possible since Ringling wheedled it away from old Charles St. Amand. It's often compared to Rodeo Drive and other famous shopping districts.

There are a variety shops, from upscale clothing stores to tourist souvenir types, and some of the city's best restaurants line up around the circle. So, explore the shops and go to dinner.

Two of the oldest on the stretch are **Café L'Europe** (431 St. Armands Circle, 941/388-4415, 11:30 A.M.–3 P.M. and 5–10 P.M. daily, $23–40) and the **Columbia Restaurant** (411 St. Armands Circle, 941/388-3987, 11 A.M.–11 P.M. Mon.–Sat., 11 A.M.–10 P.M. Sun., $8–28). Close together, both feature beautiful dining rooms and wonderful sidewalk dining, but the food's better at Café L'Europe. The Columbia opened in 1959, making it the oldest restaurant in Sarasota. (Its sister restaurant in Tampa goes one better, being the oldest restaurant in the state of Florida.) The Cuban food is authentic and dishes include the red snapper Alicante and 1905 Salad with chopped cheese, olives, and a vinaigrette. The black bean soup and pompano in parchment are good choices. Columbia is also known for its fruity sangria. As for Café L'Europe, it's a broad collection of culinary influences that's hard to pin down: The kitchen does an equally good

job with shrimp pad Thai, veal cordon bleu with luxe chanterelle mushroom risotto, and a Mediterranean chicken Kavalla that pairs chicken breast with feta, spinach, and crab.

**15 South Ristorante Enoteca** (15 S. Boulevard of Presidents, 941/388-1555, 4–11 P.M. nightly, open for lunch during high season, nightclub 7 P.M.–2 A.M. nightly, $14–34) seems to be the place to go in the area for northern Italian, and the upstairs **Straight Up Night Club** features an excellent martini bar and a diverse styles of music nightly (Latin acts, belly dancing, Caribbean tunes, a big band, you name it). The restaurant's menu will be familiar, but the dishes like grilled veal chop and garlic bruschetta are exceptional.

It's a chain, but **Tommy Bahama Tropical Café & Emporium** (300 John Ringling Blvd., 941/388-2888, 11 A.M.–10 P.M. weekdays, until 11 P.M. weekends, $20–33) is just plain fun, the food is excellent, and the drinks too good for common sense to kick in. The store downstairs carries Tommy Bahama's signature mix of tropical leisurewear and cool housewares—you have to take a flight of stairs off to the side to reach the upstairs restaurant, which has huge windows that look out on the circle. Salads and drinks are fairly pricey, but very good.

**Cha Cha Coconuts** (417 St. Armands Circle, 941/388-3300, 11 A.M.–11 P.M. daily, $8–15) is a good place to go for a drink or to grab some island-inspired dishes like coconut shrimp or a burger topped with mango chutney. Also a good place for a drink is **Hemingway's Restaurant & Bar** (325 John Ringling Blvd., 941/388-3948, 11:30 A.M.–4 P.M. daily, 4–10 P.M. Sun.–Thurs., until 11 P.M. Fri. and Sat., $15–22), but **Cork & The Bottle Shop** (29 N. Blvd. of the Presidents, 941/388-2675, 11 A.M.–10 P.M. Mon.–Sat.) is strictly for the serious wine lover. **Blue Dolphin Cafe** (470 John Ringling Blvd., 941/388-3566, 7 A.M.–3 P.M. daily, $3–9) is where to go for cheap, diner-style breakfasts with a twist (lobster Benedict, raspberry pancakes). When you're ready for some great fudge, head to **Kilwin's** (312 John Ringling Blvd., 941/388-3200, 8 A.M.–11 P.M. daily).

## Southside Village

You may be driving through Southside Village and before you have time to ask, "Hey, why are all these beautiful young professional types drinking glasses of red wine at sidewalk tables on the middle of a Tuesday afternoon?" you've passed right through it on your way downtown. Visitors don't hit this little shopping/restaurant area with frequency, which is a shame. A few of Sarasota's most contemporary restaurants are right here. Southside Village is centered on South Osprey Avenue between Hyde Park and Hillview Streets, about 15 blocks south of downtown.

Perhaps the best place in Sarasota to pick up the ingredients for a picnic is in the same block. **Morton's Gourmet Market** (1924 S. Osprey Ave., 941/364-2283, www.mortonsmarket. com, 8 A.M.–8 P.M. Mon.–Sat., 10 A.M.–7 P.M. Sun.) has the kind of fresh salads, deli items, fancy specialty sandwiches, and cooked entrées that make you press your nose up against the glass case, leaving an embarrassing smudge. Most items are fairly cheap, and you can eat on the premises or take it all out.

**Pacific Rim** (1859 Hillview St., 941/330-8071, www.pacificrimsarasota.com, 11:30 A.M.–2 P.M. Mon.–Fri., 5–9 P.M. Mon.–Thurs., 5–10 P.M. Fri. and Sat., $7–15) takes you on a very pleasant pan-Asian romp, from Thai basil curries to expertly rolled tekka maki sushi and beyond. You can play chef here and select your combinations of meats and veggies to be grilled or cooked in a wok.

Nearby **Hillview Grill** (1920 Hillview St., 941/952-0045, 11 A.M.–10 P.M. Mon.–Sat., $13–29) traffics in another melding of cuisines, this time Cajun and Creole with a bit of several other ethnic influences. It's more of a neighborhood joint, with easier prices and a relaxed setting. Try the roast chicken with red potatoes or New Zealand lamb chops with apple-mint salsa and you'll be satisfied.

## International District at Gulf Gate

Many of the better less-expensive restaurants can be found at the **Gulf Gate neighborhood**, a tiny international district that spans a three-block area from Gulf Gate Avenue to Superior Avenue, and Mall Drive around the block to Gateway Avenue. It's where to go to get a quick meal on the fly, takeout, or just something that won't break the bank. At Gateway Avenue you'll come upon the little French bistro **Le Parigot** (6551 Gateway Ave., 941/922-9115), **Pontillo's Pizza** (6592 Superior Ave., 941/921-0990), and **Rico's Pizzeria** (5131 N Tamiami Trail, 941/922-9604). After all that pizza, and for something totally different, try the pierogies at **Lucy's Polish Delicatessen** (6542 Gateway Ave., 941/926-8980). Then you'll need a beer at **Paddy Wagon** (6586 Gateway Ave., 941/925-2344). And once you hit Gulf Gate Drive, there are a couple of Chinese and sushi takeout places, a Russian joint, and a British tearoom.

## Pinecrest and Beyond

Amish cuisine. If that looks like a typo sitting there, you'll need to recall that Sarasota is a huge Amish and Mennonite winter resort. Both groups come down from Pennsylvania and the Midwest looking for sun and good Amish food, with luck on both counts. The locus of Amish activity here is in Pinecrest, where you'll see the bearded men in suspenders and wide straw hats, the women in long skirts and bonnets, all enjoying the Florida weather. While here, they eat at **Yoder's** (3434 Bahia Vista, 941/955-7771, 6 A.M.–8 P.M. Mon.–Sat., $6–14). It's been a Sarasota institution since 1975, with wholesome, rib-sticking country ham and corn fritters, turkey and gravy, meatloaf and mashed potatoes, and pies, pies, pies. Note especially the peanut butter cream pie. **Troyer's Dutch Heritage** (3713 Bahia Vista, 941/955-8007, www.troyersdutchheritage.com, 6 A.M.–8 P.M. Mon.–Thurs., 6 A.M.–9 P.M. Fri.–Sat., $5–12) is even more venerable, dating back to 1969, with sturdy, accessible buffet-style meals and a gift shop on the second floor. Another one people seem devoted to is **Sugar and Spice Family Restaurant** (4000 Cattleman Rd., 941/342-1649, 7 A.M.–9 P.M. Mon.–Sat., $8–15). All of them are closed on Sunday and serve no alcohol.

# The Keys

The northernmost of Sarasota's stretch of keys, Longboat Key is a 12-mile barrier island populated mostly by extremely upscale private residences. What you can see of the residences is showy enough, but I have a sneaking suspicion that the really incredible mansions are down all those long driveways and behind those tall hedgerows. There are only about 8,000 full-time residents, but in high season (Dec.–March), Longboat Key is where the rich and/or famous come to play a little golf and get a little sun away from the prying eyes of the public. If you are interested in seeing celebrities you can hang around at the **Longboat Key Club** or on the golf courses to catch a glimpse.

The island hasn't always been so swanky. It was the Arvida Company that laid the foundation in the late 1950s (literally, enabling construction to occur on previously loose, shifting soil) for the development of the island. Generally speaking, visitors stay in the high-rises that line the well-landscaped Gulf of Mexico Drive; residents live on the bayside in discreet, shielded estates.

Siesta Key is something else again. It's a similar eight-mile-long barrier island with beaches just as beautiful as those of Longboat Key. But Siesta is mostly casual and fun family-owned accommodations, none extremely upscale, with easy access to the beach from anywhere, fishing, boating, kayaking, snorkeling, scuba diving, and sailboarding. And at night, unlike on Longboat, these people like to party. Siesta Village has the area's most lively nightlife.

Farther south, Casey Key is eight miles long, stretching from Siesta Key on the north to Venice at the southern tip. It is almost exclusively single-family homes with just a few low-rise Old Florida beach motels. Two bridges provide access to the key, including a cool, old "swing bridge" dating back to the 1920s. Parts of the key are only 300 yards wide.

© JOSHUA LAWRENCE KINSER

**Stay near the beaches of Siesta Key for a casual and fun beach vacation with the most lively nightlife in the area.**

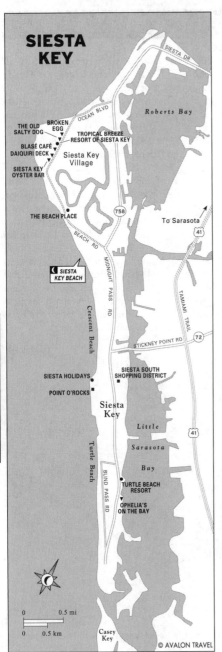

SIESTA KEY

Roberts Bay

THE OLD SALTY DOG
BROKEN EGG
TROPICAL BREEZE RESORT OF SIESTA KEY
BLASÉ CAFÉ
DAIQUIRI DECK
Siesta Key Village
SIESTA KEY OYSTER BAR

THE BEACH PLACE

To Sarasota

SIESTA KEY BEACH

Crescent Beach

MIDNIGHT PASS RD

TAMIAMI TRAIL

STICKNEY POINT RD

SIESTA HOLIDAYS
POINT O'ROCKS
SIESTA SOUTH SHOPPING DISTRICT

Siesta Key

Little Sarasota Bay

Turtle Beach

BLIND PASS RD

TURTLE BEACH RESORT
OPHELIA'S ON THE BAY

0      0.5 mi
0      0.5 km

Casey Key

© AVALON TRAVEL

The town of Venice is more like a real place than a tourist destination, in good and bad ways. The residents seem to be mostly retirees, very sociable and active. The downtown is quaint—a handful of upscale shops and galleries, a couple of restaurants, a place to get ice cream, a couple of coffee shops, and a good wine bar. There's a little community theater, of which the residents are extremely proud. Really, the biggest draw in Venice is teeth.

Every August, the Venice Area Chamber of Commerce holds the **Shark's Tooth and Seafood Festival,** with arts, crafts, food stalls, and lots of little pointy black fossils. It seems that sharks of all species shed their teeth continually. They have 40 or so teeth in each jaw, with seven other rows of teeth behind that first one waiting in the wings to mature. The average tiger shark produces 24,000 teeth in 10 years. In order to find them when they wash up on Venice beaches, stop by one of the gift shops downtown and ask for a shark tooth shovel. And once you've found a few, visit www.venice-florida.com/shark.htm to identify the species.

## SPORTS AND RECREATION
### ◖ Siesta Key Beach

We have a winner of the international whose-beach-is-better smackdown. In 1987, scientists from the Woods Hole Oceanographic Institution in Woods Hole, Massachusetts, convened to judge the Great International White Sand Beach Challenge, with more than 30 entries from beaches around the world. To this day, Siesta Key Beach remains the reigning world champ, with all other beaches too cowed, or too chicken, to demand a rematch. Its preeminence has long been known—supposedly in the 1950s a visitor from New York, Mr. Edward G. Curtis, sent a pickle jar of Siesta's sand to the Geology Department of Harvard University for analysis. The report came back: "The sand from Siesta Key is 99 percent pure quartz grains, the grains being somewhat angular in shape. The soft floury texture of the sand is due to its very fine grain size. It contains no fragments of coral and no shell. The fineness of the sand, which gives it its powdery softness, is emphasized by the fact that the quartz is a very hard substance, graded at 7 in the hardness scale of 10."

The real test can't be done with sand in a pickle jar. You need to lie on the sloping strand, run the warmed granules through your fingers, sniff the salt air, and listen to a plaintive gull overhead. That way, too, Siesta Key Beach wins—it's been named America's Best Sand Beach and ranked in Florida's Top Ten Beaches multiple years on the Travel Channel. Dr. Beach has named it in his top 10 beaches in America numerous times; *National Geographic Traveler* has also named Siesta One of America's Best Beaches. The list goes on.

## Other Beaches

The greater Sarasota area has lots of beaches to recommend. The beaches described here run from north to south.

Longboat Key has 10 miles of white, powdery beach, but most of it is accessible only to those who live there or are staying in a resort or condo. **Longboat Key Beach** is accessible at several points—at Longview Drive, Westfield Street, Mayfield Street, and Neptune Street. It's mostly underpopulated and often offers incredible sand dollar collecting. **Beer Can Island Beach,** at the very north end of Longboat Key and accessible by boat or from North Shore Road off Gulf of Mexico Drive, attracts a fair number of anglers and sun worshippers.

Then there's the aforementioned Siesta Key Beach, on the north side of Siesta Key (it is contiguous with another favorite beach called Crescent Beach—good snorkeling off this one), with white sand so reflective it feels cool on a hot day. Scientists estimate that the sand on this beach is millions of years old, starting in the Appalachians and eventually deposited on these shores. The water is shallow, the beach incline gradual, making it a perfect beach for young swimmers. There are 800 parking spots, which tend to fill up, and the lifeguard stands are painted different colors as points of reference, so you don't lose your way. The Siesta Key beaches south of a rock outcropping called Point of Rocks are not as white and soft, the

sand being shellier and grayer. **Turtle Beach,** on Midnight Pass Road near the south end of Siesta Key, is another popular beach, prized for its more private feel, large picnic shelter, and good shelling opportunities.

There used to be a small inlet that separated Siesta Key from Casey Key, an inlet called Midnight Pass that was filled in, amongst great controversy, in 1983. There have been disruptive environmental consequences to this choice, but for the visitor it means you can walk all the way on **Palmer Point Beach** from Siesta Key to Casey Key. The northern part of the beach was the former home of Mote Marine Laboratory. These days it's a quiet dune-backed beach, usually with just a few people walking and relaxing in the sand. There are neither lifeguards nor facilities. Casey Key also has **Nokomis Beach** directly west of the Albee Road Bridge, a nice average beach for the area, and **North Jetty Park** at its southernmost tip. North Jetty Park is one of the few Gulf Coast spots that draws surfers, and fisherfolk seem to congregate here, too. Boats pass through the jetties from the Intracoastal Waterway to the Gulf.

South from here you enter into the beaches of Venice, rightfully known as the place to go when you're hunting sharks' teeth. Only now you might be worried that there are loads of sharks lurking offshore waiting to gum you to death. The sharks' teeth that wash up on the beach are fossilized, floating in from a shark burial ground a few miles offshore, a deep crevice where these cold-blooded predators once went to die. In addition to these gray/black teeth, fossilized bones of prehistoric animals like camels, bison, and tapirs sometimes wash up on this beach. In local shops you can rent or buy a shark-tooth scooper, a wire rake with a mesh box that sifts the sand and shell fragments at the water's edge, leaving the teeth behind in the basket. **Venice Beach** (so different from the beach of the same name in California) is at the west end of Venice Avenue not that far from town. **Brohard Park,** at the southernmost part of Venice, is the beach of choice among anglers, with a 740-foot fishing pier on

# ANNA MARIA ISLAND

Stand at the northern end of Longboat Key and look north. You'll see another long, seven-mile strip of sandy barrier island that couldn't be much different from Longboat. Manatee County's Anna Maria Island is an island both literally and metaphorically – it is far enough south of Tampa to be removed from the city's urban hustle and bustle, and it's far enough north of Sarasota to escape being just another feather in that city's cap. It's the northernmost of the string of barrier islands that extend down to the Florida Keys, with three distinct towns spread along its length. There's the town of Anna Maria at the northern end, Holmes Beach in the middle, and Bradenton Beach at the southern end – all of them linked by their sweet, laid-back atmosphere. Three drawbridges access the island, one from Longboat Key and two from the mainland (Hwy. 64 and Hwy. 684).

Really, the little island community owes its very existence to the Fig Newton. The inventor of the "oo-ee, gooey, rich and chewy" Newton, Charles Roser, sold the recipe to Nabisco, made a fortune, and then bought up Anna Maria land and started building. (Actually, the island probably owes its existence to James Henry Mitchell, who invented the *apparatus*, a kind of funnel within a funnel, that supplies the necessary steady stream of fig jam while outside it there's a tube-like stream of dough. But, enough with the Newtons already.)

These days, there's an active year-round community as well as a robust tourist trade (for some reason you'll encounter more Danish, German, British, and Australian visitors than Americans). Tourists come for the outstanding boating, sailing, scuba, snorkeling, and fishing. Parking is the only hassle on the island, so park your car where you're staying and walk across to the beach – Holmes Beach, Anna Maria Beach, Coquina Beach, Cortez Beach, and Manatee Beach are all equally lovely stretches of white sand and blue-green water. (Manatee has the most parking and a nice picnic area.) None have lifeguards or restrooms.

It's the kind of island on which it's easy to do nothing – not because there's nothing to do, but because the pace is such that you feel entitled to easy relaxation. If your work ethic forces you to do *something*, I recommend a sunset sailing cruise with **Spice Sailing Charters** (departures from next to Rotten Ralph's Restaurant on Anna Maria Island, 941/704-0773, $25/person). The captain has a wealth of information about Florida history, fishing, and the area's recent environmental challenges.

Also worth checking out, Bradenton Beach has a newly revitalized municipal pier complex (Hurricane Charley had forced it to close in 2004). It includes a restaurant, 220-foot floating dock for free day docking, a bait house, and public bathing facilities. The 660-foot fishing pier and boater-related facilities sit at the bayside end of Historic Bridge Street in Bradenton Beach. Visitors can take advantage of watercraft transportation to the dock, but new bike lanes, sidewalks, a multiuse nature path along the beach, and a free trolley system add some other options for navigating the area.

## ACCOMMODATIONS

**Palm Tree Villas** (207 66th St., 888/778-7256, www.palmtreevillas.com, $115-195) is an inviting, warm, haven, whether it's for honeymooning couples or families. The low-rise Old Florida-style motel has been nicely refurbished, the well-appointed units clustered around a central courtyard and swimming pool. There's a great packet of literature in each villa, and the warm owners, Peggy and Ashok Sawe, are serious boosters of the area.

Another favorite on the island is **Harrington House Beachfront Bed & Breakfast** (5626 Gulf Dr., Holmes Beach, 941/778-5444, www.harringtonhouse.com, $139-359), a converted 1925 coquina-brick beachfront house. Most rooms feature French doors opening onto balconies that overlook the heated swimming pool, the beach beyond, and the Gulf beyond that. The breakfasts here are legendary (many recipes are featured in *From Muffins to Margaritas – Visit the Kitchens of Florida's Finest Inns*), there's a sweet little beach gazebo from which you watch the sunset, and the common living room is a surefire place to start lively conversations with total strangers.

### FOOD

**Beach Bistro** (6600 Gulf Dr., Holmes Beach, 941/778-6444, www.beachbistro.com, $15-40) beats much fancier restaurants in Sarasota, Tampa, and beyond for best restaurant on the Gulf Coast, according to *Zagat, Wine Spectator,* and numerous other publications. The place is quirky and cozy, with the kind of charm that comes of an independent (noncorporate) culinary vision. The food is largely excellent, and a more casual bar/café on one side is a good pick for a tasty burger. The more formal dining room is spectacular, with single long-stemmed roses adorning the center of each table. Although geared toward romantic dining, the Beach Bistro still extends real warmth and care to visiting children. For a restaurant of this caliber it isn't outlandishly pricey if you opt for the "small plates,"

which are certainly adequate if you have an appetizer as well.

Another favorite restaurant on the island is **Oma's Pizza** (201 N. Gulf Dr., Bradenton Beach, 941/778-0771, $8-15), a seriously delicious pizza, big and cheesy with a thin crust. The lasagna is good, too. For more everyday dining, it's hard to go wrong with the barbecue at **Mr. Bones** (3007 Gulf Dr., Holmes Beach, 941/778-6614, $6-14), and it also has fairly good Indian food – go figure. And you pick your beer from a coffin in the reception area. Then there's the newly refurbished **Rotten Ralph's** for fish and chips and an excellent blackened grouper sandwich. You can pull your boat up to the dock and place your order.

For more information about the island, contact **Anna Maria Island Chamber of Commerce** (5313 Gulf Dr. N., Holmes Beach, Florida 34217, 941/778-1541) and they'll send you a great packet of information and maps.

**SARASOTA COUNTY**

the property for public use. Dogs are allowed at **Paw Park** at South Brohard Park, with a fenced area, a small dog beach, and dog showers. Farther south, near Venice's little airport, **Casperson Beach** is really the locus of shark's tooth mania. Truth is, it's harder to find teeth than it used to be, partly because city boosters have replenished the sand on the beach with sand from an offshore sandbar. It's a very pretty beach left in its natural state, with people surf casting and red-shouldered hawks swooping above the shorebirds.

### Golf

In the early 1920s, John Ringling purchased major acreage on the south end of the Longboat Key. He constructed a golf course and planted Australian pine trees along Gulf of Mexico Drive; he eventually abandoned the construction of a luxurious Ritz-Carlton. With this legacy, the **Longboat Key Golf Club** (301 Gulf of Mexico Dr., 941/387-1632, resort courses,

greens fees $42–142) offers several remarkable golfing experiences to guests (and their guests' guests). Opened in 1960, the Bill Mitchell–designed Islandside Course (par 72, 6,792 yards, course rating 73.8, slope 138) features 18 holes of crisp, up-and-down shot-making through a 112-acre bird sanctuary filled with more than 5,000 palm trees and flowering plants. Water appears on 16 of its 18 fairways. With a more country-club feel (and where more of the private members play), the resort also has three 9-hole courses, played in three 18-hole combinations: blue/red (par 72, 6,709 yards, course rating 72.6, slope 130), red/white (par 72, 6,749 yards, course rating 72.7, slope 131), white/blue (par 72, 6,812 yards, course rating 73.1, slope 132).

### Fishing

Venice is a fairly well-known fishing destination—you'll see people wetting a line at the Venice jetties, Sharky's Pier, or Caspersen

# DICKIE VITALE'S LOCAL FAVORITES

**Dick Vitale** – Dickie V. to some – is the famous ESPN sports broadcaster who has called the greater Sarasota area home for the past 22 years. If you don't believe it, take a trip to the Dick Vitale Sports and Fitness Gym at the Boys and Girls Clubs of Sarasota County and see who stands outside in bronze.

Here is a list of his personal area favorites:

## 1. Siesta Key Beach
"I love walking that beach. I bring a lot of people there and it blows their mind – love the white sand!"

## 2. Sarasota Restaurants
"From Fleming's to Ruth's Chris Steakhouse to the Le Colonne Restaurant to the Café L'Europe," Vitale lists thoughtfully, splitting his favorites between tried-and-true chains and some of the area's independent eateries.

## 3. The Broken Egg in Siesta Key and Lakewood Ranch
Sure, it's another restaurant, but as Vitale notes, "It's my office away from home, five minutes from my house. I sit there for hours, doing all my work, my DickVitale.com articles, reading all my newspapers, and just having a blast with all the people." Sometimes for a couple of hours at a time, Vitale is known to do radio shows and TV interviews from the hangout where he is, he jokes, "the mayor of The Broken Egg." And when he gets hungry? The Dickie V turkey burger, of course.

## 4. Lakewood Ranch Country Club
The area was once owned by the founders of Schlitz Brewing Company, long given over to cattle ranching, turf farming, and citrus. In 1994, after much wrangling with the city, ground was broken on a new upscale residential development set squarely between Sarasota and Bradenton. It bears the distinction of being one of the largest master-planned communities in the state to achieve the Green Community designation by the Florida Green Building Coalition. "I live in the country club," says Vitale, "and I play tennis every day when I'm home."

## 5. Spring training at Ed Smith Stadium
"It's great to get up close," Vitale explains. The little 7,500-seat stadium provides intimate access to big-league play in a small-time venue.

## 6. Van Wezel Performing Arts Hall
"All the seats are great because it's so small, and it's got great sound," insists Vitale. The Van Wezel presents a wonderful range of

Beach. If you try your hand, expect to catch snook, redfish, Spanish mackerel, sheepshead, sea trout, and flounder, depending on the time of year. There are also lots of charter companies willing to take you deep-sea fishing out in the Gulf (grouper and snapper most of the year; kingfish, cobia, greater amberjack, and mahi-mahi seasonally). At the end of East Venice Avenue on the Myakka River, **Snook Haven Fish Camp** (5000 E. Venice Ave., 941/485-7221) has a fun riverside restaurant, boat rides, and fishing. **Reel Fast Charters** (941/650-4938, $75 sunset cruise, $425 for four hours, $600 for six hours, $725 for eight hours) takes groups out fishing as well as on nonfishing sunset cruises. And **Triple Trouble Charters** (941/484-3225, rates vary) takes small groups out from the Dona Bay Marina in Nokomis, just minutes from the Venice Inlet, on a 25-foot custom-rigged Parker for inshore and offshore fishing.

## Waterway Park
The **Venetian Waterway Park** (daylight hours, admission free) in Venice is a mixed-use linear park that features a recently completed 10-mile running trail that runs alongside the Intracoastal Waterway, ending on Caspersen Beach, one of the most beautiful on the Gulf. It's a long, winding, wheel-friendly park, good for in-line skaters, bikers, even jogging strollers.

Broadway productions, world-class dance, music, comedy, and popular acts, as well as being the home base for many of the local arts organizations. "Whether it be The Temptations, Vince Gill, or Tony Bennett, it's just phenomenal. I'm going there Wednesday night to see Frankie Valli and the Four Seasons. It's so great to know you have a place that close."

### 7. Main Street in Sarasota and Lakewood Ranch

"Both are special places to walk around, with restaurants and shops and lots of activities and music on the weekends," says Vitale. Lakewood Ranch's version dates back only to 2005 but still has an appealing range of boutique-style stores and eateries. More established, Sarasota's is lined with galleries, restaurants, and cute shops, and nearby historic Herald Square in the SoMa (south of Main Street) part of downtown on Pineapple Avenue has a fairly dense concentration of antiques shops and upscale housewares stores.

### 8. St. Armands Circle

"A tourist's delight," notes Vitale. While it's often compared to Rodeo Drive and other famous shopping districts, Vitale's affection for it is a little less highbrow: "Kilwin's ice cream is just phenomenal. I take a lot of people there. Since I try to stay away from fats, I go for the yogurt. It's romantic to walk to Lido Beach from there. Keeps your marriage going − I've been married 35 years!"

### 9. The Ritz-Carlton Sarasota and the Beach Club

The 266-room, 18-story luxury hotel right downtown has managed to blend in beautifully, as if it has always been here on the Sarasota scene. Ritz-Carlton's signature warmth and personality appeals to Vitale: "It's a great, great asset to the area. We love going there for dinner and going to listen to the great bands they have on the weekend."

### 10. Boys & Girls Club of Sarasota County

Vitale's commitment and enthusiasm on this topic are infectious: "My buddies and friends and I raised over $1 million to help build the Lee Wetherington Boys & Girls Clubs. It's always special to see young kids getting an opportunity in their lives."

Vitale's voice quiets a little as he says, "I've been lucky enough in my life to have opportunities to help kids chase their dreams. To bring a smile to a kid's face is really something."

SARASOTA COUNTY

While in Venice, visit the recently renovated **Venice Train Depot** (303 E. Venice Ave., free tours) downtown. The Mediterranean-style depot was constructed in 1927 and is listed on the National Register of Historic Places.

## SHOPPING

Shopping on Longboat Key is fairly limited: On the lush, tropically landscaped Avenue of the Flowers there's a little shopping center (525 Bay Isle Pkwy.) where you'll find a larger Publix grocery and a drugstore; at the **Centre Shops** (5370 Gulf of Mexico Dr., 941/387-3135) about mid-island, you'll find a small collection of shops selling T-shirts and resortwear, galleries, and little restaurants.

On Siesta Key there are two main shopping areas, **Siesta Key Village** on the northwest side of the key about one block from the Gulf, and **Siesta South shopping area** beginning at the Stickney Point Bridge and going south along Midnight Pass Road. Both have plenty of T-shirt-and-sunglasses shops, the shell-themed beachy giftware shops, and a few other stores not quite as touristy. Neither area boasts much in the way of high-end merchandise—galleries, antiques, or clothing.

## ACCOMMODATIONS
### Longboat Key

Longboat Key is mostly dotted with expensive high-rise condos and resort hotels that loom over the beaches. If you like a more modest scale, the **Wicker Inn** (5581 Gulf of Mexico Dr., 941/387-8344, www.wickerinn.com, cottages $980–2,996 per week) is more like it. There are 11 casual and fun Key West–style cottages set around an inviting pool and landscaped with purple hibiscus and oleander. There's a private beach just steps away and a 16-acre public park.

**◖ Colony Beach & Tennis Resort** (1620 Gulf of Mexico Dr., 941/383-6464, www.colonybeachresort.com, from $275) has been patronized over the years by George W. Bush, Tom Brokaw, Dustin Hoffman, and countless other luminaries. It's the area's oldest beach resort, with 235 luxuriously large suites, a relaxed atmosphere, two popular restaurants, private beach access, and 21 tennis courts (with 10 pros on staff). It's considered by many the nation's top tennis resort, but there are plenty of other distractions, such as a great beachfront pool and luxury spa.

The other big gun in town is **◖ The Resort at Longboat Key Club** (220 Sands Pointe Rd., 941/383-8821, www.longboatkeyclub.com, from $311). Serious golfers come for the 45 holes of the private Longboat Key Club, but there are lots of other reasons to settle into one of the 210 suites (with full kitchens) or one of 20 hotel rooms. There's a fine restaurant on-site, 38 tennis courts, bike and beach rentals, great pools, and a private stretch of white-sand beach with cabana rentals and beachside service. Despite the fact that this is an extremely upscale resort, the people who work here are friendly and personable.

Another big, but less expensive, favorite on Longboat is the **Hilton Longboat Key Beachfront Resort** (4711 Gulf of Mexico Dr., 941/383-2451, $270–495). The large, recently renovated rooms are decorated with contemporary furniture, all rooms with either two queen-size beds or one king-size. It sits adjacent to a private stretch of white-sand beach. The hotel provides free shuttle service to the shopping on St. Armands Circle.

## Siesta Key

There are not too many chain hotels and no huge resorts on Siesta Key—which is fine,

because you're more likely to have a memorable time in one of the modest mom-and-pop house rentals or small hotels. The warm, independent spirit of many of these hoteliers is apparent in the relaxed decor and easy beachside pleasures. Many accommodations on Siesta Key adopt an efficiency approach, with little kitchens, essential for keeping vacation costs down (have a bowl of cereal in the morning, then prepare yourself a great picnic lunch for the beach).

Rented by the week, the tropical garden beach cottages of **The Beach Place** (5605 Avenida Del Mare, 941/346-1745, www.siestakeybeachplace.com, $500–1,700/week) make a nice romantic or family beach getaway. There's a pool (but the beach is 30 seconds away), a tiki cabana with wet bar, beachside barbecue facilities, lounge chairs, beach cruiser bikes, and free laundry. The cottages themselves are modest but recently repainted and pleasant, whether it's the one-bedroom Coquina or Seahorse, the two-twin-bed Starfish, the large one-bedroom Sand Dollar, or the huge studio cottage called the Dolphin.

**◖ Siesta Holidays** (1015 Crescent St., 941/312-9882, www.siestaholidays.com, $425–1,450/week, depending on the season and unit) is a similar place, with two options. It has the Siesta Sea Castle directly on Crescent Beach, consisting of a large two-bedroom, two-bath apartment, and four one-bedroom efficiency apartments. The ground-level units have patios directly on the beach. Then there's the Siesta Holiday House, a little farther from the beach, with two one-bedroom apartments on the ground floor (with a big private screened pool) and two two-bedroom, two-bath apartments on the second floor. Pets are allowed in the Holiday House.

The **Tropical Breeze Resort of Siesta Key** (5150 Ocean Blvd., 941/349-1125, www.tropicalbreezeinn.com, $169–365/night) also offers a range of choices, spreading across four blocks of an attractive neighborhood between the village and the shoreline. There are one-, two-, and three-bedroom efficiencies and suites located directly on the beach as well as more privately located units in lush tropical gardens.

Each building comes with its own pool, and the property has a centrally located yoga deck. Everything is within walking distance of Siesta Key Village.

On the south end of the island, ❰ **Turtle Beach Resort** (9049 Midnight Pass Rd., 941/349-4554, www.turtlebeachresort.com, doubles from $250) is one of the area's best-kept secrets and without a doubt my favorite place to stay on Siesta Key. Reservations are harder to come by at this extremely relaxed and casual property, but the 10 clapboard cottages, each individually decorated with its own porch and featuring a very private hot tub, are worth waiting for. There are views of Little Sarasota Bay, Turtle Beach is a short walk away, and guests have free use of bikes, hammocks, canoes, kayaks, paddleboats, and fishing poles. Paddle a kayak from the dock of the resort to the quiet and secluded beach at Midnight Pass for sunset. Then paddle up an appetite on the way back and eat at Ophelia's next door for a real treat. Pets are welcome.

And just down the road a few blocks from the resort you can pull up your RV or stake out your tent and camp at the wonderful **Turtle Beach Campground** (8862 Midnight Pass Rd., 941/861-5000, www.scgov.net/turtle-beachcampground, $32 per night). The 14-acre park has 40 small but well-designed sites right on the Gulf. A small sandy path leads down to the beach and the campground keeps it fun with a boat ramp, volleyball net, horseshoe pits, and a playground. The city center of Siesta Key is a short drive down the road and has plenty of fun shops, restaurants, and bars to keep you from having to rough it too much at the campground. This place even has Wi-Fi, so if you forget your tent poles or your RV generator breaks down, you can just open your computer and order them online. I love camping and I love Siesta Key, so naturally I love this campground.

## Venice

If you've come to the Sarasota area with the express purpose of collecting sharks' teeth, then it makes sense to stay in Venice. Otherwise,

Set on Little Sarasota Bay, the Turtle Beach Resort features cottages with private hot tubs.

Venice lacks a lot of the amenities of Sarasota, Lido Key, Longboat Key, or Siesta Key, and the downtown pretty much closes up at night. There's a fairly inexpensive **Inn at the Beach** (725 W. Venice Ave., 941/484-8471, $98–159) and a **Best Western** (400 Commercial Court, 800/611-7450, $149–199), both perfectly fine.

## FOOD
### Longboat Key

One of Sarasota's most long-term love affairs has been with **Euphemia Haye** (5540 Gulf of Mexico Dr., 941/383-3633, $22–43). Hours vary by dining locale here: 5:30–10 P.M. Sunday–Thursday, 5–10:30 P.M. Friday and Saturday in the restaurant; 6–11 P.M. daily in the dessert room; 5 P.M.–midnight in the HayeLoft. Opened in 1975 on Longboat Key, the restaurant has marched to the beat of its own drum, serving far-reaching food in a tropical garden setting. It always wins top honors from local and national food magazines as well, and you need only to try the smoked salmon on buckwheat crepes, fried green tomatoes, or pistachio-crusted Key West snapper to see why. The wine list is broad, with good selections at every price point. As far as the food, prices are high and dishes are rich in the restaurant, so you can try the lighter/cheaper fare upstairs in the HayeLoft if you feel inclined. Chef/owner Raymond Arpke also offers cooking classes at the restaurant.

The other Goliath on Longboat Key is clearly the **Colony Restaurants** (1620 Gulf of Mexico Dr., 941/383-5558, dining room 11:30 A.M.–9:30 P.M. daily, Monkey Room dinner and breakfast only, bar 11:30 A.M.–1 A.M., $8–38) at the 36-year-old Colony Resort, partly for the sheer range of choices, and partly because so many local chefs cut their chops here. There's the fancy continental Colony Dining Room (opt for the skillet-seared snapper "Colony" with sun-dried tomatoes and lump crabmeat), the more casual Monkey Room and Bar, or the outside Monkey Room Patio and Bar. The Monkey Room is my kind of place and a must for party animals, the drinks tall with fun

names (screaming yellow monkey, anyone?), the views incredible, and the island-style food great with selections like classic Jamaican jerk chicken and Caribbean lobster tails. There's live entertainment nightly. The dining room serves Sunday brunch.

Located mid-key on the bay side of Longboat Key is a wonderful find, **Pattigeorge's** (4120 Gulf of Mexico Dr., 941/383-5111, 6–9:30 P.M. nightly, $16–28). Chef Tommy Klauber experiments with an East-West fusion style that somehow never seems contrived (he formerly owned a restaurant in Aspen called Gieusseppi Wong, serving Italian/Chinese food). Pattigeorge's has been around since 1998, making it another old-timer on the island. The dining room is comfortable but upscale and the views are nice—still, the main attraction is dishes like five-spice calamari with orange blossom honey-mustard, or Thai green curry grouper, or maybe a Thai chicken pizza.

### Siesta Key

Like everything else on Siesta Key, restaurants are mostly more casual here than on Longboat Key. Ocean Boulevard runs through Siesta Village, which is lined with loads of fun, laid-back, beachy bars and restaurants. Most places have outdoor seating, and many have live music at night.

When you're looking for that special romantic restaurant, only one place on Siesta Key will do. **◖ Ophelia's on the Bay** (9105 Midnight Pass Rd., 941/349-2212, 5–10 P.M. daily, $20–29), at the southern tip of the key, has a waterfront terrace that I swear the moon favors with an extra luminous show over Sarasota Bay and the mainland. The interior of the restaurant is stylish and romantic, but you have to sit outside. The chef seems to prefer sweet-and-salty combinations that combine meats with fruits (coconut- and cashew-crusted grouper with papaya jam) and salty meats with fish (black sea bass and clams pan roasted with applewood smoked bacon and leeks). It's a distinctive and memorable collection of dishes accompanied by a unique wine list. Try the macadamia nut torte for dessert. (The oyster bar next door to

# MAMA MIA

Longboat Key's one and only **Marcella Hazan** is considered by many who do not actually have Italian mothers to be the mother of Italian cooking in this country. She is the author of *The Classic Italian Cookbook, Marcella Says, Marcella Cucina, Marcella's Italian Kitchen,* and a few other Marcella books. She introduced balsamic vinegar to this country (by way of Chuck Williams, of Williams-Sonoma), and just as Julia Child's *Mastering the Art of French Cooking* was a book that many Francophile cooks slept with under their pillows, so too was Hazan's first book in 1973 the kind of cookbook that serious students of Italian cuisine eventually had to replace with a fresh copy (too much sauce gumming up the pages).

Hazan's in her 80s now, and this native of Cesenatico, Italy, has called Florida home for the past nine years. Having moved countless times ("four times across the ocean," in her words), she's feeling settled.

"Our son moved here to Florida. My husband and I only knew the East Coast of Florida and we didn't like it, so we were surprised by his move. We were in Italy, and we came down to cheer him up and we found that this place was completely different from the East Coast. We love to be near the water – we lived for 20 years in Venice with water all around – and we like the beach and the warm weather."

Hazan herself didn't cook a lick before she got married. But she learned fast. She got her start in culinary education in the 1950s, just teaching her friends the fundamentals of Italian cooking from her New York apartment kitchen.

"I was also teaching how to eat," Hazan remembers. "In Italy, people don't eat just a dish of pasta and a salad. They have different courses, but the courses are small. That was the first thing my students learned. I was teaching menus. Every menu was different, with different ingredients, so I took the students to the market, so they could see what it was they were going to use. It was very simple recipes with very few ingredients – people think it's such a production to make a meal. It was important for me to teach the feeling and the taste. I never tried to teach them presentation of a dish. That's not important to me – you have to eat it, not look at it."

It was Craig Claiborne of *The New York Times* who gave Hazan's vital and incisive spin on Italian cooking its big break in the early 1970s. Her classes became so popular that she began writing all of it down, a project that eventually became *The Classic Italian Cookbook.*

All of her books lay out the principles of Italian cooking in a no-nonsense, understandable writing style, and in the most recent (2008), *Amarcord: Marcella Remembers,* Marcella looks back on the adventures of a life lived for pleasure and teaching, that forever changed the way we eat.

It's as she says: "Music and cooking are so much alike. There are people who, simply by working hard at it, become technically quite accomplished at either art. But it isn't until one connects technique to feeling, turning it into the outward thrust of that feeling, that one becomes a musician, or a cook."

Never at a loss for an opinion, when asked which of her books Hazan favors, she seems stumped but quickly regroups.

"That's like asking which of your children you like best...*Essentials of Classic Italian Cooking* is more like a textbook, with home-cooking dishes that most people who like Italian food know about or have heard about. That book is still going very well, sold all over the world."

She once said, "I cook for flavor. Like truth, it needs no embellishment." And her recent memoir is full of both truth and flavor.

Look for her books in Sarasota's Main Street bookstores, such as **Sarasota News & Books** (1341 Main St., 941/365-6332), with new books and a nice café; **Main Bookshop** (1962 Main St., 941/366-7653), with four stories of remainders; or **Book Bazaar** (1488 Main St., 941/366-1373), selling used and out-of-print books. Hazan occasionally does book signings at these places.

Ophelia's is a wonderful place to kill a little time, and appetite, if you have to wait for a table at Ophelia's.)

Another great restaurant is **Siesta Key Oyster Bar** (5238 Ocean Blvd., 941/346-5443, 10 A.M.–midnight daily, $6–15), with the acronym SKOB on the sign out front. The sandwiches here are, in fact, called skobwiches and the swordfish or crab cake skobwich is mighty fine washed down with a house margarita while listening to a live rock band. Margaritas seem to find their foothold in Siesta Key, but if rum's more your drink, right down the way you'll enjoy the **Daiquiri Deck** (5250 Ocean Blvd., 941/349-8697, 11 A.M.–2 A.M. daily, $6–17). One of the better drinks is the Grateful Deck, a mix of raspberry liqueur, light rum, gin, vodka, raspberry juice, and sour mix. Tangy yet sweet, and very strong.

If you want to try a really good beer batter–dipped hot dog, head to the **The Old Salty Dog** (5023 Ocean Blvd., 941/349-0158, 11 A.M.–midnight Mon.–Thurs., until 1 A.M. Fri. and Sat., noon–midnight Sun., $5–15). It is an institution among locals, who come for that particular treat or a bowl of clam chowder and a beer. It's open-air, with great views, good burgers, and saucy waitresses. The beer bar is fashioned from the hull of an old boat, which adds a little nautical tilt to every drinker's voice. There's another location with the same hours at 1601 Ken Thompson Parkway (941/388-4311).

Best breakfast? That's the easiest call on Siesta Key. Anyone in town will promptly steer you to brand-new **The Broken Egg** (140 Avenida Madera, 941/346-2750, 7:30 A.M.–2:30 P.M. daily, $5–9), now located one block down from its original location. The place is such a cheery and busy scene most mornings that they opened a second location in 2005 at Lakewood Ranch. Try a Scram Sam (three eggs scrambled with smoked salmon and chives, served with tomatoes, onion, cream cheese, and a bagel) or banana-nut-bread french toast. The well-landscaped and shady patio is the place to sit.

**Blasé Café** (5263 Ocean Blvd., 941/349-9822, 9 A.M.–9:30 P.M. daily, $7–23) gives

The Broken Egg a run for its money, with expertly prepared egg dishes and a fine burger at lunch. Be sure to ask for outside seating on the wooden deck with the big palm tree in the middle (but if you're just stopping in for a drink, the bar is the seat of choice).

## Casey Key

On Casey Key, the place to eat is **Casey Key Fish House** (801 Blackburn Point Rd., 941/966-1901, 11:30 A.M.–9 P.M. daily, $5–15). Despite Hurricane Charley's best efforts back in 2004, this shambling restaurant and tiki bar still does a brisk business with people who navigate peel-and-eat shrimp while watching the sunset over picturesque Blackburn Point Marina. Casual seafood is the mainstay, and the fancier white wine–steamed mussels and almond snapper are brilliant.

## Venice

Along Nokomis Avenue (the main drag downtown) you'll find shops, diners, coffeehouses, and lunch spots—the best of which is **Venice Wine and Coffee Co.** (201 W. Venice Ave., 941/484-3667, 8 A.M.–8 P.M. Mon.–Thurs., 8 A.M.–11 P.M. Fri., 11 A.M.–11 P.M. Sat., noon–8 P.M. Sun.), a coffee shop by day and wine bar at night. To find Venice's Old Florida dining possibilities—all fun, all casual—you'll have to go farther afield. The **Crow's Nest, Marina Restaurant and Tavern** (1968 Tarpon Center Dr., 941/484-9551, 11 A.M.–11 P.M. Mon.–Thurs., until midnight Fri. and Sat., $13–32) has been feeding locals since 1976, with a fun tavern and great views of the marina, Venice Inlet, and the Intracoastal Waterway. The wine list is extensive, and the fare is the fried oysters/fried shrimp/steamed clam kind. Happy hour in the tavern is 4–6 P.M. Marina hours are 8 A.M.–7 P.M. daily.

The **Snook Haven Restaurant and Fish Camp** (5000 Venice Ave. E., past River Rd., 941/485-7221, 11 A.M.–9 P.M. daily, $9–20) has a similar vibe, only more down-home and bayou-style, right on the Myakka River (rent a pontoon boat or kayak before you eat). The burgers are good and you can count on some entertaining fellow customers and occasional live entertainment.

**Sharky's on the Pier** (1600 S. Harbor Dr., 941/488-1456, 11:30 A.M.–10 P.M. Sun.–Thurs., until midnight Fri. and Sat., $12–24) is closer to

civilization, with beach views and the day's catch offered broiled, blackened, grilled, or fried. Sit outside on the veranda and enjoy a Bait Bucket margarita that's finished off with triple sec and blue curaçao for that dark blue water look.

# Information and Services

Sarasota and vicinity are located within the **Eastern time zone.** The area code is **941.**

## TOURIST INFORMATION

The **Sarasota Convention & Visitors Bureau** (official Sarasota Visitor Information Center, 701 North Tamiami Trail, a.k.a. U.S. 41, 941/957-1877, www.sarasotafl.org, 10 A.M.–4 P.M. Mon.–Sat., noon–3 P.M. Sun.) and the **Sarasota Chamber of Commerce** (1945 Fruitville Rd., 941/955-8187, www.sarasotachamber.org, 8:30 A.M.–5 P.M. Mon.–Fri.) both offer heaping piles of reading material on the area. The former has more useful material and a more central location.

Sarasota has its own daily newspaper, the **Sarasota Herald-Tribune,** with multiple zoned editions serving the area, along with a 24-hour television news station, SNN. Local weekly publications include the **Longboat Observer,** Siesta Key's **Pelican Press,** and a business newspaper, the **Gulf Coast Business Review.** Nine magazines cover different aspects of Sarasota County, from business to the arts and the social scene.

## POLICE AND EMERGENCIES

In any emergency, dial 911 for immediate assistance. If you need the police in a non-emergency, Sarasota's Police Department

Headquarters Building is at 2050 Ringling Boulevard (941/954-7025). For medical emergencies, or problems that just won't wait until you get home, the nicest facilities are at the emergency care center at **Sarasota Memorial Hospital** (1700 S. Tamiami Trail, 941/917-9000).

## RADIO AND TELEVISION

Ten radio stations are located within Sarasota County, with 40 more stations in neighboring counties, including all major affiliates. Tune to **WFLA 970 AM** for news and talk radio; **WDDV 92.1 FM** is easy favorites. You'll find National Public Radio at **89.7 FM.**

On television, **WFLA Channel 8** is the NBC affiliate, **WTVT Channel 13** is the FOX affiliate, and **WWSB Channel 7** is the ABC affiliate. There are additional public television and local news channels.

## LAUNDRY SERVICES

One of the perks of renting a beach house is the reliable presence of non-coin-op laundry facilities on-site. Big resort hotels in Sarasota and on Longboat Key invariably offer laundry services. If you absolutely need a launderette, there are several in Sarasota, such as **All Star Laundry & Dry Cleaning** (2241 Bee Ridge Rd., 941/921-1258).

SARASOTA COUNTY

# Getting There and Around

## BY CAR

Sarasota is along I-75, the major transportation corridor for the southeastern United States. Sarasota County is south of Tampa and north of Fort Myers, 223 miles from Miami (about four hours' drive time), 129 miles from Orlando (about two hours' drive time), and about 5–6 hours from the Florida–Georgia line. If you prefer I-95, take it to Daytona Beach, then follow I-4 to I-75 before heading south.

U.S. 301 and U.S. 41/Tamiami Trail are the major north–south arteries on the mainland; the Gulf-to-Mexico Drive (County Road 789) is the main island road. The largest east–west thoroughfares in Sarasota are Highway 72 (Stickney Point Road); County Road 780, University Parkway; and (to the islands) Ringling Causeway, which takes you right to Lido Beach.

## BY AIR

**Sarasota-Bradenton International Airport (SRQ)** (6000 Airport Circle, at the intersection of U.S. 41 and University Pkwy., Sarasota, 941/359-2770) is certainly the closest, served by commuter flights and a half dozen major airlines or their partners, including Continental, Delta, Northwest, AirTran, and US Airways. Another option is to fly into **Tampa International Airport** (813/870-8700), which offers more arrival and departure choices and often better fares on flights and rental car prices. Tampa International Airport is just 53 miles north of Sarasota County via I-75 or I-275. Also check flights through **St. Petersburg-Clearwater International Airport** (although usually they aren't as frequent or as cheap as through the Tampa airport). Private planes can use the **Venice Municipal Airport** in the City of Venice, just down U.S. 41 from Sarasota.

**Alamo** (800/327-9633), **Avis** (800/831-2847), **Budget** (800/527-0700), **Dollar** (800/800-4000 domestic, 800/800-6000 international), **Enterprise** (800/736-8222), **Hertz** (800/654-3131), and **National** (800/227-7368) provide rental cars from Sarasota-Bradenton International Airport. **Diplomat Taxi** (941/355-5155) is the taxi provider at the airport.

## BY BUS AND TRAIN

Sarasota County Area Transit, or **SCAT** (941/861-5000), runs scheduled bus service 6 A.M.–7 P.M. Monday–Saturday. A $0.75 fare will take you to stops in the city and St. Armands, Longboat, and Lido Keys. **Greyhound** (575 N. Washington Blvd., Sarasota, 941/955-5735) offers regular bus service to Sarasota from Fort Myers and points north, and Miami to the southeast; **Amtrak** (800/872-7245) provides shuttle buses between the Tampa station and Sarasota.

# TAMPA

Tampa has had a huge renaissance in recent years, drawing businesses and workers in droves. They come for the warm climate, for the inexpensive housing and generally low cost of living, for the lack of state income tax. It's a safe, family-friendly town with adequate infrastructure, impressive schools, and plenty of upscale restaurants and shopping. The University of South Florida (USF), University of Tampa, and Hillsborough Community College—all large—lend a bit of youth and liveliness. And Tampa is also home to an incredible number of professional sporting teams.

The city is fairly urban to the south, where it runs into MacDill Air Force Base, which takes up the entire southern third of the Tampa peninsula and is home to the United States Central Command (coordinating all U.S. military operations in Africa and the Middle East). North of downtown, Tampa gets suburban quickly, then rural up into Pasco County.

What this means for the visitor: Tampa is centrally located, with an exceptional airport—an ideal city in which to begin or end a trip to other parts of the Gulf Coast. It contains Busch Gardens; a great zoo and aquarium; professional football, baseball, and hockey teams; and affordable accommodations and restaurants. These are perfect ingredients for a family vacation. For history lovers, Tampa is somewhat disappointing compared with other areas along the Gulf Coast; much of it is just not that old.

For centuries the sheltered Tampa Bay area was a quiet Native American fishing village. Even after Hernando de Soto sailed into the

# HIGHLIGHTS

**《 Spring Training:** Tampa Bay has both the boys of summer and the boys of spring. You can see professional baseball much of the year, with Tampa's own Rays during the regular season and the Grapefruit League's spring training at the end of February and in March (page 150).

**《 Bayshore Boulevard:** The five miles of sidewalk are bordered on one side by the wide open bay and on the other side by the fanciest historic homes on this stretch of Florida's Gulf Coast. Runners, walkers, bikers, and skaters take advantage of the amazing views and long expanse of carefully maintained walkway (page 153).

**《 Ybor City:** Once known as the Cigar Capital of the World, with nearly 12,000 cigarmakers employed in 200 factories that produced 700 million cigars a year, Tampa's Latin Quarter is one of only three National Historic Landmark Districts in Florida. Today it has something of a Jekyll and Hyde personality that offers visitors historic shops by day and the city's most vital nightlife and dining when the sun goes down (page 155).

**《 Busch Gardens:** The park's inverted steel roller coaster called the Montu won 9th place in *Amusement Today* magazine's survey of top roller coasters worldwide; its Kumba took the 19th spot. Both of these have had to move over for the SheiKra, debuted in 2005. The first diving coaster in the United States, it climbs 200 feet, then dives straight down, followed by a second 90-degree dive, an Immelmann loop, an underground tunnel, and a big splash water finale. The park is an unusual mix of thrill rides, animal attractions, and entertainment. It's a something-for-everyone approach that really works (page 156).

**《 Florida Aquarium:** An incredible Tampa attraction, this 152,000-square-foot aquarium focuses on Florida's relationship to the Gulf, estuaries, rivers, and other waterways, with a strong environmental message (page 157).

**《 Tampa Theatre:** The theater, ornately decorated to resemble an open Mediterranean courtyard, features 1,446 seats, 99 stars in the auditorium ceiling, and nearly 1,000 pipes in its mighty Wurlitzer theater organ (page 160).

LOOK FOR 《 TO FIND RECOMMENDED SIGHTS, ACTIVITIES, DINING, AND LODGING.

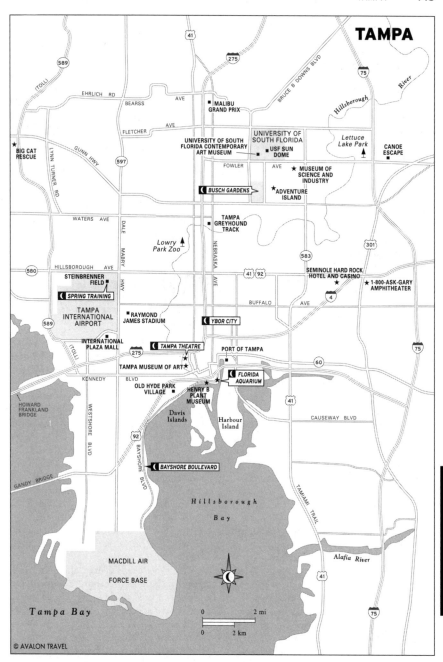

# TAMPA

- BIG CAT RESCUE
- MALIBU GRAND PRIX
- UNIVERSITY OF SOUTH FLORIDA CONTEMPORARY ART MUSEUM
- UNIVERSITY OF SOUTH FLORIDA
- USF SUN DOME
- Lettuce Lake Park
- CANOE ESCAPE
- MUSEUM OF SCIENCE AND INDUSTRY
- BUSCH GARDENS
- ADVENTURE ISLAND
- TAMPA GREYHOUND TRACK
- Lowry Park Zoo
- STEINBRENNER FIELD
- SPRING TRAINING
- SEMINOLE HARD ROCK HOTEL AND CASINO
- 1-800-ASK-GARY AMPHITHEATER
- TAMPA INTERNATIONAL AIRPORT
- RAYMOND JAMES STADIUM
- YBOR CITY
- INTERNATIONAL PLAZA MALL
- TAMPA THEATRE
- PORT OF TAMPA
- TAMPA MUSEUM OF ART
- FLORIDA AQUARIUM
- HOWARD FRANKLAND BRIDGE
- OLD HYDE PARK VILLAGE
- HENRY B PLANT MUSEUM
- Davis Islands
- Harbour Island
- CAUSEWAY BLVD
- BAYSHORE BOULEVARD
- *Hillsborough Bay*
- MACDILL AIR FORCE BASE
- *Alafia River*
- *Tampa Bay*

0    2 mi
0    2 km

© AVALON TRAVEL

ROADS: EHRLICH RD, BEARSS AVE, FLETCHER AVE, BRUCE B DOWNS BLVD, Hillsborough River, GUNN HWY, LYNN TURNER RD, FOWLER AVE, WATERS AVE, DALE MABRY HWY, NEBRASKA AVE, HILLSBOROUGH AVE, BUFFALO AVE, KENNEDY BLVD, WESTSHORE BLVD, BAYSHORE BLVD, GANDY BRIDGE, TAMIAMI TRAIL

HIGHWAYS: 41, 275, 589, 597, 580, 41, 92, 583, 301, 4, 75, 60

TAMPA

bay in 1539, the area went largely untouched by whites for more than 200 years. Dutch cartographer Bernard Romans named the Hillsborough River and the upper arm of Tampa Bay in 1772, in honor of Lord Hillsborough, British secretary of state for the colonies. The United States purchased Florida from Spain in 1821, with traders setting up shop along what is now downtown Tampa in 1855.

It wasn't until Henry B. Plant extended his railroad into Tampa in 1884 and started a steamship line from Tampa to Key West to Havana, Cuba, that the city really began to grow. In 1891, Plant built the Tampa Bay Hotel, which launched the city as a winter resort for the northern elite. Around the same time, O. H. Platt purchased 20 acres of land across the Hillsborough River, creating Tampa's first residential suburb, Hyde Park (named after Platt's hometown in Illinois). Hyde Park was, and still is, the residential area of choice for many wealthy citizens. Many of the 19th-century bungalows and Princess Anne–style cottages are still occupied today, and the Old Hyde Park Village collection of boutiques and restaurants is one of the city's biggest draws.

Don Vicente Martinez Ybor, an influential cigar manufacturer and Cuban exile, moved his cigar business from Key West to a scruffy stretch of land east of Tampa in 1885. His first cigar factory drew others, and the Spanish, Italian, German, and Cuban workers who settled here to work in the area's more than 200 cigar factories created a vivacious Latin community known as Ybor City. The area is now designated one of three National Historic Landmark Districts in Florida, with a mix of historic buildings, artisan shops, restaurants, and nightclubs.

When the United States declared war on Spain in 1898, Tampa was the port of embarkation for troops headed to Cuba. A vital colonel named Theodore Roosevelt organized his Rough Riders at the Tampa encampment. Not longer after that, another Tampa neighborhood, Davis Islands, developed during the Florida land boom. Two little islands off

© JOSHUA LAWRENCE KINSER

**Tampa's skyline is a shape-shifter, with loads of new high-rises going up in recent years.**

downtown Tampa, where the Hillsborough River empties into Hillsborough Bay, became booming real estate developments. Today, the islands are home to an airport, Tampa General Hospital, and more than 100 of the original homes.

Growth continued apace through the Roaring Twenties, slowing, as it did everywhere, during the Great Depression. Since then, Tampa hasn't been buoyed by the tourist dollar to the degree other Gulf Coast cities have, and thus has been less susceptible to the ups and downs of Florida travel (first 9/11, then the walloping hurricane season of 2004, then the BP oil spill of 2010, counterbalanced by Europeans' enthusiasm about the weakness of the dollar).

Unlike other urban centers along the Gulf, there are no beaches in Tampa to speak of. For beaches, you need to drive over the causeway to St. Pete or Clearwater (about 30 minutes from downtown Tampa). Still, Tampa offers visitors all of the amenities that have made it such a sought-after place to live.

# PLANNING YOUR TIME

How long you spend vacationing in Tampa largely depends on whether you have kids in tow. Not a city known for its urbane cultural amenities or even one-of-a-kind nature experiences, Tampa is a paradise for kids. Obviously, the big kahuna is Busch Gardens, but that's just Day One. There are at least four or five other attractions worthy of a day of family focus.

Many people choose to visit Orlando's Disney attractions and then tack on a day or two at Tampa's Busch Gardens. While this is a perfectly fine strategy (Orlando's only an hour away), it seems like too much of a good thing. After a few days of Disney, come to Tampa and rent a canoe, go to the zoo, visit the science museum, and then head over to Clearwater for a day of leisurely beach time.

As with much of the Gulf Coast, the fall and early spring are the most enjoyable weather-wise, with days in the low 80s and very dry. The summer is unrelentingly hot and humid, right through each afternoon's huge thunderstorm.

# Sports and Recreation

## LETTUCE LAKE PARK

If you're looking to get out in nature, head to Lettuce Lake Park (6920 E. Fletcher Ave., near the I-75 exit, 813/987-6204, 8 A.M.–6 P.M. daily, $2 per vehicle), just east of the University of South Florida. It's a stone's throw from urban sprawl, but don't hold that against it. The dense wilderness shelters a 3,500-foot-long raised boardwalk and a recently rebuilt tower overlooking the Hillsborough River, a perfect place from which to spy on tall wading birds, gators lurking amongst cypress knees in the swamp, or even delicate orchids and other epiphytes nestled in the trees' crooks. Rent a canoe for a closer look at the creatures that call this tannin-tinged water home, hike the fully accessible boardwalk or dirt trails (no dogs on the boardwalks), then settle in for a picnic at one of the waterfront shelters, equipped with barbecues. A kids' playground, restrooms, and water fountains make this wilderness park much more comfortable.

## CANOEING

You want to see big gators? Great blue herons, river otters, turtles, and more fish than you can string on a lifetime of lines? Paddle down the gently flowing Hillsborough River in a 16,000-acre wildlife preserve called **Wilderness Park.** You can rent canoes or kayaks and head out on your own, choosing from six different self-guided day trips. All paddling adventures start at Canoe Escape (9335 E. Fowler Ave., 0.5 mile east of I-75, 813/986-2067, www.canoeescape. com). Whether you go on a guided tour or on your own, call ahead. Staff will equip you, give you maps and paddling pointers, then take you over to your debarkation point (all paddles are downstream) and establish a pickup time.

The Sargeant Park to Morris Bridge Park trip is a two-hour paddle, 4.5 miles long, with 70 percent shade and alternating sun and shade. Morris Bridge Park to Trout Creek Park is a two-hour, four-mile paddle, with 80 percent shade and a little full sun at the end. From Trout Creek Park to Rotary Park it's five miles of full-sun paddling, about two hours, whereas Sargeant Park to Trout Creek Park is a longer, 8.5-mile paddle with the first 75 percent in the shade. Morris Bridge Park to Rotary Park is a long, nine-mile route, and Sargeant Park to Rotary Park is for experienced paddlers only, with 14 miles of river to paddle.

Self-guided rentals are $22–32 per paddler for a tandem canoe or kayak depending on the trip (a child under 12 can usually fit as a center passenger). A solo kayak ranges $42–52. Prices include shuttle fee, paddles, and life vests. If solo paddling seems daunting, Canoe Escape offers a 4.5-mile interpreted guided tour for $75 per person. I'd recommend this for the newcomer to the area because the guides' vast

TAMPA

## TAMPA GOLFING

Tampa has a couple of dozen public and semi-private courses for the visitor to try. Many of them are open to the public but located in Tampa's swankier northeast residential developments. Here are a handful of the area's top public courses:

**Babe Zaharias Golf Club**
11412 Forest Hills Dr., 813/631-4374, www.babezahariasgc.com
18 holes, 6,244 yards, par 70, course rating 68.9, slope 121
Greens fees: $18-37

**Heritage Isles Golf & Country Club**
10630 Plantation Bay Dr., 813/907-7447
18 holes, 6,976 yards, par 72, course rating 73.2, slope 132
Greens fees: $25-47

**Rocky Point Golf Course**
4151 Dana Shores Dr., 813/673-4316, www.rockypointgc.com
18 holes, 6,444 yards, par 71, course rating 71.7, slope 122
Greens fees: $19-38

**Rogers Park Golf Course**
7910 N. Willie Black Dr., 813/356-1670, www.rogersparkgc.com
18 holes, 6,802 yards, par 71, course rating 72.3, slope 125
Greens fees: $15-42

**TPC Tampa Bay**
5300 West Lutz Lake Fern Rd., Lutz, 813/949-0091
18 holes, 6,898 yards, par 71, course rating 73.6, slope 135
Greens fees: $59-132

**University of South Florida Golf Course (also called "The Claw")**
4202 E. Fowler Ave., 813/632-6893
18 holes, 6,863 yards, par 71, course rating 74.2, slope 132
Greens fees: $26-40

**Westchase Golf Course**
11602 Westchase Golf Dr., 813/854-2331
18 holes, par 72, 6,699 yards, course rating 72.6, slope 131
Greens fees: $25-89

knowledge of the local flora and fauna enrich the trip immeasurably.

## GOLF

Tampa has a couple of dozen public and semi-private courses for the visitor to try. Many of them are open to the public but located in Tampa's swankier northeast residential developments.

If you are thinking about picking up the sport, the **Arnold Palmer Golf Academy** at the Saddlebrook Resort (5700 Saddlebrook Way, Wesley Chapel, 800/729-8383) teaches golfers of all skill levels. Classes combine classroom and practice time with course play. The New Player Academy and all the other packages include accommodations, 18 holes of golf a day, instruction, meals, and use of resort facilities. There are two 18-hole Palmer-designed championship courses on the property, as well as 45 tennis courts in the four Grand Slam surfaces (the resort is also home to the **Hopman Tennis Program**).

About 25 miles south of Tampa, the **Ben Sutton Golf School** (809 N. Pebble Beach Blvd., Sun City Center, 800/225-6923) was the first American school devoted to golf instruction. There are two-, three-, four-, and six-day courses. (The school's second location opened in Christmann's Windham Resort in Windham, New York in 2006.)

## SPECTATOR SPORTS

DirectTV has something called the Sports Fan Passion Index. Tampa Bay sports fans have made it near the top of that list, fanatical for their professional sporting franchises. Why shouldn't they be this way? There are the

Tampa Bay Buccaneers for football, Tampa Bay Lightning for hockey, Tampa Bay Rays for baseball (not to mention spring training for the New York Yankees, Philadelphia Phillies, Toronto Blue Jays, and their own Rays spread around the Bay Area), Tampa Bay Storm pro arena football (five-time world champs), and the gamut of University of South Florida Bulls athletics.

## Tampa Bay Buccaneers

**Raymond James Stadium** (4201 N. Dale Mabry Hwy.) is a wonderful venue in which to see Tampa's beloved Buccaneers (813/350-6500, www.buccaneers.com) play. Raymond James Stadium, completed in 1998, holds more than 66,000 fans—52,000 in general seating—but tickets sometimes sell out for the season opener and other big games. Tickets for individual games are sold in person at TicketMaster outlets, on the phone at 813/287-8844, and by visiting www.ticketmaster.com, not at the stadium or the Bucs' ticket office. Tickets for the 16 regular-season games September–December are $55 for general admission; special seats range from $400 on down. The $168.5 million stadium features Buccaneer Cove, a 20,000-square-foot replica of an early 1800s seaport village, complete with a 103-foot-long, 43-ton pirate ship that blasts its cannons (confetti and foam footballs) every time the Bucs score. Well, six times for a touchdown, once for an extra point, twice for a safety or two-point conversion, and three times for a field goal.

Raymond James also plays host every New Year's Day to football's **Outback Bowl** (Raymond James Stadium, 813/287-8844, 11 A.M. kickoff, $65). The game matches the third-pick team from the SEC and the third-pick team from the Big Ten Conference and is the culmination of a weeklong festival in Tampa.

## USF Bulls

The powers that be at University of South Florida have made a judgment call in the past few years. They want the university to be big league, no longer a workhorse state school with a preponderance of commuting students.

They've thrown money into the effort, constructing state-of-the-art academic buildings and housing, hiring prestigious senior faculty and promising junior profs. But maybe the single biggest indicator is the **football team:** The USF Bulls (800/462-8557, game schedule varies, individual tickets $20–31) have gone from nonexistence to Division I-AA Independent to I-A to Conference USA, and into the Big East Conference in 2005. For the spectator, this means real college football is played during the fall, also at Raymond James Stadium (4201 N. Dale Mabry Hwy.).

The community has been quick to embrace this shift, ramping up attendance drastically. In 2009, the Bulls averaged 52,553 fans per game at Raymond James. The Bulls broke their existing attendance record of 49,212 four times in the 2007 season, culminating in 67,018 people attending the USF-West Virginia game, the largest non–Super Bowl crowd the stadium has ever seen.

Bulls' **basketball** has also been notched up in recent years, resulting in the team moving to the Big East conference. Home games are played at the **USF Sun Dome** (4202 E. Fowler Ave., 800/462-8557, tickets $18).

## Tampa Bay Storm

The local Tampa Bay Storm arena football team, five-time ArenaBowl champs, plays at the **St. Pete Times Forum** (401 Channelside Dr., 813/301-6600, upper level tickets $10–35, lower $35–150). Arena football is played on an indoor padded surface 85 feet wide and 50 yards long, with eight-yard end zones. There are eight players on the field at a time, and everyone plays both offense and defense, with the exception of the kicker, quarterback, offensive specialist, and two defensive specialists. It's a dynamic game in a more intimate space, and the Storm provides a good introduction to the game, having made it to the playoffs for 16 consecutive seasons.

## Tampa Bay Lightning

The 21,000-seat, $153 million **St. Pete Times Forum,** on Tampa's downtown waterfront, is

# LIGHTNING

Almost nobody is killed by alligators in Tampa. Hardly anyone is even roughed up by them. Lightning is much more deadly in Florida. In fact, about 50 people are struck by lightning each year in the state. Most of them are hospitalized and recover, but there are about 10 fatalities annually. The Tampa area is the Lightning Capital of the United States (Rwanda is the lightning capital of the world), with around 25 cloud-to-ground lightning bolt blasts on each square mile annually. The temperature of a single bolt can reach 50,000°F, about three times as hot as the sun's surface.

The problem is the tropical afternoon thunderstorms each summer, about 90 of them electrical storms. Short-lived but intense, the storms' clouds are charged like giant capacitors, the upper portion of the cloud positively charged and the lower portion negatively charged. Then, current flows between the negative cloud bottom and the top or, in the case of cloud-to-ground lightning, the positively charged earth's surface. This discharge of current substantiates the adage "opposites attract," and bolts, sheets, ribbons, and, rarely, balls of lightning hit the ground.

There's not much you can do to ward off lightning except to avoid being in the wrong place at the wrong time. The summer months of June, July, August, and September have the highest number of lightning-related injuries and deaths. Usually lightning occurs during daylight hours, with the highest concentration between 3 P.M. and 4 P.M., when the afternoon storms peak. Lightning strikes usually occur either at the beginning or end of a storm and can strike up to 10 miles away from the center of the storm.

Still, nine out of 10 people survive being struck. As long as the electrical surge is not to your brain, you are likely to be treatable. A lightning strike will often singe and burn a person's skin or clothes, but even when the electrical surge stops a victim's heart, emergency rooms have a high success rate of restarting the ticker.

## TIPS

- Stay vigilant and go inside as soon as clouds darken and thunderstorms develop.

- If the time between seeing the lightning flash and hearing the thunder is less than 30 seconds, take shelter.

- Stay away from the Gulf, pools, lakes, or other bodies of water.

- Avoid using a tree or other tall object as shelter. Lightning usually strikes the tallest object in a given area.

- Stay away from metal objects (bikes, golf carts, and fencing are bad, but a car's rubber tires render the automobile's interior a safe retreat).

- The safest place to be during an electrical storm is inside and away from windows and electrical appliances.

also home to Tampa's professional hockey team, the Tampa Bay Lightning (813/301-6600, game times vary, tickets $15–349). Stanley Cup champions in 2004. Its season runs October–April.

## ◖ Spring Training

Tampa is also home to Major League Baseball's **Tampa Bay Rays.** Their first season was 1998. The Rays (formerly the Devil Rays) play at **Tropicana Field** in St. Petersburg (1 Tropicana Dr., St. Petersburg, 888/326-7297, game days vary, times usually 2:15 or 7:15 P.M., tickets $7–20). As a concession to summer temperatures and humidity in these parts, the ballpark has a dome roof (which is lit orange when the Rays win at home) and artificial turf.

Things will hopefully be changing for the Rays soon—in the off-season at the end of 2007, they announced that they were in negotiations to potentially build a new $450-million, 35,000-seat, open-air baseball stadium at the site of Progress Energy Park/Al Lang Field, site of their current spring training facility on the St. Petersburg waterfront. However, the deal fell through due to funding and location issues. The Rays still continue to work on getting a new ballpark built, but the future at this point is uncertain and for now they will continue to play at the Tropicana.

The Rays team was the first major league franchise to train in its home city since 1919, when the St. Louis Cardinals and Philadelphia Athletics trained at home. In the past for spring training the Rays played at **Progress Energy Park, Home of Al Lang Field.** Now the Tampa Bay Rays call the **Charlotte Sports Park** (2300 El Jobean Road, Port Charlotte, 941/766-1133, www.tampabayrays.com, $15–31) their new spring training home. The stadium has a 7,000 person capacity and a natural grass field and received a $27.2 million renovation to bring it up to modern standards for the Rays.

Even with the departure of the Rays, the Grapefruit League's spring training remains a serious draw for sports fans each March. Since 1988, the **New York Yankees** have based their minor league operation, spring training, and year-round headquarters for player development in Tampa. Modeled after the original Yankee Stadium in the Bronx, **Steinbrenner Field** (1 Steinbrenner Dr., off N. Dale Mabry, 813/875-7753, www.steinbrennerfield.com, $15–31) has been the Yankees' home since 1996. The complex houses a 10,000-seat stadium with 13 swanky luxury suites, a community-use field, and a major league practice field. It's also the home of the **Florida State League Champion Tampa Yankees** (New York Yankees–Florida State League Single "A" Affiliate) and the **Hillsborough Community College Hawks** baseball team.

Other spring training venues require only a short drive: the **Philadelphia Phillies** play at **Bright House Networks Field** in Clearwater; the **Boston Red Sox** play in **City of Palms Park** and the **Minnesota Twins** play at **Hammond Stadium,** both in Fort Myers; the **Toronto Blue Jays** play at **Knology Park** in Dunedin; the **Baltimore Orioles** play at **Ed Smith Stadium** in Sarasota; and the **Pittsburgh Pirates** play at **McKechnie Field** in Bradenton.

# Sights

## MUSEUMS

You wouldn't think a midsized city art museum could spark so much controversy. And it's not the good kind of controversy: an exhibit of Robert Mapplethorpe's provocative photos, say, or Jeff Koons's Cicciolina sculptures or anything else that used to get Jesse Helms hot under the collar. For years, the **Tampa Museum of Art** (120 West Gasparilla Plaza, 813/274-8130, www.tampamuseum.org, 11 A.M.–7 P.M. Mon.–Wed. and Fri., 11 A.M.–9 P.M. Thurs., 11 A.M.–5 P.M. Sat and Sun., $10 adults, $7.50 seniors, $5 students and children over six, children under six free) has been poised to go somewhere, but no one seems to agree on its destination. The original Grand Plan, drafted in 2002 by celebrated architect Rafael Vinoly, was scrapped when the proposed 125,000-square-foot structure crept up from $46 million to a staggering $76 million. The city pulled the plug. After that, the museum board and Mayor Iorio tussled: She wanted to move the museum to the old courthouse; they wanted to keep the complex location along the Hillsborough River. Nobody won.

The next plan, in 2005, aimed to relocate the museum to Rivergate Tower at 400 N. Ashley. Subsequently, a low appraisal of the tower nixed that deal. Then in November 2007 things seemed to fall into place. Everyone agreed on a site: in Curtis Hixon Park, adjacent to the Poe Garage overlooking the Hillsborough River. And they agreed on an architect: Stanley Saitowitz from San Francisco. And they agreed on a plan: a

# PASCO COUNTY

Naked people. That got your attention. The sleepy, landlocked, mostly residential county to Tampa's north, Pasco County, has at least a day's worth of a unique brand of fun, definitely worth a side trip, a couple of meals, and maybe even an overnight at one of the area's most upscale spa/golf/tennis resorts.

But back to the buff. **Lake Como Family Nudist Resort** in the town of Land O' Lakes is the area's original nudist community, started in 1947. Since then, Pasco County has become a hotbed of naturist activity, with six all-ages nudist communities and recreational activities (until recently there was naked bowling at the local lanes – the question is, if you're wearing rented bowling shoes, are you really nude?). These days the biggest player is the 120-acre **Caliente Resort and Spa** (21240 Gran Via Blvd., Land O' Lakes, 800/326-7731). Stop in and poke around, unless you're too chicken.

Another Pasco original requiring a little bit of courage is **Skydive City** (4241 Skydive Ln., off Chancey Rd., 813/783-9399, www.skydivecity.com, $199, plus $95 if you want the video documenting your whole experience) in Zephyrhills. The town has been a world-famous "drop zone" since the 1960s, with a world meet (in the trade, it's called a boogie) in 1972. Why here? According to owner T. K. Hayes, "It's in the middle of nowhere. It's really about the people – Zephyrhills is the largest skydiving place in the world." Tandem jumping (where a rookie jumps physically harnessed to an instructor) has opened skydiving up to people who never would have had the opportunity – the elderly, people with disabilities – really, anyone can do it.

If jumping out of an airplane sounds doable: It takes about an hour to prepare, with a 20-minute briefing. The whole experience is a three- to four-hour adventure, with free fall at 120 mph for about a minute from 13,500 feet, followed by up to six minutes of steering with the parachute open. Hayes says he's never had a student fatality or serious injury (solo students have a higher rate of injury, especially on the landing), very few students lose their lunch, and, he says, "No one comes down and says they wish they'd never done that."

After that, take it down a notch and enjoy a walking tour of downtown **Dade City.** In the rolling hills of eastern Pasco County, the town has more than 50 antiques stores, gift shops, and boutiques. Stop into the historic

120,000-square-foot complex, with phase one consisting of 60,000 square feet; the city throwing in $18.5 million of community investment tax funds and the rest raised by the museum.

The new facility opened on February 6, 2010—hosting changing exhibitions ranging from contemporary to classical, and showcasing its permanent collection of Greek and Roman antiquities, 20th- and 21st-century sculpture, paintings, photography, and works on paper.

The **Henry B. Plant Museum** (401 W. Kennedy Blvd., 813/254-1891, www.plantmuseum.org, 10 A.M.–5 P.M. Tues.–Sat., noon–5 P.M. Sun., $10 adults, $7 students and seniors, $5 children under 12, open Jan.–Nov.) is housed in the dramatic hotel railroad magnate Henry B. Plant built in 1891 at a cost of $2.5 million, with an additional $500,000 for furnishings. Its 511 rooms were the first in Florida to be outfitted with electricity. It operated as a hotel until 1930 and now houses the University of Tampa. The museum consists of opulent restored rooms with original furnishings that provide a window on America's Gilded Age, Tampa's history, and the life and work of Henry Plant. The best time to see it is at Christmastime, when the rooms are bedecked for the season with elaborately trimmed trees, lush greenery, antique toys, and Victorian-era ornaments.

University of South Florida is an enormous institution, casting its imposing shadow on the cultural scene of Tampa. The visitor, however, may have little reason to walk around the less-than-picturesque campus. A visit to the **University of South Florida Contemporary**

1909 Pasco County Courthouse and look at the sweet collection of artifacts from the turn of the 20th century. And then have a slice of history with a slice of pie at **Lunch on Limoges** (14139 Seventh St., 352/567-5685, www. lunchonlimoges.com, $12-18). It's a charming throwback to a former era of structured and unhurried lunching, with a daily-changing menu served on Limoges china by nice old waitresses in nurses' uniforms. Excellent chocolate cake, but I don't like that a steep "minimum order" is required to dine here.

Not far from downtown and usually taking about an hour, **The Pioneer Florida Museum** (15602 Pioneer Museum Rd., 352/567-0262, www.pioneerfloridamuseum.org, 10 A.M.-5 P.M. Tues.-Sat., $6 adults, $5 seniors, $2 students and children 6-18, children under 6 free) consists of nine period buildings dating back to 1878. There's the John Overstreet House, the Lacoochee School, and the Enterprise Methodist Church, all displaying period furniture, clothing, toys, tools. There's also a spooky collection of miniature big-eyed dolls of Florida's first ladies.

If there's time, take a tour around **New Port Richey's Main Street** (www.newportrichey-mainstreet.com, tours 9 A.M.-noon, $10) and then board a boat and ride the **Pithlachascot-tee River** to see historic homes once owned by Gloria Swanson, Thomas Meighan, and Babe Ruth. Then walk around **Centennial Cultural Park**, which contains the Pasco Fine Arts Council, the Centennial Library, and the 1882 Baker House, one of the oldest structures in Pasco County. If you're hungry, stop in at waterside **Catches** (7811 Bayview St., 727/849-2121).

If you're thinking about bedtime now, **Saddlebrook Resort & Spa** (5700 Saddlebrook Way, 800/729-8383, $300-600) is really Tampa's nicest four-star resort hotel, only it's in the sleepy Pasco town of Wesley Chapel. It has 800 guest rooms, all beautiful, pools, tennis, the Palmer and the Saddlebrook golf courses (and the Arnold Palmer Golf Academy), and a variety of dining options (if you eat on the Tropics Terrace you can see nesting wood storks). If this is too rich for your blood, **Azalea House** (37719 Meridian Ave., 352/523-1773, $65-79) is a sweet bed-and-breakfast with just a few rooms in Dade City.

For more information about Pasco County, visit www.visitpasco.net.

---

Art Museum (4202 E. Fowler Ave., 813/974-4133, 10 A.M.-5 P.M. Mon.-Fri., 1-4 P.M. Sat., free admission) is a good excuse to drive around the university before parking at the small gallery. USFCAM maintains the university's art collection, comprising more than 5,000 artworks. There are exceptional holdings in graphics and sculpture multiples by internationally acclaimed artists, such as Roy Lichtenstein, Robert Rauschenberg, and James Rosenquist, who have worked at USF's Graphicstudio. Contemporary photography and African art are also represented. The museum also hosts USF student art shows and oversees public art projects on campus.

## ( BAYSHORE BOULEVARD

Bayshore Boulevard may or may not be the world's longest continuous sidewalk, but it borders Tampa Bay for nearly five miles without a break in the gorgeousness. Joggers, walkers, skaters, and bikers dot its length, which goes from downtown through Hyde Park. Lining the fanciest homes in Tampa, the boulevard was named one of AAA's Top Roads for its panoramic views. If you don't feel like walking it, it's Tampa's signature drive. (Also, Tampa Preservation has an excellent driving tour of Hyde Park and a walking tour of part of the neighborhood geared for younger travelers; for copies call 813/248-5437.)

## BIG CAT RESCUE

The world's largest accredited sanctuary for big cats, Big Cat Rescue provides a permanent retirement home to over 200 animals (12802

COURTESY OF BIG CAT RESCUE

The Big Cat Rescue is home to over 200 exotic animals, including a rare snow leopard.

Easy St., across from Citrus Park Town Center down a dirt road next to McDonald's, 813/920-4130, www.bigcatrescue.org). For the visitor, the center offers tours, outreach presentations, animal interaction, and the opportunity to spend an evening in the heart of the sanctuary. Regular tours run at 3 P.M. Monday–Wednesday and Friday and 10 A.M. and 1 P.M. Saturday and Sunday; a children's tour is at 9 A.M. Saturday. Prices vary by tour: regular tour $25 (for ages 10 and over), children's tour $10, feeding tour $50, and Big Cat Adventure $100. On the last Friday of each month, register for the Wild Eyes at Night tour (8 P.M.), in which guests roam the grounds equipped with flashlights that illuminate the hundreds of shining eyes in the cat enclosures. Or be a zookeeper for a day with the all-day Big Cat Adventure. You'll get an education in animal husbandry, care, and feeding, and if you plan it for the last Friday of the month you can combine it with the exciting nighttime tour.

## BIG RED BALLOON SIGHTSEEING ADVENTURES

Big Red Balloon Sightseeing Adventures (8710 W. Hillsborough Ave., 813/969-1518, www.bigredballoon.com, 6–10 A.M. daily, year-round by reservation only, weather permitting, $185 adults, $160 children) takes you up, up, and away in a beautiful hot-air balloon, and all you have to bring is a camera and your loved ones. Meet before dawn at a restaurant on the commerce strip of Dale Mabry (**Mimi's Café,** 11702 N. Dale Mabry), whereupon you are whisked into the Red Balloon van and taken to your agreed-upon launch site (there are more than 30 in the greater Tampa area from which to choose). Once inflated, the solid red balloon, the largest in the southeastern United States, is 8.5 stories tall and contains 210,000 cubic feet of air. The balloon, which comfortably accommodates eight passengers, takes a one-hour sunrise flight at up to 1,000 feet, drifting over New Tampa, southeast Pasco County, Lutz, and Land O' Lakes. A champagne toast followed by a hearty breakfast back at Mimi's is included in the price.

After landing, there is a champagne toast in the field, where the pilot recites a traditional balloonist prayer, "The winds have welcomed you with softness, the sun has left you with warm hands, you have flown so high, and so well, that God has joined you in your laughter, and set you gently back again into the loving arms of Mother Earth." Feel free to join in.

## ◖ YBOR CITY

Cigarmakers Vicente Martinez-Ybor and Ignacio Haya moved their cigar factories from Key West to Tampa in 1886, essentially settling 40 acres of uninviting scrubland northeast of the city. A railroad, a port, and a climate that acted as a natural humidor—Tampa had all the ingredients for cigar success. Soon other cigar factories joined suit until there were 140 cigar factories in the area producing 250 million cigars a year. The new Cigar Capital of the World became home to Cuban, Spanish, and Italian immigrants who worked the factories. These workers, both men and women, would hand-roll several kinds of tobacco into the signature shapes and sizes while listening to "lectors" read aloud great works of literature and the day's news. (For a window into this world, read Nilo Cruz's Pulitzer Prize–winning drama, *Anna in the Tropics,* which depicts a Cuban-American family of cigar makers in Ybor City in 1930.)

The area flourished until the early 1960s, when embargos against Cuban tobacco and declining cigar consumption (coincident with

## CIGAR BASICS

Want to try a cigar but don't know the first thing? Tampa's a good place to begin. Even before you light up, a cigar's visual specifications can give clues to its character. The outer wrapper's color indicates a great deal about a cigar's flavor. A **maduro** wrapper is a rich, deep brown, imparting a cigar with deep, strong flavors. A **claro** wrapper, on the other hand, is a light tan and lends little additional flavor to a cigar. There are essentially six color grades. Roughly from lightest to darkest, these are: **candela** (pale green), **claro, natural** (light brown), **colorado** (reddish brown), **maduro,** and **oscuro** (almost black).

Shape is another central factor in cigar selection. Among **parejos,** or straight-sided cigars, there are three basic categories. A **corona** is classically six inches long, with an open foot (the end that is lighted) and a closed head (the end that is smoked). Within this category, **Churchills** are a bit longer and thicker, robustos are shorter and much thicker, and a **double corona** is significantly longer. **Panetelas,** the second category, are longer and much thinner than *coronas,* and the third category, **lonsdales,** are thicker than *panetelas* and thinner and longer than coronas.

**Figurados** comprise the other class of cigar, which spans all of the irregularly shaped types. This includes torpedo shapes, braided **culebras,** and pyramid shapes that have a closed, pointed head and an open foot.

A cigar band is generally wrapped around the closed head of a cigar. Its original function was to minimize finger staining, not to identify brands. Nonetheless, on the band you will find the name a manufacturer has designated for a particular line of cigars – names like Partagas, Macanudo, Punch, and Montecristo. Keep in mind that after 1959, many cigar manufacturers fled Cuba to open shop elsewhere, taking their brand names with them. Thus, a brand name does not always betray a cigar's country of origin.

For neophytes lighting up for the first time, a milder cigar may ease you in. The Macanudo Hyde Park is a mild smoke, as is the Don Diego Playboy Robusto or Lonsdale. For a fuller-bodied cigar, the Punch Diademas and the Partagas Number 10 are both popular. If you're looking for a robust, ultra full-bodied taste, you might try the Hoyo de Monterrey Double Corona. The best way to discover your own personal tastes is to stop into a tobacconist or cigar-friendly restaurant and have a chat.

TAMPA

the ascendance of the cigarette as the smoke of choice) caused the market to dry up. Today Ybor City is one of only three National Historic Landmark Districts in Florida, with redbrick streets, wrought-iron balconies, and old-timey globe streetlamps.

During the day visitors can still see cigars being hand-rolled and munch a Cubano sandwich (invented here, some say), while at night Ybor is the city's nightlife district, drawing 40,000 visitors on weekends to dine at sidewalk cafés and drink and dance at nightclubs. Whether you explore during the day or at night, park your car in one of the many parking lots or garages (metered parking is strictly enforced 24 hours) and walk around or take the Ybor City trolley. You can still see little cigar shops and Latin social clubs mixed in with tattoo parlors and restaurants along La Setima (Seventh Ave.).

The **Ybor City Museum State Park** (1818 E. Ninth Ave., 813/247-6323, www.ybormuseum.org, 9 A.M.–5 P.M. daily, $4 adults, children under six free) contains photographs, cigar boxes, and other artifacts of the neighborhood's rich history. The museum also offers walking tours on Saturday mornings at 10:30 A.M. ($6, including museum admission) and cigar-rolling demonstrations. Another book, *The Immigrant World of Ybor City: Italians and Their Latin Neighbors in Tampa, 1885–1985* (Florida Sand Dollar Books) by Gary Mormino and George E. Pozzetta (University Press of Florida, 1998), is a wealth of information. Another good one is called *Urban Vigilantes in the New South: Tampa, Florida 1886–1936* (Florida Sand Dollar Books) by Robert P. Ingalls (University Press of Florida, reprint edition, 1993).

But still, you may get a more three-dimensional look at Ybor just by walking around: Walk by the La Union Marti-Maceo mural (226 Seventh Ave.), pick up a copy of *La Gaceta* (the neighborhood's Spanish-language weekly for the past 75 years), and walk by the restored former cigar workers' casitas on your way to get a Cubano sandwich, or buy a cigar at **Metropolitan Cigars** (2014 E. Seventh Ave., 813/248-3304, 9:30 A.M.–6:30 P.M.

Mon., 9:30 A.M.–8 P.M. Tues.–Thurs., 9:30 A.M.–9 P.M. Fri., 10:30 A.M.–9 P.M. Sat., noon–3 P.M. Sun.), a 1,700-square-foot walk-in humidor.

## FAMILY-FRIENDLY ATTRACTIONS

Of all the Gulf Coast cities, Tampa has the most lavish smorgasbord of kid-friendly attractions. This probably reflects the demographics of Tampa in recent years—it's a family town, wherein weekends are devoted, after Little League/soccer games/getting the car washed, to multigenerational outings to Busch Gardens, Adventure Island, the zoo, the aquarium, or the area's many sporting events.

### C Busch Gardens

How many people can say they rode on a Python, a Tidal Wave, and a Congo River Rapid all in one day? You can join the ranks of the thrill-seeking elite with a quick trip to Busch Gardens Tampa. Busch Gardens is half high-energy amusement park and half first-class zoo. With somewhat of a personality disorder, this is the only park I know where you can alternate between petting zoos and twisting, turning, high-speed roller coasters.

**Rides for Little Kids:** The amusement park has a huge section geared to children 2–7 years old (in a Dragon-centric part of the park to the far left when you're looking at the map, near **Stanleyville,** as well as in sections near the **Congo** and in **Timbuktu**). This is one of the biggest parks I've seen where annoying height limitations keep you from riding if you're *taller* than the marker.

And therein lies a slight conceptual flaw: Hyping it fiendishly for days, parents bring their toddlers for their first taste of the intoxicating chills and thrills of the midway—mini tilt-a-whirls, little roller coasters, real training-wheels rides. The children are strapped in and then the terror sets in. Some scream, others go dead white with their lips flattened. Parents stand on the ground, waving furiously and shouting encouragement while the children persevere, around and around.

**Rides for Big Kids:** Major coasters are the biggest draw for those over 48 inches tall (for Montu, SheiKra, and Kumba it's 54 inches) and with no serious health problems. The rides at Busch Gardens are either little-kiddie or pee-your-pants huge. The roller coasters, in descending order of excellence: The **Montu** at the far right of the park is one of the tallest and longest inverted roller coasters in the world. You are strapped in from above, so your feet dangle while you travel at 60 mph through 60-foot vertical loops. The **SheiKra** has got an incredible 90-degrees-straight-down thrill at the beginning, an underground tunnel, speeds of 70 mph, and water features late in the ride. The ride is a little short, so in 2007 it went floorless to add another level of thrill. **Kumba** is third best, with a full three seconds of weightlessness, an initial 135-foot drop, and cool 360-degree spirals. It offers good speed, a long ride, and one of the world's largest vertical loops. The **Python** has a double spiraling corkscrew and gut-lurching 70-foot plunge, but it's also a very short ride—over in seconds. And the **Gwazi** is for purists—an old double wooden coaster, it's got that tooth-rattling charm as it barrels over the boards in 7,000 feet of track.

Beyond the coasters, the **Tidal Wave, Stanley Falls,** and **Congo River Rapids** boat ride are guaranteed to fully saturate you, so time them for the hottest part of the day and not right before you go see the cool 3-D movie called *Pirates 4-D.* I am not sure what this fourth dimension is, but it's still a lot of fun.

**Animal Attractions:** Busch Gardens contains more than 2,700 animals. Colorful lorikeets will land on your shoulder in the aviary called **Lory Landing,** and there's a **Birds of Prey** show. The best animal attraction is the **Serengeti Plain,** which takes up the whole right half of the park—you see it all by getting on the Serengeti Express Railway (or the Skyride or a Serengeti Safari). Ostriches may race the train, and there are big cats and huffing rhinos. It's thrilling *and* a wonderful opportunity to sit down a spell and regroup.

In spring 2008, the park opened **Jungala.** Set in the Congo area, the four-acre attraction has guests mingling with exotic creatures, exploring a village hidden deep in the jungle, and connecting with the inhabitants of the lush landscape through up-close animal interactions, multistory family play areas, rides, and live entertainment.

**The Details:** Busch Gardens is expensive ($64.95 adults for the day, $54.95 children 3–9, children 2 and under free), so is it worth it? Definitely. It is a wonderful full-day extravaganza for people of any age (if you don't like rides, go to Beer School, where you can learn about the process of making beer and then get what you really came for—free samples). Busch Gardens can entertain you for a full two days, but if you do just one day everyone will be clamoring for more. A 14-day, five-Park Orlando FlexTicket ($234.95 adults, $199.95 kids) is a good deal if you have the stamina to hit SeaWorld Orlando, Universal Studios Florida, Islands of Adventure, and Wet 'n' Wild along with Busch Gardens.

Hours change seasonally: In the winter, it's generally open 9:30 A.M.–6 P.M. daily; in the summer 9 A.M.–10 P.M. daily. If you visit in the summer, count on heavy rains in the afternoon. Bathrooms are plentiful and clean, there are scads of strollers to rent, the food is much better than it needs to be (Zambia Smokehouse serves good ribs and chicken), and there's even a dog kennel to watch your pet while you enjoy the park. The park (888/800-5447, www.buschgardens.com) is at the corner of Busch Boulevard and 40th Street, eight miles northeast of downtown Tampa. Parking is an irritating additional $9, with a free shuttle that takes you from the 5,000-spot parking lot to the park's entrance.

## ◖ Florida Aquarium

The 152,000-square-foot Florida Aquarium (701 Channelside Dr., 813/273-4000, www.flaquarium.org, 9:30 A.M.–5 P.M. daily, $19.95 adults, $16.95 seniors, $14.95 children under 12) is smart, focusing on the waters of Florida. It doesn't contain an exhaustive catalog of the world's aquatic creatures, but it tells a very compelling story about Florida's relationship to the Gulf, estuaries, rivers, and other waterways. There are some exotic exhibits (the otherworldly sea dragons, like seahorses mated with philodendrons), but the best parts are the open freshwater tanks of otters, spoonbills, gators, Florida softshell turtles, and snakes. The aquarium manages to have a very strong environmental message in its natives-versus-exotics exhibits, but it's all fun, never seeming heavy-handed. There's also a wonderful big shark tank, a colorful coral grotto, and a sea-urchin touch tank. It's a small enough aquarium that three hours is plenty of time, and not so crowded that kids can't do a little wandering on their own. Regularly scheduled shows involve native Florida birds and small mammals, as well as shark feeding (in fact, the aquarium offers "swim with the fishes" wetsuit dives into the shark tank for the stalwart). A cell phone audio tour may be the coolest thing yet.

After perusing the marinelife within the eye-catching, shell-shaped building, you can take your newfound knowledge out on the bay with one of the aquarium-run **Wild Dolphin Ecotours** (813/273-4000, $21.95 adults, $19.95 seniors, $17.95 children under 12). Tampa Bay is home to more than 400 bottlenose dolphins. Tickets are available at the aquarium box office the day of the tour only, when you'll head out in a 64-foot, 49-passenger Caribbean catamaran, watching all the while for dolphins, manatees, and a huge number of migratory birds.

## MOSI

You spent a day riding the rides at Busch Gardens, then a day with the fishes at the aquarium, next what? The third day is Tampa's **Museum of Science & Industry** (4801 E. Fowler Ave., 813/987-6000, www.mosi.org, 9 A.M.–5 P.M. Mon.–Fri., 9 A.M.–6 P.M. Sat. and Sun., $20.95 adults, $18.95 seniors, $16.95 children 2–12), a wonderful resource for local schools, family vacationers, or local parents. It's a sprawling modern structure that contains 450 hands-on activities grouped into learning areas. There's some unique and fun stuff like the Gulf Coast Hurricane Chamber, which blows air at an incredible speed to simulate standing

the IMAX theater dome at MOSI

COURTESY OF VISIT FLORIDA

in the eyewall of a hurricane, and the High Wire Bicycle, the longest high-wire bike in a museum, which allows visitors to pedal while balanced on a one-inch steel cable suspended 30 feet above ground. The Amazing You exhibit teaches all about the human body. The museum has an IMAX dome and—get this—the admission price to the museum includes one free viewing of an IMAX film. The museum hosts traveling exhibits as well. Through interactive exhibits, film, and immersion experiences, guests explore the principles of simple mechanics, optics, electromagnetism, math, and psychology.

If you time your visit to allow some cooler temperatures, the free-flying butterfly garden is a treat, with microscope viewing, magnifying glasses, and chemistry stations.

## Lowry Park Zoo

This zoo has recently made the overt decision to take it to the Big Time, going mano a mano with San Diego and the other big zoo kahunas. To this end, it imported four African elephants and created a huge habitat for them. (The previous elephant program was curtailed years ago when a trainer was killed by a panicked pachyderm.)

At the Lowry Park Zoo (1101 W. Sligh Ave., 813/935-8552, www.lowryparkzoo.com, 9:30 A.M.–5 P.M. daily, $20.95 adults, $18.95 seniors, $15.95 children 3–11), habitats are naturalistic and nicely landscaped, but they are still designed for maximum viewing. All told there are around 2,000 native and exotic

the butterfly exhibit at MOSI, a family favorite

animals (white tiger cubs are a big draw), organized into reasonable housing developments, such as Wallaroo Station and Safari Africa. Lots of shade provided by big tropical plants seems to keep all species comfortable, even in the fairly substantial summer heat. One of the zoo's highlights is its Manatee and Aquatic Center, one of only three hospitals and rehabilitation facilities in the state of Florida for sick sea cows. Also, Tampa's Lowry Park Zoo and Sunline Cruises have come together to present the first-ever River Odyssey Ecotour on the Hillsborough River ($14 adults, $10 kids).

### Adventure Island

Adjacent to Busch Gardens but only open mid-March–October is Adventure Island (4500 Bougainvillea Ave., 813/987-5660, www.adventureisland.com, $41.95 adults, $37.95 children 3–9, children 2 and under free). Hours and days of operation vary here, and the park is closed during the winter. It's a 30-acre water park, with slides, corkscrews, waterfalls, a monstrous 17,000-square-foot wave pool, and a child's play area. There are 50 lifeguards on duty, but it's still only appropriate for the truly water-safe. There's also a championship white-sand volleyball complex. If you buy a ticket to Busch Gardens, you can combine it with a ticket here for a discount.

### Malibu Grand Prix

If they've been really, really good, take them to Malibu Grand Prix (14320 N. Nebraska Ave., 813/977-6272, www.grandprixtampa.com, 10 A.M.–10 P.M. weekdays, until midnight weekends, $5–12, depending on the activity). It's got killer miniature golf with lots of windmills, pagodas, and water play, Grand Prix–style go-cart racing, batting cages, and a frenetic game room that features that interactive dance video game on which even good dancers look spastic (a fun spectator sport).

### Glazer Children's Museum

Very young children (up to 10) will be more suited to an afternoon at the Glazer Children's Museum (110 W. Gasparilla Plaza, 813/433-3861, www.glazermuseum.org, 10 A.M.–5 P.M. Mon.–Fri., 10 A.M.–6 P.M. Sat., 1–6 P.M. Sun., $15 adults, $12.50 seniors and military, $9.50 children). In kind of a miniature outdoor city, it has over 170 exhibits in 12 themed areas with hands-on exhibits about different kinds of work and play (a cruise ship, a mini-theater, a giant telescope, grocery store, etc.). Find out what you should be when you grow up.

### Dinosaur World

If your kids or yourself are dinosaur-obsessed, it is your duty to get in the car and drive about a half hour east of Tampa to an otherwise agricultural town called Plant City. It is the winter strawberry capital of the state, but among the strawberry fields lurks Dinosaur World (5145 Harvey Tew Rd., Plant City, 813/717-9865, www.dinosaurworld.net, 9 A.M.–6 P.M. daily, $12.75 adults, $10.75 seniors, $9.75 children 3–12, children 2 and under free). There are 150 huge models (well, maybe 149, because one disappeared a while back—now, there's a trophy) of prehistoric beasts arrayed in a huge subtropical garden. Having recently spent time in the dinosaur exhibit at the Museum of Natural History in New York, I have a sneaking suspicion that Dinosaur World isn't preoccupied with strict accuracy (for instance, we don't really know about dinosaur coloring, but these ones all the mottled greeny-brown made popular in movies). In addition to the dinos, there are spooky fake caves to explore and an archaeological dig/sandbox area. This is best for kids under seven.

TAMPA

# Entertainment and Events

## MUSIC, THEATER, AND CINEMA

Tampa's heavy hitter for performing arts is the **Tampa Bay Performing Arts Center** (1010 N. W.C. MacInnes Pl., one block off Ashley St., 813/229-7827 or 800/955-1045, www.tbpac.org, times and ticket prices vary). It's a huge arts complex housing four distinct theaters, in which audiences can see Opera Tampa (the resident company), the Florida Orchestra, comedies, dramas, cabaret, dance, music, alternative theater, children's theater, and an annual Broadway series. Most local arts series and events find a home at the performing arts center—Arte 2005, Tampa Bay's Festival of Latin American art, Patel Conservatory's Tampa Bay Youth Orchestra Spring Concert—you name it, the curtain goes up here.

A few years ago, Tampa welcomed the **1-800-ASK-GARY Amphitheater** (formerly known as the Ford Amphitheater, 4802 U.S. 301 N., 813/740-2446, times and ticket prices vary), a state-of-the-art venue for 30–40 big-league music concerts a year. At an expense of $23 million, the outdoor open-air theater was constructed with huge video screens, a 7,200-square-foot stage, 9,900 reserved seats, and room for 10,500 more on the lawn; shortly afterward, big space-age sound shields were erected, to the relief of the neighbors. It's gorgeous, like a huge circus tent mated with the Millennium Falcon. There are enough bathrooms and lots of fairly tasty food options.

## ◖ Tampa Theatre

Tampa has its share of multiplexes, but skip the 20-screeners in favor of two hours in the dark at the Tampa Theatre (711 Franklin St., 813/274-8981, www.tampatheatre.org, times vary, $8). Built in 1926, it's a beloved downtown landmark with an acclaimed film series, concerts (Gordon Lightfoot, Keb Mo, Bright Eyes—it's a wide range), special events, and backstage tours. The motion picture palace's interior is vintage with statues and gargoyles

and intricately carved doors. Many believe that the theater is haunted by the ghost of Foster Finley, who spent 20 years as the theater's projectionist. So if you feel a hand in your popcorn, it may not be your seatmate's. Sometimes the films shown are classics, complete with Wurlitzer, other times it's more indie; look online for the schedule. Theater concessions include excellent popcorn, sophisticated candies, and beer and wine. Interesting fact: It was the first public building in Tampa to be equipped with air-conditioning.

## FESTIVALS

The biggest party in Tampa comes at the beginning of February with the **Gasparilla Pirate Fest** (www.gasparillapiratefest.com), a fun celebration over 100 years old in honor of legendary pirate José Gaspar, "last of the buccaneers," who terrorized the coastal waters of West Florida during the late 18th and early 19th centuries. The weekend festivities get under way when 1,000 people in pirate costume sail into downtown on a fully rigged pirate ship, a replica of an 18th-century craft that is 165 feet long by 35 feet across the beam, with three masts standing 100 feet tall. The ship is met by a flotilla of hundreds of pleasure crafts intent on "defending the city." The upshot is that pirates take over Tampa for a while, like Mardi Gras, only with more "argh, me matey" and eye patches accompanying the beads and buried treasure. The length of Bayshore Boulevard is lined with bleachers for the occasion, musical acts sprout on stages all over town, and there's general merriment and carousing.

In the past few years there's been "reel" big news in February with the launch of the **Gasparilla Film Festival** (813/514-9962, www.gasparillafilmfestival.com) in 2006. Tampa's always had its share of wonderful, smaller film festivals, but Tampa remained the largest city in the country without a big

# CRUISING

The Port of Tampa is said to be the fastest-growing cruise port in North America, with a passenger count going from 200,000 in 1998 to more than a million in recent years. Cruise lines seem to beget cruise lines, with newer and larger vessels steaming into the downtown Channelside port all the time. It started with Carnival and Holland America cruise lines back in 1994, but these days a number of lines head out of Tampa on four-, five-, and seven-day itineraries.

Tampa now homeports seven vessels from four cruise lines: Carnival Cruise Lines, Holland America, Royal Caribbean, and Norwegian Cruise Lines.

Carnival has three ships in Tampa. The *Legend* has seven-day cruises to the western Caribbean. The *Inspiration* offers four- and five-day cruises to the Caribbean, and the *Paradise* offers five-day cruises to the western Caribbean.

*Jewel of the Seas* and the *Radiance*, two luxury cruise liners operated by Royal Caribbean International and homeported at Tampa, offer four- and five-day cruises to the western Caribbean.

Holland America Lines' *Ryndam* offers passengers seven-day itineraries of the Caribbean and Mexico.

Norwegian Cruise Lines' *Norwegian Star* has seven-day cruises to the western Caribbean.

The Port's cruise terminals include customer-friendly information areas, superior security, full passenger amenities, and a covered on-terminal parking garage, at $14 per day (no reservations are needed). Valet services are also available. The port is located in close proximity to the interstate highway system. For directions to cruise terminals, call 813/905-7678.

---

annual film festival. The festival takes place at the end of February at venues in and around Ybor City. Over five days more than 40 films are screened in a variety of genres—what they are calling Latin Panorama (films with a Latin twist), New Horizons (films that directly focus on the arts), Fun and Fear (a mix of comedies and horrors), short films, and special screenings of featured American indie films. Then spice it all up with a handful of industry panel discussions, VIP parties, glamorous dinners, and celebrity sightings.

Also in mid-February is the **Florida State Fair** (813/621-7821, www.floridastatefair.com), a 12-day salute to the state's best in agriculture, industry, entertainment, and foods on a stick. Also in February there's a county fair, the

**Plant City Strawberry Festival** (813/752-9194, www.flstrawberryfestival.com), with a huge midway and lots of strawberry cookoffs. Plant City is known as the Winter Strawberry Capital of the World, and these sweet babies are delicious.

The second biggest party is not unlike Gasparilla for its focus on wild costumes and wilder revelry. **Guavaween** is the city's Cuban-style Halloween celebration, held October 30. Riffing on the fact that Tampa was nicknamed The Big Guava, the celebration features the Mama Guava, who has sworn to take the "bore" out of Ybor City. Really, after the parade is over, it's a big excuse to drink too much and wander the streets of Ybor City in preposterous attire.

TAMPA

# Nightlife

## YBOR CITY

Ybor City is where people come out to party in Tampa. During the week there are few bars with throbbing music drifting out onto the street—it's more about dining weekdays. Forget date night on the weekend; then, it's a place you rove with buddies, looking up trouble.

Fairly young people head to the all-disco DJ **Platforms** (1625 N. Seventh Ave., 813/241-6603, 9 P.M.–3 A.M. Wed.–Sat., cover usually $5); also drawing a young crowd, **Club Skye** (1509 E. Eighth Ave., 813/247-6606, 1 P.M.–3 A.M. Mon.–Sat., cover varies, no cover before 11 P.M. on Sat.) is what's on the horizon for Tampa's party nights. Whether you're here for College Ladies' Night, International Night, or DJ nights, Skye is the party to beat in Ybor. Although only certain nights are technically Naughty School Girl Nights, every night has plenty of sexy post-collegiate girls, especially when the club runs costume nights or competitions.

**Coyote Ugly** (1722 E. Seventh Ave., 813/228-8459, 5 P.M.–3 A.M. Tues.–Sat.) aims older, not more mature, and is often just about the biggest party in Ybor City, presided over by the most audacious bartenders to ever wield a shot glass. If you have to ask what a body shot is, you're ripe for a hard life lesson from one of Coyote's devilish (and usually gorgeous) bartenders. Just like in the movie (which in turn was based on a bar in NYC), all-female bartenders drag the unsuspecting up on the bar for some raunchy drinking, dancing, and whatever. The bare-bones room is festooned with discarded brassieres from exuberant all-ages patrons.

**Czar Vodka Bar** (1401 E. Seventh Ave., 813/247-6838, www.myspace.com/czarvodkabar) is a located in the atmospheric Pleasuredome/Tracks/El Goya building. Vodka drinks are de rigueur at Czar, with two rooms with dance floors and video screens (the side room is called Cyberia) with nice booths and a super swank chill-out room.

If music and drinking aren't your objective, stop into the **Tampa Improv** (1600 E. Eighth Ave., 813/864-4000, hours vary, $20) for an evening of live stand-up with mostly local/regional acts.

**The Rare Olive** (1601 E. Seventh Ave., 813/248-2333, $3) is a good place to end a night on an adult note, maybe with a martini, a cigar, and a little live jazz. The **Green Iguana** (1708 E. Seventh Ave., 813/248-9555) is another bar for grown-ups: good drinks, perfectly acceptable food, and audible conversation.

## HYDE PARK

There's lots of good nightlife to be had in this sophisticated South Tampa neighborhood. Head to **The Rack** (1809 W. Platt St., 813/250-1595, 4 P.M.–3 A.M. Mon.–Fri., noon–3 A.M. Sat. and Sun., $6–10) for eight ball and tekka maki. You don't see the kind of serious players who bring their own Schon or Predator cues, but there's respectable play at most of the tables in the hip, low-light, leather-couched space. It usually hosts a late 30s crowd.

There's a lot of Irish zeal on and around Azeele. If you like your music—or your flirting—with a heavy brogue, head to everyone's favorite quaint Irish bar, **Dubliner Pub** (2307 W. Azeele St. 813/258-2257). **Four Green Fields** (205 W. Platt St., 813/254-4444) is another legendary Irish pub, with lots of regulars and lively conversation. The french fry basket is a bargain and could feed a small nation. **MacDinton's Irish Pub & Restaurant** (405 S. Howard Ave., 813/251-8999, 4 P.M.–3 A.M. Mon.–Fri., 10 A.M.–3 A.M. Sat. and Sun., $7–10) is another Irish entry, with a killer black and tan, a warming Irish coffee, and a fair representation of Irish staples, from rib-sticking, mashed-potatoey shepherd's pie to corned beef and cabbage. This is absolutely the biggest scene in Tampa, with lines down and around the block on weekend nights.

## VICINITY OF TAMPA

**Skipper's Smokehouse** (910 Skipper Rd., 813/971-0666, 11 A.M.–11 P.M. Tues.–Fri., opens at noon on Sat. and 1 P.M. on Sun., $8–14) and **Bahama Breeze** (3045 N. Rocky Point Dr. E., 813/289-7922, roughly 11 A.M.–midnight Sun.–Thurs., until 2 A.M. Fri. and Sat., $8–22) could not be more different, but both are worthy of the drive time. The former,

in northern New Tampa, is the city's favored indoor-outdoor live blues venue, part classic Florida style and part islandy/Key West. The latter is a tropical-themed singles hangout with a huge waterside deck from which you can view a great sunset.

# Shopping

## OLD HYDE PARK VILLAGE

Tampa's downtown doesn't really have a retail center. For that, you need to visit Hyde Park. It's not vast, but the outdoor shopping area along Hyde Park's West Swann Avenue, South Dakota Avenue, and Snow Avenue is the most appealing shopping destination in town, especially when the weather's nice. There's a large covered parking lot, free to shoppers, and a nicely landscaped plaza at the center. Pottery Barn and Williams-Sonoma are among the bigger stores, with Ann Taylor, Brooks Brothers, Anthropologie, Talbots, and Tommy Bahama. Top restaurants include the Cal-Ital Wine Exchange, the indoor-outdoor, Sinatra-addled Timpano Italian Chophouse, and a slick pan-Asian bistro called Restaurant B.T. In the summer, Old Hyde Park Village (813/251-3500, store hours vary) hosts a free evening movie series, the classic films projected outside on a huge screen.

## INDOOR MALLS

With anchor stores Neiman Marcus and Nordstrom, **International Plaza** (2223 N. West Shore Blvd., 813/342-3790, 10 A.M.–9 P.M. Mon.–Sat., noon–6 P.M. Sun.), opened in 2001, gets the nod for fanciest shopping. A handful of usual mall stores (J. Crew, Banana Republic, Ann Taylor) are spiffed up by their proximity to 200 other specialty shops like Tiffany & Co., Jos. A. Bank, Louis Vuitton, Montblanc, Gucci, and Coach. Really, it's the most upscale assembly of stores in any shopping center on the Gulf Coast, served by an open-air village of restaurants called Bay Street, all in a

location minutes from the airport and downtown. And during the Christmas season the Neiman Marcus store really goes all out with decorations.

About a minute from International Plaza, **Westshore Plaza** (250 Westshore Plaza, 813/286-0790) features more than 100 similarly fancy specialty shops and 4 major department stores, including a Saks Fifth Avenue. It contains a 14-screen AMC Theater and restaurants like Maggiano's Little Italy, PF Chang's, and The Palm.

Located across the street from USF, **University Mall** (2200 E. Fowler Ave., 813/971-3465) is a typical indoor shopping center with mostly familiar mall stores, a 16-screen movie theater, and a standard food court.

Fairly far from where most visitors stay, **Westfield Shopping Town, Brandon** (459 Brandon Town Center Dr., 813/661-5100) and **Westfield Shopping Town, Citrus Park** (8021 Citrus Park Town Center, 813/926-4644) are both enjoyable malls with the full gamut of small shops and anchors, mostly serving the local community. Citrus Park is a little nicer, with a 20-screen Regal Cinema.

And if you want to get some great deals on name brands, you need to drive south on I-75 for 40 minutes until you reach the **Prime Outlets** in Ellenton (5461 Factory Shops Blvd., Ellenton, 941/723-1150). There, you'll find Bose, Ann Taylor, Nine West, Samsonite, DKNY, Black & Decker, Villeroy & Boch, Nike, Sak's Off Fifth, Wilson Leather, Polo Ralph Lauren, and Waterford/Wedgwood—all offering deep discounts.

## OTHER SHOPPING

**Channelside Bay Plaza** (615 Channelside Dr., 813/223-4250), the entertainment center on Tampa's downtown waterfront adjacent to the Florida Aquarium and the cruise terminal, has a few stores to investigate— a wine shop, Antonio's Cigars, Qachbal's Chocolatier, and a couple of galleries. And shopping along **Seventh Avenue in Ybor City,** Tampa's Latin quarter, will yield some interesting finds. It's a little grittier, with a few vintage clothing shops, a fair amount of racy lingerie, GBX Fashion Shoes, and a funky Urban Outfitters.

# Accommodations

Tampa's hotel scene is stymied by one thing: Tampa has no beaches. Although it's on the water—with the active Port of Tampa and waterside residential communities like Davis and Harbour Islands—there is no possibility for a luxury resort hotel or charming bed-and-breakfast just steps from the waters of Hillsborough Bay. For that kind of experience you must head over the bay to St. Pete or Clearwater.

Still, Tampa has a preponderance of pleasant, fairly priced accommodations, spread around the greater Bay Area, from the Latin Quarter of Ybor City to the Westshore business district or the Tampa Convention Center, to near Busch Gardens and the University of South Florida.

## UNDER $50

For when you're looking for a wild experience at a tame price, **Gram's Place** (3109 N. Ola Ave., 813/221-0596, www.grams-inn-tampa. com, hostel rates $22.50, room rates $34–68) in Ybor City will surely fit the bill. It's eccentric, with a different music theme (jazz, blues, rock) in each of the private suites and youth hostel–style bunks. All rooms come with a music menu of CDs. The hostel part looks like a railroad car fashioned around a 100-year-old train depot. The rooms are set in two circa-1945 cottages and share an oversized in-ground whirlpool tub, a BYOB bar in the courtyard, and a multitrack recording studio. Lest you are imagining some cool old Grandma jamming in the recording studio with a bunch of longhairs, the "Gram" in question is Gram Parsons, once a member of the Byrds and the Flying Burrito Brothers, the deceased musician responsible for that great song, "Grievous Angel," that Emmylou Harris made famous.

## $100-200

For a different kind of experience in Ybor City, head to the historic 【 **Don Vicente de Ybor Historic Inn** (1915 Republica de Cuba, 813/241-4545, www.donvicenteinn.com, $159–169), constructed in 1895 by Cuban patriot Vicente Martinez Ybor. The boutique hotel's 16 guest rooms contain four-poster beds and also broadband, voicemail, and in-room desks. Even if you don't stay here, the magnificent grand salon is worth peeking at.

Nearby, the **Bonita Casitas de Ybor** (1813 & 1815 E. Fifth Ave., 813/334-1857, $100–200) offers two charming private guest cottages with full kitchens and two bedrooms each.

If you want to stay near USF or Busch Gardens and MOSI, there are a handful of reasonably priced chains. **La Quinta Inn Tampa Near Busch Gardens** (9202 N. 30th St., 813/930-6900, $74–104) is adjacent to Busch Gardens's entrance, with 144 nicely appointed rooms with roomy bathrooms, good lighting, large desks, and computer-friendly dataport telephones. There's also a good-sized pool. The USF hotel of choice is **Embassy Suites** (3705 Spectrum Blvd., 813/977-7066, $179–314) across the road. It's a tall, suites-only hotel with a soaring atrium. Rooms are nice, with spacious living rooms, private bedrooms with either a king-size or two double beds and two TVs in every room. Although the rooms cost a little more, included in the price is a very nice daily cooked-to-order breakfast buffet and the manager's reception, where you get a free cocktail and some chips in the early evening.

If you prefer independently owned hotels, the **Tahitian Inn** (601 S. Dale Mabry Hwy., 813/876-1397, www.tahitianinn.com, $95–169) is a lovely, two-story, family-run motel that had a huge remodel in 2003, yielding 60 Tahitian-theme (dark wood, tropical accessories) moderately priced rooms and 20 executive suites, a lovely pool with tiki huts and hammocks, and the Serenity Spa with massage and Tahitian hot stone treatments. There's also a lovely little on-site café with patio seating near a koi pond. The location is close to I-275 and lots of commerce.

## OVER $200

Numerous hotels cluster along Rocky Point Drive and Cypress Street, just a couple of minutes from the airport, Westshore business district, and Tampa Convention Center. These hotels have lots of business amenities and often offer significantly cheaper rates on the weekend. Of the chains, there's **DoubleTree Hotel Tampa Airport Westshore** (4500 W. Cypress St., 813/879-4800, www.tampadoubletree.com, $233–309), **Courtyard by Marriott Tampa Westshore** (3805 W. Cypress St., 813/874-0555, $249–279), the **Holiday Inn Express and Suites Rocky Point** (3025 N. Rocky Point Dr., 813/287-8585 $209–259), among many others, all with water views of the bay and with pools and other amenities.

For a more independent approach in the same location, try **Sailport Waterfront Suites** (2506 N. Rocky Point Dr., 813/281-9599, $129–229), a four-story, all-suites hotel (all rooms have a queen-size sleeper sofa in the living room, convenient for families) with full-size kitchens, barbecue grills, outdoor heated pool, lighted tennis court, and fishing pier.

A little pricier, the **Grand Hyatt** (2900 Bayport Dr., 813/874-1234, www.grandtampabay.hyatt.com, $339–419) is another big hotel near the airport that caters mainly to the corporate traveler. There are 445 deluxe

© JOSHUA LAWRENCE KINSER

After you party like a rock star, you can find a hip place to crash at the Seminole Hard Rock Hotel and Casino.

guest rooms and suites, including 38 Spanish-style casita rooms and 7 casita suites in a secluded area at the south end of the property, which is set in a 35-acre wildlife preserve on the shores of Tampa Bay. The Hyatt contains two of the best restaurants in town, Armani's and Oystercatchers.

The **Seminole Hard Rock Hotel and Casino** (5223 Orient Rd., 866/502-7529, www.seminolehardrockhoteltampa.com, $249–359) is the huge luminous tower that rises up in the middle of nowhere off of I-75. With an illuminated 12-story tower that shifts colors, the signature huge guitar at the entrance, a 90,000-square-foot casino, and popular restaurants like Floyd's and Council Oak, it's like a little piece of Vegas right here in Tampa. The complex opened in 2004 and has been swamped with casino and overnight guests ever since. The 250 guest rooms and suites have a hipster art deco design, with

TAMPA

COURTESY OF INTERCONTINENTAL TAMPA

The InterContinental Tampa offers stylish and upscale accommodations well suited for business travelers and couples.

unique extras like Tivoli stereo and CD systems and ultraluxury beds. The most luxurious part is the pool area, with cascading fountains and cool private cabanas with televisions and refrigerators. The Seminole Indian Tribe is currently seeking approval from the state of Florida to green-light an $800 million expansion for the Hard Rock that will purportedly bring another 20- to 22-story tower to the site with 1,000 new rooms, 50,000 square feet of meeting and convention space, a 2,000-seat music venue, a new swimming pool, and a new parking garage with 6,000 spaces. So, look for there to be plenty of gambling options in the future.

One of Tampa's nicest luxury hotels is the **Renaissance Tampa Hotel International Plaza** (4200 Jim Walter Blvd., 813/877-9200, $339–389) near the Westshore business district at the International Plaza mall. The lavish decor is reminiscent of a Mediterranean villa. The hotel's not small, with 293 guest rooms on eight floors, but the service is personal and attentive, and it seems especially geared to the repeat-business, high-end business traveler.

The **InterContinental Tampa** (4860 W. Kennedy Blvd., 813/286-4400, www.intercontampa.com, $329–479) is a business traveler's dream. The 323 rooms, 17 junior suites, four business suites, and two presidential suites feature fresh decor, feather-top mattresses with luxurious linens, functional working areas, flat-screen TVs, and iPod docking stations. The hotel offers 21,000 square feet of flexible meeting space, wireless high-speed Internet throughout the entire hotel, fitness center, full-service concierge program, and a rooftop pool with views of the bay and city. The hotel also has a Shula's Steak House and Shula's No Name Lounge, which offers the best steaks in town. They also offer impressive sports packages for select games including transportation to and from the stadiums.

# Food

Maybe it's Tampa residents' deep streak of loyalty, maybe their plodding constancy, but marketing geniuses have determined that Tampa is the perfect test market for new chain restaurant concepts. They are trotted out here, and if they fly, launched upon the rest of the country. For this reason, Tampa is the home base of numerous national and regional chains—Hooters, Durango Steakhouse, Beef O' Brady's, Checkers, Hops Restaurant Bar and Brewery, Shells' Seafood Restaurant, Carrabba's, and Outback Steakhouse. (Outback is also the mastermind behind chains Lee Roy Selmon's, Fleming's Prime Steakhouse, Bonefish Grill, and Roy's.)

You will find more Chili's, Macaroni Grills, T.G.I. Friday's, and Bennigans restaurants than you could possibly patronize. For this reason, only the unique, discrete, more-or-less independently owned restaurants that are the exception to the rule in Tampa are covered here.

## HYDE PARK

This is the upscale part of town. It's a historical residential district, serviced by the Old Hyde Park Village of high-end shops and the long stretch of South Howard Avenue, or SoHo, where some very good restaurants are located.

## Asian

Picking out just a handful along Restaurant Row is difficult. For casual dining, **(** **Water, Unique Sushi** (1015½ S. Howard Ave., 813/251-8406, $8–12) is a Japanese-inspired seafood joint and a late-night hangout for the neighborhood. Water specializes in rice paper–rolled sushi (no nori) paired with punchy sauces and dynamic side dishes. A minimalist design aesthetic and a no-reservations policy cannot douse the enthusiasm for vibrant combos like unagi, banana, and avocado. Its sister restaurant next door, **Ciccio & Tony's,** is also a favorite around here for thin-crust pizzas and California-style wraps. The same company has **The Lime** (915 S. Howard Ave., 813/868-5463) down the block, a super lively hangout for fresh Mex and good 'ritas.

**TC Choy Asian Bistro** (301 S. Howard Ave., 813/251-1191, 11:30 A.M.–2:30 P.M. and 5:30–10 P.M. Mon.–Thurs., until 11 P.M. Fri., 11 A.M.–3 P.M. and 5:30–11 P.M. Sat. and Sun., $8–18) serves authentic Cantonese cuisine and noonday dim sum (and an assortment of other pan-Asian dishes) in a stylish, open space with big tables perfect for large parties.

## Spanish

If you're in the mood for Spanish tapas, Hyde Park has two laudable purveyors. **Sangria's Spanish Tapas Bar & Restaurant** (315 S. Howard Ave., 813/258-0393, 5 P.M.–midnight Mon.–Thurs., until 2 A.M. Fri. and Sat., $6–25) is a sweet little place with pitchers of sangria, a good Spanish tortilla, and lots of great shrimp in garlic. Not on the row, but off on the more upscale waterside Bayshore, the late-night **Ceviche Tapas Bar & Restaurant** (1502 S. Howard Ave., 813/250-0203, 5–10 P.M. Sun. and Mon., until midnight Tues.–Sat., $12–26) serves its namesake citrus-cured fish, sea scallops with manchego, and a variety of compact dishes with olives and almonds, all in a sleek nightclub atmosphere.

## Casual

A thin-crust pizza hotshot by day, **(** **Pane Rustica** (3225 S. MacDill Ave., 813/902-8828, 8 A.M.–6 P.M. Tues., 8 A.M.–10 P.M. Wed.–Sat., 8 A.M.–3 P.M. Sun., $6–22) from Wednesday to Saturday hosts some of the fanciest Cal-Ital dinners around, with full table service and a well-selected short wine list. You can still opt for one of those delicious thin-crust pizzas (maybe one with gorgonzola and sweet caramelized shallot, or perhaps ricotta salata with olive tapenade and sun-dried tomatoes), or even a laid-back burger with brie and roasted red peppers. Don't miss Kevin and Karyn Kruszewski's awesome cookies, cakes, and other housemade desserts.

## Fine Dining

After 15 years of being at the forefront of

Tampa's restaurant scene, B. T. Nguyen may have reached her pinnacle in **Restaurant B.T.** (1633 W. Snow Ave., 813/258-1916, 11:30 A.M.–9:30 P.M. Mon.–Thurs., until 10:30 P.M. Fri. and Sat., $8–29, 11 A.M.–3 P.M. Sun.), located dead center in Old Hyde Park Village. Classic Vietnamese and French dishes are innovatively presented in the stylish, indoor/outdoor dining room. Trained as a sommelier, Nguyen has created an exceptional wine list and a short list of cocktails, which explains the locale's popularity as an evening gathering place.

It's the biggest gorilla of them all on the Tampa dining scene, the restaurant known around the world. It's on what is now a somewhat run-down stretch of South Howard, but **Bern's Steak House** (1208 S. Howard Ave., 813/251-2421, 5–11 P.M. daily, reservations recommended, $17–100) fans are undeterred. It's a more-than-50-year-old landmark, with a wine list that could break a toe and a menu that so thoroughly explains dishes that it can sometimes seem a bit exaggerated. Waiters go through a grueling years-long apprenticeship, resulting in a staff that could, and does, quote verbatim from the offerings. Steaks are so thoroughly described that it wouldn't be surprising to hear the eye color, hat size, or hobbies of the cows in question. It's prime beef, aged and nurtured in Bern's own meat lockers, and you, the customer, dictate the size, cut, cooking temperature, and many other details. You gotta go to Bern's and after dinner take the tour of the kitchen and wine cellar.

Then head upstairs to 🌒 **The Harry Waugh Dessert Room at Bern's Steak House.** Nothing prepares you for it. People tell you, "You dine in individual hollowed-out wine casks." Someone says, "There are individual wall-mounted radios to set the mood at your table." You hear a rumor about an accordionist, maybe something about flambéing waiters. The romantic date-night possibilities of this dessert-only upstairs of Bern's (named after a wine-writing crony of Bern himself) are endless. If that's not enough, there's Chocolate-Chocolate-Chocolate. That's actually the name of the chocolate-shellacked cylinder packing chocolate cheese pie, chocolate mousse, and chocolate cheesecake into one deadly package.

If Bern's doesn't sound like your cup of tea, try the more contemporary approach at the affiliated **SideBern's** (2208 W. Morrison Ave., 813/258-2233, 5–10 P.M. Mon.–Thurs., until 11 P.M. Fri. and Sat., closed Sun., $18–32). The kitchen turns out great dim sum and world-beat small plates. The daily-changing selection of breads is absolutely knockout (curry sesame flatbread, kalamata and fig loaf).

Not among the 35 or so restaurants along South Howard, but still considered in Hyde Park, **Mise en Place** (442 W. Kennedy Blvd., 813/254-5373, 11:30 A.M.–2:30 P.M. and 5:30–10 P.M. Tues.–Thurs., until 11 P.M. Fri., only 5–11 P.M. Sat., $15–32) is a romantic, intimate spot near the University of Tampa. The weekly changing menu ranges from pizza with chorizo, roast corn, chilies, and manchego to mole spice–rubbed seared tuna with purple potatoes, vanilla bean pineapple salad, and a prickly pear habanero vinaigrette. They also take great care to accommodate folks with special diets.

## DAVIS ISLAND

Nestled in the charming business district of Davis Island, opinions on the best tables at **220 East** (220 E. Davis Blvd., 813/259-1220, 11 A.M.–10 P.M. Mon.–Thurs., 11 A.M.–11 P.M. Fri. and Sat., $13–18) are divided—out front at one of the handful on the patio, or inside at one of the deep green booths. The restaurant stays pretty busy. The wait staff is exceptionally friendly, serving fairly priced, casual meals that range through American, Asian, or even Cajun dishes.

Across the street and equally good, **Estela's** (209 E. Davis Blvd., 813/260-0192, 11 A.M.–10 P.M. weekdays, until 11 P.M. weekends, $5–9) is known for excellent carne asada (a rib-eye with lots of thinly sliced onions in a lime sauce, served with a cheese enchilada and refried beans) and chocolate tacos.

## YBOR CITY

Party central in Tampa, the century-old cigar-rolling center of town exhibits little of its Cuban heritage these days. The main drag is

Seventh Avenue, closed off to cars on weekend, which is really nice to be able to party and walk around without having to worry about traffic around you. It gets really packed on the weekend with younger partiers looking to drink and enjoy dancing and live music in the clubs of the area. During the week, the area is calmer—a better time to try out one of the many restaurants that range all over the map.

Start your adventure at **Centro Ybor** (1600 E. Eighth Ave., 813/242-4660, www.centroybor.com, 11 A.M.–11 P.M. Sun.–Thurs., until 2 A.M. weekends), a shopping, dining, and entertainment complex right at the pulsing heart of the neighborhood. The **Fresh Mouth** (813/241-8845, 11 A.M.–11 P.M. Sun.–Thurs., until 2 A.M. weekends) is the place to get a solid burger, on the plaza level at the grand staircase. **Samurai Blue Sushi and Sake Bar** (813/242-6688, 11:30 A.M.–midnight Mon.–Fri., 5 P.M.–1 A.M. Sat., 5–11 P.M. Sun., $9–26) is another big, lively joint, but this one serves sake bombers, "spontaneous combustion rolls," and other unique spins on Japanese bar staples.

**Tampa Bay Brewing Company** (plaza level under Muvico, 813/247-1422, www.tbbco.com, 11 A.M.–midnight Mon. and Tues., 11 A.M.–2 A.M. Wed.–Sat., 1 P.M.–midnight Sun.) recently moved from elsewhere in Ybor to anchor the Centro, a welcome addition. There's good live music, excellent proprietary brews (try the Redeye Ale), and a fresh American bistro menu.

Named for the irritable and poisonous gila monster, **Adobe Gilas** (813/241-8588, 11 A.M.–2:30 A.M. Mon.–Sat., noon–2:30 A.M. Sun., $5–10) is more a drinking establishment, a fun place in which to pick your poison and let it rip. Think you can handle a 64-ounce margarita? Feel free to attempt it amongst these consummate 'rita professionals. Food runs to dips and chips, so the draw is the rustic indoor-outdoor space and abounding good cheer. After this, regroup at the Centro Ybor movie theater across the plaza.

Beyond Centro Ybor, the neighborhood's restaurants are spread along many blocks on Seventh Avenue. Nearly at the end of the

---

## THE CUBANO

In Tampa, the Cubano is the king of sandwiches, or should I say the earl of sandwiches? It starts with the bread. If you've eaten anywhere in Ybor City, you've probably eaten Cuban bread. But why not go to the source? Rumor has it **La Segunda Central Bakery** (2512 N. 15th St., 813/248-1531, www.lesugundabakery.com, 8:30 A.M.–5 P.M. Mon.-Fri., 7 A.M.–3 P.M. Sat., 7 A.M.–1 P.M. Sun.) churns out 6,000 Cuban loaves daily.

You only need one loaf, in the form of the archetypal Cubano sandwich. The loaves themselves are about 36 inches long, with a zipper-like seam down the top. The third-generation owners of La Segunda have reason to be proud of their bread's thin, flaky crust and soft, pillowy interior, even more so when piled high with roast pork and Genoa salami (a strictly Tampa twist), Swiss cheese (some say Emmentaler), sour pickles, and spicy mustard – the whole thing warmed and flattened in a special hot press. Outside crisp, inside warm and a little gooey. It's perfection.

---

strip of commerce you'll find the **Columbia Restaurant** (2117 E. Seventh Ave., 813/248-4961, 11 A.M.–10 P.M. Mon.–Thurs., until 11 P.M. Fri. and Sat., noon–9 P.M. Sun., $21–30), which bears the distinction of being the oldest restaurant in Florida (started in 1905) and the nation's largest Spanish/Cuban restaurant (13 rooms extending one city block). The food's not exceptional these days, but the experience is worth it. Some of these waiters have been here a lifetime, the many rooms manage to stay packed, and there are stirring flamenco shows Monday–Saturday nights.

People-watching is a popular pastime in Ybor City. For the best sidewalk seat in town, pull up a chair at ◖ **Bernini** (1702 E. Seventh Ave., 813/248-0099, 11:30 A.M.–10 P.M. Mon.–Thurs., until 11 P.M. Fri., 4–11 P.M. Sat., 4–9 P.M. Sun., $10–24). It's set in the historic Bank of Ybor City building and serves Cal-Ital cuisine—salmon carpaccio and filet mignon with white truffle. It generally attracts an older crowd than the bars and clubs around it.

## CHANNELSIDE

Channelside is located dockside at the Port of Tampa where all the cruise ships come in. The shopping/dining/entertainment complex has a big movie theater with IMAX; a fun, upscale bowling alley; small, mostly independently owned shops; and about a dozen restaurants.

Head first to the bowling alley–restaurant **Splitsville** (615 Channelside Dr., 813/514-2695, 4 P.M.–1 A.M. weekdays, 11 A.M.–3 A.M. Sat., 11 A.M.–1 A.M. Sun., $7–18). Spares, strikes, whatever: It's good food, a whimsical environment, and the coolest bowling shoes ever. The decor sets you straight with oversized "bowling pin" columns, red velvet ropes, and 12 faultless lanes, and the food is excellent bar snacks.

The best food in the complex is at **Tinatapa's** (615 Channelside Dr., 813/514-8462, www.tinatapas.com, 4–10 P.M. Mon.–Fri., noon–2 A.M. Sat., noon–10 P.M. Sun., $12–20). Barcelona mosaics and logs for rafters give the spare, round room a decidedly Euro feel. It serves Spanish-esque small plates like baked goat cheese with tomato sauce and salmon. The flavors are fresh and bold and the prices are low.

The newest Channelside addition inherited space from the short-lived Signature Room (an homage to the original, at the top of Chicago's Hancock Building). Also an homage, the new **Gallagher's Steak House** (615 Channelside Dr. #203, 813/229-8000, 11 A.M.–10 P.M. Mon.–Sun., $21–40) is the fifth franchise that pays tribute to the historic New York flagship steak emporium. It's an enjoyable corner spot with a masculine interior serving well-marbled prime rib and justifiably famous potatoes (a baked potato meets a French fry halfway).

**Stump's Supper Club** (615 Channelside Dr., 813/226-2261, 4–9 P.M. Thurs., 4 P.M.–3 A.M. Fri., 3 P.M.–3 A.M. Sat., noon–9 P.M. Sun.) is fun for live music and **Howl at the Moon** (615 Channelside Dr., 813/226-2261, 8–10 P.M. Wed. and Thurs., 8 P.M.–3 A.M. Fri., 3 P.M.–3 A.M. Sat., 3–9 P.M. Sun.), has a dueling piano bar.

## INTERNATIONAL PLAZA

Tampa's fanciest mall (there's a Louis Vuitton store next to a Gucci store) is also home to good restaurants (all 2223 N. Westshore Blvd., 813/490-5288). It contains **The Cheesecake Factory, California Pizza Kitchen, Earl of Sandwich,** and **The Capital Grille** (813/830-9433), for when you want to splurge on a $40 dry-aged steak. The mall's Bay Street is a Caribbean-themed pedestrian promenade lined with several good restaurants.

**Café Japon** (813/874-8619) boasts Tampa's longest sushi bar and unique and fun specialty rolls. Casual, friendly and independently owned, it doesn't have the corporate slickness of many of the Bay Street offerings. **The Grape** (813/354-9463) is a lively girls' night hangout where ladies drink glasses of wine amongst a sea of shopping bags. The wine bar's menu includes a tasty spinach salad and a really good chocolate fondue.

Best bets for a drink: **Bar Louie** (813/874-1919), where Tuesday nights it's $1 burgers; there are 40 beers on tap. **Blue Martini** (813/873-2583) is for when you aim to go the martini route, with a menu that leans to small plates (seared tuna, hummus and pita chips). There's also an elevated stage behind the bar to see live rock.

For casual, family-friendly quickies, there's **TooJay's Original Gourmet Deli** (813/348-4101) and hamburgers at **Champps Restaurant & Bar** (813/353-0200).

Another great restaurant is **Pelagia Trattoria** (4200 Jim Walter Blvd., 813/313-3235), located on the main level in the Renaissance Tampa Hotel, Bay Street. Chef Fabrizio Schenardi serves Mediterranean-inspired dishes: breakfast brings special items like waffles with cappuccino mousse and walnuts; at lunch, crunchy fried olives stuffed with three meats; and for dinner, rack of lamb with fig-port sauce. It's the most beautiful hotel restaurant in all of Tampa that also has an express lunch menu that gets people in and out lickety-split.

## NEW TAMPA

Everyone's favorite restaurant in New Tampa—the mostly residential area northeast of downtown—is **Ciccio's Lodge** (16019 Tampa Palms Blvd., 813/975-1222, 11:30 A.M.–10 P.M. daily, $8–20). Most nights it teems with families devoted to this health-conscious neighborhood favorite. Ciccio's serves thin, crunchy New York–style pizzas topped with interesting picks like caramelized eggplant and goat cheese, while a turkey club "chop chop" pairs turkey breast with high-protein soy bacon bits, ripe tomato, crisp lettuce, and yellow rice.

The same crew recently opened **The Lime** (915 S. Howard Ave., 813/979-LIME, 11 A.M.–10 P.M. daily, $6–15). Not far from there, the new Greek **Acropolis Bar & Grill** (14947 Bruce B. Downs Blvd., 813/971-1787, 11 A.M.–3 A.M. daily, $6–15) offers late hours, lively fun, and people yelling "opa" regularly.

New Tampa, as the name indicates, is all new. The upside is that things are clean, pristine, hygienic; the downside is that there's no sense of history, no gritty, time-worn ambience. If you are jonesing for something that seems older than a decade or so, ◖ **Skipper's Smokehouse** (910 Skipper Rd, Tampa, 813/971-0666, 11 A.M.–10 P.M. Tues.–Sun., $4.99–14.99), has the ambience of a place 10 times its age. It's Tampa's best live music venue (blues, alt rock, Tuvan throat singers, the gamut), with concerts held outdoors under the canopy of a huge, moss-festooned live oak. It has a lively 30s-and-up bar scene (and a mighty fine mojito). A ramshackle restaurant serves a wonderful blackened grouper sandwich, gator nuggets, and black beans.

## VICINITY OF TAMPA

When you want to get a sense of Tampa's scale, distance, and scope, you have to dig deep into your wallet and head to **Armani's** (6200 Courtney Campbell Causeway, 813/207-6800, 6–10 P.M. Mon.–Thurs., until 11 P.M. Fri. and Sat., $24–39) atop the Hyatt Regency Westshore. It's the undisputed top special-occasion restaurant in town, partly for the view, partly for the solicitous service, and partly for the scaloppine Armani (thin-pounded veal sautéed with wild mushrooms and cognac in a truffle sauce) or the grilled duck breast stuffed with liver pâté and dried cherries in a vanilla sauce. The wine list is extensive, with an emphasis on California and French wines. **Oystercatchers** (2900 Bayport Dr., 813/2076815, 11:30 A.M.–10 P.M. daily, $18–35) is the hotel's No. 2 restaurant, just remodeled, a lovely seafood joint with water views and town's best brunch. It offers exceptionally fresh seafood in a beautiful and upscale but still comfortably casual waterfront setting. The outdoor dining area with personal and romantic fire pits right on the waterfront can be reserved upon request. For dinners choose between dishes like wood-grilled Gulf snapper served with tuxedo orzo and baby vegetables or lobster and mascarpone ravioli with lobster bisque and roasted organic mushrooms. And you have got to try the smoked sea salt on bread and butter. You'll never look at a dinner roll the same way again.

One of the innovative Hawaiian-fusion restaurants founded by acclaimed chef Roy Yamaguchi, **Roy's** (4342 W. Boy Scout Blvd., 813/873-7697, 5:30–10 P.M. Mon.–Thurs., until 10:30 P.M. Fri. and Sat., until 9 P.M. Sun., $19–30) is another expense-account favorite in Tampa. An exceptionally good deal can be had with the three-course dinner for $35. It may start with a grilled Hawaiian satay skewers, then segue to grilled tiger shrimp with asparagus, finishing up with Roy's signature melting hot chocolate soufflé.

In the upscale neighborhood of Carrollwood, Andrea and Michael Reilly's little **Michael's Grill** (11720 N. Dale Mabry, 813/964-8334, 11 A.M.–9 P.M. Mon.–Thurs., until 10 P.M. Fri. and Sat., $15–27) has become an institution, as much for the warm greeting and neighborly service as it is for the friendly patio and spare, brasserie-style dining room. You can eat your French onion soup or penne Bolognese at the bar and take in all the drama of the bustling open kitchen, but the crowd through the French doors and out on the patio always seems to be having more fun. You can also head next door to Borders Books after dinner for a browse.

Also in Carrollwood and new in 2007, **Grille One Sixteen** (15405 N. Dale Mabry,

813/265-0116, 11 A.M.–9 P.M. Sun.–Thurs., until 10 P.M. Fri. and Sat., $18–39) has made waves with its hip-like-Miami design. Chef James Maita has a strong New American approach with a world-beat inspired menu.

For a great steak, head to **Malio's Prime** (400 North Ashley Dr., 813/223-7746, 11 A.M.–10 P.M. Mon.–Thurs., until 11 P.M. Fri., 5–11 P.M. Sat., 4–9 P.M. Sun., $21–37). It opened downtown in Rivergate Tower, only in name similar to a historic restaurant Malio Iavarone ran on Dale Mabry. It has prime steaks served in a soaring-ceilinged dining room with banks of riverside windows. In a similar vein, **Council Oak** (5223 North Orient Rd., 813/627-7628, 5–10 P.M. Sun.–Thurs., until midnight Fri. and Sat., $24–40) opened with much fanfare as part of the Seminole Hard Rock Hotel & Casino. Smack in the center of the gaming excitement, it mainly serves seafood and steaks, all well prepared and offered by an extremely knowledgeable wait staff.

Some of the old guard are fairly far-flung: **The Palm** (205 Westshore Plaza, 813/849-7256, 11:30 A.M.–10 P.M. Mon.–Fri., 5–11 P.M. Sat., 4–9 P.M. Sun., $21–37), one of 25 in the chain, features prime Angus steaks and caricatures of Tampa Bay–area politicians and personalities on the wall. **Shula's** (InterContinental Tampa, 4860 W. Kennedy Blvd., 813/286-

4366, 11:30 A.M.–2 P.M. Mon.–Fri., 5:30–10 P.M. Mon.–Thurs., until 10:30 P.M. Fri. and Sat., until 9:30 P.M. Sun., $22–38), not surprisingly given coach Don Shula's hand in it, features decor that is all in tribute to the Miami Dolphins. It's the most elegant and enjoyable experience with football you are ever likely to have. They begin the meal with the menu hand painted onto a Miami Dolphins football. It was a fun, novel, and clever beginning to dinner that sparked conversation immediately. Everything at Shula's is large. The steaks are some of the most well seasoned and prepared steaks I've ever had, and they're huge. You can even get a 48-ounce porterhouse. The slabs of butter are large. The salads are wonderfully oversized. Servers bring out all the available cuts on a tray and let you select which one you want. The wait staff is exceptional, and Shula's serves exemplary mixed drinks—well, at least a great gin Collins. **Charley's Steakhouse** (4444 W. Cypress St., 813/353-9706, 5–9:45 P.M. Sun.–Thurs., until 10:45 P.M. Fri. and Sat., $30–44) has more fat, grilled steaks, and California wines. Some of the selections include five-pepper encrusted filet mignon with pesto, roast garlic mashed potatoes and oak-grilled vegetables, or shrimp and scallop scampi with a side of grilled asparagus and a baked potato.

# Information and Services

Tampa is located within the **Eastern time zone.** All telephone listings are within the **813 area code** unless otherwise indicated. If you're trying to call the other side of the bay (Clearwater, Dunedin, St. Petersburg), the area code is **727,** but you don't need to dial a 1 before it.

## TOURIST INFORMATION

Tampa Bay and Company's **Visitor Information Center** is in the waterfront Channelside entertainment complex (615 Channelside Dr., Ste. 108A, 813/223-1111,

www.visittampabay.com, 9:30 A.M.–5:30 P.M. Mon.–Sat., 11 A.M.–5 P.M. Sun.) at the Port of Tampa. It provides lots of brochures and information on attractions, events, and accommodations.

Tampa's daily newspaper is the **Tampa Tribune** (813/259-7711), with kiosks most places. The **St. Petersburg Times** (727/893-8111, www.tampabay.com) also covers the greater Tampa Bay area. **Creative Loafing** (813/739-4800, www.creativeloafing.com), the city's free alternative weekly, has great entertainment schedules, restaurant reviews, and a view into local politics. For quick and easy info on events, attractions, and restaurants, visit www.tampabay.citysearch.com. There are also numerous magazines: *Tampa Bay Magazine* covers the city of Tampa, *New Tampa Style* only covers the northern suburbs of the city, and there are many glossy freebies in Hyde Park.

## POLICE AND EMERGENCIES

In any emergency, dial 911 for immediate assistance. If you need police assistance in a nonemergency, visit or call the **Tampa Police Department** (411 N. Franklin St., 813/231-6130). The police department operates three districts that serve the greater Tampa Bay area—they will assign your problem to the proper district. Tampa has several hospitals equipped with emergency rooms: If you have a medical emergency in the Hyde Park area, go to **Memorial Hospital of Tampa** (2901 Swann Ave., 813/873-6400). In Carrollwood, visit the **University Community Hospital Carrollwood** (7171 N. Dale Mabry Hwy., 813/558-8068). In the Westshore area, go to **University Community Hospital** (2223 N. West Shore Blvd., 813/971-6000). In the downtown area, make your way to **Tampa**

**General Hospital** (2 Columbia Dr., 813/844-7000) near the causeway to Davis Island.

## RADIO AND TELEVISION

Of the local radio stations, my favorite is **WMNF 88.5 FM,** which has a huge following for its independent and eclectic programming—tune in and you'll hear salsa, or maybe Hawaiian slack-key guitar, or maybe a little alt-country. It has a snuggly relationship with Skipper's Smokehouse, and together they sponsor many of the city's best concerts. For a nonthreatening mix of light rock, turn to **WMTX 100.7 FM, 107.3 FM The Eagle** is hits of the 1970s, and for sports talk turn to **WDAE 1250 AM.**

On the television, if you're looking for the FOX affiliate, turn to **Channel 13,** for NBC turn to **WFLA Channel 8,** for ABC turn to **WFTS Channel 28,** and for CBS turn to **WTSP Channel 10.**

## LAUNDRY SERVICES

If you find yourself in need of coin-op laundry, head to **B & W Coin Laundry** (4810 E. Busch Blvd., 813/987-9847) or **Tampa Coin Laundry** (1613 E. Dr. Martin Luther King, 813/248-5588). Most big hotel chains offer laundry services.

# Getting There and Around

## BY CAR

Both I-75 and I-275 travel north–south, but I-75 skirts the edge of Tampa while I-275 travels through the city and over the bay. Both connect to I-4, which travels east–west, connecting Tampa Bay to Orlando and the east coast of Florida.

Once in town, from north to south, Bearss, Fletcher, Fowler, and Busch Boulevards are the big east–west roads. Dale Mabry and Bruce B. Downs are the biggest north–south roads. This all sounds fairly simple, but once you get downtown in Tampa you really need a map to find your way out. There are lots of one-way streets, and the highway on-ramps are a

bit difficult to find. The Busch Gardens area and USF lie between I-75 and I-275 northeast of downtown. The airport is just southwest of downtown.

## BY AIR

**Tampa International Airport** (5503 W. Spruce St., 813/870-8700) is perhaps the best midsize airport in the country—clean, easily traversed, with good signage and efficient staff. With one of the best on-time records around, it's Florida's third-busiest airport, located just seven miles southwest of downtown Tampa. It's serviced by Air Canada, AirTran Airlines, American Airlines, British Airways, Cayman

Airways, Continental Airlines, Delta Airlines, Freedom, Frontier Airlines, JetBlue, KLM, Midwest, Northwest Airlines, Southwest Airlines, Spirit Airlines, Ted, United Airlines, US Airways, and WestJet.

Located on the airport premises, **Avis** (800/831-2847), **Budget** (800/527-0700), **Dollar** (800/800-4000 domestic, 800/800-6000 international), **Enterprise** (800/736-8222), **Hertz** (800/654-3131), and **Thrifty** (800/847-4389) provide rental car service. Tampa has unbelievably good deals on rental cars from the airport—celebrate by upgrading to something stylin'.

## BY BUS AND TRAIN

Taxi service from the airport to downtown is about $18. Tampa is a call destination, not a flag destination. Most hotels offer shuttle service to the airport and major attractions.

**Amtrak** (800/872-7245) and **Greyhound** (800/231-2222) both service Tampa, with stations downtown. Amtrak operates out of historic Tampa Union Station, offering north–south connections as well as links to nationwide rail travel.

Within the city, **Hillsborough Area Regional Transit Authority** (813/623-5835, www.hartline.org, $4 unlimited ride all day) provides intercity bus service, with 207 buses on 26 routes, nine trolleys, and eight electric streetcars. The In Town Trolley runs north and south through downtown and connects to the TECO Line Streetcar System, which runs from downtown to the Channel District/Port and Ybor City. Still, Tampa is so spread out that it's not a city in which to be without a car.

# PINELLAS COUNTY

In some ways, Henry Ford's affordable $400 Model T foreshadowed the real estate boom in St. Petersburg in the early 1920s. It was the beginning of road-tripping, folks hopping in the car in search of sun, sand, and a little fun. They found the peninsula that hangs down Florida's west side like a thumb, the east side of it nestled against the placid Old Tampa Bay, its west side flanked by sandy beaches and the Gulf of Mexico. People liked what they saw. They bought up land, building big resort hotels, affordable motels, and homes.

Before the hordes of sun worshippers came, what is now Pinellas County had a diverse set of visitors-turned-residents. As was so common along the Gulf Coast, the original pre-Columbian Native American settlers were killed and run off upon the arrival of Hernando de

Soto and other Spanish conquistadores in the 1500s. Long after that, there came an intrepid Frenchman, Odet Philippe, who established a large orange grove near Safety Harbor in 1842; just after that came the Scottish merchants who settled Dunedin, the Russian immigrants who worked the Orange Belt Railroad and named St. Petersburg after their Russian hometown, and finally the Greeks, who came to harvest the area's rich sponge beds around 1900.

Today, **St. Petersburg** is Florida's fourth-largest city, the anchor of Pinellas County. Combined with neighboring Tampa, it's the largest market in the state. It's had another boom period in recent years, an influx of high-tech businesses drawing younger families and driving down the median age (the area until the 1990s was more of a retirement

# HIGHLIGHTS

**Fort De Soto Park:** More than just the site of a fort built to protect Tampa during the Spanish American War, the park features over seven miles and 1,136 acres of pristine coastal environment to explore (page 179).

**Honeymoon Island and Caladesi Island Beaches:** There are some wonderful choices for sun and sand, so why settle for just one when you can opt for the double whammy of Honeymoon and Caladesi, a pair of white-sand barrier islands flanking Dunedin north of Clearwater? Caladesi is accessible only by ferry from Honeymoon Island (page 180).

**Sunken Gardens:** It puttered along as a kitschy Old Florida attraction for years, until the city of St. Petersburg restored the four-acre tropical gardens to their former glory (page 181).

**Sunshine Skyway Fishing Piers:** Another local bridge has been repurposed. Sunshine Skyway Fishing Piers is the world's longest fishing pier, with a tremendous concentration of sportfish lurking in the deep waters below. You can rent fishing gear on the pier (page 184).

**Salvador Dalí Museum:** The famous Spanish surrealist is honored in a sleek museum of his work and the work of those inspired by him (page 188).

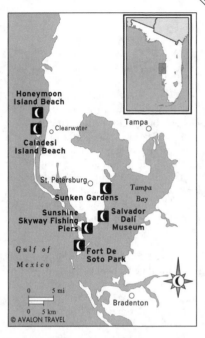

LOOK FOR ◖ TO FIND RECOMMENDED SIGHTS, ACTIVITIES, DINING, AND LODGING.

community). The city's downtown—on the Bay, mind you, not the Gulf—has seen lots of new growth, from pricey condos to the $40 million BayWalk shopping complex.

Here's a tricky fact you must get used to around here: St. Pete Beach is not just the shortened name for St. Petersburg Beach. St. Petersburg is the big city adjacent to Old Tampa Bay, which looks out across at the big city of Tampa. **St. Pete Beach,** on the other hand, is an autonomous barrier-island town to the south and west of St. Petersburg. St. Pete Beach is really on Long Key, although you'll seldom hear that used. It stretches seven miles

from Pass-A-Grille on the south to Blind Pass on the north, before Treasure Island. Also, the city of **Clearwater** is on the mainland, but **Clearwater Beach** is on a barrier island connected by Memorial Causeway.

The Gulf beaches are 20 minutes from downtown St. Petersburg across the peninsula. More than 20 little towns dot the coastline in Pinellas County, St. Pete and Clearwater Beaches being perhaps the favorites for family vacations. Clearwater Beach offers a wide, inviting shore, serious beach volleyball, and lots of nightlife and casual seafood restaurants. The Jolley Trolley whisks visitors from their hotel

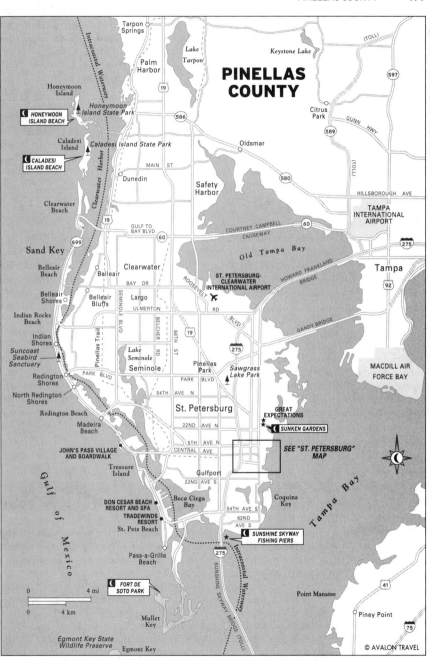

through town and right to the beachside Pier 60, something like the center of town.

Clearwater and St. Pete Beaches aren't the only strands that draw accolades—**Caladesi Island State Park,** accessible only by boat to the north of Clearwater Beach, is often rated one of the top 10 beaches in the country, as is **Honeymoon Island.**

## PLANNING YOUR TIME

Pinellas County is a peninsula, with Tampa Bay to the east and the Gulf of Mexico to the west. Its location, adjacent to Tampa, but with the benefit of long and wonderful beaches, makes it an ideal home base for a lengthy Gulf Coast stay, especially for families. Even Disney World is a fairly convenient 90 minutes to the east. The sights and attractions are more compelling on the Tampa side of the bay (Busch Gardens, lots of professional sports), and these are easily accessed by either the Howard Frankland Bridge (I-275) or the Courtney Campbell Causeway (Hwy. 60). In high-season traffic, the drive can be 45 minutes.

Where you stay depends on your priorities: The city of St. Petersburg lies on the bay side of the peninsula. It has more history, more of a sense of place and sophistication than the beach towns along the Gulf side. There are romantic bed-and-breakfasts, fine restaurants, and cultural attractions. Clearwater Beach and St. Pete Beach on the Gulf side have the densest concentrations of beachside accommodations—in Clearwater this often means tall resort hotels

and condos right on the beach; in St. Pete Beach it's low-rise motels that date back a few decades. The communities in between these two—Belleair and Belleair Beach; Indian Rocks Beach and Indian Shores; Redington Shores, North Redington Beach, and Redington Beach; Madeira Beach; and Treasure Island—are fairly residential, but with pockets of beachside hotels/motels/rentals. The whole Gulf side is really composed of a series of tiny barrier islands connected to the mainland by causeways—it may not be totally clear to you when driving, but spend a little time with the map so you know whether you're looking at boats bobbing on the Intracoastal Waterway, Boca Ciega Bay, Clearwater Harbor, or the Gulf.

The peak season typically runs November–May. It's a little more spread out than elsewhere among the Gulf Coast's beach spots, partly because American families on spring break come in March and April, and lots of European travelers fill in the time around that. In the summer the waters here are so warm as to be slightly offputting. September and October are great times to visit. In October, added enticements include the beloved annual **Clearwater Jazz Holiday** (727/461-5200, www.clearwaterjazz.com) during the third week of the month, with four days of free world-class jazz in Coachman Park. There's also the local **Stone Crab Festival** during that same time. In June, on the other hand, the **Taste of Pinellas** (www.allkids.org) is a big bash catered by all the best local restaurants.

# Sports and Recreation

## BEACHES

The beaches of Clearwater and St. Pete are textbook stretches of white sand and clear, warm Gulf water, with lots of comfy beachside hotels and waterside amenities for families. The area is home to a couple of world-class beach destinations, the kinds of places that often make Dr. Stephen Leatherman's (Dr. Beach has been ranking America's beaches for 12 years) annual top 10 list.

First, a fairly urban city beach, **Clearwater Beach** (west on Hwy. 60), the only Pinellas County beach with year-round lifeguards (9:30 A.M.–4:30 P.M. daily) is a long, wide stretch offering showers, restrooms, concessions, cabanas, umbrella rentals, volleyball, and metered parking. **Pier 60,** where the beach meets the causeway, is the locus of lots of local revelry and activity—during the day it's a heavily trafficked fishing pier, while at

© GRASSA VICTORIA/123RF.COM

relaxing under umbrellas and canopies on Clearwater Beach

night the focus is **Sunsets at Pier 60,** a festival that runs nightly two hours before sunset to two hours past sunset, with crafts, magicians, and musicians all vying with the showy sunset display over the Gulf of Mexico for your attention. Pier 60 contains a covered playground for the little ones, who will also like catching the bright red Jolley Trolley ($1.25 to ride) from Clearwater Beach and heading back to your hotel, downtown, or to Sand Key.

Clearwater Beach has a few rules to follow: No alcohol on the beach. Swim within the "safe bathing limit" area, extending 300 feet west of the high water line and clearly marked by buoys or pilings. Personal watercraft and boats are not allowed within this line.

Clearwater Beach is just the warm-up, just to get your feet wet, so to speak. The area's other best beaches require more of a commitment and are more of a full-day adventure.

## Fort De Soto Park

South of St. Petersburg, Fort De Soto Park (3500 Pinellas Bayway S., Tierra Verde, 727/893-9185, www.fortdesoto.com, open daylight hours, free) is 1,136 unspoiled acres with seven miles of beaches, two fishing piers, picnic and camping areas, a small history museum, and a 2,000-foot barrier-free nature trail for guests with disabilities, set on five little, interconnected islands. The fort itself is in the southwest corner of Mullet Key, and there's a toll ($0.85) on the bridges leading into the park. The islands were once inhabited by the Tocobaga and visited by Spanish explorers. It was surveyed by Robert E. Lee before the Civil War, and during the war Union troops had a detachment on both Egmont and Mullet Keys. The fort was built in 1898 to protect Tampa Bay during the Spanish-American War and is listed on the National Register of Historic Places. And during World War II, the island was used for bombing practice by the pilot who dropped the bomb on Hiroshima. But you thought we were talking about beaches, right?

Well, exploring the old fort is part of what makes this experience special, drawing more than 2.7 million visitors annually.

After checking out the four 12-inch seacoast rifled mortars (the only ones of their kind in the United States), head on to one of the two swim centers, the better of which is the North Beach Swim Center (it has concessions). At the beach, you're likely to see laughing gulls, ibis, and ospreys, as well as beach sunflowers and beach morning glories peeking out from the sea oats. Fishing enthusiasts can choose between the 500-foot-long pier on the Tampa Bay side or the 1,000-foot-long pier on the Gulf side. Each has a food and bait concession.

Once in the park, take a right at the stop sign, go one mile, and on the right look for **Topwater Kayak** (3500 Pinellas Bayway S., Tierra Verde, 727/864-1991, 9 A.M.–5 P.M. daily, last rental at 3:30 P.M.). It rents canoes and kayaks and issues maps of the area. Single kayaks rent for $23 for one hour, $29 for two hours; canoes cost $30 for one hour, $40 for two hours. Bike rentals are available inside the park at $6 an hour or $20 a day (cash only). Numbered signs along the shore mark a 2.25-mile kayak trail through Mullet Key Bayou.

Fort De Soto Park has the best camping in the area, with campsites directly on the Gulf. Camping is $33 per night (RV spots $40), but here's the rub for visitors. Most of the 235 campsites require reservations, which must be made *in person* far in advance. I figure it's a way to give locals the benefit of first dibs. There are a handful of walk-in campsites available, but they are hot commodities. All sites have water and electrical hookups, and there are modern restrooms, dump stations, a camp store, washers/dryers, and grills. Pets are allowed in Area 2, and some of the spots are directly on the water. Be advised, the resident raccoons are more skillful than most, able to pick cooler locks and unwrap lunch meat with ease.

## Honeymoon Island and Caladesi Island Beaches

Honeymoon Island and Caladesi Island are a double whammy, perfectly suited to visiting back-to-back. In fact, the two islands were once part of a single larger barrier island, split in half during a savage hurricane in 1921. Together,

they offer nearly 1,000 acres of mostly undeveloped land, not too changed from how it looked when Spanish explorers surveyed the coast in the mid-1500s.

The Tocobaga were the first known residents of Honeymoon Island, with ventures in more recent centuries having been quashed by deadly hurricanes. First known as Sand Island, then more inelegantly as Hog Island, it got its current name in the 1940s when marketing people tried to pitch it as a retreat for newlyweds, with little palm-thatched bungalows and cottages. It didn't quite take, foiled also by World War II, and the island went through several changes of hands before becoming a state park.

After a huge beach renourishment project in 2007, Honeymoon Island (1 Causeway Blvd., at the extreme west end of Hwy. 586, Dunedin, 727/469-5942, 8 A.M.–sunset daily, admission $8 for up to eight people per car, single driver $4, pedestrians and bicyclists $2) offers visitors all kinds of fun activities, but especially good is the fishing—you're likely to catch flounder, snook, trout, redfish, snapper, whiting, sheepshead, and, occasionally, tarpon. The island is home to 208 species of plants and a wealth of shore and wading birds, including a few endangered bird species. There is also a popular pet beach worth visiting for those traveling with their pets.

Caladesi, directly to the south of Honeymoon, is accessible only by boat (hourly ferry service available from Honeymoon, 727/469-5918, 8 A.M.–sunset daily, $12 adults, $6 children) and is the wilder of the two islands. There's the state park marina and swim beach right near where the ferry lets you off, but the rest of the island remains undeveloped. The Gulf side of the island has three miles of white-sand beach (this is the part that always makes the top rankings of beaches), and the Tampa Bay side has a mangrove shoreline and seagrass flats. So, Gulf side for swimming and beach lolling, the bay side for birding and wildlife-watching.

If you're a strong kayaker or sailor, you might take advantage of the kayak and sailboat rentals on the causeway near Honeymoon Island. Once on Caladesi, there's a 3.5-mile canoe trail starting and ending at the south end of the marina that leads paddlers through mangrove canals and tunnels and along seagrass flats on the bay side of the island.

Two cautions about Caladesi: Don't miss the last ferry or you'll be in a real pickle. And if you have brought a dog over to the dog beach at Honeymoon, it's a shame but Caladesi doesn't allow pets on the ferry (if you go by private boat, pets are invited on leash).

### Other Beaches

**St. Pete Beach** has a lot of low-rise pastel motels and its fair share of high-rise hotel towers. For some reason you'll run into a lot of European travelers here; it has a livelier vibe than many Gulf Coast beaches, but not quite the spring break magnitude of Panama City Beach and other popular party spots. It is a popular destination for families, and the resorts and hotels in the area commonly provide great children's amenities and entertainment to keep them occupied and having a good time.

The beach itself is long and wide, mostly as a result of sand restoration projects, with plenty of room to spread out and find a private patch of sand on the gulf. There are concessions, picnic tables, lots of parking, showers, and restrooms. In all, you'll have a very nice day at the beach.

There are a bunch of good beaches along **Sand Key,** which contains eight communities between John's Pass and Clearwater Pass. **John's Pass Beach** at the southern end of Sand Key and north for a couple of miles in **Madeira Beach** is beautiful sand and good fishing. Going north, the beaches in **Redington Beach** have limited public access but are pretty. Still farther north, **Indian Rocks Beach** has good public access and a party vibe, with lively beach bars. Bypass the beaches in **Belleair,** as access and amenities are very limited, in favor of an afternoon at **Sand Key County Park** (north end of Gulf Blvd. at Clearwater Pass, 727/588-4852), which has lifeguards, playgrounds, cabana rentals, and lots of wide, white-sand beach.

## GARDENS AND PARKS
### ◖ Sunken Gardens

Sunken Gardens (1825 Fourth St. N., St. Petersburg, 727/551-3102, www.stpete.org, 10 A.M.–4:30 P.M. Mon.–Sat., noon–4:30 P.M. Sun., $8 adults, $6 seniors, $4 children 2–11) was snatched from the jaws of death in 1999 and nursed back to health under the careful ministrations of the city of St. Petersburg. It was nothing a little nurturing and $3 million couldn't fix. It's a four-acre plot of land, much of it over 100 years old. There are 50,000 tropical plants and flowers, demonstration gardens, a 200-year-old oak tree, cascading waterfalls, and flamingos.

It's more than a garden—it's St. Petersburg's most beloved Old Florida attraction. In 1903, a plumber named George Turner, Sr. bought the property, which contained a large sinkhole and a shallow lake. By dint of effort and a huge maze of clay tile, he drained the lake and prepared the soil for gardening. He sold the tropical fruit he grew here at a roadside stand, but folks liked walking through the tranquil greenery so much that he started charging admission. By 1935 the garden was officially opened as Turner's Sunken Gardens (because of the former lake and sinkhole, the whole thing sits down low in a basin), attracting approximately 300,000 visitors per year. It was followed by some other attractions: the World's Largest Gift Shop and the King of Kings Wax Museum.

But, as is common for these kinds of Florida attractions, its business fell off as more upscale attractions became popular in this area among visitors. It poked along until the city felt compelled to help, also restoring the gift shop/wax museum space to its former glory (children's museum **Great Explorations** is housed here). If you're only able to visit one attraction here, make it Sunken Gardens. It is beautiful, and a definite slice of local history—a must if you can tear yourself away from the beach.

### Other Gardens and Parks

For an outdoors experience, drive up to **Brooker Creek Preserve** (1001 Lora Ln.,

Tarpon Springs, 727/453-6800, www. friendsofbrookercreekpreserve.org, trail open sunrise–sunset daily). It's an 8,500-acre wilderness in the northern section of the county near Tarpon Springs. Currently, its environmental education center offers four miles of self-guided hiking trails at the southern end of Lora Lane off of Keystone Road, about a half mile east of East Lake Road. The preserve also offers guided hikes every Saturday (reservation required, 727/453-6800) and hosts the annual **Run in the Woods** in April, the area's only walk/run that is completely cross-country through beautiful backwood pinelands and prairies.

Extending along the west side of Tampa Bay in Pinellas County, **Weedon Island Preserve Cultural and Natural History Center** (1800 Weedon Island Dr., St. Petersburg, 727/453-6500, www.weedonislandcenter.org, preserve open sunrise–sunset daily, cultural center open 10 A.M.–4 P.M. Wed.–Sun., free) is hard to classify exactly. Weedon Island Preserve is a group of low-lying islands in north St. Petersburg that as long as 10,000 years or so ago was home to Timucuans and Manasotas. The largest estuarine preserve in the county, it is also home to a large shell midden and burial mound complex. Visitors to the cultural center can see artifacts excavated from the site by the Smithsonian in the 1920s in exhibits designed collaboratively by anthropologists, historians, and Native Americans.

But you can't spend all your time at the cultural center watching videos about the art and history of the early peoples of Weedon Island—the park has a four-mile canoe trail loop, a boardwalk and observation tower, three gentle miles of hiking trails, a fishing pier (snook, redfish, spotted trout), and waterfront picnic facilities. Weedon Island Preserve Center offers guided nature hikes every Saturday and regularly scheduled guided canoe excursions (registration 727/453-6506).

Accessible only by ferry or private boat, at the mouth of Tampa Bay, **Egmont Key State Wildlife Preserve** (southwest of Fort De Soto Beach, St. Petersburg, 727/893-2627, www. floridastateparks.org, 8 A.M.–sundown daily,

free) makes a great day trip. There aren't a lot of facilities on the island, which is wild except for the ruins of historic **Fort Dade** and brick paths that remain from when it was an active community with 300 residents. You'll see the 150-year-old working lighthouse (constructed in 1858 to "withstand any storm" after a first one was ravaged by two hurricanes in 1848 and 1852), gun batteries built in 1898, a pretty stretch of beach, and lots of gopher tortoises and hummingbirds. There is no camping on Egmont Key.

Owned by the state of Florida and maintained by the Manatee County Conservation Lands Management team, **Snead Island** (941/776-2295, 8 A.M.–sundown daily, free) is just east of Egmont Key, and another good opportunity to get out into the wilderness of this area—15 miles of it bordering shoreline along the Gulf and the lovely Manatee River. The park is favored by hikers because of its variety of trails and loops, with occasional boardwalks hugging the waterways. To get there, take Hwy. 41 into Palmetto, turn right on 10th Street W., and follow signs to the island.

The west end of Snead Island is home to **Emerson Point Park** (at the end of 17th St., Palmetto, 941/776-2295, 8 A.M.–sundown daily, free), worth tacking on to your adventure—the park's 195 acres of salt marshes, beaches, mangrove swamp, lagoons, grass flats, hardwood hammocks, and semi-upland wooded areas are viewable from a well-maintained eight-foot-wide shell path, as well as more rustic walking and biking paths. Manatee County has poured money into this park in recent years such that master gardeners convene here regularly for guided walking tours of the varied plant and animal life. Call 941/722-4524 for the tour schedule.

Of special note to Native American historians, Emerson Point Park is home to the **Portavant Temple Mound** (east end of 17th St. W., Snead Island), an impressive mound complex. Walkways and boardwalks take you over and around a huge 150-foot flat-top temple mound and several horseshoe-shaped shell middens. Interpretive markers explicate the site.

**Anclote Key Preserve State Park** (1 Causeway Blvd., Dunedin, 727/469-5942, 8 A.M.–sundown daily, free) is a similar island preserve accessible by boat, only this one offers primitive camping and is pet-friendly. During nesting season, rangers ask pet owners to keep their pets on the southeast end, as protected nesting birds take up residence in the north.

## BIKING AND RUNNING

The best way to get oriented in the greater Tampa Bay area is to take a bike ride. **Northeast Cycles** (1114 Fourth St., St. Petersburg, 727/898-2453, $20/day, nice road bikes $50/day) will rent you bikes, and a rack for an additional $10 so you can load them up and take them wherever you like, as will **Chainwheel Drive**, with two locations (1770 Drew St., Clearwater, 727/441-2444; and 32796 U.S. 19 N., in Palm Lake Plaza, Palm Harbor, 727/786-3883, 10 A.M.–7 P.M. Mon.–Fri., 10 A.M.–5 P.M. Sat., $20/4 hours for hybrid, $26/4 hours for road bike).

Now that you've got the bikes, you may want to visit one of the popular bike trails, the 34-mile-long **Pinellas Trail** (ranger 727/582-2100), one of the longest linear parks in the southeastern United States, running essentially from St. Petersburg up to the sponge docks of Tarpon Springs. A rails-to-trails kind of deal, the original rail track was home to the first Orange Belt Railroad train in 1888 and is now a well-maintained, 15-foot-wide trail through parks and coastal areas for bikers, in-line skaters, and joggers. There is a free guide to the Pinellas Trail, available at the trail office, area libraries, and the Pinellas County Courthouse Information Desk (it can also be downloaded at www.pinellascounty.org—click on Location Maps under Multimedia and Maps). It lists rest stops, service stations, restaurants, pay phones, bike shops, and park areas along the trail.

## BIRDING

Every October Pinellas County hosts the annual **Florida Birding Festival & Nature Expo,** to which 3,000 avid birders flock. They come to hear a dynamic array of speakers and attend seminars, but mostly they come to tramp around on field trips to some of the region's top birding and wildlife areas. They come to look for some of the state's rarer bird species, like the reddish egret, little burrowing owls, and the Florida scrub jay, the only bird species unique to Florida.

If you're an avid birder or would like to learn more about birds, here's what you do: Go to the **Great Florida Birding Trail** website (www.floridabirdingtrail.com) and print out the *West Section* guide to the birding trail, which lists 117 sites in 21 counties. Many important birding sites are in Pinellas County.

**Brooker Creek Preserve** and **East Beach** at Fort De Soto Park are both wonderful for birding. Beyond these, **Shell Key** (shuttle and charter boat access only, located at the southern end of Pass-A-Grille channel, just west of Tierre Verde), an undeveloped 180-acre barrier island in the area, is an important place for wintering and nesting seabirds and shorebirds, with more than 100 species sighted. **Boyd Hill Nature Preserve** (1101 Country Club Way S., St. Petersburg, 727/893-7326, 10 A.M.–7 P.M. Tues.–Fri., 7 A.M.–6 P.M. Sat., 10 A.M.–6 P.M. Sun., $3 adults, $1.50 children) is 245 acres of pristine Florida wilderness, with five distinct ecosystems—hardwood hammocks, sand pine scrub, pine flatwoods, willow marsh, and the Lake Maggiore shoreline. This may be my favorite, as it is incredibly convenient, just minutes from downtown, but nonetheless feels far from the madding crowds. Precious green space in an urban landscape, it is an important stopover on the Atlantic Flyway—165 bird species have been observed here. You can camp at Boyd, and there's a small educational center with exhibits on the five ecosystems.

Another spot on the Great Florida Birding Trail, also lauded by the National Audubon Society, is **Sawgrass Lake Park** (7400 25th St. N., immediately west of I-275 in Pinellas Park, St. Petersburg, 727/217-7256, environmental center 727/526-3020, 7 A.M.–sunset daily, free). Thousands of birds migrate through the park during the fall and spring. A one-mile elevated boardwalk winds through a maple swamp and oak hammock. There's an observation tower with views of the park's swamps, canals, and lake, where you're likely to see wood storks, herons, egrets, and ibis in addition to gators and turtles. The park has naturalist-led nature tours and field trips, and its Anderson Environmental Center contains a large freshwater aquarium and exhibits on the area. My only caution is that during the wet months it can get a bit flooded in this park.

If you find an injured bird in your wandering, call **Suncoast Seabird Sanctuary** (18328 Gulf Blvd., Indian Shores, 727/391-6211), one of the country's largest nonprofit wild bird hospitals. With a new hospital facility, the sanctuary rescues and releases hundreds of birds each year into the wild. The sanctuary also offers a free tour at 2 P.M. Wednesday and Sunday, meeting at the beachfront deck.

## FISHING
◖ **Sunshine Skyway Fishing Piers**

It must have been a sight to see. In 1990, Hardaway Constructors of Tampa and a demolition team from Baltimore joined forces to perform the largest bridge demolition in Florida history. They were doing away with the 1954 Sunshine Skyway Bridge, a 15-mile crossing from St. Petersburg to Bradenton. From a long causeway on both sides, the steel bridge had a steep cantilever truss, 750 feet wide and with 150 feet of clearance above the water.

It wasn't enough clearance.

There had been some indication that this could happen—at least five freighters or barges were roughed up by this bridge, most of them with minor damage (the Coast Guard cutter *USS Blackthorn* met with disaster, but it was just west of the bridge and was weather-related).

But it was during a violent storm on May 9, 1980, at 7:38 A.M., when Captain John Lerro's visibility was nil, that the empty phosphate freighter *Summit Venture* slammed into the No. 2 south pier of the southbound span. It

## SMOKIN'

Here's a tricky scenario. You're on a great Gulf Coast vacation, the weather's perfect, you're feeling relaxed, so you decide to do a little charter fishing. You're out on the boat, you feel a yank, and there's a 40-pound greater amberjack on your line. You work a while and haul in a couple more of those and a whole mess of 20-inch Spanish mackerel. What a great day. My question: Now what? Are you going to take that fish cooler back to the Radisson and stink up the joint?

Here's what to do: You go to **Ted Peters Famous Smoked Fish** (1350 Pasadena Ave., South Pasadena, 727/381-7931, 11:30 A.M.-7:30 P.M. Wed.-Mon., $10-20, no credit cards) and they'll smoke them for you for $1.50/pound. They can even make kingfish taste good, and that's saying something. They fillet them, throw them over a smoldering red oak fire in the smokehouse, then package them up for you to take. (The smoked fish keeps for 4-5 days in the fridge.)

And if you don't have fish to smoke, still go to Ted Peters. It's been an institution for more than 50 years in Pinellas County, prized for its laid-back style and inviting picnic tables. The main attraction is obviously the smoked fish – the smoked fish spread with saltines is good, and the salmon and mullet are excellent. However, Ted Peters also produces some legendary cheeseburgers and potato salad (no fries here). This beer-drinking establishment gets very busy in high season and closes early.

knocked 1,261 feet out of the center span, the cantilever, and part of the roadway into Tampa Bay. Thirty-five people on the bridge at the time perished, most of them in a Greyhound bus headed for Miami. The only survivor had his truck land by chance on the deck of the *Summit Venture*.

One of the worst bridge disasters in history, it prompted the design, funding, and building of a new Sunshine Skyway Bridge. At a cost of $245 million, it's the world's longest cable-stayed bridge, with a main span of 1,200 feet and a vertical clearance of 193 feet. The four-mile bridge opened for business in April 1987, equipped with a bridge protection system involving 36 large concrete bumpers (oddly called dolphins) built to withstand impact from rogue freighters and tankers up to 87,000 tons traveling at 10 knots.

So, you probably think I'm leading up to saying, "It's a gorgeous bridge, a real local landmark, you gotta drive over this thing." It's all true, but it's only a part of the story. During the demolition of the old bridge spans, portions of it were preserved as fishing piers and the rubble piled alongside to form fish-friendly artificial reefs.

Since the original bridge span was built, fisherfolk have been bragging about the variety of game they catch: shark, tarpon, goliath grouper, kingfish, Spanish mackerel, grouper, sea bass. It's strange, because usually you have to be in a boat in order to have water deep enough for many of these species. Anglers have caught 1,000-pound tiger sharks from the bridge, traffic honking behind them. And now, with the artificial reefs adding extra enticement to the fish, the Sunshine Skyway Fishing Piers are killer fishing spots.

There's a 0.75-mile-long North Pier and a 1.5-mile-long South Pier—together said to be the world's longest fishing pier. You can drive your car onto the pier and park it right next to your fishing spot, parallel parking on the left lane, with room for cars to drive and walkways on either side of the span. There are restrooms on both piers, and bait shops sell live and frozen bait, tackle, drinks, and snacks. They also rent rods. The North Pier has a large picnic area next to the bait shop.

To get there, head south on I-275 toward Bradenton. The North Pier (727/865-0668) is about a mile past the toll ($1). To reach the South Pier (941/729-0117), continue over the bridge and follow the signs. There is a $3 per vehicle charge, plus $2 general admission, $1.50 seniors, $1 children 6–11, children under 6 free. *You don't need a fishing license to fish off the piers.*

So, yeah, drive over the new bridge—its bright yellow paint freshened in 2007—but, more importantly, wet a line on the remnants of the old one.

## SPECTATOR SPORTS
### Baseball

**Tropicana Field** (1 Tropicana Dr., St. Petersburg, 727/588-4852, game days vary, times usually 2:15 or 7:15 P.M., tickets $5–32) is currently home to the Tampa Bay Rays (formerly the Devil Rays). The Rays played their first season here in 1998, and since then it has been named the second most fan-friendly stadium in the major leagues, according to a fan survey by Sports Travel Inc. On the other hand, loads of people complain about it: As a concession to summer temperatures and humidity in these parts, the ballpark has a dome roof (which is lit orange when the Rays win at home) and artificial turf. Out of season, Tropicana Field hosts other athletic events, conventions, trade shows, concerts, and other entertainment, with a seating capacity of 43,773.

**Between spring training and the Tampa Bay Rays taking the field at Tropicana Field, there is definitely not a shortage of baseball excitement in this area.**

For spring training, the Rays until 2008 played locally at **Progress Energy Park, Home of Al Lang Field.** Now, the Rays relocate each spring to the Charlotte County Sports park, a grass-surface park with a 7,000-person seating capacity located a couple of hours south in Port Charlotte. Don't fret, though, because there's other spring training action nearby. Spring training games are all month in March, and tickets usually go on sale January 15. The **Philadelphia Phillies** have been training at Bright House Networks Field (601 Old Coachman Rd., Clearwater, 727/442-8496, game days vary, times usually 1:05 or 7:05 P.M.,

tickets $15–32) in Clearwater since 1948. It's a great venue, with a tiki-hut pavilion in left field, a kids' play area, group picnic areas, party suites, and club seats. The **Toronto Blue Jays** also have spring training in the area, playing at Knology Park, formerly Dunedin Stadium (311 Douglas Ave., Dunedin, 727/733-0429, game days vary, times usually 1:05 P.M., tickets $13–24). Built in 1990, it's a smaller ballpark in a fairly residential area (you end up paying almost as much for parking as for your ticket). There are upper and lower sections, the upper section having a slight overhang, which can be cooling during warm day games.

# Sights

## ART MUSEUMS

The arts are booming in St. Petersburg, especially those visual. The recently opened **Chihuly Collection at the Arts Center** is a beautiful showcase for the Seattle glassblower's eccentric work. **The Arts Center** (719 Central Ave., 727/822-7872, 9 A.M.–5 P.M. Tues.–Sat., free admission) has a ton going on in its 5,000 square feet of gallery space, divided up into six small galleries, plus classroom space for ceramics, painting, drawing, digital imaging, photography, printmaking, jewelry making, metalworking, and sculpture classes.

In 2008, the **Museum of Fine Arts** (255 Beach Dr. NE, St. Petersburg, 727/896-2667, www.fine-arts.org, 10 A.M.–5 P.M. Tues.–Sat., 1–5 P.M. Sun., $16 adults, $14 seniors and students, $10 children 7–18, children 6 and under free) unveiled its much-anticipated Hazel Hough Wing. It started with a gangbuster exhibition of works that have been rarely on view or in some cases, never before displayed at the MFA. Featuring works by such noted artists as Renoir, Leger, Pissarro, Matisse, Faberge, Chuck Close, and James Rosenquist, it showcased just how marvelous the museum's collection is. Right on the waterfront adjacent to Straub Park, the museum contains the full gamut of art from antiquity to the present day. The collection of 4,000

objects includes significant works by Cézanne, Monet, Gauguin, Renoir, Rodin, Henri, Bellows, and O'Keeffe. Its permanent collection's strength is 17th- and 18th-century European art, and the museum has a lovely garden as well.

If you have the stamina for more art, a couple of small community venues are located around Pinellas County. The **Gulf Coast Museum of Art** (12211 Walsingham Rd., Largo, 727/518-6833, www.gulfcoastmuseum. org, 10 A.M.–4 P.M. Tues.–Sat., noon–4 P.M. Sun., $8 adults, $7 seniors, $4 students, free for children under 12) is in the Pinewood Cultural Park and features contemporary art by Floridian artists from 1960 on. The center also offers classes and workshops for children and adults in ceramics, metalworking, painting, sculpture, photography, and drawing.

**Beach Art Center** (1515 Bay Palm Blvd., Indian Rocks Beach, 727/596-4331, 9 A.M.–4 P.M. Mon.–Thurs., 9 A.M.–noon Fri.) is another sweet nonprofit arts center with classes for locals in fine arts and crafts. It also has two small galleries set up in the old American Legion Hall. In a similar vein, the **Dunedin Fine Arts Center & Children's Art Museum** (1143 Michigan Blvd., Dunedin, 727/298-3322, www.dfac.org, 10 A.M.–5 P.M. Mon.–Fri., 10 A.M.–2 P.M. Sat., 1–4 P.M. Sun.)

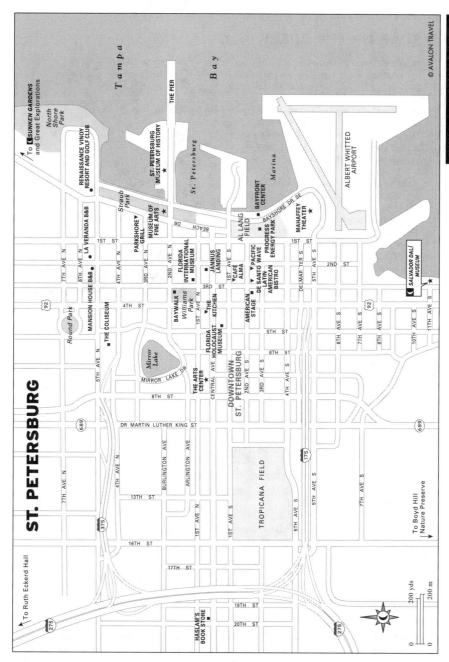

© AVALON TRAVEL

# ST. PETERSBURG

**To Ruth Eckerd Hall**

**To** SUNKEN GARDENS **and Great Explorations**

North Shore Park

*Tampa Bay*

RENAISSANCE VINOY RESORT AND GOLF CLUB

THE PIER

ST. PETERSBURG MUSEUM OF HISTORY

*St. Petersburg*

Straub Park

PARKSHORE GRILL

LA VERANDA B&B

MUSEUM OF FINE ARTS

MANSION HOUSE B&B

THE COLISEUM

Round Park

Marina

BAYFRONT CENTER

ALBERT WHITTED AIRPORT

AL LANG FIELD

MAHAFFEY THEATER

PROGRESS ENERGY PARK

FLORIDA INTERNATIONAL MUSEUM

JANNUS LANDING

CAFÉ ALMA

PACIFIC WAVE

DE SANTO

BAYWALK

Williams Park

THE KITCHEN

AMERICAN STAGE

LATIN AMERICAN BISTRO

SALVADOR DALÍ MUSEUM

FLORIDA HOLOCAUST MUSEUM

THE ARTS CENTER

DOWNTOWN ST. PETERSBURG

Mirror Lake

MIRROR LAKE DR

DR MARTIN LUTHER KING ST

BURLINGTON AVE

ARLINGTON AVE

TROPICANA FIELD

To Boyd Hill Nature Preserve

HASLAM'S BOOK STORE

BEACH DR

BAYSHORE DR SE

CENTRAL AVE

**To Boyd Hill Nature Preserve**

200 yds

200 m

# SOAK UP THE GREEK

**Tarpon Springs,** a coastal town 15 miles due north of Clearwater, has quite the past. John Corcoris, a sponge diver from Greece, brought his capabilities along with his sponge-diving equipment (a rubber suit and a heavy copper helmet to which air was pumped via hose) to Tarpon Springs around 1900. Soon, he persuaded friends and family, sponge divers all, to relocate from Hydra and Aegena, Greece, to this little Florida backwater.

Soon a booming town of Greek restaurants, Greek Orthodox churches, and Greek festivals was born, centering on the sponge industry. Tarpon Springs was the largest U.S. sponge-diving port in the 1930s, but a sponge blight and new synthetic sponge technology caused business to dry up.

The town is still more than a third Greek, with a nice "Old Florida" touristy charm and several fine restaurants. Sponges are everywhere, most of them imported from more sponge-rich far-flung lands.

Take an afternoon to see the museum **Spongeorama** (510 Dodecanese Blvd., 727/943-2164, 10:30 A.M.–6 P.M. Mon.-Sat., 11:30 A.M.–6 P.M. Sun., free), and the sponge docks, shop a little, and have dinner.

Out on the main drag, Dodecanese Boulevard, there are seven blocks of shops and

COURTESY OF VISIT FLORIDA

In the 1930s the sponge industry was prosperous, bringing in millions of dollars annually.

restaurants. Before you settle on a place to eat, stop into nearby **St. Nicholas Church** (18 Hibiscus St., 727/937-3540), made of 60 tons of Greek marble once on display at the Greek exhibit at the first New York World's Fair. The

---

has four galleries, studio classrooms, a children's museum, the Palm Cafe, and gallery gift shop. The exhibits are often the work of students.

## ◖ Salvador Dalí Museum

Perhaps the most popular art museum in Pinellas County is the Salvador Dalí Museum (1000 Third St. S., St. Petersburg, 727/823-3767, www.salvadordalimuseum.org, 10 A.M.–5:30 P.M. Mon.–Wed. and Fri.–Sat., until 8 P.M. Thurs., noon–5:30 P.M. Sun., $17 general, $14.50 seniors, $12 students, $4 children 5–9, children 4 and under free), the world's most comprehensive collection of permanent works by the famous Spanish surrealist master, with other exhibits relating to Dalí.

He himself is as recognizable as his "paranoiac-critical" paintings. Maybe only Van Gogh in his post-ear-incident self-portrait is more reliably identified than Salvador Dalí, with his long, waxed mustache and extreme arched eyebrows. Upon moving to the United States in the 1940s, Dalí made himself the lovable eccentric who introduced the average American to surrealism and the average American really liked it.

The Salvador Dalí Museum is a dense concentration of his surrealist works, what he described as a "spontaneous method of irrational knowledge based on the critical and systematic objectivation of delirious associations and interpretations."

The museum is wonderful—a great space

church is a copy of the Byzantine Revival St. Sophia in Constantinople, with beautiful Czech chandeliers and stained glass. If you happen to be here in January, time a visit for Epiphany on the 6th – this church is the center of the biggest Epiphany celebration in the country. Festivities move from the church to nearby Spring Bayou, where young Greek men dive for a cross that has been blessed and thrown into the water.

If the weather's nice, you may want to stroll along one of the well-maintained paths in nearby **Anclote River Park** (1119 Baileys Bluff Rd., Holiday, 727/938-2598, open dawn-dusk daily, free admission). The park boasts an easy two-mile roundtrip trail, as well as fishing access, a boat ramp, playground for the kids, a swimming beach, and picnic facilities. It's also a notable destination for birders – favored for its resident reddish egrets, black-bellied plovers, and osprey nests. Actually, it's part of a cluster of parks on the Great Florida Birding Trail, along with the nearby **Key Vista Nature Park** (2700 Baileys Bluff Rd., Holiday, 727/938-2598, open dawn-dusk daily, free admission), which has even more diverse natural habitats, from fresh- and saltwater marshes to pine uplands and tidal flats, all the better for observing species like loons, buffleheads, eagles, and migratory warblers.

So now you're hungry. Everyone has a different favorite Greek restaurant here. A favorite is **Hellas** (785 Dodecanese Blvd., 727/943-2400, 11 A.M.-10 P.M. daily, $10-20), a lively spot with a full bar and a wonderful Greek bakery attached to it. The best entrée is slowly braised tomatoey lamb shanks, served somewhat mysteriously atop spaghetti. There are addictive garlic shrimp, nice gyros in warm Greek pita, and a delicious Greek salad that comes with a scoop of potato salad hidden in its midst. Others swear by **Mykonos** (628 Dodecanese Blvd., 727/934-4306, 11 A.M.-10 P.M. daily, $10-20) for the lamb chops, Greek meat loaf, and slightly more upscale atmosphere. Still, **Mama's** (735 Dodecanese Blvd., 727/944-2888, 11 A.M.-10 P.M. daily, $7-14) often gets the nod for casual, family-friendly booths and delicious but messy chicken souvlaki sandwiches. If you're visiting on a Saturday night, head over after dinner to the bouzouki club called **Zorba** (508 W. Athens, 727/934-8803), for some zesty belly-dancing and an ouzo.

For more information about Tarpon Springs, contact the **Tarpon Springs Cultural Center** (727/942-5605) or the **chamber of commerce** (11 E. Orange St., 727/937-6109, www.tarponsprings.com).

where the work is described and presented very well. Even if you don't care for what you have seen of his work in books and prints, it is an incredible experience to see the original works in their larger-than-life sizes. And if you have never experienced his works at all, the museum is almost sure to make you a fan.

## HISTORY MUSEUMS

The **Florida Holocaust Museum** (55 Fifth St. S., St. Petersburg, 727/820-0100, www.flholocaustmuseum.org, 10 A.M.–5 P.M. daily, $14 adults, $12 seniors, $10 college students, $8 students under 18) is the third largest of its kind in the United States. Some of the museum is devoted to the memory of millions of innocent people who suffered, struggled, and died in the Holocaust. It also showcases only loosely linked exhibits such as the work of Czech artist Charles Pachner (who lost his whole family during the war), or the mixed-media paintings, sculptures, and installations of contemporary French artist Marc Ash.

**St. Petersburg Museum of History** (335 Second Ave. NE, St. Petersburg, 727/894-1052, www.spmoh.org, 10 A.M.–4 P.M. Wed.–Sun., $9 general, $7 seniors and students, $5 children 7–17) is one of the oldest historical museums in the state, with family-friendly displays and exhibits depicting St. Petersburg's past. It was remodeled and enlarged in 2005, with a local history exhibit that contains a Native

American dugout canoe, an exact replica of the world's first scheduled commercial airliner (it flew out of St. Petersburg), and lots of other interesting exhibits.

Beyond these, the history buff can visit the restored homes and buildings of the **Heritage Village** (11909 125th St. N., Largo, 727/582-2123, www.pinellascounty.org, 10 A.M.–4 P.M. Wed.–Sat., 1–4 P.M. Sun., free admission). It's a living history museum with people in period costume, spinning, weaving, and acting out other period activities. Most of the 25 structures date back to the late 19th century. If you go to Heritage Village, make a day of it and visit the **Florida Botanical Gardens at Pinewood Cultural Park** (12175 125th St. N., Largo, 727/582-2100, 7 A.M.–7 P.M. daily, free admission to gardens), where you can take a tour through gardens led by a local master gardener. You walk 1.5 miles, it takes 1.5 hours, and you learn all about Florida gardening. The approaches can be vastly different—there's a rose garden, a beach garden, a tropical courtyard, a topiary garden, a bromeliad garden, and more. On a nice day, it's a wonderful spot.

## AQUARIUMS

Just over the bay in Tampa, the Florida Aquarium usually gets most of the visitors. **Clearwater Marine Aquarium** (249 Windward Passage, Clearwater, 727/441-1790, 9 A.M.–5 P.M. Mon.–Thurs., 9 A.M.–7 P.M. Fri.–Sat., 10 A.M.–5 P.M. Sun., $15 adults, $11 seniors, $10 children 3–12) is a smaller, more modest facility. Reopened in 2008 after some major renovations, it's a working research facility and home to rescued and recuperating marine mammals (dolphins, whales, otters, etc.). For the visitor, the thrust is education, with hourly animal care and training presentations and exhibits on animal rescue, rehabilitation, and release—and how the public can help to protect and conserve endangered marinelife. The aquarium offers on-site feeding and care programs for interested guests and operates a daily two-hour-long **Sea Life Safari** (25 Causeway Blvd., Slip #58, Clearwater Beach, 727/462-2628, $23 adults, $20 seniors,

$15 children) that takes visitors around the Clearwater estuary and Intracoastal Waterway, with commentary by a marine biologist.

Smaller, more like a really big pet store, the **Konger Tarpon Springs Aquarium** (850 Dodecanese Blvd., Tarpon Springs, 727/938-5378, www.tarponspringsaquarium.com, 10 A.M.–5 P.M. Mon.–Sat., noon–5 P.M. Sun., $7.75 adults, $5.75 children, children 3 and under free) has a 120,000-gallon main tank aquarium with more than 30 species of fish, including nurse sharks, bonnet head sharks, snook, tarpon, and protected Jewfish (also known as goliath grouper). The best time to visit is shark or alligator feeding times: alligators at 12:30 P.M. and 3:30 P.M., sharks at 11:30 A.M., 1 P.M., 2:30 P.M., and 4 P.M.

## NATIVE AMERICAN SITES

Pinellas County's rich Native American heritage is not very noticeable today—but there are a couple of sites that command quite a bit of enthusiasm among historical travelers. Called both the **Safety Harbor Mound** and the **Philippe Park Temple Mound** this platform mound is set in a beautiful county park (2525 Philippe Pkwy., Safety Harbor, 727/669-1947, 7 A.M.–sunset daily, free). The mound is located behind shelter number two and is described with interpretive markers. The large mound complex is believed to be the village of Tocobaga, for which the Tocobaga are named. It is said that in 1567 Pedro Menéndez de Avilés, the founder of St. Augustine, visited this Tocobaga village. For a little more insight, two miles south of Philippe Park is the **Safety Harbor Museum of Regional History** (329 S. Bayshore Dr., 727/726-1668, www.safetyharbormuseum.org, 10 A.M.–4 P.M. Tues.–Sat., 1–4 P.M. Sun., free), which contains artifacts from the Weedon Island, Safety Harbor, and Mississippian periods.

Seeing more Tocobaga handiwork requires only a short drive to the **Pinellas Point Temple Mound** (7 A.M.–sunset daily, free). The large flat mound, topped by a comfy bench, is all that remains of a sizeable village. To get there, head east on 62nd Avenue S. and turn south onto 20th Street, which ends at the mound.

## FAMILY-FRIENDLY ATTRACTIONS

The No. 1 kids' draw is the beach, hands down. All the beaches of Pinellas County are enormously kid-centric, with amenities, snacks, bathrooms, and all the necessities for a day of seaside bliss. When you need a break from beachcombing and sandcastle building the area has lots of other lures.

Bilgewater Bill, Mad Dog Mike, Gangplank Gary, and the other pirates will greet you with an "argh, me matey" on the deck of **Captain Memo's Original Pirate Cruise** (25 Causeway Blvd., Dock 3, Clearwater Beach, 727/446-2587, www.captainmemo. com, 10 A.M., 2 P.M., and sunset cruises daily, $39 adults, $31 seniors, $26 children), a two-hour pirate cruise on a fancy bright red pirate ship. In a similar vein, **John's Pass Village & Boardwalk** (12901 Gulf Blvd. E., just between Madeira Beach and Treasure Island, 727/423-7824, www.thepirateshipatjohnspass.com, 11 A.M., 2 P.M., and sunset daily, $33 adults, $23 for children 2–20, children under 2 free) offers a **Pirates at the Pass** cruise on a fully kitted-out pirate ship. You'll engage in water pistol battles and treasure hunts and listen to pirate stories.

John's Pass Village is home to a large commercial and charter fishing fleet, as well as art galleries, restaurants, and boutiques along a waterfront boardwalk. Families also seem to enjoy the dolphin tours out of John's Pass and into scenic Boca Ciega Bay. A couple of companies offer these—**Hubbard's Sea Adventures** (departs from John's Pass boardwalk, 727/393-1947, www.hubbardsmarina.com, 1 P.M., 3 P.M., and 5 P.M. daily, $17 adults, $8 children 11 and under) brings you face to face with the bay's abundance of wildlife.

Farther south, **Dolphin Landings** (4737 Gulf Blvd., behind the Dolphin Village Shopping Center, St. Pete Beach, 727/367-4488, www.charterboatescape.com, sailing times vary, $25–35) conducts two-hour dolphin-watch cruises and longer three- to four-hour trips to Shell Key, an undeveloped barrier island. The scheduled trips and private charters are conducted on one of 40 locally owned sailboats, pontoon boats, and deep-sea fishing yachts.

After spending time at Sunken Gardens, give the kids their due next door at **Great Explorations** (1925 Fourth St. N., St. Petersburg, 727/821-8992, www.greatexplorations.org, 10 A.M.–4:30 P.M. Mon.–Sat., noon–4:30 P.M. Sun., $9 general admission, $8 seniors, children 1 and under free). The hands-on science center has lots of slick educational exhibits on things like the hydrologic cycle or ecosystem of the estuary. Many of the exhibits are best appreciated by late elementary-aged kids (let's say kids up to about 11), but exhibits such as Gears and the Laser Harp have appeal even to little kids. If your family enjoys hands-on science museums, head over to Tampa's MOSI for a bigger dose. This makes a fun afternoon, though, especially when capped by an ice cream at Coldstone Creamery, craftily located on the premises.

The artistically inclined kid might enjoy visiting Dunedin Fine Art Center, which contains the **David L. Mason Children's Art Museum** (1143 Michigan Blvd., Dunedin, 727/298-3322, www.dfac.org, 10 A.M.–5 P.M. Mon.–Fri., 10 A.M.–2 P.M. Sat., 1–4 P.M. Sun.), a gallery space for children. This smaller part of the museum provides hands-on activities that assist families in understanding and appreciating the work of Florida artists exhibited in the galleries. Even if you spend your time in the art center and not the children's museum, the scale is such that it's not intimidating or boring for kids.

If you're looking for something a little more exciting, **Celebration Station** (24546 U.S. 19 N., Clearwater, 727/791-1799, www.celebrationstation.com, noon–9 P.M. Sun.–Thurs., noon–midnight Fri., 10 A.M.–midnight Sat., tokens $10/roll, different prices for activities) brings you go-carts, bumper boats, games, miniature golf, batting cages, laser tag, and pizza.

# Arts and Entertainment

## MUSIC

A couple of big venues host a range of performances. **Ruth Eckerd Hall** (1111 McMullen Booth Rd. N., Clearwater, 727/791-7400, www.rutheckerdhall.com, times and prices vary) is the locus for much of the area's lively arts activity. The 2,200-seat space was designed by the Frank Lloyd Wright Foundation 25 years ago and the space still looks fresh, the sound still full and lush (acoustically, it had a fairly recent overhaul). It's home to the **Florida Orchestra** (mailing address 244 Second Ave. N., #421, St. Petersburg, FL 33701, 813/892-3331, www.floridaorchestra.org), which is the top regional orchestra, performing more than 130 concerts annually here, at the Mahaffey Theater, and elsewhere. Beyond symphonic music, Ruth Eckerd hosts pop acts, visiting theater, and other performing arts. (Its educational wing, the **Marcia P. Hoffman Performing Arts Institute,** features a 182-seat Murray Studio Theatre, three studio classrooms, four private teaching studios, a dance studio and rehearsal space, and an arts resource library.)

The **Mahaffey Theater at the Progress Energy Center** (400 First St. S., St. Petersburg, 727/892-5767, www.mahaffeytheater.com, times and prices vary) changed entirely in 2004 when it was determined that its Bayfront Center Arena was no longer viable in the marketplace. The arena was demolished at the end of that year, opening up space for the current Mahaffey Theater renovation. The $20 million project more than doubled lobby size, adding guest amenities and expanding ballroom capacity and versatility. The signature component of the renovated theater is a three-story glass-curtain wall and glass-enclosed atrium that overlooks the city's beautiful downtown waterfront. A lovely theater, it hosts the Broadway Across America series, many performances of the Florida Orchestra, jazz, ballet, opera, the circus, and contemporary performers as well. The Mahaffey is directly on the waterfront, within walking distance of shopping, some of the area's finest restaurants, and many of the downtown museums.

A smaller venue for rock and contemporary acts, **Jannus Landing** (220 First Ave. N., 727/565-0550, www.jannuslandingconcerts.com, times and prices vary) is supposedly the oldest outdoor concert venue in Florida. From jam bands like Medeski, Martin, and Wood to Linkin Park to Lucinda Williams—it all sounds great from a spot in the outdoor courtyard. It's bigger than a nightclub, with bigger acts, but there's still a cool club vibe and usually a 30s-and-up crowd.

The historic **Coliseum** (535 Fourth Ave. N., 727/892-5202, parking area on the left $4, times and prices vary) was built in 1924 and purchased by the city of St. Petersburg in 1989. It has updated up the beautiful space and reopened it as a multiuse facility, hosting a range of events from a Florida Orchestra pops concerts to the Toronto All Star Big Band to an exotic bird show.

## THEATER

At the top of the dramatic arts heap in Pinellas County, **American Stage Theatre Company at the Raymond James Theatre** (163 Third St. N., St. Petersburg, 727/823-7529, www.americanstage.org, curtain usually 7:30 P.M. Tues.–Thurs., 8 P.M. Fri. and Sat., weekend matinees 3 P.M., tickets $22–35) is Tampa Bay's oldest professional theater, with a six-play season on the main stage plus children's theater, educational outreach, and the annual Shakespeare in the Park festival.

In its 32nd year in 2010, American Stage entered into a partnership with St. Petersburg College and built a brand new state-of-the-art building in the heart of downtown St. Petersburg, facing Williams Park only four blocks from the original location. The theater has expanded its audience capacity to 182 and added two large lobbies. There is free parking at the nearby Synovis Bank during performances.

The main-stage season shows breadth, reaching from August Wilson's *Gem of the Ocean*, to the classic whodunit *Sleuth*, and Shakespeare's greatest tragedy, *Hamlet*. The Family Series is a good deal, with single tickets $7. Until the new theater opens, American Stage productions are performed at the midsize, 800-seat **Palladium Theater** (253 Fifth Ave. N., St. Petersburg, 727/822-3590).

For local community theater, several companies are worth checking out, all with reasonable ticket prices. Throughout its 83 years as Florida's oldest continuously operating community theater, **St. Petersburg Little Theatre** (4025 31st St. S., St. Petersburg, 727/866-1973, www.splt.org, curtain 8 P.M. and 2 P.M. matinees, $20 musicals, $18 nonmusicals, $10 students) has presented up to six community productions per season, split fairly evenly between musicals, comedies, and dramas. It's usually crowd-pleasers like *Noises Off* or Neil Simon's *Brighton Beach Memoirs*. **Francis Wilson Playhouse** (302 Seminole St., Clearwater, 727/446-1360, www.franciswilsonplayhouse.org, curtain 8 P.M. and 2 P.M. matinees, $26 musicals, $21 nonmusicals) is another venerable community playhouse, having opened in 1930. The intimate, 182-seat theater showcases eight comedies and musicals *(Sweet Charity, Auntie Mame)* per season and a family-oriented program in December.

In the little town of Gulfport on Boca Ciega Bay, the **Catherine Hickman Theater** (5501 27th Ave. S., Gulfport, 727/552-2222) hosts Gulfport Community Players community theater productions and Pinellas Park Civic Orchestra concerts.

The little **Beach Theatre** (315 Corey Ave., St. Pete Beach, 727/360-6697, www.beachtheatre.com) is another local gem, hosting an opera series, lectures, art-house movies, and films about music (with an appropriate accompanying band).

# Accommodations

## CLEARWATER
### $100-250
Built in 1897 by railroad magnate and west-central Florida pioneer Henry Plant, the 292-room **Belleview Biltmore Resort & Spa** (25 Belleview Blvd., Clearwater, 727/373-3000, www.belleviewbiltmore.com, $89–800) is a historical retreat from the beach bustle of Clearwater, situated high on a coastal bluff. The property, recently purchased by Legg Mason Real Estate Investors is currently closed, undergoing a $100 million renovation. It is expected to reopen in 2012.

### Over $250
On the opposite side of the historical spectrum, the first new resort to be built on Clearwater Beach in 25 years, the **Sandpearl Resort** (500 Mandalay Ave., Clearwater, 727/441-2425, www.sandpearl.com, $299–759) is extremely impressive. The combined resort and condominium project features a 253-room hotel, a full-service spa, upscale dining, state-of-the-art meeting and event space, 117 condominium units, and 700 feet of Gulf of Mexico beachfront. Rooms have an open, airy feel with balconies, high ceilings, and upscale, comfortable furnishings and fixtures. Fifty suites, located on the top two floors of the resort, offer one- and two-bedroom floor plans.

## ST. PETERSBURG
### $100-250
Especially for romance seekers, **La Veranda Bed and Breakfast** (111 Fifth Ave. N., St. Petersburg, 727/224-1057, $99–250) is wonderful for couples as it's right near the heart of downtown St. Petersburg, but still quiet and romantic. It's set in a 1910 mansion surrounded by wide wraparound porches and beautiful tropical gardens, its suites including canopy beds, antiques, and Oriental rugs. Each

suite opens directly onto the large veranda. Just up the block is a similar inn called **Mansion House Bed and Breakfast** (105 Fifth Ave. NE, St. Petersburg, 727/821-9391, www. mansionbandb.com, $139–250). There are 12 rooms set in two Craftsman-style houses, one of which is thought to have been built between 1901 and 1904 by St. Petersburg's first mayor, David Mofett. A courtyard in between the houses is perfect for a little reading or downtime. And the pool on the property is a plus.

## Over $250

The **( Renaissance Vinoy Resort & Golf Club** (501 Fifth Ave. NE, St. Petersburg, 727/894-1000, www.renaissancehotels.com, $249–600) was built by Pennsylvania oilman Aymer Vinoy Laughner in 1925. At $3.5 million, the Mediterranean Revival–style hotel was the largest construction project in Florida's history. Painstakingly restored in 1992 at a cost of $93 million, the resort is incredible. There are 360 guest rooms and 15 suites, many with views of the marina. The hotel also has a spa, a lovely pool with a waterfall, five restaurants, tennis courts, and an 18-hole golf course designed by Ron Garl. It hosts its own marina and is listed on the National Register of Historic Places.

# ST. PETE BEACH
## $150-250

For families, the **TradeWinds Island Resorts** (5500 Gulf Blvd., St. Pete Beach, 727/367-6461, www.tradewindsresort.com) is the way to go. The resort offers families a variety of accommodation choices, comprising the TradeWinds Island Grand ($168–457) and the Sandpiper Hotel and Suites ($149–226), and whichever one you choose includes playtime privileges at the other. The Island Grand is the fancier, a four-diamond property with soaring palms, a grand lobby, and really attractive rooms. Sandpiper would be my choice with little ones. The whole complex offers multiple pools, something like a dozen places to eat and drink, multiple fitness centers, tennis

courts everywhere, a pedal-boat canal meandering through the grounds, and a wide, private expanse of beach. Right out the back of the properties you can rent equipment for snorkeling or fishing, and try your hand at parasailing, waterskiing, and water scooters. The kids' program (KONK, Kids Only, No Kidding!) is tremendous, with seasonal programs like the Swashbucklin' By the Sea pirate package, in which you get to meet Redbeard and walk the plank. For adults there is a lively nightlife to be found among the many bars and restaurants and an on-site Beef O'Brady's Sports Bar where you can catch the big game. A great way to meet other people at the resort is to join the exceptionally fun TradeWinds pub crawl and visit all five of the on-site bars for a drink. One of the best features of this resort is that the restaurants and bars are mostly affordable for a resort environment.

**( Sirata Beach Resort** (5300 Gulf Blvd., St. Pete Beach, 727/363-5170, www. sirata.com, $139–370) used to be connected to the TradeWinds but is now an independent, family-run midsize hotel, with a range of kids' programs and activities. It's the kind of place that locals in Tampa take their family for a weekend of R&R, as is the very nearby **( Alden Beach Resort** (5900 Gulf Blvd., St. Pete Beach, 727/360-7081, www.aldenbeach-resort.com, $150–269), which is an attentively staffed, family-owned beach resort of 149 suites, especially favored by kids. It has tennis, volleyball, two pools (a little far from the beach, so the walk back and forth takes time for little ones), and a video game room. Rooms on the pool side are significantly cheaper than on the Gulf side.

## Over $250

For something more upscale, the huge, unmistakably pink **Don CeSar Beach Resort & Spa** (400 Gulf Blvd., St. Pete Beach, 727/360-1881, www.doncesar.com, $240–559) is a landmark in St. Pete and a longtime point of reference on maritime navigation charts. Named after a character in the opera *Maritana*, the Don CeSar hosted F. Scott Fitzgerald and wife Zelda, Clarence Darrow, Al Capone, Lou Gehrig, and countless other celebrities. Originally opened in 1928, the property was commandeered by the military during World War II and eventually abandoned. These days, it's a Loews hotel, with 340 lovely rooms, fishing, golfing, tennis, and the soothing Beach Club & Spa. Even if you don't stay here, make sure to take the tour and stop in for ice cream at its old-fashioned ice cream parlor.

## SAFETY HARBOR
### $150-250

Another piece of history, but I'm not sure if I'm buying this one, is claimed by **Safety Harbor Resort and Spa** (105 N. Bayshore Dr., Safety Harbor, 727/726-1161, www.safetyharborspa. com, $99–311). About a zillion places along the Gulf Coast profess to be what Spanish explorer Hernando de Soto identified as the Fountain of Youth. Is it the mineral pools here at this 50,000-square-foot spa and tennis academy? The waters are mighty nice either way, filling

three pools and used in the spa treatments. The resort is also home to a tennis academy, a fine-dining restaurant called 105 North, and an upscale salon. The 189 guest rooms and four suites are spacious and offer nice views of Tampa Bay.

## PALM HARBOR
### Over $200

For golfers, **Westin Innisbrook Golf Resort** (36750 U.S. 19 N., Palm Harbor, 727/942-2000, www.ininnisbrookgolfresort.com, $159–579) is a 900-acre property just north of Clearwater. It has four top-ranked golf courses, 11 tennis courts, six swimming pools (including the super kids-oriented Loch Ness Monster Pool), a children's recreation center, several restaurants, and 60 acres with a series of jogging and cycling trails. Rooms are all suites, with fully equipped kitchens. Its Copperhead Golf Course stretches more than 7,300 yards long and is home to the PGA Tour's PODS Championship.

# Food

Pinellas County is awash in restaurants, most of them fun and casual, many of them worthy of recommendation. Because the area is densely populated and traffic can get fairly impacted during high season, you're more likely to grab a bite near where you're staying or near the beach from which you're departing. For this reason, I'm listing the restaurants in the Clearwater–St. Petersburg area geographically, from north to south. There are, on the other hand, those restaurants that are worth a drive in traffic, what restaurateurs call "destination restaurants." I'll describe these first.

## FINE DINING

In keeping with the glitz of the historic Vinoy, its restaurant, **Marchand's Grill** (Renaissance Vinoy Resort, 501 Fifth Ave. NE, St. Petersburg, 727/894-1000, 6:30 A.M.–10 P.M. daily, $18–35), has undergone some major

changes. Its entrance now shows off the central Vinoy Bar, new velvet armchairs have been added, and a small wine cellar room provides an intimate dining space for four. But perhaps the biggest change is the chef and the dining concept: One side used to be Marchand's, with a Mediterranean menu, the other the Terrace Room, focusing on American-style seafood. Now it's all Marchand's. The kitchen has wisely kept the seafood focus, but dishes reflect a more Mediterranean approach. If you want to pull out all the stops at the Vinoy, **Fred's** is even more of a splurge, but you have to be a member or a resort guest to enjoy it.

The ⦅ **Cafe Ponte** (off Ulmerton Rd. in the Icot Center, 13505 Icot Blvd., Clearwater, 727/538-5768, www.cafeponte.com, 11:30 A.M.–2 P.M. Mon.–Fri., 5:30–10 P.M. Tues.–Thurs., until 11 P.M. Fri. and Sat., $18–36) features Chef Chris Ponte, who trained at

Taillevent in Paris and studied at Johnson & Wales and the Cordon Bleu. His upscale restaurant in the Icot Center is located in a strip-mall and the setting may confound would-be diners, but a single meal will set them straight. The kitchen prepares offerings such as a rich mushroom soup with a spoon of truffle cream and a crispy whole snapper with mango, mint, macadamia nuts, and ginger-vanilla rum sauce.

Downtown St. Petersburg's **Pacific Wave** (211 Second St. S., St. Petersburg, 727/822-5235, 5–10 P.M. Mon.–Thurs., until 11 P.M. Fri. and Sat., $16–30) has "date night" written all over it. The strengths of the menu are traditional sushi and sashimi, but also Japanese- and Pacific Rim–inspired cooked dishes (special emphasis on Pacific fish from Hawaii) and an appealing short wine and cocktail list. The place is a real treat; servers are polished and show a deep knowledge of the menu's ingredients and flavors.

**Salt Rock Grill** (19325 Gulf Blvd., Indian Shores, 727/593-7625, www.saltrockgrill.com, 4–10 P.M. Sun.–Thurs., until 11 P.M. Fri. and Sat., $15–37) is fairly mobbed every night. No worries if you have to wait, though, as a drink on the front deck is perfect on a warm night. The menu has enticing seafood like pan-seared scallops and salmon Oscar, as well as expertly prepared steaks aged in-house and grilled over a super hot natural oak and citrus wood pit fire. It's more formal than most beachside spots around here, and the locals love it.

**Maritana Grille at the Don CeSar** (3400 Gulf Blvd., St. Pete Beach, 727/360-1882, www.doncesar.com, 5:30–10 P.M. Sun.–Thurs., until 11 P.M. Fri. and Sat., $18–40) has a great chef's table for groups up to eight, at which executive chef Eric Neri is put through his Floribbean-cuisine paces, from marmalade-roasted Gulf red snapper served with pea vines or grilled filet mignon with truffled mashed potatoes and candied shallots. The restaurant's interior is incredible, the patrons surrounded by 1,500 gallons of saltwater aquariums and indigenous Florida fish.

## DUNEDIN AND OLDSMAR

A fun place to start casually dining in Pinellas County is **Bon Appetit** (148 Marina Plaza,

Dunedin, 727/733-2151, 11:30 A.M.–9 P.M. Mon.–Thurs., until 10 P.M. Fri. and Sat., 11 A.M.–8:30 P.M. Sun., $12–35). It's in the Best Western Yacht Harbor Inn and Suites and owners Peter Keuziger and Karl Heinz Riedl manage to add a definite style to the seafood-heavy menu, whether it's garlic mussels steamed in sauvignon blanc or the season's freshest stone crabs with only a squeeze of lemon and butter. The thing is, you don't have to pay the big prices—guests can watch the dolphins play as the sun sets out on the water and not break the bank if they dine at the Marine Café adjacent to the restaurant. It's a different menu from the fancier sibling, but a single sheet of signature dishes from the main restaurant is available outside.

Downtown Dunedin has been reinvigorated with restaurants and cafés in recent years. For casual Mexican, go to **Casa Tina** (365 Main St., 727/734-9226, 11 A.M.–10 P.M. Sun.–Thurs., until 11 P.M. Fri. and Sat., $7–15). It's lively, with an eye-catching color scheme, and the food is a little less heavy than many local Mexican joints—that said, try the wild mushroom quesadilla.

About as family friendly, **Kelly's Restaurant** (319 Main St., Dunedin, 727/736-0206, 8 A.M.–10 P.M. Sun.–Thurs., until 11 P.M. Fri. and Sat., $8–18) has a comfort food menu that leaves no stone unturned, from eggplant-portobello-tomato Napoleons to butternut squash ravioli. It's a kids' kind of joint, very friendly and accommodating.

If you're looking to dine at a "nouvelle" restaurant, meaning a place that has high prices for small portions artistically arranged on the plates, **The Black Pearl** (315 Main St., 727/734-3463, 5–9:30 P.M. daily, $18–30) next door is perfect for you. Try the cedar-planked salmon or the crab imperial.

Around since 1993 in Dunedin, **Ivory Mandarin Bistro** (2192 Main St., Dunedin, 727/734-3998, 11:30 A.M.–9:30 P.M. Mon.–Thurs., 11 A.M.–10 P.M. Fri. and Sat., $8–25) has slowly accrued a wall's worth of accolades and "best of" awards along with its devoted clientele. Crisp linens and Chinese floral prints give make the place feel more formal, but the menu reads like a greatest-hits list of Cantonese-American dishes. That means hot and sour soup, juicy pork spare ribs, sweet-tangy orange beef, and pan-fried chow fun noodles.

## CLEARWATER

Clearwater has a fairly dense concentration of good restaurants. But really, you owe it to yourself to go to the original **Hooters** (2800 Gulf-To-Bay Blvd., 727/797-4008, 11 A.M.–11 P.M. Sun.–Thurs., until midnight Fri. and Sat., $8–20). Almost 25 years old, the original pleasant, ramshackle, sports-oriented joint has spawned an international empire and airline. It's a family restaurant, really, with good chicken wings offered in a variety of styles and sauces. Only it's a family restaurant in which all waitresses are wearing flesh-colored pantyhose under orange nylon short-shorts.

By the way, a cooter is a red-bellied turtle that was historically serious eats for early Floridians. That's why **Cooters Raw Bar and Restaurant** (423 Poinsettia Ave., 727/462-2668, www.cooters.com, 11 A.M.–11 P.M. Sun.–Thurs., until midnight Fri. and Sat., $9–20) is called that. A fun place with good steamed crab legs and fried grouper.

My Clearwater favorite is (( **Carmelita's** (5042 E. Bay Dr., 727/376-4800, 11 A.M.–9:30 P.M. Sun.–Thurs., until 10 P.M. Fri. and Sat., $7–14). Each of the three legendary locations serves up the same zingy-spicy green enchiladas to eat with a potent margarita. Also great is the St. Petersburg location (5211 Park St. N., 727/545-2956).

**Lenny's Restaurant** (21220 U.S. 19 N., 727/799-0402, 6 A.M.–3 P.M. daily, $5–12) is the hands-down winner for breakfast, for the Jewish staples of blintzes, knishes, and latkes.

Evening partying is to be found all around, in tiki huts and outdoor decks along the Gulf beaches. One bar, though, is worth mentioning: (( **O'Keefe's Tavern and Restaurant** (1219 S. Fort Harrison Ave., Clearwater, 727/442-9034, 11 A.M.–2 A.M. daily, $7–14). It is the bar to beat for St. Patrick's Day. A good-times, pint-or-three shambling Irish pub, its history goes back to the 1960s when it was

O'Keefe's Tap Room, a history still visible despite the many additions and remodelings. A white brick exterior gives way to a comfortable series of rooms decked out with lots of green accents and Irishobilia. The brogue-required bartenders are fast and furious with the beers (more than 100 offerings) and the all-ages crowd is unified by their affection for the place. Once known for its "seven-course Irish dinner" (that's six beers and a potato), O'Keefe actually serves pretty good fare.

## INDIAN ROCKS BEACH AND REDINGTON SHORES

**Crabby Bill's** (401 Gulf Blvd., Indian Rocks Beach, 727/595-4825, www.crabbybills.com, 11:30 A.M.–11 P.M. daily, $8–22) is a family-owned regional chain that has made a name for itself with family-style seating, group singing, seafood cookery, and flowing beverages.

An institution since 1978, the **Lobster Pot** (17814 Gulf Blvd., Redington Shores, 727/391-8592, 4:30–10 P.M. Mon.–Thurs., until 11 P.M. Fri. and Sat., 4–10 P.M. Sun., $13–28) is a comfortable, casual seafood place with neat lobster traps on the wall. Seafood is straightforward but fresh; it's the place to try local grouper or stone crab in season.

## ST. PETERSBURG

Remember, downtown St. Petersburg's on the east side of the peninsula, not on the Gulf, but on Old Tampa Bay. There are several wonderful picks here—definitely the densest concentration of fine dining in Pinellas.

Downtown St. Petersburg owes a bit of its hipness to trendy downtown gathering spots like **Cafe Alma** (260 First Ave. S., 727/502-5002, 11 A.M.–3 P.M. Mon.–Fri., 4:30–10 P.M. Mon.–Thurs., until midnight Fri. and Sat., $16–25). Open from lunch to late night, the atmosphere sets the mood for the Mediterranean-inspired dishes. Entrées include Spanish-inflected paella alongside traditional French bouillabaisse and peppercorn-crusted Hudson Valley duck breast served atop a sweet corn pancake. While lunchtime brings business diners, at night the vibe is decidedly more festive. Or maybe it's because of **Parkshore Grill** (300 Beach Drive NE, 727/896-9463, 11 A.M.–10 P.M. Sun.–Thurs., until 11 P.M. Fri. and Sat.), with its outside patio within sight of the Museum of Fine Arts. The bar is lively but stylish, and the menu leans to very smart spins on contemporary American cuisine, with pan-seared scallops, lobster pasta, and great mixed drinks.

**The Kitchen** (409 Central Ave., 727/895-3300, 7 A.M.–8 P.M. Mon.–Fri., 9 A.M.–5 P.M. Sat., 9 A.M.–3 P.M. Sun., $4–10) is about as inviting as it gets. Margaret Guidicessi set about to create a gourmet food market where she could improvise a little each day. The room is anchored by huge glass cases of cold salads, pastries, and desserts, plus inserts of entrées. Beyond the menu of big sandwiches, the offerings change: There are eggplant dishes, grains (bulgur, couscous, quinoa), cold marinated shrimp, roasted peppers, lots of good olives. Go in, point to something, and you can have a taste before you decide.

Opened in 2007, **De Santo Latin American Bistro/Push Ultra Lounge** (128 Third St. S., 727/895-6400, 5–11 P.M. nightly) is about the trendiest nightspot around, and mid-2008 celebrity chef Jeannie Pierola took over in the kitchen, offering a hip menu of regional Mexican.

For a simple burger, go to **El Cap** (3500 Fourth St. N., 727/521-1314, 11 A.M.–11 P.M. Mon.–Sat., until 10 P.M. Sun.), and for classical French, *tres cher,* the place is **Chateau France** (136 Fourth Ave. NE, 727/894-7163, 5–11 P.M. Mon.–Sat., $27–100), set in an stylishly renovated St. Petersburg mansion.

## GULFPORT

Gulfport has exploded on the dining scene in the past few years, with worthwhile restaurants lining several blocks. Among local favorites are **Elements Global Cuisine** (3121 Beach Blvd., 727/343-9894, 5:30–9:30 P.M. Mon.–Sat., $16–24) and **Pia's Trattoria** (3054 Beach Blvd. S., 727/327-2190, 11:30 A.M.–2:30 P.M. and 5–9:30 P.M. Mon.–Sat., $8–20). At Elements, owners Jose Luis and Catherine Pawelek offer a short globe-trotting menu that includes dishes like Kona-braised short ribs with a coffee or Kahlua rub served with

gorgonzola polenta. Jose Luis's Argentine heritage is apparent in the hearty, flavorful grilled flank steak entrée, slices cooked in a citrus-based sauce with garlic and parsley. There is also Indonesian-Thai-inspired chicken and veggie stir fry or portobello ravioli with a coconut milk curry. Most of the tables are on the outdoor patio covered with a chickee thatch. The menu's short, the same at lunch and dinner and mostly pressed panini and pastas topped with a variety of simple sauces.

And then there's **La Fogata** (2832 and 2838 Beach Blvd. S., 727/327-4200, 5:30–10 P.M. Tues.–Sun., $35 and $45) You pay one price, either for the full *churrascaria* meat service or just the salad buffet, the offerings ranging from seared tuna with wasabi to Thai shrimp salad with cilantro and red onion. Then servers start coming around with the Brazilian-style meat on skewers, prepared over hardwood mesquite, seasoned with sea salt and not much else. There is also a lounge attached to the back called Bellini, which offers a short tapas menu.

## ST. PETE BEACH

If you can go to just one place in St. Pete Beach, get the blackened grouper sandwich at ⟨ **The Hurricane** (really on Pass-A-Grille Beach, 807 Gulf Way, 727/360-9558, 11 A.M.–9:30 P.M. Sun.–Thurs., until 10 P.M. Fri. and Sat., $8–24). I don't care if the place seems a little touristy; give me a grouper fillet, seasoned with red and black pepper and lots of salt, add in some tomato and lettuce on a bread roll, and that's as good as it gets in Pinellas County. There's a nice bar adjacent to the restaurant and a rooftop sundeck up top for watching the sunset.

On the other hand, if you go only to The Hurricane, then you'll miss out on the orange-pecan French toast or the creamed chipped beef on toast for breakfast at **Skyway Jack's Restaurant** (2795 34th St. S., 727/867-1907, 5 A.M.–3 P.M. daily, $5–10). It's a classic around here, moved once because it was on the approach to the Skyway Bridge and got pushed out to make room for more lanes. Stick with regular breakfast food or the smoked mullet and you won't be disappointed.

# Shopping

**The Pier** (800 Second Ave. NE, St. Petersburg, 727/821-6443) is really the heart and soul of visitor activity in St. Petersburg, looking like an inverted pyramid, or the good guys' home base in a sci-fi movie. You can rent bikes, grab a rental rod and reel and fish off the end, depart from the Pier on a sightseeing boat charter, see a flick at the 20-screen movie theater, visit the little aquarium, dine in the family-friendly food court, or browse the complex's many shops. It's not high-end stuff—there's a pet accoutrement store, an entertainment-celebrity collectibles shop, candle store, T-shirt stores, and that kind of thing.

**BayWalk** (125 Second Ave. N., St. Petersburg, 727/895-9277, www.yourbaywalk. com) is the much more upscale shopping destination in St. Petersburg, not far away. It's right downtown, with an indoor-outdoor array of shops (some independents, some chains like Ann Taylor and Chico's), mid- to high-priced restaurants with a number of cuisines available, and outdoor entertainment on the main stage. It also has a 20-screen movie theater.

Florida's largest new and used bookstore merits a couple of hours of browsing, especially if the weather is inclement (a rarity). **Haslam's Book Store** (2025 Central Ave., St. Petersburg, 727/822-8616, www.haslams. com, 10 A.M.–6:30 P.M. Mon.–Sat.) is now owned by the third generation of the same family, with more than 300,000 volumes. In a world populated increasingly by Borders and Barnes & Noble, it's refreshing sometimes to hang out in an independently owned bookstore. Haslam's has a large number of rare books, and they seem to be really into science fiction.

# Information and Services

Clearwater and St. Petersburg are located within the **Eastern time zone.** The area code is **727,** but here's the annoying thing: Right over the causeway in Tampa the area code is 813. So, you need to dial the area code, but you don't precede the phone number by dialing 1.

## TOURIST INFORMATION

**St. Petersburg/Clearwater Area Convention & Visitors Bureau** (13805 58th St. N, Ste. 2200, Clearwater, 727/464-7200) is not wildly convenient, but its website is tremendous (www.floridasbeach.com). **St. Petersburg Area Chamber of Commerce** (100 Second Ave. N., Ste. 150, 727/821-4069, www.stpete. org, 9 A.M.–5 P.M. Mon.–Fri., 10 A.M.–4 P.M. Sat., noon–4 P.M. Sun.) has a decent walk-in site with brochures and maps.

The various chambers of commerce have their own websites: Tarpon Springs (www. tarponsprings.com), Clearwater (www.clearwaterflorida.org) and Clearwater Beach (www.beachchamber.com), and Dunedin (www.dunedin-fl.com), among others. For outdoors information, there's **Clearwater Parks** (www.clearwater-fl.com—drop down to Parks & Recreation under Browse City Departments), **Florida Parks** (www.floridaparks.com), **Pinellas County Parks** (www. pinellascounty.org—go to Parks under Online Services A-Z), and **St. Petersburg Parks** (www.stpete.org—choose Parks under Select a Department).

St. Petersburg's largest newspaper is the **St. Petersburg Times** (490 First Ave. S., St. Petersburg, 727/893-8111). You'll see kiosks everywhere.

## POLICE AND EMERGENCIES

In an emergency, dial 911. If you need medical assistance, the area has several large hospitals with good emergency care: **St. Petersburg General Hospital** (6500 38th Ave. N., St. Petersburg, 727/384-1414) and **St. Anthony's Hospital** (1200 Seventh Ave. N., St. Petersburg, 727/825-1100) in the south of the county, and **Suncoast Hospital** (2025 Indian Rocks Rd., Largo, 727/581-9474) in northern Pinellas County. For a nonemergency police need, contact the **St. Petersburg Police Department** (1300 First Ave. N., St. Petersburg, 727/893-7780).

## RADIO AND TELEVISION

Because it's a big metropolitan area, Tampa and St. Pete have an enormous number of radio stations between them. There's independent radio at **WMNF 88.5 FM,** light rock at **WMTX 100.7 FM,** and NPR and classical at **WUSF 89.7 FM.**

For local television programming, **Bay News 9** is Bright House Networks' 24-hour local news station, **WFLA Channel 8** is the local NBC affiliate, **WTSP Channel 10** is the CBS affiliate, **WTVT Channel 13** is the FOX affiliate, and **WFTS Channel 28** is the local ABC affiliate.

## LAUNDRY SERVICES

Many of the larger hotels offer laundry service, as do most marinas in the area. If you find yourself in need of coin-operated laundry in St. Petersburg, try **Wash N' Go Laundry** (4154 Haines Rd. N, 727/209-0573) or **The Gardens** (3501 Central Ave., 727/323-0146). To the north in Clearwater, there's 24-hour laundry at **Thompson's Dry Cleaners and Laundry** (1713 Drew St., 727/461-2589).

# Getting There and Around

## BY CAR

Pinellas County is easily accessible from major interstates along the Midwest (I-75) and Northeast (I-95) corridors, as well as Orlando (I-4). I-275 serves the western portions of the Tampa–St. Petersburg area, including downtown Tampa, St. Petersburg, and Bradenton. It starts in the south at I-75 in Bradenton and extends up through St. Petersburg and Tampa, connected by two major bridges (Sunshine Skyway in the south and Howard Frankland Bridge to the north) before reuniting with I-75 at Lutz. I-75, by contrast, skirts both cities and acts as a bypass to southwest Florida and the Gulf Coast.

Once in Pinellas, Clearwater is in the north along the Gulf, St. Petersburg is in the south along the bay. To reach St. Petersburg from Clearwater, head south on U.S. 19A, a slow, densely trafficked mess. Farther east, the regular U.S. 19 cuts down through the center of the peninsula to St. Petersburg.

In St. Petersburg, streets are set up in a grid pattern, with avenues running east–west and

streets running north–south. Central Avenue divides north and south St. Petersburg, with the numbered avenues on either side—it's tricky, though, as to the left of Central there's First Avenue North, to the right it's First Avenue South. There are some sections of town that are all one-way streets, so you may make a lot of little squares while driving.

From St. Pete Beach all the way up through Clearwater, all you need to know is that Gulf Boulevard (Hwy. 699) runs right up the coast and through each little town. The city of Clearwater is on the mainland, but Clearwater Beach is on a barrier island connected by Memorial Causeway.

## BY AIR

The area is served by two midsize, easily traversed airports. **Tampa International Airport** (5503 W. Spruce St., 813/870-8700) was recently ranked by *Condé Nast* as the seventh best airport worldwide, located just over the bridge and causeway from St. Petersburg and Clearwater and about 30–45 minutes from beachfront accommodations. Domestically, it is serviced by AirTran Airlines, America West Airlines, American Airlines, Continental Airlines, Delta Airlines, Delta Express, Frontier Airlines, JetBlue Airways, Midwest Express Airlines, Northwest Airlines, Song Airways, Southwest Airlines, Spirit Airlines, Ted, United Airlines, and US Airways. International carriers include AirCanada, British Airways, Cayman Airways, and American Eagle.

You'll probably fly in and out of Tampa, unless you're coming from Canada. But there's also **St. Petersburg-Clearwater International Airport** (14501 Roosevelt Blvd., Clearwater, 727/531-1451), served by American Trans Air and USA 3000 Airlines; Canadian airlines CanJet, Air Transat, Sunwing, and Jetsgo Airlines; and Seacoast Airlines to Key West.

**Alamo** (800/327-9633), **Avis** (800/831-2847), **Budget** (800/527-0700), **Dollar** (800/800-4000 domestic, 800/800-6000 international), and **National** (800/227-7368) provide rental cars from both airports.

## BY BUS AND TRAIN

**Amtrak** (800/USA-RAIL, www.amtrak.com) offers service into nearby Tampa and other surrounding areas. Some services even allow you to bring your car with you. Also, **Greyhound Bus Line** (800/229-9424, www.greyhound.com) provides regular service into St. Petersburg (180 Ninth St. N., 727/898-1496). If you stay in Clearwater, it's easy to ditch your rental car and use the **Jolley Trolley** (727/445-1200, www.clearwaterjolleytrolley.com, $1.25) or the **Suncoast Beach Trolley** (727/540-1900, $2 per ride, $4.50 all day) to get around. **Pinellas Suncoast Transit Authority** (727/540-1900) also has a fairly extensive busing system ($2 per ride, $4.50 all day) around the city.

# THE NATURE COAST

The Nature Coast is the rebuttal to Orlando's Disney slickness. The area is known as "Mother Nature's theme park," and if you're looking to spend your vacation fishing, exploring the outdoors, or just getting to a laid-back and off-the-beaten-path coastal town, the Nature Coast doesn't disappoint. Nothing here is marketed, packaged, or sanitized by public relations specialists. It's rural, with the majority of the area set aside as parkland, preserves, reserves, and animal refuges.

In the weathered fishing villages along the coast and the quaint little inland towns, you're likely to see a spiffy fishing boat in every driveway. Residents stay for the affordable living, for the area's easy live-and-let-live tolerance, for the unhurried pace, and—for many, the most important reason—the fish. And that's

pretty much why visitors come, too. People drive here to see manatees, black bears, and wading birds; to catch fish; and to dive, kayak, or simply contemplate the area's wealth of waterways. There are no white-sand beaches crowded with bikini-clad college kids, no swanky nightclubs with throbbing VIP rooms. From north of Clearwater all the way to the Big Bend (where the Florida peninsula tucks west into the Panhandle), there are precious few multiplexes, museums, or fancy cultural attractions. All that would get in the way of enjoying one of the least-developed stretches of Florida's Gulf Coast.

## PLANNING YOUR TIME

The Nature Coast has more than 700 square miles of scenic driving. The main highway

# HIGHLIGHTS

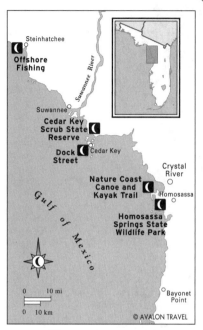

◖ **Nature Coast Canoe and Kayak Trail:** Imagine how the Native Americans or early Spanish explorers saw this area, from the seat of a canoe or kayak along the backwaters of this 17-mile paddling trail. Hernando de Soto, on his quest for gold, was said to have paddled waters in this area in the summer of 1539 (page 207).

◖ **Homosassa Springs State Wildlife Park:** Find out why *Rodale's Scuba Diving* awards the area the Best Place to See Large Animals title. The manatee is the goliath in question, and you can see it up close in the underwater "fishbowl" at this wildlife park (page 208).

◖ **Cedar Key Scrub State Reserve:** Walk this rare ecosystem to catch a glimpse of the threatened Florida scrub jay and endangered burrowing owls (page 215).

◖ **Dock Street:** Stroll around Dock Street on Cedar Key any time of day and enjoy the shops, galleries, and restaurants along the wooden boardwalk. Join the anglers and pelicans on the pier to watch the sunset (page 220).

◖ **Offshore Fishing:** Roughly 62 miles of Gulf Coast, 106 miles of rivers, and 19,111 acres of lakes, and that's just in Citrus County alone. This is fishing country. There are lots of trophy fish in these waters – tarpon, redfish, bass – so you and your fish smile for the camera (page 222).

LOOK FOR ◖ TO FIND RECOMMENDED SIGHTS, ACTIVITIES, DINING, AND LODGING.

through the area is U.S. 19. From south of Spring Hill, the long strip runs through small towns with a high number of boat dealers, fishing guides, and bait shops. North of Crystal River, U.S. 19 gets rural, with only the occasional mailbox and long driveway leading back to someone's private slice of heaven. Along the way you'll see osprey hunting overhead and cross an incredible number of waterways worth exploring. When traveling in this area it is highly recommended to travel with a boat in tow or a canoe strapped to the roof of the car. It is one thing to see these amazing rivers, creeks, and bays from the shore, but the experience of getting into a boat and exploring them in depth is not to be missed. Besides, this is the best way to get to all those tucked away pockets of fish.

**Weeki Wachee Springs, Homosassa,** and **Crystal River** are located directly along U.S. 19. To get to any of the little towns perched along the Gulf's edge—**Yankeetown, Cedar Key, Suwannee,** and **Steinhatchee,** from south to north—you have to drive west on

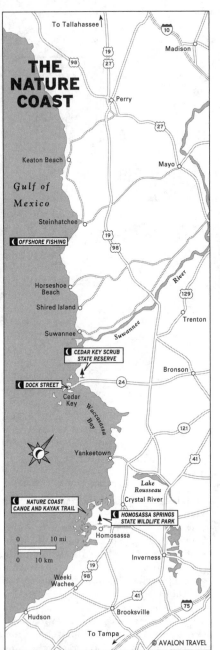

THE
NATURE
COAST

To Tallahassee
Madison
Perry
Keaton Beach
Gulf of Mexico
Mayo
Steinhatchee
OFFSHORE FISHING
Horseshoe Beach
Shired Island
Trenton
Suwannee
CEDAR KEY SCRUB STATE RESERVE
Bronson
DOCK STREET
Cedar Key
Waccasassa Bay
Yankeetown
Lake Rousseau
Crystal River
NATURE COAST CANOE AND KAYAK TRAIL
HOMOSASSA SPRINGS STATE WILDLIFE PARK
Homosassa
Inverness
Weeki Wachee
Hudson
Brooksville
To Tampa

0    10 mi
0    10 km

© AVALON TRAVEL

Anglers come from all over the world to fish the exciting tarpon of the Nature Coast.

rural two-lane roads. None of these can be reached one from the other, except by boat or by driving back east, rejoining U.S. 19, and then more driving.

Weeki Wachee Springs is well worth a day trip, especially for families, either as an add-on to seeing Tarpon Springs farther south, or an addition to a trip to elsewhere on the Nature Coast. Since manatee viewing is best early in the morning, and fishing trips usually head out fairly early as well, it makes sense to stay over a night in Crystal River or Homosassa. Cedar Key and Steinhatchee, partly because they're harder to get to and partly because they're so charming, are each worth a couple of days of exploration.

# Weeki Wachee to Crystal River

Florida is home to 700 freshwater springs, 33 of them first magnitude, meaning they discharge at least 100 cubic feet of water per second. Several of these first-magnitude springs are along the Nature Coast, a huge draw for swimmers and divers. It wasn't always such an easy sell, though. Weeki Wachee Springs, dutifully pumping 170 million gallons of crystal-clear water a day, languished as a tourist attraction until 1947, when a local entrepreneur figured out a way to lure the crowds: mermaids. Its underwater mermaid show is the kind of Old Florida attraction that makes people misty-eyed about the good old days. The town of Spring Hill owes its existence to the spring and its water park—not surprisingly, allies rallied as the park's commercial success waned and the mermaids beseeched Spring Hill to "Save Our Tails." At the end of 2007, its landlord, the Southwest Florida Water Management District, and the state of Florida agreed to make Weeki Wachee a state park. It was added to the state park system on November 1, 2008. Let's hope that saves those tails well into the future.

Farther north, the manatee is the 800-pound gorilla. But even bigger. Local cynics refer to these gentle mammals as "cash cows," and indeed the sea cows bring in a sizable revenue stream to the little towns of Homosassa and Crystal River. Upwards of 400 West Indian manatees make this their winter home, drawn by the warm waters of the seven spring-driven rivers that meet here at the Gulf of Mexico. Were it not for the manatees, both towns would still be on the map as fishing destinations. The area's anglers and manatee advocates make uneasy bedfellows, however: Many fisherfolk feel that overzealous Save the Manatee legislation has put unnecessary strictures on boating here.

Older than Crystal River by a good bit, Homosassa has more charm and the greater reputation as a fishing draw. The Calusa and the Seminole tribes were the first to inhabit the area, but after the Civil War, families escaping the conflict and its aftermath settled many of the smaller islands, carving out a hardscrabble life of subsistence farming and fishing (often the little keys were named for the families who lived there). As real communities developed, commercial fishing became the mainstay, with the local catch transported north to Cedar Key by sailing sloop and, later, by railroad.

By the end of the 19th century, this rural area had developed a mighty reputation among sportsmen, and in 1886 a group of financiers bought up much of the swampy riverfront property on the Homosassa River. Extensive land filling, highway projects, and a major marketing blitz in the 1920s failed to draw many serious investors and residents. And it remains pretty much that way today: a few thousand people drawn by beautiful rivers, unmanicured wilderness, and fish.

## SPORTS AND RECREATION
### Buccaneer Bay
If you've been entranced by the lip-synching mermaids of Weeki Wachee Springs, you'll be inspired to try some of your own aquatic tricks at the adjacent Buccaneer Bay water park (6131 Commercial Way, Spring Hill, 352/592-5656, 10 A.M.–4 P.M. daily, $26 adults, $12 children 6–12, children 5 and under free). Pure, cold spring water laps against a tiny white-sand beach while families zoom down the flume rides and water slides or hang out on the floating dock. It's a safe place to let kids roam free (lots of strict, eagle-eyed lifeguards make sure of that), and when they're exhausted you can trot off to the riverboat cruise, petting zoo, and sweet animal show. Weeki Wachee Springs also hosts two-day mermaid camps, in which kids are taught the finer points of mermaidhood (352/592-5656, ext. 30, $200).

When you're ready to get away from the crowds, head for the rear of the water park parking lot and follow the arrows for **canoe rental** (352/592-5666, $30 single-seat kayak, $35 two-seat kayak or canoe). It takes about

## THE SILVER KING

Homosassa is the place. Any fly fisher will tell you, this little Old Florida town is where the big tarpon congregate, for no reason anyone can fathom. The current world record – 202.8 pounds – was caught right here. But you won't find annual tarpon tournaments broadcast from here on ESPN2. It's a low-key endeavor, with patience often yielding nothing but sunburn. On any given day, you'll see the river dotted with 25 or 30 flat boats navigated with push poles in a hushed silence of profound concentration, everyone waiting to see one roll along the surface in water depths of 5-25 feet. People come from all over the world to the Nature Coast to sight fish, spin casting or fly-fishing for these behemoths before releasing them gently into the warm, clear waters. Tarpon begin to run the last weeks of April and fade out in July. What many consider the Super Bowl of fishing, tarpon fishing requires a special $50 tag to keep one, and some serious know-how. If you catch one – using live crabs, baitfish, or hand-tied flies – the initial jumps and runs of that hooked fish are very exciting.

If you want to try your hand at chasing giant tarpon on the Gulf or, even better, fly-fishing with light tackle in the backwaters from Homosassa to Cedar Key, try **Captain Rick LeFiles** (Osprey Guide Services, 6115 Riverside Dr., Yankeetown, 352/447-0829, $350 for a day of reds and trout, $400 for tarpon) or fourth-generation Homosassa **Captain William Toney** (352/621-9284, www.homosassainshorefishing.com, half day $300, full day $400 for 1-2 people, $50 each additional person).

three hours to paddle this serene stretch of the Weeki Wachee River, and when you've finished they'll pick you up and bring you back upstream by van. Bring lunch or a beverage: There are spots along the river where you can hop out on a sandy beach, swim, and relax.

### Golfing

Golfers will be sorely tempted to sneak away while their families visit Weeki Wachee Springs. The big kahuna of courses in these parts is the famous Tom Fazio–built **World Woods** (17590 Ponce de Leon Blvd., Brooksville, 352/796-5500, www.worldwoods.com, greens fees $50–130), just minutes away in Brooksville. It's a 45-hole complex with challenges for every golfer. Begin the day warming up on one of the hugest driving ranges you've ever laid eyes on (23 acres). From there, you can bone up on the nine-hole short course featuring seven par 3s and two par 4s, and then attempt either the 18-hole Pine Barrens, modeled after the great Pine Valley, or the stately and refined Rolling Oaks parkland course, an homage to Augusta National.

### Swimming with the Manatees

The West Indian manatee is still listed as an endangered species, but the population has rebounded tremendously in the past few years in this area. Manatee season is October 15–March 31, but you'll spot them all year long. Kings Bay in Crystal River has the densest concentration, but the Blue Waters area of the Homosassa River is a little less trafficked by boats, thus a bit quieter. Either way, you can swim with these gentle mammals from the distance that suits you (up close their size is unsettling—just remember they are herbivores, with blunt teeth so far back in their heads that you could, were it legal, hand-feed them with no worries). **Manatee Tour & Dive** (4 NE Fifth St. on Citrus Ave., Crystal River, 888/732-2692, www.manateetouranddive.com, $29 for tour, $20 for gear) offers two-hour manatee swim and snorkeling trips suitable for the whole family in the waters of Crystal River, and scuba trips in Crystal Springs and Kings Spring, an underwater cavern praised for its excellent visibility, size, and potential for underwater photography (thousands of saltwater fish congregate at the cavern's two exits).

COURTESY OF VISIT FLORIDA

Diving and snorkeling the cool, crystal-clear waters of the abundant springs in this area are the perfect ways to beat the summer heat.

**Sunshine River Tours** (352/628-3450, www.sunshinerivertours.com, $50) has a similar range of guided ecotourism escapades in Homosassa. If a manatee swim and snorkel tour doesn't sound like a good way to take to the waters, you can try your hand at scalloping (July 1–Sept. 10) or just enjoy a boat ride to follow the river out to the Gulf of Mexico.

## Canoeing, Kayaking, and Boating

During the warm months when manatees are a little scarce elsewhere in Crystal River and Homosassa, head to **Chassahowitzka National Wildlife Refuge** (accessible from Rd. 480 off U.S. 19, south of Homosassa, 352/563-2088, 8 A.M.–sundown daily, no fee), where they seem to congregate. And during the colder months you're likely to spot endangered whooping cranes that make this their winter home. There are no walking trails at the refuge, but there is a small

visitors center that will quickly connect you with a commercial boat tour or rental. The 30,500 acres of saltwater bays, estuaries, and brackish marshes are home to nearly 250 species of birds, 50 species of reptiles and amphibians, and at least 25 species of mammals. You can't camp here, but several miles east of the refuge you'll find **Chassahowitzka River Campground** (352/382-2200), which has a nice canoe and boat launch of its own.

### ◀ NATURE COAST CANOE AND KAYAK TRAIL

This trail is 17 miles long, beginning in the north on the Salt River off Crystal River (near the Marine Science Station on Hwy. 44). Follow the markers on the Salt River south to the Homosassa River. From here, the trail goes east on the Homosassa River a few hundred feet to a little stretch of water called Battle Creek, and then it jags to the south through Seven Cabbage Cut to the mouth of the Chassahowitzka River. The calm, protected waters of this estuarine ecosystem, part of the Great Florida Birding Trail, is home to ospreys, cormorants, wood storks, and loads of other wading birds.

To rent kayaks and canoes, go to **Aardvark's Florida Kayak Company** (707 N. Citrus Ave., Crystal River, 352/795-5650, $35 singles, $45 tandem, closed Mon. and Tues., but will open by prior arrangement). But if paddling out on your own sounds daunting, **Riversport Kayaks** (5297 S. Cherokee Way, Homosassa, 352/621-4972) leads tours along this trail, as well as great paddling along the Halls River and even overnight camping trips with an experienced and knowledgeable guide. They also offer a lunch-and-paddle special that combines a kayak or canoe rental with a gift certificate to the Riverside Crab House good for dinner, lunch, or just drinks ($45 single kayaks, $55 two-seat kayaks or canoes).

## Birding

The area's salt marshes, hammocks, uplands, forest and prairie, freshwater marshes, swamps, lakes, and rivers provide a variety

THE NATURE COAST

of habitats, which in turn draw a variety of birds. Hundreds of bird species call this area home, and birders can observe them via boating along waterways, driving trails, and walking trails all over Citrus County. Roseate spoonbills, great blue herons, ibis, and other wading birds; ospreys, bald eagles, and other birds of prey; shore birds, wetland birds, and beach birds are all on view. March–May is a good time to see colorful mating plumage. One of the largest undeveloped river delta–estuarine systems in the United States, the **Lower Suwannee National Wildlife Refuge** (16 miles west of U.S. 19 on County Rd. 347, 352/493-0238) was established in 1979 in an effort to protect and maintain a rare ecosystem. The park is bisected by the Suwannee River, its tributary creeks fringed with majestic cypress (this part is best seen from the one-mile River Trail). Be sure to visit the upland area dotted with scrub oak and pine, and then explore some of the 26-mile stretch of tidal marshes along the Gulf.

Birders also gravitate to the **Withlacoochee Bay Trail** (from U.S. 19, turn east on the Sunset Parkway Rd., 352/447-1720), a five-mile walking trail from Felburn Park Trailhead to the Gulf. The child-friendly, two-mile looped **Eco Walk Trail** (5990 North Tallahassee Rd., 352/563-0450) can be reached by taking U.S. 19 north to just before Seven Rivers Hospital, then turn left onto Curtis Tool Road for the Eco Walk trailhead, which is at the intersection of Curtis Tool and Tallahassee Road. **Fort Island Trail** (5 miles west of U.S. 19 on Fort Island Trail) is a flat, paved, nine-mile trail that ends at Fort Island Trail Beach. All of these parks are open 8 A.M.–sunset, and admission is free.

## Motorcycling

And if you need a break from all that outdoors activity, you can hop on a hog and play *Easy Rider* at the **Harley-Davidson Shop of Crystal River** (1785 S Suncoast Blvd., 352/563-9900). Sportsters, Big Twins, and V-Rods are all for rent for $150 a day for those over 21 with a valid driver's license.

## SIGHTS
### ◖ Homosassa Springs State Wildlife Park

Manatees, so famous in these parts, can weigh up to 2,000 pounds and are often seen feasting on algae and barnacles. You'll catch sight of them most often during cooler months, December–March, in the Suwannee River or at Manatee or Fanning Springs State Parks. From boat or shore, look for swirly "footprints" on the water's surface or torpedo-like shapes ambling across the shallow bottom. If you want a guaranteed viewing, stop into Homosassa Springs State Wildlife Park (4150 S. Suncoast Blvd., Homosassa, 352/628-5343, 9 A.M.–5:30 P.M. daily, $15 adults, $5 children 6–12), where you can see these marine mammals several ways. Visitors are loaded onto pontoon boats and shuttled through the canopied headwaters of the Homosassa River to a refuge for injured manatees and other animals. Alternatively, at 11:30 A.M., 1:30 P.M., and 3:30 P.M., a manatee program allows you to watch guides wade out to feed stubby carrots to a slow-moving swarm of these creatures, many etched with outboard motor scars from run-ins with boats. Afterward you can walk down to the glass-fronted Fishbowl Underwater Observatory and see eye-to-eye with the gentle giants and the park's other indigenous aquatic creatures. (Mysteriously, the park hosts a hippo named Lucifer—a washed-up animal actor—that former governor Lawton Chiles declared an honorary Florida native.)

### Yulee Sugar Mill Ruins and Vicinity

David Levy Yulee was the man responsible for bringing the Atlantic and Gulf Railroad to Cedar Key in 1860—putting Cedar Key on the map. When Florida became a state in 1845 he was the state's first U.S. senator, and he had another sweet business on the side: By 1851, his mill on the Homosassa River employed more than 1,000 people, producing sugar, syrup, and molasses. Yulee was imprisoned briefly for siding with the Confederacy during the Civil War, and his mill was permanently closed. Now the

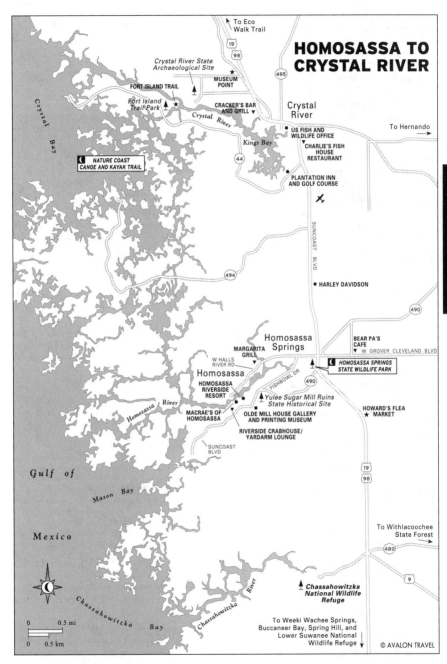

# HOMOSASSA TO CRYSTAL RIVER

To Eco Walk Trail

19
98

495

Crystal River State Archaeological Site
★ MUSEUM POINT

FORT ISLAND TRAIL

Fort Island Trail Park ★

Crystal River

CRACKER'S BAR AND GRILL ▾

Crystal River

US FISH AND WILDLIFE OFFICE

To Hernando

Kings Bay

CHARLIE'S FISH HOUSE RESTAURANT

44

NATURE COAST CANOE AND KAYAK TRAIL

PLANTATION INN AND GOLF COURSE

Crystal Bay

SUNCOAST BLVD

THE NATURE COAST

494

HARLEY DAVIDSON

490

Homosassa Springs

MARGARITA GRILL ▾

BEAR PA'S CAFE
▾ W GROVER CLEVELAND BLVD

W HALLS RIVER RD

Homosassa

HOMOSASSA RIVERSIDE RESORT

FISHBOWL DR

HOMOSASSA SPRINGS STATE WILDLIFE PARK

490

Homosassa River

Yulee Sugar Mill Ruins State Historical Site

HOWARD'S FLEA ★ MARKET

MACRAE'S OF HOMOSASSA

OLDE MILL HOUSE GALLERY AND PRINTING MUSEUM

RIVERSIDE CRABHOUSE/ YARDARM LOUNGE

SUNCOAST BLVD

Gulf of

Mason Bay

Mexico

19
98

To Withlacoochee State Forest

480

9

Chassahowitzka National Wildlife Refuge

To Weeki Wachee Springs, Buccaneer Bay, Spring Hill, and Lower Suwanee National Wildlife Refuge ↓

Chassahowitzka River

Chassahowitzka Bay

0    0.5 mi
0    0.5 km

© AVALON TRAVEL

**Yulee Sugar Mill Ruins State Historical Site**
(352/795-3817, 8 A.M.–sundown daily, no fee) is hardly more than a huge stone chimney and the bones of a partially restored 40-foot-long structure that houses steam boilers, crushing machinery, and large cooking kettles. Visitors walk on a short path through the six-acre site tagged with interpretive plaques, and there is a small nearby picnic area with grills. To reach the site, take U.S. 19 to the town of Homosassa Springs, then turn west onto County Road 490 West (Yulee Drive). Proceed for approximately 2.5 miles to the park.

If the Yulee Sugar Mill doesn't sound like quite enough to make you detour from U.S. 19, right down the block is a nice museum/café called the **Olde Mill House Gallery & Printing Museum** (10466 W. Yulee Dr., 352/628-1081, 10 A.M.–3 P.M. Tues.–Sat., free admission, tours by appointment). Presided over by Jim Anderson, the little museum explores the history of printing, focusing on the letterpress era. The café sells very tasty authentic Cubano sandwiches and black beans and rice. And if you want to get even more return on your mileage investment, continue west on County Road 490 just a bit until you reach **Historic Old Homosassa,** a collection of craft and gift shops, restaurants, and one of the oldest residential communities on Florida's Gulf Coast.

## Howard's Flea Market

Heavy shoppers will be a little left out by the Nature Coast's meager retail options. There is a mall in Crystal River (1801 NW U.S. 19, 352/795-2585) with the usual stores, such as Sears, Waldenbooks, and Payless, and Cedar Key's Dock Street is host to the kinds of shell-themed giftware and handicrafts stores found in many little seaside towns. For a real local bit of excitement, sift through the 300 or so booths at Howard's Flea Market (6373 S. Suncoast Blvd., Homosassa Springs, 352/628-3532, 7 A.M.–1 P.M. Fri., 7 A.M.–3 P.M. Sat.–Sun.). To safeguard against rain and muggy weather, the market is enclosed, with vendors selling leather goods, antiques, tools, fishing gear, and even pets. A bird aviary and

food vendors (good barbecue and excellent old-fashioned root beer) make it fun for the whole family.

## Crystal River State Archaeological Site

In 200 B.C., this was a happening spot. Florida's Native Americans came from all over to bury their dead and to participate in ceremonies and trade activities. People estimate that, for 1,600 years, roughly 7,500 Indians visited these 14 acres every year. Today, Crystal River State Archaeological Site (3400 N. Museum Point, Crystal River, 352/795-3817, park open 8 A.M.–sundown daily, visitors center 9 A.M.–5 P.M. daily, admission $3 per vehicle) is still hosting a fair number of visitors to the banks of the Crystal River. They come to see the six mounds built by what are now referred to somewhat prosaically as the pre-Columbian mound builders. After viewing an eight-minute interpretive video and seeing the small museum's exhibit chronicling the archaeological excavations begun in 1903, you'll be better equipped to walk a paved, half-mile loop and marvel at the mounds, studded with shells, bones, jewelry, and pottery from early civilizations. The park also has a very interesting dugout canoe exhibit and a Sifting for Technology interactive exhibit. With the latter, there are biweekly programs for the general public in which participants use sifting screens and other archaeological tools to recover artifacts from the spoils of a dredged boat slip.

## ENTERTAINMENT AND EVENTS
### Festivals

The average year-round temperature along the Nature Coast is 70°F, with an average of 294 days of sunshine. That means it's pretty all year, but you might want to schedule a visit to correspond to one of the local festivals.

In January, Crystal River hosts the three-day **Florida Manatee Festival** (call the Citrus County Chamber of Commerce at 352/726-2801) with free manatee-sightseeing boat tours, crafts, food, entertainment, and, best of all for

## TAIL SPIN

The job requirements are tough: a winning smile, powerful athleticism, and a great body. Now add to that the ability to hold one's breath for 2.5 minutes. Florida is home to a variety of rare aquatic creatures, but perhaps none are so singular as the 21 mermaids and mermen who swim through their daily choreographed show at **Weeki Wachee Springs** (6131 Commercial Way, Spring Hill, 352/596-2062, 10 A.M.-4 P.M. daily, $26 adults, $12 children 6–12, which includes admission to Buccaneer Bay). Weeki Wachee is open year-round but Buccaneer Bay is closed during the winter months and reopens in mid-March.

In 1947, former U.S. Navy frogman Newton Perry thought of a way to bring added draw to one of the United States' most prolific freshwater springs. More than 170 million gallons of 72°F water pour dramatically into the Weeki Wachee River daily. Perry's notion was to make the spring more attractive by adding a school of beautiful mermaids – to this end, he taught a group of powerful swimmers to breathe through submerged air hoses supplied by an air compressor, the upshot being a remarkable 30- to 45-minute, entirely underwater extravaganza.

Conceived in the heyday of MGM's trademark aquatic musical spectaculars starring Esther Williams, the show at Weeki Wachee Springs is nonetheless a family affair. There are plenty of ogling opportunities, but these bathing beauties are put through their paces in a show that usually draws from past Disney movies such as, unsurprisingly, *The Little Mermaid* and *Pocahontas.*

The audience sits in a small underground amphitheater in front of a four-inch-thick plate-glass window, behind which the blue waters of the springs teem with fish, turtles, eels, and women in oversized, shimmering tails who twirl, undulate, and lip synch on cue. Many of the mermaids have been with the show for decades, a fact that can be ascertained with a quick look through photos and memorabilia in the small Mermaid Museum (a wall of fame includes early sea nymphs cavorting with Elvis and Don Knotts), opened to commemorate the show's 50th anniversary in 1997.

After getting your picture taken with a mermaid, it's off to the rest of the 200-acre family entertainment park, Florida's only natural spring water park. This includes a flume ride at Buccaneer Bay, a low-key Birds of Prey show, petting zoo, and jungle river cruise.

Past years had been hard for the attraction, with the mermaids and supporters launching Save Our Tail efforts. The upshot is that Weeki Wachee Springs became a Florida state park in 2008. For a truly wonderful record of the attraction's history, pick up a copy of Lu Vickers' *Weeki Wachee, City of Mermaids: A History of One of Florida's Oldest Roadside Attractions,* if only for the historic pictures.

**THE NATURE COAST**

you parrot heads, a Jimmy Buffet sound-alike contest. Fins up! The **Cedar Key Arts and Crafts Festival** (www.cedarkeyartsfestival.com) in April is known as a hot place to find new talent. It's a big fun arts show with lots of crafts for sale. The Homosassa River is home to a number of fishing tournaments worth watching: The annual **Cobia Tournament** (call MacRae's Bait and Tackle at 352/628-2602 or Barramundi Corp at 352/628-0200) is in mid-June and the famous **Southern Redfish Tour** (www.redfishtour.com) comes a few weeks later in July. Cedar Key has recently begun a Fourth of July **Clamerica Festival** (352/543-6346, www.cedarkey.org/clamerica) with live music, clam hunts, clam-shucking demonstrations, clam bag races, and so forth. And the third weekend in October, the **Cedar Key Seafood Festival** (call Thelma McCain at 352/543-5436 or visit www.cedarkey.org/events.php) draws 30,000 people for two days of seafood gluttony (book a room far in advance for this one). A few years back, the whole Nature Coast launched an annual celebration at the end of October called the **Nature Coast Birding and Wildlife Experience** (352/543-5600).

Concentrated most heavily in the Cedar Keys and along the Suwannee and Waccasassa rivers, the festival included dozens of ways for families to enjoy nature, free of charge. And the second weekend in November, the **Homosassa Arts, Crafts, and Seafood Festival** (www.homosassaseafoodfest.com) whips up chowders and soft-shell crabs for the masses.

## ACCOMMODATIONS

People are drawn to the Nature Coast for a raw view into the natural world. They come with rods and reels, their boats topped with gas and canoes packed to the brim with stocked coolers and camping gear. As a result, this swath of Florida is complete with RV parks, campgrounds, and fish camps that run from rough wooden cabins to affordable and simple motels. In nearly all the small towns that dot U.S. 19 or the little roads west to the Gulf, you can bet on finding a clean room in a casual and unique independently owned motel where the amenities are whatever is happening out on the river, bay, or spring.

But in addition to these or the more upscale lodgings listed here, the area provides opportunities to indulge a lot of people's fantasy of endless, tranquil mobility: a stay on a houseboat. You can go "way down upon the Suwannee River" with a 44-foot houseboat rented from **Miller's Marine & Suwannee Houseboats** (County Road 349, Suwannee, 352/452-7349, $599 for two days including weekends, $1,199 for a week, www.suwanneehouseboats.com). The houseboats rent by the day or week, sleep up to eight, and are equipped with showers, bathroom facilities, linens, full kitchens, and cookware. The owners take renters on a warm-up cruise to teach them the basics, then you're on your own with 70 miles of river, countless springs, and an up-close view of the area's wildlife.

We got the anchor stuck, saw a bald eagle, fished from the comfort of our beds, scratched chigger bites, and generally pretended we were Huckleberry Finn.

### Under $100

For RV travelers, there are 398 picturesque sites set on 80 acres at **Elite Resorts at Crystal**

You can go way down the Suwanee River with Miller's houseboats.

COURTESY OF VISIT FLORIDA

River (275 S. Rock Crusher Rd., Crystal River, 352/795-1313, $35). Formerly known as Rock Crusher Canyon RV Park, it contains a 7,000-seat outdoor amphitheater that has welcomed Willie Nelson, Three Dog Night, and Joan Jett, as well as some humongous RV rallies. Also in Crystal River, with lakeside ($30) and canalside spots ($37) that include your own boat dock space, **Crystal Isles Resort** (11419 W. Fort Island Trail, Crystal River, 352/795-3774) is a 30-acre RV resort not far from the Fort Island Trail Beach. For inexpensive and pleasant waterside accommodations in Cedar Key, try **Sunset Isle RV Park/Motel** (11850 Hwy. 24, 352/543-5375, www.cedarkeyrv.com, RV campsites start at $25, motel rooms start at $50).

In Crystal River you'll find many of the inexpensive chains, such as **Best Western Crystal River Resort** (614 NW U.S. 19, Crystal River, 352/795-3171, $70–120), with its own marina and excellent fish/dive shop; **Quality Inn** (4486 N. Suncoast Blvd., Crystal River, 352/563-1500, $58–90); **Days Inn** (2380 NW U.S. 19, Crystal River, 352/795-2111, $65–100); and **Econo Lodge** (2575 NW U.S. 19, Crystal River, 352/795-9447). Most cater to visiting anglers and ring in somewhere around $75, many without a lot of bells and whistles beyond a computer in the lobby to check email. But for a more authentic experience, spend just a bit more and head for one of the independently owned places.

The area right around Weeki Wachee Springs has a lot of suburban sprawl, so it isn't the best vacation spot on the Nature Coast, but if you really want to be near this particular spring the **Quality Inn Weeki Wachee** (6172 Commercial Way, Spring Hill, 352/596-2007, $79–99) is your best bet. It's right across the street from the spring and its water park, with 116 rooms in a nice two-story building.

## Over $100

**Homosassa Riverside Resort** (5297 S. Cherokee Way, Homosassa, 352/628-2474, www.riversideresorts.com, $65–210), is the oldest resort along the Homosassa River.

Many rooms have full kitchens, so you have dining flexibility, but the on-site restaurant and lounge are definitely worth a visit. From the hotel you can arrange a manatee-awareness tour, kayak and canoe rentals, airboat rides, and other adventures.

Presided over by Gator MacRae, **MacRae's of Homosassa** (5290 S. Cherokee Way, Homosassa, 352/628-2602, $85–125) is the rustic angler's pick, with a series of log cabin–like squatty structures and old-fashioned rockers on the front porches. The 12 rooms and 10 efficiencies are equipped with kitchens, and there are laundry facilities on the premises. Its riverside marina offers boat rentals, a bait shop, and fishing charters.

Also in the "something different" category, **Nature's Resort Campground and Marina** (10359 W. Halls River Rd., Homosassa Springs, 352/628-9544, www.naturesresort-fla.com, $100 for the cabins, $35–45 for an RV site, $28 per campsite) has cabins; several hundred RV campsites; tent camping; canoe, kayak, and pontoon boat rentals; a marina; a country store; hiking trails; a pool; restaurant; and a marina bar on 97 lush acres along the Halls River. Oh, and there's a band shell that hosts country and gospel acts when the weather accommodates.

The Nature Coast doesn't offer the abundance of golfing opportunities of elsewhere in Florida. If you're jonesing to tee off, the **Plantation Inn and Golf Resort** (9301 W. Fort Island Trail, Crystal River, 352/795-4211, www.plantationgolfandspa.com) boasts a par-72, 18-hole championship course and a nine-hole executive course for training and practice, in addition to manatee snorkeling tours, guided scuba diving, and 145 guest rooms (with 12 golf villas and six condos). Given all the amenities and glitz, room rates are a fairly reasonable $124–350 (which includes greens fees).

The **Izaak Walton Lodge** (One 63rd St., Yankeetown, 352/447-2311, www.izaakwaltonlodge.com, call for rates) is one of the few reasons to get off U.S. 19 and amble down County Road 40 to Yankeetown. Named for the English biographer and author of the 1653 book, *The*

*Compleat Angler,* the small inn has a serene setting on the banks of the Withlacoochee River. The restaurant was rebuilt after a fire destroyed the original structure in 1999, but the lodge was not. It is currently undergoing a renovation and reconstruction. The renovation of the restaurant is the first phase of the Izaak Walton Lodge and Marina and will include the dining room and bar on the first floor, a multitiered dining terrace, and banquet and meeting facilities on the second floor. The second phase of the development will include a bed-and-breakfast attached to the restaurant, a general store, art gallery, resort-residential units, and boat slips along the riverfront.

If you want something nice in a romantic kind of way, **Pine Lodge Country Inn** (649 Hwy. 40 W., Follow That Dream Parkway, Inglis, 352/447-7463, www.pinelodgefla.com, $110–160) is a bed-and-breakfast with four rooms, built in the 1940s and situated in the natural settings of Inglis. Located right at the Levy and Citrus county lines, it's along the picturesque Withlacoochee River.

# FOOD
## Weeki Wachee
The town of Spring Hill, where Weeki Wachee Springs resides, has a couple of fun family-friendly places in which to refuel after a grueling day at the water park. **Boston Cooker** (5375 Spring Hill Dr., Spring Hill, 352/684-6000, 11:30 A.M.–9 P.M. weekdays, until 10 P.M. Fri. and Sat., $10–20) is the go-to place for Maine lobster, scrod, Ipswich clams, and all things New England seafood. **Nellie's Restaurant** (6234 Commercial Way, Spring Hill, 352/596-8321, 6 A.M.–8:30 P.M. daily, $7–19) is an old favorite for lunches of cottage pie or chicken-fried steak, and dinners of pot roast and meat loaf.

For something a little nicer, **Bare Bones Fish & Steakhouse** (3192 Shoal Line Blvd., Hernando Beach, 352/596-9403, $22–35) is presided over by owners Tom and Karen McEachern and features hand-cut Black Angus steaks and an array of Gulf seafood. The low, blue-shuttered building has a warm, wood-paneled dining room and a broad menu. Start with fried asparagus with chipotle ranch dip, then maybe the onion-crusted wild salmon with basil and brandy cream or the Bare Bones Signature rib eye, chargrilled and topped with mushroom-burgundy sauce.

## Homosassa
The south shore of the Homosassa River, accessible from Halls River Road, is host to a memorable place. Dinner at **Riverside Crabhouse** (5297 S. Cherokee Way, Homosassa, 352/621-5080, 11 A.M.–9 P.M. weeknights, until 10 P.M.weekends, breakfast 8–10:30 A.M. Sat.–Sun., $9–17) is a relaxed and casual joint specializing in two-foot platters heaped with sweet corn, hush puppies, scallops, soft-shell crab, steamed blue crab, clams, catfish, and a little gator tail. Thursday night is all-you-can-eat crab night, $17 for the really good garlic version. The attached Yardarm Lounge and the outdoor Monkey Bar tiki lounge are great places from which to spy on the four mostly tame monkeys who live on a tiny island a stone's throw away. After a few drinks, it's easier to come up with some creative theories as to *why* there are monkeys on Monkey Island.

**Dan's Clam Stand** (7364 W. Grover Cleveland Blvd., Homosassa, 352/628-9588, 11 A.M.–8 P.M. Mon.–Sat., $8–15) is no-frills but makes a mean clam chowder, a serviceable lobster roll, and a fine fried grouper sandwich. If you don't love seafood, the buffalo wings are hot and tasty. And **Bear Pa's Café** (7449 W. Grover Cleveland Blvd., Homosassa, 352/628-4100, 6 A.M.–2 P.M. Tues.–Sun., $8–10) is the place to try the local breakfast: fried cornmeal-crusted mullet with cheese grits.

For nightlife in Homosassa, locals go to **Margarita Grill** (10200 W. Halls River Rd., Homosassa, 352/628-1336) for the obvious, attempt a little karaoke at the **Dunbar's Old Mill Tavern** (10465 W. Yulee Dr., Homosassa, 352/628-2669), or have a leisurely riverside beer at **The Shed at MacRae's** (5300 S. Cherokee Way, Homosassa, 352/628-2602).

## Crystal River

In Crystal River, people tend to send visitors to **Charlie's Fish House Restaurant** (244 NW U.S. 19, Crystal River, 352/795-3949, 11 A.M.–9 P.M. daily, $9–16) for the views of the river and the simply prepared local fish, as well as oysters and stone crab claws (you eat only the claws because fisherfolk haul 'em up, yank off one claw, and throw them back to grow another). The restaurant has a substantial boat dock for waterborne diners.

**Cracker's Bar and Grill** (502 NW Sixth St., Crystal River, 352/795-3999, 11 A.M.–11 P.M. Mon.–Thurs., until midnight Fri. and Sat., until 10 P.M. Sun., $6–13), just up the block, is a locals' hangout with a commitment to big portions and providing something for everyone. The menu is vast, with burgers, nachos, and such alongside sautéed scallops and shrimp. Live entertainment has things hopping in the tiki bar and deck on the weekend, with karaoke many nights. Tie your boat up to one of the restaurant's 14 slips, or hop on the restaurant's water taxi and see some of Kings Bay.

For nightlife, the young folks gather at **Gabby's** (Crystal River Mall, 1801 NW U.S. 19, 352/563-5666), which recently tripled in size, while the older, classic-rock crowd patronizes **Gypsy's Den** (155 SE U.S. 19, Crystal River, 352/564-9595).

# Cedar Key

They say in Cedar Key it takes two hours to watch *60 Minutes*. There's only one road in and out of town; there's no movie theater, no Starbucks, and no fast food. In fact, there's no fast anything.

But it wasn't always that way. Back in the 1880s, Cedar Key was the busiest port in Florida, with a population of around 5,000. It was founded in 1842 by Judge Augustus Steele as a seaside resort colony for prosperous plantation owners, but a wealth of local cedar trees quickly transformed the town into the foremost producer of pencils (Eberhard-Faber, Eagle, and others) in the country, and a relatively deep harbor made Cedar Key the natural choice as the first Gulf port and the terminus for David Yulee's cross-state Atlantic and Gulf Railroad in 1860.

A flattening 10-foot tidal surge from a hurricane in 1896, followed by other bad luck (fire, poor civic planning, reckless consumption of natural resources) crippled the little town, and when Henry Plant finished his own competing railroad, linking more cosmopolitan Tampa to Florida's east coast, it was the nail in Cedar Key's cedar coffin.

Today, the constellation of tiny islands that juts three miles out into the Gulf of Mexico is inhabited by fewer than 900 year-round residents. Florida's 1995 net ban law ended the bustle of commercial fishing fleets. What that leaves are all the charms Judge Steele saw back in 1842: an abundance of birds, fish, and other wildlife; beautiful sunsets; and a profusion of dappled creeks and rivers that flow into the warm Gulf. Recently Cedar Key has become home to a substantial resident artist community, which has brought color to the town. It hasn't lost the rough-edged, casual environment that makes Cedar Key an easygoing pleasure, though. It is still the kind of place where the only locals who seem impatient are the pelicans on the Dock Street pier, hoping to steal some angler's unguarded bait stash.

## SPORTS AND RECREATION
### ◖ Cedar Key Scrub State Reserve

See some scrub before it vanishes. Okay, so scrub doesn't sound too sexy, but a scrub is an austere local plant community characterized by the dominance of shrubs (whereas forests are dominated by trees, prairies by grasses), and it is one of the fastest disappearing habitats in Florida. In the wet months, rainwater and wind rush through, cutting

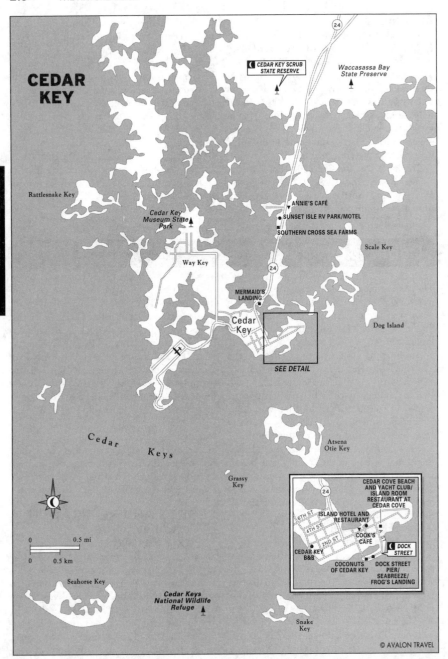

CEDAR KEY

Waccasassa Bay
State Preserve

CEDAR KEY SCRUB
STATE RESERVE

Rattlesnake Key

Cedar Key
Museum State
Park

ANNIE'S CAFÉ

SUNSET ISLE RV PARK/MOTEL

SOUTHERN CROSS SEA FARMS

Scale Key

Way Key

MERMAID'S
LANDING

Cedar Key

Dog Island

SEE DETAIL

C e d a r    K e y s

Atsena
Otie Key

Grassy
Key

0        0.5 mi

0        0.5 km

Seahorse Key

Cedar Keys
National Wildlife
Refuge

Snake
Key

CEDAR COVE BEACH
AND YACHT CLUB/
ISLAND ROOM
RESTAURANT AT
CEDAR COVE

ISLAND HOTEL AND
RESTAURANT

6TH ST

4TH ST

COOK'S
CAFÉ

2ND ST

DOCK
STREET

CEDAR KEY
B&B

COCONUTS
OF CEDAR KEY

DOCK STREET
PIER/
SEABREEZE/
FROG'S LANDING

© AVALON TRAVEL

channels in the loose soil; when it's dry, fires sweep in and burn the scrub to the ground. And then those scrappy little shrubs grow again. Extremely hot in summer, the arid, sandy terrain is home to the Florida scrub jay and a bunch of other tough nuts of the animal world. Cedar Key Scrub State Reserve (six miles northeast of Cedar Key on Hwy. 24, 352/543-5567, 8 A.M.–sundown daily, no fee) consists of 12 miles of very beautiful marked walking trails. It's dramatic in a very quiet way. Pets are welcome on leash.

## Fishing

Cedar Key has lots of ways to make you feel "reel" talented. Freshwater anglers can wet a line in the 3,657-acre **Lake Rousseau/ Withlacoochee River** area to bag bluegill, redear sunfish, catfish, black crappie, or largemouth bass. For saltwater fishing, the waters of **Cedar Keys National Wildlife Refuge** and the **Lower Suwannee National Wildlife Refuge** teem with spotted sea trout, redfish, and sheepshead. And **Waccasassa Bay Preserve State Park** provides both freshwater and saltwater fishing opportunities.

## Canoeing, Kayaking, and Boating

Designated a refuge by President Hoover way back in 1929, the **Cedar Keys National Wildlife Refuge** (352/493-0238) encompasses approximately 800 acres and is composed of 13 barrier islands in the Gulf of Mexico. The refuge is home to as many as 200,000 birds, making it a hot spot for bird-watchers. To protect the area's wildlife and fragile ecosystems, the refuge is accessible only by boat (time your trip for high tide, otherwise the shallow mud and grass flats can slow your progress), and all of the islands' interiors are closed to the public, except Atsena Otie Key, the easiest island to access. You can paddle out from Cedar Key and collect shells, identify birds, picnic, and take pictures all year-round. It's worth the effort of getting there—egrets, white ibis, cormorants, herons, pelicans, and anhingas make it a genuine avian convention out there.

Part of Seahorse Key, including the lighthouse,

is leased by the University of Florida as a Marine Research Laboratory and classroom and is closed to the public. A few days each year, the Refuge and University host an open house where the public is invited to visit the lighthouse. Formed as a giant kidney-shaped sand dune, Seahorse Key rises to a height of 52 feet, the highest point on the state's west coast. It was a military hospital and detention center for captured Indians during the Seminole Wars, with a decommissioned lighthouse built in 1855. Visitors, when they are allowed, are asked to pack out anything they take onto the islands and to refrain from removing any island animals, vegetables, or minerals.

If you don't think you can get out to view the islands under your own power, there are the **Island Hopper cruises** (352/543-5904, $21 adults, $15 children) run out of the city marina, where you can also rent pontoon boats, skiffs, kayaks, and canoes (for kayaks and canoes, call 352/949-0200). You can also rent canoes and kayaks from **Kayak Cedar Keys** (across from the Gulf Cart Co., First and A streets at the Cedar Key Beach and Park, next to the Marina, Cedar Key, 352/543-9447, www.kayakcedarkeys.com, $25–40).

If you don't want to go out on your own, **Brack Barker's Wild Florida Adventures** (P.O. Box 626, Williston, FL 32696, 352/528-3984, tour lengths and prices vary) leads kayak tours from Shell Mound near Cedar Key to the estuaries and coastal islands of the Lower Suwannee National Wildlife Refuge; out to Atsena Otie; exploring the coastal marshes of Steinhatchee; and along the Waccasassa River.

Adjacent to Cedar Key Scrub State Reserve, the **Waccasassa Bay State Preserve** (352/543-5567, 8 A.M.–sundown daily, no fee) is also accessible only by boat. (Boats can be launched from C40 in Yankeetown, C326 in Gulf Hammock, and Cedar Key.) This 32,777-acre coastal wilderness area consists of salt marsh scattered with wooded islands, themselves striated with more than 100 tidal creeks that flow into the estuary. Once here, visitors enjoy fresh- and saltwater fishing, canoeing, primitive camping, and checking

# CATCH OF THE DAY

No matter the time of year, there's something fishy along the Nature Coast. But just what are you likely to catch? When can you catch it? How many of 'em can you keep? And why should you go to the effort?

## AMBERJACK, GREATER

**When:** Caught year-round, this Atlantic species is often caught way offshore.

**Limit:** 1 fish per person, minimum size requirement of 28 inches to the fork of the tail

**Fun Factor:** They're a big, strong fish, offering a wonderful pull and feisty runs to the bottom.

## COBIA

**When:** They have a spring run and a late-fall run but are generally caught in spring.

**Limit:** 1 fish per person, 33-inch minimum

**Fun Factor:** Exceptional pullers, they will readily bite. They prefer to hang out near structures like pilings or channel markers.

## FLOUNDER

**When:** Caught year-round

**Limit:** 10 fish per person, 12-inch minimum

**Fun Factor:** A smaller species than the Atlantic version (often under 10 inches), they are excellent table fare, but cleaning them is tricky.

## GROUPER (BLACK OR GAG)

**When:** Caught year-round, but they swim way out in the summer. They move inshore fall and winter, in as little as 6 feet of water.

**Limit:** 2 fish per person (all other grouper species 5 per day), 24-inch minimum (all other grouper species have a 20-inch minimum)

**Fun Factor:** People love their fight and flavor so much that the big ones are mostly fished out. You'll find lots under 22 inches.

## JACK CREVALLE

**When:** Caught year-round, they school in the summer months.

**Limit:** No limits

**Fun Factor:** The thuggish brute that hangs out in the dark alley, it's the toughest fighting fish in the Gulf. No good to eat.

## KINGFISH

**When:** Caught year-round, but better in late winter

**Limit:** 2 fish per person, 24-inch minimum

**Fun Factor:** With lots of fight, they are beautiful, long, silvery fish that taste terrible. They tend to hunt in schools.

## MANGROVE SNAPPER

**When:** Caught year-round

**Limit:** 5 fish per person, 10-inch minimum

**Fun Factor:** One of the smaller snappers, it rarely exceeds 5 pounds. Find them around docks and piers. Watch out – they bite. Also called gray or mango snapper.

---

out the local population of bald eagles, black bears, and manatees.

## Biking

At the turn of the 20th century, steamships won out over the railroad as preferred freight and passenger carriers in this area. As in so many parts of the country, this left miles of abandoned track, which have slowly been repurposed to meet the needs of outdoor enthusiasts. The 32-mile paved **Nature Coast Trail State Park** (U.S. 19 just south of downtown Chiefland, 352/493-6072, 8 A.M.–sundown daily, no fee) links several wildlife and recreation areas together, including **Fanning Springs State Park** and **Andrews Wildlife Management Area.** The various trails wind along the Suwannee River, ranging in length from 4.3 miles up to 10 miles, with trailheads in the downtowns of five communities, including Cross City (near County Rd.); Old Town (adjacent to the Old Town Fire Station); Fanning Springs (near the Agricultural Inspection Station); Trenton (two blocks off Main St. at

## MULLET

**When:** Caught year-round
**Limit:** 50 per person, no size limit
**Fun Factor:** This is a the fish you see that jumps out of the water frequently. You cast net for them because they prefer vegetation and won't eat your bait fish, or you can use cane poles and dough balls of white bread.

## REDFISH

**When:** Caught year-round
**Limit:** 1 fish per person, 18-inch minimum, 27-inch maximum
**Fun Factor:** The bread-and-butter fish in this area, they are delicious table fare and good fighters, especially 22-35 inches in size. They have become the new inshore/shallow water tournament fish of choice. Also called red drum.

## SEABASS, BLACK

**When:** Caught year-round
**Limit:** 10 fish per person, 11-inch minimum in Gulf, 12-inch minimum in Atlantic
**Fun Factor:** Extremely small in this area, they are generally too small to keep. More of an offshore and Atlantic species.

## SHEEPSHEAD

**When:** Caught year-round, but easier to get in winter
**Limit:** 15 fish per person, 12-inch minimum
**Fun Factor:** With jailhouse stripes, it's not

surprising they're bait thieves. They hang out near barnacle-crusted structures. Good table fare but a little on the bony side.

## SPANISH MACKEREL

**When:** Caught spring through fall
**Limit:** 15 per person, 12-inch minimum
**Fun Factor:** Caught on very light tackle, they are generally under 5 pounds, travel in large schools, and are easy to catch. Most locals smoke them.

## SPOTTED SEA TROUT

**When:** Caught year-round, season closed November and December in southern areas, February in northwest regions
**Limit:** 5 fish per person, 15-inch minimum, 20-inch maximum (and you can keep one over 20 inches per day)
**Fun Factor:** One of the most abundant fish in the area, they like the grass flats. The commercial netting ban has increased their numbers recently.

## TARPON

**When:** Caught April, May, and June
**Limit:** 2 fish per person
**Fun Factor:** A protected species, they require a $50 tag to keep one, and the only reason to keep one is to set an IGFA world record, which happens a lot around here. People fly-fish for tarpon, the most explosive of inshore species.

the railroad depot); and Chiefland (near the railroad depot two blocks beyond downtown). This makes it easy to enjoy a ride and finish up with lunch or dinner in one of these sweet inland towns.

Bikes can be rented at **Suncoast Bicycles** (322 N. Pine Ave., Inverness, 352/637-5757, $15–25). There are also group rides that leave from the store most days and the store's website, www.suncoastbicycles.com, contains great local cycling routes in pdf format. Or, right downtown in Cedar Key, the **Gulf Kart**

**Company** (A St. at First, across from City Park, 352/543-5300, www.gulfkart.com) rents golf carts that seat 2–4 people ($50 for two people all day, $70 for four, $30 for four hours for two people, $40 for four—a really fun way to move around the island).

## SIGHTS
### Southern Cross Sea Farms

You could call Cedar Key "Clamelot" if you wanted. It's a backbreaking, difficult business that requires the salty seadog's perseverance and grit combined with a huge amount of scientific knowledge. All you need to know is that the town is the nation's No. 1 producer of farm-raised littlenecks, available for your delight year-round. But if you want to learn more, sweet-talk your way into Southern Cross Sea Farms (12170 Hwy. 24, Cedar Key, 352/543-5980, www.clambiz.com). They don't give official tours, but if you show an interest, they'll walk you through the process, from the saltwater larvae tanks thick with silt (which, under a microscope, is millions of perfect clams, each 60 microns in size) to the clam nursery and out to the clam bags sunk in the Gulf, where the bivalves spend 18 months maturing. Interesting clam tidbit: All are born male. It is at maturity that 50 percent become female.

## ◖ Dock Street

Cedar Key might be lean on attractions, but that's part of the attraction. Cedar Key is made up of a series of small barrier islands, but the commercial and residential parts of town are clustered on Way Key. And on Way Key, the place to be is Dock Street.

The fishing pier is the center of the action, where anglers, pelicans, and onlookers enjoy the sunset over the wide wooden boardwalk. On the weekends a little live music wafts out from Seabreeze or Frog's Landing, along with the aromas of just-caught seafood getting its culinary due. The couple of blocks of Dock Street that fan out on either side of the pier are crowded with gift shops, galleries, restaurants, and bars—a rewarding stroll at any time of the day.

## Cedar Key Museums

St. Clair Whitman invented tools and gizmos for the Standard Manufacturing Company in the early 1900s, but more importantly, he was a persistent collector. He accumulated antique glassware, old bottles, photographs of Cedar Key, and an incredible number of seashells. The **Cedar Key Museum State Park** (12231 SW 166 Ct., Cedar Key, 352/543-5350, 10 A.M.–5 P.M. Thurs.–Mon., admission $2), in Whitman's house restored as it was in its 1920s heyday, proudly displays all his collections. But it's more than just a sweet little museum in which to see his treasures. Exhibits

© JOSHUA LAWRENCE KINSER

Head to Cedar Key's downtown Dock Street as the sun goes down and your hunger rises.

provide insight into the Timucuans who once inhabited this stretch of coast, as well as Cedar Key's 19th-century history as a center for pencil manufacturing and fiber broom and brush manufacturing. Docent-led tours are offered 1–4 P.M. Save this for an afternoon when the weather is gloomy or the fish aren't biting.

There are more opportunities to explore Cedar Key history at the **Cedar Key Historical Museum** (609 Second St., Cedar Key, 352/543-5549, 1–4 P.M. Sun.–Fri., 11 A.M.–5 P.M. Sat., $1 adults, $0.50 children) right downtown. Housed in one room of a former private residence circa 1871, the museum tells the story of Cedar Key through historic photos and a somewhat idiosyncratic assortment of memorabilia, as well as displays of Native American artifacts, minerals, and woodworking tools. It's worth checking out, especially if one of the guides are available to talk about the glory days of the local lumber, pencil, and fishing industries. Although it's a little pricey ($4.50), the brochure for a self-guided historical walking tour of downtown is a great short course on the area. Also, across the street from the museum is a quirky bookstore called **Curmudgeonalia** (Second St. and D St., 352/543-6789, 9 A.M.–5 P.M. daily) that offers a great collection of birding, naturalist, and offbeat Florida history books.

## ACCOMMODATIONS

New on the scene, **◖ The Faraway Inn** (Third & G Streets, 888/543-5330, www.farawayinn.com, $75–160) is set within a quiet, attractive residential area away from traffic and nightlife, but within a short five-minute walk past Victorian and traditional Cracker homes to restaurants, convenience stores, shops, boat launches, the public beach, and the city dock. Faraway Inn was built in the early 1950s on the original site of the 19th-century Eagle Pencil Company Cedar Mill. The inn has little freestanding efficiencies and cottages as well as more motel-like accommodations. It's pet-friendly.

**Cedar Cove Beach and Yacht Club** (192 Second St., 352/543-5332, www.

cedarcove-florida.com, $109–185) has more upscale amenities than most properties in this area. All rooms are fully equipped efficiencies with private balconies and access to a heated pool and an extensive fitness facility.

A stop on the town's historical district walking tour, the **Cedar Key Bed and Breakfast** (810 Third St., 352/543-5050, www.cedarkeybandb.com, $99–175) was built in 1880 as a home for Eagle Pencil Company employees. Today, it's a comfortable six-room inn with a very nice breakfast.

## FOOD

Cedar Key has a handful of very good restaurants, especially when it comes to fresh seafood. **Annie's Café** (just over the causeway on Hwy. 24, 352/543-6141, 6:30 A.M.–4 P.M. most days, until 8 P.M. weekends, $4–8) is a local favorite for bird-watching over breakfasts of mullet, grits, sliced tomato, and a freshly made, steaming biscuit. Another breakfast joint, **Cook's Café** (434 Second St., 352/543-5548, 6:30 A.M.–2 P.M. daily, $8–10), is right downtown and allows pets on the patio if they're well behaved. Built in 1859, the **Island Hotel and Restaurant** (Second St. and B St., 352/543-5111, 6–9 P.M. Tues.–Sun., $15–24) is purportedly haunted by 13 ghosts, particularly during grisly weather. Even if you don't believe the story of the restless spirit of a murdered former owner, you'll enjoy the hearts of palm salad, the crab bisque, or just a drink in the friendly bar.

For more upscale waterside dining, head to the **Island Room Restaurant at Cedar Cove** (10 E. Second. St., 352/543-6520, www.islandroom.com, 5–10 P.M. Mon.–Fri., 8 A.M.–10 P.M. Sat.–Sun., $14–28) for Chef Peter Stefani's house-grown veggies and greens or bread pudding with bourbon sauce. After dinner, if you're not quite ready to turn in, head over to Dock Street for a game of pool, darts, or some game viewing at **Coconuts of Cedar Key** (330 Dock St., 352/543-6390, www.coconutsofcedarkey. com) or a drink with the locals at **Frog's Landing** (420 Dock St., 352/543-9243,

11 A.M.–10 P.M. Thurs.–Sun.) or **Seabreeze** (310 Dock St., 352/543-5738). And if you want something different, order Seabreeze's signature salad, a mix of lettuce, hearts of palm, peach, pineapple, and dates, topped with a scoop of peanut butter ice cream.

Opened in 2007 and owned by Peter Stefani of the Island Room, **Dock Street Depot** (490 Dock St., 352/543-0202, 11 A.M.–10 P.M. daily, $8–15) serves very good seafood jambalaya and shrimp Creole along with a menu of other seafood, fried or broiled.

## Steinhatchee

If you're really looking to get out into the wilderness of this region, you can get deeper into the backcountry in Steinhatchee (STEEN-hachee), pop. 1,500. It's 33 miles north of Cedar Key on U.S. 19 and about a dozen miles west on Highway 51. The fishing and hunting is incredible here. The trout, redfish, and wild game have kept things jumping around here since the mid-1800s. The mouth of the Steinhatchee River, called Deadman's Bay, was home to thousands of Native Americans who came for the exceptional fishing and beautiful environment. Hunters and fisherfolk have been following suit ever since. In recent years Steinhatchee's appeal has broadened, thanks in large measure to a Georgian entrepreneur named Dean Fowler.

Fowler's place, Steinhatchee Landing Resort, has drawn accolades from an array of travel magazines in recent years. This hasn't picked up the pace around here—in fact, at his place the posted speed limit is 9 mph. Why, you ask? "If it was 10, no one would pay it any mind," says Fowler. It's that kind of folksy, down-home sensibility that makes Steinhatchee such a joy to explore.

The Steinhatchee River—along with the Suwannee, Wacissa, Econfina, Fenholloway, and St. Marks rivers—has emptied its rich contents here into the Apalachee Bay of the Gulf of Mexico for centuries. The shallow bay's gentle, gradual slope and fertile grass flats have made it a world-class fishing destination and a summer scalloping hot spot. It's a place where everyone has a big fish story and the time to tell it right, a place where "live bait and cold beer" sound like two of the central ingredients in happiness.

## SPORTS AND RECREATION
### Scalloping

Beginning July 1 and ending September 10, the scalloping season brings thousands of visitors to the little town of Steinhatchee. You need a recreational saltwater fishing license (888/347-4356, www.wildlifelicense.com, $17 for a three-day license) before you can wade out into the grassy shallows to scoop up the sweet bay bivalves. Each harvester is limited to two gallons of whole scallops or one pint of shucked meat per day. Pack a snorkel, swim shoes, and a mesh bag for your catch.

### ◖ Offshore Fishing

Folks visiting this area most often spend their time, and considerable money, on half-day or full-day charters out into the Gulf in search of amberjack, kingfish (not the best tasting, but a beautiful sportfish), redfish, cobia, and grouper. Black grouper limits are five per person per day, and they must be at least 22 inches long. **Big Bend Charters** (352/498-3703, www.bigbendcharters.com) takes groups of up to six far out on offshore ($870) or nearshore ($600) trips, or a "thrill" fishing trip that targets a range of species ($990).

Farther in, spotted sea trout, catfish, and redfish can be coaxed out of the grass flats of Deadman's Bay or the slow-moving Steinhatchee River. Kingfish travel through Steinhatchee spring and fall to stay in the perfect water temperature (72°F or so), and the town is a legendary trout and redfish fishery in the wintertime when the fish move up into the river. Freshwater fishing can be accomplished dockside or from a rented canoe, but it's more fun in a shallow-draft boat with a motor: A 24-foot deck boat with a 200-horsepower Yamaha motor with a bimini will run you $150 per half day plus fuel at the **River Haven Marina** (1110 Riverside Dr. SE, Steinhatchee, 352/498-0709, www.riverhavenmarinaandmotel.com). First-timers should hire a guide (it's an eminent place to learn saltwater fly-fishing techniques), but if you're striking out on your own, head to one of the local marinas (Sea Hag, River Haven, or Gulf Stream) and listen carefully to suss out the latest hot spots and irresistible baits. (Tip: Wear sunglasses with polarized lenses so you can see into the water more effectively.)

## Diving

*Rodale's Scuba Diving* magazine is always heaping kudos on the Nature Coast, and scuba devotees come from all over to try cave and freshwater diving in the crystal-clear waters. Many of the draws are north and east of Steinhatchee and Cedar Key.

Along the Santa Fe River in High Springs, **Ginnie Springs** (from U.S. 19 head northeast on Hwy. 47, 386/454-7188, www.ginniesprings.com) may be one of the most popular freshwater dive sites in the world, a place Jacques Cousteau once characterized as "visibility forever." Certified cave divers will also have heard of its Devil's Eye/Ear cave system. If you're diving for the first time, Ginnie Springs is perfect—no waves or breaking surf, no boats to contend with. There's a noncertification guided Discover Scuba Diving program (386/454-7188, $99 per student).

There are also two first-magnitude springs, **Manatee Springs State Park** (on Hwy. 320 west of Chiefland, 352/493-6072) and **Fanning Springs State Park** (U.S. 19, Fanning Springs, 352/463-3420), 10 minutes from each other and 30 minutes northeast from Cedar Key. Situated in a 2,075-acre park, Manatee Springs produces 117 million gallons of clear blue water daily, a haven for manatees, fish, wading birds, scuba divers, and swimmers alike. There are two spots for excellent cavern and cave diving, **Manatee Spring** itself and

**Catfish Hotel Sink.** You can camp, fish, boat, and hike in the park as well, but for a quick day trip the boardwalk through cypress swamp to the Suwannee River is a must-see. At Fanning Springs, which releases about 50 million gallons of water a day, swimmers and snorkelers explore the 20-foot-deep spring basin fed by two springs, Big Fanning and Little Fanning. Fanning Springs also has a cool boardwalk to the river, a nature trail, volleyball, and picnic facilities.

And a little farther away on Highway 3 in the town of Williston, there are two diving draws: Visitors to **Devil's Den Resort & Springs** (5390 NE 180th Ave., 352/528-3344, www.devilsden.com, general admission $9, dive fee $37, gear rental $71) descend wooden steps through a rock tunnel to a floating dock, and then the dive begins about 40 feet down with swim-throughs, nooks, and crannies to explore. One of the safest cavern dives in the state is the nearby **Blue Grotto** (3852 NE 172nd Ct., 352/528-5770, www.divebluegrotto.com, dive fee $37), a limestone sink with heavy-duty guidelines and platforms down to the 100-foot depths.

Farther south, if you want to get a sense for the history of the Suwannee River steamboat era, you can dive to see the **City of Hawkinsville Underwater Archaeological Preserve** (western bank of the Suwannee River, Old Town, accessible only by boat, 850/245-6444). Built in 1896 for the Hawkinsville Deep Water Boat Lines, the steamboat was used on the Suwannee River for the booming lumber industry before it ceased operation in 1922. Today, divers can explore the intact 141-foot hull of the sunken steamer, swimming along the long deck of the vessel to the stern paddlewheel alongside the area's more intrepid fish.

For diving equipment and services, options are plentiful. **American Pro Diving Center** (821 SE Hwy. 19, Crystal River, 352/563-0041), **Bird's Underwater** (320 NW Hwy. 19, Crystal River, 352/563-2763, www.birdsunderwater.com), and **Steve's Scuba & Snorkeling** (669 NE Hwy. 19, Crystal River, 352/795-1551) all have good reputations in the area.

## Beaches

Of all the hundreds of miles of Florida's Gulf Coast, the Nature Coast offers the most limited beach access, much of it unsuitable for swimming. Tiny barrier islands and shallow grassy flats protect the coast from getting buffeted by Gulf winds and surf but also preclude the soft, white sand of elsewhere on the Gulf Coast. If you want to make a day of it, your best bet is **Keaton Beach,** a neat little beach town 17 miles north of Steinhatchee. Families and fisherfolk are drawn to the wide natural public beach, the 700-foot fishing pier, and the large boat ramp. The trick is getting there: Follow U.S. 19 north through Cross City, go approximately 11 miles, turn left onto Highway 358. At the flashing light, stay to the right and once you go through Jena, turn right. Go over the bridge, turn left at the stop sign, and at next stop sign turn right. Go another 17 miles and turn left at the stop sign.

Beyond that, Cedar Key has a fair amount of private beach, but public access is limited to the downtown **city park** next to a colorful kids' playground on Second Street. The bay here is very shallow and muddy, due to the outflow of numerous creeks and rivers, and the sand is rocky and hard on bare feet. A better bet is to head out to **Fort Island Trail Beach** (from U.S. 19, turn west on Fort Island Trail and drive 10 miles). This Gulf-side beach is about 1,000 feet long, with a new fishing pier, concessions, and picnic facilities. A lifeguard is on duty Memorial Day–Labor Day, and the beach is open daylight–9:30 P.M.

## ACCOMMODATIONS

**⟨ Steinhatchee Landing Resort** (228 NE Hwy. 51, Steinhatchee, 352/498-3513, www.steinhatcheelanding.com, $146–506) is as upscale as it gets along the Nature Coast. Its 35 acres are dotted with dozens of individual one-, two-, and three-bedroom Victorian and Florida Cracker cottages, most equipped with French country furniture and oversized spa tubs. There's a new swimming pool and patio area, and it accepts pets up to 28 pounds.

The same folks own the nearby 17-room, budget-friendly **Steinhatchee River Inn** (1111 Riverside Dr., Steinhatchee, 352/498-4049, www.steinhatcheeriverinn.net), where the rates range seasonally $89–119.

## FOOD

The dining scene is dominated by **Fiddler's Restaurant** (1306 Riverside Dr., 352/498-7427, http://fiddlersrestaurant.com, 6 A.M.–10 P.M. daily, $10–20), a sprawling, lively spot populated by men swapping big fish stories and tucking into fried grouper (you can bring your own cleaned catch and have them cook it up). **Roy's** (100 First Ave. SW, 352/498-5000, www.roys-restaurant.com, 11 A.M.–9 P.M. daily, $13–16), a local favorite for 38 years, doesn't serve any booze but has an exhaustive salad bar, fried seafood, and fat burgers that keep people happy. **Lynn-Rich Restaurant** (202 15th St. SE, 352/498-0605) offers a familiar range of breakfast selections and sandwiches at lunch.

# Information and Services

The Nature Coast is located within the **Eastern time zone.** The area code is **352.**

## TOURIST INFORMATION

**Citrus County Chamber of Commerce** has three offices (401 Tompkins St., Inverness, 352/726-2801; 28 NW U.S. 19, Crystal River, 352/795-3149; and 3495 S. Suncoast Blvd., Homosassa, 352/628-2666), each of which stocks racks of local brochures and pamphlets; all are open 8:30 A.M.–4:30 P.M. Monday–Friday, until 1 P.M. Saturday. For more information about local events, pick up the *Citrus County Chronicle* ($0.25), the largest daily in the county. There's also an easy-to-use online version at www.chronicleonline.com.

**Cedar Key Chamber of Commerce** (618 Second St., 352/543-5600, 10 A.M.–1 P.M. Mon., Wed., and Fri.), right down the block from the city hall and library, has limited hours and limited offerings. Each Thursday you can pick up the *Cedar Key Beacon* ($0.50), the little island newspaper that directs you to events and activities.

For other tourist information and maps of the area, contact **Florida's Pure Water Wilderness** (352/463-3467, www.purewaterwilderness.com). Birders will want to check out the award-winning website, www.citrusbirdingtrail.com, which catalogs birding opportunities on virtually every trail in the area.

## POLICE AND EMERGENCIES

The **Crystal River Police Department,** the largest along the Nature Coast, is in back of city hall (123 NW U.S. 19, 352/795-4241).

In the event of a medical emergency, **Seven Rivers Regional Medical Center** (6201 N. Suncoast Blvd., Crystal River, 352/795-6560) has emergency services, as does **Nature Coast Regional Hospital** (125 SW Seventh St., Williston, 352/528-2801). For anything major, you may want to head to **North Florida Regional Medical Center** in Gainesville.

## RADIO AND TELEVISION

**WXCV "Citrus" FM 95.3** broadcasts popular music and information about the Nature Coast; for news, tune in to **WFSU FM 88.9** out of Tallahassee; **WKTK FM 98.5** out of Gainesville pumps out easy 1970s, 1980s, and 1990s rock (and is the station to turn to for info on suspected flooding); **WJUF FM 90.1** sends out classical, jazz, and folk; and **WRGO FM 102.7** gives you oldies from Cedar Key.

On the television, **WCJB CH 20** is the ABC affiliate out of Gainesville and Ocala. Also out of Gainesville and Ocala, **WOGX CH 51** is the FOX affiliate.

## LAUNDRY SERVICES

Catering to fisherfolk, many of the Nature Coast's motels, hotels, fish camps, and campgrounds offer laundry facilities. But if you need a coin laundry, try **Crystal Center Laundromat** (648 SE U.S. 19, Crystal River, 352/795-0979).

## FISHING LICENSES

If you haven't planned ahead, fishing licenses can be purchased on the fly at the Kmart in Crystal River or the Wal-Mart in Homosassa.

# Getting There and Around

Florida's Nature Coast is west of I-75 and is accessible by the north–south corridor of U.S. 19. If you happen to be piloting your own small plane, Cedar Key has a single 2,300-foot hard-surfaced runway, but this is uncontrolled airspace. The closest commercial airports are **Gainesville Regional Airport** (approximately one hour away, 352/373-0249), with service provided by Continental, Delta, and US Airways, and **Tallahassee Regional Airport** (also one hour away, seven miles north of Tallahassee, 904/891-7800), with service provided by Continental, Delta, and US Airways. **Orlando International Airport** (407/825-2001) and **Tampa International Airport** (813/870-8700) are both approximately 1.5

hours away by car, both offering many more commercial flights.

**Alamo** (800/327-9633), **Avis** (800/831-2847), **Budget** (800/527-0700), **Dollar** (800/800-4000 domestic, 800/800-6000 international), and **National** (800/227-7368) all provide rental cars from these airports.

Most of the Nature Coast is accessible by car or boat only. There is no public transportation to speak of besides two southbound and two northbound Greyhound buses that stop daily in Crystal River and Chiefland—but once you've arrived, you still need a car to get around. From south to north, Spring Hill (the town in which Weeki Wachee Springs lies), Homosassa, and Crystal River are lined up adjacent to each other right along U.S. 19. To get to Cedar Key, head north on U.S. 19 and then 23 miles southwest on Highway 24, the only road in and out of town (much of which is a quite rural two-lane highway until you cross the causeway into town). Steinhatchee is 33 miles north of Cedar Key on U.S. 19 and then 12 miles west on Highway 51.

Driving in Florida during the summer months can be especially challenging, with periods of heat and humidity and tremendous thunderstorms occurring almost every afternoon. It pays to have your car equipped with a first-aid kit, jumper cables, flashlight with new batteries, a jack, and cellular phone (although cell phone service can be spotty in the more rural communities).

# TALLAHASSEE

A Florida anomaly in many ways, Tallahassee has none of the manic fun-in-the-sun energy of beach towns on the peninsula or even out the state's Panhandle. It's a rooted place with a sense of history, and much more Southern in manner than any of the state's other urban centers. It's counterintuitive, but farther south on the Florida peninsula (Tampa, Sarasota, Naples) it hardly seems like the American South at all. But here in Tallahassee, a scant 20 miles from the Georgia border, you'll hear the fluid and relaxed sound of the Southern accent; you can order tall glasses of sweet iced tea and find rocking chairs on the deep porches of beautiful houses. Even the area's landscape is different from the rest of Florida, with rolling hills, oak-canopied roads, red clay, and dogwood, magnolia, oleander, and confederate jasmine blossoms.

Tucked in the foothills of the Appalachian Mountains, at the juncture of Florida's Panhandle and peninsula (an area called the Big Bend), Tallahassee hasn't always been the capital. It was a compromise. When the east and west Florida territories combined in 1822, officials shuttled between the western capital of Pensacola and the eastern capital of St. Augustine. State officials felt it was a bit too far to travel and decided to relocate the capital at a hilly, forested spot between the two cities. Tallahassee was chosen in 1824.

Hardly a stylish urban center at that time, the capital began as an agricultural community with land that proved rich enough to support crops like cotton, corn, and sweet potatoes. Yet, after the Civil War, many of Tallahassee's large plantations were repurposed as hunting lodges.

© JOSHUA LAWRENCE KINSER

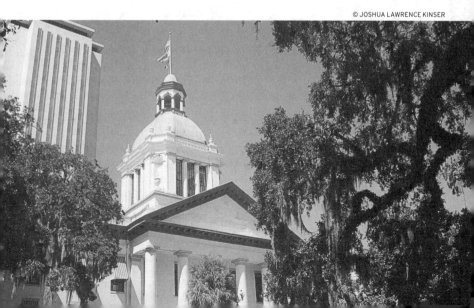

# HIGHLIGHTS

**◖ Big Bend Saltwater Paddling Trail:** Extending 60 miles along the Gulf Coast, the Big Bend Wildlife Management Area is home to hundreds of bird and animal species as well as a meandering 105-mile mapped kayak and canoe trail (page 231).

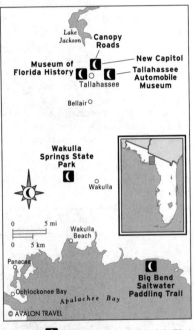

**◖ Wakulla Springs State Park:** What do *Airport '77* and *Tarzan's Secret Treasure* have in common? They were both filmed in the lush wilderness surrounding these crystal-clear springs, which pump 600,000 gallons of water per minute (page 233).

**◖ Canopy Roads:** Five official canopy roads radiate out from downtown Tallahassee, the gnarled live-oak tunnels festooned with lacy Spanish moss. They make a wonderful driving tour, culminating in a visit to Bradley's Country Store out on Centerville Road (page 234).

**◖ New Capitol:** The sleek edifice sticks out like a glamorous modern thumb against the low-rise Tallahassee skyline. To orient yourself, head to the 22nd-floor observatory level before taking the guided tour of this center of state government (page 234).

**◖ Museum of Florida History:** The Old Capitol, now home to the Florida Center for Political History and Governance, is one of the five sites that this downtown historical museum comprises, a good place to get your bearings in Florida's capital (page 236).

**◖ Tallahassee Automobile Museum:** A new addition to Tallahassee, the museum is laudable for both its incredible collection (the hearse that carried Lincoln, the Batmobile) and its progressive use of solar panels (page 237).

LOOK FOR ◖ TO FIND RECOMMENDED SIGHTS, ACTIVITIES, DINING, AND LODGING.

Growth was slow but steady right through the Depression, the wars, and until today. Some of the population is accounted for by the presence of Florida State University, Florida A&M (Agricultural and Mechanical) University, and Tallahassee Community College. FSU has a total enrollment of 33,971, FAMU has 12,126 students, and the community college boasts another 11,966—that's a lot of youthful energy in a city of roughly 150,000 people.

As with any college town, the schools bring academic and cultural amenities to the area. Add to that the presence of state government, the good manners of the South, and abounding natural beauty and it's a recipe for a beautiful, restful vacation. Kids may be less than enthralled with tours of restored 19th-century plantation homes and picturesque canopied roads, but there are enough outdoor activities and natural enticements to provide fun for all ages.

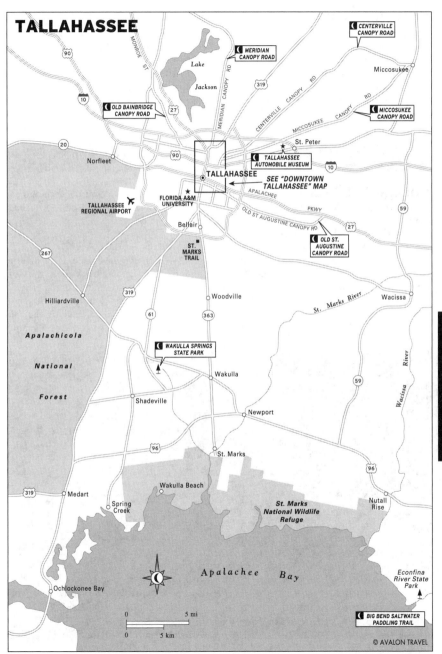

# TALLAHASSEE

90

MONROE ST

Lake
Jackson

( MERIDIAN
CANOPY ROAD

( CENTERVILLE
CANOPY ROAD

Miccosukee

319

10

( OLD BAINBRIDGE
CANOPY ROAD

27

MERIDIAN CANOPY RD

CENTERVILLE CANOPY RD

MICCOSUKEE CANOPY RD

( MICCOSUKEE
CANOPY ROAD

20

Norfleet

90

St. Peter

( TALLAHASSEE
AUTOMOBILE MUSEUM

10

● TALLAHASSEE

SEE "DOWNTOWN
TALLAHASSEE" MAP

TALLAHASSEE
REGIONAL AIRPORT

★ FLORIDA A&M
UNIVERSITY

APALACHEE

PKWY

59

Bellair

OLD ST AUGUSTINE CANOPY RD

27

267

■ ST.
MARKS
TRAIL

( OLD ST.
AUGUSTINE
CANOPY ROAD

Hilliardville

319

Woodville

St. Marks River

Wacissa

*Apalachicola*

61

363

*National*

( WAKULLA SPRINGS
STATE PARK

59

*Forest*

⛺ Wakulla

Wacissa River

Shadeville

Newport

96

St. Marks

96

319

Medart

Wakulla Beach

Spring
Creek

*St. Marks
National Wildlife
Refuge*

Nutall
Rise

Ochlockonee Bay

*Apalachee Bay*

Econfina
River State
Park

0        5 mi

0        5 km

( BIG BEND SALTWATER
PADDLING TRAIL

© AVALON TRAVEL

TALLAHASSEE

## PLANNING YOUR TIME

The city makes a wonderful weekend get-away, or a several-day add-on to another Gulf Coast destination. Timing a trip to Tallahassee is fraught with difficult choices. It's a city with four distinct seasons, unlike much of Florida where there seem only to be two. All year-round it's pleasantly moderate: In December the average high temperature is about 65°F, with five inches or so of rain. In the summertime, the temperature hovers in the low 90s and it can rain nearly nine inches a month. There are numerous local events and festivals worth considering, not to mention the extreme excitement that is a Seminoles home game.

# Sports and Recreation

## COLLEGE FOOTBALL

**Doak Campbell Stadium** (bordered by Stadium Dr., Pensacola St., and Gaines St., 850/64-GO-FSU, http://seminoles.colleg-esports.com, $19–36 tickets, which sell out far in advance) is the site of an incredible amount of school spirit. The **Florida State University Seminoles** play here, and die-hard fans on game days transform Tallahassee into a scene of high-energy celebration. The most difficult tickets to get are those against their longtime rivals, Virginia Tech and the Florida Gators. Call for a schedule of games, dates, and times.

## BEACHES AND PARKS

Tallahassee isn't on the coast exactly, making it a bit of an outlier in a book about the Gulf Coast. But all you have to do is hop in the car and drive less than an hour to hit a bunch of wonderful beaches and parks along the wild Big Bend area, an area sparsely populated by

Tallahassee comes alive when there is a home game for the Seminoles.

COURTESY OF FLORIDA STATE SPORTS INFORMATION/MIKE OLIVELLA

humans and dense with subtropical plants and wildlife.

## St. Marks National Wildlife Refuge

St. Marks National Wildlife Refuge (1255 Lighthouse Rd., St. Marks, 850/925-6121, sunrise–sunset daily, $5 per vehicle) is one of the oldest refuges in the National Wildlife Refuge System (established in 1931), with 68,000 acres of protected coastal land. The coastal marshes, islands, tidal creeks, and estuaries of seven north Florida rivers can be explored by boat or by foot. Stop in first at the visitors center (8 A.M.–4 P.M. Mon.–Fri., 10 A.M.–5 P.M. Sat. and Sun.) to get an overview of what there is to do and see in the park.

The refuge has 75 miles of trails, including a 50-mile segment of the Florida National Scenic Trail, but there are wonderful short walking trails as well: the Plum Orchard Pond Trail (0.3 mile), Headquarters Pond Trail (0.25 mile), and Lighthouse Levee Trail (0.5 mile—the St. Marks Lighthouse is still in use today), and the Mounds Interpretive Trail (1 mile), which offers a diversity of habitats for birdwatching and wildlife-viewing. Hiking here is less pleasant in the summer months, when you might opt to explore via a driving tour with the air-conditioning on.

The park is a magnet for birders, who come for the myriad wading birds as well as the ospreys, red-cockaded woodpeckers, kestrels, redshouldered hawks, and bald eagles. The refuge is open to fishing year-round and hunting in season. There are restrooms at the Refuge Visitor Center, Mounds Trail, and Otter Lake Recreation Area, and picnic facilities are next to Mounds Trail and at Otter Lake.

## ◖ Big Bend Saltwater Paddling Trail

Birders also enthuse about the **Big Bend Wildlife Management Area**'s Hickory Mound Impoundment (from Tallahassee, take U.S. 98 east, turn right on Cow Creek Grade, and go six miles to the check station, 850/488-5520). The list of birds that hang out here includes wading birds, ospreys, swallow-tailed and Mississippi kites, bald eagles, and a whole lot of birds I've never even heard of (buffleheads, gadwalls, American wigeons). This area is just one of the five areas, along with Spring Creek, Tide Swamp, Jena, and Snipe Island, that make up the Big Bend Wildlife Management Area. It extends about 60 miles along the Gulf Coast, with Tallahassee approximately 40 miles north of the northernmost part, all of it a gorgeous wilderness explored by bike, horseback, foot, or—the best way—by kayak. The 105-mile Big Bend Saltwater Paddling Trail is open September–June. To order the $15, 40-page paddling guide for the trail, call 850/488-5520 or go online at http://myfwc.com. It details seven designated primitive campsites, exclusively for trail users, spaced 10–14 miles apart (requiring permits).

Canoes and kayaks can be rented in Tallahassee at **The Wilderness Way** (3152 Shadeville Rd., 850/877-7200, www.thewildernessway.net, single kayaks or canoes $30 per day, $150 per week; tandem kayaks or canoes $35 per day, $175 per week), which also leads nature-based canoe and kayak tours around the Panhandle; and **Blue Water Scuba and Travel Center** (2320 Apalachee Pkwy., 850/656-3483).

## Maclay State Gardens

New York financier Alfred Maclay designed a garden where both native and exotic plants of Florida grow together on the grounds of his Tallahassee winter home. Maclay State Gardens (3540 Thomasville Rd., 850/487-4556) has stunning formal gardens, designed to be at their height of beauty during the winter and early spring (when Maclay and his family would have been in residence). Visitors can walk the gardens ($6 adults, $3 children) or enjoy the park's nature trails, boating, swimming, fishing, and picnicking. The park is open 8 A.M.–sunset daily, the gardens 9 A.M.–5 P.M. daily, overstreet trails 8 A.M.–6 P.M. daily, and the Maclay House 9 A.M.–5 P.M. daily January–April. Parking is $4.

# PANACEA AND SOPCHOPPY

It's a competition for the two best names in Florida. These little colorful towns are both in Wakulla County south of Tallahassee between Carrabelle and Crawfordville, along U.S. 98 near Apalachee Bay and the Gulf of Mexico, and tucked between Apalachicola National Forest and the St. Marks Wildlife Refuge.

Panacea was developed as a tourist resort more than 100 years ago by residents looking to market the incredible local springs. These days it's a sweet town of about 1,000 people, with seafood shops along the main street.

You can also visit Anne and Jack Rudloe's **Gulf Specimen Marine Laboratory** (222 Clark Dr., 850/984-5297, 9 A.M.–5 P.M. Mon.–Fri., 10 A.M.–4 P.M. Sat., noon–4 P.M. Sun., $7.50 adults, $6 seniors, $5 children 3-11). The Rudloes are both marine biologists and authors of well-known books on Florida natural history and marinelife. The independent non-profit environmental center and aquarium is open to the public, enabling visitors to get a peek at green shrimp, scarlet sponges, comb jellyfish, and other local marinelife in a sea-grass meadow or on a limestone outcrop in a collection of seawater tanks and aquariums. It's a "small is beautiful" approach to aquatic creatures.

There's a tiny airport in Panacea, really just a grassy landing strip, out of which a few enterprising pilots take small charters. Show up and ask around and you might get a pilot to zip you over to Dog Island for the day.

The first weekend in May draws more than 20,000 people to Panacea for the **Blue Crab Festival.** At night in the summer, the thing to do in these parts is to go swimming in the Gulf when the water's **bioluminescence** lends an eerie shimmer to the dark water. Totally safe (after all, it's just the chemical-based light produced by a whole bunch of marine organisms), the gleam seems to echo the zillions of stars visible in the Panacea or Sopchoppy night sky.

For dinner in Panacea, the obvious choice is **Angelo's** (on pilings over Ochlockonee Bay on U.S. 98 on the east side of the bridge, 850/984-5168, 4:30-10 P.M. Wed. and Thurs., until 11 P.M. Fri. and Sat., noon–10 P.M. Sun.). Destroyed in the storm surge from Hurricane Dennis a couple of years ago, it's back with a vengeance in a sturdier structure, with just-caught fish and great views. Or else hit **Posey's Beyond the Bay** (1506 Coastal Hwy., 850/984-5799) for topless oysters or smoked mullet, or enjoy the restorative comforts at the **Coastal Restaurant** (1305 Coastal Hwy., 850/984-2933) before bunking down for the night at the **Panacea Motel** (1545 Coastal Hwy., 850/984-5421).

In Sopchoppy the biggest industry is raising worms. Worm "grunters" pierce loose soil with a wooden stake called a stob. Once the stob is driven into the soil it gets rubbed with a flat piece of metal called the bat. The vibrations in the ground drive the big earthworms out, where they are scooped, packaged, and sold for bait. To see how it's done, there's an unbelievable nine-minute movie about it on YouTube.

This is such a compelling calling that the town of about 500 holds a well-attended **Worm Gruntin' Festival** each April. The second-biggest festival comes in June with the **June Jam** of mostly local musicians performing in the square.

**George the Potter** is a beloved local attraction, with a studio down a dirt road south off of U.S. 319 just east of Sopchoppy (110 Suncat Ridge, 850/962-9311). Look for his sign. He makes lovely bowls and mugs, and has a savvy self-promoting bumper sticker that says "Been to Sopchoppy met the Potter."

Then think of camping in Sopchoppy at the **Myron B. Hodge City Park** (Sheldon St. and Park Ave., 850/962-4611).

Sopchoppy is the nearest town to Alligator Point, and between those two towns there's a strange prevalence of **white squirrels.** There are many lyrical myths about how and why these creatures got here. A great many **monarch butterflies** also appear here in September and October in their migration south to Mexico. During the fall the beaches can be dotted with these beautiful butterflies.

## ◀ Wakulla Springs State Park

Wakulla Springs are said to be the world's largest and deepest freshwater springs, in which the water temperature remains a fairly constant 70°F. The springs have been the site of lots of Hollywood filming because of their wild, untouched jungle feel, just 15 miles south of Tallahassee. They were a tourist attraction long before Johnny Weismuller slipped into his loincloth to star as Tarzan or Ricou Browning donned the rubber suit for the film *Creature from the Black Lagoon*. In fact, as a teenager Browning was a lifeguard at Wakulla Springs and put on underwater shows for the glass-bottomed boat tours (he helped develop the underwater hose-breathing that has made the mermaid show at Weeki Wachee Springs a hit for so long).

That same glass-bottomed boat tour is a must-see today at Wakulla Springs State Park (550 Wakulla Park Dr., Wakulla Springs, 850/926-0700, 8 A.M.–sundown daily, $6 per vehicle entrance to the park, $8 tour for adults, $5 children under 12). The 30-minute tours, offered only when the water is clear, provide a glimpse into the clear 125-foot depths, but more than that they offer a window into north Florida's past. The people who lead the tours give excellent narration as you explore the mysteries and history of this magical place. Oh, and a high-jumping fish named Henry is involved. The park offers a 60-minute riverboat tour that takes a different route, but I'd opt for the former if it's running.

In the past few years, Wakulla has also become home to numerous manatees, with seven manatees, including two calves, remaining in park waters year-round.

The park also contains a wonderful six-mile nature trail, picnic facilities, swimming (only in designated areas, as it's gator country), and the stately **Wakulla Lodge** (850/224-5950, $95–150) for overnight guests. The lodge was built in 1937, with 27 rooms, each individually decorated with antiques and period furniture. The lodge also has a nice restaurant called the Ball Room Restaurant—order the navy bean soup or the fried chicken. And make sure to

Take a glass-bottom boat ride at Wakulla Springs for exceptional manatee viewing.

© JOSHUA LAWRENCE KINSER

**TALLAHASSEE**

check with the lodge during the slow season for incredible rates and specials, like the couples special usually offered Sept.–Feb. that includes dinner for two at the Ball Room Restaurant, a boat tour for two, and a night's stay at the lodge for $99.

Flowing from Wakulla Springs nine miles to the St. Marks River are the crystal-clear waters of the **Wakulla River.** Along the Spanish moss–trimmed cypress lining the river's banks you'll see abundant wildlife, from manatees, otters, and eagles to numerous waterfowl. Several boat ramps provide access to the river, a perfect day's paddle by kayak or canoe. **TNT Hideaway** (6527 Coastal Hwy., Crawfordville, 850/925-6412) is a small, family-owned business with 20 canoes and 20 kayaks, offering guided tours on the Wakulla River (and also off-the-beaten-path tours to St. Marks Lighthouse and Wildlife Refuge, Spring Creek, Aucilla River, Sopchoppy River, and Ochlockonee River). If your aim is to spot a manatee, the weekly *Wakulla News* carries a manatee-watch section that gives all the specifics of recent sightings.

After a day at the springs or along the river, you can bunk down at the **Sweet Magnolia Bed & Breakfast** (803 Port Leon Dr., St. Marks, 850/925-7670, $85–185) or at one of the area's campgrounds: **Ochlockonee River State Park** (four miles south of Sopchoppy on U.S. 319, 850/962-2771, $18) or **Holiday Campground** (14 Coastal Hwy., Panacea, 850/984-5757, around $30, depending on family size).

## GOLF

Just for comparison's sake, Naples and Tallahassee are roughly similar in size. In Naples, there are 90 or so public, resort, and semiprivate golf courses within a 30-minute drive of each other. In Tallahassee, cut that number down—way down. There are fewer than 10 courses in the capital city. This isn't a luxury golf retreat destination with acres of rolling greens. There are no resort-level courses that draw professional golfers here, but that doesn't mean you can't play, mostly for a very fair price.

The city of Tallahassee's Park & Recreation Department manages two city-owned golf courses. **Hilaman Park Municipal Golf Course** (2737 Blair Stone Rd., 850/891-2560, greens fee with cart $25–35). It's a par-72, 18-hole course purchased by the city in 1981 and refurbished. The park also offers a swimming pool, tennis courts, racquetball and squash courts, driving range, and golf pro shop. The second one is **Jake Gaither Municipal Golf Course** (801 Tanner Dr., 850/891-3942, greens fee $15–22, cart additional) a par-36, nine-hole course. Tee times are offered on the weekend, with open play during the week.

The **Seminole Golf Course** (2550 Pottsdamer St., 850/644-1790, greens fee $20–50) has had a recent $7 million upgrade, improving the quality of play on this 1962-vintage course. But the area's most celebrated semiprivate course, **SouthWood Golf Club** (3750 Grove Park Dr., 850/942-4653, www.southwoodgolf.com, $25–75), is what has golfers excited. Fred Couples said, "Without a doubt, the land at SouthWood is one of the most ideal settings Gene and I have ever had the opportunity to work with. We had the perfect palette from which to sculpt the course—rolling hills and wide open pasture lands combined with stands of awesome moss-draped live oaks."

And for a relaxed day of golf outside the city, head west to the little town of Quincy. The **Golf Club of Quincy** (2291 Soloman Dairy Rd., Quincy, 850/627-9631, $35–45) is a quiet course of rolling hills and tree-lined fairways.

# Sights

## ◖ CANOPY ROADS

Five official canopy roads radiate out from downtown Tallahassee—Old St. Augustine, Miccosukee, Meridian, Centerville, and Old Bainbridge. It is mandatory that visitors steer their vehicles through at least one of these moss-draped live-oak tunnels. Narrow, curvy and full of leafy greenness, these 60 miles of road were the work of plantation owners. The roads follow earlier trails forged in the 16th century by Spanish missionaries, but their antebellum purpose was to provide shade for travelers on their long journeys to the Gulf of Mexico. It is not much different today. All local maps indicate the canopy roads. If you choose Old St. Augustine Road, look for the **stump-carving work** of chainsaw artist John Birch. And if you head out on Centerville, stop in and pick up sausages at old-time **Bradley's Country Store** (10655 Centerville Rd., 850/893-1647).

## ◖ NEW CAPITOL

The New Capitol building (Apalachee Pkwy. and Monroe St., 850/488-6167, 9 A.M.–5 P.M. Mon.–Fri., free admission) is hard to miss downtown, a sleek modern building providing visual contrast to the classic domed Old

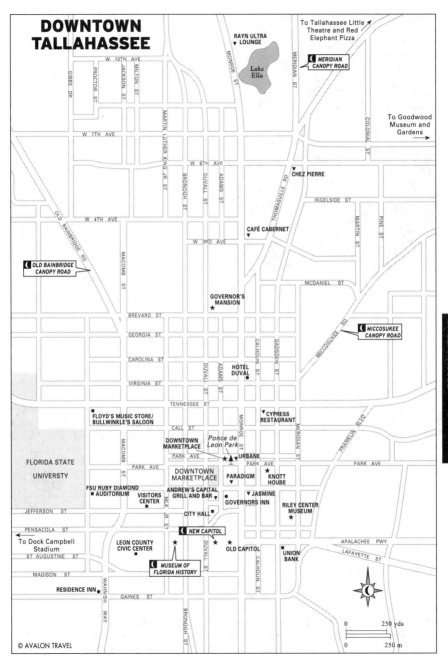

# DOWNTOWN TALLAHASSEE

© AVALON TRAVEL

TALLAHASSEE

© JOSHUA LAWRENCE KINSER

Take a slow drive down one of Tallahassee's beautiful canopy roads.

Capitol next door. At the top of the New Capitol, on the 22nd floor, there's an observatory level from which one can see all the way to Georgia, 20 miles away. The new building was completed in 1977 and became the center of state government business. Guided tours are available on the hour. The **Governor's Mansion** (700 N. Adams St.) offers tours during the holiday season, legislative session, and by appointment. (The Governor's Mansion curator coordinates all tour requests and may be contacted at 850/922-4991.)

Around the new and old capitol complex there's a 10-block historical district worthy of a long stroll, with beautiful historic homes and Southern style.

## MUSEUMS AND HISTORIC HOMES

Because the area is fairly historically rich, a number of small museums examine certain periods and elements of Tallahassee's past.

### ◖ Museum of Florida History

Start with the Museum of Florida History (500 S. Bronough St., 850/488-1484,

9 A.M.–4:30 P.M. Mon.–Fri., opening at 10 A.M. on Sat. and noon on Sun., free admission). It actually has five different sites: the Main Gallery, the Old Capitol, the Union Bank, Mission San Luis de Apalachee, and the Knott House, which each highlight a different period of Florida history. It's a large assortment of nearly 44,000 items, but if you're patient, and you read the signage and literature, there's a wealth of interesting history and information to learn. Movie posters, quilts, furniture, cigar box labels, citrus labels, governors' portraits, Civil War flags, Seminole basketry—it's all arrayed and annotated to give you a slice of the area's cultural history.

Head to the museum's **Old Capitol** site (400 S. Monroe St. at Apalachee Pkwy., 850/487-1902), in a stunning original 1845 building with red candy-striped awnings and a stained-glass dome, housing exhibits on the state's political history, constitutions, and the history of the building. The building has pretty much been restored to its 1902 appearance and now houses the Florida Center for Political History and Governance. It's a good way to get a comprehensive multimedia instruction on the state's history, and visitors get to hang out in the Governor's Suite, State Supreme Court, and Senate and House chambers.

The **Knott House** (301 E. Park Ave., 850/922-2459, 1–4 P.M. Wed.–Fri., 10 A.M.–4 P.M. Sat.) construction dates to 1843, but it's the Knott family who lived there from 1928 on that gave it its flavor. It's a typical striking Victorian home, with all original furnishings. But here's the thing: Luella Knott, the matron of the house, wrote rhyming verse about items of furniture all over the house. Her poems, many of them with strong temperance themes, hang from these items of furniture today.

The **Union Bank** (Apalachee Pkwy. at Gadsden St., 850/561-2603) part of the museum houses artifacts and documents on black history.

**Mission San Luis** (2020 and 2021 W. Mission Rd., 850/487-3711, 10 A.M.–4 P.M. Tues.–Sun., free admission) is a living history museum at the site of a Franciscan mission to the Apalachee Indians circa 1656. While many people know about the missions of California and the Southwest, the Florida missions were earlier and there were more than 100 of them. Mission San Luis has a visitors center and an orientation exhibit that presents text and an audio tour in both English and Spanish.

## ( Tallahassee Automobile Museum

For something totally different, head to the new Tallahassee Automobile Museum (6800 Mahan Dr., 850/942-0137, 8 A.M.–5 P.M. Mon.–Fri., 10 A.M.–5 P.M. Sat., noon–5 P.M. Sun., $16 adults, $12 seniors, $11 students, $7 children), opened in early 2008. Get this: It's got a 1931 Duesenberg, the first Prowler and Viper to roll off the line, three Batmobiles, and the list goes on. At an estimated construction cost of $25 million, the two-story museum is vast, necessary to house one of the world's largest car collections.

## Other Museums

Spanish explorer Panfilo de Narvaez liked it here. So much so that he hyped the place after his 1528 visit, prompting Hernando de Soto and his 600 men to come back to this area at the confluence of the Wakulla and St. Marks rivers in 1539. By 1679, the Spanish governor of Florida constructed a fort here (destroyed almost immediately by pirates). Only modestly deterred, the Spanish built a second wooden fort here in 1718, then a third fort made out of stone in 1739—after which, occupation of the fort seesawed back and forth between the Spanish and British, ending in 1821 when Florida was ceded to the United States. Eventually a federal marine hospital was constructed by the U.S. government at the site, using stones from the Spanish-built fort, providing care for victims of yellow fever (once a serious epidemic in this swampy, mosquito-ridden wilderness). In the Civil War, the Confederates took control of the fort, renaming it Fort Ward. Built on the foundation

COURTESY OF TALLAHASSEE AREA CVB

The Tallahassee Automobile Museum features over 50 antique and classic cars, including the hearse that carried Abraham Lincoln to his funeral.

TALLAHASSEE

of the old marine hospital, **San Marcos de Apalache State Historic Site** (148 Old Fort Rd., St. Marks, 850/925-6216, 9 A.M.–5 P.M. Thurs.–Mon., admission $2) has a little visitors center and museum containing exhibits and artifacts of Gulf Coast history, while a walking trail meanders through the ruins of the historic fortification.

For an extremely kid-friendly look at Florida history, the **Tallahassee Museum of History and Natural Science** (3945 Museum Dr., 850/576-1636, www.tallahasseemuseum.org, 9 A.M.–5 P.M. Mon.–Sat., 12:30–5 P.M. Sun., $9 adults, $8.50 seniors, $6 children) has a range of entertaining exhibits seldom seen under one roof. The 52-acre museum features a natural-habitat zoo for indigenous wildlife (Florida panthers, red wolves, river otters, black bears), an environmental science center, an 1840s plantation house, an 1880s farmstead, an African-American church and schoolhouse dating to the 1850s, and 20 acres of walking trails. It's fun to wander through the birds of prey aviary and the hands-on Discovery Center. The museum is in heavy rotation with school groups and hosts many outreach events throughout the year.

For a look into the area's African-American history, stop into the **Riley Center Museum** (419 E. Jefferson St., 850/681-7882, 10 A.M.–4 P.M. Mon.–Fri., tours $2 adults, $1 children). The center has an oral history program and a multicultural outreach program. It also serves as a resource center for those doing African-American genealogical work.

For more insight into Tallahassee's plantation era, **Goodwood Museum & Gardens** (1600 Miccosukee Rd., 850/877-4202, 10 A.M.–3 P.M. Mon.–Fri., 10 A.M.–2 P.M. Sat., free admission to gardens, $6 for museum) is a restored plantation house with 13 outbuildings set on 19 acres of lawns, heirloom gardens, and large, moss-draped live oaks. The main house, built around 1840, has been restored to its 1920s look (check out the beautiful frescoed ceiling), surrounded by a skating rink, a reflecting pool, water tower, and carriage house with stables. Like the Tallahassee Museum of History and Natural Science, it's the kind of indoor-outdoor museum you stroll your way through. Tours, scheduled 10 A.M.–4 P.M. Monday–Friday, are a good way to get a snapshot of antebellum life in these parts.

# Entertainment and Events

## MUSIC AND THEATER

The presence of Florida State University brings a definite liveliness to town. The university usually has a visiting artist series every year, along with special events and three theaters to serve the well-regarded FSU theater program. Check the student newspaper *FSView & Florida Flambeau* (or visit www. fsunews.com) or the *Tallahassee Democrat* for performances at the Main Stage, The Lab, and the Studio Theatre on campus. The university's Music School also hosts more than 400 performances a year, including the Artist Series and the Kaleidoscope faculty chamber music series (check www.music.fsu.edu for concert schedules).

The **Leon County Civic Center** (505 W. Pensacola St., box office 850/222-0400, times and prices vary) sees lots of entertainment over the year, from Florida State Seminoles basketball to six traveling Broadway musicals each year and concerts that range from Ted Nugent to Boston Pops.

The **Tallahassee Symphony Orchestra** (FSU Ruby Diamond Auditorium, Westcott Building, corner of College Ave. and Copeland St., 850/224-0461, www.tsolive.org) is a professional company including music faculty from Florida State University, music graduate students, and professional musicians from the community. The orchestra puts on an annual Masterworks Series in addition to holiday concerts and performances for children and teenagers. Less professional but a lot of fun (and all concerts are free), the **Big Bend Community Orchestra** is an all-volunteer community orchestra that performs mostly at Lee Hall Auditorium on the Florida A&M University campus.

**The Tallahassee Ballet** (218 E. 3rd Ave., 850/224-6917, www.tallahasseeballet.com) stages 11 performances each year, drawn mostly from local amateur dance talent with the occasional guest professional making an appearance. At Christmastime, this usually means *The Nutcracker,* with a couple of other family-friendly ballet classics to round out the season.

There is no professional theater company in Tallahassee, but one of the area's oldest community theaters, **Tallahassee Little Theatre** (1861 Thomasville Rd., 850/224-8474, performances 8 P.M. Thurs.–Sat., 2 P.M. Sun., $20 adults, $16 for student and seniors) stages mainstream dramas and musicals *(A Funny Thing Happened on the Way to the Forum, Damn Yankees).* There is also a second, more experimental coffeehouse series. The **Quincy Music Theatre** (Leaf Theatre, 118 E. Washington St., Quincy, 850/875-9444), about 15 minutes west of Tallahassee, is in its 23rd year of production. Its mainstay is family-friendly musicals *(Gypsy, Jesus Christ Superstar, Babes in Toyland),* with a seasoned community cast and a pretty 400-seat theater.

## CINEMA

For mainstream movies, a clean, bright **AMC 20** at the Tallahassee Mall (2415 N. Monroe St., 850/386-7873) has lots of family-friendly first-run films; **Movies@Governor's Square** (1501 Governor's Square Blvd., 850/878-

7211) offers mainstream movies with a minimum of teen junk; **Miracle 5** (1815 Thomasville Rd., 850/224-2617) balances the offerings with five screens of foreign, artsy, and indie flicks (it's also home to the Tallahassee Film Club); and **Movies 8** (2810 Sharer Rd., 850/422-0051) gives you all the current mainstream films.

So you could go spend a lot of time at Tallahassee's multiplexes, but then you'd miss out on a local institution, the **Student Life Cinema** (in the Student Life Building on the FSU campus, 942 Learning Way, 850/644-4455, www.fsu.edu). Parking won't be easy, but it's fun to sit with a bunch of rowdy undergraduates (they get in for free; you have to pay $4) and watch *High Noon* or *Casablanca.*

## FESTIVALS

The middle of February has become increasingly busy during Tallahassee's **Seven Days of Opening Nights** (850/644-6500, www.sevendaysfestival.org) annual fine- and performing-arts festival, which draws big national and local stars. Equally well attended is April's **Springtime Tallahassee** (850/224-5012, www.springtimetallahassee.com), a city festival with parades and a giant arts and crafts jubilee, and December's **Market Days Tallahassee** (www.marketdays.org), a downtown fine arts sale and festival.

Seafood lovers can time a trip for the **Blue Crab Festival** (www.bluecrabfest.com) in Panacea in May or the **Florida Seafood Festival** (www.floridaseafoodfestival.com) in November in Apalachicola, while music lovers can attend the bluegrass **Swamp Stomp** (www.tallahasseemuseum.org/swamp-stomp) at the Tallahassee Museum of History and Natural Science in July.

# Nightlife

Maybe it's just the influence of a large university in its midst, but at night, Tallahassee tears it up. For live music, **Floyd's Music Store** (6661 W. Tennessee St., 850/222-3506, usually 8 P.M.–2 A.M., cover $6–12) is where to go when you want to hear hard rock and pop acts. When you're more interested in listening to the blues, head to **Bradfordville Blues Club** (7152 Moses Ln., off Bradfordville Rd., 850/906-0766, 8 P.M.–2 A.M. Fri. and Sat.). Just ease your car down the tiki torch–lined dirt road and you'll hear the one-room cinderblock juke joint before you see it. Blues greats have played in this little rural club, called the BBC, nestled in an old oak grove. Then there's **The Moon** (1105 E. Lafayette St., 850/878-6900), a club with multiple-personality disorder, in a good way. Fridays it's called Stetson's On The Moon and is a country-western bar with line dancing and mechanical bulls. Saturdays you'll find a pretty standard dance club, with a slightly older crowd (no T-shirts, sneakers, or ball caps allowed); Wednesday night is college night, when the average age in attendance drops precipitously. There's karaoke in the Silver Moon Lounge; whether that's a threat or a promise is up to you.

Established in 1979, **Bullwinkle's Saloon** (620 W. Tennessee St., 850/224-0651) has been a Florida State institution for most of that time. It's another rowdy college bar with DJs some nights, live bands on others. Things get ugly on nights when it's $5 for all you can drink 9 P.M.–1 A.M. with a student ID (usually Wednesday).

The crowd looking for a trendy bar in which to drink cocktails and martinis will appreciate **Rayn Ultra Lounge** (1660 N. Monroe St., 850/841-1100), an upscale Miami-style dance club. Saturdays it's a young professional crowd and Thursdays it seems more college-age. The Raynforest VIP lounge is available for rental and bottle service. And for when you're tired of all that dancing and just want a bit of friendly conversation over a glass of wine, try **Paradigm** (115 W. College Ave., 850/224-9980), a hip bar that attracts legislators during session and FSU students throughout the year.

College towns are by default sports bar towns. **AJ's** (1800 W. Tennessee St., 850/681-0731, 11 A.M.–2 A.M. daily) is a college-student hangout, especially on Tuesday nights. There are coin-op pool tables and gigantic beers called "big daddies." **4th Quarter Bar & Grill** (2033 N. Monroe St., 850/385-0017, 11 A.M.–2 A.M. daily) has 17 televisions tuned to different games and lots of regulars enjoying the sports action.

There are a few good pool halls in Tallahassee, too: The most fun is **Snookers** (1861 W. Tennessee St., 850/224-8644), with good drink specials and really well maintained pool tables. There's also **Halligans** (1698 Village Square Blvd., 850/668-7665) and **Pockets** (2810 Sharer Rd., 850/385-7665).

# Shopping

At **Governor's Square Mall** (1500 Apalachee Pkwy., 850/219-9996) JCPenney, Sears, Macy's, and Dillard's are the big anchors, with plenty of your usual mall stores like Auntie Anne's Pretzels and Limited Too filling the space in between. The **Tallahassee Mall** (2415 N. Monroe St., 850/385-7145) has more than 15 restaurants, along with the Gap, Barnes & Noble, and a 20-screen AMC 20 movie theater.

The weekly **Downtown Marketplace** (Ponce de Leon Park, Monroe St. at Park Ave., 850/224-3252, 8 A.M.–2 P.M. Sat., March–Nov., free admission) is framed as a farmers market, but for the visitor, the live music, chef demos, children's storytelling, and author appearances steal the show.

Some of the area's most delicious shopping requires a drive to the northern town of **Havana,** which, true to its name, was once a locus of cigar manufacturing. When that business dried up, Havana was not much of anything. It was when trailblazing Tallahassee antiques shop owners Henderson and Lee Hotchkiss bought up a block of downtown in 1983 that the town's luck started to change. The pair began selling and leasing store spaces to other antiques dealers, with the idea that if there were a certain critical mass, the sleepy little town would become an antiques shopping destination. Their calculation seems to have worked, as now the town has nearly 100 dealers of antiques, fine arts, and crafts. The center seems to be at **Antique and Design Center** (104 N. Main St., 850/539-1555), with room after room of antiques, wall hangings, gifts, and art. Also worth checking out are the **Florida Art Center & Gallery** (208 First St. NW, 850/539-1770), **Wanderings** (312 First St. NW, 850/539-7711), **Nicholson Farmhouse & Shops** (200 Coca Cola Ave., off State Rd. 12, three miles west of town, 850/539-5931), **First Street Gallery** (204 First St. NW, 850/539-5220), and **Planters Exchange** (204 Second St. NW, 850/539-6343).

If you time your visit correctly, you can visit Havana during April's MusicFest, a fairly elaborate lineup of acts, food, and crafts. Havana also hosts a Bead and Jewelry Fest and a Pumpkin Fest, both in October.

# Accommodations

Tallahassee has lots of affordable chain hotels and basic motels to accommodate the regular influx of college parents and government workers in session. What it doesn't have are very many resort hotels, golf-and-spa destinations, or upscale inns.

For something completely different if you're traveling to Tallahassee from the east, stay in the only yurt on the Gulf Coast at **Torreya State Park** (2576 N. W. Torreya Park, Bristol, 850/643-2674, $40/night). A yurt is a portable, round, canvas structure traditionally used by the nomadic peoples of Northern Asia. The yurt, found right outside of Tallahassee, is not as traditional as nomadic peoples may have used and thankfully it is more modern. It has air conditioning, wood deck flooring, a ceiling fan, bed, dresser, and a very interesting sky light in the top of the structure, as well as an exceptionally friendly raccoon named Steve that lives in a nearby tree; Steve has become somewhat of a celebrity in the park. It is an extremely affordable and fun way to stay near Tallahassee, highly recommended for those wanting to make that transition from modern accommodations to camping or the ecotourist. The yurt is surrounded by the rolling hills and steep bluffs of the state park, which runs alongside the Apalachicola River. The yurt also has a large deck with picnic table, a fish-cleaning station, and a very enjoyable fire-ring area with charcoal grill. The park features historic tours of the plantation home on the property and has hot showers, restrooms, a campground equipped for tent and RV campers, and a very cozy gathering room with wood-burning stove. Make camping reservations online at www.reserveamerica.com.

## UNDER $50

Hotel and motel rates start right around $50 in Tallahassee. If you want to chisel a few dollars off your room rate and don't much care about amenities, drive down Apalachee Parkway or North Monroe Street and check out the signs for the numerous small chains along both sides. You'll see Quality Inn, Howard Johnson, Hampton Inn, and other familiar brands.

## $50-150

Best Western has two properties locally, the **Best Western Pride Inn & Suites** (2016 Apalachee Pkwy., Tallahassee, 850/656-6312, $70–90) and the **Best Western Seminole Inn**

(6737 Mahan Dr., Tallahassee, 850/656-2938, $60–80). Both are geared to the business traveler, with pleasant rooms and executive suites and a complimentary continental breakfast. The former is closer to town, Florida State University, and the capitol. The latter is directly off I-10 at Exit 209A.

The **Hotel Duval** (415 N. Monroe St., Tallahassee, 850/224-6000, $100–200) is much more upscale, with greater amenities, and it's in the historic downtown district. It was formerly the Park Plaza Hotel until Marriott bought it and quickly completed a multimillion-dollar renovation. The face-lift brought a new, hip vibe to the hotel, along with tech upgrades such as iPod docking stations, flat screen TVs, and free Wi-Fi. In the process they received the green lodging designation from the State of Florida. It also added a Shula's Steakhouse and redesigned its suites with a variety of color schemes. You can browse through the colors and choose the scheme you would like. The hotel features 116 guest rooms, an exercise room, sauna, business center, and six meeting/banquet rooms, with a complimentary airport shuttle.

A little out of the way, the **Staybridge Inn & Suites** (I-10 E., 1600 Summit Lake Dr., 850/219-7000, $139–229) is a very nice new property in the area, pet-friendly with apartment-like suites featuring kitchens, flat-screen televisions with HBO, in-room computers with free wireless connection, iPod docking stations, and a 24-hour business center.

And if you're traveling to Wakulla Springs, you might want to stay at the new **Wildwood Resort** (3896 Coastal Highway 98, Wakulla, 800/878-1546, $89–120). The nature and golf resort is one of the few lodges in the state to become a Certified Green Lodge by the Florida Department of Environmental Protection. The resort features an 18-hole golf course, 71 rooms and suites, a fitness center, and pool all near the St. Marks National Wildlife Refuge, the Apalachicola National Forest, and Wakulla Springs State Park. There is also an on-site restaurant and bar called the Wildwood Bistro, as well as indoor and outdoor meeting space that can accommodate up to 200 people.

## OVER $150

The undisputed finest accommodations to be had in Tallahassee are found at the **Governors Inn** (209 S. Adams St., Tallahassee, 850/681-6855, www.thegovinn.com, $139–289). It's half a block from the capitol building right downtown, with complimentary continental breakfast, cocktails, turndown service, and valet parking. Each of the 40 rooms and suites is named for a past Florida governor. It has antebellum charm, with creaky wood stairs and wood-burning fireplaces. The coolest rooms are the loft suites with circular staircases up to the bedroom.

Opened in 2007, the **Residence Inn** (600 West Gaines St., 850/329-9080, $159–209) offers spacious suites as well as complimentary area shuttle service and breakfast buffet.

# Food

## BREAKFAST AND LUNCH

The problem with starting a visit to Tallahassee at **Another Broken Egg** (3500 Kinhega Dr., 850/907-3447, www.anotherbrokenegg.com, 7 A.M.–2 P.M. Tues.–Sun., $6–15) is that your expectations for the remainder of the trip may be unreasonably high. It's a small regional chain, but they do things right, with beignets, excellent cinnamon rolls, crab-filled omelettes,

blackberry grits, and lots of coffee served in these great earthenware mugs.

For a quick lunch on the fly (either eat-in or takeout), **Crispers** (1241 Apalachee Pkwy., 850/656-4222, 10:30 A.M.–10 P.M. Mon.–Sat., 11 A.M.–8 P.M. Sun., $6–8) has good soups, gumbos, and chowders, as well as nice salads. **Hopkins' Eatery** (1700 N. Monroe St., 850/386-4258, 1415 Market St., 850/668-

0311, 1208 Capital Circle SE, 850/325-6422, 11 A.M.–9 P.M. Mon.–Fri., 11 A.M.–5 P.M. Sat., $7–12) has three locations, each of which has an enjoyable patio on which to enjoy fat specialty sandwiches.

The **Red Elephant Pizza and Grill** (1872 Thomasville Rd., 850/222-7492, 11 A.M.–10 P.M. daily, $7–23) has become the local favorite, with outstanding pizza and a nice family-friendly vibe.

## AMERICAN

C **Andrew's Capital Grill & Bar** (228 S. Adams St., 850/222-3444, 11:30 A.M.–10 P.M. Mon.–Sat., $8–30, valet parking) has been a Tally downtown landmark since 1997, with a sandwich "express line" weekdays for government types (some of these locals have been immortalized with sandwiches named after them). At night, the terrace is the place to be, whereupon you can dig into meatloaf with brown mushroom sauce or a cumin-crusted pork loin. Downstairs is **Andrew's 228,** the more upscale counterpart, with an incredible bilevel dining room. Prices are steeper, and the menu includes a variety of Italian-inspired items: butternut squash and walnut ravioli, seafood fra diavolo, and tempura oysters (fine, those aren't Italian, but they're tasty). Andrew's also boasts a very busy after-work happy hour scene and a classic martini for $6.

By day an excellent gourmet shop, **Clusters & Hops** (707 N. Monroe St., 850/222-2669, 1–11:30 P.M. Mon.–Sat., $9–21) becomes a stylish small restaurant in the evenings, serving the likes of Madeira-marinated mushrooms served with red pepper and goat cheese polenta between puff pastry, or a great warm apple pie with caramel sauce.

**Food Glorious Food** (Betton Place, 1950 Thomasville Rd., 850/224-9974, 11 A.M.–2:30 P.M. and 5:30–9:30 P.M. daily, $14–35) has always had wonderful, if eclectic, food (apricot-balsamic glazed chicken with honey mashed sweet potato and green beans, chilled Thai coconut soup with tempura shrimp and sake, Cuban roast pork with black beans). Opt for a seat in the softly lit courtyard.

## BOILED P-NUTS

There are stands that dot all the back roads of the rural Florida Panhandle. Each has a hand-lettered sign that touts the glories of the green peanut. The outskirts of Tallahassee are P-nut Central, so you owe it to yourself to stop.

Technically, boiled p-nuts are supposed to be the fresh, green nuts, so look for them in the fall. They're hawked all year-round, but these tend to be garden-variety peanuts, sold to the unsuspecting. There are four species of peanuts – Valencia, Spanish, Virginia, and runners. Northern Florida peanuts tend to be southern runners, with a medium-sized nut, two to a pod.

The raw peanuts are boiled in the shell for several hours, then a huge amount of salt is added to the water and the whole mess is boiled some more. Then the peanuts sit in the brine until a customer pulls up. They are then drained and sold to enthusiasts by the quart at the road's shoulder. Soft, and salty, and a little damp, they are the perfect companion for light beer; you must eat them warm and eat them right away, as you pull away from the p-nut stand, the shells forming a huge detritus pile in the front seat as you start thinking about where you're going to stop for that beer.

A local institution, **The Wharf** (3507 Thomasville Rd., 850/668-1966, 4:30–9:30 P.M. Tues.–Sun., $10–20) prepares Southern-style seafood and runs a catering business called Manna Catering that seems to crop up frequently at local functions.

There are some good restaurants in Tallahassee hotels—**Marie Livingston's Steakhouse** (adjacent to Holiday Inn, 2705 Apalachee Parkway, 850/562-2525, 11 A.M.–2 P.M. and 5–9 P.M. Mon.–Thurs., until 10 P.M. Fri. and Sat., $15–21) for standard steak, chops, and baby-back ribs, and the **Monroe Street Grill** (Ramada Inn, 2900 N. Monroe St., 850/386-1027, 6:30 A.M.–2:30 P.M.

and 5–10 P.M. daily, lunches under $10, most dinners under $20) for prime rib and a huge salad bar.

## ETHNIC

Ask around for Italian, and everyone will steer you to **Anthony's** (Betton Place, 1950 Thomasville Rd., 850/224-1447, 11 A.M.–2 P.M. Mon.–Thurs. and 5–9 P.M. Mon.–Sun., brunch 11 A.M.–2 P.M. Sun., $17–30). It's not a conspiracy, exactly, but a local habit. It has the warmth and charm of an old favorite with a comfortable dining room and worn menu covers that are a classic sign of a long-running popular restaurant that has stood the test of time.

At **Jasmine** (109 E. College Ave., 850/681-6868, 11:30 A.M.–10:30 P.M. Mon.–Fri., noon–10:30 P.M. Sat. and Sun., $9–17) you'll find sushi and a little bit of Italian food. Try the chicken and brie sandwich on a toasted baguette and then the peanut butter pie for dessert. The sushi is offered in familiar combinations. Jasmine is popular with downtown professionals for lunch, does a brisk happy-hour business, and then attracts College Avenue partiers in the evening. Another Japanese dining experience can be found at **Osaka** (1690 Raymond Diehl Rd., 850/531-0222, 5–10 P.M. Sun.–Thurs., until 10:30 P.M. Fri. and Sat., $17–26). It's a Japanese steakhouse with hibachi chefs who make very good food.

Tallahassee has more than its share of inexpensive Mexican restaurants, the best of which is **El Tapatio** (1002 N. Monroe St., 850/224-0351, 11 A.M.–10 P.M. Mon.–Thurs., until 11 P.M. Fri. and Sat., until 9 P.M. Sun., $7–10), with burritos, tacos, and enchiladas.

## SEAFOOD

There are lots of mom-and-pop fish joints in Tallahassee that are rich in Southern fried fish. For an enjoyable sit-down experience, **Crystal River Seafood** (2721 N. Monroe St., 850/383-1530, and 1968 W. Tennessee St., 850/575-4418, 11 A.M.–9 P.M. daily, until 10 P.M. Fri. and Sat., $10–25) is a homey family restaurant with fried fish, hush puppies, and sweet tea. **Barnacle Bill's** (1830 N. Monroe St.,

850/385-8734, 11 A.M.–11 P.M. daily, $12–22) is more the place to go for steamed seafood, topless oysters, and cold beers. I hesitate to recommend it because it's a chain, but locals really like their **Bonefish Grill** (3491-7 Thomasville Rd., 850/297-0460, 4–10:30 P.M. daily, $12–30). The spins on simple grilled fish are fresh, and the restaurant interior is very inviting.

## FINE DINING

Where locals take out-of-town guests for special occasions, **Café Cabernet** (1019 N. Monroe St., 850/224-1175, 5 P.M.–2 A.M. Mon.–Sat., small plates $8–9, entrées $16–22) has lived a long and impressive life. With a 500-label cellar and 30 pours by the glass, wine is a focus here. It's a fairly busy meeting place, where you'll see locals slicing into a wasabi-dusted tuna steak with gingered green beans and green curry lo mein or pecan-crusted chicken glazed with a brandy blueberry sauce.

**Capital Steak House** (Holiday Inn Select, 316 W. Tennessee St., 850/222-9555, 6 A.M.–11 A.M. and 5–10 P.M. daily, $15–33) is more of a straight steakhouse idiom. The best part about it is the gallery of photos that tell the story of Florida State and Florida A&M universities' histories. Great drinks, too.

When Tallahassee has something to celebrate—anniversaries, new jobs—**Chez Pierre** (1215 Thomasville Rd., 850/222-0936, 11 A.M.–10 P.M. daily, until 2 A.M. Fri. and Sat., $24–35) gets the business. It's usually the top winner in annual "best of" magazine articles, with French/continental cuisine that has many admirers. But in addition to a pine-nut and sun-dried tomato–crusted rack of New Zealand lamb, or a cedar-planked salmon, Chez Pierre serves a great hamburger. Another perennial local award winner is **Georgio's** (3425 Thomasville Rd., 850/893-4161, 4–10 P.M. Mon.–Sat., $18–35). An elegant place, it serves rich American/continental dishes like Charleston she-crab soup and blue crab–stuffed Gulf red snapper.

**Cypress Restaurant** (320 E. Tennessee St., 850/513-1100, 5–10 P.M. Tues.–Sat., about $8 for little dishes, $18–27 for big dishes) has imaginative takes on Southern regional cooking. Chef-proprietor David Gwynn has a super version of shrimp and grits. The wine list is thoughtful (largely American boutique wineries), and the decor is very nice but still relaxed and casual.

One of the hottest restaurants to come to Tallahassee in recent years is ( **Urbane** (115 E. Park Ave., 850/422-2221, 5–10 P.M. Tues.–Sat., $14–34). Chef-owner Bruce Pollett serves up a seasonal contemporary American menu that includes small plates such as southwestern shrimp cake with roasted corn–black bean salsa and smoked pepper aioli, or lobster shiitake mushroom pancakes with coconut curry. If you're in the mood for something more substantial, head for blue-corn fried catfish with jalapeño-vinegar-infused collard greens, or pan-seared duck breast with roasted pear–and–sweet potato hash and wilted spinach.

# Information and Services

Tallahassee and vicinity are located within the **Eastern time zone.** The area code is **850.**

## TOURIST INFORMATION

For information or trip-planning assistance and rates before you arrive, call the **Tallahassee Area Convention and Visitors Bureau** (106 E Jefferson St., 850/606-2305 or 800/628-2866). Once here, your first stop for information should be the **visitors center** (Apalachee Pkwy. and Monroe St., 850/413-9200) on the first floor of the West Plaza entrance of the New Capitol building. The gentleman who runs the center, Don Hardy, is a wealth of local lore and history. He'll equip you with maps and a plan and send you on your way.

Tallahassee has its own daily newspaper, the *Tallahassee Democrat.* You will find kiosks all over the downtown area, for a price of $0.50. It's a Gannett paper, printed mornings, with a super weekend entertainment section. There's also an African-American weekly called the *Capital Outlook* published every Thursday, and the *FSView,* the twice-weekly student newspaper covering Florida State University.

## POLICE AND EMERGENCIES

In any emergency, dial 911 for immediate assistance. If you need the police in a nonemergency, contact the **Police Department** (234 E. 7th Ave., 850/891-4200). Tallahassee has two hospitals equipped to care for patients in need of emergency medical care: **Capital Regional Medical Center** (2626 Capital Medical Blvd., 850/325-5000) and **Tallahassee Memorial Hospital** (1300 Miccosukee Rd., 850/431-1155).

## RADIO AND TELEVISION

Spinning the dial on your car radio, you'll encounter public radio at **WFSM 89.1 FM,** classical at **WFSU 91.5 FM,** classic rock at **WWFO 99.9 FM,** and country at **WAIB 103.1 FM.** If you really want to listen like a local, turn to the cool college stew of genres played on **WVFS 89.7 FM,** the Florida State independent station.

Leon County's television offerings include **WCTV Channel 6,** the CBS affiliate; **WFSU Channel 11,** the PBS affiliate; and **WTXL Channel 27,** the ABC affiliate.

## LAUNDRY SERVICES

Undergraduates and coin laundries go together like pizza and beer—there's the **Northwood Coin Laundry** (1700 N. Monroe St., 850/385-9121) and the **Laundry Basket Coin Laundry** (2256 W. Pensacola St., 850/575-4278) for starters.

# Getting There and Around

## BY CAR

The main access road in and out of town from the east or west is I-10. From Gainesville, it's about 120 miles west, the easiest route I-75 north to I-10 west. From Pensacola at the westernmost edge of the state, it's four hours east to Tallahassee. To reach the Gulf of Mexico and the little coastal towns along the Panhandle, take U.S. 319 south to U.S. 98.

Once in town, you need to know that the main north–south road is Monroe Street, which is also the east–west dividing line for addresses. The downtown is bounded by Tennessee Street to the north, Van Buren Street to the south, the FSU campus to the west, and Magnolia Drive to the east. FSU is about 0.75 mile west of Monroe Street, and Doak Campbell Stadium (where the Seminoles play football) is on the southwestern part of campus. Florida Agricultural & Mechanical University (FAMU, pronounced fam-YOU) is just south of downtown, bordered by Canal Street on the north and Perry Street on the south.

## BY AIR

**Tallahassee Regional Airport** (3300 Capital Cir. SW, 850/891-7800) is 10 miles southwest of downtown and is serviced by six national/regional airlines including Delta and USAir. There's also a small air charter service called **Flightline Group, Inc.** (3256 Capital Cir. SW, 850/574-4444), which has its own aviation support center, charter/rental aircrafts, flight school, and fueling and repair.

**Alamo** (800/327-9633), **Avis** (800/831-2847), **Budget** (800/527-0700), **Dollar** (800/800-4000 domestic, 800/800-6000 international), **Enterprise** (800/736-8222), **Hertz** (800/654-3131), and **National** (800/227-7368) provide rental cars from the airport.

## BY BUS AND TRAIN

Following Hurricane Katrina, **Amtrak** service to Tallahassee was terminated and the station closed.

Within the city, **StarMetro** (C.K. Steele Plaza, 111 W. Tennessee St., 850/891-5200, $1) is a pretty extensive public transit system with 31 routes, university shuttles, and Dial-A-Ride services for the elderly and people with disabilities. **Yellow Cab** (850/580-8080) provides 24-hour passenger or package transportation, with wheelchair accessibility and charter van service. From the airport to downtown is about a $20 cab ride.

# THE FORGOTTEN COAST

Despite its name, the area between Panama City and St. Marks may be the most memorable region on the Gulf Coast. More overlooked than forgotten, this region was disregarded by tourists for the greater part of the 1900s due to its unpalatable mix of industrial development and lack of infrastructure across large spans of wilderness. Then the paper mill that was located west of Port St. Joe came down in 2003 and the area slowly transformed into a desirable tourist destination. In today's climate where ecotourism and natural beauty are often high on travelers' lists, the Forgotten Coast has experienced record numbers of tourists visiting the pristine beaches, waterways, forests and towns. It seems the Forgotten Coast has been remembered.

These days, the Forgotten Coast is best known for its protected lands (87 percent of the region is national or state park), top-rated and underpopulated beaches, sweet oysters, affordable cost of living, and its pristine waters. The waters of Apalachicola Bay and the Apalachicola River Watershed are considered so important economically and ecologically that Apalachicola Bay is designated as a State Aquatic Preserve and the Apalachicola National Estuarine Research Reserve, located at the mouth of the Apalachicola River, one of only 25 such sites designated by the NOAA. The lower Apalachicola watershed is also designated as a UNESCO Biosphere Reserve.

As a reflection of its economic importance, environmental value, and ecological health, Apalachicola Bay is one of the most productive bays in the United States. It alone provides

# HIGHLIGHTS

**◖ Apalachicola Estuary Tour:** Take a guided boat trip through the Apalachicola National Estuarine Research Reserve to see some of the 308 species of birds, 186 species of fish, and 57 species of mammals that call this fertile estuary home (page 252).

**◖ St. Joseph Peninsula State Park:** Dr. Beach knows a few things. Scientifically considering sand, surf, shells, and such, Dr. Stephen Leatherman has taken it upon himself to bestow annual kudos on the country's best beaches. A funny-shaped barrier peninsula near Cape San Blas, St. Joseph Peninsula State Park rightfully made it to the top of his rankings a while back (page 253).

**◖ Self-Guided Historic Walking Tour:** Go back in time to an era of antebellum grace and charm with a leisurely stroll in downtown Apalachicola. More than 200 of the buildings and homes downtown made the National Register of Historic Places, and many of them are open annually for tours (page 256).

**◖ Florida Seafood Festival:** You'll gain a robust appreciation for Apalachicola's beloved eastern oysters in November at the annual Florida Seafood Festival held in Battery Park (page 258).

**◖ Tupelo Honey:** Make sure to stop by one of the few operating tupelo honey apiaries in the world and sample some of the prized, greenish-tinted, sweet treat. The apiaries around Wewahitchka produce honey from the blossom of the tupelo tree, which grows nowhere else on the planet but the Apalachicola River Basin (page 259).

**◖ St. George Island State Park:** The Forgotten Coast has another top beach contender, this one taking up the eastern nine miles of St. George Island. A nighttime beach walk on St. George reveals one of the darkest night skies in the United States (telescope optional) and the mystery of baby loggerhead turtles flapping their way back out to sea under a luminous moon (page 264).

**◖ Biking St. George Island:** If you're staying on the Plantation (western) side of the island, stop in town for a cool ice cream cone and then continue along the roadside path until you reach the state park at the island's eastern end (page 265).

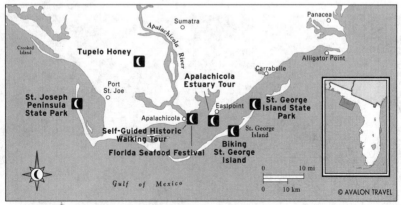

LOOK FOR ◖ TO FIND RECOMMENDED SIGHTS, ACTIVITIES, DINING, AND LODGING.

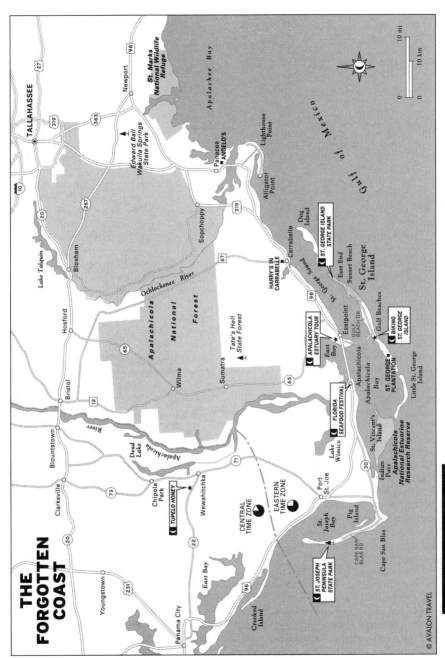

# THE FORGOTTEN COAST

© AVALON TRAVEL

90 percent of the oysters consumed in Florida and supports extensive shrimping, crabbing, and commercial fishing industries. The Apalachicola watershed has the greatest number of freshwater fish species in Florida and the highest density and diversity of amphibian species in North America. Most importantly, perhaps, the clean waters and healthy seafood populations provide incomparable outdoor recreation opportunities and support a culture and a way of life that is rapidly disappearing in Florida and across the nation as our waters become increasingly less productive.

And from about A.D. 1000, before it was "forgotten," the region was home to the Apalachee Native American Tribe. Prior to European contact, there were an estimated 50,000 Apalachees living in widely dispersed villages. In 1528, Pánfilo de Narváez was the first European explorer to make contact with the Apalachees. He arrived in the region after the Native Americans living in the Tampa Bay area told him he could find gold here.

The European presence eventually took its toll on the Apalachees from continual war and contagious diseases introduced by the explorers. Under Colonel Moore from South Carolina, an expedition in 1704 nearly wiped out the entire Apalachee population, and by 1758 the population fell to barely over 100. In 1764, the remaining Apalachee migrated into Louisiana and settled on Red River, where 250 to 300 Apalachee descendants live today.

A turning point for the region took place in the early 1800s when the town of **Apalachicola** was founded by cotton and lumber magnates to provide an accessible port for the South's cotton plantations. Cotton warehouses were quickly erected—at one point the town had 43 warehouses, making it the third-largest cotton port on the Gulf Coast.

Then during the Civil War, the shipping industry foundered (a blockade sealed off the harbor; railroads became ubiquitous). Residents responded by looking to the fertile Gulf waters for new revenue sources. From the 1870s until the early 20th century, Apalachicola's sponge-diving industry ranked third in the state after

Greek émigrés began harvesting sponges there. Timber and turpentining proved lucrative land-based endeavors around the same time. Historians say the demand for turpentine in the early 1900s was comparable to our reliance on petroleum today.

During World War II the area was used as a training camp and after the war, as the market for turpentine abated, independent-minded fishermen began harvesting the abundant seafood from the generous Apalachicola Bay and River.

As with other rural spots along the Gulf, the Forgotten Coast doesn't offer everything to everyone: There are no amusement parks, few malls, even fewer fast-food restaurants. Yet, this is the appeal for folks who seek a more natural and adventurous Florida experience. The region reaches back to Florida's past, a time before most of the landscape became resorts and vacation homes seemingly overnight.

Where you set up your base camp is a matter of preference—the historic port of Apalachicola is jam-packed with restored Georgian and Victorian homes and cotton warehouses converted into antiques shops and mouthwatering seafood restaurants. **St. George Island,** on the other hand, is an unparalleled barrier island retreat, with hundreds of beachfront rentals ranging in size and price. And **Eastpoint** on the mainland or **St. Joseph Peninsula** is where to go if you're here to fish, camp, paddle, boat, or otherwise explore the unforgettable outdoor adventures of the Forgotten Coast.

## PLANNING YOUR TIME

The Forgotten Coast, roughly speaking, is bounded on the west by Mexico Beach and on the east by St. Marks. From west to east, it includes the communities of St. Joe Beach and Port St. Joe, Simmons Bayou, Cape San Blas, Indian Pass, Apalachicola, St. George Island, Eastpoint, Carrabelle, Ochlockonee Bay, and Panacea. The best way to explore is by car, and the communities worthy of most of your attention are Apalachicola and St. George Island. (Apalachicola will hold your interest for a minimum of a weekend, and St. George

Island rentals, at least during high season, are mostly by the full week.) For tent camping, RV camping, and paddling, St. Joseph Peninsula State Park's Shady Pine campground sits right on the Gulf of Mexico and is one of the best on the Gulf Coast. Eastpoint, Carrabelle, and Apalachicola are the main hot spots for fishing trip guides and services in the surrounding bays, rivers, and offshore in the Gulf.

The area is served by U.S. 98; while sometimes slow and congested, it is a picturesque roadway that stretches 300 miles along the northwest Florida Panhandle coast. An easy way to explore the Apalachicola River Basin and Apalachicola National Forest is take State Road 12, also known as the Apalachee Savannahs National Scenic Byway. It begins in Bristol, Florida, and winds alongside the Apalachicola River for most of the way before veering into the heart of the National Forest. Driving south from Alabama and Georgia, you can make time along east–west I-10, but it's about 65 miles to the north. Sooner or later you've got to hook up with U.S. 98 and slow down.

Which suits the area. The beaches of St. George Island, Cape San Blas, St. Vincent's Island, and St. Joseph Peninsula State Park often make people's lists of top beaches in the United States. There are lighthouses, dunes towering up to 30 feet high anchored by sea oats and magnolia trees, miles of white sand dotted with perfect sand dollars, and hardly another person in sight.

High season here is very different from that in the rest of coastal Florida. It stays cooler here than elsewhere on the Gulf, making it a little chilly in the winter and more than tolerable in the summer. Summer is the peak, with rental prices jumping substantially on beach houses on St. George and hotel rooms in Apalachicola. Many beach houses book as far as a year in advance during the summer months. If you are more impulsive, try off-peak times to get a room on the fly. Spring and fall are gorgeous on this stretch of the coast, especially for camping and paddling trips (but watch out, Easter week tends to be a difficult reservation).

## Apalachicola

Say it with me: apa-LATCH-ee-CO-la. The locals shorten it to Apalach and, more so than many places along the Gulf Coast of Florida, they have strong Southern accents. The population here is roughly 3,000, but Apalachicola has the cultural opportunities of a much larger city and a coastal Southern charm only found in these smaller Gulf-front communities. Here you'll find Georgian and Victorian homes settled in along wide avenues, shaded by moss-covered live oaks and a civic pride in the citizens that reflects the area's long and proud history.

It was a booming port city in the 1830s and 1840s, yet the demise of steamboat travel at the end of the Civil War in some ways froze the town—it never grew much bigger or more populous. For the visitor today, this means beautiful houses on wide, tree-lined avenues,

fine restaurants, and a pace that harkens back to the 1840s. For one of the finest examples of the classy homes in the area, make sure to tour the Orman House; the former home of cotton merchant Thomas Orman is now designated as a state park and open to the public.

Some of the homes in Apalachicola may seem the worse for wear, but just ask the locals about the string of powerful hurricanes they have experienced in the last two decades and it will become clear as to why many of the homes are in need of repair. Glancing at pictures of the flooding and destruction that took place during and after Hurricane Dennis in 2005 will surely give most of us an appreciation for the power of these storms and the resilience of the Apalachicola community.

And if you ask the locals what brings most people to Apalachicola, most will say it is

THE FORGOTTEN COAST

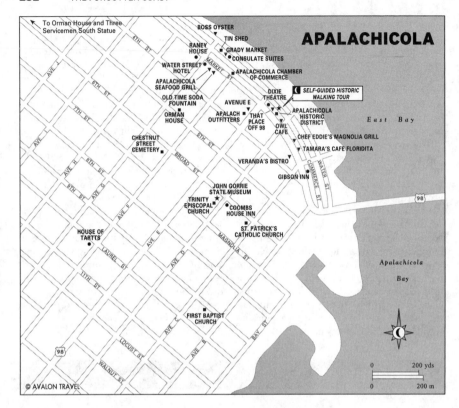

oysters. In fact, the plentiful and nutrient-rich oysters found in the area are believed to have attracted the first Native American inhabitants, as evidenced by the ancient oyster shell mounds they left behind throughout the region. Today Apalachicola is the hub of an oyster industry that provides 90 percent of the oysters consumed in Florida and 13 percent of the oysters consumed in the United States. Some of the very first pictures of the area show steamrollers crushing oyster shells for the first road beds and the roads lined with oyster packaging and canning houses.

So while you're in town get out on the water with a local guide and pull your own fresh oysters right out of Apalachicola Bay. Shuck the oyster on the bow of the boat. Throw it raw right on a cracker with a little horseradish, cocktail sauce, and a squeeze of fresh lemon juice and be part of a culinary history dating back thousands of years. Or at least have a couple of oysters on the half shell served on ice at one of the many restaurants that dish up the fresh seafood harvest of Apalachicola.

## SPORTS AND RECREATION
### ( Apalachicola Estuary Tour

Apalachicola Bay is one of the most productive estuarine systems in the Northern Hemisphere (an estuary is where a river meets the sea, where freshwater meets saltwater). You might get a sense for this while touring the **Apalachicola National Estuarine Research Reserve** (108 Island Drive, Eastpoint, 850/670-4783, 9 A.M.–5 P.M. Tue.–Fri., free admission) and its affiliated **Nature Center.**

The reserve is said to house 1,162 subspecies of plants, 308 species of birds, 186 species of fish, and 57 species of mammals. Much of it is inaccessible unless you have a boat, and stomping around in some parts is discouraged except for those conducting long-term research, education, and stewardship programs. A new Nature Center opened in November 2010 and is located on Apalachicola Bay at the foot of the St. George Island Bridge in Eastpoint. It is an excellent outing for the whole family. The new 4,800-square-foot visitors center offers educational exhibits and information, as well as aquariums of local fish and turtles, surrounded by a bay-front park complete with picnic pavilions and an outdoor amphitheater. You're likely to see dolphins, crabs, turtles, snakes, a variety of fish, ospreys, and eagles during a stroll around the visitors center and the surrounding Apalachicola Bay shore park.

A remarkable way to explore the estuary is by taking a tour with **Journeys of St. George Island** (850/927-3259, www.sgislandjourneys. com, $250–450). The guides here will take you shelling on a remote island in Apalachicola Bay before exploring the estuary accompanied by fascinating commentary as you wander upriver, through the marsh, and into the swamps.

## ◖ St. Joseph Peninsula State Park

Dr. Beach, really a guy named Stephen Leatherman, conducts an annual ranking of American beaches, rating them by water temperature, number of sunny days, color of sand, algae, smell, pests, and about 40 other criteria. No kidding around—this is serious. And one beach that keeps showing up on his top 10 list is St. Joseph Peninsula State Park (8899 Cape San Blas Rd., Port St. Joe, 850/227-1327)—it was No. 1 in 2002. Projecting seven miles out into the Gulf, this barrier peninsula is reachable from the mainland across Apalachicola Bay and via Cape San Blas. Sand blows up across the beach and lodges in sea oats to produce exceptionally tall dunes (30–40 feet), the water is a sparkling aquamarine and hovers around

84°F in summer, the surf is gentle, and the 2,500-acre beach park is never crowded.

And here's what Dr. Beach has to say about the local sand:

*The sand is nearly pure quartz crystal. While most noncarbonated (noncoral) beaches are composed of 15 to 20 different types of sand, the Panhandle beaches are like a bar of Ivory soap – 99.44 percent pure. The remarkable purity of the Florida Panhandle sand is related to its geologic history. Like most all beaches along the East and Gulf Coasts, the Panhandle sands came from the wearing down of the Appalachian Mountains, which brought an array of different minerals to the shore. But unlike other coastal areas, the rivers stopped bringing any new sand for tens of thousands of years. During this long period of time, wave action has ground the particles down to size. Quartz, being the most resistant mineral commonly available on the face of the earth, is the only type of sand grain left as the other minerals were ground down to dust.... What we find on the Panhandle beaches today is quartz sand crystal at its terminal size, meaning that all the grains are nearly the same size (well sorted in geologic terms).*

It's not all beach, though. The park includes a large expanse of heavy pine forest that is home to bobcats, deer, raccoons, and rattlesnakes, as well as bald eagles, ospreys, and endangered peregrine falcons. In the fall hawks and monarch butterflies perch for a while on their migration along the Yucatan Express to Mexico. And in July and August you'll find visitors hunkered down along the bayside looking for sweet scallops.

There are no hotels in the park, although there are eight loft-style, furnished cabins on the bay side of the park that were refurbished in 2007 (they accommodate 5–7 people, $100/ night) and 119 campsites with water and electricity available in two areas: Gulf Breeze sites are more open (better for RVs and big cars), and Shady Pines area is more secluded and shaded ($24 per night in either spot). You can also primitive camp on the peninsula ($4/person/night, reservations a must). A trail winds its way across the peninsula, and backpackers can hike back to designated camp areas and also camp right on the beach. Fires are permitted in some areas and the primitive campsites are great to utilize for overnight or other long-distance paddling trips in St. Joseph Bay. There is also a boat ramp and marina located near the entrance to the park ($3/day). The boat ramp is free for overnight guests, who are permitted to leave their boat moored at the marina.

On your way to the park you might want to stop off to visit **Cape San Blas's lighthouse.** On the site of two former brick lighthouses (beach erosion is tough on these kinds of structures—in fact, the nearby Cape St. George Lighthouse fell down in 2006), the current iteration is a picturesque iron tower.

## Barrier Islands

The Forgotten Coast's barrier islands serve to separate Apalachicola Bay from the Gulf of Mexico, acting as shock absorbers to protect the mainland from howling winds, vicious storms, and rogue waves. In addition to that, these little islands make for fabulous and varied exploration.

Birding, shelling, surf fishing, beach contemplation—these are the offerings on **Dog Island** to the east of St. George Island, accessible by water taxi from Carrabelle. It's also known as a refuge for loggerhead and leatherback turtles. A handful of people really do live on the island, and there's a single funky hotel called the **Pelican Inn** (800/451-5294, $300 for two nights, $395 for three, $595 for four, $850 for seven, pets welcome for an additional $10/day) with eight studio units that each sleep up to four people. But be advised—there are no stores, no restaurants, really no other amenities on the island.

It used to be that St. George Island was 28 miles long. In 1954, the Army Corps of Engineers carved out an artificial channel to create two separate barrier islands (this was primarily to make it easier for the shrimpers to get out to the Gulf). The larger is still St. George Island, and the smaller, boomerang-shaped island is known locally as **Little St. George Island** and more formally as **Cape St. George State Reserve.**

Little St. George can be reached only by private boat—a very worthwhile excursion. The nine-mile-long island was purchased by the state of Florida in 1977 under the Environmentally Endangered Lands program as part of the Apalachicola National Estuarine Research Reserve to protect it from development and to contribute to the protection of Apalachicola Bay. It's remote, wild, and populated only by an idiosyncratic assortment of creatures.

Originally established for waterfowl, the reserve's aim has broadened to protect a range of endangered species: You'll see bald eagle nests in pines along the island's freshwater marshes; loggerhead sea turtles nest on the white-sand beaches; wood storks and peregrine falcons are frequent visitors; and indigo snakes burrow in the dunes.

Little St. George is open to the public for swimming, fishing, birding, and hiking. Primitive camping is permitted at designated sites at West Pass and Sike's Cut (at either end of the island; call 850/653-8063 with your dates and number of people). Fires are permitted at the campsites, but no live wood can be cut.

You have to book your own shuttle to get over to **St. Vincent Island,** to the west of Little St. George. **Captain Joey Romanelli** (850/229-1065) will take you out on his 27-foot pontoon boat, departing from the end of Indian Pass Road. The whole island constitutes the **St. Vincent National Wildlife Refuge,** with 12,358 acres of dunes and woods.

In 1990, the island became a haven and breeding ground for endangered red wolves. These solitary animals once roamed the Southeast, but habitat loss reduced their numbers such that there were a mere 100 confined to a small area of coastal Louisiana and Texas. The wolves (bigger than a coyote, smaller than a gray wolf) now populate St. Vincent, and when pups are weaned they are taken to reintroduction facilities around the country.

Before becoming a refuge, the island was used as a private hunting and fishing preserve. Previous exotic-minded owners introduced Southeast Asian elk called sambar deer (big guys, they weigh up to 600 pounds, as opposed to the native white-tailed deer that weigh in at a modest 100 or so pounds) to the island, and they can be spotted to this day. There are native white-tails here too, and a fair number of other species (lots of rattlers, so beware) on what is one of the 500 refuges in the national system. You can bring a bike with you on the shuttle or just hike the trails and beaches of the island.

## Fishing

Apalachicola Bay, Apalachicola River, and the Gulf of Mexico each provide stellar fishing experiences for the rookie or serious angler. There are dozens of charter providers in the area, but a handful of names come up time and again when you ask for locals' recommendations: **Captain Charlie's Charters** (850/653-6482, $400–500 for bay area fishing trips, $850–1250 for offshore fishing) leads offshore fishing groups, sightseeing and shelling expeditions, oystering adventures, and, in season, tarpon trips; **Backwater Guide Service** (850/899-0063, $375 half day, $500 full day) takes people bass fishing or fly-fishing on the river on a 17-foot homemade wood boat and offers sightseeing trips on the Apalachicola River, shelling trips to the barrier islands, and dolphin-watching tours; marine biologist Chip Bailey takes anglers out on a 23-foot SE Parker center console with his **Peregrine Charters** (850/653-2204, $350 half day, $450 full day); and the **Robinson Brothers Guide Service** (850/653-8896, $550) gets the nod for both "skinny water" fishing (that's shallow water, where anglers stand on the bow of a flats boat with their fly rod or spinning rod—usually all catch-and-release) as well as bay fishing with live bait in a little bigger boat in deeper water. Tommy and Chris Robinson's knowledge of the area is impressive.

COURTESY OF THE APALACHICOLA CHAMBER OF COMMERCE

Hire a local fishing guide and reel in a redfish like this 30-pounder from Apalachicola Bay.

The more independent-minded angler may want to rent a boat on his or her own. **Seahorse Water Safaris** (340 Marina Dr., Port St. Joe, 850/227-1099) rents pontoon boats holding 10 people for you to take out on St. Joseph Bay ($190 half day plus fuel costs).

If finfishing leaves you cold you may want to experience oystering. **Book Me A Charter** (P.O. Box 333, Apalachicola, FL 32329, 850/653-2622, www.bookmeacharter.com, $350 half day) takes up to four clients out on an oysterboat, demonstrating how to tong, cull, and harvest oysters from legal harvest areas (you get to take the bivalve bounty home with you). They also offer in-shore and offshore fishing trips led by experienced local guides.

## Diving

Scuba enthusiasts have a few excellent options in the area (including some nice artificial reef diving and clam-covered rock ledges in St. Joe), but the most celebrated wreck dive can be found 105 feet down, 20 miles south of Cape San Blas. Undulating with packs of curious amberjack, barracuda, snapper, and rays, the **Empire Mica** lies in disarray on the floor of the Gulf. A British oil tanker built in 1941, the ship was en route from Houston to England on June 29, 1942, when two German submarine torpedoes ignited the 12,000 tons of oil it was carrying. The ship went down in a series of fiery explosions, killing 33 men on board. Today, the bow section of the 479-foot-long ship is intact, as are 60–80 feet of deck, the metal getting lacy and thin. **Killfish Custom Charters** (Port St. Joe, 850/527-7901, $150 per person with three air tanks) provides wonderful all-day trips to the *Empire Mica* or to the *Exxon Template,* another favorite local dive 32 miles off of Apalachicola. **Seahorse Water Safaris** (850/227-1099) offers diving trips (prices vary by trip and duration) and guided snorkel tours, if scuba seems too hardcore ($25 plus $10 gear rental).

## Forests

Here's how the story goes: A guy named Cebe Tate once entered a vast swamp in search of a Florida panther that was killing his livestock. Gone for seven days and nights, when Tate emerged with his trusty hunting dog, shaken and thirsty, he announced, "My name is Cebe Tate, and I just came from Hell!" That's how **Tate's Hell State Forest** (access the forest from U.S. 98, County Road 67, or Hwy. 65, 850/697-3734) got its ominous name. It's 185,000 acres between the Apalachicola and Ochlockonee rivers, much of it suitable for hiking and biking. There's an observation tower at the **Ralph G. Kendrick Boardwalk** from which visitors can look out over a dense stand of rare dwarf, or hatrack, cypress, many of them 150 years old and only 15 feet tall. A number of endangered or threatened species call Hell home, including the bald eagle, red-cockaded woodpecker, gopher tortoise, and Florida black bear.

The forest contains 35 miles of rivers, streams, and creeks available for canoeing, boating, fishing (boat launch at Cash Creek and other sites), and primitive camping. The **High Bluff Coastal Trail** is a wonderful hiking path that's part of the Florida Division of Forestry's Trailwalker Program, its trailhead located on U.S. 98, four miles west of Carrabelle.

To the north, abutting Tate's Hell State Forest, is **Apalachicola National Forest** (850/643-2282, www.fs.fed.us/r8/florida), the largest national forest in Florida. The area was largely destroyed at the turn of the 20th

century by the timber and turpentine industries, but since 1936 it's been allowed to percolate unharassed and now has the largest red-cockaded woodpecker population in the world. Much of the forest is difficult to get to, but there are a few nice day hikes easily accessible: the 4.5-mile-long **Wright Lake Trail,** the 6-mile-long **Trail of Lakes,** and the 5.4-mile-long **Leon Sinks Geological Area Trail.** Mountain bikers will head to the **Munson Hills Off-Road Bicycle Trail,** in the eastern part of the forest, and the 16-mile paved **St. Marks Trail,** which is part of a rails-to-trails program that passes through the forest and terminates in the town of St. Marks. For serious backpackers and more remote hiking, there's also a 68.7-mile section of the **Florida Trail** running through the forest that's a designated part of the Florida Statewide Greenways and Trails System. For a trail map and more information, visit www.florida-trail.org.

## SIGHTS
### ◖ Self-Guided Historic Walking Tour

Stop in at the **Apalachicola Chamber of Commerce** (122 Commerce St., Apalachicola, 850/653-9419) for a copy of the self-guided historic walking tour map. More than 200 of the regal old homes in Apalachicola are listed on the National Register of Historic Places. Not all of them are in mint condition, but an hour or two of walking, gawking, and reading the brochure is a great way to get to know the downtown area.

There is a handful of little historic churches: **Trinity Episcopal Church** (79 Sixth St., 850/653-9550) dates all the way back to when Andrew Jackson was president and Florida was still a territory. It was actually built of white pine in New York and shipped down to Apalachicola—the white Greek Revival church is the sixth-oldest church in the state of Florida, the second-oldest church still holding services. Not far away, there's the **First Baptist Church** (46 Ninth St., 850/653-9540), originally built on the corner of Sixth Street and Avenue H, and the Romanesque **St. Patrick's Catholic Church** (27 Sixth St.,

# ICE, ICE, BABY

Ice cube museum. Hmm. Are you imagining a very cold room containing, maybe, a piece of the berg that sank the *Titanic*, a cube from Dean Martin's final cocktail, or the original "fly-in-the-ice cube" novelty gag? *Buzz!* Thanks for playing, and we have some very nice consolation prizes for you today.

Apalachicola luminary **John Gorrie** is known in the history books as the father of air-conditioning and ice manufacturing, recipient of the first patent for mechanical refrigeration in 1851. A tiny, charming museum in a little historic house tells the Gorrie story.

By the time the young doctor arrived in town in 1833, Apalachicola was bustling as the third-largest port on the Gulf, shipping cotton to Europe and New England. During his time in town, Gorrie served as mayor, postmaster, city council member, bank director, and founder of Trinity Church. But all that civic-mindedness pales when compared to his medical work. Yellow fever was a menace in those years, no one linking the terrifying sickness to those swarms of pesky mosquitoes that plagued these swampy, humid, low-lying floodplains. In addition to chills, headache, muscle aches,

vomiting, and backache, the onset of the illness was marked by high fever. Gorrie posited that bringing the fever down was essential to prevent the shock, bleeding, and kidney and liver failure that often led to death.

As cold temperatures were hard to come by in these parts, he set about making some. His idea is one used in today's refrigeration: Cooling can be achieved through the rapid expansion of gases. He built a machine with two pumps that condensed and then rarefied air. He cooled the air all right, but the machine kept clogging with ice cubes. There's no evidence that his invention saved any lives, and Gorrie died unable to market his apparatus.

The little **John Gorrie State Museum** (46 6th St., Apalachicola, 850/653-9347, 9 A.M.-5 P.M. Thurs.-Mon., $1) contains a replica of Gorrie's ice machine, built from his specs. There are also wonderful exhibits on the history of the area, from its days as a cotton port to sponge diving and oyster harvesting. The museum interpreters are a real wealth of knowledge and are willing to expound at length on Apalachicola lore.

---

850/653-2100), built in 1929 (although the congregation goes back to 1845, the first structure was destroyed in a big fire that consumed 70 downtown buildings in 1846).

The historic homes are even more compelling, several of them tourable inside and out (and each May there's a fling-open-the-doors tour of historic homes, $12 per guided tour). As part of a Florida state park, the **Orman House** (177 Fifth St., 850/653-1209, 9 A.M.-5 P.M. Thurs.-Mon., $2), the original 1838 home of cotton merchant Thomas Orman, is open to the public. There is an hour-long narrated tour of the Federal and Greek Revival two-story house, the wood for which was cut and measured near Syracuse, New York, and shipped to Apalachicola by sailboat around the Florida Keys. The majestic, columned **Raney House** (46 Ave. F, 850/653-1700, 1–4 P.M. Sun.–Fri., 10 A.M.–4 P.M. Sat., free

admission) dates to the same year, the home of David Greenway Raney and family. The interior is now a little museum run by the Apalachicola Area Historical Society.

## Chestnut Street Cemetery

Dating prior to 1831, historic Chestnut Street Cemetery (U.S. 98 between Sixth St. and Eighth St.) contains many Confederate soldiers, the world famous botanist Dr. Alvin Wentworth Chapman, and many victims of yellow fever. The broad range of surnames speaks to the town's early diversity (Spanish and French settlers, shipwreck victims). To some spooky, to others just peaceful, the little urban cemetery contains beautifully carved funerary art tucked in the dappled shadows cast by gnarled old live oaks shrouded with Spanish moss.

THE FORGOTTEN COAST

## Dixie Theatre

If you're looking to determine whether Apalachicola's on the wax or wane, the Dixie Theatre (21 Ave. E, 850/653-3200, performances usually 8 P.M. Fri. and Sat., 3 P.M. Sun.) is a pretty optimistic sign. Built in 1912, it was the locus of cultural activity—stage performances, then silent pictures, then the talkies—in the county for decades. It foundered in the late 1960s, but recent boosters have gotten it back up and running. The original building's decrepitude led to some ingenious restoration and re-creation. In 1998 the building was completed, with a facade that looks much like it did in 1912, and the original ticket booth painstakingly restored. There's now a winter repertory theater season, and it shows the occasional ragtime piano show or big town gala.

## ENTERTAINMENT AND EVENTS
### ☾ Florida Seafood Festival

Apalach and surrounding towns are the undisputed eastern oyster capital of the world. The oyster industry began in the later part of the 19th century, and by 1896 there were three oyster-canning factories shipping something like 50,000 cans of oysters daily (the first time canning was attempted in Florida). The Oyster industry in Apalachicola harvested 2.5 million pounds of oysters in 2009, worth $6.1 million, according to the Florida Fish and Wildlife Conservation Commission.

Naturally, oysters provide the foundation for the area's biggest annual party. The Florida Seafood Festival (888/653-8011, www.floridaseafoodfestival.com) is actually the oldest maritime festival in the state, drawing thousands each year during the first weekend in November. There are oyster-shucking and -eating contests, parades, arts and crafts, musical entertainment, and a running race—but clearly the big draw is pot upon pot of just-caught seafood in a multitude of preparations.

## Big Bend Saltwater Classic

The other big annual draw is the Big Bend Saltwater Classic (850/216-2272) fishing tournament in Carrabelle in June, an opportunity to see more than 700 serious anglers competing for big prizes in a weekend event that benefits the Organization for Artificial Reefs.

## SHOPPING

The nine square blocks that make up downtown Apalachicola offer plenty of options for shopping. Retailers are spread amongst repurposed brick and tin cotton warehouses and early-1900s cottages. Located across from the docks, the **Grady Market** (76 Water St., 850/653-4099) seems to be the locals' pride and joy, a 19th-century ship's chandlery made over to house about a dozen boutiques and galleries (including that of black-and-white photographer Richard Bickel). A block from there is a more eccentric spot called the **Tin Shed** (170 Water St., 850/653-3635), specializing in antique nautical items like Japanese fishing floats, captains' telescopes, compasses, and ships' bells.

**Avenue E** (15 Ave. E, 850/653-1411) is a fairly priced shop offering antiques and reproduction pieces, a small assortment of children's clothing, gifts, lamps, folk art, and marine-themed interior accessories. **BLUE beach + home** (31 Ave. E, 850/653-8778) is another nearby upscale home store with plenty of cool beach-themed housewares.

If you're looking for crystal jewelry, lotions, gowns, wraps, and accessories head to **Riverlily** (78 Commerce St., 850/653-2600). Nearby, there's **The Oystercatcher** (79 Market St., 850/653-1616), a rather funky boutique chockfull of denim, dresses, swimwear, and jewelry. Also an interesting spot, **Petunia** (14 Ave. D, 850/653-9144) has a small collection of gifts and apparel for pets and their people.

**Forgotten Coast Outfitters** (94 Market St., 850/653-9669), an authorized Orvis dealer, is where you can purchase clothing and gear for camping and fly-fishing. For a larger selection of rods and reels and fly-fishing tackle you can head over to **Apalach Outfitters** (29 Ave E, 850/653-3474, 11 A.M.–6 P.M. daily). It opened in the storefront that used to house Dolores' Sweet Shop and carries a full line of outdoor clothing and footwear with brands like North Face, Patagonia, and Prana. A couple of doors down is **Chez Funk** (88 Market St., 850/653-3885) where you can browse the antiques, "trash art," and painted furniture.

## ❰ Tupelo Honey

*She's as sweet as tupelo honey*
*She's an angel of the first degree*
*She's as sweet as tupelo honey*
*Just like honey from the bee.*

Just what was Van Morrison singing about, anyway? He was comparing his sweetie to a rare honey, thought by connoisseurs to be among the world's finest. Prized for its flavor and for the fact that it never granulates, tupelo honey is produced by bees that cavort in the tupelo gum trees that grow with gusto along the Apalachicola River. Harvested for two short weeks in late April, tupelo honey was featured in the Peter Fonda vehicle *Ulee's Gold*.

The locus of tupelo production is in Wewahitchka, the only place in the world the honey is produced commercially. The process starts when bees are placed on elevated platforms along the river's edge. The bees then swarm the tupelo blossom–laden swamps and return with their treasure. The resulting honey is a pale amber color with a slight greenish cast, its flavor delicate and distinctive. Because it costs more to produce, tupelo is more expensive than many other honeys. But listen to Van the Man—this is the good stuff. The recent crisis in honeybees as a result of the Colony Collapse Disorder, combined with Georgia's water shortage (resulting in slightly less freshwater in Florida), means tupelo honey may be an endangered commodity.

Regardless, every spring at Lake Alice Park in Wewahitchka, folks gather to celebrate the apian masterpiece. For years the **Tupelo Festival** took place the third week in April during the tupelo pollinating time, but in recent years it's been moved to the third weekend in May to coincide with when the keepers scoop the honey from the hives. There's

Visit David Smiley at Smiley Apiaries and pick up a bottle of his prized tupelo honey.

© JOSHUA LAWRENCE KINSER

entertainment, arts and crafts, kids' activities, and a whole lot of things containing tupelo honey, from lotions to snacks.

If you're looking for some honey to take back home with you, many shops in the area stock it, but you can also call the ones who tutored Peter Fonda on beekeeping for the film, **L.L. Lanier & Son's Tupelo Honey** (850/639-2371), or stop by the extremely friendly **Smiley Apiaries** (850/639-5672) and buy a bottle right from Donald Smiley's front porch.

## ACCOMMODATIONS
## $50-150

Pretty much nothing in Apalachicola runs under $50, but the **Best Western Apalach Inn** (249 U.S. 98 W., 850/653-9131) and the **Rancho Inn** (240 U.S. 98 W., 850/653-9435) both ring in around $70–130, right next to each other in a convenient location. The former offers complimentary hot breakfast and an outdoor pool, and children 17 and under stay free. The latter accepts pets for a $10 fee.

**The Gibson Inn** (51 Ave. C, 850/653-2191,

The Gibson Inn is a sprawling cypress and pine Victorian inn with a picturesque cupola.

$90–175), on the National Register of Historic Places, had some major cosmetic surgery in 1985, but it still has the antebellum dignity that comes of wide wraparound porches, four-poster beds, antiques, and slowly revolving ceiling fans. This gracious tin-roofed Victorian right downtown (built in 1907 as a hotel, never a private residence) contains 30 rooms, each different. Suited well for romance-seekers and history buffs; the Gibson Inn does allow pets in certain rooms.

In a similarly Victorian vein, but even more spruce, is the sunny yellow **Coombs House Inn** (80 Sixth St., 850/653-9199, $89–229), built in 1905 by a lumber magnate. The three-story mansion has high ceilings, an ornate and creaky oak staircase, nine wide fireplaces that perennially exude the homey smell of recent wood smoke, and a slew of historical photos. Guests in the 20 antique-bedecked rooms enjoy a pleasant breakfast, weekend evening wine receptions, and use of the inn's bikes, umbrellas, and beach chairs. If the quiet and rarefied

chintz-and-doilies bed-and-breakfast experience isn't your idea of fun, you can still tour the Coombs House after checking out the Chestnut Street Cemetery across the street as part of a whirlwind local history lesson.

If you're looking for a little more privacy, the **Raney Guest Cottage** (46 Ave. F, 850/653-9749, $140/night, $907/week) is a quaint house that dates back to around 1835 (all the town records burned around 1900, so most dates are pure conjecture and sleuthwork), one of the oldest buildings in Apalachicola. Sit on a rocker or the hand-crafted swing on the wraparound porch and sip a glass of ice-cold sweet tea, or walk the block into town (two to the river). It's definitely charming, and the historic house is all yours, with two cozy bedrooms, two baths, dining room, kitchen, screened back porch, two gas-burning fireplaces for the nippy north Florida winters, washer/dryer, and grill. Similar, **House of Tartts** (50 Ave. F, 850/653-4687) is another restored guesthouse with three private rooms.

New to Apalachicola in 2007, **Water Street Hotel & Marina** (329 Water St., 850/653-3700, www.waterstreethotel.com, $169–199) offers 30 suites and a 20-slip marina (a floating dock servicing boats up to 55 feet) blocks from the center of downtown Apalach. Despite a turn-of-the-20th-century vibe, it still boasts all the contemporary bells and whistles (wireless Internet, in-room movies), with enough space to make it very family-friendly.

## Over $150

Then again, you could stay at the **Consulate Suites** (76 Water St., 850/927-2282, $155–315) and pretend you're visiting dignitaries. Prior to the Civil War, when Apalachicola had its commercial heyday, the French consulate was located in the second story of the bustling Grady Building, a ship's chandlery. The Grady Building was renovated several years back and transformed into a breezy shopping attraction of galleries and gift boutiques. Above it are four apartment-sized luxury suites with 11-foot tin ceilings and lots of exposed brick. Three of the four suites overlook the river, and all have balconies and sleep four people (not a bad deal when compared to two rooms in an inn or hotel).

# FOOD
## Oyster Bars

**(** **Boss Oyster** (125 Water St., 850/653-9364, 11:30 A.M.–10 P.M. daily, $10–25) seems to be the oyster palace to beat (tagline: Oysters All Ways 'n' Oysters Always). Topped with the sensible (a squeeze of lime, a splash of tequila, and a dash of Tabasco) and the nearly obscene (envision a broiled oyster stacked with bacon, jalapeños, colby, and a splash of hot sauce), the local oysters are briny bliss. A lively family-oriented crowd, nightly drink specials, and a casual Apalachicola River–side setting keep it full. Try the heads-on shrimp; roll up your sleeves and don't be fussy. And if you advocate topping an oyster with something out of the ordinary, tell the staff and they just might name a dish after you.

Those in the other camp are staunch adherents of the slippery bivalves at **Papa**

**Joe's Oyster Bar and Grill** (301 B Market St., at Scipio Creek Marina, 850/653-1189, 11:30 A.M.–10 P.M. Mon.–Thurs., 5–9 P.M. Fri. and 5–10 P.M. Sat., $6–20). It's another waterside seafood-and-steak joint with a serious emphasis on local oysters, raw or broiled.

About 17 miles west of Apalachicola, the absolute must-eat destination is the **(** **Indian Pass Raw Bar** (8391 County Road C-30A, Indian Pass, 850/227-1670, noon–9 P.M. Tues.–Sat., $4–8). It is always a party in this shambling roadside shack (recently buffed up somewhat), every vinyl stool filled with someone vigilantly watching as the oyster shucker works his or her magic at the end of the bar. Raw on the half shell is best, but the garlic butter and parmesan baked version is a delicious spin on these briny beauties. Grab your own drink from the cooler and be sure to order the key lime pie (and kids, this place serves a killer corn dog).

## Lunch

Former PGA-money winner Mike Keller owns **That Place off 98** (17 Ave. E, 850/653-9898, 11 A.M.–9 P.M. daily, $10–22). Formerly called That Place on 98, Keller has relocated his restaurant into the heart of downtown Apalachicola, right next door to the Dixie Theater. It is a comfortable, casual oyster joint with an upbeat feel. Hands down, this is the best bowl of seafood gumbo in town—I went back two days in a row just to get another bowl of this tasty traditional Cajun soup that is anything but skimpy on the seafood. It has quickly become one of the most popular seafood restaurants in Apalachicola, with an extensive lunch and dinner menu that features all local seafood and those delicious oysters on the half shell.

**Apalachicola Seafood Grill** (100 Market St., 850/653-9510, 11:30 A.M.–4 P.M. Mon.–Sat., $8–15) seems mighty proud of its fried fish sandwich—"largest in the world," although that may be a little gastronomic hyperbole—which may explain why the restaurant under the town's only traffic light has kept 'em coming since 1903.

# EASTERN OYSTERS

Franklin County has historically harvested 90 percent of the state's oysters and 13 percent of the nation's. More than 1,000 people in the county make their living in the oyster business. To give you a sense of quantity, in recent years the U.S. oyster haul has been roughly 30 million pounds of meat – about 75 percent of that eastern oysters, or *Crassostrea virginica*, the species that is shown off to finest effect right here in Apalachicola.

Currently, a number of things threaten the Florida oysters. The BP oil spill of 2010 reduced the numbers of oysters harvested during the summer harvest season. Some oyster distributors in the region reported that their oyster supply was down by as much as 70 percent at the height of the oil spill, between June and September 2010. Also, an increase in the price of oysters and consumer fear over oil contamination has caused a reduction in sales for the region's number one seafood export item.

The second, even more serious, is drought in Georgia to the north. Reduced water flows down the Apalachicola River mean saltwater encroachment upriver into the estuaries, where the gulf seafood spawns. Some estimates put the Apalachicola oysters at half dead right now due to lack of freshwater, with the east and west ends of Apalachicola Bay the hardest hit. Let's hope this $200 million-a-year regional industry can bounce back.

Found all around the Gulf of Mexico and up the eastern seaboard all the way to Canada, eastern oysters have historically flourished in the bay, which encompasses the waters of St. George Sound and St. Vincent Sound and is renewed constantly by the nutrient-rich freshwater of Apalachicola River. It's this balance of fresh- and saltwater that seems to act as some kind of magic growth serum. Oysters grow fast and sweet here, reaching marketable size in less than two years (in colder climates it can take as long as six years). The 210-square-mile

estuary is shallow, 6–9 feet deep at low tide, with oysterers skimming along in small boats to scoop up their harvest from the bottom with long-handled tongs.

Local oysters are carefully monitored and husbanded. The Department of Health Services, the EPA, and other agencies test for water purity and natural threats such as red tide. In addition, the Department of Agriculture and Consumer Services has sponsored extensive efforts to restock oyster shell in the bay to create new oyster bars, and even to "plant" more than 100,000 bushels of adult and juvenile oysters on public oyster reefs in the bay. These transplanted oysters are taken from waters where harvesting is not allowed or where growth is poor and relocated to approved waters where conditions are more favorable for oysters to healthfully grow to market size. The ultimate aim: enhancing oyster production and ensuring oyster quality.

You know that expression, "That which doesn't kill you makes you stronger"? A few bad oysters have given these bivalve mollusks a bum rap, but oysters are quite good for you. A dozen rings in at approximately 110 calories, rich in iron, copper, and iodine and high in calcium and vitamin A. Around here they are sold by the dozen, half bushel, peck, or bushel, graded according to size: The largest marketed are "selects" and the average are "standards." Look for oysters that close tightly when handled. They'll live in a cold fridge for more than a week (cover them loosely with a damp cloth, never in an airtight container). If you buy them already shucked, use them right away and don't freeze them.

While you're in Apalachicola, throw caution to the wind and try them on the half shell. If you aren't in the mood to challenge fate by eating them raw, they are a treat eaten fried, baked, steamed or broiled – that's paradise on the Forgotten Coast.

Another longtime lunch favorite is **The Owl Café** (15 Ave. D, 850/653-9888, 10:30 A.M.–3 P.M. and 5:30–10 P.M. Mon.–Sat., 11 A.M.–3 P.M. Sun. brunch, $18–24). The café features black-and-white photos by local photographer Richard Bickel on the walls (if you like his work, local shops carry his latest book, *Apalachicola River: An American Treasure*), pretty wood floors, a second floor, and an adjacent wine room. The high-ceilinged clapboard building is a replica of the original, lost to fire in 1911. Again, seafood is the strong suit, from the black grouper with garlic, capers, and artichokes to seafood pastas. The chicken Caesar salad is also not to be missed, and the wine list merits some perusal.

The **Old Time Soda Fountain** (93 Market St., 850/653-2606, 10 A.M.–5 P.M. Mon.–Sat., $4–9) will satisfy your hankering for malts, floats, ice-cream sodas, and diner-style sandwiches. It's a 1950s-style, stools-at-the-counter relic that was once the town's drugstore. And if you just need a wireless Internet venue, enhanced by a deep Venezuelan coffee, head to **Café Con Leche** (234 Water St., 850/653-2233, 8 A.M.–5 P.M. Mon.–Sat.), recently relocated to the Grady Market building.

## Fine Dining

Boss Oyster's sister restaurant, **Caroline's Dining on the River** (123 Water St., 850/653-8139, 7 A.M.–10 P.M. Mon.–Sat., $16–24) adopts more of a fine-dining mindset, but the same straightforward, fish-centric American food sense. Presided over by Caroline Maddren, it's in the Apalachicola River Inn and is the place to luxuriate in a lengthy Sunday brunch (opt for the oyster cakes or zingy shrimp Creole heaped over buttermilk biscuits). As with most places around here, the oysters and fresh finfish get the nod—you can watch the shrimp and fish boats tooling by outside with the day's catch.

## Ethnic/Eclectic

While seafood—oysters in particular—dominates this area, a few restaurants give their marine creatures a little twist.

**Tamara's Cafe Floridita** (71 Market St., 850/653-4111, 8 A.M.–11 A.M. for breakfast, until 10 P.M. for lunch and dinner Tues.–Sun., $12–20) is where local seafood gets Caribbean and South American inflections, such as paella or a pecan-crusted grouper with a creamy jalapeño sauce, everything served with black beans and rice. Wednesday nights are the best times to take a group—it's tapas night, with classics like shrimp sautéed with lots of garlic and a Spanish tortilla, all the little dishes very affordable.

At **Chef Eddie's Magnolia Grill** (75 Market St., 850/653-8000, 5–10 P.M. Tues.–Sun., closing earlier in the off-season, $16–24), you'll find seafood like down on the bayou. In a sweet 1880s bungalow, Eddie Cass sends out sophisticated oak-grilled rib eye steaks, a New Orleans–style seafood gumbo redolent of all the succulent local catches, and a no-holds-barred death by chocolate cake. There is a very fairly priced wine selection drawn mostly from Napa, Sonoma, and Burgundy.

## Cocktails

If you're looking for a fancy wine bar in town, head to **Veranda's Bistro** (76 Market St. and Ave. D, 850/653-3210, 11 A.M.–10 P.M. daily, $8–25). The place has a great view and the menu has been considerably expanded in recent years with dinner selections like ginger seared salmon steak with an apricot mustard glaze and fried oysters served in a Creole remoulade. For lunch you can choose among a large selection of salads, soups, and sandwiches like the pepper-encrusted tuna with caramelized onion wakami salad or a fried green tomato B.L.T. The selection of wines by the glass is impressive. The second story is a good place to end a day or take in a sunset.

# St. George Island

The new St. George Island Bridge in Franklin County was officially opened in 2004. It is 4.1 miles long, cost $71 million, and took three years to construct. It is the largest Design-Build effort ever undertaken by the Florida Department of Transportation and the third-largest bridge in Florida.

So what, you say? The old bridge certainly did the job of shuttling vacationers and residents from the mainland fishing village of Eastpoint to the narrow, wooded barrier island of St. George Island. The new bridge, though, is a rock-solid testament to the island's recent growth, burgeoning affluence, and rampant optimism. East of St. Vincent Island, St. George shelters Apalachicola Bay and St. George Sound, both productive bodies of water for commercial fishing and sportfishing. The whole eastern end of the island is taken up with the 1,900-acre St. George Island State Park, which contains some of the most pristine and underpopulated white-sand beaches in Florida, first-class fishing, and fabulous beaches. St. George has got it all *right now*, and only a lucky few seem to know about it.

For much of its 5,000-year tenure, the island has been inhabited mostly by the avian, the reptilian, and a few small mammals. Humans swooped in in the early 1900s to harvest the sap from the island's slash pines (used to make turpentine). The island's dunes were used for training exercises during World War II, but it's been mercifully underutilized since then.

In 1970, a Tallahassee real estate developer named John R. Stocks bought up much of the island, then sold Little St. George and the east end, now the state park, to the state of Florida. His company, Leisure Properties, then started selling five- and eight-acre tracts like hotcakes. Growth was quick in what is now the Plantation area, but strict environmental rules keep the sight lines low and the water views spectacular. There are still only around 700 year-round residents, but thousands flock to the island for luxurious beachfront house and condo rentals during the summer months.

## SPORTS AND RECREATION
### ◖ St. George Island State Park
It's officially called the Dr. Julian G. Bruce St. George Island State Park (1900 E. Gulf Beach Dr., 850/927-2111, open 8 A.M.–dusk daily, $6 per vehicle), but most people around here just call it the state park. And what a state park it is. The land was acquired for the park in 1963, and the completed park facilities opened to the public in 1980. Imagine 1,900 acres of wind-swept, sea oat–fringed dunes, gorgeous enough and underpopulated enough to make most aficionados' lists of best beaches in the United States. The whole east end of the island is state park land, so officially it's the longest beach of any beachfront state park in Florida—nine miles of white sand.

The water is warm, shallow, and calm enough for hours of swimming (sorry, surfers). The beaches seem to be stocked with perfect shells by the local chamber of commerce, and the abundant fish are often biting. Along the beach you'll see starfish and sand dollars, jellyfish, loggerhead sea turtle nests during the summer, and hardly another person. And when you get tired of all that perfect white sand, there are nature trails through the pine flatwood forest and live oak hammocks.

The park has no lifeguards or concessions, so bring your own picnic provisions and toys. There are, however, six sets of rustic wood-beamed pavilions with sheltered picnic tables, water fountains, outside showers, and bathrooms. It is illegal to walk through the sea oats along the high sand dunes—walk from the parking area out to the beach only along the weathered wooden boardwalks. Be on the lookout for the burrowing ghost crab, its semi-transparent carapace and huge eyes making it a wild sight (they can also run up to 10 mph). In the woods you might glimpse raccoons and a fair number of snakes and diamondback terrapins.

Anglers most often catch whiting, but you'll see them reeling in flounder, redfish, pompano, sea trout, and Spanish mackerel as well. (A saltwater fishing license is required.) Birders, on the other hand, train their sights on osprey, eagles, snowy plover, least tern, black skimmer, and willet.

RV and tent camping is permitted in the 60 pine-shaded campsites ($24) in the forests on the bay side set behind the dunes. The campground features a dump station, flush toilets, and nature trails. The maximum stay is 14 nights; there are sites to camp with pets. There are also primitive campsites at Gap Point for those who wish to hike in along the 2.5-mile trail, which meanders from the bay through the pine flatwood forest to the campground. As with all Florida state parks, reserve campsites at www.reserveamerica.com. Boat ramps are located at the Youth Camp Area and East Slough, and kayaks are available for daily rental.

## Loggerhead Turtles

St. George Island is said to have one of the darkest night skies in the continental United States, making it a favorable place for stargazing. While a lot of this is merely a byproduct of low population density, some of it is by design. Franklin County adopted the Lighting Ordinance for Marine Turtle Protection in 1998, which restricts house lights, streetlights, and even flashlight use on the island.

Florida beaches are home to 90 percent of the loggerhead sea turtle nests in the southeastern United States, the largest population in the Western Hemisphere and one of the two largest in the world. St. George Island provides habitat for loggerhead, green, and leatherback turtles. Every year, starting around May 1, would-be mother loggerheads travel tremendous distances to come ashore here to nest (scientists think they return to the beach on which they were born). It's been shown that lights on and around beach homes can distract the mothers from their task and disorient the hatchlings enough to make them crawl inland instead of toward the sea, making them easy snacks for their many predators.

Currently, all seven sea turtle species are listed as either threatened or endangered, and the five species that swim in the Gulf of Mexico and nest on its shores, including the loggerheads, are declining in numbers. What can you as a visitor do to aid the nesting sea turtles? At the very least, if you've rented a beach house, keep outdoor house lights off as much as possible and pull your shades at night to minimize window light pollution on the beaches. Beyond that, you can call Apalachicola Bay and River Riverkeepers (850/670-5470) or Bruce Drye, the local permit holder for sea turtles (850/927-2103), to report disoriented hatchlings or injured or stranded turtles.

If your visit to St. George Island coincides with nesting season (May–Oct.), you can take a night beach walk in the hopes of glimpsing mother sea turtles crawling ashore—they leave a distinctive, filigreed track in the sand—or the hatchlings clumsily flapping their way back out to sea. A single female loggerhead builds as many as three or four nests in a single season, laying about a hundred eggs in each one—it's quite a sight to see the little guys struggling to meet the sea, but resist the impulse to take flash photographs. And if you're compelled to help, you can volunteer with St. George Island Volunteer Turtlers to find, mark, and protect turtle nests incubating in the warm sand. Call the Estuarine Reserve (850/670-4783) to ask about volunteer efforts.

## 🄲 Biking St. George Island

It's hard to say, but perhaps the single nicest thing about St. George Island is its bike accessibility and nearly ubiquitous paved bike paths. All the way from the Plantation side (west end) to the state park at the east end, there are straight, flat roadside paths for bicyclists, and miles of off-roading possibilities as well. Bikes can be rented from **Island Adventures** (105 E. Gulf Beach Dr., 850/927-3655, $10/day). If you're absolutely opposed to physical exertion, you can rent golf carts at **Jolly Roger Beach Shop** for $125 per day (139 West Gorrie Dr., 850/927-2999). It also offers surfboard rentals for $35 per day and kayak rentals for $45 per day.

Book a paddling tour with Journeys of St. George Island and explore the Apalachicola River, Estuary, and Bay.

## Birding

The shores and inland areas of St. George Island and the sheltered harbor of Eastpoint are rife with birding possibilities. In the latter, loons, gulls, and waterfowl play host to a number of vagrant bird species in the fall.

If you're attentive, from the bridge linking Eastpoint with St. George Island you'll see the nests of large colonies of least terns and black skimmers April–July. As its name implies, the least tern is the smallest of the terns, weighing about one ounce (don't confuse them with the medium-sized gull-billed terns, with their heavy black bills and short forked tails, that also occasionally hang out here).

Florida birders also boast of the area's abundance of Sprague's pipit (although these little guys are hard to see, usually choosing to hang out in fields of short grass) in the late fall, and in the winter it's not uncommon to see the common goldeneye in nearby water.

Walking the shores of St. George Island, you'll view American oystercatchers, spotted sandpipers, ruddy turnstones, willets, sanderlings, several kinds of plovers, and loads of other shorebirds. And driving down the island's many wooded dirt roads yields a wealth of sightings in the spring and fall—bald eagles nest here, and in the fall you're apt to see sharp-shinned hawks, peregrine falcons, northern harriers, and American kestrels.

In the early spring, the youth campsite's oak hammock at St. George Island State Park is a good place to spot newly arrived migratory birds, maybe even something as rare as a Connecticut warbler. Continuing to the end of the park's paved road and walking out to the beach, you may be treated to the sight of plucky little snowy plovers. In the winter, northern gannets are sometimes seen in the park or in offshore waters.

If you want to view many of the area's 200 species of birds—or even if you have your heart set on seeing one specific feathered treasure— you may want to arrange a bird-focused kayak trip with guides at **Journeys of St. George Island** (www.sgislandjourneys.com, 850/927-3259). They offer a large variety of family ecotours and kids-only trips, including dolphin watches, shark fishing adventures, a Bounty of the Bay tour (tong for oysters, pull in blue crab traps, net cast for mullet), and fishing trips both in the Bay and offshore. Ecotours, fishing trips, guided paddling trips, and boat cruises range in price $30–450. The kayak tours on the Apalachicola River are a great deal at $50 for three hours (only $30 for children). Journeys has a very well organized and comprehensive website that clearly and thoroughly explains all of the prices and descriptions of its various trips.

## SHOPPING

Not known for its shopping, St. George boasts a couple of gas stations, a handful of bikini and boogie board shops, and a preponderance of ice-cream scoop stands (most of these with prices that reflect a little isolation inflation). If you have the urge to shop and don't feel like heading back over the bridge to Apalach, meander over to **Island Outfitters** (235 E. Gulf Beach Dr., 850/927-2604), where you can peruse resort wear along with the latest in saltwater fishing tackle, rods, reels, and accessories. Island Outfitters is also the place to charter a boat or rent a 19-foot Carolina skiff or catamaran so you can explore the barrier islands and the Apalachicola River and its tributaries. **Sometimes It's Hotter Seasoning Company** (37 E. Pine Ave., 850/927-5039) is a unique local institution and a nice place to pick up dried herbs and herb blends for barbecuing or the folks back home. Not far from there, **Island Emporium** (160 E. Pine St., 850/927-2622) is a two-story souvenir shop of collectibles, beachwear, and sandcastle-building supplies.

If you arrived on-island without your beach essentials, the nearby **St. George Island Beach Chair Rentals** (137 E. Pine St., 850/670-4536) rents beach umbrellas ($15/day), kayaks ($15/ hour for a two-seater), surf boards ($10/day), and other necessities and offers free delivery to any St. George Island rental unit. It also rents catamarans, larger sailboats, and personal watercraft (like Jet Skis).

## ACCOMMODATIONS

On St. George, hotel or inn accommodations are only sensible if you are staying very briefly or are traveling alone or as a couple. Families tend to rent one of 800 beach cottages or houses on the island, most offered by the week (and, off-season, by the weekend). Some of these houses are absolutely enormous, a super opportunity to convene several generations of your family or several families together under one roof. Pets are often allowed, and many homes have private pools, game rooms, and tremendous kitchens for preparing the daily catch.

## Vacation Rentals

◖ **Resort Vacation Properties** handles many of the upscale rental houses (850/927-2322, www.resortvacationproperties.com), with wonderfully detailed descriptions and photos of properties on their website. They deal with properties all over the island but seem to have a special lock on the large houses in the Plantation, the private community on the western end of the island. Other realtors that traffic in properties all over the island include **Collins Vacation Rentals** (800/683-9776, www.collinsvacationrentals.com) and **Suncoast Realty** (800/341-2021, www.uncommonflorida.com). Beyond picking your price range (they go from $1,000/week up to more than $5,000 for some of the more luxurious ones), there are lots of other factors to consider, such as whether to be on the Gulf or bay side, how close to town you want to be, and the kind of neighborhood in which you feel most comfortable.

### ST. GEORGE PLANTATION

This is a gated community stretching from the Gulf to the bay on the island's west end, with slow, winding roads and lots of speed bumps to keep the pace leisurely. Homes are all distinctive in terms of architecture, amenities (many with spa or pool), and decor, but the general vibe is luxury. It's mostly large, three-story homes that sleep eight or more. Something to consider here is that the farther toward the west end of the island you settle, the longer the drive is to get a gallon of milk back in town.

Within the Plantation is an even more exclusive and secluded area called The Bluffs. It's two quiet cul-de-sacs of luxury homes, each with spectacular views of the Gulf and Apalachicola Bay beyond towering 25-foot dunes.

### GULF BEACHES AND EAST END

The four miles in the center of the island are called the Gulf Beaches area. In this, the first populated area on the island, the architectural styles are all over the map, from little Cracker cottages to huge windswept wooden structures on stilts kitted out with widow walks. Not as fancy as those at the Plantation, the homes have the benefit of being a quick bike ride into town for ice cream or a video rental. Going east, the two miles before you get to the state park are called, not surprisingly, East End. This is less densely populated, with comfortable-looking houses widely spaced, mostly up on high stilts with great beach access. In the

East End area, there are also townhouses in a community called 300 Ocean Mile. It is very close to the state park, and rentals, while not so fancy, are fairly affordable.

## SUNSET BEACH
This is a densely packed gated community of Spanish terra-cotta tile-and-stucco villas. It looks like a condo village, with big parking lots that take away from the beachside location. The beaches in this area also seem less picturesque, and with less vegetation than elsewhere on the island. One advantage of Sunset Beach is that it has easy access to the state park, which is great.

## Camping
**St. George Island State Park** (1900 E. Gulf Beach Dr., 850/927-2111, $24 per day) offers 60 campsites with electric and water hookups for RV and tent camping. Reserve far in advance with ReserveAmerica (800/326-3521, www.reserveamerica.com). Primitive campsites are also to be had at Gap Point, a 2.5-mile backpacking hike-in site and can be reserved by calling the park office (850/927-2111). There is tents-only youth-group camping for organized groups of 6–25 campers.

## Hotels
Very affordable and geared toward families, the **Buccaneer Inn** (160 W. Gorrie Dr., 850/847-2091, $60–175) is a 1960s-style, low-rise beachfront motel. Rooms are clean and no-nonsense, with a lot of pale pastel coverlets and serviceable kitchenettes, and there's a courtyard swimming pool and a Gulf-side tiki hut.

A little fancier, the **St. George Inn** (135 Franklin Blvd., 800/927-2903, $119–189) is two blocks from the beach with clean, modest rooms. The sprawling white house, with wraparound porches affording Gulf and bay views, has been recently remodeled to include a few two-room suites and a little conference room.

## FOOD
The majority of the island is given over to beach houses, many with impressive kitchens overlooking the bay or Gulf. Thus, vacationers come prepared to dine in with some regularity. Grocery stores include a **Piggly Wiggly** (130 U.S. 98, 850/653-8768) and an **IGA** (425 U.S. 98, 850/653-9695) in Apalachicola, the former a little nicer than the latter, and the island has a pleasant little market called the **Market Place** (148 E. Pine Ave., 850/927-2808) with decent meat, deli, and groceries. Beyond that, you definitely need to patronize some of the local seafood retailers. On the island, look for the guy who parks his trailer at one of a couple intersections in town—he's got exemplary shrimp, scallops, oysters, and grouper. Or head back over the bridge to Eastpoint to the 300–500 blocks of U.S. 98. Hurricane Dennis in 2005 took a major toll on Eastpoint oystermen, destroying many of the dockside structures, and just a handful of seafood vendors remain: **Lynn's Quality Oysters** (402 U.S. 98, 850/670-8381), **Fred's Central Seafood** (322 Patton St., 850/670 8381), and **Barber Seafood** (510 U.S. 98, 850/670 8830).

## Seafood
Restaurants on the island are a little less sophisticated than those in Apalach, but that's fitting. On the beach side (the Gulf side, as opposed to the bay side of this long strip of an island), people gravitate toward the **Blue Parrot Oceanfront Café** (68 W. Gorrie Dr., 850/927-2987, 11 A.M.–9 P.M. daily, $9–25), to relax on the wide deck or sidle up to the tiki bar, enjoying beer and cocktails over an excellent po'boy sandwich or burger. Opt for the local seafood (grouper and oysters) over the imports (conch fritters and Alaskan crab, for crying out loud) and you'll navigate the menu just fine.

As an aside, often in the month of June the Blue Parrot holds the annual **mullet toss.** They build a mullet-tossing range and you pay a small fee to try your hand at flinging these slippery raw fish as far as you can. Underhanded, overhanded, football-style—there are several competition divisions: men, women, children, and free form (in which you build a mechanical device to catapult your fish to victory).

On the bay side, **Eddy Teach's Raw Bar** (37 East Pine St., 850/927-5050, lunch and dinner daily, hours change seasonally) offers up cold beer, cheap oysters, peel-and-eat shrimp, steamed clams, and decent cheeseburgers, with music on the weekends.

### Pizza and Ice Cream
On St. George, if you aren't seafood-bound, you are limited to sandwiches, pizza, an ice-cream cone, or maybe a cup of coffee. **BJ's Pizza & Subs** (105 W. Gulf Beach Dr., 850/927-2805, 11 A.M.–10 P.M. daily, $7–20) tosses good pizzas (also offered by the slice) and has a raucous game room in which to rapidly lose a pocketful of quarters. **Aunt Ebby's**

**Island Deli & Ice Cream** (147 E. Gulf Beach Dr., 850/927-3229, open 11 A.M.–5 P.M. daily March–Sept.) is the place to stop for a frozen treat after a long hot day at the beach.

### Drinks
**Harry A's** (28 W. Bayshore Dr., 850/927-3400, 8 A.M.–midnight weekdays, until 2 A.M. weekends) is just about the oldest building on the island, with the kind of wide, inviting front porch that's more and more difficult to leave after each successive beer. The tavern where locals meet visitors over a pint and some hot wings, Harry's A's brings in musical entertainment most nights and serves up straightforward bar fare like pizza, tacos, and fried seafood.

# Eastpoint

Not long ago one out of every 10 residents in Franklin County had an oyster permit. There were oyster beds out in Apalachicola Bay that people swore by, magical spots with names like Cabbage Top, Catpoint, North Spur, and West Lump. With worn wooden poles, oyster-men would tap along, waiting for the thud to sharpen as the pole hit shell. Then the tongers, men with ropy arm muscles and profound tans, heave their tongs over the side of their small wooden flats boats and get to work. Like two metal rakes hinged together scissor-style, the long-handled tongs rake the bivalves off the shallow bottoms. Pulled aboard, the oysters are sorted with a practiced eye on a culling board, with only those three inches long kept as the morning's catch.

Things are changing, though. Franklin County's gorgeous setting has drawn luxury condos and other, more lucrative, beach development, inching out some of the career oysterers. Hurricane Dennis in 2005 ravaged the oyster docks and sorting and packing facilities, rendering it an even dicier career path. Then add to that the population growth of greater Atlanta to the north—more than four million people and growing fast—which has tapped more and more water from Georgia's Chattahoochee River, a river that becomes the Apalachicola River as it heads into Florida.

Still, on the surface, Franklin County's Eastpoint maintains its gruff, fishing-village beauty, a beauty that is amplified by its own unselfconsciousness. Stop along the roadside waterfront to watch the remaining "house-men" at the wholesale seafood houses man-handle oysters, shrimp, and finfish, brusquely sorting and packing the catch into boxes or bags. It's a year-round venture, with the oyster harvest rotated seasonally from 10,000 acres of oyster beds in St. George Sound and environs. Virtually the whole length of Eastpoint's commercial district is perfumed with the briny waft of seafood docks and the sounds of WOYS FM, Oyster Radio, out of Apalachicola competing with the boisterous calls of fourth-generation oysterers getting off work for the day.

Visit soon, because all signs point to its imminent extinction. Eastpoint has never had the kind of bells and whistles that would make it a big tourist draw, just a few restaurants, a couple of rustic bars, and more oysters than you could shake a tong at.

THE FORGOTTEN COAST

# DRINKING VILLAGE WITH A FISHING PROBLEM

Rustic, quaint, even crusty – words like this were invented to describe places like **Carrabelle.** East of Eastpoint, it's still an active fishing town with shrimpers and finfishers unloading their daily catch. For just this reason, it's been the filming location for a couple of Victor Nuñez movies, including *Ulee's Gold* starring Peter Fonda and *Coastlines*, with Josh Brolin. There are still fewer than 1,200 residents, and the downtown has never been gentrified or prettied up for the tourists.

It's historically had the world's smallest **police station** (a phone booth), but the force now works outside of that Superman-esque environment. The State Forestry Division's **Carrabelle Fire Tower** on the east side of town has great views of the area, and the little **Camp Gordon Johnston WWII Museum** (1001 Gray Ave., 850/697-8575) pays tribute to the amphibious soldiers who trained here and served in WWII, Korea, and Vietnam. Camp Gordon Johnston actually covered 165,000 acres along the Big Bend, with 36 miles along the shores of the Gulf of Mexico. The area was left in its natural state for training purposes,

where thousands of soldiers learned to land the crafts that would be used on the beaches of Normandy on D-Day.

Carrabelle also boasts the **Crooked River Lighthouse** (1975 W. U.S. 98), a rickety lighthouse constructed to replace the lighthouse on Dog Island that was destroyed by hurricane in 1873. The 103-foot iron tower was built in 1985, and at the end of 2007 the Carrabelle Lighthouse Association members restored and relit the structure. **Carrabelle Beach,** just west of town, is a popular spot for picnickers and beachcombers.

What's left to do in Carrabelle? Bumper stickers describe the town as a "small drinking village with a fishing problem." You can drink and/or eat at some of the more convivial establishments around. For straight drinking, head to **Harry's Bar & Package** (306 Marine St., 850/697-9982). Have sandwiches and coffee at **Carrabelle Junction** (88 Tallahassee St., 850/697-9550), barbecue at **Hog Wild BBQ** (1593 U.S. 98 E., 850/697-2776), and a whole lot of fun at **Wicked Willie's** (600 Marine St., 850/697-8488).

## ACCOMMODATIONS

Pretty much the only game in town is **Sportsman Lodge Motel & Marina** (99 N. Bayshore Dr., 850/670-8423, $50–60), a rustic, fish camp–style motel, marina, and RV park overlooking the East Bay. It's wooded and quiet (well, except for a flock of crabby peacocks); family-friendly amenities include kitchenettes, a nice boat dock, ramp, and easy access to fishing guides and charters. Even if you aim to explore the oyster-fishing charms of Eastpoint, you have a much greater range of hotel options in nearby Apalachicola.

## FOOD

From Eastpoint, continue east to Carrabelle and you'll find **Harry's in Carrabelle** (306 Marine St., 850/697-9982, 6 A.M.–9 P.M. Mon.–Sat.) just behind the Georgian Motel,

which opens bright and early to serve the fisherfolk heading into the Gulf. It's mostly a drinking establishment, as is the later-night spot around the corner, **Wicked Willie's** (601 Marine St., 850/697-8488, 11 A.M.–10:30 P.M. weeknights, midnight on the weekends). Nurse a beer and eavesdrop on the boisterous banter of the career anglers and the weekenders. For food in Carrabelle, head for the ribs at **Hog Wild BBQ** (1593 U.S. 98 E., Carrabelle, 850/697-2776).

Even farther east, in Panacea, **Angelo's** (5 Mashers Sand Rd., 850/984-5168, 4:30–10 P.M. Mon., Wed., and Thurs., 11 A.M.–11 P.M. Fri. and Sat., until 10 P.M. Sun., $12–25) is a longstanding and justifiably famous purveyor of the local blue crabmeat (try the seafood cakes). There are waterside tables, a wide wraparound porch, and friendly locals.

# Information and Services

The Forgotten Coast is located within the **Eastern time zone.** The area code is **850.**

## TOURIST INFORMATION

*Forgotten Coastline* is a crusty, cantankerous, locals-only paper you'll see being read all over. It gives you the inside track on the area's issues, gripes, and secret treasures. There's also an online version at http://forgottencoastline.com.

Beyond that, you'll find lots of useful information on the area by visiting www.apalachicolabay.org or www.visitgulf.com. Anita Grove at the **Apalachicola Chamber of Commerce** (122 Commerce St., Apalachicola, 850/653-9419, www.apalachicolabay.org) is also a tremendous resource. Be sure to pick up the historic walking tour brochure while you're there.

## POLICE AND EMERGENCIES

For any real emergency, dial 911. For nonemergencies, there's the **Apalachicola Police Department** (1 Ave. E, 850/653-9755), the **Franklin County Sheriff's Department** (270 Hwy. 65, Eastpoint, 850/670-8500), and the **Carrabelle Police Department** (until recently it was the smallest in the United States, being located inside the phone booth in town, 1001 Gray Ave., 850/697-3691).

If you find yourself in need of a doctor during your visit, you may choose between **Franklin Family Medicine** (no emergency services, 35 Island Dr., Eastpoint, 850/670-8585, 9 A.M.–5 P.M. Mon.–Fri.) and **George E. Weems Memorial Hospital** (135 Ave. D, Apalachicola, 850/653-8853).

For your pharmacy needs, try **Buy Rite Drugs** (45 Ave. D, Apalachicola, 850/653-8825) or **CVS** (139 Ave. E, Apalachicola, 850/653-8737). Pet emergencies are best handled at **Apalachicola Bay Animal Clinic** (187 U.S. 98, Eastpoint, 850/670-8306).

## RADIO AND TELEVISION

When you're feeling musically nostalgic, tune in to **The Coast,** WFCT 105.5 FM out of St. Joe, with a mix of "favorites from yesterday and today." To seem like a real local, twist the dial to **Oyster Radio** at WOYS FM 100.5 out of Apalachicola, with daily local news, national news, hourly weather reports, and beach music (there's a sister station at 106.5 FM that broadcasts country). There are no local television stations, but out of Tallahassee, **WFSU Channel 11** is the PBS affiliate, **WTXL Channel 27** is the ABC affiliate, and **WTLH Channel 49** is the FOX affiliate.

## LAUNDRY SERVICES

Most rental houses on St. George Island have laundry facilities. If you're without access where you're staying (at an inn in Apalachicola, for instance), many of the marinas have self-serve laundries. There's also a nice little laundry in Eastpoint, **Pearl Linen** (191 U.S. 98, behind the car wash, 850/670-8703).

## FISHING LICENSES

Fishing licenses are sold in the County Tax Collector's Office and in many local bait and tackle shops, or by calling 888/347-4356. It is free for Florida residents to saltwater fish from the shore. Saltwater and freshwater annual licenses for nonresidents are each $47; a nonresident three-day pass is $17 for either saltwater or freshwater fishing.

THE FORGOTTEN COAST

# Getting There and Around

The Forgotten Coast is just west of the Big Bend (where the Florida peninsula attaches to the Panhandle), 80 miles southwest of Tallahassee, accessible by the east–west corridor of U.S. 98. If you're piloting your own small plane, **Apalachicola Municipal Airport** (850/653-2222) is a former military base (serving B-17s in WWII), with three concrete runways and fuel available. The closest commercial airports are **Tallahassee Regional Airport** (service provided by Delta, US Airways, Continental, Gulfstream, and Northwest Airlink, 850/891-7802) and **Northwest Florida Beaches International Airport** (850/763-6751), the first international airport built in the United States in a decade, 60 miles to the west. Northwest Florida Beaches Airport is served by Delta and Southwest Airlines.

**Alamo** (877/222-9075), **Avis** (800/230-4898), **Budget** (800/527-0700), **Dollar** (800/800-3665 domestic, 800/800-6000 international), and **National** (800/367-6767) provide rental cars from these airports. There is no real public transportation (no buses or trains) to speak of along this stretch of coast, so you need a car.

To reach the Forgotten Coast by car, there are several routes worth considering. From the north, if your aim is to minimize back roads, take I-75 south to Tifton, then U.S. 319 to Tallahassee, then U.S. 98 to the St. George Bridge at Eastpoint, or continue west to Apalachicola. If you're coming west from, say, Orlando, find your way to I-75 heading north; exit on U.S. 441 west at Alachua, just before Lake City, quickly changing to U.S. 27, which intersects with U.S. 98 near Perry.

By boat, on the Gulf Intracoastal Waterway from Florida's west coast, enter at St. George Sound through East Pass, between Dog Island and St. George Island, or through Bob Sikes Cut (pretty shallow). From the west, take the Intracoastal Waterway through East Bay from Panama City, then on past White City. Continue east through Wimico to the Jackson River, which leads to the Apalachicola River. Follow markers past the Railroad Bridge to Apalachicola.

# THE EMERALD COAST

Some say the emerald color of the water in this area is the result of a blue-green algae. Not true. It's just very clear water, layered over super-reflective white sand in the shallows that produces the green color—the deeper the water, the bluer it gets.

Unified by this eye-catching water color, the beaches of northwest Florida, from Pensacola Beach to the long stretch of the Beaches of South Walton and beyond to the east in Panama City Beach, offer miles of unspoiled natural beauty and a range of options for vacation fun. But they're really different options—this chapter reflects the three distinct draws, each with its own dramatically different character.

First, the **Destin** and **Fort Walton Beach** area in the westernmost part, closest to

Pensacola Beach, is the best-known destination (or Destin-ation, as so many websites pun). Incorporated as recently as 1984, the fishing village of Destin has seen enormous growth as tourism has taken off, with lots of new construction, visitor attractions, and restaurants to lure ever more people. With one of the best geographical locations for fishing on the Gulf Coast, Destin is only 30 miles inland from the 100-Fathom Curve where the best deep-sea fishing for tuna, wahoo, and blue marlin are found. The exciting Destin Seafood Festival and the Destin Fishing Rodeo, both held in October, are testaments to this region's dedication and passion for fishing. It's getting built up, but most of the beachfront is still low-rise (most believe condos will come soon enough, though). Folks visit Destin, Fort

COURTESY OF BEACHES OF SOUTH WALTON TDC

# HIGHLIGHTS

**◖ Crab Island:** Rent a boat or watercraft of some kind and attend the biggest daily impromptu lunch party in Destin on a partially submerged island north of the Destin Bridge (page 279).

**◖ Fishing in Destin Harbor:** Offshore, inshore, cobia, sailfish, wahoo – Destin is a serious fishing destination. Arrange a fishing charter to suit your interests and what's biting, and find out why Destin is often called the "World's Luckiest Fishing Village" (page 279).

**◖ Big Kahuna's Water and Adventure Park:** If the beach isn't enough to fully occupy the family, take them to Big Kahuna's Water and Adventure Park in Destin, with 25 acres of water slides, flumes, tubing, lagoons, wave pools, and more (page 284).

**◖ Seaside:** Spend a day exploring the picturesque pastel beach town of Seaside, featured in the Jim Carrey movie *The Truman Show* (page 289).

**◖ Biking Along Scenic Route 30A:** Explore the Beaches of South Walton slowly and under your own power, with a bike ride along the 19-mile paved path that follows Scenic 30A at the coast (page 292).

**◖ St. Andrews State Recreation Area:** With its luminous green water and fine white sand, the Emerald Coast has numerous beaches to recommend. This one in Panama City, at one point named "the world's best beach" by *Travel Magazine*, offers miles of Gulf-side beach as well as a broad, inviting Grand Lagoon and a 700-acre offshore barrier strip called Shell Island (page 298).

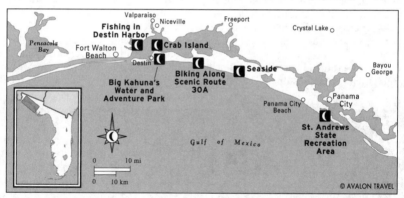

LOOK FOR ◖ TO FIND RECOMMENDED SIGHTS, ACTIVITIES, DINING, AND LODGING.

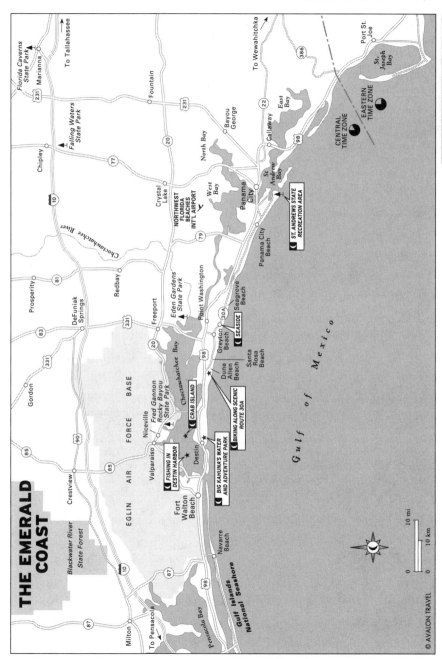

# THE EMERALD COAST

To Tallahassee

Florida Caverns State Park

Marianna

231

Falling Waters State Park

Chipley

10

Fountain

231

20

77

Crystal Lake

NORTHWEST FLORIDA BEACHES INTL AIRPORT

West Bay

North Bay

To Wewahitchka

386

Port St. Joe

St. Joseph Bay

EASTERN TIME ZONE

CENTRAL TIME ZONE

22

East Bay

Callaway

98

St. Andrew Bay

Panama City

Bayou George

Panama City Beach

**ST. ANDREWS STATE RECREATION AREA**

79

Choctawhatchee River

81

Prosperity

DeFuniak Springs

83

Redbay

331

Freeport

20

Eden Gardens State Park

Point Washington

98

30A

Seagrove Beach

**SEASIDE**

Grayton Beach

Santa Rosa Beach

Gulf of Mexico

331

Gordon

90

85

Crestview

EGLIN AIR FORCE BASE

Valparaiso

Niceville

Fred Gannon Rocky Bayou State Park

Choctawhatchee Bay

**CRAB ISLAND**

Dune Allen Beach

**BIKING ALONG SCENIC ROUTE 30A**

**FISHING IN DESTIN HARBOR**

Destin

Fort Walton Beach

**BIG KAHUNA'S WATER AND ADVENTURE PARK**

Blackwater River State Forest

10

Milton

To Pensacola

87

98

87

Pensacola Bay

Navarre Beach

Gulf Islands National Seashore

Gulf of Mexico

10 mi

10 km

© AVALON TRAVEL

Walton Beach, and Okaloosa Island to do some fishing, splash in the emerald-green water, and have a good time with the kids.

The **Beaches of South Walton** region, on the other hand, makes up a 26-mile stretch of shoreline to the east of Destin, containing 14 beach communities. These pristine beaches offer pure, clear, emerald-green water; fine, sugar-white sand; and rare coastal dune lakes; together, these create a unique and varied landscape. It's the first place in the country to receive Blue Wave Environmental Certification from the Clean Beaches Council for all 26 miles of its coastline. Mostly it's private residences in newish, forward-thinking, and ecofriendly planned communities. You won't find a lot of go-cart tracks, mini-marts, or T-shirt shops. Remember that near-perfect town in *The Truman Show?* It was shot here in Seaside—nearly all of the area's towns have this old-fashioned beach retreat style. None of this comes cheap, though. It's pricey to stay in the Beaches of South Walton, but the understated upscale environment and back-to-basics feel are exceptionally memorable.

The third section is **Panama City Beach,** about 20 miles farther east. It is best known as the biggest draw along the Gulf Coast of Florida for high school and college spring breakers. If the Beaches of South Walton sounded good, this might not be for you—and vice versa. It's mostly about crowds of people partying and enjoying themselves on the very beautiful beaches, miniature golf courses, video game arcades, and souvenir shops. It's bustling with personal watercraft and parasailers, girls in bikinis, restaurants heavily reliant on deep fryers, and partiers cruising the strip with their car windows down.

## HURRICANES

Through Hurricane Ivan in 2004, Hurricane Dennis in July 2005, and then Hurricane Katrina in August 2005 (the costliest and one of the five deadliest hurricanes in U.S. history), the Emerald Coast east from Destin was mostly unaffected. You will see very little evidence of any of these storms, although resulting dredge projects have meant that huge quantities of beach-quality sand have been dragged up for beach renourishment efforts. In fact, seven years in the making, the Beaches of South Walton Tourist Development Council completed a large-scale project that restored 26,200 feet of beach over five miles on the west end of Beaches of South Walton, in and around the Sandestin area. More than 75 feet of beach were added in these areas, creating wide, expansive beaches for the public's enjoyment.

The past few years have been an enormous growth period for the area, with new high-rise hotels going up at a rapid clip in Panama City Beach and whole new planned communities erected in the Beaches of South Walton.

## PLANNING YOUR TIME

High season along the Panhandle is summer, with rates dropping precipitously in the fall and winter. Spring break is a brief flurry around here in March and April, at its densest in Panama City Beach. But where to stay? Anglers: Go to Destin or Fort Walton Beach. If you're looking for upscale leisure with coastal beauty all around: Visit the Beaches of South Walton. Spring breakers: Get yourselves to Panama City Beach, and remember to have a designated driver. The latter is worth two days of intensive revelry, three if you have a long attention span. Many of the rentals along the 14 communities of the Beaches of South Walton have a minimum stay, some as much as a week during high season. The area could certainly occupy you for that long, with a day trip to Pensacola, another one to visit the amusements in Panama City Beach, and a third to one of the wonderful state parks here.

# Fort Walton Beach and Destin

Spanish explorer Panfilo de Narvaez landed along the Emerald Coast in 1628 to find himself a drink of water. The Creeks chased him and his men back to the boat, thirst unquenched. There's no telling, really, why up until about 50 years ago a wide swath of the Emerald Coast, from Destin to Panama City, was unsettled sand dunes and quiet green waters. Most of the growth here dates back only a few decades.

Not so of Destin and Fort Walton Beach. Okaloosa County has got roots. In 1830, New England seafarer Leonard Destin fell for the place, the first white man to settle in the area among several local Native American tribes. He lured other New England fishermen with big fish stories, and by 1845 there were 100 white residents, all employed in the fishing business. And Fort Walton Beach was a Civil War campsite, its location chosen because of its protection from the Gulf by the Santa Rosa Sound and Okaloosa Island.

During Prohibition the joint was jumping. "Entrepreneurs" like Al Capone came down to the area to hide out. Mobsters being mobsters, the area was soon dotted with hopping casinos filled with shady characters evading the law up North.

The casinos and mobsters are gone, but what's left is a beloved fishing destination, one that boasts five saltwater world records. It looks the part: Destin and Fort Walton Beach were the shooting location for *Jaws II,* both admirably portraying charming seaside resort towns.

## SPORTS AND RECREATION
### Beaches

There are 24 miles of beach—the sand a shockingly fine, white quartz that somehow made its way here down 130 miles of the Appalachian River, the water a brilliant jewel green. Nearly 60 percent of the beach around here is preserved

Destin has an abundance of beautiful and diverse beaches.

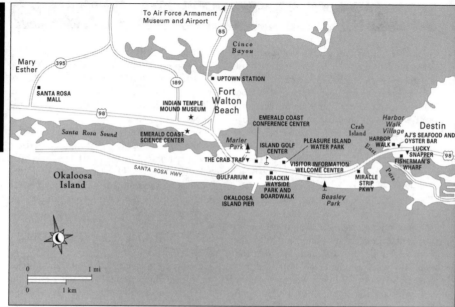

in perpetuity, or at least for a long, long time. There are five beachfront parks and 12 beach access ways along the Destin, Fort Walton Beach, and Okaloosa Island shoreline.

One of the best is the 208-acre **Henderson Beach State Park** (17000 Emerald Coast Pkwy., east of the city of Destin on U.S. 98, 850/837-7550, for camping call 800/326-3521 or visit www.reserveamerica.com, 8 A.M.–sundown daily, $4/vehicle with single occupant, $6/vehicle with up to eight passengers, $2 pedestrian or cyclist, $30 camping), which has 6,000 feet of shoreline. There's urban sprawl off to the west in Destin; in fact, the beach's entrance is just across the street from a Wal-Mart Supercenter. Once out on the coastal dunes you'd never know it—sea oats anchor the soft sand in the dunes, while the ocean's salt spray and wind cause the rosemary, magnolias, and scrub oak to grow low and horizontal, their limbs bent shoreward. During the fall the beach is dotted with colorful wildflowers, blanket flower and beach morning glory carpeting the clean sand.

At Henderson you can swim, surf fish,

picnic, bike, in-line skate, walk the 0.75-mile nature trail, or camp (the campground has 60 full-facility campsites for tents or RVs). Colored flags indicate the wave and swimming conditions—red flag means "knee deep is too deep" as there is high potential for rip currents to form, and double red flag means the water is closed for swimming.

**James Lee County Park** (3510 Scenic U.S. 98, Destin, 8 A.M.–sundown daily, free parking) is another good beach, right at the Walton/Okaloosa County line. This park has three pavilions, 41 picnic tables, nine dune walkovers, a playground, restrooms with changing rooms, and 166 parking spaces. It's a popular beach for families, with the water shallow and clear and the Crab Trap restaurant in the middle of the beach's parking lot.

Okaloosa Island has a series of beaches, really contiguous—first, the **John Beasley Wayside Park** (U.S. 98, Okaloosa Island, 1.2 miles east of Fort Walton Beach, 850/546-0342) is on the bay side of the barrier island just yards from the Okaloosa Boardwalk (an entertainment complex with clubs and restaurants). John Beasley

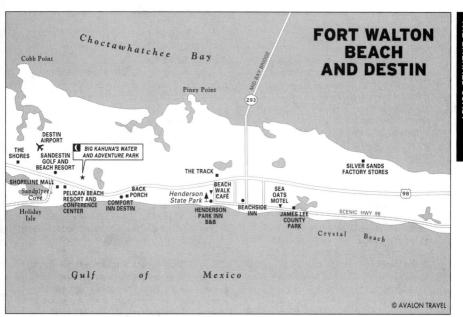

has restrooms, picnic tables, showers, changing rooms, vending machines, and lifeguards. It has fishing for trout and reds, snorkeling activity, and even a little surfing. The same can be said of the adjacent **Brackin Wayside Park and Boardwalk** (U.S. 98, Okaloosa Island, one mile east of Fort Walton Beach, 850/651-7131), which has several pavilions, 41 picnic tables, restrooms with changing rooms, a children's playground, dune walkovers to the beach, lots of parking, and fierce beach volleyball during the warmer months.

## ⟨ Crab Island

You've got an appointment to keep. To get there, you need something that floats—maybe a pontoon boat, or a glass-bottomed boat, or a fishing boat, or even a Wave Runner. You can shop at **Boogies Watersports** (U.S. 98 at the foot of the Destin Bridge, Destin, 850/654-4497) to pick up a rental that suits your budget, skill level, and personal sense of style. But you're in a hurry. It's a lunch date.

You're going to need directions, but any local can tell you how to get to Crab Island. North of

the Destin Bridge, it used to be two islands in the middle of nowhere, made of sand dredged by the Army Corps of Engineers from East Pass. It used to even be a real island with sea grass, shrubs, and seabirds. But now it's submerged a few feet and only surfaces at low tide. But it's where people congregate for a lunchtime bash. Boats pile up out there and people jump off into the three-foot shallows, eating, chatting, and drinking. Sometimes there's even live music on the back of a boat or floating vendors serving food and drinks (often an ice-cream guy) to all the folks gathered there.

## ⟨ Fishing in Destin Harbor

About 30 miles offshore (only 10 miles from Destin's East Pass), the Gulf of Mexico turns from emerald green to deep blue. It's at this point, called the 100-Fathom Curve, where you're in deep, deep water all of a sudden. This deep-water curve is closer to Destin than to any other spot in Florida, meaning a fishing charter from Dustin is the quickest way out to deep water. And it's a lucky thing, because these waters are churning with fish. In the spring there's

# BEACH BASICS

So that your day at the beach can be an, um, day at the beach, keep a few things in mind.

## BEACH HUSBANDRY

Bare coastal dunes are vulnerable to destruction by the same forces that form them: wind and waves. Dunes are built when sand blows up through beachside plantlife and is trapped, creating ever-taller mounds. These mounds in turn protect the shore during storms by washing back out to sea and decreasing the energy of the storm waves. For these reasons, do not trample, pick, spindle, or mutilate any beachside plantlife (like the sea oats). In fact, along public beach accesses, always use the **boardwalks and raised walkways** rather than tramping through the sand.

**Sea turtles** nest on the gulf beaches of Okaloosa County April–November. Recent hurricane seasons have wrought havoc on these already threatened and endangered species. Again, no spindling (it's illegal to disturb a nest or harm a turtle in any way), or even taunting. Never crowd around a turtle nest, don't impede a turtle's progress toward the water, and don't shine lights on the beaches at night if possible.

This area's beaches are all **clothing-required.** Navarre Beach used to have a lot of nude sunbathers, but federal agents have cracked down on the depravity and lawlessness that comes of lying nude on a beach towel. Be advised. Also, beaches in this area **prohibit pets,** and that goes double for nude pets. If you see animals on the beach, they probably belong to residents who have gotten special beach pet permits, available only to locals.

## BEACH SAFETY

**Jellyfish** are common to Gulf beaches. Not the big terrifying Man O' War types, but the local species' sting can still be pretty fierce. Shuffle your feet in the water to alert nearby jellyfish to your presence. In the event that you do get stung, the experts say ammonia poured on the sting relieves the pain, as does meat tenderizer and toothpaste. (Who figures these things out — is someone getting stung and then applying poultices of household products just in the name of science? — "Preparation H, yes. Mr. Clean, no.")

**Rip currents** occur in any type of weather. If caught in a rip current, swim parallel to the shore until the current weakens and you can swim in.

And although shark attacks in these waters are very infrequent, there are ways to further minimize your chances of a **shark encounter.** You're more vulnerable if you're swimming alone, and if you swim far from shore. Sharks are most active at dusk, when they have a competitive sensory advantage. They tend to hang out in areas between sandbars or steep drop-offs — use caution when swimming in these areas. As you know, sharks smell blood — if you have a wound, if you are menstruating, or if nearby fisherfolk are cleaning fish or throwing out bait, think about postponing a swim. And remove shiny jewelry before you go in — its reflective glinting looks like the sheen of fish scales to a hungry predator.

Use **sunscreen,** and lots of it. Experts say that an average-sized person should use about two tablespoons per application.

the migration of mighty cobia (you can sight fish for these) and in May come the kingfish (inshore troll). People bottom fish for grouper, red snapper, triggerfish, and amberjack year-round. In summer, when the waters warm up, it's serious marlin and sailfish (offshore troll), and wahoo and tuna (inshore troll). Destin bills itself, so to speak, as the Billfish Capital of the World. The best I can figure, based on

conversation with sometimes-taciturn fisher types, billfish is a tunalike fish species similar to marlin, sailfish, and spearfish—those fish with the big, swordlike bill. Destin is also known by some as the "World's Luckiest Fishing Village," because its waters harbor four times more types of fresh fish per season than any other Florida destination except for Key West. Supposedly, during any given season there are 20 edible species of gamefish to be found in local waters.

So you have to come here and fish. Offshore, bottom, inshore, or even surf-casting—there are lots of people around here with enormous experience willing to take you out on a saltwater charter or just hook you up with gear. In addition, the area's rivers offer freshwater fishing for catfish, bass, and bream. And many restaurants in the area are willing to cook up your fresh catch.

The price of a private charter averages $150–165 per hour, for up to six people. Many boats only accommodate six people, so make clear how many people are in your party. You can also sign up for a group charter, pooling with other people who are looking to go out (prices are the same, you just split it between all the people on the boat). Obviously, you have to find others who are simpatico, in terms of what they're fishing for and how long they want to be out.

**Destin Charter Service** (Fisherman's Wharf, Destin, 850/837-1995) is one-stop shopping, with access to 40 of Destin's best charter boats (there are more than 100 vessels for hire around here). These boats offer year-round fishing trips for individuals or groups, from four-hour trips to overnights, either on the Gulf or the bay side. **Harborwalk Fishing Charters** (next to Lucky Snapper off U.S. 98, 850/837-2343, $100/person for four hours—it's customary to tip 15 percent) is another well-regarded local charter company. Staff will clean, fillet, and bag your catch at trip's end. **Captain John Holley** (next to Lucky Snapper off U.S. 98, 850/837-4946) specializes in big fish. He has a number of marlin, cobia, and kingfish tournament wins to his credit and has been involved in many of the local billfish tournaments (they're tag and release). He was the Destin Rodeo Sportfishing Captain of the Year for nine consecutive years. Prices vary by the type of fish: cobia $1,000 full day, $600 half; trolling and live bait fishing for marlin, tuna, wahoo, mahimahi, and king mackerel $150/hour; and bottom fishing for amberjack and grouper $150/hour.

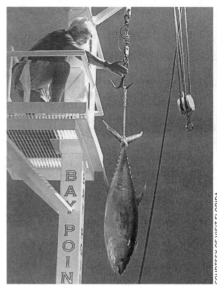

COURTESY OF VISIT FLORIDA

**Located only 30 miles from the 100-Fathom Curve, Destin is as close to deep-sea fishing as you can get on the Gulf Coast.**

If you just feel like finding your own boat and giving it a go, **Gilligan's Water Sports** (Destin Harbor, 850/650-9000) rents pontoon boats for reasonable prices ($250 full day, $175 half day), good for snorkeling, fishing, or just tooling around. You can also head out into the Blackwater, Shoal, or Yellow rivers in search of bass, bream, and catfish.

No boat is required to fish from the **Okaloosa Island Fishing Pier,** open 24 hours a day. The cost for fishing is $7 for adults and $4 for children 6–12, no license necessary. It's a 1,261-foot pier, lighted at night, with rod holders and benches built into it. You'll catch all kinds of things (including big mahi-mahi). You can also cast from the area's finger jetties, sandy shores, and the 3,000-foot **Destin Bridge Catwalk** to hook speckled trout, white snapper, and redfish. And there are stocked ponds in the area, such as the 350-acre **Hurricane Lake** in Blackwater River State Park, filled with channel catfish, largemouth bass, bluegill, and shellcracker.

When you want to find out what is biting

## EAST PASS

Originally, the Gulf of Mexico and the Destin Harbor did not connect to the Choctawhatchee Bay in this area, which posed some navigational challenges to the local fishing fleet and some flooding danger to the settlements as well. In 1926, three local, stalwart families took it upon themselves to change that. The Destins, the Marlers, and the Melvins grabbed a bunch of shovels and started digging by hand, making a two-foot-wide ditch across Okaloosa Island. Within two hours, supposedly, the trench was over 100 yards wide. A torrent of water rushed in, creating what is now East Pass. In 1935, the East Pass Bridge was built. To this day, the Army Corps of Engineers keeps close tabs on the pass, dredging it every two years or so (more in hurricane years) to ensure the water's deep enough for boats to move safely through it.

The East Pass is the only waterway connecting the Choctawhatchee Bay to the Gulf of Mexico for 60 miles in either direction (Pensacola to the west and Panama City to the east each have waterways that connect the bay with the Gulf). The East Pass is the lifeblood of the Destin fishing fleet – without it, the town would surely not be the angler's paradise that draws fisherfolk from around the world. All because of a few shovels.

and where, visit www.gulfcoastangling.com, then plan your fishing accordingly.

### Shelling and Diving

The beaches are uniformly fine white sand, and compared to the beaches to the south there are very few shells in sight. So how can the Emerald Coast be ranked as a top shelling destination? They're offshore—you have to dive for them. Giant sandbars about a mile from shore and a natural coral-encrusted limestone outcropping (the pre–Ice Age shoreline) three miles out act as natural shovels to collect perfectly formed shells—pastel lion's paws, true tulips, huge queen helmets, and Florida's signature shell, the horse conchs, are there for the picking.

The center of much of this shelling mania is **Sand Dollar City,** an artificial reef complex the county put together about a mile out. It's got six patch reefs placed in a hexagonal pattern around a single center point, the sunken 1941 tugboat called the *Mohawk Chief.* The whole area is a fish and shellfish haven, and by extension, a shelling bonanza. **Timber Hole** is another hot spot of shelling and intriguing marinelife observation (sea squirts, four-foot basket sponges, aqua and purple sea whips). It has a natural limestone reef 6–18 feet high

and 110 feet deep, as well as sunken planes, ships, and a railroad car. There are loads of natural reefs in this area, for shelling, diving, and fishing; **Amberjack Rocks** is one of the area's largest reef systems, within three miles of Destin Pass. About 80 feet deep, it is known for shelling as well as spearfishing for black snapper and amberjack. **Long Reef** features staircase ledges and is known for lobsters and shells. The area also has intriguing wrecks to explore—an air force barge, a Liberty Ship, Butler's Barge, and the rubble of the Destin Bridge. Divers here often enjoy 40–100 feet of visibility.

For safety reasons, all divers must display a free-flying, 12- by 12-inch flag with a white diagonal stripe on a red background—the diver-down flag—in the area in which the dive occurs. Divers should try to stay within 100 feet of the flag, and the flag and diver should never be in areas that might constitute a navigational hazard.

**Emerald Coast Scuba** (503-B Harbor Blvd., Destin, 850/837-0955) provides scuba instruction and charters. Many other dive shops offer theme excursions like spearfishing, deep sea, shell, and lobster, with certification classes. They will also take you out snorkeling from their boats. If you just want to snorkel on your own, you can do so from the beach at **Destin Jetties** or from the **Old Crystal Beach Pier.**

## Golf

Emerald-green waters mirrored by emerald-green golf courses. There are 1,080 holes of golf in these parts, many of the courses designed by some of the world's best architects: Robert Cupp of Jack Nicklaus fame, or Finger, or Dye, or Fazio. Many of these courses utilize the area's lush natural beauty and surrounding waterways, with contrasts of woods and wetlands, for challenging and memorably beautiful play.

The 18-hole **Regatta Bay Golf Club** (465 Regatta Bay Blvd., Destin, 850/650-7800, $59–129, par 72, 6,864 yards, course rating 73.8, slope 148) was designed by Robert Walker, winding along the shore of Choctawhatchee Bay and carved through wetlands and protected nature preserves. Another popular one, the creation of Fred Couples and Gene Bates, **Kelly Plantation Golf Club** (307 Kelly Plantation Dr., Destin, 850/650-7600, $60–140, par 72, 7,099 yards, course rating 74.2, slope 146) utilizes the Choctawhatchee Bay as well, nestled along its southern edge with rolling greens and beautiful fairways.

Acclaimed by *Golfweek* as one of the 50 Most Distinctive Development Courses in the Southeast, **Emerald Bay** (40001 Emerald Coast Pkwy., Destin, 850/837-5197, $35–105, par 72, 6,802 yards, course rating 73.1, slope 135) was designed by nationally recognized architect Robert Cupp. He said of the course, "There is no signature hole, it is—instead—a signature golf course."

At **Indian Bayou Golf and Country Club** (1 Country Club Dr. E., Destin, 850/837-6191, $30–65, par 72, 7,000 yards, course rating 74, slope 132–142) there's an assortment of Earl Stone–designed nines, the Choctaw, Seminole, and Creek, which can be played in any 18-hole combination. The Creek course, the newest, has lots of water that comes into play; the Choctaw is heavily wooded; and the Seminole has wide fairways and large greens.

Also situated on the banks of Choctawhatchee Bay, **Shalimar Pointe Golf and Country Club** (302 Country Club Rd., Shalimar, 850/651-4300, $29–59, par 72, 6,765 yards, course rating 72.9, slope 125) is a Finger/Dye–designed course that *Links* magazine accused of having "Two of the Hardest Holes on the Emerald Coast," the 11th and 17th. It is bordered by rolling white dunes and dense hammocks of pine, oak, and magnolia. Shalimar Pointe has been host to The Emerald Coast Tour.

Beyond these, there's **Shoal River Country Club, Fort Walton Beach Municipal Course,** the two courses at **Eglin Air Force Base** (available only with government ID), and the world-class courses at Sandestin.

## SIGHTS
### Museums

Located near Eglin Air Force Base's main gate, the **Air Force Armament Museum** (Hwy. 85 and Hwy. 189, seven miles north of Fort Walton Beach, 850/651-1808, 9 A.M.–4:30 P.M. Mon.–Sat., admission free) is the only facility in the United States dedicated to the display of air force armament. You'll see thousands of weapons, an educational film called *Arming the Air Force,* and photography exhibits in addition to 25 cool reconnaissance, fighter, and bomber planes. There's a B-17 Flying Fortress, an F-4 Phantom II jet, and an SR-71 Blackbird Spy Plane. The museum spans four wars in its scope—WWII, Korea, Vietnam, and Persian Gulf. Kids love the fighter cockpit simulator.

The Fort Walton Beach community has a rich Native American past, settled by a number of prehistoric tribes as far back as 12,000 B.C. The **Indian Temple Mound Museum and Park** (139 Miracle Strip Pkwy. SE, Fort Walton Beach, 850/833-9595, 10 A.M.–4:30 P.M. Mon.–Sat., closes at 4 P.M. all week in winter, $5 adults, $3 children 3–17, free for children 3 and under) provides a peek into the area's Native American history, with a thoughtfully assembled collection of southeastern Indian ceramic artifacts and an Indian Mound Temple that dates to A.D. 1400 and originally served as a religious and civic center.

It was the first schoolhouse constructed for the children of Camp Walton, later to be known as Fort Walton Beach. **Camp Walton Schoolhouse Museum** (127 Miracle Strip Pkwy. SE, Fort Walton Beach, 850/833-9595, noon–4:30 P.M. Mon.–Sat., $1) was built of native pine and oak, and when it opened in 1912 there were 15 students and one teacher. It was restored in the early 1970s and opened as an educational museum in 1976. These days, it's mostly for the benefit of local school groups, but it still makes a sweet nostalgic look at a past most of us never knew.

## Family-Friendly Attractions

A good example of the compelling science museums for kids that seem to be popping up in every town these days is the **Emerald Coast Science Center** (139 Brooks St., Fort Walton Beach, 850/664-1261, 9 A.M.–2 P.M. Tues.–Fri., 9 A.M.–4 P.M. Sat., noon–4 P.M. Sun., $6 adults, $5 seniors, $4 children 3–17) with an interesting section devoted to color and light. You can fly and land a model airplane in a mini-air tunnel, noodle with a laser spirograph or a Van de Graff generator (you know, that orb that makes your hair stand on end). There's also a nature part to the museum, with tarantulas and giant millipedes, and a human body section with presentations about the digestive system, the five senses, and the skeleton.

Opened in 1955, **Gulfarium** (1010 Miracle Strip Pkwy., Fort Walton Beach, 850/243-9046, 9 A.M.–4 P.M. daily, closes earlier seasonally, $19.25 adults, $18.25 seniors, $11.50 children 3–11, free for children 2 and under) was one of the country's original marine parks. Like a mini Sea World, it hosts Atlantic bottlenose dolphins, California sea lions, Peruvian penguins, Ridley turtles, and lots of Gulf-focused educational marine exhibits. The Gulfarium was closed for quite a while after the hurricane season of 2004, but the closure ultimately resulted in even better dolphin shows with high jumps and soccer games and a sweet sea lion show (they're not bad Frisbee players, considering the lack of opposable thumbs and

all). For a fairly hefty fee ($150), guests can also have one-on-one interactions with the dolphins. The Gulfarium also sponsors the Dolphin Project, which focuses on interaction between dolphins and children with disabilities (like autism).

## BIG KAHUNA'S WATER AND ADVENTURE PARK

Even adults get a little wide-eyed when they begin describing Big Kahuna's Water and Adventure Park (1007 U.S. 98 E., Destin, 850/837-8319, www.bigkahunas.com, 10 A.M.–6 P.M. all summer, water park closed in the winter and adventure park with weekend hours only, $36 adults, $30 children and seniors, free for children 2 and under), with more than 40 water attractions and an adventure park spread over 25 acres. Clad in your bathing suit and a smile, you can wind through caves and waterfalls (the Tiagra Falls pumps 30,000 gallons of water per minute over 250 feet of mountain granite rock). There are three rivers, speed slides, body flumes, white-water tubing, leisurely lagoons, two wave pools, four children's areas with kid-sized slides and variable-depth pools, and other exciting wet-and-wild attractions for kids of all ages. Then once you dry off, visit the attached Adventure Park attractions (be aware, it's a separate ticket price, and a steep one—it's cheaper if you get the combined all-day pass for, gulp, $48). There are 54 holes of miniature golf, a go-cart raceway, a bunch of other rides, and an arcade.

## ENTERTAINMENT AND EVENTS
### The Arts

The attractions on the Emerald Coast are mostly outdoors, where the sun, sand, and fish are. While art is not the largest draw for the Emerald Coast, it doesn't disappoint. The **Northwest Florida Ballet** (101 Chicago Ave., Fort Walton Beach, 850/664-7787) is the longest-running arts organization in northwest Florida, producing full-length semiprofessional ballets in a number of local venues, including summer ballet in the park and the requisite holiday performance of *The Nutcracker*. **Stage Crafters Community Theatre** (Fort Walton Beach Civic Auditorium, 107 Miracle Strip Pkwy., Fort Walton Beach, 850/243-1101, 7:30 P.M. and 2 P.M. matinees) is a small community troupe that puts on the familiar *(Godspell)* and the unfamiliar *(Meshuggah-Nuns)*. The **Northwest Florida State College's Mattie Kelly Fine and Performing Arts Center** (100 College Blvd., Niceville, 850/729-5382) stages plays in its large 1,600-seat main theater but also hosts dance, opera, the Northwest Florida Symphony Orchestra, and other arts events.

In visual arts, the **Arts & Design Society** (17 First St. SE, Fort Walton Beach, 850/244-1271), founded in 1956 by a group of local artists, is more of a community art outreach, with classes, lectures, and children's programs, but it also hosts monthly local, regional, and national exhibits that are worth checking out.

### Festivals
In the Destin area, there are annual events like the Spring Splash, the Billy Bowlegs Festival, and the Christmas Boat Parade—but the biggest of them all is the monthlong **Destin Fishing Rodeo** in October. There are 30 different categories of prizes, with all saltwater game fish eligible—so you'll see people fishing all over the place with a vengeance. There's a more focused, single-species event in March and April with the annual Cobia Tournaments.

## NIGHTLIFE
Destin and Fort Walton Beach can get lively, then it's quiet again to the east in the Beaches of South Walton area; still farther east in Panama City Beach it gets hopping again. Here, head dockside to **AJ's Club Bimini** (on the Destin Harbor, 0.25 mile east of the Destin Bridge, 850/837-1913, 11 A.M.–4 A.M. nightly) for a Bimini Bash, a powerful concoction of cranberry, orange, and pineapple juices with a five-rum roundhouse punch. Then try out one of the theme nights at the sprawling **Nightown** (140 Palmetto St., 850/837-6448) and groove

with the DJ. Or you could just stop in for a margarita at **Pepito's** (757 U.S. 98 E., Destin, 850/650-7734, until 4 A.M. daily), in front of the Destin Cinemas, or get crazy on the dance floor at **Harry T's** (46 Harbor Blvd., 850/654-4800, 11 A.M.–4 A.M. nightly) which recently moved to the Harbor Walk village. Opened by a big top trapeze artist, Harry T's is adorned with circus memorabilia, including a stuffed giraffe, and treasures from the sunken luxury liner *Thracia*. Then warm up with a few scales, because crowd participation is required at the dueling piano bar of **Howl at the Moon** (The Boardwalk, Okaloosa Island, 850/301-0111).

## SHOPPING
**Silver Sands Factory Stores** (10562 Emerald Coast Pkwy. W, on U.S. 98, eight miles east of Destin, near Sandestin Golf & Beach Resort Destin, 850/654-9771, www.silversandsoutlet. com, 10 A.M.–9 P.M. Mon.–Sat., 10 A.M.–6 P.M. Sun.) is supposedly the nation's largest designer outlet center. And it keeps growing. Think Off Saks Fifth Avenue, Ann Taylor, Polo Ralph Lauren, Dooney & Bourke, Tommy Hilfiger, Ellen Tracy, Adrienne Vittadini, Banana Republic, Liz Claiborne, and the like. If shoes are your thing: Nine West Outlet, Famous Footwear, Liz Claiborne Shoes, Kenneth Cole, and Cole Haan. There are more than 100 designer outlet stores within 450,000 square feet of retail space, drawing something like six million shoppers annually.

## ACCOMMODATIONS
If you want to rent a beach cottage or luxurious condominium, **Newman-Dailey Resort Properties** (12815 U.S. 98 W, Ste. 100, Destin, 850/837-1071 or 800/225-7652, www. destinvacation.com) is a well-regarded property management and vacation rental company in the area for the past 22 years. The website offers virtual tours of properties.

### $50-150
Because of spring break maniacs, most of the hotels around here don't rent to people under 25 (unless they're with an "adult"). One of the

good and bad things about the Destin area is that there aren't too many big hotels right on the beach. Most lodgings are just a bit of a drive. If you are looking for a quiet, independently owned place right at water's edge, try **Sea Oats Motel** (3420 Old U.S. 98 E., Destin, 850/837-6655, $80–105), which is a long, low-slung motel right on the sand, offering condo rentals as well.

If you're willing to hop in the car or on a bike to hit sand, there's the **Beachside Inn** (2931 Scenic U.S. 98, Destin, 850/650-6300, $80–171), with brightly colored rooms in a modest-sized low-rise hotel. The **Best Western Summerplace Inn** (14047 Emerald Coast Pkwy., Destin, 850/650-8003, $107–139) is in the heart of Destin, a quick drive to public beach access. There's a decent complimentary continental breakfast, indoor and outdoor pools with a big whirlpool, and free high-speed Internet access. **Comfort Inn Destin** (19001 Emerald Coast Pkwy., Destin, 850/654-8611, $85–145) is new and pretty deluxe for a Comfort Inn—no offense. It's got 100 rooms, nicely appointed, and two pools (one indoors).

## Over $150

There are plenty of condos right on the beach, many only renting by the week in high season. The **Pelican Beach Resort and Conference Center** (1002 U.S. 98 E., Destin, 888/654-1425, $150–206, two-night minimum much of the year) is a big, imposing cube. **Hidden Dunes Beach and Tennis Resort** (9815 U.S. 98 W., Destin, 850/837-3521, $130–600) has several ways to go, from a unit in a 20-story tower at water's edge, to luxurious three- and four-bedroom villas overlooking the private Hidden Dunes lake, to Carolina-style cottages with private screened porches, nestled in a wooded landscape. Farther east, into the Beaches of South Walton town of Seascape, the **Majestic Sun** (1160 Old U.S. 98, Destin, 850/837-8264, $102–368) is a huge condo tower with beautiful pools, tennis, and golf, all just across the street from the beach. **Sandpiper Cove** (775 Gulfshore Dr.,

Destin, 850/837-9121, $170–320) is pretty much a Destin landmark, with a 43-acre landscaped property that has its own 1,100 feet of beach. These are individually owned (and decorated) condo units, so look at the pictures before deciding what's right for you. The property has five swimming pools and three outdoor hot tubs.

The **Henderson Park Inn Bed & Breakfast** (2700 Scenic U.S. 98, 850/269-4432, www.hendersonparkinn.com, $179–199) is northwest Florida's only beachside bed-and-breakfast. Beyond the inn's lovely setting adjacent to the 208-acre Henderson Beach State Park, travelers are spoiled with tidbits like complimentary breakfast and lunch, nightly sunset glasses of wine and beer, arrival wine and fruit assortment, evening turndown service with sweets, and a stocked kitchen pantry, all included in the room price. Guests also get complimentary use of water-sports equipment, high-speed Internet access, and beach service with chair and umbrella setup.

## FOOD

The restaurants of Destin, Fort Walton Beach, and Okaloosa Island tend to focus on fish, with lots of casual oyster bars and fish shacks. There are upscale spots around, but the best places are the Southern-style casual seafood joints.

### Breakfast

Start your day, and your visit, at the **Donut Hole** (635 U.S. 98 E., Destin, 850/837-8824, 6 A.M.–10 P.M. daily, $4–12). It's breakfast all day, with sturdy baked goods and nice people.

### Casual

The ◖ **Back Porch** (1740 Old U.S. 98 E., Destin, 850/837-2022, 11 A.M.–10 P.M. daily, $10–25) is a fun cedar-shingled seafood shack, an ideal place to try your first char-grilled amberjack. The view is great—you won't mind waiting because you can hang out right on the beach while they ready a table. Also, it's a notable surf spot, so you can watch surfers paddling out hopefully to the break.

The tiki-topped **AJ's Seafood and Oyster Bar** (0.25 mile east of the Destin Bridge, Destin, 850/837-1913, 11 A.M.–midnight daily, until 9:30 P.M. in the off-season, $9–21, no reservations) is another longtime beachside visitor favorite. Overlooking Destin Harbor, AJ's Club Bimini is the place to see the sunset over a plate of Oysters AJ (oysters baked with jalapeños, Monterey jack, and bacon). AJ's charter fleet offers daily trips into shallow or deep waters to hunt for grouper, amberjack, and wahoo—the kitchen will cook your catch straight off the line. Try the fried fish sandwiches or the shrimp po'boy. Another locals' fave is **Lucky Snapper** (76 E. U.S. 98, Harborwalk Marina, Destin, 850/654-0900, 11 A.M.–10 P.M. daily, $10–24) for easy, fun seafood, with a kids' menu. You can watch the Destin fleet unload the catch of the day right outside, and there's also live music.

Don't like fish? **Fudpucker's Beachside Bar & Grill** (20001 Emerald Coast Pkwy., Destin, 850/654-4200, and Okaloosa Island, Fort Walton Beach, 850/243-3833, 11 A.M.–9 P.M. weekdays, late night menu on weekends until 2 A.M., $8–20) is the place for burgers, drinks on the deck, and some of the best bands on the beach.

In Fort Walton Beach, **The Crab Trap** (1450 Miracle Strip Pkwy., Okaloosa Island Boardwalk, Fort Walton Beach, 850/301-0959, 11 A.M.–10 P.M. daily, $7–25), nestled in the beautiful James Lee County Park and overlooking the water, graciously accommodates the sand between your toes and your unmistakable whiff of suntan oil. Grouper, tuna, and amberjack are the freshest catches, with lots of fried seafood and all-you-can-eat snow-crab legs (they're not from around here, though). It's casual, but not as casual as the nearby **Angler's Beachside Grill and Sports Bar** (1030 Miracle Strip Pkwy., Okaloosa Island, Fort Walton Beach, 850/796-0260, 11 A.M.–9 P.M. Mon.–Thurs., until 10 P.M.

Fri. and Sat., 10 A.M.–2 P.M. Sun. for brunch, $7–20). You can eat right on the boardwalk or inside with all the games on big TVs.

## Fine Dining

Some of the best food in the area is to be had from Chef Tim Creehan at the ◖ **Beach Walk Café** (The Inn at Crystal Beach, 2700 U.S. 98 E., Destin, 850/650-7100, www.beachwalkcafe.com, 5:45–11 P.M. daily, $26–54). He has won most of the awards and plaudits possible (DiRoNA Award, *Wine Spectator* award, praise from *Bon Appetit*). There are jumbo sea scallops, lightly fried and paired with grilled orange and tempura-fried softshell crab with sticky rice, stir-fried cabbage, and a tangy pineapple sauce. It's a splurge restaurant, so be prepared for an extremely hefty check.

**Louisiana Lagniappe** (775 Gulf Shore Dr., Holiday Isle, Destin, 850/837-0881, no reservations, 11 A.M.–9:30 P.M. daily Mar.–Oct., $15–26) overlooks Old Pass Lagoon and is a local favorite serving upscale Louisiana-style seafood, like pannéed fillet of grouper topped with lobster medallions, lightly covered with garlic beurre blanc. It traffics in live Maine lobsters and has a beautiful outdoor deck. It was renovated in 2008 and looks better than ever.

**Marina Cafe** (404 Harbor Blvd., 850/837-7960, 5–10 P.M. nightly, $17–28) is another special-occasion destination, moved just slightly in 2007. It's owned by Harbor Restaurant Group, which also owns Destin Chops (a good steak and chop house not far away) with a second Chops location in Seacrest Beach. There's an outdoor dining deck overlooking the Destin Harbor, but inside seating is just as nice. The menu is all over the map, with Cajun/Creole dishes, a sushi bar, and Latin-inspired dishes like citrus/adobo-rubbed yellowfin tuna with black bean lime sauce, saffron basmati rice, pickled onions, and charred tomato salsa.

# Beaches of South Walton

The Beaches of South Walton are fairly new. Obviously, the long expanses of white-sand beach have been here all along, but it's in the past 20 years that developers have set their sights on this area. Residents have kept a tight handle on growth—not out of a fear of change as much as a clear vision of how they'd like these communities to meld and enhance their natural settings. Some of it you may find contrived, like Disney for adults, but the idea of New Urbanism has really taken hold with the creation and restoration of compact, walkable, mixed-use towns. Visitors have most of what they need within walking distance of where they're staying, and the Gulf of Mexico and Choctawhatchee Bay are soothing backdrops for a very restful vacation.

Some of these 14 communities actually developed organically, while others were masterminded by architects and savvy developers. From west to east:

**Seascape** is the closest to Destin, with lakefront and golf villas in an upscale setting. **Miramar Beach** begins at the Gulf along Scenic Gulf Drive and then curves around to join Emerald Coast Parkway. It's mostly condos and private homes and is very close to the Silver Sands Factory Stores. Next up, **Sandestin,** probably the most famous of these little communities, nearly overrun with enormous luxury golf/beach resorts, but all very tasteful. The **Village of Baytowne Wharf** is here in the style of a wealthy but rustic Southern fishing village.

**Dune Allen Beach** is a quaint and quiet beach community two miles long with mostly classic wood-sided beach houses, homes on a lake, and smaller-sized condo developments. This is where the area's eight-foot-wide, off-road bike path begins, winding all the way to Inlet Beach. Fairly developed, **Santa Rosa Beach** has a number of shops and commercial bits, with some golf and beachside amenities. There's a stylish outdoor mall here with boutiques, bike rentals, medical offices, antiques

stores, a market, and a big handful of restaurants. Then there's **Blue Mountain Beach,** the highest point along the Gulf of Mexico; with wonderful views and beautiful sand, it has become attractive as an artists' retreat.

**Grayton Beach** is the oldest town between Pensacola and Apalachicola. Settled in the early 1900s, it is a tree-lined beach community of old cypress cottages and small narrow streets. There is a great bar called the Red Bar that you shouldn't miss, as well as many fine restaurants.

With Seaside to the east fully built out, builders turned not long ago to neighboring **WaterColor,** which is primarily a residential community. Many of the new stylized Cracker-style buildings are available for rent, and the town has a sleek hotel, the 60-room WaterColor Inn.

The next town over is **Seaside,** an upscale, planned beach community of pastel homes and cottages organized around a town square with an outdoor amphitheater, galleries, restaurants, and boutiques. You either love it, using words like "charming" and "picturesque," or you hate it and grumble words like "contrived" and "looks like a stage set" (which it technically was, as the shooting location for *The Truman Show*).

**Seagrove Beach** is next door to the newer and more fancy Seaside. This peaceful beach town is tucked between the coast's natural sand dunes and pine trees. Visitors can choose from rambling beach houses, cottages, or condos. The very newest, **WaterSound** is one of the fanciest, with a resort that is plopped right against a pristine coastal dune lake. Then there's **Seacrest Beach,** a newish beach community made up of cottages and condominiums hidden behind natural dunes.

One of my more favorite communities is **Rosemary Beach.** Like Seaside, it's completely planned in a very narrow architectural style, but this time it's all Caribbean-inspired homes connected to the shore by boardwalks and footpaths with a town square and an exceptional eternity pool.

And finally, **Inlet Beach** is just west of Panama City Beach (over the bridge) and next to Rosemary Beach. Named for the large lagoon on its eastern shore, Phillips Inlet, the peaceful community is known for its secluded natural areas and minimal development.

## ◖ SEASIDE

It used to be that Americans retreated during the summers to simple beachside cottages for months at a time. Every day, after you got your sunburned hide up off the porch, you biked or walked into the little town center to take in a movie or get the local gossip and an ice cream. In 1946, J. S. Smolian bought 80 acres near Seagrove Beach on Florida's Panhandle with this vision floating in his mind—a utopian summer camp for his employees. His grandson, Robert Davis, was smitten by the same vision, growing up to become a fancy developer in Miami in the 1970s. Still, the sweet, multigenerational, seaside summer village eluded him. He infected Miami architects Andres Duany and Elizabeth Plater-Zyberk with his gentle dream, and they built in their minds a fantasy town based on the northwest Florida architectural style of wood-frame cottages with peaked roofs, deep overhangs, and big windows for cross-ventilation. They traveled through Florida with sketchpads and eyes wide open.

Then they made it real in the early 1980s. They built a small town nestled against an idyllic curve along the Gulf Coast shoreline, against a wide swath of beach and mild emerald waters. There are 200 or so homes now, in a paradigm called New Urbanism situated around a town square with an amphitheater, restaurants, elegant boutiques, a repertory theater, and the beach off at the edge of it all. There's a much-lauded charter school, a chapel, and a medical arts building. It's a living laboratory—an experiment in harmonious beachside community life.

The kicker is that you can go to Seaside and visit. If you vacation here, you pull your car in, turn off the ignition, and that's the last you need of it for the duration. Everything is within walking distance in what *Time* called "the most astounding design achievement of its era." Panama City is 40 miles to the east, Destin is 20 miles to the west—but Seaside seems miles and miles from anywhere.

## Sports and Recreation

**Seaside Swim & Tennis Club** (850/231-2214, 8 A.M.–4 P.M. Mon.–Sat., until 2 P.M. Sun.) is at the center of lots of the town's activities. It offers private tennis lessons and clinics for kids and adults, shuffleboard and horseshoes, bike rentals (including trikes), and three beautiful croquet courts. There are three pools—the West Side Pool is the largest, with an adult pool at the north end of Seaside Avenue and a family pool at the northeast corner of Seaside. **Camp Seaside** is a special program for kids 5–12, with half-day or full-day crafts, sports, swimming, and other activities. It also offers a kids' night out, with dinner and a movie, and regularly scheduled free storytime in the amphitheater.

Beyond that, Seaside has nearby golf, a long biking/walking path, deep-sea fishing, hiking, kayaking, and swimming in the Gulf to keep everyone occupied.

## Shopping

Ruskin Place, named after John Ruskin, the famous supporter of 19th-century art, is the town's center for galleries, with a good coffee shop and a few other diversions. There are plenty of shops worth a bit of exploration in Seaside, but definitely check out the vessels, chandeliers, sinks, and other blown-glass art of **Fusion Art Glass** (63 Central Square, 850/231-5405, www.fusionartglass.com). **Sundog Books** (89 Central Square) is a great place in the area to spend a few hours. The current fiction is always in stock, along with plenty of art and design books.

## Accommodations

To rent a cottage at Seaside, you need only to call 888/541-0801. The tricky part comes in figuring out what you want—people have built their dream homes in Seaside, and the prices,

# EGLIN AIR FORCE BASE

Eglin Air Force Reservation in Fort Walton Beach is the largest air force base in the free world. It's the size of Rhode Island, covering 724 square miles of reservation and 97,963 square miles of water in the Gulf of Mexico. Eglin employs approximately 10,000 each of military personnel and civilians.

Unless you're in the military, much of it is off limits to you. For instance, Eglin has two 18-hole championship golf courses (850/882-2949) open year-round. The Eglin Golf Course, host of a 2000 U.S. Open qualifier, has a hill on the seventh hole so steep that the course provides a towrope to golfers. Here's an interesting tidbit: Al Capone funded the layout of this course originally. In fact, Capone's private beach hideout house is now the officers' club at Eglin.

Much of Eglin you wouldn't want to have access to if you could: Recently the Mother of all Bombs (MOAB), the most powerful nonnuclear bomb ever created, was tested at Eglin. And for years Eglin Air Force Base has been testing depleted uranium (DU), with an estimated 220,000 pounds of DU penetrators expended there since 1973.

The Air Force Armament Museum (850/651-1808, 9 A.M.-4:30 P.M. Mon.-Sat., admission free) is definitely a wonderful public part of Eglin, but it is just one of many opportunities for the visitor. The reservation covers 464,000 acres in Santa Rosa, Okaloosa, and Walton counties. If you go to the **Jackson Guard** office (107 Hwy. 85 N., Niceville, 850/882-4164) you can get an outdoor recreation permit, a comprehensive map, and a list of regulations. This allows you to explore the area's many activities – hunting, fishing, primitive camping, canoeing, and hiking part of the **Florida National Scenic Trail** (www.florida-trail.org).

**Hunting** (which accounts for 4,200 of the 12,000 recreation permits granted annually) is for deer, turkey, wild hogs, and small game, seasonally. There's a huge managed quail area, another for "planted" doves, and two duck management units totaling 78,000 acres. There's even an annual hunt open to the mobility-impaired. Fishing in the reservation is on any of 17 stocked ponds (two of them fully accessible).

**Birders** will enjoy the old-growth longleaf pine swath of Eglin reservation that is a designated part of the **Great Florida Birding Trail** (www.floridabirdingtrail.com). You may see the endangered Okaloosa darter, found in only six creek systems in the central portion of the Air Force base. It's also got the fourth-largest red-cockaded woodpecker population in the country. The area is home to more than 90 rare or listed plant and animal species.

Within the reservation there are seven miles of barrier island for swimming and canoeing, with lots of other creeks; enjoy open-water **kayaking** in the Choctawhatchee Bay, Santa Rosa Sound, or the Gulf.

The **Anderson Pond Recreation Area** (off Hwy. 85, three miles north of Niceville) is open to the public year-round, with an elevated boardwalk, a picnic shelter, a pier, and a camping area. All the facilities are fully accessible.

styles, and sizes are all over the map. There are 200 homes and cottages. It offers 400 individual accommodations, including private homes, cottages, luxury townhouses, penthouses, and beachfront hideaways. If bed-and-breakfasts are more your speed, there's a brand new **Inn by the Sea, Vera Bradley,** with nine colorful guest rooms. The website (www.lfoa.com/seaside) gives a list of accommodations with photos, virtual tours, descriptions of amenities, reserved dates, and prices.

## Food

Seaside's restaurants work as a team to satisfy most of your tastes and style. There is a large handful of restaurants within the village, with the upscale **Bud & Alley's** (2236 E. Hwy. 30A, 850/231-7327, 11:30 A.M.-9:30 P.M. daily, $25-35) serving a popular fusion of Mediterranean/coastal Southern dishes. Chef Jim Shirley brings his brand of Southern cooking to Seaside at the **Great Southern Café** (83 Central Square, 850/231-7327,

11 A.M.–9:30 P.M. daily, $10–28). The menu's regional flair includes Gulf shrimp, Apalachicola oysters, and traditional Southern vegetables. It seems like no one talks about the Great Southern Café without mentioning the Grits a Ya Ya, one of the most-ordered dishes, which offers seasoned shrimp in smoked gouda cheese grits topped with cream gravy, bacon, spinach, and mushrooms. **Dawson's Yogurt** (121 Central Square, 850/231-4770, 10 A.M.–9 P.M. Sun.–Thurs., until 10 P.M. Fri. and Sat.) is the place for yogurt, and **Cafe Rendez-Vous** (25 Central Square, 850/534-0254, 5–10 P.M. daily, noon–10 P.M. Sun.) has a delicious array of sushi rolls and crepes, not to mention the place to pick up pearl jewelry. Weird one-stop shopping, but it works.

## SPORTS AND RECREATION
### Beaches
Of the numerous beaches along the stretch, many have public beach access, with additional beach accesses located within the 14 beach communities if you're staying there. From west to east, most with access right along scenic Highway 30A, the beaches are: Miramar Beach, Legion Park, Cessna Park (on the Choctawhatchee Bay side), Dune Allen Beach, Ed Walline, Gulfview Heights, Blue Mountain Beach, Grayton Dunes, Van Ness Butler Jr., Santa Clara, Inlet Beach, and Pier and Boat Ramp 331 (bay side). Which is the nicest is hard to say; most are sparsely populated, many have small, no-fee parking lots, and several have restrooms and showers. My favorite is probably Santa Clara, with a beautiful stretch of sand and picnic facilities, but the pristine windswept dunes of Grayton Dunes make a very nice afternoon of exploration, too.

### Parks and Recreation Areas
There's a large variety of outdoor activities, so bring your most comfortable hiking shoes. At the top of the heap is **Grayton Beach State Park** (357 Main Park Rd., south of U.S. 98 halfway between Panama City Beach, near the intersection of Hwy. 30A and County Road

283, 850/267-8300, 8 A.M.–sundown daily, $5/vehicle, $2 pedestrian or bicyclist, $24–30 camping, cabin rental $110/day or $705/week), with sugar-white sand, emerald-green water, little development, and huge sea oat–covered sand dunes. Foot traffic is prohibited in the dunes and in bird-nesting areas. Despite its natural setting, there are great restaurants and accommodations in nearby Grayton Beach or Seaside. Camping is popular, with 37 campsites and 30 cabins. Make reservations early. Due to the number of endangered plants and animals found within the park (like the rare Choctawhatchee beach mouse), pets must be kept on a six-foot leash. If you visit in the fall, you may catch the thousands of monarch butterflies resting beachside during their southward migration to Mexico.

Identified as the most pristine piece of coastal property in the state, **Topsail Hill State Preserve** (7525 W. Hwy. 30A, in Santa Rosa Beach 10 miles east of Destin, 850/267-8330, 8 A.M.–sundown daily, honor $3/vehicle, $2 pedestrian or bicyclist, $42/night for RV camping, $24 tent camping, $100/night and $690/week for the bungalows) owes its existence to turpentine. More than a century ago, workers turpentined old-growth longleaf pine trees here for caulking the seams of wooden ships, a key mode of transport. Today, it's 1,600 acres of stunning Gulf-front pine forest, nature trails over mountainous sand dunes, and two freshwater dune lakes. It is one of only two remaining natural populations of the nocturnal, endangered Choctawhatchee beach mice. The park features a 140-acre RV resort as well as tent camping and nice bungalows to rent.

In the southernmost portion of Walton County, the 15,000-acre **Point Washington State Forest** (5865 E. U.S. 98, Santa Rosa Beach, 850/267-8325, 8 A.M.–sundown daily, $2/person, $20 reserved picnic space) is home to more than 19 miles of trails and boasts 10 different habitats with rare plant and wildlife species, from gopher tortoises to red-cockaded woodpeckers. For an easy day hike, the Eastern Lake Trail System was the first trail established in this forest. It consists of three double-track loop trails. The hiker or bicyclist can travel the 3.5-, 5-, or 10-mile loops. Access to the trail system is at the parking lot and trailhead on County Road 395.

Nearby, and worth a stop to see, **Eden State Gardens** (off U.S. 98 on County Road 395, just north of Seagrove Beach, 850/267-8320, 8 A.M.–sundown daily, honor $4/vehicle, guided tour $4 adults, $2 children), in historic Point Washington on the shore of Tucker Bayou, is a beautiful 1895 Greek Revival estate surrounded by gardens of azaleas, camellias, and large moss-draped live oak. This 12-acre sprawling park was once the home of lumber baron William Henry Wesley and his family. Find yourself a picnic spot on the wide, manicured lawn.

Just east of Seagrove Beach, **Deer Lake State Park** (357 Main Park Rd., off Hwy. 30A, Santa Rosa Beach, 850/231-4210, 8 A.M.–sundown daily, $3/vehicle, $2 pedestrian or cyclist) is the newest park in these parts. It has a fine beach with a new dune walkover/board-walk, from which there are great views of this dynamic dune ecosystem. North of here are acres of hiking trails worth exploring.

If you're interested in enjoying all this nature within the context of an ecotour or guided adventure, there are plenty of guides in the area. **Blue Sky Kayak Tours** (89 Lakeside Dr., Freeport, 850/368-3155) offers guided tours in different local habitats. **Choctawhatchee Delta Tours** (710 Black Creek Rd., Freeport, 850/585-0445) also offers tours of this area, departing from the 331 Bridge. **Island Winds Sailing** (801 Kell-Aire Dr., Destin, 850/699-2511) has catamarans for sailing, offering ecotours, lessons, sunset/moonlight cruises, and sand dollar excursions. And **Big Daddy's Bike and Beach** (2217 Hwy. 30A, Santa Rosa Beach, 850/622-1165) offers ecotours on bike along Highway 30A and through state forest area.

### ◘ Biking Along Scenic Route 30A

The **Timpoochee Trail** is one of the longest and most widely used paths in Walton County. The 19-mile, paved trail winds through nine of the 14 distinctive beach communities traversing

## COASTAL DUNE LAKES

Think about it for a second: When was the last time you saw a freshwater lake right up against a huge body of saltwater, just a little picturesque sea oat-fringed sand dune separating the two? It appears so gloriously natural that it's easy to overlook, but the Emerald Coast's coastal dune lakes are rare enough to be considered globally imperiled by the Florida Natural Areas Inventory. The 15 in Walton County have sister lakes in a few other spots along the Gulf Coast, then in New Zealand, Australia, and Madagascar. That's it.

These lakes were formed between 2,000 and 10,000 years ago. Coastal winds and flowing tides have kept these water havens safe, separated from the Gulf by ever-changing dune systems ranging 10-30 feet high. Intermittently, when they are swollen with rainwater, the lakes have little wandering fingers that empty out into the Gulf, meaning a canoe or kayak can paddle from freshwater to saltwater and back again without overland toting. These dune lake areas are also biologically diverse with fresh, estuarine, and marine all coexisting in this constant state of flux. Migrating birds are drawn to these coastal lakes, as well.

**Topsail Hill Preserve State Park** has the densest concentration, with Morris, Campbell, and Stalworth lakes as well as two minor unnamed coastal dune lakes on its property. For more information on the lakes at Topsail Hill Preserve State Park, contact Park Services Specialist Leda C. Suydan at 850/267-0299 or Leda.Suydan@dep.state.fl.us.

state recreational areas, state parks, dunes, and coastal dune lakes. Named after Timpoochee Kinnard, the most influential Indian chief of the Euchee Indians, the path runs along Scenic Highway 30A parallel to the Gulf of Mexico. From migrating flocks of birds to blooming wildflowers and trees, the Timpoochee Trail is full of surprises all year long. Hop off the bike for an ice cream. Rent a bike with a basket and pick up some groceries for dinner along the way—a paperback from Sundog Books, maybe a bottle of wine for the sunset.

This is road or touring bike territory. For the mountain biker, there is also a 10-mile loop in the Point Washington State Forest called the **Eastern Lake Bike/Hike Trail,** which winds through natural vegetation and wildlife habitat. A new stretch of trail goes to Seagrove, or go in the opposite direction for a scenic ride from Seaside to Blue Mountain Beach.

And then there's the **Longleaf Pine Greenway System** (850/231-5800) interlaced through several state parks and forests, with eight miles of trails through different terrain from the Gulf to Choctawhatchee Bay. Most bike shops will equip you with maps of the different cycling possibilities in the area.

Depending on where you're staying, there are several convenient bike rental shops. From west to east: **Seaside Bike Shop** (87 Central Square, Seaside, 850/231-2314, $30/day, $65/5 days), **Butterfly Bike & Beach Rentals** (3657 E. Hwy. 30A, Seagrove Beach, 850/231-2826, with Caloi off-road bikes), and **Bamboo Beach & Bicycle Company** (Rosemary Beach, 850/231-0770, $20/day, $60/week, children's bikes less).

## Fishing

**Baytowne Marina at Sandestin** is a good place to start. **Baytowne Bait and Tackle Store** (850/267-7777) provides basic boating necessities, and it's a good place to hook up with a fishing guide. Similarly, **Old Florida Outfitters** (850/534-4343), an Orvis-endorsed guide program, is a great source for specialized fishing charters, located in WaterColor's Town Center.

**Not A Dog Charters** (850/267-2514, www. notadogcharters.com) heads out from Grayton Beach; after a short boat ride you will be bottom fishing for red snapper, grouper, and trigger fish, or trolling for king mackerel. In the spring, the target is cobia right along the beach. **Yellow Fin Ocean Sports** (850/231-9024) in

Grayton will take you fishing for redfish or trout in coastal bays or head out into the Gulf for grouper, snapper, dolphin, or marlin. **Dead Fish Charters** (174 WaterColor Way #280, Seagrove Beach, 850/685-1092, www.deadfish-charters.com) specializes in Indian Pass half- or full-day trips, and inshore grouper and snapper trips in Grayton Beach.

## SHOPPING

Shopping is clustered in a handful of tasteful centers along the Beaches of South Walton. The **Market Shops at Sandestin** (9375 U.S. 98 W. at Sandestin Golf & Beach Resort, 850/267-8093) complex has 30 shops, split between kitchen ware stores, skin care, chocolates, housewares, and more. The **Shops at Grayton** (26 Logan Ln., Grayton Beach) are not as upscale, and here you'll find jewelry, clothing, and antiques. In Seaside there is **Ruskin Place Artist Colony** near the new Seaside Chapel and the rest of the 40 or so **Merchants of Seaside** (63 Central Square, 850/231-5424) for cafés, galleries, clothing, books, and gifts. Head to the Beaches of South Walton, especially Seaside, if you're looking for art. This area is increasingly a hotbed of independent art galleries.

## ACCOMMODATIONS
### Camping

The only way to slide in under $50 around here is by camping—it's warm much of the year, with nice evening breezes, lots of beach, plenty of fresh air, and not so rural that you can't go out for dinner. One of the best places in the area to camp is located in the town of Grayton Beach near Seaside at **Grayton Beach State Park** (357 Main Park Rd., south of U.S. 98 halfway between Panama City Beach, near the intersection of Hwy. 30A and County Road 283, 850/267-8300, 8 A.M.–sundown daily, $5/vehicle, $2/pedestrian or bicyclist, $24–30 camping, cabin rental $110/day or $705/week). The campground has 34 sites accommodating tents and RVs. The campground is located right on the Gulf of Mexico among trees and dunes. It has restrooms, electricity, and hot showers to rinse away those hours of swimming and wading in the salty warm waters of the Gulf of Mexico before you roast some marshmallows over an open fire with the waves of the Gulf lapping in the background.

In Sandestin you can camp on the Gulf at **Camping on the Gulf** (10005 W. Emerald Coast Pkwy., Destin, 850/837-6334, $40–91), with an activity center, fishing, cable TV, and full hookups. **Destin RV Beach Resort** (362 Miramar Beach Dr., Destin, 850/837-3529) is hands-down the nicest RV campground I have come across. The owners call it a "luxury RV resort." It is right across from the beach, with a swimming pool and a free deep-sea fishing trip with a paid stay.

You can also camp at **Topsail Hill State Park Preserve** (7525 W. Hwy. 30A, in Santa Rosa Beach 10 miles east of Destin, 850/267-8330, 8 A.M.–sundown daily, honor $3/vehicle, $2 pedestrian or bicyclist, $42 camping for RVs and $24/night for tent camping, $100/night and $690/week for the bungalows) at the Topsail Hill Gregory E. Moore RV Resort, which has the highest possible rating from *Trailer Life* and Woodall's, placing it in the top 1 percent of RV campgrounds in the nation. The campground has a stunning 156 RV sites with electricity, sewer, water, and cable. It also offers 22 tent sites with electricity. The park has a swimming pool, bathrooms, hot showers, and a camp store with water, other drinks, snacks, and camping items. A tram will give you a lift to the beach. It's definitely more set up for older RV enthusiasts, but it's a good place to tent camp as well if there aren't any sites left at Grayton Beach State Park.

You can camp on **Santa Rosa Beach** at Willows Campground (82 Veterans Rd., in Santa Rosa Beach 10 miles east of Destin, 850/267-2183, $20/night for RV camping and $15 for tent camping).

## $50-150

The **Hilton Sandestin Beach Golf Resort & Spa** (4000 Sandestin Blvd. S., Destin, 850/267-9500, www.hiltonsandestinbeach.

com, $149–259) recently completed a major renovation project and spa expansion. The hotel's Emerald Tower features the addition of granite countertops in bathrooms and tasteful new interior design elements. The lobby and the kids' play area have also been redone. In all, it's an extremely beautiful golf-and-spa resort of 598 rooms, the largest beachfront resort hotel in the northwest Florida region. There are 190 spacious standard guest rooms, 22 parlor suites, two presidential suites, and 385 junior suites that feature bunk beds with portholes in the sides for a nautical style and a private gaming system that kids will surely appreciate. The hotel has an award-winning program for children, with accessible on-site dining at Sandcastles Restaurant & Lounge, which has a great breakfast buffet in the morning. There's also a fancier restaurant called Seagar's Prime Steaks & Seafood that has a long sushi bar lining the back. The wine room located in the front of the restaurant is separated from the rest of the dining room and doubles as an intimate and private dining room. You can reserve the space for a small party or couple and hold your special occasion in a romantic setting surrounded by racks of the wine bottles that make up the restaurant's extensive wine list.

## Over $150

So many of the nicer accommodations around here are private homes or condos. There are numerous property management companies—the Beach Rental of South Walton website (www.beachrentalsofsouthwalton.com) is a good place to start surfing for what you want. It's divided by community, specializing in the more affordable ones. Many of the swankier communities have their own websites with rental information and slide shows (www.rosemarybeach.com, www.seasidefl.com). My favorite is definitely ( **Rosemary Beach** (on Hwy. 30A, in between Seacrest and Inlet Beach, 850/278-2030, www.rosemarybeach.com, roughly $200–500 per night, but many rentals are by the week), with one- to five-bedroom Gulf-front and midtown cottages for vacation

© JOSHUA LAWRENCE KINSER

The Hilton Sandestin Beach Golf Resort & Spa is a family favorite that offers sweeping views of Sandestin Beach.

rentals. All designed in a loose Caribbean style, there are family cottages, carriage houses, flats, and contemporary lofts, all connected to the shore by boardwalks and footpaths. It's a good location for families, because it's farther east than many of the communities, and thus closer to the liveliness of Panama City Beach but still out of the fray.

Then there's the **Sandestin Golf & Beach Resort** (9300 Emerald Coast Pkwy. W., Sandestin, 850/267-8150, $172–450), really the premier resort in this area, set on 2,400 beach- and bay-front acres. There are four championship golf courses, 15 world-class tennis courts, a full-service marina, water sports, charter sailing and fishing, fine and casual dining, a fancy fitness center, a professional salon and day spa, and fun children's programs. If you want to improve your game, professional golf and tennis trainers on-site use the most advanced swing analysis technology available. It's got 1,350 different rooms and accommodations, with a range of options—it's kind of like

a little city unto itself, with leisure as the town's central preoccupation.

Really, the city in question is **Village of Baytowne Wharf** (9300 Emerald Coast Pkwy. W., Sandestin, 850/267-8100, $180–800), a sweeping pedestrian village right on the beach that rents its own accommodations. There are different choices on where to stay, grouped into five resort areas: Beachfront, Beachside, Village, Bayside, and Dockside. Each of the five Florida resorts offers a unique flavor, as well as a range of rates. Included with a stay at any of the resort accommodations options are free kayak, canoe and bike rentals. The resort is also the host of many area festivals including the Sandestin Wine Festival and, my favorite, The Baytowne Beer Festival. They are also starting to host outdoor concerts with large nationally recognized acts. When I was there Vince Gill was performing on the grounds of the resort, so make sure to check the events calendar on the extensive website to see what's on the agenda.

# FOOD

All of the little communities of South Walton have their own cluster of restaurants, in a range of price points and culinary traditions. A few I would recommend include **Criolla's** (170 E. Hwy. 30A, Grayton Beach, 850/267-1267, 5:30–9:30 P.M. Mon.–Sat. Mar.–Oct., closed Mon. Nov.–Feb., $26–39), where executive chef and owner Johnny Earles sends out something called "contemporary Creole-Caribbean," which translates as pan-seared Gulf grouper with yellow corn, a black bean muneta, prickly pear mole, and a scotch bonnet–amped pineapple jam or maybe Aunt Irma's banana and pecan beignets. It's pricey, but a good choice for special occasions. **Bud and Alley's Restaurant** (2236 E. Hwy. 30A, Seaside, 850/231-5900, 11:30 A.M.–3 P.M. and 5:30–9 P.M. daily, until 9:30 P.M. weekends, closed Tues. in off-season, rooftop bar 11:30 A.M.–2 A.M., $20–28) was opened in Seaside in 1986 and named after a dog and a cat. It's a casual and unpretentious place, with a cooking style that nods to the coastal Mediterranean, Basque country, Tuscany, and the American Deep South. Oysters Seaside are baked Apalachicola beauties with shrimp, scallops, calamari, cilantro, garlic, and lime, and there are tempura-fried softshell crabs with rémoulade, or heads-on shrimp with garlic and shallots. The bar has an extensive wine list and is a great spot for conversation with the locals.

**Cafe Thirty-A** (3899 E. Hwy. 30A, Seagrove, 850/231-2166, 6–10 P.M. nightly, $12–34) is another upscale spot, with a large wine list, many selections by the glass. The menu has broad appeal, with dishes such as wood oven–roasted grouper served with baby tiger shrimp and risotto in a sweet carrot sauce or maple barbecue pork chop with fried peaches and corn mashed potatoes on the side. I'm pretty content just to slice up one of the Hawaiian-style wood-fired pizzas.

Next there's **Basmati's Asian Cuisine** (3295 W. Hwy. 30A, Blue Mountain Beach, 850/267-3028, 4:30–10 nightly, $9–28) with a full sushi bar and mostly Japanese fusion dishes served in a beautiful dining room and a nice sheltered deck.

In the Village of Baytown Wharf, you've got **Graffiti's & The Funky Blues Shack** (707 Harbor Blvd., Sandestin, 850/654-3839, 5–10 P.M. daily, $12–23), a folk art–infused restaurant and live blues club venue or **New Orleans Creole Cookery** (The Village of Baytowne Wharf, Sandestin, 850/351-1996, 11 A.M.–9 P.M. Sun.–Thurs., until 10 P.M. Fri. and Sat., $15–30)—if you've got the Nola jones, head here, especially for the barbecued shrimp and Creole bread pudding. Sandestin's signature Gulf-front restaurant is **Finz** (9300 U.S. Highway 98 W, Miramar Beach, 850/267-4800, 11 A.M.–10 P.M. Tues.–Sat., $21–34), where chef Justin Stark serves up a Caribbean- and Creole-inspired menu that includes coriander-crusted grouper, Blue Mountain lamb with jicama and mint slaw, and seared scallops in calabaza sauce.

For breakfast, top honors go to Rosemary Beach's **Wild Olives Market** (104 N. Barrett Square, Rosemary Beach, 850/231-0065, 8 A.M.–8 P.M. Tues.–Sat., 8 A.M.–5 P.M. Sun.) or **Summer Kitchen** (16 N. Barrett Square, Rosemary Beach, 850/231-6264, 7:30 A.M.–9 P.M. daily) for pastries and egg dishes; for a glass of wine, stop off at nearby **Courtyard Wine and Cheese** (66 Main St. in the Gourd Garden Courtyard, Rosemary Beach, 850/231-1219, 2–10 P.M. Tues.–Sun.), with 50 wines by the glass.

Locals have been flocking to **Cerulean's** (WaterColor Town Center, 866/426-2656, 7 A.M.–9 P.M. daily), a low-key neighborhood coffee shop, logo store, newsstand, wine bar, bookstore, and performance and art exhibit space. It's right in WaterColor Market in the heart of Town Center, an easy place to hang out and enjoy the effects of a relaxing beach vacation plus caffeine.

# Panama City Beach

Panama City Beach gets billed as the No. 1 spring break beach in the country, attracting more than 300,000 people annually. The hottest spring break places change, though. In the 1980s it was places like Palm Springs or Fort Lauderdale; for a while after that people seemed more focused on Cancún, Mazatlán, or Cabo San Lucas. Most recently Puerto Vallarta and Miami Beach are neck and neck for spring break mania.

Yet, Panama City Beach attracts a huge crowd of young people ready to throw down for spring break and has a ton of attractions to keep them entertained. The city even publishes a booklet for spring breakers that outlines the attractions in the area they are most likely to enjoy. With the same green water and white-sand beaches found elsewhere on the Emerald Coast, these beaches are more action-oriented, with volleyball, Frisbee, skim boarding, Jet Skiing, and parasailing. Although the beach is wide with a lengthy expanse of shallows, there are hundreds of natural and artificial reefs offshore—Panama City Beach ranks with Key Largo in providing some of the best diving in the country. The fishing is also good, with mackerel, flounder, redfish, and other game fish swimming through the clear waters.

At the east end of the city, St. Andrews State Park is fabulous, one of the most popular outdoor recreation spots in Florida. It contains verdant woods, sea oat–fringed sand dunes, fresh- and saltwater marshes, a lagoon swimming area, fishing jetties, hiking trails, 2.5 miles of beach, and two campgrounds. From here, you can also take a pedestrian ferry to Shell Island, an undisturbed 700-acre barrier island just across from the mainland for sunning, shelling, birding, or watching the sunset.

Outside of the beaches, the area is known for its roadside attractions like miniature golf, water-slide parks, go-cart tracks, and a marine park. The Miracle Strip, which lent Panama City Beach its name as a nickname, was a beloved amusement park—one of the area's biggest draws—but it closed in 2004.

So, we know it's packed in March and April, and tourists from Georgia and Alabama flock to PCB during the summer. But in the early fall or during May, between the hordes, Panama City Beach makes for an entertaining beachside playground, with loads of modestly priced accommodations. It's at these times that you can understand why the area has been a popular beach vacation spot for more than 40 years.

## SPORTS AND RECREATION
### Diving and Snorkeling
Panama City Beach was dubbed the Shipwreck Capital of the South by *Skin Diver* magazine. As such, this part of the warm Gulf of Mexico is an excellent home and breeding ground for all types of sealife. You'll see sea turtles, manta rays, puffer fish, sand dollars, blue marlin, horseshoe crabs, small coral, colorful sponges, and lots of other marinelife.

Of the "natural" wrecks in this area, you can investigate a 441-foot **World War II liberty ship,** a 220-foot tug called **The Chippewa,** a 160-foot coastal freighter called the **S.S. Tarpon,** the 100-foot tug **Chickasaw,** another tug called **The Grey Ghost,** and the Gulf's most famous wreck, the 465-foot **Empire Mica.** A bunch of other artificial reef projects have sunk bridge spans, barges, and the City of Atlantis (a different one). Many of these dive sites are at depths of 80–100 feet and are just a few miles offshore, and the best time for diving is April–September.

Experts say that the top five dives are the **USS Strength,** a naval mine sweeper; the **Blackbart,** a supply vessel; another supply vessel called the **B. J. Putnam;** the **Accokeek,** a 295-foot navy tug boat; and a huge aluminum **hovercraft** in 100 feet of water. If you want to rent diving equipment, **Dive Locker** (106 Thomas Dr., 850/230-8006), **Diver's Den** (6222 E Business Hwy., 850/871-6889),

**Panama City Dive Center** (4823 Thomas Dr., 850/235-3390), and the **Dixie Divers** (109 W. 23rd St., 850/914-9988) will help you out.

Snorkelers will have a better time around the **St. Andrews Jetties,** an area with no boat traffic. Nineteen feet under the surface there is an old tar barge ideal for underwater exploration. If you want to snorkel with a guide, **Island Time** (Treasure Island Marina, 3605 Thomas Dr., 850/234-7377, $35/person) offers 3.5-hour catamaran excursions, wet suits available, and **Captain Ashley Gorman Shell Island Cruises** (5701 U.S. 98, east end of Hathaway Bridge, 850/785-4878, $35/person) does swim and snorkeling tours for the whole family.

## ◖ St. Andrews State Recreation Area

St. Andrews State Recreation Area (4607 State Park Ln., Panama City, 850/233-5140, 8 A.M.–5 P.M. daily, $4 single driver, $8/vehicle 2–8 people, $2 pedestrians or cyclists, $28 camping) has rolling, white-sand dunes separated by low swales of either pinewoods or marshes. There are 2.5 miles of beach, with two different parking lots with access. You can rent bicycles during the summer at the park and explore the trails. There's a double-sided concrete boat launch for watercraft (if don't own a boat, you can take a boat tour out to Shell Island in the spring and summer, tickets at the park concession), and they rent canoes at the boat ramp (paddle around Grand Lagoon or across the boat channel to Shell Island). If you want to fish, there are two fishing piers and jetties, from which you're likely to catch Spanish mackerel, redfish, flounder, sea trout, bonito, cobia, dolphin, and bluefish. The concession stores in the park sell bait and fishing licenses, along with other beachside necessities. For hikers, there's Heron Pond Trail (starting at a reconstructed Cracker turpentine still) and Gator Lake Trail (yep, you'll see gators), both easy and well marked. And if it's all too great to leave, there are 176 campsites in the park or on the barrier Shell Island.

## Other Recreation Areas

All the other parks around here get overshadowed by St. Andrews, which is a shame. **Pine Log State Forest** (5583-A Longleaf Rd., Ebro, 850/535-2888) is a favorite locals' spot for picnicking, hiking, off-road bicycling, horseback riding, fishing, and hunting. There are 23 miles of hiking trails winding through the forest. Nearby **Point Washington State Forest** (5865 U.S. 98 E., Santa Rosa Beach, 850/267-8325) is less developed but has 19 miles of trails for mountain biking, birding, and hunting.

In general, the whole area has benefited from the recent completion of a U.S Army Corp. of Engineers beach renourishment project, Florida's longest continuous beach restoration. The $23.5 million project elevated and widened a 16.5-mile stretch of beach by an average of 30 feet, with something like a billion cubic yards of new, white sand. Besides beautifying the shoreline, the renourishment provides critical storm protection.

## SIGHTS

The biggest local thrills around here used to be at the Miracle Strip Amusement Park, which closed in 2004. Let us observe a moment of silence.

Now, the best family attraction is to be had at **Gulf World** (15412 Front Beach Rd., Panama City Beach, 850/234-5271, 9 A.M.–5:30 P.M. daily, $27 adults, $17 children 5–11, free children 4 and under), which got pumped up seriously around the millennium, with a $6.5 million expansion that netted it a state-of-the-art dolphin habitat, a new bird theater, and enclosed tropical gardens. It needed it. The marine mammal park opened in 1969 with animal shows and displays, but it also has a facility to rehabilitate stranded or injured marine animals from all over the Panhandle. As with so many of Florida's aquariums and water parks, there is a swim-with-the-dolphins option to the tune of $150 per person (also a trainer for a day program and a slumber-party option).

**Coconut Creek Mini Golf and Gran Maze**

(9807 Front Beach Rd., Panama City Beach, 850/234-2625, www.coconutcreekfun.com, 10 A.M.–6 P.M. daily, $18 one price, $10.50 just for golf, $9.50 just for gran maze—why there's no "d" on that is a mystery) has two miniature golf courses in a kind of African safari/jungle motif. The maze is the better part, built in 1987 and completely rebuilt recently. It's a huge, human-sized maze the size of a football field in which you will find disoriented children and lots of military personnel using their professional navigational skills to find the four checkpoints (for some reason, they are Fiji, Tahiti, Samoa, and Bali) essential to successfully navigating the maze. There's no shame in crawling under to get the heck out of here. Well, maybe a little shame.

**Shipwreck Island Water Park** (12201 Middle Beach Rd., Panama City Beach, 850/234-3333, www.shipwreckisland.com, 10:30 A.M.–5:30 P.M. daily during the summer, $33 50 inches and above, $28 35–49 inches, free under 35 inches, $22 seniors) is the kind of water park with long slides and flumes, a wave pool, kiddie pools—in other words, what to do if the beach isn't holding the kids' interest for another warm summer day. There is a 48-inch height restriction on two of the more exciting rides (the Rapid River Run and Tree Top Drop), and you're not allowed to bring food in from outside, or flotation devices, goggles, or masks. Little ones not yet potty-trained are required to wear waterproof swim diapers.

Need more to do? There's a **Ripley's Believe It or Not! Museum** (9907 Front Beach Rd., 850/230-6113, 10 A.M.–10 P.M. daily, $15 adults, $12 children 6–12) with all the requisite shrunken heads and scale models of the Lusitania made out of ear wax. OK, I made that one up. Nearby you'll find **Zoo World Zoological and Botanical Park** (9008 Front Beach Rd., 850/230-1243, 9 A.M.–4 P.M. daily, $15 adults, $10 children 4–11), a small and pleasant zoo. The best part is the interspecies interaction between Tonda the orangutan and T. K. the tabby cat. Little kids will really enjoy **Sea Dragon Pirate Cruise** (departs from 5325 N. Lagoon Dr., 850/234-7400, $21 adults, $17 kids, times vary, reservations highly recommended), a cruise with Captain Phil on a totally kitted out pirate ship, heavy on the "argh." **Museum of Man in the Sea** (17314 Panama City Beach Pkwy., 850/235-4101, 10 A.M.–4 P.M. daily, $5, free for children under 7) is a small but very interesting museum that delves into the history of deep sea diving and ocean exploration.

## SHOPPING
### Pier Park

Shopping, dining, and entertainment are all within easy reach at Pier Park, new in 2008. This 900,000-square-foot retail and entertainment complex sits on 93 acres in the heart of downtown across from the City Pier. Target, Panera Bread, The Grand 16-Plex Theatres, and Longhorn Steakhouse were the first establishments to open. It is anchored by a 125,000-square-foot Dillard's, JCPenney, and Jimmy Buffet's Margaritaville restaurant and nightclub, with smaller stores including Ron Jon Surf Shop, Starbucks, Ann Taylor Loft, Ulta Cosmetics, Victoria's Secret, Bath & Body Works, and more. Its open-air eateries take best advantage of gorgeous Gulf views.

Beyond that, there are little pockets of shops all over, mostly of the sunglasses-and-suntan lotion variety. You may need to stock up on bathing suits at **Beach Scene Superstore** (10059 Hutchinson Blvd., 850/233-4606), which has something like 25,000 suits to try on. If you feel the need for more extensive browsing, the **Shoppes at Edgewater** (4412 Delwood Ln., Panama City Beach, 850/234-6112) complex has a number of nice shops. Also, the Edgewater Movie Theater and Rock-It Lanes Family Entertainment Center are adjacent to the shopping center. **Panama City Mall** (at the intersection of U.S. 231, Hwy. 77, and 23rd St., 850/785-9587) is a standard enclosed mall anchored by Dillard's, JCPenney, and Sears, with stores like American Eagle Outfitters, Victoria's Secret, Kirkland's, Bath & Body Works, The Gap, and Express.

## Spas

The spa industry makes up the fourth-largest leisure industry in the United States, something Panama City Beach has jumped on with a vengeance in recent years. The toniest might be the 12,025-square-foot **Serenity at Bay Point** (850/236-6028, www.serenityat-baypoint.com), but there's also the **Spa at Majestic Beach Resort** (866/494-3364), and the **Spa at the Edgewater Beach and Golf Resort** (800/874-8686).

# ACCOMMODATIONS

It seems that all of Panama City Beach has been under construction in the past few years, with condos, resorts, hotels, town homes, and villas transforming the destination. Panama City Beach has recently completed over 30 resort and condominium projects, many big high-rises set right against the beach. Inventory has grown to an all-time high of more than 30,000 rooms. Due to the surplus of rooms in the off-season during the fall and winter months, you can find some of the best deals on the Gulf Coast right here in Panama City Beach.

## Under $50

The **Sandpiper Beacon** (17403 Front Beach Rd., 850/234-2154, $39–100) is a comfortable, family-friendly place with lots of on-site amenities for the price. It has 1,000 feet of beachfront, with parasailing, personal watercraft, and the Big Banana Ride right out the back door. There are three pools (one indoor), a lazy river ride, and twin turbo water slides, a game room, restaurant, children's playground, gift shop, and tiki bar. There are family units, with some suites sleeping up to 10 people.

**Super 8 Panama City Beach** (11004 Front Beach Rd., 850/234-7334, $39–80) is another no-frills beachside home base. It has clean rooms and very basic amenities, but get this: During March and April a deposit of $200 is required, and you have to wear *wristbands* to prove you're actually staying here and aren't just crashing the joint.

## $50-150

**Chateau Motel** (12525 Front Beach Rd., 888/84-BEACH, $119–189) is a favorite among young people, with 150 Gulf-view rooms 500 feet from the sand. It's right at the center of all the Miracle Strip excitement, with restaurants, attractions, shopping, and nightlife within walking distance. If you're under 25, they make you pay an extra $100 deposit until you pass checkout inspection.

**Days Inn Beach Hotel** (12818 Front Beach Rd., 850/233-3333, $161–179) is hopping, with 188 Gulf-front rooms and suites with private balconies. Room decor is tropical and breezy, but you'll spend most of your time outside at the seven-story volcano mountain waterfall. It's in the huge pool situated between the Days Inn and Ramada Limited. It's a scene out there, with athletic young people sipping tropical drinks and flirting shamelessly in the whirlpool.

## Over $150

Brand new and very upscale, **☾ Grand Panama Beach Resort** (11800 and 11807 Front Beach Rd., 866/621-8862, www.sterlingresorts.com, $149 and up) is a 35-acre resort cuddled against a 240-foot stretch of beach, the property featuring 299 units spread out over two beachfront towers, two pools and spas, a fitness center and two tiki bars, plus a playground, game room, and a jogging/bicycle path around the perimeter of the property. Besides its own on-site concert venue, the resort is also home to the Village of Grand Panama, a 55,000-square-foot retail center with an array of shops, services, and restaurants, including a spa and salon, a wine shop, and several clothing boutiques. Additionally, the property offers guests free high-speed Internet access, including Wi-Fi in designated outdoor and poolside areas. Guests staying at Grand Panama Beach Resort are granted exclusive access to the Sterling Club at Bay Point, featuring northwest Florida's only Nicklaus-designed golf course, the new Serenity Spa at Bay Point, tennis, dining, and a water-sports marina.

**Edgewater Beach Resort** (11212 Front

Beach Rd., 800/874-8686, $81–516) is worth the splurge, really Panama City Beach's premier resort, and very family-friendly. It had a fairly recent $21 million restoration project, which brought new luster to the 110-acre property. It's a great location on the beach, right across the street from Cinema 10 Theaters, Rock-It Lanes, miniature golf, and Shoppes at Edgewater. On-site there are two restaurants, two bars, 11 heated outdoor pools, an executive nine-hole golf course, and the 27-hole Hombre Golf Club championship course just minutes away. The rooms themselves are spread throughout a vast property, from the Gulf Front Towers to the Golf and Tennis Villas to the Windward and Leeward Suites.

Another excellent place, a bit removed from the fray, is the relatively new **Marriott's Legends Edge at Bay Point** (4000 Marriott Dr., 850/236-6000, $280–419). Each villa has a fully equipped kitchen, spacious living and dining areas, and well-appointed bedrooms. It's adjacent to the Marriott Bay Point Resort Village and situated in the midst of the Club Meadows and Lagoons Legends golf courses (designed by Bob von Hagge and Bruce Devlin in 1985, and a notoriously challenging course). The Gulf of Mexico is 10 minutes away and the Grand Lagoon of St. Andrews Bay is within walking distance.

## FOOD

In PCB you mostly get fried seafood, wings, pizza, and burgers—the sort of food you would expect from a location mostly supported by college students. Yet there are some great restaurants for all tastes. One option is to keep it simple, heading for familiar offerings like **Bonefish Grill, Carrabba's Italian Grill,** or **Ruth's Chris Steakhouse.** For a great cheeseburger, go to **Flamingo Joe's** (2304 Thomas Dr., Panama City Beach, 850/233-0600, 11 A.M.–9 P.M. daily, $8–15). It also has an addictive salsa, served warm. **Sharky's Seafood** (15201 Front Beach Rd., 850/235-2420,

11 A.M.–10 P.M. daily, $15–27) is a longstanding favorite for a good sunset, fine live entertainment in the world's largest tiki hut, and seafood-centric food.

**The Boat Yard** (5323 N. Lagoon Dr., 850/249-9273, 11 A.M.–11 P.M. daily, later on the weekend if things are hopping, $10–26) has a similar open-air feel on the docks of Grand Lagoon, with gigantic margaritas, conch fritters with hot pepper jelly and wasabi mayo, or crispy fried lobster sandwiches, and a really tasty dessert invention of creamy key lime pie dipped in dark chocolate and frozen on a stick. **J' Michaels** (3210 Thomas Dr., 850/233-2055, 11:30 A.M.–9:30 P.M. daily, $8–15) is dockside of Grand Lagoon and is the place to go for comfort food like red beans and rice.

You want to take it a little more upscale? **Angelo's Steak Pit** (9527 Front Beach Rd., 850/234-2351, 5–10 P.M. daily, closed in the winter, $14–26) always gets the nod for fat steaks grilled over aromatic hickory. It's been here since 1958 and the resident Big Gus 20,000-pound steer is practically a local celebrity.

**Captain Anderson's Restaurant** (5551 N. Lagoon Dr., 850/234-2225, 4:30–10 P.M. Mon.–Fri., open at 4 P.M. Sat., $12–35) is another serious locals' establishment, focusing on seafood. It's a waterfront favorite that's been here for years—go for the heads-on shrimp or the open-hearth whole fish.

And then, for when you really want to do something zany, maybe with the kids, maybe just because, take your appetite to **The Treasure Ship** (3605 Thomas Dr., 850/234-8881, main dining room 4–10 P.M. daily, $15–28), a full-scale replica of Sir Francis Drake's *Golden Hind,* permanently docked. Now who said this trip wasn't going to be educational? You can eat seafood, book a charter fishing boat (its online page of options is helpful, www.thetreasureship.com), or just browse through the fun pictures of people in pirate costumes.

# Information and Services

The Emerald Coast area is located within the **Central time zone.** The area code is **850.**

## TOURIST INFORMATION

The Panama City **News Herald** is the daily around here, but its parent company, Florida Freedom Newspapers, also operates the **Northwest Florida Daily News, The Destin Log, The Walton Sun,** and www.emeraldcoast.com.

To get tourist information, there are several different locations, depending on where your home base is. For Destin and Fort Walton Beach information, visit the **Emerald Coast Convention and Visitors Bureau** (1540 E. U.S. 98, Fort Walton Beach, 850/651-7131, www.destin-fwb.com). There's also the **South Walton Tourist Development Center** (25771 U.S. 331 at U.S. 98, on Santa Rosa Beach, 850/267-3511, 8 A.M.–5 P.M. daily) and the **Destin Area Chamber of Commerce** (4484 Legendary Dr. at U.S. 98, 850/837-6241, 8:30 A.M.–5 P.M. Tues.–Fri.).

For information about the Beaches of South Walton area in advance of your trip, contact the **Beaches of South Walton Tourist Development Council** (P.O. Box 1248, Santa Rosa Beach, FL 32459, 800/822-6877, www.beachesofsouthwalton.com).

In Panama City Beach, visit the **Panama City Beach Convention & Visitors Bureau** (17001 Panama City Beach Pkwy., 850/233-5070, www.thebeachloversbeach.com, 8 A.M.–5 P.M. daily) for brochures, maps, and information about attractions and accommodations.

## POLICE AND EMERGENCIES

In an emergency, dial 911. For a non-emergency police need, call or visit the **Fort Walton Beach Police Department** (7 Hollywood Blvd., Fort Walton Beach, 850/833-9546) or the **Panama City Beach Police Department** (17110 Firenzo Ave., Panama City Beach, 850/233-5000).

In the event of a medical emergency, stop into **Sacred Heart Hospital Office** (7800 U.S. 98 W., Destin, 850/278-3000) in the western part of the Emerald Coast, or in the eastern part, go to **Bay Medical Center** (615 N. Bonita Ave., Panama City, 850/769-1511).

## RADIO AND TELEVISION

There's lots of music radio in this area, heavy on rock and pop for all those spring breakers. **Beach 99.9 FM** is oldies, **Pirate Radio 94.5 FM** is rock, **92.5 FM** has country, **Sunny 98.5 FM** is soft rock, and **93.5 FM** is alt rock.

And on the television, there are two local ABC affiliates, **WMBB Channel 13** out of Panama City and **WEAR Channel 3** out of Pensacola. The CBS affiliate is **WCTV Channel 6** out of Tallahassee, the PBS affiliate is **WFSG Channel 56** out of Panama City, and the NBC affiliate is **WJHG Channel 7** out of Panama City.

## LAUNDRY SERVICES

Laundry options are at their best in Panama City Beach. There's **Flamingo Beach Laundry** (7922 Front Beach Rd., 850/234-6186) or **EBR Laundry** (11309 Hutchinson Blvd., 850/233-5331).

# Getting There and Around

## BY CAR

Ground travel is easy around the Emerald Coast, along several primary feeders: U.S. 98, U.S. 331, Highway 85, and I-10. Fort Walton Beach, the hometown of Eglin Air Force Base, is 60 miles west of Panama City and 35 miles east of Pensacola. U.S. 98 travels east–west along the Emerald Coast, edging the Gulf through Destin and Fort Walton Beach. The beach of Fort Walton Beach is actually on Okaloosa Island, a barrier island at the southern end of Choctawhatchee Bay. Destin is about five miles east on U.S. 98 (sometimes called the Miracle Strip Parkway). To get to this area from the north, take U.S. 331 south, take Highway 85 south at the Alabama/Florida line, straight into Destin and Fort Walton Beach. From I-10, exit onto Highway 85 south at the Fort Walton Beach exit.

The Beaches of South Walton communities are about 35 miles west of Panama City Beach, along Highway 30A (also called Scenic 30A and Scenic Gulf Coast Drive). Highway 30A splits off from U.S. 98 just before Highway 393 in the west and right after Panama City Beach in the east.

Panama City Beach is on a barrier island. If you're visiting, note that Panama City Beach and Panama City are two separate cities and their names should not be used interchangeably. The Hathaway Bridge crosses St. Andrews Bay and connects the two of them. U.S. 98 splits at Panama City Beach and becomes U.S. 98 in the north (also called Panama City Beach Parkway) and U.S. 98A along the beach (also called Front Beach Road).

## BY AIR

The nearest airports to Destin and Fort Walton Beach are the **Northwest Florida Regional Airport** (1701 Hwy. 85 N., on Eglin Air Force Base, 850/651-7160), a small airport serviced by Delta Airlines, American Eagle, Northwest Airlines, US Air Express, and Continental, and the new **Northwest Florida Beaches International Airport** (850/763-6751), the first international airport built in the United States in a decade and served by Delta and Southwest Airlines. A 50-minute drive to the west, the **Pensacola Gulf Coast Regional Airport** (2430 Airport Blvd., Pensacola, 850/436-5000) is the biggest airport in northwest Florida. It's not huge, serving a moderate number of flights from Air Trans, American Eagle, Continental, Delta, Northwest, and US Airways. Delta has the largest number of direct flights.

Car-rental agencies are inside the main terminal entrance at Pensacola Regional Airport across from baggage claim. **Alamo** (800/327-9633), **Avis** (800/831-2847), **Budget** (800/527-0700), **Dollar** (800/800-4000 domestic, 800/800-6000 international), **Hertz** (800/654-3131), and **National** (800/227-7368) are all on the premises. Enterprise and Thrifty are off-site.

## BY BUS AND TRAIN

The **Amtrak** (800/USA-RAIL) Sunset Limited service was not operating in this area of this writing, due to damage Hurricane Katrina caused to the tracks in New Orleans. You need wheels to get around locally. **Greyhound** (800/231-2222) has a bus station in Panama City (917 Harrison Ave., 850/785-6111), but public transportation won't get you to most places along the Emerald Coast, unless you're just hanging out on the beach in Panama City Beach.

# PENSACOLA

A culturally rich city, Pensacola has seen five flags—Spain, France, England, America, and the Confederacy—flown proudly at different historic moments in the past four centuries. The area is more widely known as a summer vacation destination—a picture-perfect beach retreat with deep turquoise waters and fine, white sand. It is also the site of numerous important forts as well as the Naval Air Station Pensacola, the launching point for the flight training of every American naval aviator, naval flight officer, and enlisted aircrew. It is home to the Blue Angels and the phenomenal, not-to-be-missed National Museum of Naval Aviation located on the Naval Air Station.

The city and the popular beach that sits on the barrier island of Santa Rosa are both much more casual than most areas along the Gulf Coast. It has plenty of upscale resorts and restaurants, but they seem to find a common thread with a laid-back, informal style that leaves pretentiousness behind and has managed to retain much of the old Florida charm that has been lost in many of the cities and beaches to the south. Pensacola is infinitely more Southern in manner than most of the areas to the south—well, maybe with the exception of Everglades City. In Pensacola you will find the hospitality that you often associate with the South and food that is a unique blend of flavors inspired by a convergence of coastal American, Spanish, and Cajun cultures. You're just as likely to find menus offering deep fried mullet with cole slaw, hush puppies and a tall glass of sweet tea as you are grilled grouper with a mango sauce served

PENSACOLA

# HIGHLIGHTS

**◖ Pensacola Beach Fishing Pier:** The pier, longest on the Gulf of Mexico, is really at the heart of festive, action-packed Pensacola Beach. You don't need a fishing license to wet a line (page 308).

**◖ Gulf Islands National Seashore:** Hurricane Ivan did its darnedest to erase this 150-mile-long string of undeveloped barrier islands back in 2004, but the windswept dunes still stand. The protected area has miles of delicate beach habitat along Santa Rosa Island, as well as Fort Pickens and other historic sights (page 308).

**◖ Historic Pensacola Village:** Stop off for sustenance at the Seville Quarter's Rosie O'Grady's before heading on to the cluster of 18th- and 19th-century museums and homes that constitute the Historic Pensacola Village (page 312).

**◖ National Museum of Naval Aviation:** Find out why Pensacola is called the Cradle of Naval Aviation at this vast and spectacular aviation museum on the grounds of the Naval Air Station Pensacola (page 314).

**◖ Sam's Fun City:** At the center of Sam's Fun City is Surf City Water Park. There are enough water slides, wave pools, and water sprayers to keep the whole family cool in the steamy Pensacola heat (page 317).

LOOK FOR ◖ TO FIND RECOMMENDED SIGHTS, ACTIVITIES, DINING, AND LODGING.

with a side of black beans and rice or a bowl of spicy New Orleans gumbo with a tray of raw oysters.

Pensacola has a long history. Native Americans left pottery shards and artifacts in the gentle coastal dunes here centuries before Tristán de Luna arrived with his fellow Spaniards in 1559. Tristán de Luna was the first to attempt a settlement in Pensacola, but violent hurricanes uprooted his attempts and sent the Spanish sailing south to St. Augustine, where they established North America's first European settlement. Even after this first exploratory settlement didn't take, Pensacola was settled by white Europeans very early on. It was one of a handful of Colonial period communities in the southeastern United States, its Seville Historic District one of the oldest and most intact in all of Florida. Within this small neighborhood is Old Christ Church, Florida's oldest church still standing in one place (1832), and St. Michael's Cemetery, deeded to Pensacola by the king of Spain in 1822. A walk through Historic Pensacola Village will give you insight into the area's history.

Pensacola has a strong military presence with Naval Air Station Pensacola and nearby Eglin Air Force Base; it is often called the Cradle of Naval Aviation. The free National Museum of Naval Aviation, the third largest in the world,

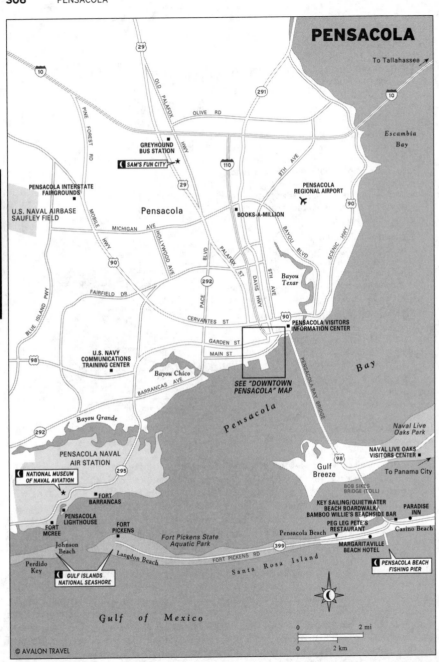

PENSACOLA

# PENSACOLA

To Tallahassee

Escambia Bay

OLIVE RD

GREYHOUND BUS STATION

SAM'S FUN CITY

PENSACOLA INTERSTATE FAIRGROUNDS

U.S. NAVAL AIRBASE SAUFLEY FIELD

Pensacola

PINE FOREST RD

MOBILE HWY

OLD PALAFOX HWY

HOLLYWOOD AVE

MICHIGAN AVE

BLUE ISLAND PKWY

PENSACOLA REGIONAL AIRPORT

BOOKS-A-MILLION

PALAFOX ST

DAVIS HWY

9TH AVE

BAYOU BLVD

SCENIC HWY

Bayou Texar

FAIRFIELD DR

PACE BLVD

CERVANTES ST

PENSACOLA VISITORS INFORMATION CENTER

GARDEN ST

MAIN ST

SEE "DOWNTOWN PENSACOLA" MAP

U.S. NAVY COMMUNICATIONS TRAINING CENTER

Bayou Chico

BARRANCAS AVE

Bayou Grande

Pensacola Bay

PENSACOLA BAY BRIDGE

Naval Live Oaks Park

NAVAL LIVE OAKS VISITORS CENTER

To Panama City

PENSACOLA NAVAL AIR STATION

NATIONAL MUSEUM OF NAVAL AVIATION

FORT BARRANCAS

PENSACOLA LIGHTHOUSE

FORT McREE

FORT PICKENS

Gulf Breeze

BOB SIKES BRIDGE (TOLL)

KEY SAILING/QUIETWATER BEACH BOARDWALK/ BAMBOO WILLIE'S BEACHSIDE BAR

PEG LEG PETE'S RESTAURANT

PARADISE INN

Casino Beach

Pensacola Beach

MARGARITAVILLE BEACH HOTEL

PENSACOLA BEACH FISHING PIER

Johnson Beach

Perdido Key

GULF ISLANDS NATIONAL SEASHORE

Fort Pickens State Aquatic Park

Langdon Beach

FORT PICKENS RD

Santa Rosa Island

Gulf of Mexico

0       2 mi

0       2 km

© AVALON TRAVEL

showcases the history of aviation through indoor and outdoor exhibits.

And then there are the beaches. Some are developed, fun, tourist beaches such as Pensacola Beach; others are more uninhabited. The Gulf Islands National Seashore cuts through this area, a 150-mile-long, discontinuous string of undeveloped barrier islands that begins at Santa Rosa Island and extends into Mississippi. Santa Rosa Island contains seven beautiful, undeveloped miles of beach, with clear water, white sandy beaches, lots of fish and wildlife, and fewer people crowding the pristine shores.

## HURRICANES

Pensacola's location on the Panhandle makes it particularly vulnerable to hurricanes. Many storms over the years have made landfall here—a number during years before storms were named, and then Hurricane Juan in 1985, the devastating Hurricane Opal in 1995, and Hurricane Ivan on September 16, 2004. It made landfall as a Category III hurricane, wreaking particular havoc around Perdido Bay and Pensacola Beach. The area's bridges and roads sustained major damage, and locals say 99 percent of the buildings in the area were damaged, with a staggering 40 percent utterly destroyed or catastrophically damaged by the 130-mph winds and 10- to 12-foot storm surge.

It's all back up to speed these days, although some road restoration in natural areas was complicated by the fact that it's a habitat for endangered species—all work must be approved by the Fish and Wildlife Service and other government bodies.

Ivan the Terrible did its darnedest (causing an estimated $13 billion worth of damage, it's the fifth costliest hurricane to ever strike the United States), but bed tax dollars have gone back to fund tourist interests in the area, and today few vestiges of the storm's wrath are apparent.

## PLANNING YOUR TIME

As on most of the Panhandle, high season is April–August. The value season runs roughly August–March. Regardless of when you'd like to visit, make reservations in advance. Visitors at the naval base tend to fill the hotels nearest it. The greater Pensacola area can occupy you for a couple of days with its historical attractions, beaches, and nature parks. If you fly into Pensacola and rent a car, think about tacking on a couple of extra days to explore the Emerald Coast area just to the east.

# Sports and Recreation

## BEACHES

There are wonderful beaches here, all of which took a beating from Hurricane Ivan in 2004 and have rebounded at different speeds. The long stretch of the **Gulf Islands National Seashore** and the **Naval Air Station Pensacola** and **Eglin Air Force Base** farther east have imposed restrictions on commercial growth. The communities in the area set quotas on density and height restrictions on new construction. Thus, the more urban beachfront areas around Pensacola aren't littered with high-rise condos and resort hotels, and there's another six miles of utterly preserved seashore in the park. Still, the area had been recovering from Hurricane Opal for nine years when it got walloped, in nearly identical ways, by Hurricane Ivan in 2004.

**Perdido Key** is the westernmost island in the long chain of barrier islands that line the Panhandle's edge, an island that Florida shares with the state of Alabama. The developed beach areas are called **Orange Beach** and **Johnson Beach** and the more natural part is **Perdido Key State Park** (15301 Perdido Key Dr., 15 miles southwest of Pensacola, off Hwy. 292, 850/492-1592, 8 A.M.–sundown daily, $3 honor system for beach, $4 for main park). The latter is open to the public, all the buildings, nature trails,

PENSACOLA

beach crossovers, and roadbeds restored since Ivan. These beaches provide some of the best swimming in the state—warm, clear water, gentle surf, long stretches of shallows. Big Lagoon State Park is located just across the bay from Perdido Key and offers tent, camp trailer, and RV sites. Then take a short drive up the road and hike the nature trails at Tarkiln Bayou Preserve State Park.

**Santa Rosa Island,** just to the east, is one of the longest barrier islands in the world, stretching 50 miles from Pensacola Bay on its western side to Choctawhatchee Bay to its east. The beaches here are all fine, white quartz sand.

### ( Pensacola Beach Fishing Pier

**Pensacola Beach** (Pensacola Beach Visitor Information Center, 800/635-4803) itself covers much of the island, with restaurants, shops, and entertainment at their highest density near the Pensacola Beach Fishing Pier—at 1,471 feet long and 30 feet above the water, the longest on the Gulf of Mexico. Crossing the two bridges from Pensacola to Santa Rosa Island, you'll be on Pensacola Boulevard—it splits left and right, but directly in front of you is Pensacola Beach. The area is rich with water-sport possibilities: parasailing, sailboarding, deep-sea fishing, Jet Skiing, and scuba diving. Pensacola Beach is open to the public, accessible by car or by ECAT bus or trolley. The fishing pier is open to the public 24 hours a day and costs $1 to walk on, $7.50 for adults to fish, children under six are free; you're likely to catch flounder, bonita, Spanish and king mackerel, and cobia. From its end you're likely to spot dolphins, sea turtles, and the occasional manatee.

At the corner of Pensacola Boulevard and Fort Pickens Road, which goes to the west, is **Casino Beach.** It is the heart of Pensacola Beach, named for an old beachside casino resort from 1933. The casino is long gone, but its beach ball water tank is still the beach's landmark. Casino Beach is home to the huge brick Gulfside Pavilion, site of numerous free concerts and events over the years. The beach has picnic tables, restrooms, restaurants, and

---

### FAST TIMES

Addicted to speed? Pensacola has a couple of ways to scratch that itch. **Five Flags Speedway** (7451 Pine Forest Rd., on Hwy. 297 a mile south of Exit 2 on I-10, 850/944-8400, www.fiveflagsspeedway.com, dates and times vary, $10-20) was built in 1956, one of the oldest established short track races still in existence. A high-banked asphalt oval, it is the fastest half-mile track in the country and home to the annual Snowball Derby (usually the first few days of December). The Snowball Derby is widely recognized as the country's premier short track Super Late Model event. The rest of the season features racing of different kinds, from the fire-breathing, fuel-injected, winged sprint cars of the United Sprint Car Series, to the Bombers, Spectators, Super Stocks, Vintage, and Pro Late Models. The track has attracted top drivers like Carl Yarborough and Rusty Wallace, and fans from all over.

**Pensacola Greyhound Track** (951 Dog Track Rd., off U.S. 98, 850/455-8595, www.pensacolagreyhoundpark.com, 7 P.M. Fri. and Sat., 1 P.M.Sat. and Sun., free admission) offers the thrill of high-speed greyhound racing and the equally thrilling attendant betting. You can watch the races from an air-conditioned restaurant/lounge called the Kennel Club or railside seats. The facility also has live and instant replay televisions throughout the complex.

---

souvenir shops. And just past the tollbooth onto the island, **Quietwater Beach,** on the Santa Rosa Sound side, is a gentle, shallow beach great for kids.

### ( Gulf Islands National Seashore

The Gulf Islands National Seashore (800/934-2600, $8 for a seven-day pass) has numerous beaches along Santa Rosa Island. At its westernmost edge is **Fort Pickens Park,** maintained by the National Park Service. Fort Pickens Road was breached by Ivan and then whomped the

Pensacola Beach Fishing Pier

next year by Dennis, but it recently reopened to the public. The road is located in a sensitive habitat for nesting sea turtles and colonial shorebirds, so be sure not to park along the sandy road shoulder. This will also help you avoid getting your vehicle stuck and keep you from getting a park ranger–administered ticket.

Historic Fort Pickens is open for self-guided tours during daylight hours only. The fishing pier is open, and Fort Pickens campground Loop A is open to primitive camping on a first-come, first-served basis for $10 per night. Campers have access to running water, grills, picnic tables, and bathrooms with cold showers. Boaters planning to camp can unload their passengers and gear near Battery Langdon, located on the bay side of the island and west of the Ranger Station dock, and hike on the bike path or Fort Pickens Road to Loop A.

The J. Earle Bowden Way (Hwy. 399) on Santa Rosa Island connects Pensacola Beach with Navarre Beach. This road was also damaged by the two recent hurricanes but is now open again.

Really within the Fort Pickens area is another beach called **Langdon Beach,** which has picnic tables, restrooms, and outdoor showers. The scenic bike path, going from Langdon Beach all the way to the fort, has been restored, as have the Dune Nature Trail and the Blackbird Marsh Nature Trail.

Also part of Gulf Islands National Seashore, **Opal Beach** is three miles east of Pensacola Beach. It is generally less populated than Pensacola Beach, offering restrooms, showers, and picnic pavilions, a great stop for hikers and bikers taking in the beautiful dune landscape between Pensacola Beach and Navarre Beach on the Seashore Trail or the South Santa Rosa Loop Trail. The Opal Beach area can also be reached by motorists via Hwy. 399, which runs parallel to the multiuse trail through the National Seashore. From Pensacola Beach, drive east toward Navarre Beach on Hwy. 399. Opal Beach will be on the Gulf side (right). From Navarre Beach, drive west toward Pensacola Beach on Hwy. 399. Opal Beach will on the Gulf side (left).

## Navarre Beach

Navarre Beach is the easternmost beach on Santa Rosa Island. It's a family-friendly beach, with bathrooms, picnic facilities, and a fishing pier. The Navarre Beach State Park is 130 acres of beach, wetlands, and scrub, a third of which is set aside for nondevelopment in perpetuity. After lolling on the beach, multiuse Seashore Bicycle Trail will carry you alongside dunes, forests, and the Gulf for a nice array of picturesque scenery.

## FISHING

The area's had some losses, but also some gains. The Three Mile Bridge over Pensacola Bay has in recent years carried traffic alongside the long-abandoned U.S. 98 bridge. The bridge, prior to Hurricane Ivan, was used by local anglers as their huge personal fishing pier. Now much of that pier lies on the bottom of Pensacola Bay. The fishing, however, has taken a huge upswing. The decommissioned aircraft carrier **USS Oriskany** was sunk as an artificial reef in the Gulf of Mexico 22.5 miles southeast of Pensacola Pass in May 2006. The navy committed $2.8 million for its preparation and deployment as a reef, the first time a ship of this size had been sunk for this purpose. The decommissioned Mighty O (32,000 tons and 911 feet), which saw action in Korea and Vietnam, sits in 212 feet of water. The *Oriskany* is the first Navy ship cleaned following the EPA's 2004 policies ensuring artificial reefs are environmentally safe.

Fisherfolk have already started to flock in greater numbers to the greater Pensacola area. A 2006 NOAA study predicts the reefed *Oriskany* will add an additional $9 million annually to the local economy. Even more enthusiastic than the anglers, though, are the divers. Divers can reach the top of the *Oriskany's* superstructure or "island" at 60 feet, while its flight deck sits in 130 feet of water, below the depth of recreational divers but well within reach of specialty divers trained in deep-water diving. With year-round warm water temperatures (mid-80s in summer and mid-60s in winter) and visibility of 60–100 feet, it's tempting to divers.

Not surprising, then, the first underwater wedding took place here. Crystal and Cooper Labenske literally took the plunge here in May 2006. Pensacola Dive Company owner Captain Ron Beermünder officiated the underwater "I Dos."

# Sights

Downtown Pensacola is awash in historical attractions, many of them clustered in one of several historic districts.

## SEVILLE SQUARE

The survivors of an early, thwarted attempt to settle Santa Rosa Island hightailed it to more solid ground and established a permanent settlement in 1752. After the French and Indian War of 1763, the British took west Florida and occupied the area, laying out a clean grid of houses. The Spanish, upon capturing Pensacola after that, kept the old town square intact but renamed the streets to reflect the new Spanish presence. So about 20 blocks of historic 18th-century to 19th-century residential and business streets have Spanish names. It's a beautiful area with a mixture of Victorian, Spanish-, and French-influenced Gulf Coast–style cottages (these are often 1.5-story houses with steeply pitched gabled roofs and a deep front porch) centered on shady Seville Square Park.

The Seville Historic District makes for a wonderful afternoon of walking. First, I encourage a stop at **Seville Quarter** (130 E. Government St., 850/434-6211, 11 A.M.–3 A.M., late night menus until 1 A.M., $10–25) for live music, food, or a few cold drinks. Within this historic complex, down an east alleyway, stop into **Rosie O'Grady's** for some Dixieland jazz dueling pianos, a

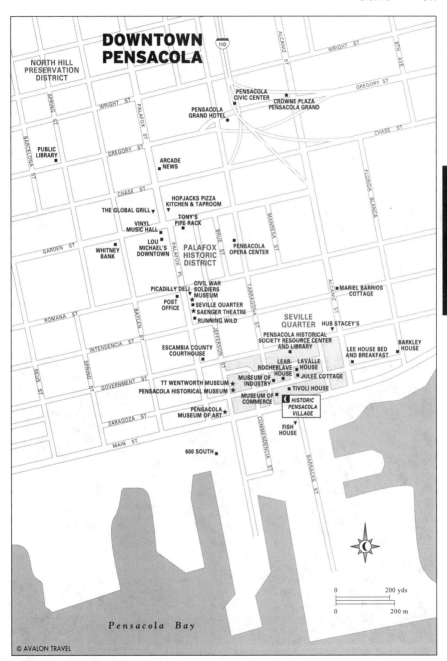

# DOWNTOWN PENSACOLA

NORTH HILL PRESERVATION DISTRICT

PENSACOLA CIVIC CENTER

CROWNE PLAZA PENSACOLA GRAND

PENSACOLA GRAND HOTEL

PUBLIC LIBRARY

ARCADE NEWS

HOPJACKS PIZZA KITCHEN & TAPROOM

THE GLOBAL GRILL

VINYL MUSIC HALL

TONY'S PIPE RACK

LOU MICHAEL'S DOWNTOWN

PALAFOX HISTORIC DISTRICT

PENSACOLA OPERA CENTER

WHITNEY BANK

CIVIL WAR SOLDIERS MUSEUM

MARIEL BARRIOS COTTAGE

PICADILLY DELI

POST OFFICE

SEVILLE QUARTER

SAENGER THEATRE

RUNNING WILD

SEVILLE QUARTER

HUB STACEY'S

PENSACOLA HISTORICAL SOCIETY RESOURCE CENTER AND LIBRARY

ESCAMBIA COUNTY COURTHOUSE

LEE HOUSE BED AND BREAKFAST

BARKLEY HOUSE

LEAR- ROCHEBLAVE HOUSE

LAVALLE HOUSE

JULEE COTTAGE

TT WENTWORTH MUSEUM

MUSEUM OF INDUSTRY

PENSACOLA HISTORICAL MUSEUM

TIVOLI HOUSE

MUSEUM OF COMMERCE

HISTORIC PENSACOLA VILLAGE

PENSACOLA MUSEUM OF ART

FISH HOUSE

600 SOUTH

0      200 yds

0      200 m

PENSACOLA

*Pensacola Bay*

© AVALON TRAVEL

Flaming Hurricane, and the historic setting—it was built in 1871 as the Pensacola Cigar and Tobacco Company. Directly across from Rosie O'Grady's is the entrance to **Lili Marlene's World War I Aviators Pub,** once the Pensacola Printing Co., which for a long time was the oldest print shop in continuous operation in the country, and the original home of the *Pensacola News Journal.* Beyond these, there are several other themed rooms in this entertainment and dining complex, outfitted with period antiques. The complex also has two inviting courtyards and a gift shop.

## ( Historic Pensacola Village

Also part of the Seville historic district, Historic Pensacola Village (850/595-5985, 10 A.M.–4 P.M. Tues.–Sat., $6 adults, $5 seniors and active military, $3 for children 4–16, free for children 3 and under) is bounded by Government, Taragona, Adams, and Alcanz streets. The village consists of 20 properties in the Pensacola National Register Historic District. Ten of these properties

are interpretive facilities open to the public: the Museum of Commerce, Museum of Industry, Julee Cottage, Lavalle House, Lear House, Dorr House, Old Christ Church, Weaver's Cottage, Tivoli House, and Colonial Archaeological trail. Do them all if you've got the stamina—the guided house tour is the way to go. House tours are included in admission price and leave from the Tivoli House at 11 A.M., 1 P.M., and 2:30 P.M.

**T. T. Wentworth Jr. Florida State Museum** (Plaza Ferdinand, free admission) is an elaborate Renaissance Revival building that houses rotating exhibits on west Florida's history, architecture, and archaeology (kids will go more willingly if you tell them there's also a shrunken head on display). The **Museum of Commerce** (201 E. Zaragoza St.) is a brick turn-of-the-20th-century warehouse containing a reconstructed 1890s-era streetscape with a toy store; leather, hardware, music, and print shops; and horse-drawn buggies. The **Museum of Industry** (200 E. Zaragoza St.) houses an exhibit depicting several important 19th-century industries in west

Take a shaded stroll through Seville Square in historic downtown Pensacola.

Florida: fishing, brick-making, railroad, and lumber. It was the most recent to reopen, featuring a variety of interactive displays teaching visitors about the area's natural resources and early industry.

The historic homes in the village include the **Lavalle House** (205 E. Church St.), an example of French Creole colonial architecture; the **Dorr House** (311 S. Adams St.), Greek Revival architecture furnished with fine antiques; and the **Lear-Rocheblave House** (214 E. Zaragoza St.), a two-story folk Victorian home with several furnished rooms. The **Barkley House** (410 S. Florida Blanca St.) is one of the oldest masonry houses in Florida, and the **Mariel Barrios Cottage** (204 S. Alcaniz St.) is owned and operated by the Pensacola Historic Preservation Society and exhibits household items and furnishings from Pensacola during the 1920s. The **Julee Cottage** (210 E. Zaragoza St.) is a museum classroom once owned by Julee Panton, a free African American woman. The **Tivoli House** (205 E. Zaragoza St.) is a reconstructed version of an 1805 boarding and gaming house and now houses the Historic Pensacola Village gift shop and ticket office.

After touring the homes, pick up the brochure for the **Colonial Archaeological Trail,** which was produced by the Archaeology Institute at the University of West Florida; it leads you through the ruins of the colonial commanding officer's house, the foundations of the officer-of-the-day's building, and the remains of what might have been a trader's home and warehouse just outside the western gate of the British fort built during the American Revolution.

Also, the **Pensacola Historical Museum** (115 E. Zaragoza St., 850/433-1559, 10 A.M.–4 P.M. Tues.–Sat., free) is in the midst of the historic village, operated by the Pensacola Historical Society. It offers changing exhibits every year on topics of local history (currently that includes the Hotel San Carlos, Pensacola commemorative glass, sailors, snapper fishing, yellow fever, the West Florida Regional Library, and slaves at Fort Pickens). It also sponsors a deliciously eerie

haunted house tour in October—see it if you can time your visit right.

## PALAFOX HISTORIC DISTRICT

Palafox Historic District is another historic area downtown, contiguous with Seville Square, only just to the west of it. It runs up Palafox Street from Pensacola Bay in the south to about Wright Street in the north. Again, it's an area of beautiful homes and historic buildings with wide brick sidewalks. It's really the commercial heart of Pensacola, and it houses a couple of the area's big cultural draws.

The **Pensacola Museum of Art** (407 S. Jefferson St., 850/432-6247, 10 A.M.–5 P.M. Tues.–Fri., noon–5 P.M. Sat. and Sun., $5 adults, $2 students and active military, free admission on Tues.) is right at its center, with a wonderful space and intriguingly diverse visiting exhibits. They range from the realistic sculptures of Duane Hanson to 20th-century Japanese printmaking. The permanent collection has minor works, most on paper, by some heavy hitters (largely 20th century) as well as lots of fine decorative glass. The museum is housed in what was the city jail 1906–1954, so there are sturdy bars on the windows.

Just around the corner you will find the **Vinyl Music Hall** (2 S. Palafoc Place, www.vinylmusichall.com, tickets $15–50) the newest music and entertainment venue in town. What was once a historic Mason Lodge has been restored and remodeled into a hip music venue and bar. The intimate general admission venue is standing room only and is starting to draw large national acts mainly in the blues and rock genres like Dr. John and the Blues Travelers, but it mostly features national and regional alternative rock artists.

## NORTH HILL PRESERVATION DISTRICT

Before you tire of all this history, another worthy walk is the North Hill Preservation District, which occupies 50 city blocks due north of the Palafox District, away from the water, bounded on the west by Reus and on the east by Palafox. On the National Register of Historic Places, the neighborhood is pretty much residential, with great examples of fully restored historic homes. You can't go inside unless you make friends, but some of the current owners are descendants of the original builders—Spanish nobility, lumber barons, French Creoles, and Civil War soldiers.

## NAVAL AIR STATION PENSACOLA

Pensacola is known as the Cradle of Naval Aviation, a bold claim that can be authenticated through an exploration of one of the many sites open to the public at the Naval Air Station Pensacola and environs. To reach the historic mainland forts and the National Museum of Naval Aviation from the north, take Exit 7 off I-10 (Pine Forest Rd., Hwy. 297), go about 1.5 miles, and take a right onto Blue Angel Parkway. Then drive 12 miles to the west gate of the Naval Air Station. (Visitors without military stickers can *depart* only from the main entrance on Navy Boulevard.)

## ◖ National Museum of Naval Aviation

If you're only going to devote time to one historic attraction in the greater Pensacola area, the National Museum of Naval Aviation (1750 Radford Blvd., NAS Pensacola, 850/452-3604, 9 A.M.–5 P.M. daily, free admission) is it. It's one of the largest air and space museums in the world, with 160 restored aircrafts representing Navy, Marine Corps, and Coast Guard aviation. There's a seven-story, glass-and-steel atrium in which four A-4 Skyhawks are suspended in formation. You can stand on the flight deck of the USS *Cabot* and fly an F/A-18 mission in Desert Storm in a motion-based flight simulator. There's an IMAX theater (it costs $6.50) with a film called *The Magic of Flight.* Or, if you want to see real-life flying, watch the **Blue Angels,** based in Pensacola, practice in an area adjacent to the museum. Practices are held most Tuesday and Wednesday mornings at 8:30 A.M., weather permitting. Follow the signs to visitor viewing and parking.

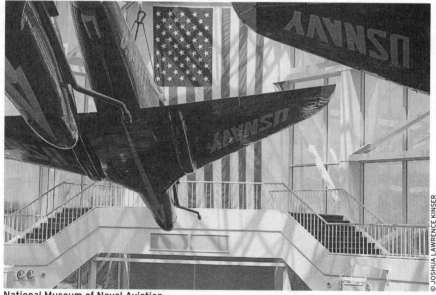

National Museum of Naval Aviation

© JOSHUA LAWRENCE KINSER

PENSACOLA

# BLUE ANGELS

Watching them reveals just how much slower sound waves are than light waves. You look up to see a tight diamond formation of blue streaking past in the sky, the combined engine noise trailing behind like a memory. The Blue Angels, at their fastest, fly about 700 mph in an air show, in a maneuver called a sneak pass, and at their slowest, 120 mph for a move called a Section High Alpha. They fly as high as 15,000 feet for vertical rolls, and as low as 50 feet from the ground during that sneak pass.

At the end of World War II, Chief of Naval Operations Admiral Chester W. Nimitz ordered the formation of a flight demonstration team to showcase the glories of Navy and Marine Corps aviation. The team was assembled and put to work, performing its first flight demonstration less than a year later. Since its inception, the team has flown for more than 400 million fans – an estimated 15 million each year. The Blue Angels flew 68 air shows at 35 air sites in the United States during the 2010 season, as the team celebrated their 23rd year of flying the F/A-18 Hornet.

The Naval Air Station Pensacola is the proud home of the Blue Angels, providing training and winter practice space for the team of talented active-duty Navy or Marine Corps tactical jet pilots. Since the Blue Angels' inception, there have been over 200 demonstration pilots, each with a minimum of 1,350 flight hours under their belts at the outset, with another 120 training flights required during winter training in order to perform a public demonstration safely. In the beginning they flew Grumman F6F Hellcats but have transitioned over the years through eight types of aircrafts – since 1986 it has been the Boeing F/A-18 Hornet (which can actually fly at speeds of about 1,400 mph, which is almost twice the speed of sound).

This type of high-speed, low-altitude flying in tight formation is not without risks – in December 2004 one of the F/A-18s crashed into the Gulf of Mexico in the shallows off Perdido Key. Miraculously, the pilot ejected safely, a little bruised but not requiring even an overnight stay at the hospital.

As part of the Blue Angels' regular season, they perform several shows in the Pensacola area (usually July 2 and around November 10), but you are welcome to attend a practice demonstration for free behind the Naval Aviation Museum at NAS Pensacola, held Tuesday and Wednesday mornings at 8:30 A.M., weather permitting. Check with the museum (850/452-3604) to confirm dates. Arrive early to sit on the bleachers and watch the warm-up acts – training jets taking off and landing. Then the main act rolls out onto the runway, the F/A-18 Hornets diving and spinning in delicate choreography for nearly an hour. At the end, some of the pilots may stop by to sign autographs and chat with the fans. An inspiring way to spend a morning in Pensacola, indeed.

A new addition, the National Museum of Naval Aviation is now one of only two locations nationwide that features four real F-14 military flight-training simulators with all actual controls. Experience mock air-to-air combat, practice carrier landings, or simply cruise over Las Vegas, Iraq, and other simulated sites during this 20-minute joyride. Paying guests (it's $25, including a cockpit orientation) get to experience the thrill of flight in these authentic flight simulators featuring the fighter jet immortalized in the 1986 movie *Top Gun.*

## Pensacola Lighthouse

Also on the grounds of the naval air station, the Pensacola Lighthouse (Hwy. 292 S) follows on the heels of other lighthouses constructed in this area. The construction of the first Pensacola lighthouse, the Aurora Borealis, was completed in 1824, the first lighthouse on the Gulf Coast and the second lighthouse in Florida. It stood at the northern entrance of the bay near the present-day Lighthouse Point Restaurant. Unfortunately, trees on Santa Rosa Island obscured the light beam to ships. The construction of the present lighthouse was begun in 1856, and it was lit January 1, 1859. At night it still shines for sailors 27 miles out at sea, 171 feet tall and with a first-order Fresnel lens. In 1965, the lighthouse was automated, obviating the need for an on-site lighthouse keeper. The Keeper's Quarters now house the Navy's Command Display Center, with an exhibit on the lighthouse and the naval air station. The tower is closed to the public, but the lighthouse grounds are open.

## The Forts

Accessed through Naval Air Station Pensacola, the historic forts in this area are actually part of the **Gulf Islands National Seashore** (mailing address 1801 Gulf Breeze Pkwy., Gulf Breeze, FL 32563, 850/934-2600). The park spans 160 miles from Cat Island, Mississippi, east to the Okaloosa Day Use Area near Fort Walton Beach. The seashore was devastated by Hurricane Ivan, but recovery is now complete.

**Fort Barrancas** sits on a sandy bluff overlooking the entrance to Pensacola Bay. This site has seen three forts—first an earth-and-log Royal Navy Redoubt in 1763, then a Spanish two-part fort with Bateria de San Antonio at the foot of the bluff and Fort San Carlos de Barrancas above. The American brick-and-mortar Fort Barrancas was mostly completed in 1846, boasting 37 guns. During the Civil War, Confederate forces held Fort Barrancas until 1862. It was rearmed in 1890 and used as a training facility briefly during the Spanish-American War, after which it was disarmed again and used as an observation and communications post until 1930. Fort Barrancas was deactivated in 1947 and lay unused until it became part of the Gulf Islands National Seashore in 1971. It was entirely restored by 1980 at a cost of $1.2 million. Today, there's a visitors center with exhibits on the history of Pensacola under five flags 1559–1971, with displays of Civil War and coast artillery artifacts. The visitors center shows a 12-minute video on the fort and offers guided tours daily.

The **Fort Barrancas-Advanced Redoubt,**

700 yards south, was built 1845–1859 to defend the Pensacola Navy Yard from overland infantry assault. It was only manned during the Civil War, at which point it was deemed obsolete. Tours are available on Saturday at 11 A.M. The half-mile Trench Trail connects the Advanced Redoubt to the Fort Barrancas Visitor Center. For information, call 850/455-5167.

The largest of the four forts built to defend Pensacola Bay, **Fort Pickens** on Santa Rosa Island sustained serious damage during Hurricane Ivan but is now reopened to the public. All buildings in the historic area were flooded to a depth of several feet, the island experienced major erosion on its south side, and the Florida Department of Transportation rebuilt sections of Fort Pickens Road, inland and north of where it used to be.

Construction of the fort was begun in 1829, completed in 1834, and then it was used until the 1940s. It is said to be the only Southern fort not captured by the Confederacy in the Civil War, and that Geronimo surrendered here in 1886, marking the end of the Apache Wars. The park has a visitors center with a great self-guided tour map of the fort. There are also regularly scheduled ranger tours and a little museum with regular interpretive programs. There is year-round camping (850/934-2622, for reservations 877/444-6777) in the area on the west end of Santa Rosa Island, as well as the Blackbird and Dune Nature Trails and a fully repaired fishing pier.

While Fort Pickens is on the western tip of Santa Rosa Island, **Fort McRee** is on a narrow bar of sand on the eastern tip of Perdido Key. Or maybe I should say it used to be there. Once used as the third point of the triangle (with Pickens and Barrancas) by the U.S. Army to defend Pensacola Bay, Fort McRee was built there 1834–1839. It was heavily damaged during the Civil War and then really leveled by hurricanes over the years. It is a great day sailing trip to the fort, where you can usually have the beach and surrounding island all to yourself and wander through the remnants of the fort and Battery 233.

## FAMILY-FRIENDLY ATTRACTIONS

There are only so many historic sites a kid can endure before reprehensible behavior sets in. Beyond the area's beaches, there are a couple of fun enticements for young ones. **The Zoo** (5701 Gulf Breeze Pkwy., 10 miles east of Gulf Breeze on U.S. 98, 850/932-2229, 9 A.M.–4 P.M. daily, $12 adults, $11 seniors, $8 children 3–11, free for children under 3) is home to something like 1,400 animals, spread across a 50-acre wildlife preserve. You can view the free-roaming animals from the boardwalk or from the cute red Safari Line train. The train ride is narrated by a guide who points out African wild dogs, giraffes, pygmy hippos, gorillas, and native wildlife. The zoo also has a tranquil Japanese garden, a gift shop, Jungle Cafe, and Whistlestop Snack Bar.

If you happen to be in town during October, the **Pensacola Interstate Fair** (6655 W Mobile Hwy, 850/944-4500) is vast, with 147 acres of rides and exhibits. Many days there is free admission, and it usually takes place the last 11 days of the month.

### ( Sam's Fun City

It's fairly small-scale compared to Disney or Busch Gardens, but Sam's Fun City (6709 Pensacola Blvd., just south of I-10 on U.S. 29, Pensacola, 850/505-0800, www.samsfuncity. com, noon–8 P.M. Sun.–Thurs., until 11 P.M. Fri. and Sat., only weekend hours during winter, $6–39) is Pensacola's amusement park. There are a bunch of midway-style rides along with go-carts, bumper boats, and miniature golf. It also has a 1,600-square-foot arena for laser tag and a huge game arcade. Sam's recently added **Surf City Water Park** with a wave pool, 15 water slides, a 1,200-foot-long endless river, spray grounds, water play structures, and kiddie pools. The on-site Bullwinkle's Restaurant is a pleasant, something-for-everyone family restaurant.

# Accommodations

## $50-150

The **Ashton Inn & Suites Pensacola** (4 New Warrington Rd., 850/454-0280, and 910 N. Navy Blvd., 850/455-4561, weekdays $70–85, weekends $80–135) serves the Naval Air Station Pensacola and NTTC Corry Station, convenient to the National Museum of Naval Aviation.

My favorite place to stay on Pensacola Beach is the ( **Paradise Inn** (21 Via de Luna Drive, Pensacola Beach, 850/932-2319, www.paradiseinn-pb.com, $70–150). Look for the sign with the colorful sun on it. It's easy to miss, but you don't want to do that. The low-rise inn is tucked away among the newer, towering hotels and condos that have sprouted up like sand spurs along the shores of Pensacola Beach. Located right on Santa Rosa Sound and a short walk to the Gulf of Mexico, the Paradise captures the essence of classic Pensacola Beach and the charm of Old Florida. It also offers some of the best waterfront rates in town. The inn's 55 recently remodeled and renovated rooms are simple but stylish and come equipped with wireless Internet, cable, refrigerators, and microwaves. They surround a casual, fun bar and restaurant run by Renee Mack, who serves a delicious mix of Southern seafood, American fare, and traditional New Orleans–inspired dishes. Renee also runs a very popular and successful catering business, and her food is found at many of the conventions, weddings, and parties around town. The prices are a real treat with most entrees below $20, but the atmosphere is the clincher. Tables are set up right in the sugar white sand under a covered pavilion with Santa Rosa Sound just a few feet away. At night, lit tiki torches add to the tropical setting. The Inn and restaurant offer a private dock for boaters who want to sail in to dinner or take a break from touring the Intracoastal Waterway for a couple nights' rest. On weekends the Paradise brings in mostly blues, reggae, zydeco, and coastal country musicians for performances on its waterfront stage and in recent years has gained a reputation as a favored entertainment venue among locals. They offer specials on rooms during weekdays, so call and check the rates before you arrive.

The **Crowne Plaza Pensacola Grand** (200 E. Gregory St., 850/433-3336, $99–150) experienced an extensive renovation in 2005. It has a fully equipped and updated gym on the second floor, an extensive library on the first floor, a heated pool, upscale dining in the 1912 Restaurant, and cocktails in the L&L lobby bar. The downtown location is convenient to the historic areas.

## OVER $150

On Pensacola Beach, it was a long time after Hurricane Ivan before hotels really rebounded. They're back now, looking better than ever and with many new ones to experience.

**Courtyard by Marriott Downtown** (700 E. Chase St., 850/439-3330, www.marriott.com, $134–169) opened at the end of 2007, a boon to visitors who wish to enjoy the charm of the downtown area. The five-story hotel features 120 spacious rooms combining comfort and functionality, including high-speed Internet access, large desks, and ergonomic chairs. Amenities include a restaurant for breakfast, large fitness room, and swimming pool with hydrotherapy spa.

You can now find out about the changes in attitudes at the Pensacola Beach latitude at Jimmy Buffet's **Margaritaville Beach Hotel** (165 Fort Pickens Rd., Pensacola Beach, 850/916-9755, www.margaritavillehotel.com, $150–300). The most recent addition to the area, Margaritaville offers very well designed tropical-themed rooms and suites decorated to capture the colors and natural environment of the Gulf of Mexico. All of the rooms have free high-speed wireless Internet and flat-screen televisions. The property features an open and airy lobby with nice, high ceilings and slowly rotating fans that circulate above the Frank and Lola Love Pensacola Café. The

Margaritaville Beach Hotel on Pensacola Beach

café serves breakfast, lunch, and dinner with your traditional American breakfast choices and their own spin on the omelette called the Cheese Omelet in Paradise. For lunch it's Cheeseburgers in Paradise and seafood dishes like seafood gumbo and grouper sandwiches. At dinner it's mostly seafood and steaks in Paradise and a great selection of less-expensive salads and sandwiches. Outside the hotel you will find a beautiful pool and a tiki bar. And when you want that Landshark beer and the namesake margarita you can head over to the Gulf-front Landshark Landing where you'll find nightly entertainment, volleyball nets, a playground, hammocks tied under palm trees, and a pared-down menu of mostly American food and, you guessed it, Cheeseburgers in Paradise and lots of Jimmy Buffet's Landshark beer on tap.

The **Hilton Pensacola Beach Gulf Front** (12 Via de Luna Dr., 850/916-2999, www. pensacolabeachgulffront.com, $109–259), previously known as The Hilton Garden Inn, is a large beachfront hotel within walking distance of water sports, shopping, dining, and nightlife. Many rooms are Gulf-front rooms and suites with private balconies. At the end of 2007, it added on a new tower with an additional 93 rooms. In addition, the property increased function space from 15,000 square feet to 30,000 square feet to accommodate corporate luncheons, conferences, and wedding receptions. H2O, its signature restaurant featuring Cajun-Asian cuisine, has also nearly doubled in size and now offers a chef's table experience as well as private and semiprivate dinning.

**Hampton Inn Pensacola Beach** (2 Via de Luna Dr., Pensacola Beach, 850/932-6800, $99–199) has 181 pleasantly outfitted rooms right on the Gulf. The property has a lively tiki bar on the west end of the hotel by the pool, with the waves of the Gulf of Mexico lapping in the background. Ring games and horseshoes are available to entertain visitors, and fun-loving bartenders can whip up any beverage you want, including specialty drinks like the Mojo, Voodoo Juice, or Island Ice Pick.

Another wonderful addition to the area, the historic **Lee House** (400 Bayfront Parkway, Downtown Pensacola, 850/912-8770, www. leehousepensacola.com, $195–245), was damaged by fire in 2001 and knocked down three years later by Hurricane Ivan. It has been resurrected as an upscale bed-and-breakfast, and the location can hardly be topped. Sitting across from Seville Square Park in the historic district of downtown Pensacola and less than a mile from the foot of the three-mile bridge that takes you over to Pensacola Beach, the Inn is close to everything you want to experience on your Pensacola visit. The owners, very well known in the area for their culinary success with their local restaurants and catering services Norma's and Norma's-On-The-Go, prepare a wonderful and very large breakfast for guests in the morning. And for those who really love to cook, you can watch Norma prepare the breakfast in the incredible open kitchen. The gathering room in the front of the inn is comfortably upscale with several plush couches and a grand piano taking center stage, where musicians provide a background for guests in the evening. The private and quiet courtyard is a wonderful spot to break for coffee and tea in the afternoon after exploring the historic homes and downtown waterfront surrounding the inn. Each of the eight suites has a unique theme, from the elegant bridal suite with a private jetted tub to the eccentric purple and leopard print room for a zany, fun atmosphere, and a more masculine nautical-themed suite.

For an upscale resort experience on Pensacola Beach visit the **Portofino Island Resort** (10 Portofino Dr., Bayfront Parkway, 877/484-3405, www.portofinoisland.com, $380–500). The property comprises five towers with over 300 suites available. Built right at the eastern end of the Gulf Islands National Seashore preserve, which extends seven miles from Pensacola Beach to Navarre Beach, the resort gives you immediate and convenient access to the large stretch of preserved beach with the most beautiful dunes in the area, as well as great flats fishing, kayaking, and boating on Santa Rosa Sound. The resort offers two- and three-bedroom suites, each equipped in an efficiency approach with kitchens, washers and dryers, a dining room, private balconies, and living room, offered with 2-, 2.5-, 3-, or 3.5-bathroom floor plans. The two-bedroom suites are spacious with over 1,300 square feet of space. The three-bedroom suites

are ultra roomy, offering over 2,000 square feet. Each tower has its own heated pool and spa. Luxurious options include having a private chef come to your suite and cook meals for you or enjoying a massage on your private balcony with sweeping views of the white-sand beaches and Gulf of Mexico stretching out behind the resort.

# Food

## DOWNTOWN

Everyone who visits Pensacola has to eat at **( The Fish House** (600 South Barracks St., 850/470-0003, www.goodgrits.com, 11 A.M.–midnight Sun.–Thurs., until 2 A.M. Fri. and Sat., $13–28) at least once, as seen on Travel Channel, *Food and Wine* magazine, and other leading media (*Wine Spectator* gave its wine list a nod). Just-off-the-docks seafood, sushi, an award-winning chef, and the Fish House Deck Bar—it's all a hit. From a fire pit conversation area and dining tables to an hors d'oeuvres menu and a bandstand with a dance floor, this 3,500 square feet of sun and Gulf breezes offers both local and regional bands serving up live music on Friday and Saturday nights. The Deck's official beer is Landshark.

Very popular with locals, at one of those "disaster café" locations that have seen a lot of restaurants come and go, **The Global Grill** (27 S. Palafox Pl., 850/469-9966, 5–10 P.M. Tues.–Sat., $7–14) offers Pensacola some of its best tapas (actually, some of its only tapas). It's a world-beat approach that includes lamb lollipops with an Israeli couscous cake and sun-dried tomato au jus, or a crab West Indies and avocado martini.

There are a few great, casual pizza joints in town. **HopJacks Pizza Kitchen & Taproom** (10 Palafox Pl., 850/497-4703, www.hopjacks. com, $7–20) offers up plush couches and a stage for local performers. Pizza is the house pride, along with 150 bottled and 36 tap beers. Take a seat inside or grab a slice and head out to the outdoor courtyard for an evening under

the stars. Located in the Old Sacred Heart Hospital building is **Ozone Pizza Pub** (1010 N. 12th Ave., 850/433-7336, $6–20), a popular choice for residents in the East Hill district. It offers calzones and pizzas with an especially wide variety of vegetable toppings, grinders, and an extensive selection of beers on tap. It usually also hosts a busy bar scene on weeknights.

And just down the road is the **Tuscan Oven** (4801 N. Ninth Ave., 850/484-6836, www. thetuscanoven.com, $7–20). They serve traditional Southern Italian thin-crust pizzas prepared in a hardwood-fired oven made of clay, brick, and pumice shipped straight from Italy. The oven and counter bar that wraps around the kitchen are the centerpiece of the cozy dining room. You can chat with the friendly owners and staff while you watch your pizza get prepared and placed in the 500-degree inferno. An outdoor patio for dining or drinking one of the wines from the selective list tops it all off for an extremely enjoyable spot to slice up some pie.

## EAST HILL

To the north a bit and east of North Hill Preservation District, East Hill has a couple of my favorite restaurants. **Jerry's Drive-In** (2815 E. Cervantes St., 850/433-9910, 11 A.M.–9 P.M. Mon.–Sat., $5–9) offers killer cheeseburgers, onion rings, and fried okra in a comfy diner setting. It's been here since the 1940s, I'm told, and still has a line at lunch (but it's not really a drive-in, it's a walk-in).

## SOMETHING FISHY

It's technically four inches over the Alabama line into Florida's Perdido Key, which took a savage lashing by Hurricane Ivan. You can't keep the irrepressible **Flora-Bama Lounge** (17401 Perdido Key Dr., Perdido Key, 850/492-0611, www.florabama.com) down, though. The longtime beachside roadhouse where fun flows as unchecked as the booze has reopened and been rebuilt to retain its original weathered and ramshackle mystique. The bartenders are famous – and there are 10 bars, along with three stages for bands, volleyball courts, an oyster bar, package store, and sprawling beachside patio.

But that's just the beginning. When it started in 1961, it was a little local bar. It's grown over the years into a huge local bar that looks as if it were built from driftwood and scraps of debris left behind by Hurricane Ivan. It also hosts the international spectacle, the annual **Interstate Mullet Toss,** whereby contestants grip deceased yet slippery fish and throw them as far as they can into the state of Alabama. It's a straight distance competition, but you definitely get style points. Football spiral, underhanded, shot put-style – practice at home with a trout or something to hone your craft.

Several hundred people compete, and nearly 30,000 people turn out to watch the third weekend in April. There's a Ms. Mullet contest, barbecue, crawfish, peel-and-eat shrimp, topless oysters, and a whole lot of cocktails to sweeten the deal. The Flora-Bama has a couple of other annual events of note, one of which is the **Polar Bear Dip** on the morning of January 1, an early morning bar-to-water mad scramble. After a bracing splash in the Gulf (many "bears" leave behind their clothing entirely), revelers go back to the Flora-Bama for some warming black-eyed peas, and if you find a dime in your peas, it's good luck for the whole year.

Not far from there is the Pensacola restaurant everyone knows about, ◖ **McGuire's Irish Pub** (600 E. Gregory St., 850/433-6789, $10–30). "Irishmen of all nationalities" sign dollar bills and staple them to the ceiling, beer is brewed on the premises, the gorgeous wine cellar has a capacity of 8,000 bottles, and you can spend an ungodly sum on a burger (accompanied by caviar and champagne). It's a hard place to describe, really, set in Pensacola's original 1927 Old Firehouse. The steaks are good, and expensive (but it's fitting because all the beef is USDA-certified prime), but it still has a wild-and-wooly Irish pub feel to it. It's vast, with 400 seats and 200 employees, sprawling through a bunch of curio-packed theme rooms. Just go—it'll be fun.

### PENSACOLA BEACH

Greatest oyster bar? My personal favorite restaurant on Pensacola Beach? It's **Peg Leg Pete's** (1010 Fort Pickens Rd., 850/932-4139, 11 A.M.–10:30 P.M. daily, $8–20), offering some of the best prices on the freshest seafood in Pensacola Beach. The little-known secret around town is that the owner of this fun, family-oriented restaurant also owns Maria's Seafood, the second-largest seafood distributor in town. The rustic and casual, pirate-themed atmosphere of the restaurant and the extensive playground make it a great place for families. The menu features a variety of local favorites and regional classics like grouper sandwiches, crab claws, and a perfect cup of seafood gumbo. Take the stairs down to the ground level and visit the "under-where?" bar, where they serve cold drinks, raw oysters, and a full menu and feature live music on the weekends.

**Flounder's Chowder House** (800 Quietwater Beach Rd., 850/932-2003, 11 A.M.–midnight daily, until 2 A.M. Fri. and Sat. in summer, $15–24) is a fun, family-oriented place. The fare is lobster, grouper, and shrimp, as well as ribs from the smoker outside. Also on the bay side, **Hemingway's** (400 Quietwater Beach Rd., 850/934-4747, 11 A.M.–9 P.M. daily,

$8–33) features an open kitchen and two levels of outdoor deck seating. The menu is island-inspired, with roasted corn and crab chowder, Key West ribs, and shrimp basted with dark rum sauce, and the drinks tend toward the tropical cocktails and beach favorites.

**Sidelines** (2 Via de Luna Dr., 850/934-3660, 11 A.M.–11 P.M. daily, $7–20) is a fun-loving sports bar.

## COCKTAILS

**The JellyFish Bar** (13700 Perdido Key Dr., 850/332-6532) may very well be the perfect spot to end a perfect day on Perdido Key. Specialty cocktails and fine drinks of all varieties take center stage; the signature drink, the jellyfish martini, involves Three Olives brand vanilla vodka, berry-infused Pucker, and Sprite, and is rimmed with honey that drizzles down inside the glass to complete the jellyfish look). Enjoy the Gulf views on the patio while sippin' on a mojito or Lost Key lemonade.

**Finnegans Wake Irish Pub & Eatery** (2100 W. Nine Mile Rd., 850/477-6600) opened in 2007 and is located in the old New Market Steakhouse. Guess the menu. Did you say shepherd's pie and bangers and mash? Good job. Live music at the indoor and outdoor bars, and good beers on tap.

# Information and Services

Pensacola is located within the **Central time zone.** It's that far west. The area code is **850.**

## TOURIST INFORMATION

Begin a visit with a stop to the **Pensacola Bay Area Convention & Visitors Bureau information center** (1401 E. Gregory St., at the foot of the Pensacola Bay Bridge, 800/874-1234, www.visitpensacola.com, 8 A.M.–5 P.M. daily) to pick up maps, brochures, and a copy of the self-guided historic-district tours. There's also a convenient **Pensacola Beach Visitors Information Center** (735 Pensacola Beach Blvd., Pensacola Beach, 850/932-1500, 9 A.M.–5 P.M. daily).

The main daily newspaper is the **Pensacola News Journal,** and there's a free city magazine called **Pensacola Downtown Crowd** that covers local restaurants and the arts.

## POLICE AND EMERGENCIES

In an emergency, dial 911. If you need medical assistance, **Baptist Hospital** (1000 W. Moreno St., Pensacola, 850/434-4011) has full emergency services, as do **Sacred Heart Hospital** (5152 N. Ninth Ave., Pensacola, 850/416-7000) and **Gulf Breeze Hospital** (1110 Gulf Breeze Pkwy., Gulf Breeze, 850/934-2000).

## RADIO AND TELEVISION

On the radio, turn to **WUWF 88.1 FM** for NPR, **WTKX 101.5 FM** for straight-ahead rock, **WTKX 101.5** for alt rock, and **WCOA 1370 AM** for local talk radio.

For local television programming, **WEAR Channel 3** is the local ABC affiliate, **WKRG Channel 5** is the CBS affiliate out of Mobile-Pensacola, **WALA Channel 10** is the FOX affiliate out of Mobile-Pensacola, **WPMI Channel 15** is the NBC affiliate out of Mobile-Pensacola, **WSRE Channel 23** is PBS, and **WBQP Channel 12** is a local independent.

## LAUNDRY SERVICES

If you find yourself in need of coin-op laundry services, try **Dave's** (4124 Mobile Hwy., 850/455-6931) or **Modern Day** (3109 W. Michigan Ave., 850/944-5151).

# Getting There and Around

## BY CAR

The major east–west roads in this area are I-10, U.S. 90, and U.S. 98. Running north–south are U.S. 29 and I-110. To get to Pensacola from I-10, you can travel south on Highway 85 into Fort Walton Beach, then west on U.S. 98 to Navarre, then west over Navarre Toll Bridge, and finally west on Highway 399 approximately 20 miles to Pensacola Beach. Or you can go south on I-110 (lots of chain motels along this stretch) or Highway 281, then east on U.S. 98, follow signs to the beaches, and finally drive over Pensacola Beach Toll Bridge into Pensacola Beach. To get to Perdido Key from Pensacola, go west on Highway 292 to Perdido and finally over Perdido Key Bridge onto Perdido Key.

In town, Palafox is the major north–south artery, and Garden Street, which becomes Navy Boulevard on the way to the naval station, runs east–west. The historic district to the waterfront is walkable; for most of the rest of the area you'll need a car. Naval Air Station Pensacola is southwest of the city, and Pensacola Beach is southeast of the city on Santa Rosa Island. Pensacola is connected to Gulf Breeze by the Pensacola Bay Bridge (also called Three Mile Bridge), which in turn is connected to Pensacola Beach by the Bob Sikes Bridge.

## BY AIR

Located in Escambia County approximately three miles northeast of the central business district of Pensacola, **Pensacola Regional Airport** (2430 Airport Blvd., 850/436-5000)

is the biggest airport in northwest Florida, but that's not saying too much. It's not huge, serving more than 100 flights daily from AirTran Airways, American, American Eagle, Continental, Delta, Northwest, and US Airways. Delta has the largest number of direct flights. It's located in the center of town at 12th Avenue—very convenient.

Taxis queue up outside the main terminal entrance at baggage claim. Car-rental agencies are inside the main terminal entrance across from baggage claim. **Alamo** (800/327-9633), **Avis** (800/831-2847), **Budget** (800/527-0700), **Dollar** (800/800-4000 domestic, 800/800-6000 international), **Hertz** (800/654-3131), and **National** (800/227-7368) are all on the premises. Enterprise and Thrifty are off-site.

## BY BUS AND TRAIN

**Amtrak** (980 E. Heinberg St., 800/USA-RAIL) has a train station in Pensacola that was still closed in 2011 due to damaged train tracks from Hurricane Katrina. **Greyhound** (505 W. Burgess Rd., 800/229-9424), however, offers fairly extensive bus service. Such a large military presence usually ensures decent public transportation. There's even a local bus line run by **Escambia County Area Transit** (850/595-3228, www.goecat.com) that includes a University of West Florida (UWF) trolley service and a Pensacola Beach trolley. All in all, it is possible to get around here without a car, but difficult, with some of the more significant attractions inaccessible via public transportation.

PENSACOLA

# BACKGROUND

## The Land

### GEOGRAPHY

Florida is bounded on the north by Alabama and Georgia, to the east by the Atlantic, to the south by the Straits of Florida, and to the west by the Gulf of Mexico. The east coast of the state is comparatively straight, extending in a rough line 470 miles long. The Gulf side, on the other hand, has a more curving and complex coastline, measuring roughly 675 miles. In all, Florida's 2,276-mile coastline is longer than that of any other state in the continental United States and contains 663 miles of beaches and more than 11,000 miles of rivers, streams, and waterways.

It's nearly pancake flat, without notable change in elevation, and young by geological standards, having risen out of the ocean 300–400 million years ago. The state of Florida has six major geographical regions, several of which are represented along the Gulf Coast. First, the **coastal lowlands** encircle the state and extend along the shores inland 10–100 miles. The most recent to emerge from the ocean, the lowlands are covered with forests of saw palmetto and cypress. To the northwest, between the Perdido and Apalachicola Rivers, the **western highlands** are hilly uplands of pine forest. The highlands offer the highest elevation in Florida—345 feet above sea level in the northwestern part of Walton County.

And farther east, between the Apalachicola and Withlacoochee rivers, the **Tallahassee Hills** is a hilly region dotted with live oak and pine forests. It gradually slopes eastward to a plain until it hits the Suwannee River.

The Gulf side of the state has numerous deep-water bays: Tampa Bay, Apalachicola Bay, Charlotte Harbor, and Pensacola Bay. There is also an abundance of rivers (Caloosahatchee, Peace, Withlacoochee, Manatee, Suwannee, Ocilla, Ocklockonee, Apalachicola, Choctawhatchee, Yellow River, Escambia, Perdido, and others) and harbors on the Gulf side, and a record-holding number of first-magnitude springs. Thus, the fishing, boating, and swimming along the Gulf Coast are legendary.

Starting in the south, the **Everglades** region consists mainly of submerged sawgrass plains. The water, about knee-deep and with a slight southward current, provides habitat to hundreds of fish species, birds, and small mammals. Some of the Everglades' water is overflow from **Lake Okeechobee,** the second-largest freshwater lake with boundaries entirely in the United States, 30 miles wide and 33 miles long.

North of the lake, extending through De Soto, Manatee, Osceola, and Brevard counties, is a vast tract of prairie land with large swamp areas. This is where much of the state's cattle is raised. North of that, in Polk, Marion, Orange, Sumter, Lake, and Alachua counties, there's a little rise along the central ridge (up to 300 feet above sea level), with large and small lakes dotting the fertile, gently rolling terrain. The **coastal plain** that runs along the length of the Gulf Coast is low-lying and sandy, skirted by a dense pine region and marshes in many parts.

Several geographical features and plant communities are common in Florida, such as barrier islands, mangrove islands, marshes, hardwood hammocks, pineland, and flatwoods.

## Barrier Islands

Barrier islands are ridges of sand that usually run parallel to the main coast (Sanibel sticks out the other way), separated from the mainland by a bay or lagoon. They are sand deposits of recent geologic origin, in much of the Gulf Coast composed of almost pure milky quartz. Delivered to the Gulf by rivers, this sand is washed and well sorted, resulting in fine, even-grained sand along many Gulf beaches. Buffering the mainland from storms and heavy surf, they are constantly being contoured and molded by wave action and wind. **Sea oats** and other beachside plants provide a little structure and foundation for dunes to develop. They capture and hold the blowing sand—thus, they are to be preserved and nurtured (there's a steep fine for trampling or messing with the sea oats on Gulf Coast beaches). **Swales** are wetlands formed on these islands where the wind has scoured out the sand down to the water table or below, and often a **maritime forest** can be found on the back side of barrier islands behind the secondary dunes.

## Mangrove Islands

Along Florida's south coast and halfway up the peninsula, mangrove swamps hug the shoreline. They create a fringing network around most islands, growing at the high-tide line and helping to stabilize the shore. In the maze of the **Ten Thousand Islands** in between Marco Island and the Everglades, you can see entire island ecosystems created by saltwater-tolerant mangroves. These trees send their roots into the shallows, filtering pollution and providing a crucial habitat for fish and wading birds.

## Marshes

Marshes make up a large area near the Gulf Coast—areas that are partially or periodically submerged land, where the water table is near the surface of the soil. Water flows into marshes and swamps from rivers, creeks, and bayous, bringing with it rich organic debris that settles and accumulates in the marshes, compacting into peat. Trees in marshes, or in the larger category of **wetlands,** get used to living in standing water. Cypress and tupelo buttress their trunks by sending up "knees" for support (and for breathing air).

In **salt marshes** there is a clear line drawn between the wetland and upland, because the salt is detrimental to the growth of so many plant species. (From Apalachicola Bay south to Tampa Bay, salt marshes are the main coastal community.) In freshwater wetlands that line is more blurred, with the wetland plants shifting subtly into upland species. In the case of **tidal marshes,** affected by the ebb and flow of tides, the demarcation line is even more pronounced. Many tidal marshes along the Gulf Coast are dominated by stands of black needle rush and saltmarsh cordgrass.

Freshwater and saltwater marshes, as well as a similar community called a **seagrass meadow,** are enormously important to Florida's fish species, providing the shelter as a "nursery" for many species, a safe haven in which to mature among the marsh grasses before adult fish go out into the predator-dense Gulf.

**Swamps,** certainly a defining feature of Florida, are just forested wetlands. About 10 percent of Florida is covered by forested wetland bordering rivers or ponds, populated by plant species that tolerate periodic high water levels. For great examples of swamps, visit Fakahatchee Strand State Preserve or Big Cypress National Park.

## Hardwood Hammocks

Hardwood hammocks may be the oldest natural community type in Florida, dating back more than 25 million years. There are **upland hardwoods** and **bottomland hardwoods,** the latter being the transition forest between a drier upland area and a wet river floodplain. Either way, the largest mature trees in a hardwood forest (laurel oak, sweetgum, Southern magnolia, and others) tend to hog all the light. The understory, the next level of stratification (trees like dogwood and shrubs like Elliott's blueberry or Florida anise), has to grab whatever light is left over. And then the forest floor (moss and ferns) lives in the low-light murk. Vines and epiphytes have to hoist themselves up on the canopy trees to gain access to light.

## Pineland

Longleaf pineland used to cover 70 million acres in the south. Sadly, Florida pineland is an endangered plant community, a habitat that must be burned regularly to thrive. The small remaining pinelands in Florida are generally so close to residential and commercial areas that regular burning programs often aren't feasible. As if that's not bad enough, invading species like the Brazilian pepper are choking other species in these delicate habitats.

**Long Pine Key** in Everglades National Park is a great example of a pineland, much of it old-growth forest. And along the northwest Panhandle, **Blackwater River State Forest,** along with Conecuh National Forest and Eglin Air Force Base, contains the largest holding of longleaf pine trees in the world. Longleaf pine is a long-lived tree, between 350 and 500 years. A mature longleaf pine forest has an open canopy that allows sunlight to flood the forest floor, resulting in a forest floor of lots of plant species and grasses.

## Flatwoods

**Pine flatwoods** (also called pine flats or pine barrens), on the other hand, are ubiquitous in Florida, historically covering almost half of the natural land area in the state. They are characterized by low, flat land, an open canopy of slash pine, and an understory dominated by palmetto prairie. Slash pine have historically been used to produce all kinds of commercial goods, from paper products to turpentine and household goods. Additionally, pine flatwoods provide important habitat for many wildlife species.

A **scrub** is a similar plant community, same pine up above with various shrubs and palmetto underneath, but scrubs are found in upland areas that are generally much harsher and drier, with no organic matter in the soil. It's an austere habitat, but home to **gopher tortoises** and the endangered Florida **scrub jay.**

## CLIMATE
## Heat and Humidity

Florida is closer to the equator than any other continental American state, located on the southeastern tip of North America with a humid subtropical climate and heavy rainfall

# GULF COAST TEMPERATURES

| City | Avg. Low (°F) | Avg. High (°F) |
|---|---|---|
| Apalachicola | 59 | 79 |
| Cedar Key | 61 | 83 |
| Fort Myers | 64 | 84 |
| Naples | 64 | 85 |
| Panama City Beach | 53 | 81 |
| Pensacola | 59 | 77 |
| Sarasota | 62 | 83 |
| St. Petersburg | 66 | 82 |
| Tallahassee | 56 | 79 |
| Tampa | 63 | 82 |

During the summer months, expect temperatures to hover around 90°F and humidity to be near 100 percent. The most pleasant times of the year along the length of the Florida peninsula fall between December and April—not surprisingly, the busiest time for tourism. Along the Panhandle, however, where temperatures are more moderate in the summer and chillier in the winter, the summer sees more tourist action.

The common wisdom is that the hard freeze line in Florida bisects the state from Ocala to Jacksonville. North of that, freezing temperatures rarely last long, and south of that it's just an hour here or there under the freezing point (with serious damage to tropical plants in years when the temperature dips low). The best approach for packing in preparation for a visit to Florida is layering—with a sweater for over-air-conditioned interiors or chilly winds, and lots of loose, wicking material for the heat.

## Rain

It rains nearly every day in the summer along the Gulf Coast—and not just a sprinkle. Due to the abundance of warm, moist air from the Gulf of Mexico and the hot tropical sun, conditions are perfect for the formation of thunderstorms. There are 80–90 thunderstorms each summer, generally less than 15 miles in diameter—but vertically they can grow up to 10 miles high in the atmosphere. These are huge, localized thunderstorms that can drop four or more inches of rain in an hour, while just a few miles away it stays dry. The bulk of these tropical afternoon thunderstorms each summer are electrical storms.

## Lightning

With sudden thunderstorms comes lightning, a serious threat along the Gulf Coast. About 50 people are struck by lightning each year in the state. Most of them are hospitalized and recover, but there are about 10 fatalities annually. Tampa is the "Lightning Capital" of the United States, with around 25 cloud-to-ground lightning bolt blasts on each square mile annually. The temperature of a single bolt can

April–November. Its humidity is attributed to the fact that no point in the state is more than 60 miles from saltwater and no more than 345 feet above sea level. If this thick steamy breath on the back of your neck is new to you, humidity is a measure of the amount of water vapor in the air. Most often you'll hear the percentage described in "relative humidity," which is the amount of water vapor actually in the air divided by the amount of water vapor the air can hold. The warmer the air becomes, the more moisture it can hold.

When heat and humidity combine to slow evaporation of sweat from the body, outdoor activity becomes dangerous even for those in good physical shape. Drink plenty of water to avoid dehydration and slow down if you feel fatigued or notice a headache, a high pulse rate, or shallow breathing. Overheating can cause serious and even life-threatening conditions such as heatstroke. The elderly, small children, the overweight, and those on certain medications are particularly vulnerable to heat stress.

reach 50,000°F, about three times as hot as the sun's surface. There's not much you can do to ward off lightning except to avoid being in the wrong place at the wrong time. The summer months of June, July, August, and September have the highest number of lightning-related injuries and deaths. Usually lightning occurs during daylight hours, with the highest concentration between 3 P.M. and 4 P.M., when the afternoon storms peak. Lightning strikes usually occur either at the beginning or end of a storm, and can strike up to 10 miles away from the center of the storm. Keep your eye on approaching storms and seek shelter when you see lightning.

Locals use the 30-30 rule: Count the seconds after a lightning flash until you hear thunder. If that number is under 30, the storm is within

# HURRICANE LINGO

## HURRICANE TERMS

- **Severe Thunderstorm** – a thunderstorm with winds 58 mph or faster or hailstones 0.75 inch or larger in diameter

- **Tropical Depression** – an organized system of clouds and thunderstorms with a defined circulation and maximum sustained winds of 38 mph (33 knots) or less

- **Tropical Storm** – an organized system of strong thunderstorms with a defined circulation and maximum sustained winds of 39-73 mph (34-63 knots)

- **Hurricane** – a warm-core tropical cyclone with maximum sustained winds of 74 mph (64 knots) or greater

- **Eye** – the "calm" center of a hurricane with light winds and partly cloudy to clear skies, usually around 20 miles in diameter (but the range is 5-60 miles)

- **Eye Wall** – the location within a hurricane where the most damaging winds and intense rainfall are found

- **Tornadoes** – violent rotating columns of air that touch the ground; they are spawned by large severe thunderstorms. They can have winds estimated 100-300 mph. A **tornado watch** means they're possible; a **tornado warning** means they're in your area.

## HURRICANE WARNINGS

- **Tropical Storm Watch** – issued when tropical storm conditions may threaten a particular coastal area within 36 hours, when the storm is not predicted to intensify to hurricane strength

- **Tropical Storm Warning** – winds ranging 39-73 mph can be expected to affect specific areas of a coastline within the next 24 hours

- **Hurricane Watch** – a hurricane or hurricane conditions may threaten a specific coastal area within 36 hours

- **Hurricane Warning** – a warning that sustained winds of 74 mph or higher associated with a hurricane are expected in a specified coastal area in 24 hours or less

## HURRICANE SCALE

- **Category I** – winds 74-95 mph with a storm surge of 4-5 feet and minimal damage

- **Category II** – winds 96-110 mph with a storm surge of 6-8 feet and moderate damage

- **Category III** – winds 111-130 mph with a storm surge of 9-12 feet and major damage

- **Category IV** – winds 131-155 mph with a storm surge of 13-18 feet and severe damage

- **Category V** – winds 155+ mph with more than an 18-foot storm surge and catastrophic damage

six miles of you. Seek shelter. Then, at storm's end, wait 30 minutes after the last thunderclap before resuming outdoor activity.

## HURRICANES

Hurricanes are violent tropical storms with sustained winds of at least 74 mph. Massive low-pressure systems, they blow counterclockwise around a relatively calm central area called the eye. They form over warm ocean waters, often starting as storms in the Caribbean or off the west coast of Africa. As they move westward, they are fueled by the warm waters of the tropics. Warm, moist air moves toward the center of the storm and spirals upward, releasing driving rains. Updrafts suck up more water vapor, which further strengthens the storm until it can be stopped only when contact is made with land or cooler water. In the average hurricane, just 1 percent of the energy released could meet the energy needs of the United States for a full year.

In Florida, the hurricane season is July–November. These storms have been named since 1953. It used to be just female names, but now male names are also being used. Really powerful hurricanes' names are retired, kind of like sports greats' jerseys.

The 2004 hurricane season was the last really destructive year in Florida, with Charley, Frances, Ivan, and Jeanne wreaking havoc on the Gulf Coast in rapid succession. In areas like Pensacola, it was several years before insurance and FEMA monies had been entirely paid out and blue roof tarps weren't common any longer. In the Charlotte Harbor area, hit by Charley, the reconstruction efforts have yielded an even more attractive destination for visitors. Although Hurricane Katrina's devastating effects are still felt in nearby Louisiana and Mississippi, the past few years have been meteorologically uneventful in Florida.

### Hurricane Safety

Monitor radio and TV broadcasts closely for directions. Gas up the car, and make sure you have batteries, a water supply, candles, and food that can be eaten without the use of electricity. Get cash, have your prescriptions filled, and put all essential documents in a large resealable bag. In the event of an evacuation, find the closest shelter by listening to the radio or TV broadcasts. Pets are not allowed in most shelters. There are designated pet shelters, but all animals must be up to date on shots. Alternatively, an increasing number of hotels and motels accept animals for a nominal daily fee.

# Flora and Fauna

The abundance of sunlight and rain and the near absence of four traditional seasons allow for the successful growth of nearly 4,000 plant species and nearly that many animals in Florida. The lower Gulf Coast's palms, the great cypress swamps, mangroves, and on the Panhandle one of the greatest forested regions in the East—Florida's plantlife is richly diverse, providing a range of habitats. Even nonnative plants and animals flourish in these lush conditions, a fact that troubles Floridian scientists as more exotic species take hold. The trade in exotic pets and plants, as well as the movement of huge numbers of people and vehicles, can intentionally or unintentionally bring new species into Florida, devastating native species and invading natural areas.

## FLORA

On March 27, 1513 (Easter Day), Ponce de Leon landed on the coast of Florida and pronounced it a "land of flowers." And it's true, mostly. Florida Gulf Coast plants—if you're from somewhere else—can either creep you out or fill you with wonderment. The subtropical climate is warm, moist, lush, with the kind of foliage in the summer for which you don't need a stop-action film in order to document growth. There are plants that grow like Audrey II in *Little Shop of Horrors*.

Fast, loose, and weird. The even greater thing is that many native and even flourishing exotic Florida plants have huge advocates and devotees.

There are avid clubs devoted to carnivorous plants, to orchids, to bromeliads, to palms (which are really not trees—despite the fact that the state "tree" is the cabbage palm). It's a gardener's state, but there's a certain humility gardeners bring to the table. It's not generally a state for regimented topiary or manicured rose gardens. Serendipity, chance, and Mother Nature's whim play a part in Florida gardening. So much is given, but, as recent hurricane seasons have shown, so much can be taken away.

## Trees

**Palm trees** are practically a Florida cliché. Also known as cabbage palm and palmetto, it's from the **sabal palm** that hearts of palm are harvested. Sabal palm grows in all conditions in the state—wet, dry, coastal, swampy— and it is from the fronds of the sabal that the Seminoles built watertight chickee roofs. In some parts of the Gulf Coast, you'll encounter **royal palm,** identified by its towering 80-foot pale gray trunk and bright, glossy crown shaft. Many of the other palm species usually associated with Florida are not native—the easily recognized **coconut palm,** the heavy-trunked **Canary Island date palm,** and the slim, statuesque **red latan palm.** You'll see them all along the Gulf Coast, but it's what they're in contrast to that gives this subtropical landscaping its own flavor.

**Mangroves** are often called walking trees because they hover above the water, their arching prop roots resembling so many spindly legs. Seeds sprout on the parent tree and drop off, bobbing in the water until they lodge on an oyster bar or a snag in the shallows. There, the seed begins to grow to a tree, the foundation of a new, tiny island. Around its roots sediment and debris build up to create a thick layer of peat upon which other plant species begin to grow. This first tree drops more seed tubules, which get stuck in the mulchy ground and create more trees. This is how islands are often created off the Gulf Coast.

There are three types of mangrove along the Gulf: The red mangrove forms a wide band of trees on the outermost part of each mangrove island, facing the open sea. The red mangrove encircles the black mangrove, which in turn encircles the white mangrove at the highest, driest part of each mangrove island. Mangroves are protected by federal, state, and local laws.

**Cypress** is another oh-so-Florida tree. Forested wetlands in the state are often dominated by cypress trees, located along stream banks and riverbanks or in ponds with slow-moving water. Bald cypresses (they aren't always bald, they just lose their leaves in winter) are the largest trees in North America east of the Rockies. They can live for hundreds of years, quietly ruminating with their roots in water, their "knees" protruding above the soil and waterline. The function of these knees, part of the root system that projects out of the water, isn't totally known, other than that they provide stability and more air for the base of these flood-tolerant trees. The Gulf Coast offers several cypress swamps to explore.

**Live oaks** are certainly not the sole custody of Florida. In all of the South these huge semideciduous trees loom, gnarled and woebegone, draped with Spanish moss (which is neither Spanish, nor a moss). The Tallahassee area is especially dense with live oak, but you'll see them all over.

The **gumbo limbo,** one of only three native tree species in North America, is common down toward the Everglades. They call it the sunburn tree, as its smooth bark peels off in sheets to reveal a red trunk color beneath. I love these trees, and I love saying their name even more.

## Sawgrass

Also a defining feature of the Everglades, sawgrass looks like smooth, soft hay. It dominates wide swaths of marshland in this area known as "The River of Grass," but sawgrass blades have little sawlike teeth along one side that make walking through it very painful.

© JOSHUA LAWRENCE KINSER

Fine examples of Florida's plant life, like this fairy orchid, can be found at the Marie Selby Botanical Gardens in Sarasota County.

## Epiphytes

"Epi" means "on" and "phyte" means "plant." Thus, an epiphyte is a plant that grows on another plant. They're sometimes called airplants because they grow above ground, in the air, roots wiggling in the breeze. Host plants support them high off the ground, where they don't need to compete for light and rainwater, and where they don't have to cope with floodwater and marauding animals. Epiphytes generally do no harm to the host plant and get their nutrients from their own photosynthesis and their own water from runoff on their host. Cardinal airplant and resurrection fern are wonderful plants to explore.

Within this category, **orchids** are probably the best known, with more genera than any other plant. They are among the most exotic and delicate flowers in the world, holding a special fascination for collectors, photographers, and hobbyists. Orchids abound in the Everglades' hardwood hammocks, marshes, pineland, and prairies. To see thousands of orchid species, visit Marie Selby Botanical Gardens in Sarasota.

**Bromeliads** are another type of epiphyte, members of the pineapple family. They use shallow roots only to anchor themselves to a tree or the ground and absorb through their leaves the water and nutrients they need from the air and from the rain. These leathery, brightly colored tropical plants often collect water in little "tanks" or between their leaves. Of Florida's 16 species of native bromeliads, 13 are not found elsewhere in the United States.

## Crops

The citrus fruit industry has been big business in the state since the 1890s when Chinese horticulturist Lue Gim Gong introduced a new variety of **orange** and a hardier **grapefruit.** Today, citrus is Florida's leading cash crop, with the state producing 90 percent of the country's orange juice (almost all Florida oranges are juiced, not sold whole). Florida is second only to Brazil in orange juice production, and it is the world leader in grapefruit production.

There are about 750,000 acres of citrus groves in the state and more than 100 million citrus trees, mostly in the lower two-thirds of the state. There are about 40 citrus packinghouses and 20 citrus processing plants in Florida. It is estimated that the growing, packing, processing, and selling of citrus generates a $9 billion per year impact on Florida's economy—not surprisingly, the orange blossom is the state flower.

Recent cold snaps that devastate the season's yield have posed a major threat to this Florida industry and the estimated 76,000 jobs in the citrus industry or related businesses.

Beyond citrus, though, Florida is the "winter salad bowl," providing 80 percent of the fresh vegetables grown in the United States during January, February, and March. The Gulf Coast is responsible for lots of tomatoes, peppers, and strawberries—Plant City near Tampa is the state's strawberry capital.

There are also exotic tropical fruits and vegetables grown along the Gulf Coast, from smooth-skinned avocados the size of softballs to mangoes (Lee County), guavas, lychees, sapotes, cherimoyas, and others.

## FAUNA
### Fish

No other state in the United States and few other countries boast a more varied marine environment. Florida has hundreds of species of fish crowding its waters. There's the Atlantic and the fertile Gulf of Mexico with its

## GREAT GUIDES TO FLORIDA WILDLIFE

### BIRDS

Tekiela, Stan. *Birds of Florida Field Guide*. Minnesota: Adventure Publications, 2005. It's a great small-sized book organized by bird color. This makes it easy to narrow things down when you've just spotted a flash of wing color in your binoculars.

Maehr, David. *Florida's Birds: A Field Guide and Reference*. Sarasota, FL: Pineapple Press, 2005. For birders and rookies alike, birds can be quickly identified in this book via picture (pretty ones with birds grouped by similar species), text, or index. Maps indicate when migratory birds are present or breeding, and where.

Even better than these books, though, is the sand- and waterproof *Florida's Gulf Coast Birds* flip map illustrated by Ernest C. Simmons (visit www.floridabooks.com if you can't find it in area bookstores). It puts birds into rough groups – wading birds, shore birds, wetland birds, birds of prey, etc. And another great resource is the spring and fall bird migration tables at www.birdnature.com.

### FISH

Arnov, Boris. *Fish Florida: Saltwater/Better than Luck – The Foolproof Guide to Florida Saltwater Fishing*. Houston, TX: Gulf Publishing, 2002. This is a fairly good beginner book: It describes a kind of fish, let's say amberjack, then tells you how it fights (fiercely); appropriate tackle, whether you're spinning or plug casting or fly-fishing; and technique for live bait or light tackle casting. It also gives catch and size limits and other regulations.

Dew, Gregory. *The Barefoot Fisherman's Guide to the Emerald Coast: From Gulf Shore, Alabama, to Apalachicola, Florida*. Birmingham, AL: Crane Hill Publishers, 1999. Flip to Chapter 3, which enumerates 40 or so fabulous fishing spots on this gorgeous stretch of coast, and what you're likely to catch there.

### MAMMALS

Adams, Alto. *A Florida Cattle Ranch*. Sarasota, FL: Pineapple Press, 1998. You'll learn about Cracker cows, scrub, and the hardscrabble world of Florida ranching.

Maehr, David. *The Florida Panther: Life and Death of a Vanishing Carnivore*. Washington, D.C.: Island Press, 1997. The author makes these endangered cougars spring to life in their last frontier in the Big Cypress National Preserve and around the Okaloacoochee Slough.

hundreds of bays, sounds, inlets, and brackish marshes. But there are also freshwater rivers, lakes, estuaries, and numerous other marine environments.

The **Panhandle** has long stretches of white-sand beaches and ocean that quickly drops off to deep water—boaters in 70 feet of water can often see bathers on the beach. The area is also home to bountiful estuaries (where rivers meet the sea) tucked behind long, narrow barrier islands.

From **Apalachicola** to the **Big Bend,** estuaries are protected by oyster bars and rocky islands. Here the water depths drop off very gradually. Off the Suwannee River and St. Marks Light, ordinary outboard motorboats can run aground more than three miles from shore. This area has few beaches and is dominated by marshes with vast seagrass beds. Farther south along the Gulf, anglers enjoy a number of exciting species, from huge **tarpon** to tasty **grouper, cobia,** and the fabled **snook.**

In much of this area, freshwater fishing is most productive in the spring while sportfishing is good all year. But you need a license. An annual nonresident saltwater or freshwater fishing license is $47, a seven-day license is $30, and a three-day license is $17. You need to figure out what you're fishing for before you purchase your license, but either way the revenue generated by the sale goes to the Florida Fish and Wildlife Conservation Commission.

---

Sobczak, Charles. *Alligators, Sharks & Panthers: Deadly Encounters with Florida's Top Predator – Man.* Sanibel, FL: Indigo Press, 2006. It chronicles grisly attacks, but with an underlying environmentalist's message about humans mucking about in creatures' natural habitats.

### BUTTERFLIES

Daniels, Jaret. *Butterflies of Florida Field Guide (Our Nature Field Guides).* Gainesville, FL: Adventure Publications, 2003. It's a lovely field guide with great pictures and not-too-Latin text.

### SHELLS

Williams, Winston. *Florida's Fabulous Seashells: And Other Seashore Life.* Tampa: World Publications, 1988. It's light enough to pack in your beach bag, with good color photos and interesting text about the marine animals.

Witherington, Blair and Dawn. *Florida's Seashells.* Sarasota, FL: Pineapple Press, 2007.

### WHERE TO FIND GOOD FLORIDA WILDLIFE BOOKS

**Haslam's Book Store** (www.haslamcorp.com) is a St. Petersburg institution and one of the best bookstores in Florida, while in Tampa **Inkwood Books** has a broad Florida nature, wildlife, and gardening section.

**Pineapple Press** (www.pineapplepress. com) is the best local small press, producing a handful of books on Florida each year, all of high caliber and many with an environmental bent.

The **University Press of Florida** (www.upf. com), the consolidated publishing efforts of all of the Florida state universities, groups Florida books by helpful categories (environment, people, arts, and artifacts).

**Florida Plants Online Bookstore** (www. floridaplants.com) indeed lists lots of excellent books on local flora, but its reach also extends to fauna, highbrow literature, and books for young readers.

For rare or out-of-print books, **Grove Antiquarian** (www.abebooks.com) traffics in preowned books specializing in South Florida and the Caribbean.

The bookstore at **Everglades National Park** (www.nps.gov) features a long reading list of Everglades-centric books. And way up in Cedar Key there's **Curmudgeonalia,** which proffers a discerning collection of birding, naturalist, and offbeat Florida history books.

There are also numerous shellfish species: **scallops** in Steinhatchee, **oysters** in Apalachicola, **stone crabs** in Everglades City, **clams** in Cedar Key, and delicious **Florida blue crabs** all over the state.

## Birds

With 500 bird species, both those native to the state and those that migrate here, the Gulf Coast is a bird lover's paradise in a range of habitats. Mangrove estuaries are home to many species of **egrets, herons,** and numerous other **wading birds. Waterbirds** occupy interior wetlands, and countless **shorebirds, terns,** and **gulls** populate the white-sand beaches. Unique to the state, the **Florida scrub jay** lives in a small patch of scrub-oak habitat; **ospreys** and **bald eagles** make their large nests all along the Gulf Coast. In the woods you can find **red-shouldered hawks** and endangered **red cockaded woodpeckers.** In backyard ponds you'll see the long, sinuous neck of the **anhinga**—what Native tribes called "snakebirds"—they stand in a confident-looking stance with their wings stretched out to dry them after a dive for fish. You'll spot **white pelicans,** the second-largest flying bird in North America, sailing low over the Gulf waters, while high above a **frigate** is barely a speck. Your hair might stand up on end when you hear the nagging cry of a **little blue heron** and you may be startled by the trilling call of the enormous **sandhill cranes** that stroll around in small family groups of three.

It's serious birding country, with loads of expert birders to lead you through the prime birding spots. There are numerous birding festivals along the Gulf Coast, and the **Great Florida Birding Trail** (www.floridabirding-trail.com) for when you want to get out into the wilderness alone.

## Large Mammals

After the alligator, the **West Indian manatee** is the Florida Gulf Coast's most famous animal. A manatee is a large, gray aquatic mammal with a body that tapers to a flat, paddle-shaped, beaverlike tail. Completely herbivorous, they are gentle and slow moving, found in shallow rivers, estuaries, saltwater bays, canals, and coastal areas. Manatees are migratory, meaning they move around and are concentrated in the warm Florida waterways in the winter. Most of their time is spent traveling, resting, and eating—they can consume 10–15 percent of their body weight daily in vegetation (and that's a lot, since adult males weigh 800–1,200 pounds). They have no known predators, but habitat destruction and collisions with watercraft propellers have kept this species on the endangered list (although at the end of 2007 the U.S. Fish and Wildlife Service discussed downgrading its status to threatened). There are an estimated 3,500 West Indian manatees left in the United States, many of them convened along the Nature Coast in Homosassa and Crystal River in the winter. Manatees are protected under federal law, and the Florida Manatee Sanctuary Act of 1978 states: "It is unlawful for any person, at any time, intentionally or negligently, to annoy, molest, harass, or disturb any manatee." It's a steep fine and imprisonment, so look but don't touch these guys. In many waterways on the Gulf Coast there are reduced boat speed zones for manatee protection.

Another locally protected animal is the **Florida panther.** They're called the Florida panthers, but really they once roamed throughout the Southeast from east Texas to the Atlantic and north to parts of Tennessee. Overhunting, loss of habitat, and reduction of their primary prey reduced their population to just a handful living in southern Florida in pinelands and mixed swamp forests. Fewer than 100 remain in Florida, making them one of the rarest and most endangered mammals in the world. A subspecies of cougar that has adapted to the subtropical environment of Florida, they are still to be found occasionally in Fakahatchee Strand State Preserve and Big Cypress National Preserve, where there is a 26,400-acre **Florida Panther National**

**Wildlife Refuge.** The Florida Fish and Wildlife Conservation Commission monitors panther activity using radio telemetry collars. Florida panthers are tawny and brown with cream or white undersides; adult males average 130–160 pounds with an average length of 6–8 feet.

Cattle was first introduced to North America in 1521, when Ponce de Leon landed on the Gulf Coast. He brought a small herd of Andalusian cattle, the descendants of which might be the foundation stock of Florida's **piney-woods cattle.** Spanish missions had herds of cattle, and the Native Americans learned to raise cattle from the Spanish. British and Creek invasions of Spanish Florida in 1702 and 1704 destroyed the Spanish herds, but the Seminoles kept their own herds intact. During the English occupation of Florida, the British brought their own longhorn and shorthorn cattle, which eventually bred with the surviving Andalusians, resulting in a tough, compact cow weighing a scant 600 pounds. A speckled brindle pattern, sharp horns, and a cranky disposition still define the Florida piney-woods cow. Cows used to roam the state free, branded or earmarked for owner identification. In order to round them up, Florida cattlemen would crack long whips to get them moving. Some people say it is this that caused rural Floridians to be called Crackers.

## Reptiles and Amphibians

There are so many sexy, exciting wild animals in Florida, from alligators to roseate spoonbills, that the little everyday animals often get short shrift. The Gulf Coast is Lizard Central, with several species duking it out for dominance. The **Cuban knight anole** was introduced into Florida in the 1950s. These guys and the **brown anole** are hardy and aggressive (although not in any way harmful to humans), and they have displaced the native **green anole** along the Gulf Coast. The green anole is still the top lizard species in the state's interior.

Turtles are also plentiful in Florida, with 26 different species. Of the species that prefer dry land, there is the **Florida box turtle** common to upland scrub and marshes. They can live up to 100 years but are now protected and fairly uncommon. The **gopher tortoise** you'll see in upland scrub areas. They are protected but occur throughout the state. **Florida snapping turtles** can get up to 70 pounds and are common throughout the state, whereas **alligator snapping turtles** are only to be found along the Panhandle. Both have powerful jaws and could snap a finger in half. The **Florida soft shell turtle** can be found throughout the state; it has a rubbery shell to allow it to bury itself in the sand as well as swim very fast. The **Florida cooter** lives in large ponds, canals, slow-moving rivers, and lakes—it's historically a delicacy among Floridaians, and occasionally you'll still find it on menus on the Gulf Coast.

Over 33 species of frogs inhabit the state of Florida, from the exotic **giant marine toad** once imported to control cane beetles to the ubiquitous **Cuban tree frog,** which has displaced many local frog species and has a pretty noxious skin toxin—as well as a fair number of snakes. The snake that seems to worry everyone is the **Florida cottonmouth**—almost always near water, reaching up to six feet, and highly venomous. You'll often encounter them sunning themselves on semisubmerged logs along southern Gulf Coast rivers, whereas Florida's **eastern diamondback,** the largest and most dangerous local snake, is more common in palmetto flatlands and pine woods. **Black racers** are much more common, most of them fairly small despite their potential to grow to six feet. Common in many Florida gardens, they're nonvenomous but they can still bite if cornered.

## Spiders and Insects

There are loads of big spiders in Florida, too. One of the coolest is the really large **golden silk spider** common to wooded areas or groves, but there are excellent brightly colored **jumping spiders** that don't build webs but instead hunt for their prey and pounce on the unsuspecting. The **black and yellow**

# ALLIGATORS

In his excellent memoir, *Totch, A Life in the Everglades,* Totch Brown describes a gator's sounds:

> Gators make three different sounds. One is the "grunt" used by young gators in distress to call their mothers. When you pick up a baby gator it'll start grunting every time. The mother will come to this sound right away. (With practice, you can imitate this "grunt" and often fool a grown gator into coming to you.)
>
> Then there's a blowing sound gators make when they're more or less hemmed up, or cornered and are good and mad.
>
> The third sound is the gator bellow – a bloodcurdling sound that can be heard for miles across the Everglades. When one gator bellows, usually another will answer.... When a 12-foot gator bellows, he raises his head up as high as possible, his mouth wide open, and with a full breath, lets out his air. It's a sight to be seen! The bellowing is generally in mating season, the late spring, when the rains are about to start. The gators seem to be asking Mother Nature for a drink of water.

I've seen a gator bellow, his head tipped way back. To me he didn't seem like he was asking anybody for anything other than to buzz off. It's a noise that has the kind of effect as your first viewing of *Jaws.*

Alligators were first listed as an endangered species in 1967, their numbers threatened by hunting and habitat loss. Then the American alligator was removed from the endangered species list in 1987 after the U.S. Fish and Wildlife Service pronounced a complete recovery of the species. I'll say – conservative estimates put the population at over one million in Florida, Louisiana, Texas, and Georgia. Because they can tolerate brackish water as well as freshwater, they can be found in rivers, swamps, bogs, lakes, ponds, creeks, canals, swimming pools, and lots of Florida golf courses.

The American alligator is the largest reptile in North America (distinguished from the American crocodile by its short, rounded snout and black color). They can live 35–50 years in the wild, 60–80 years in captivity. The average adult male is 13 feet in length (half of the length taken up by the tail), although they can grow up to 18 feet long. Bulls are generally larger than females, weighing 450–600 pounds.

They're everywhere in Florida, and they eat just about anything. Usually that means lizards, fish, snakes, turtles, even little gators, but they'll also enjoy corgi and chicken terrier yorkie.

Florida residents have learned to be blasé about gators. They're an everyday part of living in this subtropical climate. But things are changing. Sanibel Island may be leading the way for a new stance on gators in the state. In the past six years several people have died in alligator attacks across the state, with several in Sanibel. It's hard to be as sanguine about gator-human relations when women are getting chomped while pruning their gardens.

The problems are not just a function of large numbers – people feed the gators and thus the alligators have gotten chummy and less fearful of humans, and vice versa.

So now new policies are being put in place. In many spots along the Gulf Coast, if gators get large (over eight feet) they are taken away and "processed." Smaller ones get relocated. The jury is out on this interspecies relationship.

## STAY SAFE

Alligators are cold-blooded (literally, maybe figuratively). It's a good survival tactic because they don't need to eat as much or as often as their warm-blooded counterparts. In fact, they can't eat unless their internal body temperature is 90 degrees. Thus, they don't eat all winter, and in the spring can be seen in the midmorning basking on the banks in a sunny spot. They're hungry and ready to mate in April and May – a good time to steer especially clear. In the summer the females lay their eggs in a nest (up to 70 eggs) and cover them, then the eggs incubate for 65 days. (As a cool aside, alligators lack sexual chromosomes, so that sex is determined by the temperature at which eggs incubate. Between 90 and 93 degrees they're all male, between 87 and 89 degrees they're female.) The mom stays close, carrying the freshly hatched babies to the water. Even after they're swimming around, mama is protective for up to the first two years (supposedly she can hear their cry for help up to a mile away). Still, it's said only 1 in 10 alligators lives through the first year.

So, to review:

- Don't feed the gators. And if you see others doing so, give them a hard time.

- Don't bother the babies or come between a mother and her young.

- Don't bug them during their cranky spring mating season.

- Closely supervise kids playing in or near fresh or brackish water. Never allow little kids to play by water unattended. The same goes for pets. In fact, just don't let your dog swim in fresh or brackish water in Florida, period.

- Alligators feed most actively at dusk and dawn, so schedule your lake or river swim for another time.

- They don't make good pets. They are not tamed in captivity, and it's illegal.

- If you are bitten, seek medical attention, even if it seems minor. Their mouths harbor very infectious bacteria.

- If you see a big one that seems especially interested in humans, call the local police nonemergency number.

- Don't throw your fish scraps and guts back into the water when fishing. This encourages gators to hang around boats and docks.

### A LITTLE FLORIDA GATOR HUMOR

An old codger in Florida owned a large farm with a big pond in the back. He had it fixed up pretty nicely, with a picnic table, a shady fruit orchard, a little fishing dock.

One evening the farmer decided to go down to the pond and have a look around. He grabbed an old five-gallon bucket to bring back some fruit.

As he neared the pond, he heard voices, with shouting and laughter. As he came closer he saw it was a bunch of young women skinny-dipping in his pond. He made the women aware of his presence and they all went to the deep end.

One of the women shouted to him, "Sir, we're not coming out until you leave!"

The old man frowned. "I didn't come down here to spy on you ladies swimming naked." Holding up the bucket, he said, "I'm here to feed the alligator."

Moral: Old men can still think fast.

COURTESY OF NAPLES, MARCO ISLAND, EVERGLADES CVB

**argiope spider** is another distinctive and fairly common Gulf Coast species—they build big webs with zipperlike zigzag bands of silk at the center.

There are two species of **fire ants** in Florida, the red imported fire ant and the tropical or native fire ant. Either way, their sting is a nasty shock. They form loose, sandy mounds on the ground, and when perturbed they swarm out of their house to bite you, leaving raised white or red welts that really hurt and itch for days. Be aware of where you're standing while visiting Florida, avoiding mounds of loose dirt at all costs.

# History

## THE GULF COAST'S NATIVE AMERICANS

Twenty-five thousand years before the birth of Christ, small tribes of primitive hunters crossed the Bering Strait from Asia to the Americas. Generation after generation traveled southward until these hunters arrived in what is now Florida—perhaps one of the last places on continental North America to be inhabited by humans. Warm and mild of climate, the waters teeming with fish, Florida was a hospitable home for early nomadic Paleo-Indians (circa 12,000 B.C. to 7500 B.C.). They built small huts of animal fur and lived off the land's bounty, fishing the bays and streams. In the time 1000 B.C. to A.D. 1500, the tribes developed advanced tools and pottery-making skills. And by A.D. 1500 Florida's natives were divided into large groupings, most ethnologically and linguistically related to the Creek family. Each grouping was divided further into small independent villages. Conservative estimates put the total numbers of Native Americans in Florida at 100,000 at that time.

In northwest Florida the **Apalachee** of the Tallahassee Hills, in between the Suwannee and Apalachicola Rivers, and the **Timucuans,** their dominion ranging more in the center of the Florida peninsula, between the Aucilla River and the Atlantic and as far south as Tampa Bay, brought farming skills to the area. They cultivated squash, beans, and corn, hunting to supplement their meals with meat. Highly organized and hierarchical tribes, they lived in great communal houses and had an absolute ruler (who was assisted by a shaman and a council of noblemen) and a delineated pecking order. They also built elaborate burial and temple mounds, the ruins of which can still be seen.

Along the southwest Gulf Coast the **Calusa** dominated, feared because of their fierceness. They were tall, with long flowing hair and simple garb consisting only of breechclouts of tanned deerskin. They were not farmers, living instead off the bounty of the local waters and the wealth of the nearby woods. Forty Calusa villages spread along the Florida Gulf Coast, with Mound Key near the mouth of the Caloosahatchee River the largest village. They had only primitive tools, but the Calusa built huge mounds of shell and deep moats to protect their villages of raised, thatch-roofed huts. They practiced sacrificial worship and exhibited little interest in the Spaniards' missionary overtures.

Franciscan friars fared better in bringing Catholicism to the Timucuans and the Apalachee, just as the Spanish soldiers were granted permission to steal from the native peoples. The missionaries taught the natives to read and write, and they became more like Spaniards, leaving their villages to build houses in St. Augustine or carrying corn along the Camino Real connecting St. Augustine with the Tallahassee area.

Both tribes lost numbers to diseases brought by the Spaniards, and then more to the British who tried to raid the Spanish missions and gain control of Florida. The British brought the Yamasee Indians from South Carolina, and together they destroyed the mission buildings and took many of the natives as slaves. In 1763, when the Spanish ceded Florida to the British, the Spanish departed the fort at St. Augustine and took the remaining Indians to Cuba. While the Calusa were less amenable to coexisting peacefully with the Spanish, they met the same fate, dying out in the late 1700s. Enemy tribes from Georgia and South Carolina began raiding the Calusa territory; some Calusas were captured and sold as slaves, and the rest seem to have died of diseases such as smallpox and measles.

The **Seminoles** were originally of Creek stock, hailing from Georgia and Alabama. They moved into Florida during the mid-1700s, occupying the spaces indigenous Florida Indians had left behind. They, too, ended up being annihilated by disease and the Spanish, British, and American settlers. Their refusal to withdraw to reservations resulted in the Seminole Wars of 1835–1842. By the end of the war, 4,420 Seminoles had surrendered and been deported to the west. Another 300, however, defied every effort of the United States government, retreating to the backwoods of the Everglades to hide out. Many of their descendants occupy the area to this day. According to 2000 census data, 581 tribes, bands, and groups are represented in the state's Native American population of 117,880.

In recent years, the Seminole tribe, headquartered in Hollywood, Florida, has assumed a higher profile, with more noncontiguous reservations than any tribe in North America and lucrative gaming casinos getting more buff by the year.

## SPANISH EXPLORATION

The southernmost state in the United States, Florida was named by **Ponce de Leon** upon his visit in 1513, clearly taken with the lush tropical wilderness. This expedition, the first documented presence of Europeans on the U.S. mainland, was ostensibly "to discover and people the island of Bimini." On the return voyage he rounded the Dry Tortugas to explore the Gulf of Mexico, entering Charlotte Harbor. He soon realized that Florida was more than a large island. Near Mound Key he encountered the fierce Calusa people, and while on Estero Island repairing his ship he narrowly escaped Calusa capture. Eight years later he returned and headed to the Calusa territory with 500 of his men, aiming to establish a permanent colony in Florida. In an ensuing battle with the Calusa, Ponce de Leon was pierced in the thigh by an arrow and carried back to his ship. He never returned again.

Many of the subsequent explorers' missions were less high-profile. In 1516, **Diego Miruelo** mapped Pensacola Bay. In 1517, **Alonso Alvarez de Pineda** went the length of the Florida shore to the Mississippi River, confirming Ponce de Leon's assertion that Florida was not an island. In 1520, **Vasquez de Ayollon** mapped the Carolina coast (which at the time Spain claimed in the vast region they called "Florida").

**Panfilo de Narvaez** was a veteran Caribbean soldier, hired by Spanish authorities in 1520 to overthrow Hernán Cortés's tyrannical rule. After a lengthy imprisonment by Cortés, Narvaez went back to Spain and obtained a grant to colonize the Gulf Coast from northern Mexico to Florida. Together with **Cabeza de Vaca,** an armada of five ships, and 400 soldiers, Narvaez landed north of the mouth of Tampa Bay in 1527. Spanish–Native American relations deteriorated quickly during this period; the Spaniards' ruthless hunt for gold and riches met with violence on the part of the Indians.

Narvaez ordered his ships back to Cuba, while a band of men headed northward to the Panhandle in search of gold. Empty-handed, Narvaez finally returned to the Gulf at St. Marks. Assuming Mexico to be only a few days' journey to the west, Narvaez had five long canoes constructed, which capsized in a storm off the coast of Texas. Narvaez drowned, and only Cabeza de Vaca and four others survived. This little band traveled 6,000 miles and in 1536 reached Mexico City to report on their ill-fated mission.

## SPANISH, FRENCH, AND ENGLISH COLONIZATION

Then came **Hernando de Soto.** In the spring of 1539 he sailed for Tampa Bay with seven vessels, 600 soldiers, three Jesuit friars, and several dozen civilians with the intent of starting a settlement. Where he went exactly is a topic of much debate: Some say he landed in Manatee County; others believe it was in Charlotte Harbor. Like many of the conquistadores before him, de Soto was attracted to the stories of Indian riches to the north, so he sent his fleet back to Cuba, left only a rudimentary base camp on the Manatee River, and set off inland from the coast. He and his men never found what they sought, moving ever northward into Georgia, South Carolina, Tennessee, Alabama, Mississippi, and Arkansas, where he died of fever.

There were religious missions to the state during the same time—Dominican priest **Father Luis Cancer,** three additional missionaries, and a Christianized Indian maiden named Magdalene arrived on the beaches outside Tampa Bay in 1549. Given the Native Americans' experience with white men, it's probably no wonder that Father Cancer was quickly surrounded and clubbed to death. The survivors in his party hightailed it back to Mexico to put the skids on future missionary proposals for Florida.

In 1559, the viceroy of Mexico decided a settlement on the Gulf was essential in helping shipwrecked sailors and to discourage French trading visits. He hired **Tristán de Luna** to establish this colony. With 1,500 soldiers and 13 ships, de Luna landed at Pensacola Bay. De Luna's poor leadership led to the group becoming scattered, five ships being destroyed, and a period of near starvation for the settlers. They gave up and went home. (As an aside, in 1992 the Florida Bureau of Archaeological Research found the remains of a colonial Spanish ship in Pensacola Bay that might have been one of de Luna's sunken ships.) Following this, King Philip II of Spain announced that Spain was no longer interested in promoting colonial expeditions into Florida.

French Protestant Huguenots prepared to challenge Spain's sovereignty in Florida. Another failure, really. **Jean Ribault,** France's most lauded seaman of the time, set sail for Florida on April 30, 1562, establishing a colony at Port Royal, South Carolina, that year. It didn't work out, and somehow on his return to Europe England's Queen Elizabeth had him arrested for establishing a French colony in Spanish territory. Spaniard **Pedro Menéndez de Avilés,** a much-celebrated naval commander, took up where Ribault left off, establishing what is thought of as the first European settlement, in St. Augustine, Florida, in 1565.

The history of Florida during the first Spanish administration (1565–1763) centers along the east coast of the state, specifically around St. Augustine. The English neighbors to the north periodically attempted to capture the Florida territory (Governor Moore of South Carolina made an unsuccessful attempt in 1702, Governor Oglethorpe of Georgia invaded Florida in 1740), and in 1763 Spain ceded Florida to England. They, in turn, did an equally incomplete job of populating the country and developing its resources, especially in light of the increasingly aggressive Native American tribes. The British controlled Florida 1763–1781, at which point the Spanish occupied it again 1783–1821. But in 1821 the Spanish government ratified a treaty turning over Florida to the United States.

## STATEHOOD, CIVIL WAR, AND RECONSTRUCTION

After the signing of the Adams-Onis treaty ceding Florida to the United States in 1821, Andrew Jackson was appointed military governor of the territory. Florida's present boundaries were established, with Tallahassee as the new capital and William P. Duval as its first territorial governor. It was a plantation economy, with settlers expanding ever southward and crowding out the Seminole Indians. Florida was admitted to the Union in 1845, the 27th state. After Abraham Lincoln's election to the presidency in 1860, Florida's proslavery stance led to it seceding from the Union in 1861 and joining the Confederacy. Florida furnished salt, cattle, and other goods to the Confederate army. Relative to population size, Florida furnished more troops than any other Confederate state, participating in the campaigns of Tennessee and Virginia. Florida was represented in the higher ranks of the Confederate service by Major-Generals Loring, Anderson, and Smith, and Brigadier-Generals Brevard, Bullock, Finegan, Miller, Davis, Finley, Perry, and Shoup. Florida was represented in the Confederate cabinet by Stephen H. Mallory, Secretary of the Navy. The most notable Civil War engagement fought in Florida was the battle of Olustee (February 20, 1864), a Confederate victory.

After the war, a new constitution was adopted, the Fourteenth Amendment ratified, and Florida was readmitted into the Union in 1868. It took a decade or so for the state to establish social, educational, and industrial health. The state's general level of poverty led to four million acres of land being sold to speculative real-estate promoters in 1881. The discovery of rich phosphate deposits in 1889 improved the state's economy, as did its increasing popularity as a winter resort destination.

## FLORIDA'S FIRST BOOM

Along with the phosphate mining in the southwestern part of the state, agriculture (especially citrus) and cattle ranching brought wealth to Florida, as did wealthy tourists who came to relax in the state's natural beauty and mild climate each winter. In the 1870s, steamboat tours on Florida's winding rivers were a popular attraction. Sponge diving around Tarpon Springs, cigar-making around Tampa—industry was booming in the later part of the 19th century even along the less-populated Gulf Coast.

The boom had its roots in the railroad and in road construction, industries that blossomed as a result of the state legislature's passage of the Internal Improvement Act in 1855. It offered cheap or free public land to investors, particularly those interested in transportation. On Florida's east coast, **Henry Flagler** was responsible for the Florida East Coast Railway, completed in 1912 and linking Key West all the way up the eastern coast of Florida. After making his money with Standard Oil, in retirement he realized that the key to developing the state of Florida was to establish an extensive transportation system. His biggest contribution might have been converting all of the small railroad lines he purchased to a standard gauge, allowing trains to travel the whole length without changing track.

## On the Gulf Coast

Another Henry worked his magic on the other coast of Florida. **Henry B. Plant** was largely responsible for the first boom period along the Gulf, using his railroad to open vast but previously inaccessible parts of the state. Henry Plant's rails extended south from Jacksonville along the St. Johns River to Sanford then southwest through Orlando to Tampa. The Plant Investment Company bought up several small railroads with the aim of providing continuous service across the state, his holdings eventually including 2,100 miles of track, several steamship lines out of the port of Tampa, and a number of important hotels. The University of Tampa now occupies the lavish hotel Plant built at the terminus of his line. This new rail line not only provided passengers with easy access but also gave citrus growers quick routes to get their produce to market.

Around the same time, in 1911, **Barron Gift Collier** visited Useppa Island off the Fort Myers coast and fell in love with the subtropical landscape. Over the next decade he bought up more than a million acres of southwest Florida, making himself the largest landowner in the state. His holdings stretched from the Ten Thousand Islands northward to Useppa Island and inland from Naples into the Everglades and Big Cypress. He invested millions of dollars to convert this vast wilderness into agricultural land and a vacation paradise (some would say a dubious gift to the state). His real gift, however, was his completion of the state's Tamiami Trail, a road that exists even today, linking Tampa with Miami. In gratitude, the state created Collier

County in his honor in 1923, with Everglades City as the county seat.

The Roaring Twenties were good to Florida. With more Americans owning cars, it became the hip thing to visit the Sunshine State on vacation. Land speculators bought up everything, parcels being sold and resold for ever-increasing amounts of money. Great effort was expended to drain the Everglades and Florida swampland to create even more viable land for homes and agriculture. The land frenzy reached its peak after World War I in 1925, but a swift bust followed the next year due to a major hurricane, then another one in 1928, and then the Great Depression.

## CUBAN REVOLUTION

Located 90 miles south of Key West, Cuba has always been closely connected with the affairs of Florida, and vice versa. Under Spanish rule in the late 1800s, Cuban relations with Spain deteriorated, and in 1868 the two countries went to war, with 200,000 Cuban and Spanish casualties. In 1898, the Spanish-American War focused the country's attention on the Gulf Coast city of Tampa, the primary staging area for U.S. troops preparing for the war in Cuba.

During the war, many prominent Cubans fled to Key West, including Vicente Martinez Ybor, who opened a cigar factory, the El Principe de Gales, in Key West in 1869. (He eventually relocated the factory to a scrub area east of Tampa in 1886, once Henry B. Plant had completed rail service to aid in shipping and importation. This first factory begat a huge cigar industry in Tampa, with 200 factories at its peak.)

The war lasted only a few months after American involvement. Cuba was relinquished to the United States in trust for its inhabitants by the signing of the Treaty of Paris on December 20, 1898. Spanish rule ended January 1, 1899, and U.S. military rule ended May 1, 1902.

Cuban history after that continued to be fractious: Thomas Estrada Palma was the first president of the new republic, but he was ousted in 1906. Again, a provisional American government ruled, then withdrew in 1909. There was a period of prosperity, another revolt, and then General Gerardo Machado was elected president in 1925 and reelected in 1928. During his second term he suspended the freedoms of speech, press, and assembly and was forced to flee the country in 1933.

Colonel Fulgencio Batista y Zaldivar, who controlled the army, was elected president in 1940. During his term, Cuba entered World War II on the side of the Allies. Batista was defeated in 1944 by Grau San Martin, and then in 1948 Carlos Prio Socarras was elected president—but he was overthrown by Batista in 1952. Mayhem ensued, but Batista wasn't taking no for an answer. There continued to be strong anti-Batista resistance, and in 1959 Batista resigned and fled the country. Fidel Castro set up a provisional government with himself as premier. Political refugees from the Cuban revolution poured into Florida by the thousands.

Not long after came the Cuban Missile Crisis of October 1962, precipitated by the Soviets installing nuclear missiles in Cuba. Soviet field commanders in Cuba were authorized to use tactical nuclear weapons unless President John F. Kennedy and Premier Nikita Khrushchev could reach an understanding.

In 1980, more than 100,000 Cuban refugees came to the United States, mostly through Florida, when Castro briefly opened the port of Mariel to a flotilla of privately chartered U.S. ships, and in the early 1990s Florida received refugees from the military coup in Haiti and another wave of refugees from Cuba in 1994. Many of the Cuban expatriates live in Miami and environs, less so on the Gulf Coast. Still, the Cuban influence is robustly felt in areas such as Tampa's Ybor City.

## MODERN FLORIDA

While it was the first state to be settled by Europeans, Florida might be the last state to have entered fully into modernity. It remained more or less a frontier until the 20th century, with the first paved road not until 1920. It was really World War II that changed things in the state, prompting a period of sustained growth that lasted more than 50 years. Immigration to the state has resulted in a real diversity of ethnic groups, with a dense concentration of Cubans in the Miami area and Mexicans throughout the state.

Tourism has been responsible for much of the growth in modern times, with a serious assist from Walt Disney World, the biggest tourist destination on the planet. There are more hotel rooms in Orlando than in New York City, I kid you not. The beaches have continued to draw multitudes of tourists, and the beaches of the Northwestern part of the state have seen a recent surge of interest with locations such as Seaside and Destin becoming increasingly popular vacation destinations.

However, recently the state has witnessed an onslaught of both natural and human-induced disasters, both physical and economic, that have been at least partly responsible for the first population decrease in the state since the 1940 war boom days. Between the years of 2008 and 2009 the state saw a decrease in population by more than 56,000 people. The hurricane season of 2004 was the first blow that caused many people to rethink their desire to live on the welcome mat for most U.S. hurricanes. And then insurance costs skyrocketed and got people really considering heading for the hills of greener pastures in other states. To put it into perspective, according to the *New York Times,* homeowner insurance rates in

Florida have as much as tripled since the 2004 storm seasons.

Just as much of Florida was starting to recover from the brutal 2004 storms, the bottom fell out of the housing market. In October 2010, Florida ranked second in states with highest number of foreclosures. It is estimated that in 2010, 1 in 167 homes in Florida were foreclosures. (The leader was Nevada where an astounding 1 in 69 homes were foreclosed.) In Florida, foreclosures made up more than 30 percent of home sales for 2010. And then on April 20, 2010, the Deepwater Horizon well exploded off the coast of Louisiana, killing 11 rig workers and releasing, over a three-month period, an estimated 185 million gallons of crude oil into the Gulf of Mexico. Eventually, some of the oil made its way onto the Gulf Coast of Florida, most of the oil that impacted Florida washing onto the shores of the Northwestern beaches from Pensacola to just West of Port St. Joe. The deep and lasting impacts of oil spill are still unknown as scientists scramble to study the marinelife, people, and economies that have been affected by the disaster, but the immediate impacts have been enormous and unfathomably diverse, from the loss of lives and the incalculable impacts of stress on Floridians to the economic losses of tourism and the fishing industry, to name a few. The well was finally capped around July 15, and slowly the areas most impacted by the spill are recovering.

# Government and Economy

## STATE GOVERNMENT

In 1968, Florida adopted a new state constitution. The governor is elected for a term of four years, and the legislature has a senate of 40 members and a house of representatives of 120 members. The state also elects 23 representatives and 2 senators to the U.S. Congress and has 25 electoral votes.

Historically, the majority of Florida citizens voted Democrat. However, the population

explosion that Florida experienced between 1950 and 2008 brought an increasing number of Republicans, leaving the state approximately evenly split between the two parties. It's because of that, combined with its large number of electoral votes, that Florida is considered by political analysts to be a key swing state in presidential elections.

North Florida and the length of the Panhandle has mostly supported Republican candidates over the past 16 years, despite the fact that there are plenty of registered Democrats—the thought is that there are many Democrats who, for whatever reason, have failed to change their registration. Leon, Jefferson and Gadsen counties, all grouped together around Tallahassee, are dominated by Democrats. The population in Naples and southwest Florida are predominately Republican. Broward and Palm Beach Counties on the east coast have pockets of Democrats who consistently vote for the most liberal candidate running, while the Cubans equal them in numbers and vote mostly Republican. Tampa, once strongly Democratic, is now much more heavily Republican.

Florida has had an inconsistent voting pattern that seems somewhat unrelated to voter political party affiliation. It's the state that elected Democrat Bob Graham in five consecutive statewide elections. Florida elected Nixon in 1968 and 1972, but Carter in 1976, Reagan in 1980 and 1984, Bush in 1988 and 1992, Clinton in 1996, George W. Bush in 2000 and 2004, and then Obama in 2008.

As for state government, Democrat Lawton Chiles, elected governor in 1990 and reelected in 1994, was succeeded by Republican Jeb Bush, elected in 1998 and reelected in 2002, followed by Republican Charlie Crist (attorney general under Bush), elected in 2006. Republican Rick Scott was elected governor in 2010, with Jennifer Carroll as lieutenant governor, Pam Bondi as attorney general, and Jeff Atwater as CFO.

## FLORIDA INDUSTRY

Florida spent its early years luring industry here with big tax breaks and incentives, sometimes even free land. A relatively inexpensive labor force, rich natural resources, a general antiunion government, and no state income tax has brought many waves of takers. The deep-water ports along the Gulf prompted shipbuilding booms as far back as the 1830s, with industries like cotton shipping utilizing the calm open water, connecting rivers and Intracoastal Waterway.

Tallahassee is the modern seat of government in Florida.

Today, tourism is the state's number one industry, plain and simple. From January 1 through December 31, 2008, more than 84.2 million people visited Florida, according to data released by Visit Florida, the state's marketing arm. It's an approximately $65.2 billion business, with 41,000 restaurants, 4,700 hotels and accommodations, and some of the world's top tourist attractions (Walt Disney World, Kennedy Space Center, and did I mention Walt Disney World?).

Agriculture has also played a mighty role in the commercial well-being of the state. In 2008 (the last available statistics), Florida ranked first in the value of oranges, grapefruit, tangerines, sugarcane for sugar and seed, squash, watermelons, sweet corn, fresh-market snap beans, fresh-market tomatoes, and fresh-market cucumbers, with receipts of $1.4 billion. It also ranked third in fruit and nuts with receipts of over $3 billion; second in the United States in the value of production of strawberries, bell peppers, and cucumbers for pickles; and fourth in the production of honey. Horticultural products (meaning plants and floriculture) are big business, too, hiking up total state agricultural revenues past $6.8 billion.

Cattle ranches and dairy farms are dense in

the middle of the state, and from Gulf waters commercial fishers haul millions of pounds of fish and shellfish, and sportfishers haul millions more. The lumber industry is still going strong in some parts of the state, while high-tech companies have flocked to the St. Petersburg/Tampa area recently, drawn by good weather and low housing costs.

Along with many environmentally sound businesses and industries, Florida, like most of the United States, has seen its fair share of environmentally damaging industries from timber and turpentining to paper mills and chemical plants. It wasn't until the Clean Water Act in 1972—which regulates the discharge of pollutants into U.S. waters and makes it illegal for industry to discharge pollutants without a permit—that industry in Florida was forced to regulate and control its release of contaminants. The state is continually improving the level of pollutants in waterways and air, but the Gulf states (Florida, Texas, and Louisiana in particular) are still among the top offenders for allowing permit violations for high-hazard chemicals.

The BP oil spill of 2010 took a serious toll on state visitation, especially along the Northern Panhandle portion of the Gulf Coast, and the entire Gulf Coast is still recovering from the disaster. BP pledged $20 billion to help with recovery efforts, but the dispersing of the funds has been slow. At the time this book was published, six months after the oil spill, BP had dispersed at least 185 million gallons of oil into the Gulf of Mexico but less than $1 billion of the pledged $20 billion into Gulf Coast communities impacted by the disaster.

## FLORIDA'S MILITARY

There are currently 13 active military installations in Florida. This follows a 2005 shakeup at the hands of the U.S. Department of Defense when they announced their preliminary 2005 Base Realignment and Closure list (it recommended closing 33 major bases and realigning, either enlarging or shrinking, 29 others). Though shrinking, the military has in recent years been the state's third top economic sector

behind tourism and agriculture, with 64,500 people employed in the armed forces directly.

Many of the bases and two of the unified commands are along the Gulf Coast. **U.S. Central Command** (CENTCOM) is at MacDill Air Force Base in Tampa and is responsible for U.S. security interests in 25 nations that stretch from the Horn of Africa, through the Gulf region, and into Central Asia. The command was activated in January 1983 as the successor to the Rapid Deployment Joint Task Force. A few years after that, in 1987, **U.S. Special Operations Command** (USSOCOM) was established as a unified combatant command also at MacDill, composed of army, navy, and air force special operations forces. Its mission is to support the geographic commanders-in-chief, ambassadors, and their country teams and other government agencies by preparing special operations forces. Its annual budget is nearly $5 billion, 1.3 percent of the overall defense budget.

Of Florida's naval bases, **NAS Pensacola** (Escambia County), **Saufley Field** (Escambia County), **NAS Whiting Field** (Santa Rosa County), and **Panama City Naval Surface Warfare Center** (Bay County) are along the Gulf Coast. Of Florida's air force bases, **Eglin AFB** (Okaloosa County), **Hurlburt Field** (Okaloosa County), **MacDill AFB** (Hillsborough County), and **Tyndall AFB** (Bay County) are on the Gulf Coast.

But Florida's defense industry goes beyond its military installations; Florida ranks fourth in the largest dollar volume of Department of Defense prime contracts awards received by private-sector companies.

## EDUCATION IN FLORIDA

The issue in the forefront of education in Florida is funding. In the past several years, public schools have been receiving funds well below the national average as a result of widespread deficits and budget cuts. Many education interest groups such as the Florida Education Association have been promoting and lobbying for a one percent sales tax increase to be implemented over a three-year period that will directly benefit the under-funded schools of the Florida public education system. At the same time public schools are battling with funding issues, students and parents are wrestling with skyrocketing tuition costs at Florida' colleges and universities.

Florida's tuition on average is in fact lower than most states in the nation. It ranks 48th in the nation in the cost of in-state tuition for college. On average students still pay over $7,000 a year for higher education and overall 49 percent of students in Florida graduate from college with an average of $20,766 of debt, according to data provided by The Project on Student Debt. Across the nation tuition costs increased 4–7 percent for the 2010 school year; currently Florida State colleges are looking to pass legislation that will allow them to increase tuition by a whopping 15 percent. When you combine these high costs of education, the staggering amount of debt with which students graduate, and a struggling economy with an unemployment rate in August 2010 of 12.4 percent, you end up with a pretty rough deal for the class of 2011.

Another funding issue has long plagued the Florida education system—teachers' salaries. Florida now ranks number 28 in teacher salary, but increases in salary have been slow and mostly unimpressive. In 2009 teachers' salaries increased by only $16 to an average salary of $46,938, which still trails the national average by $5,508. The lower-than-average salaries for teachers has partly resulted in a low retention rate in the teacher workforce, with more than 40 percent of teachers in Florida leaving their jobs in the first five years. The loss statistics are even higher in low-income schools.

Florida's public schools have also had a hard time competing on a national level. Recently reports that came out evaluating Florida schools in 14 categories found the state exceptionally below the national average in three categories. Florida has been well below the average on nationally standardized tests, the amount of funding per student, and college readiness. However, it is a mixed picture as the recent report by *Education Week* ranked Florida's public school system 8th overall in the nation. Also,

Florida is implementing legislation to reduce class size and increase the number of teachers in state schools. The state has also recently been awarded up to $700 million through a grant from the Race to the Top program, which funds projects to turn around low-performing schools and implement standards for testing and assessments.

Florida also ranks among the lowest in the country in spending per student (39th out of 50 states, according to the U.S. Census Bureau's 2009 Education Finance Report). For example, between 2007 and 2008, the state spent a total of $9,039 per pupil. But the problems also seem to be as much about ideology as dollars and cents. The state has failed to prioritize the education of its students, as much at the elementary school levels as at the college level.

## ENVIRONMENTAL ISSUES

When talking about environmental issues on the Gulf Coast of Florida, the issues related to and surrounding the Gulf Oil Spill of 2010 overshadow all others. The spill started when the Deep Water Horizon well off the coast of Louisiana exploded on April 20, 2010. It killed 11 workers who were present on the rig at the time and, according to a *New York Times* report, started releasing more than 60,000 barrels of oil a day into the Gulf of Mexico. When the well was finally plugged on July 15, 2010, it had released an estimated 53,000 barrels of oil a day into the Gulf. According to the Flow Rate Technical Group appointed by BP and the Coast Guard to estimate the extent of the spill, the total volume of oil released into the Gulf over the three months the well was leaking is believed to be at least 205.8 million gallons of crude oil. On September 19, 2010, the relief well was finally completed and the Coast Guard declared the well to be officially "dead." In early 2011, scientists were still finding an abundance of oil on the sea floor of the Gulf of Mexico within a 1.5-mile radius around the well.

What the oil spill has meant for the ecosystem in the Gulf of Mexico is still largely unknown as the long-term effects of the largest oil spill to take place in the Gulf of Mexico are studied and documented. Scientists are just now starting to gather information on the impacts of the oil spill, but initial information published has painted a very grim picture for the health of the environment in the Gulf and surrounding region.

On April 23, 2010, the U.S. Coast Guard began receiving reports that oil was washing up in Wildlife Refuges and the seafood grounds on the Louisiana Coast. By June 21, 36 percent of federal waters in the Gulf of Mexico were closed for fishing, totaling nearly 67,000 square miles and detrimentally impacting the fishing industry in the region. It is estimated that the initial impacts of the oil spill have cost the fishing industry along the Gulf Coast over $2.5 billion. Currently, it has been shown that over 20 percent of the juvenile bluefin tuna were killed by the oil spill, a species that has declined by 80 percent over the past 30 years. Even more frightening numbers are found in the volume of dead sealife collected since the beginning of the disaster. There are more than 8,000 species inhabiting the area impacted by the oil spill, including more than 1,200 fish, 200 birds, 1,400 mollusks, 1,500 crustaceans, four sea turtle species, and 29 marine mammals. According to the U.S. Fish and Wildlife Deep Water Horizon Fish and Wildlife Collection Report released on July 5, 2010, 4,678 dead animals had been collected, including 4,080 birds, 525 sea turtles, and 72 dolphins and other mammals.

Currently, what also has many residents and scientists concerned are the dispersants that were used in fighting the oil spill. More than 1 million gallons of chemical dispersant were released into the Gulf of Mexico directly at the wellhead source in an effort to break up the oil before it reached the surface. Robert Diaz, a marine biologist at the College of William and Mary recently said on dispersants, "The dispersants definitely don't make oil disappear. They take it from one area in an ecosystem and put it in another." And University of South Florida researchers are finding that the dispersed oil is having a toxic effect on the phytoplankton and bacteria in the Gulf of Mexico—the microscopic plants that make up the basis of the food chain here. The EPA and NOAA have openly stated that they support the claim that dispersed oil is no less toxic than the oil alone. Most experts can agree, however, that the true impacts of the BP oil spill will not be known for decades to come.

Apart from the oil spill of 2010, there are many complex and far-reaching environmental issues in Florida, from declining amphibian populations to an abundance of superfund sites, paper mill water contamination, saltwater intrusion in the Everglades and other areas, and the quickly disappearing Florida Panther population, to name but a few. Millions of acres have been bulldozed to make way for strip malls, condo developments, and all those beautiful golf courses and theme parks. It's the same story that is told of most recently developed natural settings. And with more than 125,000 new residents moving to Florida every year from 1950 to 2008, something had to give.

For instance, recent drought in Georgia has meant that the Army Corps of Engineers has repeatedly withheld water to accommodate the water needs of greater Atlanta. Downstream along the Apalachicola River and Apalachicola Bay, the resulting salinity (less freshwater in an estuary means a greater percentage of saltwater) may mean the end of the state's oyster industry, not to mention the destruction of endangered species like Florida sturgeon and several kinds of mussels.

Still, the state's commitment to the environment elevates the situation from hopeless. There's been an enormous grassroots effort in the past decade in Florida that has largely moved into the mainstream after the BP oil spill, of regular people who have stood up against offshore drilling and supported the protection of the abundant and beautiful natural resources that are so directly tied to the quality of life and economy of everyone in the state. If their efforts are successful, the state's natural treasures, as well as its fishing and tourism industries that make up such a large portion of the Gulf Coast's economy might be preserved, restored, and possibly even strengthened.

# People and Culture

## DEMOGRAPHICS

Florida ranks fourth in the United States in population, behind California, Texas, and New York. In 2009, the population was estimated to be 18,537,969 (up from 9,746,961 in 1980). If you count Tampa/St. Petersburg/Clearwater as a single metropolitan area, it beats Miami for sheer numbers—2,733,761 versus 2,500,625 at the last census in 2009. On the Gulf Coast, the other most populous areas are Fort Myers/Cape Coral (218,876), Tallahassee (172,574) Sarasota/Bradenton (105,998), Pensacola (53,428), and Naples (21,653). Until 2008, nearly 1,000 people were moving to Florida every day. Then, in 2009, Florida experienced the first decrease in population since 1950. Still, the fastest-growing part of the state is the central interior, particularly the corridor along I-4, which connects the Tampa Bay area through Orlando to Daytona Beach in the east.

## Age

Florida's age distribution over the past decade has changed very little regarding those 65 years and older. In 1990, there were 3,281,220 Floridians aged 65 and older (17.7 percent of the total population), whereas in 2009 the census counted 3,188,531 in this group (17.2 percent of the total). So the percentage and number of those over 65 has only slightly declined.

The Gulf Coast, especially the area around Tampa, has gotten younger in recent years. For instance, the youth population (those age 0–19) has shown increasing growth rates over the last 30 years, from 15.5 percent 1970–1980 to 20.31 percent in 2010.

The median age is at its lowest all along the northern border of the state, where it meets Georgia and Alabama all the way out the Panhandle. There's another dense concentration of youth around Miami and Tampa (sister city St. Petersburg, famously a retirement destination, has also shifted younger, demographically). The oldest parts of the state, citizenry-wise, are Sarasota, Naples, and along the Nature Coast.

## Race

The population of the Gulf Coast is still primarily white (21.6 percent nonwhite in 2009), with the greatest ethnic diversity in the Tampa Bay area. The African American population is twice that of the Latino population along the northern border of the state (along the Panhandle and the Alabama and Georgia borders), while in the southern part of the state, close to Miami, the correlation flip-flops. The state's Latino population reached 21.5 percent in 2009.

## Religion

In modern times, the Gulf Coast is primarily Christian. Jewish retirees don't, for whatever reason, settle along the Gulf Coast, with the exception of Sarasota (3–6 percent Jewish, as compared to the east coast of the state from Coral Gables up through Palm Beach, which is roughly 13–15 percent Jewish). The southernmost part of the state is predominantly Catholic, as is the area just north of Tampa up through what is known as the Nature Coast. Most Floridians are Protestant, with the number increasing the closer you get to the northern border of the state.

## SNOWBIRDS

First, what's a snowbird? It's a temporary resident in Florida, someone who comes from a colder, less hospitable winter climate to bask in the Sunshine State all winter. Snowbirds are usually of retirement age, or nearing it. But let's get more specific: New Yorkers account for 13.1 percent of Florida's temporary residents, followed by Michiganders at 7.4 percent, Ohioans at 6.7 percent, Pennsylvanians at 5.8 percent, and Canadians at 5.5 percent. The average length of stay is five months. If Florida has roughly 7 million households, there are an estimated 920,000 temporary residents during

# WHO YOU CALLING A FLORIDA CRACKER?

That's a good question, really. Many Florida historians are devoted to the theory that the term Florida Cracker originated with the area's cow hunters. As Jesse Otis Beall describes it in the book *Cracker* by Dana Ste. Claire:

*Well, people didn't know what cracker meant and they thought it was just a slang word, you know, for a person. But it was named after the whip, I think, the crackin' whip, as the cowhunters come in. There wasn't cowboys in those days, there was cowhunters, and they used those whips and we'd say, 'Yep, here comes the Crackers.' That's where the word comes from. I'm always a callin' myself a Cracker.*

Pretty convincing. This hypothesis goes back as early as 1810, with John Lambert's *Travels Through Lower Canada, and the United States of North America*. But a lot of historians aren't buying it, weighing in instead on the side of a different theory entirely. Even Florida cow hunter historian Joyce Peters believes that Florida Crackers were called such because of their diet – a poor, rural people, they had trouble rounding up enough calories. Cracked corn fit the bill, as it could be roughly stone ground and then made into a paste with water or fat, baked into a hard "cracker," and then either eaten as hard tack or reconstituted in a stew.

Still others say, yes, cracked corn is implicated, but in a more nefarious way. These Florida backwoodsmen were known to operate moonshine stills, stills that fermented cracked corn mash into a blisteringly alcoholic "white lightning."

Other theories that may or may not hold water: The people were named after the "crackerbox" shape of their simple log houses. Or, they were originally called *cuaqueros*, or Quakers, by the Spaniards who confused them for a colony of Quakers who settled early on in Florida. And the speculations go on.

The book *Cracker* wanders all over trying to figure out what one is exactly, but you have to wait until the glossary until it cuts to the chase: "Cracker – a self-reliant, independent, and tenacious settler of the Deep South, often of Celtic stock, who subsisted by farming or raising livestock and, as a general rule, valued personal independence and restraint-free life over material prosperity. Cracker settlers provided a spirited foundation for the peopling of the rural South and Florida."

These days Florida Cracker is still something a Floridian can call him- or herself, and with pride, but it's not a moniker to go slinging around lightly. There are still Florida Crackers along the Gulf Coast, and you'll probably know one when you see one.

---

the peak winter months and another 170,000 during the late summer.

## CIRCUS PERFORMERS AND CARNIES

Most people connect Sarasota with the circus. It was in 1927 when Sarasota became an official circus town, with John Ringling bringing his Ringling Bros. and Barnum & Bailey Circus's winter quarters to Sarasota, giving the calm Florida town a bit of spectacle. Many of the little people who starred in the circus retired in Sarasota (in specially built small houses in an area known as "Tiny Town").

Still, Sarasota doesn't get the title "Showtown USA." That high honor goes to another Gulf Coast town.

**Gibsonton,** or Gibtown as it's often affectionately called, was made famous as a wintering town for sideshow and circus performers as well as garden-variety carnies. Many of them retired permanently to Gibtown and have, in recent years, died off, but they leave the town with a colorful history. It's in Hillsborough County, south of Tampa on U.S. 41 near the town of Riverview.

Gibsonton was home to Percilla "Monkey Girl" Bejano and her husband Emmitt "The

Alligator Skin Man" Bejano (billed as the "World's Strangest Married Couple" on sideshow midways all over). There was Jeanie the Half Girl, Al the Giant, and Grady "Lobster Boy" Stiles, Jr. (from a long line of people with ectrodactyly, or "lobster claw" syndrome); Stiles committed murder but got off with probation because prison wasn't equipped to handle him, only to be murdered himself some years later. The conjoined twin Hilton sisters (different Hilton sisters) ran a fruit stand here. Melvin "Rubber Face" Burkhart was the most recent to die, in 2001. His most famous routine was to shove an ice pick and a five-inch nail into his nose.

Gibtown has a post office counter that accommodates little people, and its zoning laws allow residents to keep elephants and circus animals in trailers on their front lawn. Still, it is home to the **International Independent Showmen's Association** (6915 Riverview Dr., 813/677-3590) and a bar called **Showtown USA Lounge** (10902 U.S. 41 S., 813/677-5443) that has rollicking karaoke on the weekend. An historic eatery called **Giants Camp Restaurant,** opened by Al Tomaini (eight feet, four inches tall) and his wife, Jeanie (two feet, six inches tall), sadly, closed in 2006.

Even if you can't fit it into your trip, you can get a sense of Gibtown if you can get your hands on the "Humbug" episode of the *X-Files* (season two), in which Mulder and Scully travel to Gibsonton to investigate the death of Jerald Glazebrook, the Alligator Man. In the episode you'll meet Jim Jim, the Dog-Faced Boy, and the Enigma, who is covered in blue puzzle-piece tattoos and eats glass. Also, there is a 65-minute documentary called *Gibtown* that is hard to find, but worthwhile.

Gibsonton is also home to the largest tropical fish farm in the country, **Ekkwill Waterlife Resources** (800/237-4222, www.ekkwill.com).

## MOVIES SET ON THE GULF COAST

Florida has been a film location just about as long as there've been movies. Today it is ranked third in the country for film production based on revenue generated. The climate, the scenery, the dense and tropical foliage—it has all sparked the imagination of countless directors, cinematographers, and actors, standing in for far-flung lands on several continents. The earliest Florida films aren't anyone's flights of fancy, however, but the 1898 newsreels of U.S. troops in Tampa during the Spanish-American War.

The Museum of Florida History in Tallahassee has a collection of movie posters from films shot in the state. The following are some featured in this collection, and an idiosyncratic assortment of others, all shot along the Gulf Coast.

*Hell Harbor* (1930), the first full-length "talkie" to be made in the state, was shot in Tampa and depicts the story of the descendants of pirate Henry Morgan. *A Guy Named Joe* (1944), starring Spencer Tracy as a WWII pilot who dies and becomes the guardian angel of a young pilot in love with Tracy's girlfriend, was also shot in Tampa at Drew and MacDill air fields.

The Marx Brothers' *The Cocoanuts* (1929) may well be set in Miami, it's not totally clear, but it revolves around Florida's first land boom. *The Yearling* (1946) is also educational and an absolute classic starring Gregory Peck; it's based on the Newbery award–winning book by Marjorie Kinnan Rawlings and was nominated for seven Oscars. Parts of the film were shot at Rawlings's homestead in Cross Creek.

Then we get into some real camp faves, from *Mr. Peabody and the Mermaid* (1948), a William Powell film shot at Weeki Wachee Springs with local mermaids, to *Beneath the 12 Mile Reef* (1953), the story of a Greek sponge diver from Tarpon Springs who falls in love with a girl from the rival Key West sponge divers. The king of Gulf Coast films, *Creature from the Black Lagoon* (1954), was filmed in Wakulla Springs and Tarpon Springs and was followed by two sequels.

Directed by Cecil B. DeMille and starring Betty Hutton, James Stewart, and Charlton Heston, *The Greatest Show on Earth* (1952) was

# FAMOUS FLORIDIANS

It's an incomplete list, but these people, along with O. J. Simpson, Oprah Winfrey, Janet Reno, Clarence Thomas, and Rush Limbaugh, were born and raised in the Sunshine State or at least called it home for a long while.

- **Baseball players:** Buster Posey, Steve Carlton, Dwight Gooden, Barry Larkin, Sammy Sosa

- **Football players:** Emmitt Smith, Mike Ditka, Joe Namath, Daunte Culpepper, Mike Astott, Warrick Dunn, Tony Dungy, Chris Simms

- **Tennis players:** Jennifer Capriati, Martina Hingis, Anna Kournikova, Ivan Lendl, Martina Navratilova, Monica Seles, Andy Roddick, Serena and Venus Williams

- **Wrestlers:** Hulk Hogan, Rick Flair, Dwayne "The Rock" Johnson, Joannie "Chyna" Laurer, Randy "Macho Man" Savage

- **Actors:** Johnny Depp, Kelsey Grammer, Sidney Poitier, Butterfly McQueen, Burt Reynolds, Ben Vereen, Faye Dunaway, Buddy Ebsen, River Phoenix, John Travolta

- **Writers:** Harriet Beecher Stowe, Marjorie Kinnan Rawlings, Zora Neale Hurston, Ernest Hemingway, Carl Hiaasen, Stephen King

- **Artists:** John James Audubon, Winslow Homer

- **Singers:** Jim Morrison, Pat Boone, Jimmy Buffet, Frances Langford, Gloria Estefan, Enrique Iglesias, Lenny Kravitz, Tom Petty, Bo Diddley, Backstreet Boys, *and* some of 'N Sync, the brothers Gibb, Beyoncé Knowles, Jennifer Lopez, Scott Stapp

- **Military Figures:** Joseph W. Stilwell (Army general), Daniel James (Air Force general)

## FAMOUS NAMES IN FLORIDA HISTORY

- Pedro Menendez de Avilás: founder of St. Augustine

- William Pope du Val: first territorial governor

- Osceola: Seminole Indian leader

- David Levy Yulee: one of Florida's initial U.S. senators (first Jewish-American senator)

- Henry B. Plant: famed Florida railroad baron of the late 19th century, on the Gulf Coast

- Henry Flagler: builder of the East Coast Railway, which connected the whole east coast of Florida

- Hamilton Disston: bought four million acres in central Florida and created a canal system

- Thomas Edison and Henry Ford: inventors (well, they both just lived here part-time, but they left a big mark)

- John Ringling: circus entrepreneur

- Barron Collier: southwest Florida landowner and builder of Tamiami Trail

- A. Philip Randolph: labor leader

---

filmed at the Barnum & Bailey headquarters in Sarasota and required all the actors to do their own stunts.

Elvis spent a little time on the Gulf Coast in Pasco County filming *Follow That Dream* (1962)—not a great film. And Christopher Plummer, Gypsy Rose Lee, and Burl Ives got to hang out in the Everglades for the making of Nicholas Ray's *Wind Across the Everglades* (1958), a story about the hardscrabble life in the wilds of South Florida.

Victor Nuñez has done a few excellent movies set along the Gulf Coast, from *A Flash of Green* (1988), based on the novel by J. D. MacDonald about corruption in Sarasota, to *Ruby in Paradise* (1993), a small film about a young woman, played by Ashley Judd, set on the Panhandle. Then he did the Peter Fonda pic

*Ulee's Gold* (1997), a Panhandle family drama about beekeepers, and another not widely released Florida pic called *Coastlines.*

Peter Weir's *The Truman Show* (1998), starring Jim Carrey, was set in the scary-perfect Panhandle town of Seaside; Volker Schlondorff's crime drama *Palmetto* (1998) is set in and around Sarasota; and Spike Jonze's *Adaptation* (2002), a loose interpretation of Susan Orlean's book *The Orchid Thief*, takes place in the mangrove swamps of the Everglades.

John Sayles's *Sunshine State* (2002) is set in a fictional town in Florida, which might be the east coast, but it describes the conflicts of early Floridians and new developers so well that it's worth seeing. Kids will recognize Florida as the setting for *Hoot* (2006), Carl Hiaasen's environmental flick filmed in Boca Grande.

# ESSENTIALS

## Getting There

### BY AIR

Tampa International Airport is the largest airport on the Gulf Coast, with 550 flights per day and ranked in 2007 by the U.S. Department of Transportation as second nationwide in on-time performance for arrivals and departures. Southwest Florida International Airport in Fort Myers has also experienced enormous expansion in the past few years. And the Northwest Florida Beaches International Airport outside of Panama City is the best way to fly into the popular beaches of South Walton County; opened on May 23, 2010, it is the first international airport to be built in the United States in over a decade.

Generally, the most direct routes and cheapest fares can be found through these airports, but it's worth pricing flights through Orlando, which is an hour east of Tampa (mostly from Orlando International Airport, but there is a second airport that is increasingly popular for international travelers called Sanford International Airport). Gulf Coast airports are, from north and west to south:

- **Pensacola Regional Airport** (3 miles northeast of Pensacola, 850/435-1746)
- **Okaloosa County Air Terminal** (1 mile east of Destin, 850/651-7160)
- **Northwest Florida Beaches International**

© NICKOLAY KHOROSHKOV/123RF.COM

**Airport** (20 miles northwest of Panama City, 850/763-6751)

- **Hernando County Airport** (40 miles north of Tampa, 352/799-7275)
- **St. Petersburg Clearwater International Airport** (7 miles southeast of Clearwater, 813/531-1451)
- **Tampa International Airport** (5 miles west of downtown Tampa, 813/870-8700)
- **Sarasota Bradenton International Airport** (3 miles north of Sarasota, 941/359-5200)
- **Venice Municipal Airport** (0.5 mile south of Venice, 941/485-9293)
- **Charlotte County Airport** (3 miles southeast of Punta Gorda, 941/639-1101)
- **Southwest Florida International Airport** (10 miles southeast of Fort Myers, 941/768-1000)
- **Naples Municipal Airport** (2 miles northeast of Naples, 941/643-0733)

## From Europe

Most international flights on the Gulf Coast arrive and depart out of Tampa or Southwest Florida International in Fort Myers. Additional international flights arrive in Miami, Orlando, and Key West. British Airways, KLM, and Lufthansa offer direct flights, as do American carriers American, Delta, United, and Northwest. (From Canada, Air Canada has flights to Tampa and Fort Myers.)

## Cheap Fares

All of the online travel resources (Kayak, Orbitz, Travelocity, Expedia, etc.) offer last-minute specials and weekend deals on travel. The way to get a good fare in advance on air travel or hotel rooms is by traveling outside of peak season. That period is different for different parts of the Gulf Coast (each chapter gives the approximate peak season dates in its introduction). For instance, peak season on St. George Island is the middle of the summer, while in Naples summer is the least desirable

time to visit, thus the cheapest. Spring break in March and April seems to be the most expensive time to visit much of the Gulf Coast, but bear in mind that in the off-season, hours for restaurants and attractions are sometimes more limited.

## BY CAR

The main arteries into Florida include I-95, which crosses the Florida-Georgia border just north of Jacksonville and hugs the east coast of the state all the way down, and I-75, which runs south from Georgia through the state's middle, then works its way west to the coast just south of Tampa. I-4 extends southwest across the state from Daytona through Orlando and then connects to I-75 in Tampa. On the Panhandle, I-10 is the big east–west road, which can be accessed from the north by U.S. 29, U.S. 231, or U.S. 19.

## BY BOAT

If you're traveling to Florida by boat, you probably have a host of chart maps and navigational tools at your disposal. A paragraph in this book is hardly going to keep you afloat. However, I do want to put in a plug for the **Gulf Intracoastal Waterway.** Most boaters are familiar with the 1,090-mile, toll-free East Coast channel that is the Intracoastal Waterway (ICW), linking Norfolk, Virginia, to Miami, Florida, through gorgeous sheltered waters. Well, the Gulf has one too, extending about 1,300 miles from Carrabelle, Florida, to Brownsville, Texas. (And there's a noncontiguous section of the waterway connecting Tampa Bay with the Okeechobee Waterway.) The Gulf Intracoastal Waterway follows a course of sheltered bays, rivers, and canals along the Gulf of Mexico, perfect for recreational cruising. The sheltered Gulf waters aren't as punishing as the Atlantic Ocean, but still the Gulf Intracoastal Waterway makes for varied and scenic cruising.

Speaking of cruising, the **Port of Tampa** is a huge home port for a variety of cruise lines (Carnival, Royal Caribbean, Celebrity, Holland America, and Crystal Cruises).

Nearly a million passengers pass through its cruise terminals each year on their way to days upon the wide-open sea, shuffleboard, and cocktails on the Lido deck. (For the single funniest essay on cruise ships ever written, read the title essay in David Foster Wallace's *A Supposedly Fun Thing I'll Never Do Again.*) So, another vacation itinerary might be taking a cruise, followed or preceded by an exploration of Florida's Gulf Coast.

# Getting Around

## BY CAR

Florida's Gulf Coast is an ideal destination for those with a poor sense of direction. There are only a few major roads you have to master, and even the urban areas are mostly laid out in a grid (except Tampa, where driving visitors are known to browbeat the map-reading visitors in the passenger seat). On the Panhandle, I-10 runs inland east to west, while at the coast the major east–west road is U.S. 98. U.S. 98 curves all the way around the Big Bend of the Panhandle into the Florida peninsula, where it is also called U.S. 19. U.S. 19 extends along the coast all the way down to St. Pete. I-75 is the huge north–south artery on the Gulf Coast side of the Florida peninsula, stretching from where it enters the state at Valdosta, Georgia, all the way south to Naples, where it jogs across the state to the east along what is called Alligator Alley. One of the more famous north–south routes in Florida is U.S.41, also known as the Tamiami Trail, which extends from Tampa down to Naples, where it, too, shoots east across the state (significantly south of I-75). The Tamiami Trail and I-75 run parallel, fairly close together—which you choose depends on your preference: I-75 has the speed; Tamiami Trail has the charm.

### Car Rentals

**Alamo** (800/462-5266), **Avis** (800/831-2847), **Budget** (800/527-0700), **Dollar** (800/800-4000 domestic, 800/800-6000 international), **Enterprise** (800/736-8222), **Hertz** (800/654-3131), and **National** (800/227-7368) provide rental cars from most of the major airports on the Gulf Coast. You pay a small premium for the convenience of picking up and dropping off at the airport, and you pay significantly more if you pick up a car in one city and drop it off in another. Most rental car companies insist that the driver be at least 21 years old, some even older than that—be sure to have your driver's license and a major credit card (even if you aim to pay cash, the rental companies want a credit card for their own peace of mind) with you, or you're walking.

Whether to accept a rental agency's insurance coverage and waivers depends on your own car insurance—before leaving home, read your own car policy to determine if it covers you while renting a vehicle. Also, some credit cards cover damages to many basic types of rental cars, so it's worth checking into that as well. If you decline the insurance, rental car companies hold you totally responsible for your rental vehicle if damaged or stolen. The rental agency's insurance may add $12–30 per day to your bill.

### Hitchhiking

Florida is not a great hitchhiking state. The law reads: No person shall stand in a roadway for the purpose of soliciting a ride. Clearly, you can't stand *in the road* to thumb a ride, but there's nothing that says you can't stand on the shoulder. Still, police officers don't like it and most people won't pick you up. However, you will still see people thumbing on the highway, and in all the years I have lived in Florida I have never seen anyone get arrested for attempting to hitchhike or heard of anyone landing in the slammer or issued a ticket as a result of attempting it. However, hitchhiking is very dangerous. Standing on the side of the road while vehicles careen past you going over 70 miles an hour is dangerous enough. Add the risk you take when you get into a confined space with a stranger who could be extremely dangerous and possibly carrying a weapon and the danger is greatly compounded. In short, it is not recommended to hitchhike anywhere. There are places, like Hawaii, for example, where hitchhiking is a regular and accepted practice, but Florida is not one of these locations.

## BY BUS

**Greyhound** (800/231-2222, www.greyhound.com) service has gotten spottier in recent years, but there are still regular routes that run from Naples up through Fort Myers, then up to Tampa and St. Petersburg, and all the way around the Big Bend of the Panhandle to Tallahassee, Panama City, and Pensacola. If traveling by Greyhound is new to you, here's some general information: There are no assigned seats (do not, under any circumstances, take the seats adjacent to the bathroom—it's olfactory suicide), no smoking, no pets, no meal service (but there are regular meal stops so you can jump out and buy something). There are no reservations, so you just buy a ticket and show up. Stopovers at any point along the route are permitted if you've paid a regular fare. The driver gives you a notation on your ticket, or a coupon, and you can get back on whenever you like.

Who rides the bus these days? The elderly, the military, the poor, and people who just don't fly. Regular patrons include children who wish they were somewhere else, and their parents, who also wish their children were somewhere else. There are better ways to see the state.

## BY TRAIN

Train service is limited along the Gulf Coast. **Amtrak** (800/872-7245, www.amtrak.com) offers service exclusively up the eastern side of the Florida peninsula and Orlando, with the exception of the Gulf Coast city of Tampa and environs. To give some idea of price, the three-hour trip from Orlando to Jacksonville is $23 one-way. Amtrak service has been greatly improved over the past few years. It now offers free Wi-Fi service on select trains, and there is always more legroom on the train than on a plane. Unfortunately, much of Amtrak's service that once existed throughout the length of the Panhandle has been out of commission since Hurricane Katrina destroyed the tracks in New Orleans in 2005. There do not appear to be plans to restore this service any time soon. Make sure to check with Amtrak about the availability of any route before you make your travel plans.

# Tips for Travelers

## FOREIGN TRAVELERS
### Visas

Unless you're coming from Canada, you need a valid passport and a tourist visa (a Non-Immigrant Visitors Visa B1, for business, or B2, for recreation). Keep your passport in a safe place, and make a copy of the passport number and other critical information and keep it elsewhere.

### Money

U.S. currency looks pretty fancy these days, with watermarks, lots of anticounterfeiting devices, and large heads, but working with dollars is fairly simple—there's the $1, the $5, the $10, the $20, and, less common, the $50. The $100 bill is very seldom used and very seldom accepted without a lot of scrutiny. (The old, small-head bills are still good, don't worry.) In coins, pennies ($0.01) are pretty much only good for wishing wells; then there's the nickel ($0.05), the dime ($0.10), the quarter ($0.25), and the more rare 50-cent piece ($0.50) and golden dollar ($1) coins.

Money can be exchanged at a very limited number of airports (Tampa, Orlando, Fort Myers) on the Gulf Coast. Exchange money before you arrive, or use U.S. travelers checks. For the most part, if you have a Visa or

MasterCard, put all of your accommodations, restaurant meals, and attractions expenditures on that—an easy way to keep track of how you spent your money on vacation.

## Electricity

The United States uses 110 to 120 volts AC, as opposed to Europe's 220 to 240 volts. For the most part, Gulf Coast hotels will have hair dryers for your use, so leave yours at home. If you have other electrical devices for which you need a converter, bring one from home.

## Telephone Basics

Each urban area along the Gulf Coast has its own area code of three numbers that must be dialed if calling from outside. For example, the area code in Tampa is 813, but you needn't dial it if you're calling within the area code. If you're dialing another area code, you must first dial 1, then the three-digit area code, then the seven-digit phone number. Since the telephone industry was deregulated, calling long distance from pay phones can be a total crapshoot, costing a different amount depending on the carrier. Public pay phone pricing is no longer regulated by the Florida Public Service Commission, but prices should be clearly marked, with local calls usually $0.50. If you don't have a cell phone that works in Florida, you're better off getting a prepaid international calling card. Hotels also charge by the call, so making calling-card calls is often more cost-effective.

Be aware that in the past five years cell phones have rendered the pay phone an endangered species. At the end of 2007, AT&T announced that they will sell all 60,000 pay phones they operate and many other companies are following suit.

## Tipping

Service-sector workers expect a tip. It's only in name a "gratuity," meaning an elective gift. It's how they make the bulk of their money. Fifteen percent is pretty much the minimum, whether it's at a restaurant, a hair salon, or in a taxi. Tip bellhops about $1 per bag; tip the valet parking attendant $1–2 every time you get your car. Tip a good waiter or bartender 18–20 percent. But here's some tricky stuff: If the hairdresser or tour operator is the owner of the business, a tip can sometimes be seen as an insult. Crazy stuff. Keep lots of small bills at the ready for all these situations, but don't ever tip at the movies, a retail shop, the gas station, or at the theater, ballet, or opera.

## Metric Conversions

The United States had a failed attempt at going metric in the 1970s. So, you need to know that one foot equals 0.305 meters; one mile equals 1.6 kilometers; and one pound equals 0.45 kilograms. Converting temperatures is a little trickier: To convert Fahrenheit to Celsius temperatures, subtract 32 and then multiply the result by 0.555. Got it?

# ACCESS FOR TRAVELERS WITH DISABILITIES

The more developed and sophisticated parts of the Gulf Coast (Sarasota, Naples, Tampa) are very accessible to travelers with disabilities. As one would expect, the more remote and rural areas may not have ramps, accessible bathrooms, and other amenities. You may want to consider buying a copy of *Wheelchairs on the Go: Accessible Fun in Florida* (727/573-0434, www.wheelchairsonthego.com, $19.95 plus $3 shipping), Florida's only access guide for visitors who use canes, walkers, or wheelchairs. The 424-page paperback covers wheelchair-accessible and barrier-free accommodations, tourist attractions, and activities across the state.

**Society for Accessible Travel & Hospitality** (212/447-7284, www.sath.org) provides recommendations and resources to help travelers with disabilities plan their vacations, and **Able Trust** (888/838-2253, www.abletrust.org) offers helpful links to disability resources throughout Florida.

Most major car-rental companies have hand-controlled cars in their fleets (give them 24- to 48-hours' notice to locate one). If you need to rent a scooter or wheelchair during your visit, **ScootAround** (888/441-7575, www.scootaround.com) is a mobility enhancement company with scooter and wheelchair rental service in a number of Gulf Coast cities.

Diabetic travelers can call the **American Diabetes Association** (800/342-2383, www.diabetes.org) to get a list of hospitals that provide services to diabetics, or log on to **Dialysis Finder** at www.dialysisfinder.com.

The **American Foundation for the Blind** (800/232-5463, www.afb.org) provides information on traveling with a dog guide.

## TRAVELING WITH CHILDREN

The Gulf Coast is the kind of destination suited to a rambling family car trip. But how to face the open road with a carful of antsy travelers? As with a NASA launch, it's all about careful planning and precise execution. Consider yourself lucky that this doesn't mean devising zero-gravity suits and dehydrating food—you just have to keep your astronauts comfortable, fed, and entertained. To that end, consider carrying a master list of all that you've packed. Although it sounds pretty meticulous, it helps to see where your gaps are, it allows you to easily keep track of things from car to motel to final destination, and if you generate this list on the computer, it can be used as the basis for future trip lists.

The list should be divided into categories: clothes and equipment (these are the things that go in the trunk, to be exhumed at your final destination) and the stuff that makes or breaks your travel time—food, entertainment, and car comfort. Older kids can each be put in charge of a category checklist as the car gets loaded.

For smaller kids, always take a change of underpants or diapers inside the car with you, rather than in the trunk with the luggage. For older kids, encourage a layered approach to dressing—when one child is chilly, donning another layer may be preferable to making everyone endure the car heater.

Think of packing foods that nature has already prepackaged—bananas, oranges, hard-boiled eggs. Avoid things with sauces or drip-potential, chips coated with the dreaded nacho cheese orange goo, or things that crumb too easily. And for drinks, carry a large, plastic, spill-proof cup for each child. This way,

you can get juices at convenience stores but you won't be at the mercy of those wide-mouthed, splash-prone glass bottles in the car. Alternatively, bring a bevy of frozen juice boxes. You won't have to wait in line for sodas and the juice boxes will be nice and cold during the first leg of a trip.

The sight of the golden arches fills most kids with joy and most parents with dread. Fast food is the most common pitfall on long car trips, a wasteland of fat, salt, and sugar. To avoid the tortures of drive-through (it's everywhere, after all), you have to stand firm. Finding other food can be an adventure on long trips. On the Gulf Coast, this is easy: Get off the highway and hunt down an old-fashioned diner, one with counter stools, a good jukebox, and a short-order cook who makes the perfect grilled cheese. In preparation for your trip, research the indigenous foods of the areas you'll be passing through. Use the Internet to print out pictures and histories of each city's culinary highlights.

When traveling in the car with small children, allow more time to reach your destination. Count on stopping every hour to stretch your legs and run around. Churches are good stopping spots if rest areas aren't available, as they often have open, grassy areas and playgrounds. Traveling at night or during nap times is a good way to make up time. Put blankets, pillows, and any necessary stuffed animals in the back seat at the ready.

Your local party goods and dollar stores are perfect places to find inexpensive new forms of amusement. Wrap each new toy as a gift, to make the excitement last. Caveat: Do not buy travel games with small pieces sure to get lost immediately under the back seat. Maze books, magic-pen books, stickers, a magnetic puzzle of the U.S., even car bingo can keep everyone entertained. For long car trips, the book *Miles of Smiles* is filled with car games. Picture-puzzle books (like *I Spy* and *Where's Waldo*) can be made into games as well: One person names an object for the rest to find in the picture.

Even if you eschew the plugged-in feel of video games, iPods, or DVDs in the car, bringing a stereo headset for each child allows everyone to listen to their first choice, whether that's Fergie or *Good Night Moon*. You can even make your own books on tape: Record your child's favorite stories on audiotape and then they can have the stories "read" to them in the car.

Bring lap desks and art supplies for projects. Dated spiral-bound drawing pads can be a nice way to chronicle a trip, with each child keeping the finished pad (parents can annotate as instructed). Encourage older kids to journal with a cool pad and a set of gel pens.

## TRAVELING WITH PETS

More and more hotel chains are accepting people's canine companions (other pets, from pot-bellied pigs to naked mole rats, are a harder sell). Best Western, Motel 6, Holiday Inn, and even swanky chains such as Four Seasons often accept pet guests for an additional fee. To get good information, pick up a copy of *The Dog Lover's Companion to Florida*, by Sally Deneen and Robert McClure, or visit www.petswelcome.com.

Flying with your pet to and from Florida can be problematic, as most major airlines have an embargo against pets as checked baggage during the summer months (any day in which the outdoor temperature might reach 90°F), and even for small pets that fit under an airplane seat, the airlines only allow one pet per cabin. The ASPCA strongly discourages pets as checked baggage.

Dogs are prohibited on many walking trails in Florida, as well as most beaches. There are designated dog parks and dog beaches all over the Gulf Coast. Pensacola, Panama City, Tallahassee, Tampa, St. Petersburg, Sarasota, and Fort Myers all have designated dog beach parks with amenities such as fenced play areas, dog water fountains, and poop bags. Be aware that in much of the Gulf Coast's wilderness areas, poisonous snakes and alligators pose more of a threat to your dog than to you.

## TRAVELING ALONE

Beach walking, fishing, kayaking, even the area's many cultural attractions—all the offerings of the Gulf Coast are well suited to traveling alone. The only exception to that is backwoods camping in the Everglades or deep wilderness. Be extremely careful to give rangers your exact schedule and detailed whereabouts. Beyond that, I've traveled the length of the Gulf Coast by myself and have not experienced a single troubling episode. I wouldn't hesitate to recommend the Gulf Coast as a spot for quiet, solo travel—except, perhaps, during colleges' spring breaks, and then I would recommend it for loud, lively, social partying.

### Spring Break Fever

Because school schedules vary across the country, spring breakers arrive in Florida at different times. Some come as early as late February, but March and April are the months most colleges and schools release for spring break. Students focus most of their attentions on certain key cities along the eastern coast of the state (Daytona Beach, Miami Beach), but along the Gulf Coast, Panama City Beach and down by Key West are the big draws.

## GAY AND LESBIAN TRAVELERS

Miami's South Beach and Key West are the locus of lots of gay travel. Nowhere on the Gulf Coast is the nightlife as trendy, but that said, nothing on the Gulf Coast seems unsuitable for gay or lesbian travel. As with most places, the more rural the area, the more likely any discernible difference is likely to prompt unwanted notice. The Gulf Coast's wealth of outdoor activities seems suitable for any orientation, as do the restaurants and accommodations. It's a fairly nightlife-impoverished area regardless of your orientation, so you may spend your evenings curled up with a good book.

A good resource is the **Gay, Lesbian & Bisexual Community Services of Central Florida** (407/228-8272, www.glbcc.org) for welcome packets and calendars of events, or the **International Gay & Lesbian Travel Association** (800/448-8550, www.traveliglta.com, $250 annually to join) for a list of gay-friendly accommodations, tours, and attractions.

# Health and Safety

Despite what it might look like in the backcountry of the Everglades, Florida is a modern, developed kind of place, with good emergency services and medical care pretty much all over the Gulf Coast. From Tampa to Sarasota you'll see more medical facilities, pharmacies, and billboards for MRI scanners than nearly anywhere else, a remnant of the area's recent past as a mostly retirement-age destination (as the Bob Dylan song says, "it's younger than that now").

Still, you want to do what you can to stay healthy during a visit here. The sun is probably the biggest underestimated foe. **Sunburn** can be wicked, so be sure to slather with at least an SPF of 30, and because you'll be in and out of water, and sweating in the steamy humidity, opt for waterproof or water-resistant cream such as Banana Boat Sport Sunblock Lotion (waterproof/sweatproof, SPF 30). Even better, one of my favorite finds on the Gulf Coast, Avon now makes an SPF 30 Skin So Soft cream with a DEET-free bug repellent in it to cope with the Gulf Coast's other big bully, the **mosquitoes.** DEET-based products are more effective in preventing mosquitoes from landing on you, but I hate to have that poison sitting on my skin all day. Lather up with the Avon product, then apply a DEET-based spray only if the mosquitoes are bad. Mosquitoes in Florida don't carry any diseases such as malaria, but their itching bites can certainly be preoccupying.

Another burning subject is **fire ants.** If you see loose, sandy mounds on the ground, do not stand in them. These little devils get incensed at the foot in their house and swarm up your shoe and beyond to bite and leave raised white or red welts that really hurt and itch for days. There is no known treatment for their bites, but I have found that if you douse the bites with aftershave or just plain alcohol, it helps reduce the itching substantially, though maybe not the burning.

The Gulf Coast's water is perfectly safe to drink, although it tastes a little funky in some areas. A much safer bet is the food. On the Gulf Coast you'll find one great seafood restaurant after another. Make sure to try some of the most adventurous local foods when you're on the Gulf Coast, as they are usually the most memorable and tasty. Become the Sir Edmund Hillary of food. When asked "Why did you eat that?" answer back a gravelly "Because it was there." So, try the oysters, clams, whatever, raw on the half shell with a splash of Tabasco. For some, though, this is truly dangerous. Pregnant women, young children, the elderly, or anyone with an immune system problem should order all seafood baked, broiled, steamed, or fried. The bacteria *Vibrio vulnificus* can, at the very least, ruin your vacation. For a list of safe and sustainable flat fish, California's Monterey Bay Aquarium's website (www.mbayaq.org) has a useful seafood watch section.

Many travel articles suggest getting **medical travel insurance.** If you have medical insurance, though, that's probably all the coverage you'll need. The best emergency rooms are listed in each chapter, and you can always dial 911 (a number used nationwide to contact local emergency medical, fire, or police personnel) or the Centers for Disease Control and Prevention (800/311-3435, www.cdc.gov) for information on health hazards by region.

# Information and Services

## MAPS AND TOURIST INFORMATION

### Maps

**Visit Florida** (www.flausa.com) sends a great map of the whole state with its Visit Florida literature. (And, as always, AAA members should raid the free-map smorgasbord that is their divine right.) The state's tourism office also has several welcome stations near Florida's border (one north of Pensacola on I-10, one off U.S.231, one in Tallahassee, one in Jennings off I-75, and one on the state's east coast on I-95) that give out good state and regional maps. Some cities (Apalachicola, Naples) can be navigated with only the Xeroxed map the desk clerk at the hotel hands out; just follow the yellow highlighter marks. In other cities (Tampa), you need a real map. And if you're traveling alone, don't be chintzy—buy the laminated flip map to the area; its ease of use in the car may keep your wheels on the road.

A portable GPS is an absolute godsend for the frequent road tripper. Unlike the built-ins, it can be stowed in luggage and plugged into every rental car. Garmin, TomTom, and Magellan all make affordable portable versions (some that have mp3 connectivity and fit in your purse or backpack).

### Tourist Offices

Tourist office addresses are listed at the end of each chapter. Most convention and visitors bureaus have extremely helpful websites at this point, and many will send you a vacation package of information, maps, and coupons free of charge.

### Photo Development

With regular 35mm film, developing film along the way is a snap at one-hour photo places and most big drugstores. If you've gone digital, don't worry about photo development until you get home (uploading onto a website like Shutterfly or Snapfish is a cheap way to get prints made and to digitally share your trip with everyone). That said, you need to bring an adequate amount of memory for the length of your trip. Digital memory cards are not affected by airport security X-rays, so bring extras. And don't forget extra batteries and your battery charger.

## COMMUNICATIONS AND MEDIA

### Mail

Mail service within the United States generally takes 2–3 days, except during the Christmas holiday season when all bets are off. Within Florida, post takes about two days to get anywhere (you speed things up if you use the full nine-digit zip code). A first-class stamp currently costs $0.44.

### Telephone

If you are calling long distance, dial 1, and then the three-digit area code followed by the seven-digit phone number. If calling from abroad, the international code for the U.S. is 1. Within the United States, the 800, 888, 877, and 866 area codes are toll-free, meaning they cost you nothing to dial.

### Fax

Most hotels and motels will send and receive a fax for a fee, and multipage documents can be sent at any copy shop.

### Internet Access

This is changing so fast on the Gulf Coast that it's probably fruitless to weigh in. Even budget hotels offer in-room dataports or wireless Internet connection now, and many low-tech coffee shops and cafés sport the Wi-Fi Hotspot sticker in the window for wireless Internet connections. Even if you're not packing a laptop on your trip, you can check web-based email from almost any hotel or motel, often for no fee.

## Newspapers and Magazines

Regional and city newspapers are listed at the end of each chapter. There are many great daily papers in the area. The major metro papers in the area include the *St. Petersburg Times,* a left-of-center daily, and the *Tampa Tribune,* a more conservative publication. Other papers of note include the *Naples Daily News,* the *Tallahassee Democrat,* and the *Pensacola News Journal.*

## Television

Nearly every hotel, motel, and inn on the Gulf Coast has cable TV now, providing scores of channels to click your way through. Local television stations are listed at the end of each chapter (along with their network affiliates). Most accommodations on the Gulf Coast have wireless or wired Internet access. Some are still charging for it, and surprisingly some are asking quite a bit for the service. While traveling the Gulf Coast I ran into some hotels that were asking as much as $1 per minute for Internet access. Make sure to ask about Internet use fees before making your reservations.

# RESOURCES
## Suggested Reading

### THE PARADISE COAST
#### Travel Guide

Molloy, Johnny. *A Paddler's Guide to Everglades National Park.* Gainesville: University Press of Florida, 2000. Paddling the Everglades is daunting, plain and simple. There are things in there that can kill you, others that can merely maim. This book well describes 53 designated paddling routes, camping spots, places to avoid, and wind and tide problems. Molloy is a serious outdoorsman who has written a handful of well-regarded paddling and camping books for Florida and Colorado.

#### Memoir

Brown, Loren G. "Totch." *Totch: A Life in the Everglades.* Gainesville: University Press of Florida, 1993. It's my very favorite book about this area, told in glorious vernacular by the original Everglades renegade. A seasoned tall-tale teller, Totch harkens back to his days in the Ten Thousand Islands, moonshining, selling gator hides, fishing, smuggling dope, and any other thing he thought might be fun, or lucrative, or both. It's memoirs like this that clinch southwest Florida as this country's final frontier.

#### Nonfiction

Douglas, Marjory Stoneman. *The Everglades: River of Grass.* Sarasota, FL: Pineapple Press, 50th anniversary edition, 1997. Originally published in 1947, this was a book that actually changed the world. At the time the Everglades were a worthless swamp that developers were scheming about draining, damming, etc. The publication of this straightforward natural history, heavy on the flora, fauna, and indigenous people, galvanized President Harry Truman to sign the controversial order protecting more than two million acres as Everglades National Park. Douglas has been called the Queen of the Everglades, and her descriptions of the Native Americans, pirates, runaways, and ne'er-do-wells who populated the 'Glades is as compelling as it ever was.

Orlean, Susan. *The Orchid Thief: A True Story of Beauty and Obsession.* New York: Ballantine Books, 2000. This was the book that the film *Adaptation* was loosely based on. *New Yorker* staffer Susan Orlean wrote an incredible piece on John Laroche, an orchid chaser who was arrested with three Seminole Indians in 1994 carrying contraband rare orchids and epiphytes from the Everglades. Orlean expanded upon the story, writing this book that reveals a whole world of eccentric and brilliant obsession. The Wild West feel of the Everglades and swampy environs is clear, and the story is at times hilarious and moving. It is definitely one of my favorite books on the area, and you can also learn a lot about orchids. Be careful, though—you might just become obsessed.

Zimmerman, Stan. *A History of Smuggling in Florida: Rum Runners and Cocaine Cowboys.*

Charleston, SC: The History Press, 2006. Wander through the Ten Thousand Islands and it becomes clear: This would be a good place to hide, or to get lost, or both. It's this geographic anomaly, plus Floridians' general sense of subversive fervor, that makes Florida a natural spot from which or to which to smuggle drugs, booze or other contraband.

## Fiction

Matthiessen, Peter. *Killing Mister Watson.* New York: Vintage, reprint edition, 1991. It's a trilogy, along with *Lostman's River* and *Bone by Bone,* that paints a vivid picture of the early settlers living at the edge of civilization in the Ten Thousand Islands and the Everglades. Drawn from bits of historical fact, Matthiessen creates a fictionalized oral history set in Chokoloskee and other little mangrove islands. Edgar J. Watson, who is said to have gunned down the outlaw Belle Starr, came here to elude the law but instead faced the rough frontier justice of his fellow fugitives. It's an absolute must-read if you plan to spend any time in Everglades City. At age 81, Matthiessen collapsed the three stories into one book (as he originally intended) and released the revision as a 890-page novel called *Shadow Country.* For this work he received his second National Book Award.

## LEE COUNTY
### Nonfiction

Smoot, Tom. *The Edisons of Fort Myers.* Sarasota, FL: Pineapple Press, 2004. Lots of biographies cover Edison's public life as a world-famous inventor, but this one explores the big loves of his life: Mina Miller and Fort Myers, Florida. It's an especially fun read preceded or followed by a visit to the Edison estate.

Turner, Gregg. *Railroads of Southwest Florida.* Charleston, SC: Arcadia Publishing, 2000. Turner's written a ton about Florida railroads, so he's something of an expert on the rails. This book covers Henry Plant, the Florida

Southern Railway, and all the other railway endeavors that prompted accelerated growth in this part of Florida. The writing isn't super exciting, but there's a lot of good information here. He has a newer one called *Florida Railroads in the 1920s* (2006) about the "Big Three's" race in the state.

Witherington, Blair and Dawn. *Florida's Living Beaches: A Guide for the Curious Beachcomber.* Sarasota, FL: Pineapple Press, 2007. It packs in 822 items, 983 color images, and 431 maps describing the state's plants, animals, minerals, and artificially created objects. A handy paperback identification guide.

## Fiction

Hiaasen, Carl. Where do you even put Carl Hiaasen in a guide about the Gulf Coast? He's everywhere in south Florida, bigger than a novelist, bigger than a *Miami Herald* columnist. He's like a rock star around here (good because he owns a Fender Strat that Dave Barry helped him pick out), with so many titles it's hard to pick which ones to list. The most recent is *Star Island,* New York: Grand Central Publishing, 2010, before that *Scat, Downhill Life, Flush, Nature Girl, Skinny Dip, Basket Case, Sick Puppy, Lucky You, Stormy Weather, Strip Tease, Native Tongue, Skin Tight, Double Whammy,* and *Tourist Season.* He has a penchant for two-word titles and writes mostly about south Florida. He likes to write about smart hookers with a heart of gold, finds tough-guy baldies especially amusing, and is a bulldoggish environmentalist. In addition to his novels, Hiaasen has also published two collections of his newspaper columns, *Kick Ass* and *Paradise Screwed,* and an anti-Disney book called *Team Rodent.*

Wayne White, Randy. *Sanibel Flats.* New York: St. Martin's Press, 1991. Randy Wayne White was a fishing guide at Tarpon Bay on Sanibel for 13 years. A prolific mystery novelist, he writes mostly about this part of southwest Florida, with numerous novels featuring super tough-guy Doc Ford solving various mysteries *(Black Widow, Hunter's Moon, The Deadlier Sex, Cuban Death-Lift, The Deep Six, The Heat Islands, The Man Who Invented Florida, Captiva, North of Havana, The Mangrove Coast, Ten Thousand Islands, Shark River, Twelve Mile Limit, Everglades, Tampa Burn,* and *Dead of Night).* In all his books, Florida is one of the main characters, described in all its glory. Wayne White is a columnist for *Outside Magazine* and *Men's Health,* and he's written lots of other books of essays and such, including *Batfishing in the Rain Forest* and a fish cookbook.

# SARASOTA COUNTY
## Photography

Evans, Walker. *Walker Evans: Florida.* Los Angeles: J. Paul Getty Trust Publications, 2000. Everyone knows Walker Evans's gutsy, gripping Depression-era photographs. But for six weeks in 1942, Evans focused his lens on Sarasota for *Mangrove Coast,* a book by Karl Bickel. These are some of the wonderful photos he took during that time of the circus's underbelly, old people, railroad cars, and decrepit Florida buildings. Text is by novelist Robert Plunket.

## Nonfiction

Apps, Jerry. *Tents, Tigers, and the Ringling Brothers.* Madison: University of Wisconsin Press, 2006. Apps writes pretty much exclusively about Wisconsin. But this story started there, in Baraboo, Wisconsin to be exact. A wonderful history of the Ringling Circus and the seven brothers who made the "Greatest Show on Earth" from scratch. It's got great photos of early circus life.

# TAMPA
## Travel Guide

Murphy, Bill. *Fox 13 Tampa Bay One Tank Trips With Bill Murphy.* St. Petersburg: Seaside Publishing, 2004. An offshoot of a television segment Murphy does, the books showcase 52 Florida-based adventures that are all within a full tank of Tampa. It's lots of off-the-beaten-path attractions, all worthy of your time, from Pioneer Florida Museum in Dade City to the excellent camping at Fort De Soto Park in Pinellas County.

## Drama

Cruz, Nilo. *Anna in the Tropics.* Theatre Communications Group, 2003. This play won Cruz the Pulitzer Prize for drama in 2003. It is a romantic drama, loosely a retelling of Tolstoy's *Anna Karenina,* that depicts a Cuban-American family of cigar makers in Ybor City (Tampa) in 1930. It tells the story of the factory's new lector, a person hired to read aloud great works of literature and the day's news to the cigar workers. A beautiful stage play—keep your eyes open for any performances of it during your visit to Florida.

# PINELLAS COUNTY
## Nonfiction

Klinkenberg, Jeff. *Seasons of Real Florida.* Gainesville: University Press of Florida, 2004. *St. Petersburg Times* writer Klinkenberg may have invented the term "Real Florida," which means the Old Florida, without Disney, fancy golf courses, or really anything glamorous. This book is an assemblage of largely humorous essays he's written for the paper that tell great stories about the people, flora, and fauna in west-central Florida. Another collection of essays entitled *Pilgrim in the Land of Alligators* was published in 2008 by the University Press of Florida.

## Fiction

MacDonald, John. *Condominium.* New York: Fawcett, reissue edition, 1985. For most of his life MacDonald was considered a pulp fiction writer, and prolific, who spent more than half his life in west-central Florida, first in Clearwater, then in Sarasota and Siesta Key. This book still seems fresh, especially in light of 2004's hurricane season. The setting is Golden Sands, a Sunbelt condo in the path of Hurricane Ella. It's a multicharacter disaster book, think *The Towering Inferno* or something like that. (*Cape Fear,* by the way, was based on a MacDonald book.)

# THE NATURE COAST
## Nonfiction

Warner, David T. *Vanishing Florida: A Personal Guide to Sights Rarely Seen.* Montgomery, AL: River City Publishing, 2001. I love this book, written by a guy who sounds like a dead ringer for Ernest Hemingway (Papa features occasionally in the book, so maybe Warner fancies a resemblance himself). Some of this book appeared as features in *Sarasota* magazine—mostly it's chapter-long ruminations and odes to small towns along the Gulf Coast (especially good chapters on Cedar Key and other parts of the Nature Coast), with lots of drinking and womanizing thrown into the mix.

## Fiction

Cook, Ann. *Trace Their Shadows.* San Jose, New York, Lincoln, and Shanghai: Mystery and Suspense Press, 2001, and *Shadow Over Cedar Key.* San Jose, New York, Lincoln, and Shanghai: Mystery and Suspense Press, 2003. As a baby the author was the model for the original Gerber baby (daughter of cartoonist Leslie Turner who drew the famous baby head in 1928), but as an adult she has turned to mystery writing. The cool thing about these books is the setting—they are easy, beachy reads with plucky reporter Brandy O'Bannon having exciting adventures all over charming Cedar Key.

# TALLAHASSEE
## Travel Guides

Edel, Andrew. *Historic Photos of Tallahassee.* Nashville, TN: Turner Publishing Co., 2007. Hundreds of historic black-and-white photos tell the tale of Tallahassee's pedigreed past as a cultural center in the South, delving into government, education, and events throughout the city's history.

Robinson, Erik. *Tallahassee.* Charleston, SC: Arcadia Publishing, 2003. It's a straight forward photo and text history of the capital city, written by the man who has been the curator at the Museum of Florida History for 20 years. It's good foundation information for the historical traveler.

# THE FORGOTTEN COAST
## Nonfiction

Cerulean, Susan, ed. *Between Two Rivers.* Tallahassee: Red Hills Writers Project, 2004. If you can find it—give it a serious college try—you'll be mesmerized by this anthology of 29 writers telling stories about the rich cultural and environmental landscapes of the Red Hills and northern Gulf Coast. (The two rivers in question are the Aucilla to the east and the Apalachicola to the west.) The Red Hills Writers Project is a group of mostly Florida writers with a serious nature and ecological bent to their writing. Editors include Susan Cerulean (biologist, activist, and writer of *Book of the Everglades* and *Wild Heart of Florida*), Southern author Janisse Ray *(Ecology of a Cracker Childhood, Wild Card Quilt),* and Tallahassee poet Laura Newton (poetry editor of the *Apalachee Review*).

Rudloe, Jack. *The Living Dock of Panacea.* New York: Alfred A. Knopf, 1977. Rudloe is one of the contributors to *Between Two Rivers.* He's a longtime Florida naturalist, director of Gulf Specimen Marine Laboratory, and author of nine or so books on the area. He's big into turtles *(Time of the Turtle, Search For The Great Turtle Mother),* but this older book (recently reprinted with a new introduction and called just *The Living Dock*) is a great rumination on the Gulf Coast's marine life, told from the author's floating dock in the tiny fishing community of Panacea.

# THE EMERALD COAST
## Travel Guides

Hollis, Tim. *Florida's Miracle Strip: From Redneck Riviera to Emerald Coast.* Jackson, MS: University Press of Mississippi, 2004. This is a nostalgic look at the area that is now fairly glamorous Panama City Beach, Fort Walton Beach, Destin, and Pensacola Beach, with lots of fun descriptions of the campy Old Florida attractions that used to bring people here—like Castle Dracula and the Snake-A-Torium. It's got lots of cool vintage photos and postcards.

## Fishing

Dew, Gregory. *The Barefoot Fisherman's Guide to the Emerald Coast: From Gulf Shores, Alabama, to Apalachicola, Florida*. Birmingham, AL: Crane Hill Publishers, 1999. It's a little techie, with lots of talk about tackle and rigs, so the beginning angler might just be interested in Chapter 3, which enumerates 40 or so fabulous fishing spots on this gorgeous stretch of coast. Dew also gives great information on all of the species you're likely to catch here, and then what to do with them if you aim to eat 'em.

Hoskins, Jim. *Fishing the Local Waters: Gulf Shores to Panama City*. Gulf Breeze, FL: Maximum Press, 2006. A guide to angling in Florida's Gulf Coast waters, written by two local fishermen, includes LORAN coordinates for 50 tried-and-true spots. Even for the rookie it's a valuable book because it gives a listing of guides and services in the area.

# PENSACOLA
## Nonfiction

Pensacola Historical Society. *Pensacola in Vintage Postcards*. Charleston, SC: Arcadia Publishing, 2004. It's just a packet of postcards, but a riffle through will give you a sense of the way Pensacola used to be.

# CHILDREN'S BOOKS ABOUT THE GULF COAST
## Travel Guides

DeWire, Elinor. *Florida Lighthouses for Kids*. Sarasota, FL: Pineapple Press, 2004. Great pictures and fun stories about Florida's 33 lighthouses (many on the Gulf Coast)—it

gives kids something to read in the car and a way to participate in the process of planning a trip.

Lantz, Peggy and Wendy Hale. *The Young Naturalist's Guide to Florida*. Sarasota, FL: Pineapple Press, 2006. Again, this gives kids a fun window through which to see the kooky plants and animals of the state, with information on careers in the environmental field.

## Fiction

DiCamillo, Kate. *Because of Winn Dixie*. Cambridge, MA: Candlewick Press, 2001. Now a major motion picture, this book about 10-year-old India Opal Buloni and her ugly dog Winn-Dixie (named for where she found him) has captured the attention of lots of families. It's a great story, set in a fictional town of Naomi, Florida (I like to think it's modeled on someplace down toward Port Charlotte). Opal's had kind of a hard life, so it might be too much for a really sensitive kid.

George, Jean Craighead. *Everglades*. New York: HarperTrophy, reprint edition, 1997. Geared toward littler kids (maybe 5–8), it tells the story of a man poling through the Everglades and teaching his five young passengers about the 'Glades' sawgrass, hundreds of species of animals, and fragile ecosystem. It's not as preachy as it sounds—the environmental message is light and Wendell Minor's illustrations are wonderful. Newbery medalist Jean Craighead George has written lots of wonderful children's books with the Florida wilderness at their centers—older kids might like the ecomystery *The Missing 'Gator of Gumbo Limbo*, New York: HarperTrophy, 1993.

Hiaasen, Carl. *Hoot*. New York: Knopf Books for Young Readers, 2002. Geared for readers 9–12, this Newberry-honor book by Florida great Carl Hiaasen does double duty. As with many of Hiaasen's novels there's a heavy environmental message (this one about protecting rare burrowing owls and their habitat), but it also tells an exciting tale of new kid Roy Eberhardt who moves to Coconut Grove and gets mixed up in a crazy ecological adventure with Mullet Fingers and bully-beater Beatrice in a fight against Mother Paula's All-American Pancake House. A middle-school mystery, the language and plot are edgy. A second book, *Flush,* New York: Knopf Books for Young Readers, 2005, follows a similar formula: Misunderstood teen iconoclast takes a stand and helps preserve the environment in the face of adults' scheming machinations.

Hogan, Linda. *Power.* New York: W.W. Norton & Company, 1999. In an area that was once populated exclusively by Native tribes, it's exciting to read about what life must have been like before all the development. This is a coming-of-age story about a 16-year-old Native American girl named Omishito, who witnesses the killing of a sacred animal, the Florida panther. It is based on a true story.

Konigsburg, E. L. *T-backs, T-shirts, Coat and Suit.* New York: Aladdin, 2003. A more contemporary book from the author of the classic Newberry winner *From the Mixed-Up Files of Mrs. Basil E. Frankweiler,* this one tells the story of 12-year-old Chloe who spends the summer in Florida with her wild aunt Bernadette, who drives a commissary van and sells junk food at roadsides. For ages 9–12.

Rawlings, Marjorie Kinnan. *The Yearling.* New York: Simon Pulse, 50th edition, 1988. Rawlings wrote 10 books while a resident in Cross Creek, Florida, the most popular of which was *The Yearling,* which won a Pulitzer Prize in fiction in 1939. It tells the story of scrappy young Jody Baxter and his pet fawn Flag, who together roam the Florida scrublands wrestling big swamp gators and cavorting with bear cubs. Rawlings's second-best book is called simply, *Cross Creek* also with the same earthy Florida Cracker dialect.

Smith, Patrick D. *A Land Remembered.* Sarasota, FL: Pineapple Press, 1998. Beginning with Tobias MacIvey's arrival in Florida in 1858, this young-adult historical novel tells the story of three generations of Floridians carving out a hardscrabble life for themselves in the wilds of central Florida. This sweeping story is rich in Florida history.

# Internet Resources

## GENERAL GULF COAST
### Visit Florida
### www.flausa.com

For a good introduction to the Gulf Coast, contact the state's official tourist information organization, Visit Florida (or call 888/7-FLA USA), for a copy of its excellent annual *Visit Florida* guide, the *Florida Events Calendar,* or *Florida Trails.* Online resources include a number of electronic travel guides (for which you can order printed versions if you prefer). Visit Florida also has a 24-hour multi-lingual tourist assistance hotline at 800/656-8777.

### Florida Secrets, The Insider's Guide to Unique Destinations
### www.florida-secrets.com

The graphics have a cheese factor and it's heavy on the advertising, but the site is a treasure trove of little-known destinations in Florida, divided up on the Gulf Coast by southwest, west-central, eastern, and western Panhandle.

## FISHING
### Fish We Catch in Florida
### www.redfishhunter.com/fish

If you're looking for a no-nonsense description of what you're likely to catch, what they look like, how to nab them, and then whether they're worth eating, this is the site for you.

### Florida Fishing
**www.floridafishing.com**
It's a clearinghouse of fishing guides, fishing charters, and fishing captains in the state, divided by region.

## CAMPING
### Florida Association of RV Parks & Campgrounds
**www.floridacamping.com**
It's an easy-to-use comprehensive database of Florida campgrounds, including amenities information for each site. You can also go on this website and order a print version of the guide. To make reservations at a Florida state campground (or in any state), however, you must utilize www.reserveamerica.com.

## PARKS AND FORESTS
### Florida State Parks Department
**www.floridastateparks.org**
Find a park, its affiliated camping and lodging, or get a bead on what events are coming up along the Gulf Coast. The site also has maps and directions to Florida's state parks, and it runs an amateur photo contest of state park photography.

### Florida Trail Association
**www.florida-trail.org**
The Florida Trail Association is a nonprofit that builds, maintains, promotes, and protects hiking trails across the state of Florida, especially the 1,400-mile Florida Trail. From this site you can download all kinds of trail maps and park brochures.

## SPORTS
### Florida Sports Foundation
**www.flasports.com**
The foundation usually posts the "Grapefruit League" Florida spring-training baseball schedules on its website late in January. Another way to find out about spring training for your favorite team is by visiting the website of Major League Baseball (www.mlb.com).

## THE PARADISE COAST
### Naples, Marco Island and Everglades Convention & Visitors Bureau
**www.paradisecoast.com**
A slick website for the area, it features convenient charts for local accommodations, a round-up of attractions and recreation in the area, as well as well-written background on the area. The only thing that's missing here is detailed restaurant info.

### Guide to Southwest Florida
**www.florida-southwest.com**
Naples and Marco Island enticements are laid out in categories, and the restaurant write-ups here are fairly reliable.

## LEE COUNTY
### Lee County Visitor and Convention Bureau
**www.fortmyers-sanibel.com or www.leeislandcoast.com**
One of the most professional-looking sites around from a convention bureau, its information is helpful, current, and entertainingly written. There are short essays on local attractions, and a nice section called "ask an expert" that creates a live chat environment in which to talk to a local authority.

### Charlotte Harbor and the Gulf Islands
**www.pureflorida.com**
This area gets short shrift due to its proximity to more well-known vacation destinations. Still, as the website shows, Charlotte Harbor has loads to do and abundant natural beauty. It has an easily downloadable list of local accommodations.

## SARASOTA COUNTY
### Sarasota Convention & Visitors Bureau
**www.sarasotafl.org**
The convention and visitors bureau's award-winning site is about as user-friendly as they

come, with easily sortable menus of restaurants, accommodations, outdoor attractions, and more. The excellent feature stories on the area's lures are written by local travel writers. The site is offered in English, Spanish, and German. A second site, discovernaturalsarasota.org, focuses exclusively on the natural draws of the area, including beaches, parks, gardens, and historic sites.

### Anna Maria Island Chamber of Commerce
**www.annamariaisland.info**
Too far from Tampa in the north and too far from Sarasota to its south, Anna Maria Island doesn't really get covered in other, bigger regional websites. This one doesn't have as many bells and whistles as other sites, but it's got all the basics of where to stay, what to do, and where to eat.

## TAMPA
### Tampa Bay Convention and Visitors Bureau
**www.visittampabay.com**
This is a good site for background on the Bay Area as well as travel strategies and accommodations.

### Creative Loafing
**http://tampa.creativeloafing.com**
The local alternative weekly newspaper has a great website. The writing is provocative and witty and covers politics, arts and entertainment, local events, and regional news.

## PINELLAS COUNTY
### St. Petersburg/Clearwater Area Convention & Visitors Bureau
**www.floridasbeach.com**
Very similar to the Tampa Convention and Visitors Bureau site, this one focuses, not surprisingly, on the beaches. It's easy to book a room from this site, and it features excellent downloadable maps.

### St. Petersburg Times
**www.tampabay.com**
The daily metro paper covers local as well as national news. It has a good website, and the paper's movie, book, and pop music reviews are notably good.

## THE NATURE COAST
### Citrus County Tourist Development Council
**www.visitcitrus.com**
This is a very interactive site with a wealth of information on Homosassa, Crystal River, and environs. It's a good site from which to choose a manatee snorkeling trip or fishing charter.

### Cedar Key Chamber of Commerce
**www.cedarkey.org**
The chamber's site is a fine resource for information specifically about Cedar Key, especially good for local events.

### Steinhatchee Landing Resort
**www.steinhatcheelanding.com**
Steinhatchee is one of the Gulf Coast's least-known destinations, and generally the web doesn't help much to illuminate. This is the best site about the area, a site brought to you from the most popular upscale resort on the Nature Coast. The recreation section is very helpful in planning a trip.

## TALLAHASSEE
### Tallahassee Area Convention & Visitors Bureau
**www.visittallahassee.com**
This site has all the info you might need to plan a great trip to the capital city, with easy downloadable pdfs of brochures and maps, and carefully written descriptions of restaurants, attractions, and accommodations. It has special sections devoted to people coming for the legislative session as well as those moving to Tallahassee.

### Tallahassee Democrat
**www.tallahassee.com**
The local newspaper's website is the place to go for special-event information, including Florida State University sporting events.

# THE FORGOTTEN COAST
## Forgotten CoastLine Online
### www.apalachicolabay.com

My favorite resource for Forgotten Coast-obilia, it's the website for a monthly tabloid of the same name, heavily impacted by local Chuck Spicer. It's quirky and opinionated, like a good little local paper should be.

## Apalachicola Bay Chamber of Commerce
### www.apalachicolabay.org

It's a little more straight forward and no-nonsense than the Forgotten CoastLine site, but it has good background information on the area and a list of chamber members that actually provides guidance when you're choosing a fishing charter or beach house rental.

# THE EMERALD COAST
## Beaches of South Walton
### www.beachesofsouthwalton.com

About as nice as a site like this can be, this resource well describes the dozen-plus little communities that make up the area, providing useful insight into where to eat, what to do, and where to stay. (Seaside has its own website, www.seasidefl.com, that is even more impressively stylish.)

## Emerald Coast Convention & Visitors Bureau
### www.destin-fwb.com

A fairly serviceable site that explores the areas of Destin, Fort Walton Beach, and Okaloosa Island. The best feature is the lodging locator, in which you can sort by a long list of amenities.

## Panama City Beach Convention & Visitors Bureau
### www.thebeachloversbeach.com

For information specifically on Panama City Beach, this is the best resource. It offers lots of spring break–specific material during the months of March and April. From the site you can also order a 96-page vacation guide that provides helpful and accurate information about activities, entertainment, accommodations, and dining.

# PENSACOLA
## Pensacola Bay Area Convention & Visitors Bureau
### www.visitpensacola.com

All there is to do in Pensacola, Pensacola Beach, and Perdido Key is outlined in an organized fashion, with a special emphasis on the historical and military attractions.

# Index

# List of Maps

# Acknowledgments

I'd like to thank Laura Reiley, author of the first and second editions of *Moon Florida Gulf Coast,* and everyone at Avalon Travel, especially Kathryn Ettinger, Grace Fujimoto, and Domini Dragoone for all their help and for making this project possible and so much fun. I'd also like to thank my parents and brothers for their support and helpful ideas. I had an excellent traveling companion, fact checker, and proofreader while writing this book: Thank you, Jessica Nile, for all of your encouragement, support, hard work, and excellent piña coladas. I could not have done it without you.

I'd also like to thank the following people for their time and expertise during the researching of this book: Sarah Brazwell at Sandestin Golf and Beach Resort; Kelly Grass Prieto at Hayworth Creative; Anita Grove of the Apalachicola Bay Chamber of Commerce; Lee Rose of Lee County Visitor and Convention Bureau; Hue Reynolds at the Florida Department of Education; Bob Thomas at Florida State University; Katie Kole at Visit Tallahassee; Michelle Moran at Sunstream Resorts; Shannon Hagen of the Beaches of South Walton Tourist Development Council; Sandee Harraden at North American Canoe Tours and the Ivey House in Everglades City; Laura A. Lee of the Pensacola Bay Area Convention & Visitors Bureau; Alissa Hopkins at the Morean Arts Center; Josh Hall at the St. Pete and Clearwater Convention & Visitors Bureau; Jamie Veronica at the Big Cat Rescue in Tampa; JoNell Modys of the Greater Naples, Marco Island & Everglades City CVB; Lindsay Bennett at the Panama City CVB; Kelly Robinson of Visit Florida; and all the great, fun people I met traveling across the Gulf Coast of Florida.

# www.moon.com

DESTINATIONS | ACTIVITIES | BLOGS | MAPS | BOOKS

**MOON.COM** is ready to help plan your next trip! Filled with fresh trip ideas and strategies, author interviews, informative travel blogs, a detailed map library, and descriptions of all the Moon guidebooks, Moon.com is all you need to get out and explore the world—or even places in your own backyard. While at Moon.com, sign up for our monthly e-newsletter for updates on new releases, travel tips, and expert advice from our on-the-go Moon authors. As always, when you travel with Moon, expect an experience that is uncommon and truly unique.

**MOON IS ON FACEBOOK—BECOME A FAN!**
**JOIN THE MOON PHOTO GROUP ON FLICKR**

# MAP SYMBOLS

| | | | |
|---|---|---|---|
| ▰▰▰ Expressway | Ⓒ Highlight | ✕ Airfield | ⚲ Golf Course |
| ═══ Primary Road | ○ City/Town | ✈ Airport | Ⓟ Parking Area |
| ▰▰▰ Secondary Road | ◉ State Capital | ▲ Mountain | ⬛ Archaeological Site |
| ▫▫▫ Unpaved Road | ⊛ National Capital | ✦ Unique Natural Feature | ⛪ Church |
| - - - Trail | ★ Point of Interest | | |
| ·········· Ferry | • Accommodation | ℳ Waterfall | ⛽ Gas Station |
| ▰▰▰ Railroad | ▼ Restaurant/Bar | ⧫ Park | Glacier |
| ▰▰▰ Pedestrian Walkway | ▪ Other Location | Ⓣ Trailhead | Mangrove |
| ▥▥▥ Stairs | ⋀ Campground | ✗ Skiing Area | Reef |
| | | | Swamp |

# CONVERSION TABLES

°C = (°F - 32) / 1.8
°F = (°C x 1.8) + 32
1 inch = 2.54 centimeters (cm)
1 foot = 0.304 meters (m)
1 yard = 0.914 meters
1 mile = 1.6093 kilometers (km)
1 km = 0.6214 miles
1 fathom = 1.8288 m
1 chain = 20.1168 m
1 furlong = 201.168 m
1 acre = 0.4047 hectares
1 sq km = 100 hectares
1 sq mile = 2.59 square km
1 ounce = 28.35 grams
1 pound = 0.4536 kilograms
1 short ton = 0.90718 metric ton
1 short ton = 2,000 pounds
1 long ton = 1.016 metric tons
1 long ton = 2,240 pounds
1 metric ton = 1,000 kilograms
1 quart = 0.94635 liters
1 US gallon = 3.7854 liters
1 Imperial gallon = 4.5459 liters
1 nautical mile = 1.852 km

# MOON FLORIDA GULF COAST

Avalon Travel
a member of the Perseus Books Group
1700 Fourth Street
Berkeley, CA 94710, USA
www.moon.com

Editor and Series Manager: Kathryn Ettinger
Copy Editor: Valerie Sellers Blanton
Production Coordinator: Domini Dragoone
Graphics Coordinator: Sean Bellows
Cover Designer: Domini Dragoone
Map Editor: Mike Morgenfeld
Cartographers: Kat Bennett, Suzanne Service,
   Mike Morgenfeld
Indexer: Greg Jewett

ISBN: 978-1-59880-716-5
ISSN: 1556-0309

Printing History
1st Edition – 2005
3rd Edition – July 2011
5 4 3 2

Text and maps © 2011 by Avalon Travel.
All rights reserved.

Laura Reiley wrote the first and second editions of
*Moon Florida Gulf Coast.*

Some photos and illustrations are used by permission
and are the property of the original copyright
owners.

Front cover photo: St. George Island State Park, at
the end of the barrier island and surrounded by
Apalachicola Bay and the Gulf of Mexico © Getty/
The Image Bank/James Randklev.

Title page photo: Courtesy of Lee County CVB.
Front color photos: pgs. 4 & 7 (top left) Courtesy
   of Naples, Marco Island, Everglades CVB; pg. 5 ©
   kalenkov/123rf; pgs. 6 (top), 7 (top right & bottom
   right), 9, 12, 18 & 21 Courtesy of Visit Florida, pg.
   6 (bottom) © Natalia Bratslavsky/123rf; pgs. 7
   (bottom left) & 13 © Elena Kouzmina/123rf; pg. 10
   Courtesy of Tallahassee Area CVB; pg. 11 © Anatoliy
   Lukich/123rf; pg. 14 © Andrew Zarivny/123rf;
   pg. 15 © Rich & Galina Leighton/123rf; pg. 16 ©
   Stacey Lynn Payne/123rf; pg. 17 © Alcinoe; pg.
   20 © Joshua Lawrence Kinser, pg. 22 © Stefan
   Ekernas/123rf; pgs. 23 & 24 Courtesy of Lee
   County CVB.

Printed in Canada by Friesens

## KEEPING CURRENT

If you have a favorite gem you'd like to see included in the next edition, or see anything
that needs updating, clarification, or correction, please drop us a line. Send your
comments via email to feedback@moon.com, or use the address above.

MO●N HANDBOOKS

# FLORIDA
# GULF COAST

JOSHUA LAWRENCE KINSER

# FLORIDA GULF COAST